Computer-Supported Cooperative Work

Springer
Berlin
Heidelberg
New York
Barcelona
Budapest
Hong Kong
London
Milan
Paris
Santa Clara
Singapore
Tokyo

Uwe M. Borghoff Johann H. Schlichter

Computer-Supported Cooperative Work

Introduction to Distributed Applications

With 203 Figures and 18 Tables

Springer

Prof. Dr. Uwe M. Borghoff

Institute of Software Technology
University of the Federal Armed Forces Munich
Werner-Heisenberg-Weg 39
85579 Neubiberg, Germany

borghoff@informatik.unibw-muenchen.de

Prof. Dr. Johann H. Schlichter

Department of Computer Science
Technical University of Munich
Arcisstr. 21
80333 Munich, Germany

schlichter@in.tum.de

Library of Congress Cataloging-in-Publication Data applied for

Die Deutsche Bibliothek - CIP-Einheitsaufnahme

Borghoff, Uwe M.:
Computer supported cooperative work : introduction to distributed applications/Uwe M. Borghoff; Johann H. Schlichter. - Berlin; Heidelberg; New York; Barcelona; Hong Kong; London; Milan; Paris; Singapore; Tokyo: Springer, 2000

ACM Computing Classification (1998): H.5.3, H.4.1, C.2.4, D.2.9, D.2.12, F.1.2, K.4.3, K.6.4

ISBN 978-3-642-08631-1

Springer-Verlag is a part of Springer Science+Business Media

Printed in Germany

Cover Design: Künkel + Lopka, Werbeagentur, Heidelberg

Preface

The terms groupware and CSCW (computer-supported cooperative work) have received significant attention in computer science and related disciplines for quite some time now. This book is a revised and extended version of the 2nd edition of the German textbook *"Rechnergestützte Gruppenarbeit: Eine Einführung in verteilte Anwendungen"*. It has two main objectives: first, to outline the meaning of both terms, and second, to point out both the numerous opportunities for users of groupware and the risks of applying such systems. The book intends to introduce an area of distributed systems, namely the computer support of individuals trying to solve a common problem in cooperation with each other but not necessarily having identical work places or working times.

Computer-supported cooperative work is an interdisciplinary application domain. It can be viewed as a synergism between the areas of distributed systems and (multimedia-) communication on the one hand and between those of information science and socio-organizational theory on the other hand. Thus, the book is meant to help students of all these disciplines, as well as users and developers of systems which have communication and cooperation within groups as top priorities.

Structure of the book. The book is divided into three main parts. The first part contains two chapters and introduces distributed systems and computer-supported cooperative work (groupware). Many of the fundamental principles of distributed systems play an important role in CSCW. Therefore, in **Chapter 1** we briefly introduce these principles as they are relevant to the understanding of the distribution aspects of CSCW. We discuss the key concept of transparency and typical communication mechanisms such as information sharing, message exchange, bi-directional communication and producer-consumer interaction. Moreover, as part of the discussion of the widely-accepted client-server model, we introduce the remote procedure call (RPC) as a means of processing service requests. We describe in detail RPC properties, the structure of RPC messages, and the fundamental mechanisms of RPC languages. Additionally, we also introduce object-oriented systems and show how objects of such systems can be distributed among the different participating sites. The description of distributed applications focuses on group communication and the design of distributed applications built according to the ODP framework.

Contemporary literature is overflowing with technical terms defining various aspects of computer-supported cooperative work. In **Chapter 2** we introduce these terms and discuss them with respect to practical teamwork support. In addition to demonstrating typical usage scenarios and their characteristics, we also present several classification models, in particular the time space taxonomy. When dealing with the so-called application level classification, we discuss message systems, group editors, electronic meeting rooms, conferencing systems, shared information spaces, intelligent agents, and coordination systems. Furthermore, we investigate factors which contribute to the success or failure of groupware systems. Research and experiments with computer-supported cooperative work in real environments support this work. The results of these studies demonstrate how groupware should be designed and how CSCW concepts should be validated. With Lotus Notes we present one of the most successful groupware systems.

The second part of the book is subdivided into three chapters and deals with some basic concepts of computer-supported cooperative work, including group processes, concurrency control, and replication. The group process is a fundamental CSCW concept which specifies the goals and structure of the team as well as the progress of the cooperation between team members. In **Chapter 3** we discuss the centralized, the distributed nonreplicated, and the distributed replicated group process models. After an introduction to a general cluster model, we explain strategies for distributing information within and between clusters. Special attention is given to possible structures of asynchronous team interaction. The management of a shared context is a further basic CSCW aspect we deal with, focusing on the WYSIWIS (what you see is what I see) concept and the support of group awareness. Possible architectures of groupware systems conclude the chapter. Issues are window sharing, conferencing components and conference managers, as well as collaboration aware systems.

In **Chapter 4** we look into concurrency control concepts. We discuss optimistic approaches for concurrency control as well as approaches with locking, floor-passing, transactions, and operation transformations. In **Chapter 5** we look deeper into replication issues and introduce more sophisticated approaches for concurrency control such as voting and coding schemes as well as the grid protocol. These schemes have the advantage of an enormous improvement as far as the availability of replicated data is concerned, while the consistency is guaranteed even during network partitioning. For comparison and classification purposes we develop some criteria for evaluating the possible use of each scheme.

The third part of the book, which contains four chapters, addresses application classes of computer-supported cooperative work. In **Chapter 6** we deal with communication systems and shared information spaces. The architecture and functionality of a typical email system is discussed. Further attention is directed towards synchronous communication as exemplified by video conferences. We also present an information management approach to support the work on shared information in the context of workgroups. We discuss an architecture for hypermedia systems, the hypertext abstract machine, and the Dexter reference model which facilitates the interoperability between different hypermedia systems. The navigation problem in large information spaces and hypertext-specific solutions are presented. The IBIS method provides functions to systematically structure the problem solving information. Finally, we present the information space of the Campiello system, a community support system for tourist applications.

A workflow specifies a set of coordinated activities which represent a so-called business process within a company or an organization. In **Chapter 7** we deal with workflow management systems, a particular kind of groupware intended to support groups of people involved in the execution of business processes. A workflow management system coordinates and monitors group activities by handling both causal and temporal interdependencies and the execution context. After a brief introduction to some basic concepts of workflow management we discuss the functionality and a possible architecture of workflow management systems. Various coordination models (e.g., the customer-performer model) are discussed as well as the conversation model which is derived from linguistics. Based on the concept of a conversational network we present the conversation systems Coordinator and Domino, along with the activity management system Tacts. Besides the standardization activities within the Workflow Management Coalition (WfMC), we discuss adaptive workflows which handle exceptional situations in flexible ways.

Chapter 8 deals with systems for workgroup computing focusing on the cooperation between people working in a team. We investigate distributed document systems and provide an overview of existing group editors. Using the examples of Iris and DistEdit, we introduce typical problem areas of group editors. We demonstrate why highly structured documents, along with logical document views, are advantageous to the handling of joint authoring scenarios and to the management of shared documents. Concepts for version and history management are discussed. Moreover, undo-operations in the context of group editors are considered in detail.

Chapter 9 discusses various aspects of multiagent systems applied for intelligent coordination of agent-based computer-supported cooperation as required in groupwork. After an initial classification and description of the most important features of agents, we introduce aspects for modeling distributed multiagent systems and the cooperation between agents. We explore three basic approaches for distributed problem solving: the contract net protocol which is based on the exchange of semistructured messages, an agent-based information brokerage, and distributed meeting scheduling. Finally, we discuss the actor model by Hewitt.

Usage of the book. This book is based on two lectures – "Distributed Applications" and "Computer-Supported Cooperative Work" –, regularly held by J. Schlichter at the Technical University of Munich, Germany, since the winter of 1991/92, as well as on the lecture "Distributed Information Management" held by U. Borghoff at the Technical University of Munich, Germany, and the University of the Federal Armed Forces Munich, Germany. Between 1985 and 1989 J. Schlichter was a member of the Document Systems Group of the Xerox Research Center, Webster, NY. Between 1994 and 1998 U. Borghoff was with the Xerox Research Centre Europe (formerly Rank Xerox Research Centre) in Grenoble, France. Their work there was quite influential to the content of the book. Furthermore, the results of the five months sabbatical which J. Schlichter spent at the Xerox Research Centre Europe as well as relevant publications by U. Borghoff in the field of agent-based cooperation have been taken advantage of.

Chapters 1 and 2 may be used as material for a two hour weekly introductory lecture on the basics of distributed applications. Should time be more restricted, Sect. 1.6.5, 1.6.6 and 1.7.4 may be skipped. For a three-hour weekly lecture on synchronous and asynchronous techniques of distributed applications, you may wish to use the Chapters 3, 4, 6–9. In case of limited time, Sect. 3.2, 3.3, 8.3 and 9.6 may be omitted. On first reading of the book one might skip Chapter 5, since the solutions outlined therein are meant to enrich special lectures or advanced seminars on the topic of distributed synchronization (e.g., distributed operating systems and distributed databases).

Computer-supported cooperative work being a rather newly established topic within computer science, we cannot provide the reader with references to advanced textbooks in each chapter. We have, therefore, collected a rather extensive – albeit long – bibliography at the end of the book. The reader may consult the referenced literature on details of the introduced methods and concepts.

Acknowledgements. The description of Tacts in Sect. 7.2.6 has been supplied by Gunnar Teege. The group editor Iris as introduced in Sect. 8.2.3 has been implemented as part of several master theses. Our thanks go to Franz Bauernfeind, Thorsten Gesing, Michael Koch and Anke Mäkiö, as well as to Kathrin Möslein for her preparatory work on the interpretation of the term CSCW. Our special thanks go to Evelyn Gemkow for typing and translating parts of the manuscript and always eagerly working away on even roughly outlined paragraphs. The sketches at the beginning of each chapter were drawn by Julia Schlichter. We are also most thankful for her careful proofreading of the entire manuscript. Last but not least, we would like to express our gratitude towards our publisher Hans Wössner of Springer-Verlag as well as towards the reviewer of the first German edition, Christoph Bussler, for their appreciated comments which have highly contributed to the quality of the book.

Computer-supported cooperation during the production of the book. The writing of the book itself is a good example for computer-supported cooperative work. The co-authors have dealt with a shared task (namely the book) while they were both locally distributed (initially, in France and Germany), and temporally distributed (due to different working rhythms). It goes without saying that the overall production of the book was highly cooperative. During several face-to-face sessions the general procedures were first agreed upon, and later the particulars were repeatedly refined before being eventually fixed. For information transfer, various means of communication were deployed, ranging from telephone and Fax to email, file transfer and the world wide web. Sketches of figures for the co-author's opinion were sent via Fax, whereas email and file transfer constituted the backbone of the distributed cooperation. Between August and December 1994 alone (work on the 1st German edition), approximately a thousand emails were sent, partly with enormous information volume (as in some 130 postscript figures). This transmission volume was, however, grossly surpassed during the phase of complete revision of the book between June 1996 and April 1997. Consolidated versions of individual chapters were regularly compressed and filed away in the world wide web where they were offered to the co-author for file transfer. The final text processing was performed in Munich where the full and consistent formatting information was always available. During the work on this English edition, the authors used the system BSCW (Basic Support for Cooperative Work) by the German National Research Center for Information Technology (GMD). The authors have not yet given up hope that a European information highway will be installed and accessible for some future cooperation in a form which would allow cooperation methods as offered by distributed group editors in a better and more efficient way than at present.

Munich, Germany, June 2000

U.M.B.
J.H.S.

Table of Contents

Part I. Introduction to Distributed Systems and Computer-Supported Cooperative Work

Part II. Basic Concepts of Computer-Supported Cooperative Work

Part I

Introduction to Distributed Systems and Computer-Supported Cooperative Work

1. Fundamental Principles of Distributed Systems

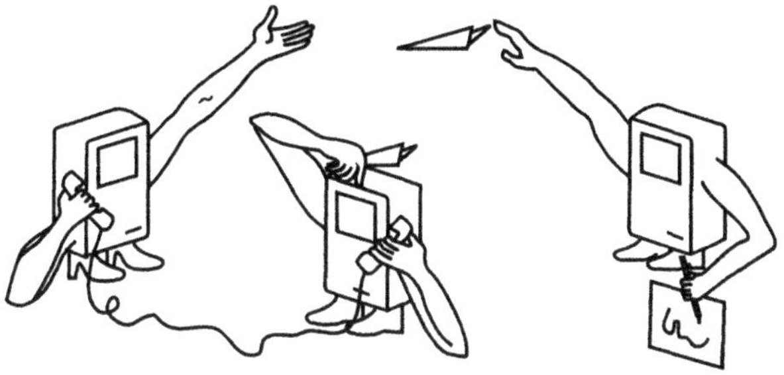

Many of the fundamental principles of distributed systems play an important role in computer-supported cooperative work (CSCW). Therefore, this chapter briefly introduces these principles as they are relevant to an understanding of the distributed character of CSCW.

We discuss the key concept of transparency as well as typical mechanisms of communication such as information sharing, message exchange, bidirectional communication, producer-consumer interaction, and the well-known client-server model. As part of the discussion of the client-server model, we introduce the remote procedure call (RPC) as a means for processing service requests. We describe, in detail, RPC properties, the structure of RPC messages, and the fundamental mechanisms of RPC languages.

Furthermore, we introduce object-oriented systems and show how objects of such systems can be distributed among the different participating sites. Here, we briefly mention the concepts of the famous tuple space model as well as that of so-called Linear Objects. As part of the description of distributed applications, we focus on group communication and the design of distributed applications built along the ODP framework.

Finally, we present a survey-like introduction to the problem of resource allocation and resource assignment, respectively, in distributed systems.

1.1 Introduction

The continually increasing significance of distributed systems is a result of various factors. Firstly, the costs of VLSI technology (e.g., processor and storage units) has been decreasing dramatically over the years. Secondly, networking technology with high bandwidth is now available at almost all locations at low cost. Moreover, applications in a wide variety of relevant domains (e.g., collaborative information spaces, workflow management, telecooperation, autonomous agents) are flourishing. These applications, in contrast to traditional centralized systems, provide adaptive, user-customizable graphical user interfaces and support cooperation as well as joint information access among geographically dispersed user communities.

All of the above application domains share the concept of distribution. For a precise understanding of what we mean by distribution, we distinguish between the following five fundamental methods of distribution: hardware components, load (mostly controlled by the underlying subsystem), data (seen during data generation as well as during their usage within an application), control (e.g., operating system), and processing. An example of processing distribution is the distributed execution of an application. In the following, we will concentrate mainly on the latter three methods of distribution, with a particular focus on processing distribution.

Distributed systems possess a series of interesting properties. The existence of multiple functional units, for instance, allows dynamic assignments of resources to different, independent execution threads. Typically, these (physical and logical) functional units are distributed, and at the same time, linked through an interconnecting network. An operating system controls, integrates and homogenizes the components of the functional units. Individual functional units may have their own local operating system instance. Communication between the functional units serves synchronization purposes and guarantees consistency among mutually dependent execution threads. Other characteristics of distributed systems are cooperative autonomy during the interaction among the physical or logical functional units, independence of functional units during partial failures, as well as a high degree of transparency. Transparency will be discussed in some detail in Sect. 1.2.

Two perspectives highlight the strengths of distributed systems that are heavily exploited during the design of particular CSCW applications: in contrast to a centralized system, a distributed system might be more economical, might provide higher throughput, might better support distributed applications (such as CSCW applications), might support seamless replication techniques, and might outperform any centralized system as far as scalability is concerned. When compared to mainframes, the economical advantage of distributed systems can be brought down to the better price-performance ratio of microprocessors. Replication brings about advantages such as increased availability. The failure of a single component within the distributed system can be masked, i.e., the distributed system as a whole will still work properly as long as the components are not directly dependent upon each other. A distributed system can incrementally be augmented, in terms of components and functionality.

In contrast to isolated workstations, a distributed system supports sharing of common resources (e.g., file systems, printers) and allows for sophisticated ways of communication (e.g., email, video conferencing). Furthermore, a distributed system makes better use of the functionality and the flexibility of workstations. As an example, load might be distributed among unused but available sites.

Although we have seen a couple of advantages of distributed systems, there are obvious disadvantages. In addition to dependencies as far as performance and reliability of the underlying network are concerned, we see dependencies from (invisible) components and functional units of the distributed system. A very satirical description of this was given by L. Lamport who was once heard to say: "A distributed system is one that stops you from getting any work done when a machine you've never heard of crashes." Network support is of a high complexity. The installation of an adequate network management system is a must. Limitations of network activities may lead to bottlenecks for communication and information exchanges. Another risk is security. A distributed system offers more portals for intruders. Communication with untrusted sites is quite problematic. Very often, a compromise must be reached between easy access to remote data and strict security control. In Unix, for example, the ".rhosts" are introduced to support a comfortable and automatic (unchecked!) login to remote nodes. Obviously, this opens up an immense security risk. Version control is another problem area in distributed systems. Here, we not only see a risk in versioning files but also in versioning components and functional units being the constituents of the distributed system. Most CSCW applications try to ignore this disadvantage, some of them – as we will see later – are more or less successful in this endeavor.

Last but not least, there is a disadvantage concerning the complexity of the installed software realized in the distributed system. This software should take into consideration communication among distributed sites and, most importantly, potential failures during execution at these sites (e.g., node[1] crashes, link failures, network partitioning). Testing and debugging of such a software is complex, time consuming, and difficult. It is a tough job to provide adequate test suites and test environments. In practice, therefore, we see mostly real-life tests.

1.2 Transparency

For a better exploitation of resources within a distributed, heterogeneous network – without significant changes of the existing software platform –, a

[1] A node may be a single machine or a cluster of machines.

high degree of transparency is necessary. Without a doubt, transparency is seen as one of the key enablers for and one of the key concepts of a successful distributed system implementation. When speaking of a better exploitation of resources, we are referring to access to remote files and devices, economic usage of hardware and software components, distributed computation, and execution of processes at less loaded sites.

1.2.1 Levels of transparency

In contrast to Lamport's rather ironic description of a distributed (operating) system, Tanenbaum and v. Renesse (1985) presented a more serious definition:

> "A distributed operating system is one that looks to its users like an ordinary centralized operating system but runs on multiple, independent central processing units (CPUs). The key concept here is transparency. In other words, the use of multiple processors should be invisible (transparent) to the user."

The following brief survey gives the highlights of the most significant levels of transparency we have encountered for distributed system design.

We speak of *location transparency* when a user accessing a particular resource need not necessarily know the location of this resource within the network in order to access it. Not knowing the location of a particular resource implies that all accesses to such a resource are realized via a simple location-independent name of the resource. Figure 1.1 shows an example of a printing device that is accessed by a user by simply stating its name, while ignoring the fact that this device is not attached to the user's workstation. Aspects of location transparency include the fact that the name of a resource contains neither the location where it resides at the moment nor the location where the resource was created.

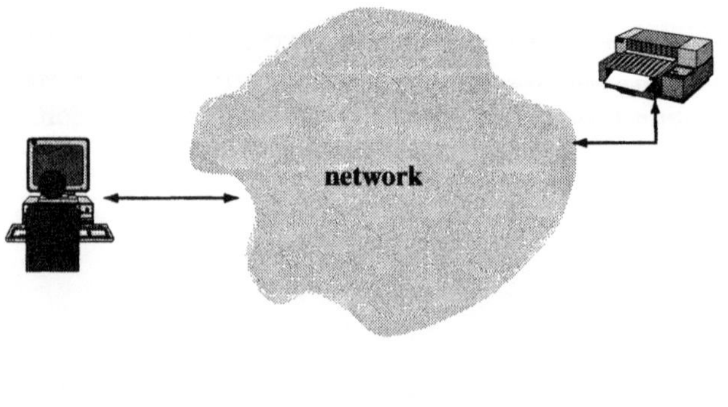

Fig. 1.1. Example of location transparency

More precisely, we can define three levels of location transparency. In level 0, a user might identify separate computing systems that are able to communicate with each other via networking applications. In level 1, there might be some applications that hide an environment of multicomputing systems from the user. While level 0 is mostly achieved in networks consisting of heterogeneous subsystems (e.g., remote login, file transfer), a level 1 implementation of location transparency veils the fact that the user gets her functionality through multiple interconnected computing systems. However, the user is still aware of working with a distributed system. A "remote who" command might still reveal the names of the set of users who are logged into various sites at the same time. Finally, in level 2, network-wide services for shared resource usage might hide the existence of multiple interconnected computing systems.

Access transparency provides access to local and remote resources in exactly the same way. A well-known example of access transparency is given in the world wide web. Here, the concept of a uniform resource locator (URL) provides this kind of transparency.[2] Figure 1.2 illustrates the way in which a user accesses two different files (one stored locally, one stored remotely) transparently. The term device transparency is also seen in the literature when referring to transparent accesses to locally or remotely located devices.

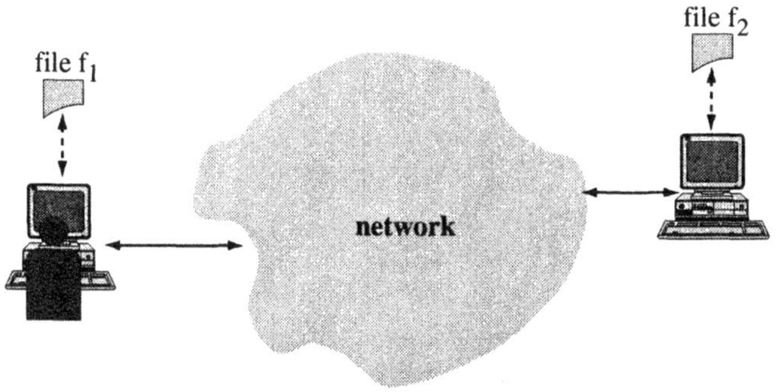

Fig. 1.2. Example of access transparency

For reasons of availability, resources might be replicated. If a user is unaware of whether a resource is replicated or not, *replication transparency* is provided. In Fig. 1.3 an individual file exists in two replicas. If a user invokes a **read** command for this file, either of the two replicas might be selected to be read. In principle, for a user, there is only a single logical file that consists

[2] Note, however, that URLs do not support location transparency because they code the location of the resource into the resource locator. This causes complications when resources are relocated. Many of the readers may have encountered the problem of dangling links to no longer existing resources. A way out of this dilemma, i.e., providing access transparency and location transparency at the same time was attempted in the world wide web by introducing uniform name locators (URNs). A URN works just like a URL but does not code the location into the name locator.

of two replicas. A variety of protocols have been proposed that deal with the problem of consistency among replicated files. Chapters 4–5 focus on these protocols in some detail.

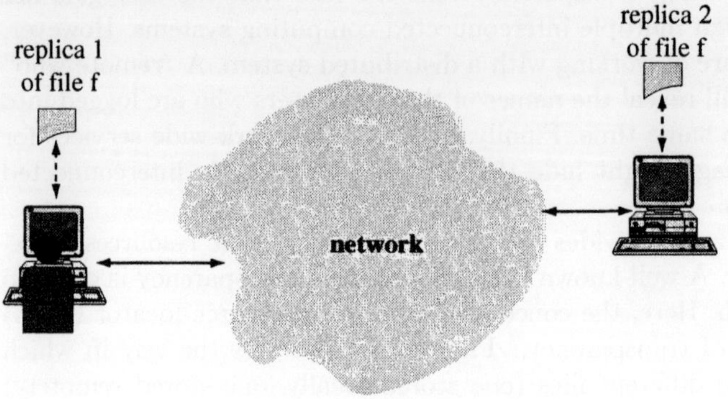

Fig. 1.3. Example of replication transparency

Distributed systems that mask link failures or node crashes are said to provide *failure transparency*. For instance, if files are replicated the crash of an individual file server does not prohibit access to the remaining replicas of the file on other unharmed file servers.

The problem of synchronization of parallel and concurrent accesses to shared resources increases when the resources and the users accessing these resources are geographically dispersed. We speak of *concurrency transparency* when the needed control of synchronization is embedded into the distributed system implementation.

Migration transparency provides a solution to the problem of relocation of resources in distributed systems. Resources may migrate from one node to another without influencing the correct behavior of running applications. A reason for this kind of relocation is an improved load balancing. Resources migrate from overloaded to less loaded sites. In many implementations, this implies a homogeneous system or so-called machine transparency. However, the implementation of the migration transparent components is independent of the target environment (i.e., of the environment in which the components will eventually be processed). More precisely, the type of processor and the operating system variant at the target environment are unimportant. Section 1.6 details this problem area in the context of object-oriented distributed system design.

A special case of migration transparency is host migration transparency. The correct behavior of an application is not influenced by the migration of its host from one subnetwork to another. Host migration transparency is extremely useful for mobile workers who connect their laptops (i.e., the hosts) to different subnetworks while traveling. Their hosts support the same environments, the same applications, and the same look-and-feel, no matter where the mobile workers are currently connected to the network. Internet technology (e.g., browsers, portals, ubiquitous user profiles) supports this kind of transparency. CSCW applications benefit substantially from host migration transparency. Here, we also distinguish between off-line and on-line migration. While off-line migration simply means that a host being disconnected from a specific subnetwork is unable to send or receive data from the network, on-line migration means that a host remains connected while migrating (e.g., through wireless communication). Off-line migration implies a so-called stand-alone mode of operation – the typical mode of operation for laptops. During migration, all data (e.g., a local replica of a file) are stored locally, updates cannot be propagated to the remaining replicas until the user reconnects to the network. Consequences for the network-wide consistency of the data are self evident.

Execution transparency implies that processes may be processed on different runtime systems. A user may choose the execution location of her processes according to some criteria of efficiency. Processes may migrate within the distributed system freely (i.e., processes may run at remote sites without an explicit recompilation phase). Processes are implicitly adapted to a new runtime system. In the case of migrating a running process to another site, the current process context migrates as well. Obviously, this kind of transparency level is costly, especially in the case of the migration of a running process. However, languages that are compiled to a worldwide accepted virtual machine format, or interpreted scripting languages are important steps towards the realization of this kind of transparency level. The Java virtual machine could be a potential platform of the former, J. Ousterhout's Tcl, or General Magic's Telescript could be seen as early attempts for the latter.

Performance transparency allows for dynamic reconfiguration of the system to improve the overall system performance when changes in load characteristics are detected.

Scalability transparency supports extensions and enhancements of the system or the applications without the need of modifications to the system structure or changes to the application algorithms. In distributed system design this is one of the most essential transparency levels. Incremental enhancements and extensions are key features of distributed systems in general.

If components of an application are implemented in different programming languages, *language transparency* is of great help. In this case, interaction between components of an application are independent of the languages used to implement the components. Figure 1.4 illustrates the case of a calendar system with the functionality of insertion and deletion of calendar information. Inferences such as "when did the last project meeting take place?" are also handled correctly.

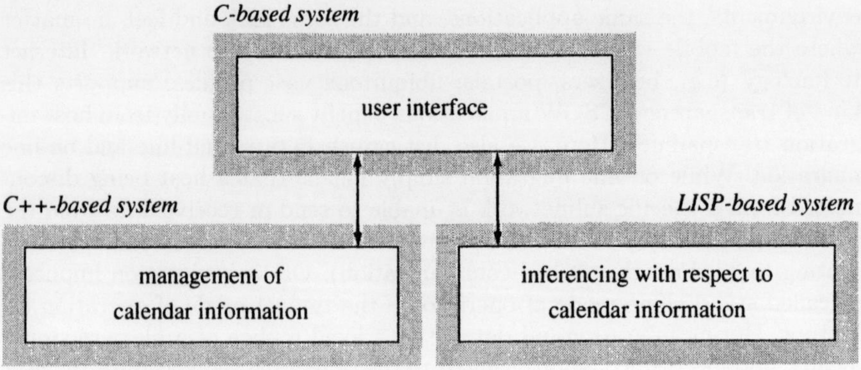

Fig. 1.4. Example of language transparency

A major goal of most distributed systems, especially of distributed file or operating systems, is the realization of a rich set of transparency levels.

1.2.2 Transparency levels of existing systems

Over the years, a variety of distributed (file and operating) systems have been developed. Comprehensive surveys are given by Borghoff (1992), Svobodova (1984), and Tanenbaum and v. Renesse (1985).

One of the first systems providing access transparency in a Unix environment was the Newcastle Connection. It introduced the concept of a super-root (Brownbridge et al. 1982).[3] Another widely used distributed file system providing location as well as access transparency has been marketed by Sun Microsystems, Inc., namely the Network File System (NFS).

Many other system approaches have focused on other levels of transparency. Succinct overviews in the area of distributed file and operating systems are given by Borghoff (1992). From this book we have taken Table 1.1 in a slightly condensed and modified form.

1.2.3 Problems with transparency in CSCW

The above discussion shows that an application designer may implement a rich set of transparency levels. But is a rich set of transparency levels appropriate for all classes of applications? The answer is probably yes for distributed systems like distributed file or operating systems where users should not feel the distribution at all. The answer is definitively no for computer-supported cooperative work. Here, the levels of transparency must be carefully selected. We may want to provide location and access transparency but

[3] We can see a vestige of the super-root concept in the coding of the uniform resource locator (URL). The "//" right after the protocol specification and the colon can be interpreted as a condensed super-root, e.g., http://www.telekooperation.de/cscw/.

Table 1.1. Selected transparency levels of distributed file and operating systems

System	Main reference	Levels of transparency: location	replication	concurrency	failure
Accent	(Rashid and Robertson 1981)	*			*
Amoeba	(Tanenbaum et al. 1991)	*		*	*
Andrew/AFS	(Satyanarayanan et al. 1985)	*	*	*	
Argus	(Liskov 1985)	*			*
Athena	(Balkovich et al. 1985)	*			
BirliX	(Härtig et al. 1986)	*	*	*	*
Cedar	(Gifford et al. 1988)	*	*	*	*
Clouds	(Dasgupta et al. 1988)	*		*	*
Cronus	(Schantz et al. 1986)	*	*		
DACNOS	(Eberle and Schmutz 1986)	*		*	
Domain	(Levine 1987)	*			
Dunix	(Litman 1986)	*			
Eden	(Almes et al. 1985)	*	*		*
Emerald	(Black et al. 1986)	*			
Grapevine	(Schroeder et al. 1984)	*	*		
HCS	(Notkin et al. 1988)	*			
Ibis	(Tichy 1984)	*	*	*	
Locus	(Popek and Walker 1985)	*	*	*	*
Mach	(Acetta et al. 1986)	*			*
Newcastle	(Brownbridge et al. 1982)	*			
Nexus	(Tripathi 1987)	*			*
NFS	(West 1985)	*			
Pulse	(Wellings 1985)	*	*		
RFS	(Rifkin et al. 1986)	*			
Saguaro	(Andrews et al. 1987)	*	*		
SOS	(Shapiro 1986)	*			*
Sprite	(Ousterhout 1987)	*	*	*	
V	(Cheriton 1988)	*			
VAXclusters	(Kronenberg et al. 1986)			*	*

no strict concurrency transparency. Section 8.2.3 describes an application where a carefully chosen subset of transparency levels has been achieved.

1.3 Mechanisms for Communication

In the following, we will discuss some mechanisms for communication, namely information sharing, message exchange, and the producer-consumer interaction (pipe mechanism). Information sharing is a variant of implicit communication whereas the other two are variants of explicit communication. We will discuss the client-server model as well as object-oriented communication in Sect. 1.4 and Sect. 1.6, respectively. We will briefly introduce group communication in Sect. 1.7.1.

1.3.1 Information sharing

If components of a distributed application communicate through shared integrated information management, as schematically depicted in Fig. 1.5, we refer to this as information sharing.

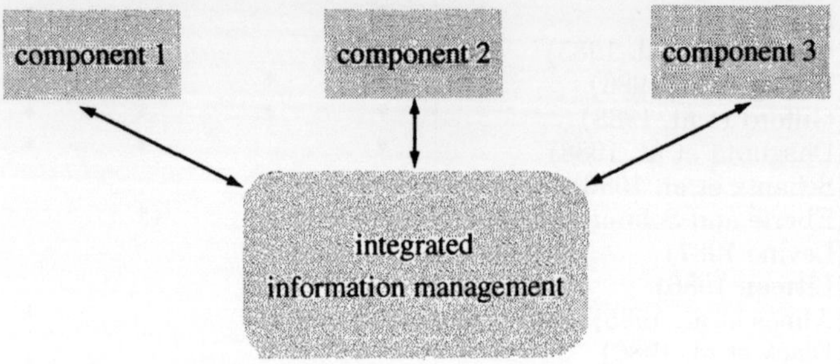

Fig. 1.5. Information sharing

As an example, think of a shared, possibly replicated file system that is distributed across a set of nodes. There is no direct communication among the components of the distributed application. All communication is through the shared file system. A common data model as well as a common understanding of the semantics of the data are essential. Concurrent accesses are synchronized, and in many cases, a transactional scheme is implemented. An example of information sharing can be found in many CASE[4] tools where the tools communicate solely through a shared database.

Since the purist approach of information sharing might be too restrictive for some of the CSCW applications, many designers provide additional direct communication among the components of the distributed application. Figure 1.6 illustrates such an approach.

1.3.2 Message exchange

Interprocess communication (IPC) as found in centralized systems can be achieved in distributed systems through message exchange between a sender and a receiver.

Messages consist of a message head and a message body (the content of the message). The message head contains the sender's specification, a message identifier, the message type, and a specification of the receiver. This specification of the receiver may consist of a receiver's name, a mailbox, a port number, or a socket. Sockets are mainly used in connection with a host address which leads to a location-dependent specification of the receiver. Using

[4] Computer Aided Software Engineering.

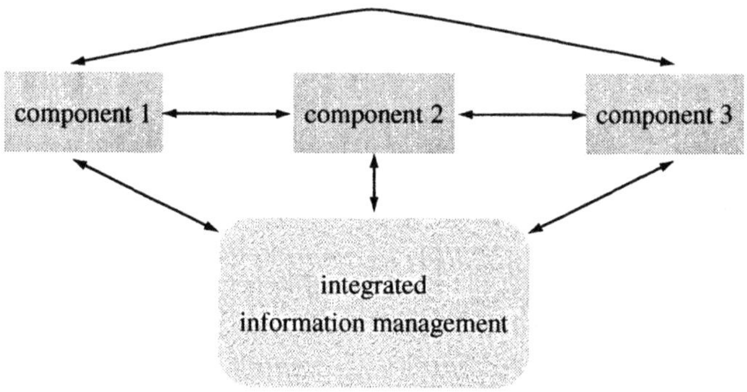

Fig. 1.6. Information sharing plus direct communication

names instead of sockets, location independence can be achieved by introducing a so-called name service that maps a name to a real host address (see Sect. 1.4.3). The message body is comprised of a set of data objects that are either structured or semistructured (see Sect. 6.1).

The basic functionalities of a message system are firstly, sending of a message to a receiver, given as operation **send**(message M) **to** receiver R, and secondly, receiving a message from a sender and transferring the corresponding message into a buffer.

To better compare the idiosyncrasies of this communication, it is instructive to consider the sending and the receiving sites separately. If we assume that a sender has invoked an operation **send**(message M) **to** receiver R, then the receiver invokes an operation of the form **receive**(message M, sender S, buffer B).

Sender's view. In the sender's view, we will distinguish between asynchronous and synchronous message exchanges, as well as the so-called remote-invocation send.

Asynchronous message exchange allows a sender to resume its processing immediately after a message is put forward into a message queue. To avoid manipulation before and during message transmissions, the message queues are managed by the message system itself. A sender does not wait until the receiver has processed the message. A **receive** operation indicates that the receiver is interested in receiving a message. The arrival of such a message leads to passive or active notification at the receiver's site. In the case of passive notification, a receiver repeats the invocation of the **receive** operation to check whether a message has arrived. When active notification is achieved, the receiver gets a callback from the message system once the message has arrived. The callback leads to an interruption of the current activity at the receiver's site. Two variants of active notification exist. The first variant specifies a data structure into which arriving messages are inserted, the second variant specifies a procedure or a script that will be executed upon reception of a message.

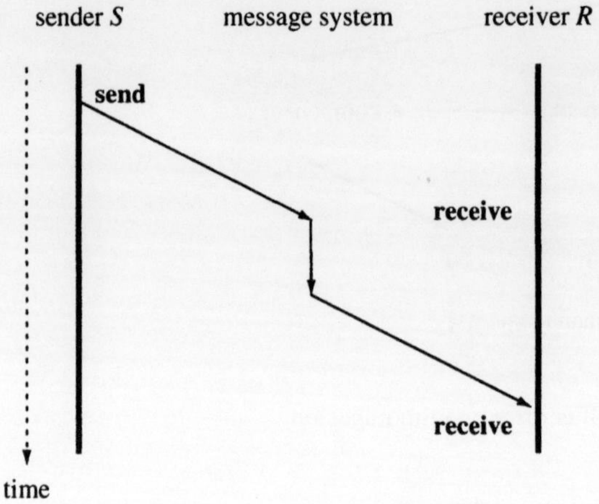

Fig. 1.7. Asynchronous message exchange

Figure 1.7 illustrates how a receiver repeats the invocation of the **receive** operation until a message arrives.

Asynchronous message exchange has three main advantages. Firstly, it is useful in the context of real-time applications, especially during situations where a sender must not be blocked. Secondly, it supports parallel execution threads at the sender's and the receiver's sites. Finally, it can be used for event signaling purposes.

Unfortunately, asynchronous message exchange has some weaknesses. Managing the message queue and dealing with buffer overflows as well as access control problems are some areas where failures can occur. Problematic are also receiver failures and moreover, the way in which the sender is notified of these receiver failures. Note that the sender is not suspended. When the sender is notified of failures in the context of messages which it may have previously submitted, the sender may possibly be in the middle of another calculation and may prefer not to be interrupted. A correct design of a message system is a difficult task. The failure behavior depends heavily on buffer sizes, buffer contents, and the time behavior of the exchanged messages.

Synchronous message exchange blocks a sender until the receiver has effectively received the message. In analogy, the receiver is blocked until the message is stored into the receiver's buffer. Figure 1.8 illustrates this approach. Note, however, that a failure of the receiver may lead to an infinite blocking of the sender.

To remedy this drawback, we need some sort of decoupling of sender and receiver. One option is to associate a timeout with every **send** operation, another option creates subprocesses for sending a message. The second option can be achieved by using lightweight processes, also called threads.

When using remote-invocation send, a sender suspends execution until the receiver has received and processed a submitted request that was delivered as part of the message. The receiver informs the sender about the (successful)

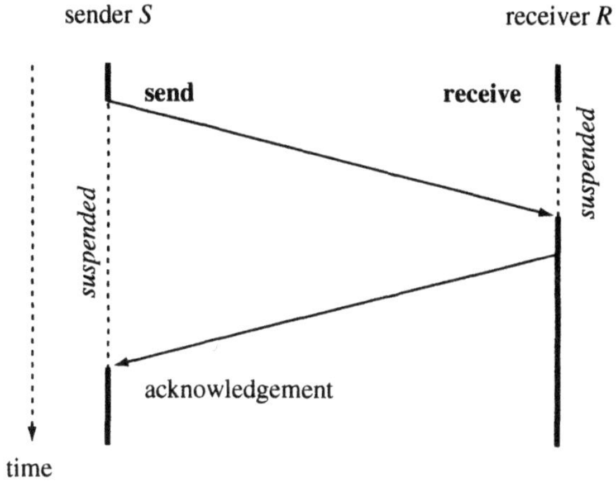

Fig. 1.8. Synchronous message exchange

processing of the operation as seen, for instance, in an RPC (remote procedure call). If an additional message exchange is necessary for the successful processing of the submitted request (e.g., another remote-invocation send), then this method is rather time-consuming. If the receiver wants to communicate with the sender through a different communication port (i.e., not the port from which the sender is waiting for the answer), then we have to deal with the problem of deadlocks. Sender and receiver may end up in a cyclical blocking state, and therefore cannot answer over the expected ports.

Receiver's view. The reception of a message can be classified into three cases, namely the conditional reception, the reception with timeout, and the selective reception.

In the case of the conditional reception, the resumption of execution by the receiver is dependent upon the existence of an arriving message. A precise description of this situation appears in the algorithm below.

Code fragment (Operation **receive***).*
function receive(message M, sender S, buffer B): errorcode;
  if ($\exists$ message M **of** sender S) **then**
    copy message M into buffer B;
    return true
  else return false;

If the expected message of a sender has arrived, the function **receive** returns **true**, otherwise it returns **false**.

In the case of the reception with timeout, the receiver is blocked either until a message is received from a sender or until a timeout occurs. The following algorithm depicts this situation.

Code fragment (Operation **receive** *– variant using timeout).*
function receive(message M, sender S, buffer B, timeout t): errorcode;

wait until (∃ message M **of** sender S **or** timeout t);
if (∃ message M **of** sender S) **then**
  copy message M into buffer B;
  return true
else return false;

In the case of selective reception, the receiver specifies a set of sender names (e.g., using explicit names or wildcards). For each name, the receiver may specify an individual procedure or script for processing corresponding messages. As soon as a message by a specified sender arrives, the corresponding procedure or script is executed. The sender selection is either arbitrary, predefined, or user-customizable. An arbitrary selection is a random, unspecified selection method. A predefined or user-customizable selection method, for instance, might select messages according to the sequence of message arrivals or according to message priorities. In CSCW applications, user-customizable selection is heavily used. For example, a user may want to assign a script to any message sent by a particular user agent. Let us assume this user agent is a bargain finder that compares best offers for a given item searched by the user. If this item is only available before an expiration date, the user may want to get this timely information forwarded to her mobile phone, pager, or some other device specified within the script. Another example for user-customizable selection may occur in a project team. A project member may decide that messages sent by team members should reside within the mailbox over the week-end without further notification, while messages sent by the project leader should immediately be handled in some way, for example, again using a script similar to the one described in the previous example.

1.3.3 Bidirectional communication

Bidirectional communication supports information flow from sender to receiver and vice versa. Typically, this provokes a request-answer scheme as the pattern for the message exchange. The request consists of the name of a requested service operation together with the needed parameters. The answer contains the result the receiver has obtained by executing the requested service operation using the submitted parameters. If lost request and answer messages can always be detected, a bidirectional communication is said to be reliable.

Any communication between a sender and a receiver is subject to losses of request messages, losses of answer messages as well as crashes (and restarts) of the sending or receiving sites. Therefore, the literature distinguishes between different call semantics.

1. Under an at-least-once semantics, the requested service operation is processed once or several times. Figure 1.9 shows executions of the requested service operations for a first and a second request[5] which could

[5] The answer for the first request has been lost; see symbol ⊗.

be different. Therefore, an at-least-once semantics is ideal only for idempotent service operations that always produce identical results without side-effects.

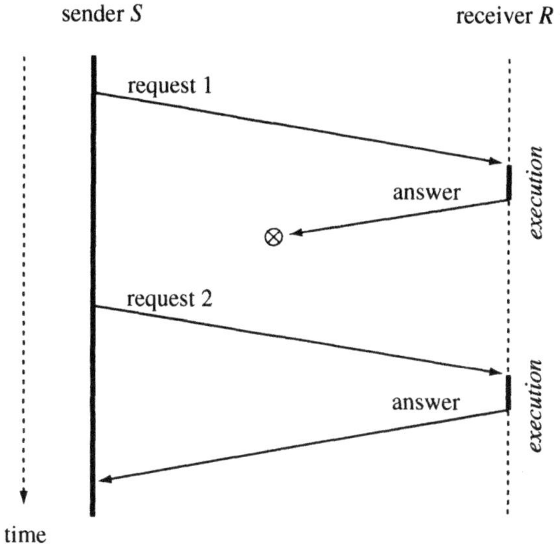

Fig. 1.9. Temporal sketch of a request-answer scheme under an at-least-once semantics

2. Under an exactly-once semantics, the requested service operation is processed exactly once. That implies, that repeatedly sent requests – due to timeouts at the sending site – have to be detected, and handled, at the receiving site.
   The receiver keeps a list of current requests. Each request in the list is tagged with a unique identifier. Requests are not deleted from the list until the sender has acknowledged the correct reception of the result submitted by the receiver. Repeatedly sent requests for the same service operation are answered with the result of the first successful service operation. In any case, the receiving site does not process the same request twice. This is illustrated in Fig. 1.10 where the reception of the third request results in answering with the result obtained from processing the second request.
3. Under a last semantics, the requested service operation is processed once or several times, however, only the last processing produces a result and, potentially, some side-effects.
4. Finally, under an at-most-once semantics, the requested service operation is processed once or not at all. If the service operation is processed successfully, the at-most-once semantics coincides with the exactly-once semantics. The renunciation of a repeatedly sent request after a timeout at the sending site, for instance, supports this kind of semantics. In this

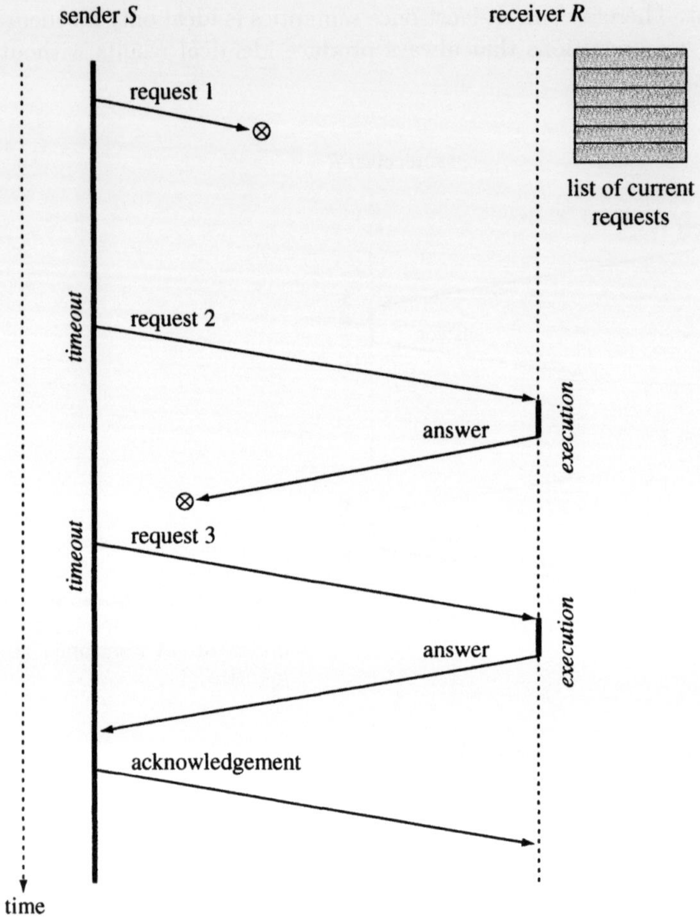

Fig. 1.10. Temporal sketch of a request-answer scheme under an exactly-once semantics

case, moreover, the request submission is encapsulated into a transactional scheme. A series of requested service operations are to be executed atomically (i.e., either the entire series of requested service operations are successful or none at all).

1.3.4 Producer-consumer interaction

Figure 1.11 depicts a producer-consumer interaction, also called fire-and-forget interaction. After an invocation of the consumer, the producer resumes its execution immediately (and is not suspended). Producers do not expect results from the consumers. As a consequence, both producer and consumer run in parallel and fully concurrently.

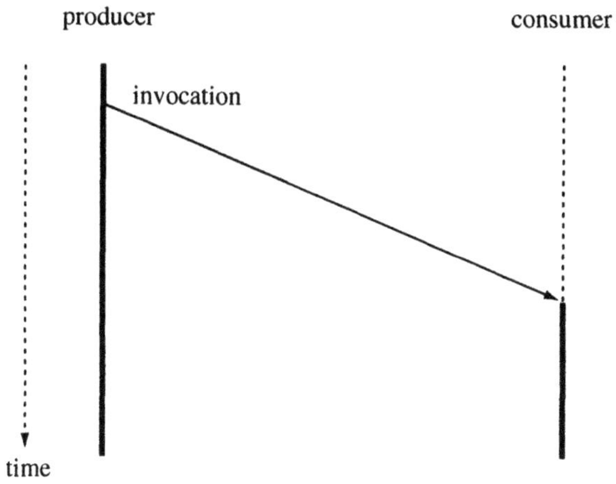

Fig. 1.11. Producer-consumer interaction

Using multicast, an invocation can be submitted to multiple consumers at the same time. A special case is the so-called pipe mechanism where, in analogy to pipes in Unix, a consumer reads from a pipe (some sort of shared data space, realized, for instance, as an ordinary file), whereas a producer writes onto the pipe. If the pipe is empty, consumers cannot perform a read operation. If a pipe is not realized as an ordinary file, the pipe could be set up with a maximal buffer capacity. In this case, if the pipe is full, producers cannot perform a write operation. When limiting the buffer capacity of a pipe to a single message, synchronization and sequentialization are easy to achieve between the concurrently running producers and consumers.

1.4 Client-Server Model

We can see a trend in system software design to provide needed functionality by means of user processes. The client-server model together with its applications support this trend. A good example is the operating system Mach that displaces functionality from the system kernel to user processes (Acetta et al. 1986).

The client-server model implements a sort of handshaking principle, i.e., a client invokes a server operation, suspends operation (in most of the implementations), and resumes work once the server has fulfilled the requested service.

As shown in Fig. 1.12, the client suspends execution while the server tries to fulfil the requested service (note, however, that nonblocking implementations of the client-server model exist; see Sect. 1.3.2). In many cases the requested service does not produce a real result, e.g., a service operation that simply updates a database entry. In this case, the client-server model

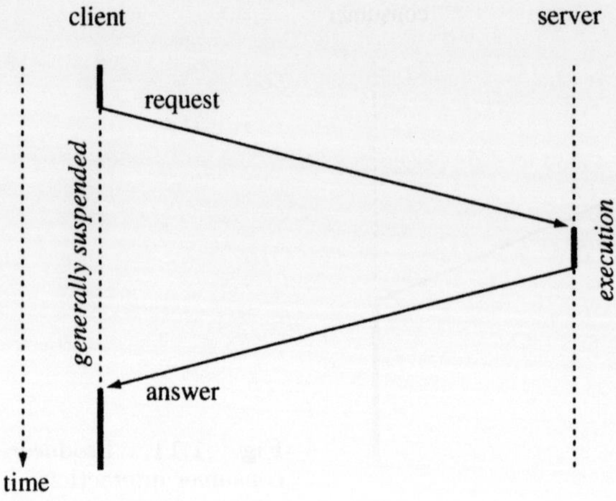

Fig. 1.12. Client-server model

allows for empty result messages (acknowledgments) to notify the client of a successful fulfillment of the service.

Centralized servers that manage access to shared resources in a distributed environment may become bottlenecks. Furthermore, centralized servers are also problematic, since server crashes result in an unavailability of the shared resources managed by these servers. Again, as we will see, replication techniques can ameliorate this disadvantage.

Setting up the interaction between a client and a server can be expensive. Therefore, most implementations of the client-server model choose a simple request-answer protocol, with the most famous instance known as remote procedure call (see also Sect. 1.5). The request-answer protocol is built on top of a transport layer. As widely used (lower layer) transport, we find either the user datagram protocol (UDP) or the transmission control protocol (TCP). Both protocols are members of the Internet protocol stacks.

In general, a transport protocol realizes the (peer-to-peer) transport of a message between two communicating processes. UDP is a connectionless transport protocol that neither supports flow control, guarantees correct sequencing of delivered messages, nor assures that all messages will be delivered. It should be clear that UDP works best for reliable networks, while for unreliable networks, UDP puts a lot of additional burden on protocols of the next higher levels. TCP, on the other hand, is a connection-oriented transport protocol where the two communicating processes are seen as connected in a virtual circuit. TCP supports flow control and other features needed for unreliable networks. For the interested reader, Tanenbaum (1996) gives an in-depth introduction to this topic of computer networks.

1.4.1 Terms and definitions

Most of this section is devoted to technical terms and their definitions. It should be clear to the reader by now that we have used so far technical terms at different levels of abstraction. Remember, for instance, the terms sender and receiver in the sense of pure message exchanging entities, or client and server in the sense of entities acting in some specialized protocol.

According to Svobodova (1984) it is worth while to distinguish between server and service. Thus, we now examine terms such as client, service, and server. Figure 1.13 shows the relationship between these three terms.

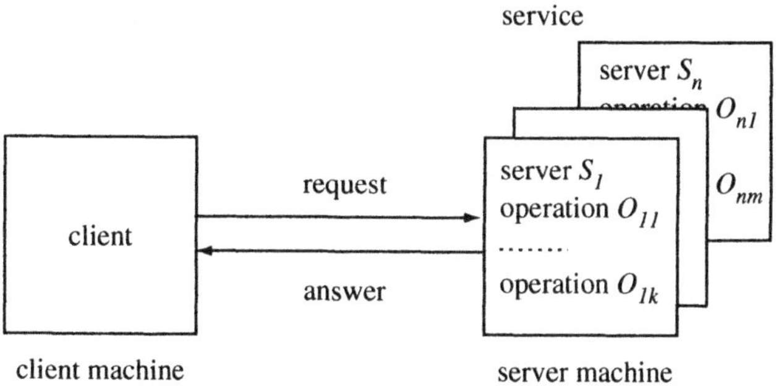

Fig. 1.13. Client, service and server

Definition 1.4.1 (Client). *A client is a process (some say, an application) that runs on a client machine and that typically initiates requests for service operations. Potential clients are a priori unknown. Rather, clients are user processes, and as such created, maintained, and killed dynamically.*

Definition 1.4.2 (Service). *A service is a piece of software that provides a well-defined set of services. This piece of software may run on one or multiple (server) machines.*

Definition 1.4.3 (Server). *A server is a subsystem that provides a particular service to a set of a priori unknown clients. A server executes a (piece of) service software on a particular server machine. Obviously, a single server machine can host multiple server subsystems. The services provided to the clients can also be handled through a combination of multiple servers. This situation implies a more complex interaction scheme and needs well-adapted protocols.*

The server subsystems can be realized as dedicated processes. Essentially, these permanently running dedicated processes execute the following loop, also called the server loop.

Code fragment (Server loop).
while true do
  wait until a service operation is requested by a client C;
  execute requested service operation;
  send(answer) **to** client C;

Typically, a client is embedded into an application. The client is mostly realized via library calls as shown in Fig. 1.14.

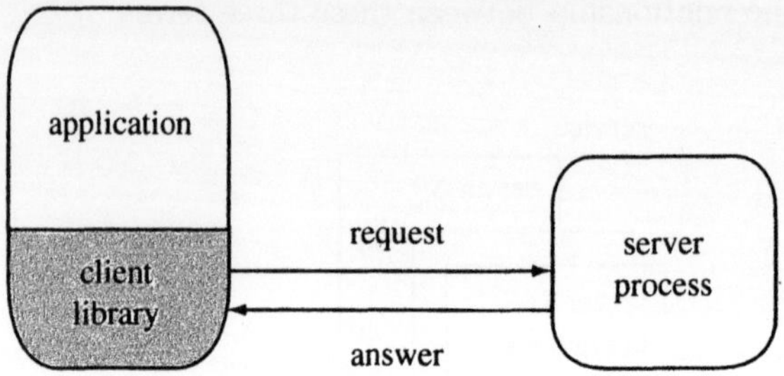

Fig. 1.14. Embedding a client into an application

As a rule, the client machine (e.g., workstation or laptop) and the server machine are separated. They communicate through either a local area network, a modem connection, or some other link. In the rare case of an identicalness of client and server machine, communication can be established as interprocess communication (IPC).

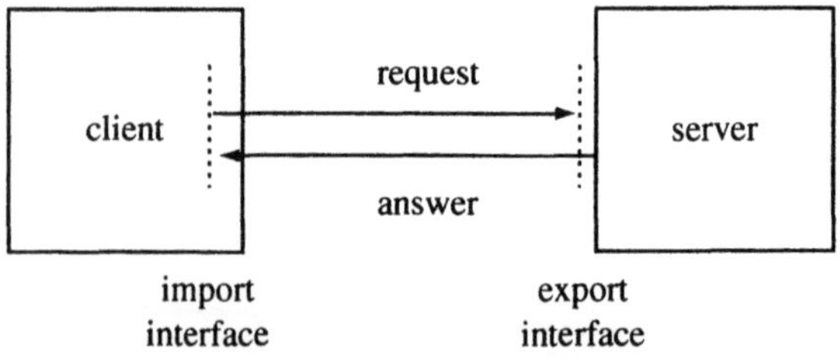

Fig. 1.15. Interface between client and server

Figure 1.15 sketches the interface between client and server. The client interface (i.e., the import interface) is responsible for representing the server within the client as well as for preparing the parameters (i.e., marshalling) and sending the request message to the server subsystem. Furthermore, it prepares the interpretation of the result that is extracted from the answer message submitted by the server (i.e., unmarshalling).

The server interface (i.e., the export interface) is responsible for representing all potential clients within the server. It accepts client requests for service operations, interprets the parameters, invokes the requested service operations, and finally, prepares (and sends) the answer message containing the result of the service operation.

1.4.2 Client-server communication

The logical foundation of the communication of the client-server model is seen as a many-to-many communication style, i.e., a client may communicate with many servers, and a server may communicate with many clients. It is quite common that this style of the many-to-many communication is split into (i) a many-to-one communication fragment for requests (here, many clients send requests to a particular server subsystem), (ii) a one-to-many communication fragment for answers (here, a particular server subsystem provides results to many clients), and (iii) a simple one-to-one communication fragment for further communication between an individual client and an individual server subsystem.

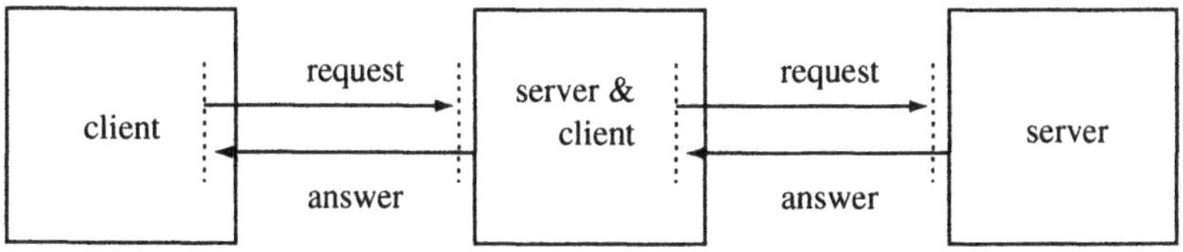

Fig. 1.16. Client and server as part of a single subsystem

Figure 1.16 should indicate that it is particularly easy to design a subsystem that is client and server at the same time.

In a client-server application, it is convenient to distinguish between the following three components: presentation, execution, and data storage (e.g., a database). The distinction between different implementation concepts of client-server applications comes from the location in which these components reside, i.e., either within the client or the server subsystems, or when dealing with distributed (and possibly replicated) components, within both client and server.

Table 1.2 illustrates the four possible cases. In case 1 the components presentation and execution are at the client site whereas the database resides at the server site. Access to the remote data storage can be achieved, for instance, through Sun's NFS. In case 2 the component execution (together with the database) is now held remotely at the server site. The component presentation either resides completely locally, or part of it resides remotely at the server site. A remote presentation allows, as in the X-window system, a presentation on a workstation that is not the workstation where the execution is currently running. The server site may already perform a sort of preparation of the presentation information. Returning to our example of the X-window system, we find ways to display the same information at different

Table 1.2. Concepts for client-server applications

Client	presentation execution	presentation	presentation	presentation execution	presentation execution (with local database)	presentation execution database
Server	database	presentation execution database	execution database	execution database	execution (with local database) database	database
	case 1	case 2	case 2	case 3	case 3	case 4

workstations at the same time. For data inputs, this variant needs a so-called pseudo-window server that sequentializes the different input streams (see also Fig. 3.17, p. 179). In case 3 we see a cooperative distributed execution among individual modules of an application. This cooperative distributed execution makes an application a distributed application. Here, besides distributing the execution component to the client and the server sites, the database could also be distributed. Finally, in case 4 this latter distribution of the database is the main focus. Possibly, the distribution could end up with a local and a remote replica of the entire database stored at the client and the server site respectively. If the entire database has been replicated, or even if just some relevant parts of the database have been replicated, updates concerning replicated data must then be propagated to both the client and the server site. This increases network traffic and makes the protocols more complex and more expensive, especially when replication transparency is desired.

1.4.3 Processing requests for service operations

Since clients and servers have different life spans, and since requests for service operations are not equally distributed among the clients, servers manage these requests in a queue. Queued requests are processed by the server either through a single dedicated server process or through cloning new server processes per request. The latter case can be implemented using a threading package, i.e., lightweight processes.

To further explain these ideas we shall briefly describe all three variants.

1. Figure 1.17 illustrates the first variant where a single dedicated server process is in charge of processing requests for service operations. This process continuously waits for request entries in the queue (compare also the server loop described earlier), and then processes them one by one. Since requests are processed in sequential order, this variant is not very efficient. This brings us back to a problem stated at the beginning of the discussion. Since there exist services that can only be handled through a

combination of multiple servers, the single dedicated server process may have to invoke other server subsystems to handle a particular request. In this case, the server process is suspended, no activity other than waiting for the answer of the invoked server subsystem is possible. Thus, the server can become a bottleneck. In addition, this variant also prohibits an interruption of the processing of the current request when a higher prioritized request appears in the queue. Very often, a pure sequential order is not what is needed. Instead, an ordering based on priorities of the requests together with an effective interrupt handling are necessary and are in fact seen in modern state of the art in client-server implementations.

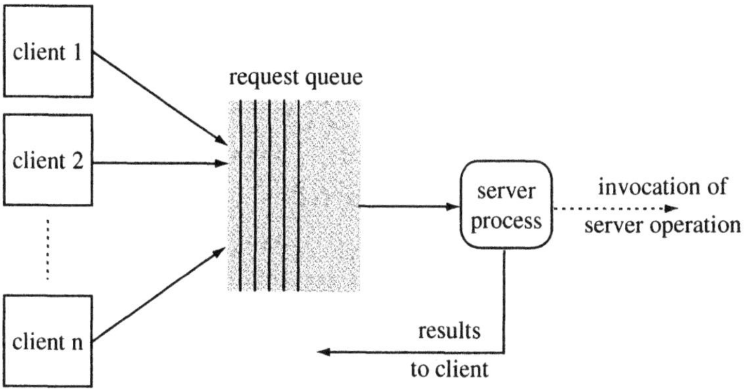

Fig. 1.17. Processing requests for service operations through a single dedicated server process

2. Figure 1.18 illustrates the second variant where every incoming request is handled by a new server process. Each of the cloned server processes runs in separate address spaces. After having answered the request, these processes are killed. A dispatcher waits for request entries in the queue and creates a new server process when necessary. Although this variant outperforms the first variant, it is still quite expensive. Furthermore, if accesses to shared persistent variables have to be synchronized, this variant may aggravate a parallel processing of multiple requests.
   To improve runtime efficiency, a so-called process pool can be initialized. A process pool is a set of processes that are created in advance. In the beginning these processes sleep. The number of processes created in advance depends on hardware properties, especially on main memory. If a new request arrives in the queue, a sleeping process is assigned to this request, until there are no more sleeping processes in the pool. If all sleeping processes have been used up, new processes are cloned and put into the pool. Some finagling is needed to avoid an inflation of process clones. The main advantage of preinitializing a process pool lies in the

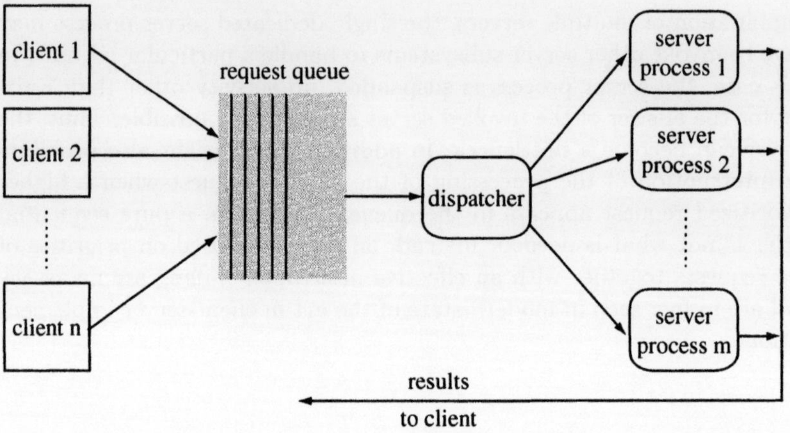

Fig. 1.18. Processing requests for service operations through cloning of server processes

start-up phase. Process creation is costly and time-consuming. It is by far faster to set a sleeping process running than to create a new process on demand. This improvement of runtime efficiency has the disadvantage that is consumes more space within the main memory.

3. In the third variant, every incoming request is handled by a new lightweight process. This variant has been successfully demonstrated in the distributed operating system Mach. Compared to the previous variants, accesses to shared persistent variables can be synchronized more easily. As a consequence, lightweight processes may allow for a very fine-grain parallelism.

Lightweight processes (threads) possess the following advantages. They run in the same address space, need less state information (e.g., process stack and program counter), and allow for a lighter and faster scheduling. Due to the shared address space, lightweight processes may share variables. Every lightweight process can be seen as a single sequence of control. Parallel sequences of control bring about real parallelism when executed on multiprocessor hardware.

File service. A file service provides (remote) centralized data storage facilities to clients distributed among a network. The most important service operations include the following. The operation **read***(file, displacement, nbytes)* returns a data block of a given number of bytes from a given file starting at a given position. In analogy, the operation **write***(file, displacement, data block, nbytes)* writes a given data block of a given number of bytes to a given file starting at a given position. The operation **length***(file)* returns the length (typically, given as the number of bytes) of a given file. The operation **create***(name)* creates a file under a given name, whereas the operation

delete*(file)* deletes a given file. The operations **write**, **create** and **delete** do not return result data. Instead they return an acknowledgment.

When location transparency is provided, the parameter *file* is mapped (using a name service) to the correct file server and the correct file system on this server.

States of a server subsystem. Within the different classes of server subsystems, Corbin (1991) differentiates between stateless and state-dependent subsystems.

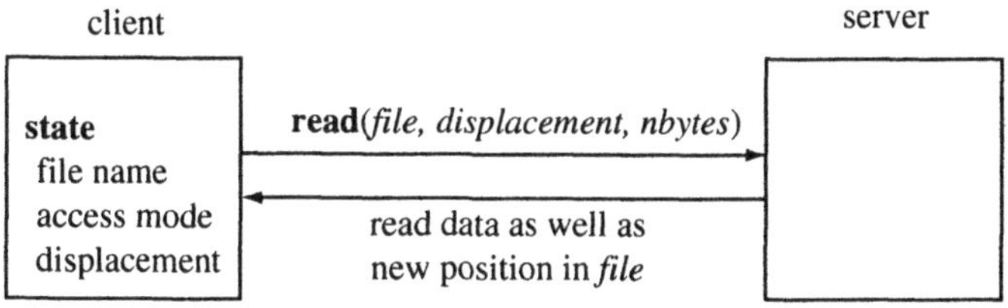

Fig. 1.19. Stateless server subsystems

As shown in Fig. 1.19, stateless server subsystems do not manage any state information about their clients. Since each client request is self-contained and no state information can be lost, a crashed server can be restarted without dealing with state reinstallments. However, communication is less efficient because each client request needs additional parameters such as the file name or the displacement, i.e., the position within the file where a read or a write service operation should take place. Programming at the client site becomes more complex.

A familiar example of a stateless file server subsystem is Sun's NFS.

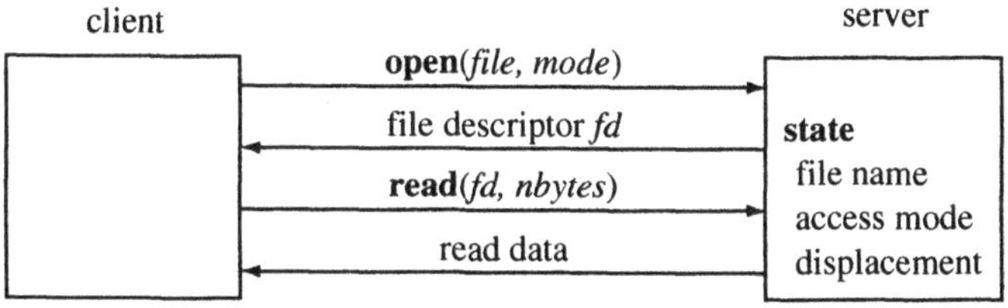

Fig. 1.20. State-dependent server subsystems

As shown in Fig. 1.20, state-dependent server subsystems manage state information about their clients. As a consequence, programming at the client site becomes less complex. Most state-dependent (file) server subsystems provide an additional service operation, namely the operation **open***(file, mode)*. This operation opens a file either in mode read or write, and returns a file descriptor (in our example, the file descriptor is coded as fd). Communication is more efficient because parameters such as file name and mode need only be communicated once, when opening the file. Displacement information is kept at the server site, i.e., a client simply requests the service operation **read** *(fd, nbytes)* and the server subsystems then know which data blocks have already been read. Obviously, programming at the server site is now more complex. What would happen, for example, should a client crash? In this case, the server subsystem would detect these orphan requests and the corresponding invalid state information of the crashed client.

Name service. A name service, also called a directory service, provides (remote) centralized name management facilities to clients distributed among a network. We have already mentioned the advantage of a name service for location transparent accesses. But what are these names that are managed by a name service? Names refer to certain objects in the network such as files, server subsystems, services, workstations, devices (e.g., printers and scanners), and users.

An example for the management of login information about users (e.g., passwords) is Sun's Yellow-Pages server.

A name service is needed in a wide variety of distributed applications, such as when searching for a particular service provided somewhere in the network.[6] For this reason, server subsystems usually register their export interface at a name server. Clients can thus easily find out about the right server or servers for a particular service request. If the name service knows more than one server subsystem, a client may decide on one based on criteria such as proximity, quality of service, or costs. As an example, let the requested service be the printing of a file. If the name service knows a nearby black-and-white printer for A4 with 300dpi, and a color printer for A4 and A3 with 1200dpi in an office across the street, the client may choose the right one according to her needs.

In a nutshell, name servers manage a list of names. Such a directory entry might be stored in a data structure as given below:

Code fragment (Directory entry).

```
class directory_entry
    name                  /* Name of the object as parameterized in a client
                             request.                                        */
    address               /* Address of the object within the network, e.g.,
                             host number concatenated with communication
                             port number.                                    */
    access_information    /* This access information may limit access to the
                             object for particular clients.                  */
    attributes            /* Additional attributes of the object.            */
```

[6] In the context of object-oriented systems we speak of so-called object servers. A object server manages, just like a name server, objects, their location, and meta information about them.

operations /* Operations that can be applied to directory entries, e.g., **insert, delete, update, read.** */

Time service. A time service provides a synchronized system-wide time for all nodes in the network. This is a good example of a case in which a server becomes a client of another server. A file server, for instance, may become a client requesting a time service in order to create correct timestamps for file accesses.

Other services. It is fairly universally recognized that distributed applications require the above discussed fundamental services such as file, name, or time services. For CSCW applications, however, more specific services are necessary. Some of the most prominent services of this kind include Web-based brokering services, services for shared workspaces, services for joint or group authoring, workflow management services, agent-based services for user communities, or (group) document management services. These services serve as the foundation for some of the most interesting classes of CSCW applications. We will dedicate individual chapters of this book to these classes of CSCW applications. As an example for agent-based services for user communities, suppose that members of a particular community provide a user profile where they state what interests, preferences, and past experiences they have. The user profile can then be exploited by a set of service operations. One of the service operations may determine other users in the community sharing the same profile, or more precisely, having good correlation with the requester's profile. The Firefly system, which will be described in a later chapter, was one of the most successful systems to provide such a service. The success of Firefly and the overall importance of groupware of its kind were demonstrated by the recent purchase of Firefly by Microsoft, and by the fact that other well known companies have announced products and services in this domain of recommender systems.

1.5 Remote Procedure Call (RPC)

A remote procedure call (RPC) is a generalization of the standard procedure call as provided in many higher programming languages such as Ada, C, or Pascal. An RPC is syntactically as well as semantically embedded into a programming language.

Birrell and Nelson (1984) define an RPC as a synchronous flow of control and data passing scheme achieved through procedure calls between processes running in separate address spaces where the needed communication is via "small" channels (e.g., a local area network). They were called small channels in contrast to local interprocess communication facilities which were, at the time of the RPC invention, orders of magnitude broader in bandwidth than networked communication channels.

The beauty and the main success of an RPC lies in the fact that neither the client nor the server assume that the procedure call is performed over a network, i.e., that messages and fancy protocols are involved. Both of them just execute a standard procedure call. Before we will discuss how this is achieved, let us look again at the way the RPC works from the outside. The flow of control as well as the data passing scheme are synchronous, i.e., the client – after having called the procedure – suspends execution, and waits for the procedure, in reality for the server, to return the result. To avoid endless blocking phases due to the crashing of servers or to the unreliability of networks, timers are set. Timeouts free the suspended clients and allow them to react properly with regard to these kinds of problems.

Figure 1.21 shows a temporal sketch of an RPC.

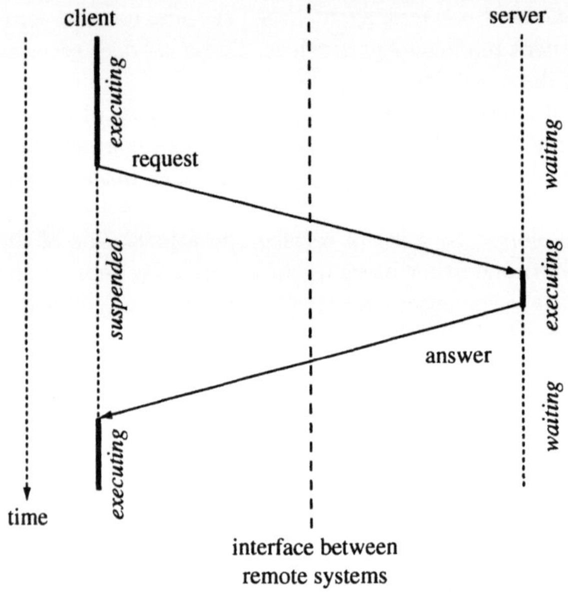

Fig. 1.21. Temporal sketch of an RPC

Seen from the outside, the main domains of difference between an RPC and a local procedure call are: address space, runtime environment, and life span. In an RPC, client and server do not share address spaces, do not possess a common runtime environment, and have different life spans. Not having shared address spaces – and not assuming network-wide unique memory addresses – an RPC cannot provide access to shared global data. As a rule, the call-by-reference parameter-passing scheme is not realistic. Not having a common runtime environment can prohibit access to shared variables. Having different life spans causes problems for the provided call semantics. Tay and Ananda (1990) thoroughly discuss this topic.

1.5.1 RPC properties

For an application programmer, local and remote procedure calls can be coded in the same way. Type-checking of parameters and results occurs during the compilation phases. If the communication between clients and servers were achieved through the low-level primitives **send** and **receive** type-checking would not be as easily achieved. An RPC frees an application programmer from packaging the parameters into a message. Unfortunately, an RPC does not support all parameter-passing schemes. While traditional local procedure calls apply parameter-passing schemes such as call-by-value and call-by-reference, the latter is not realistic for remote procedure calls. A way to bypass this limitation is through the so-called call-by-copy/restore scheme, i.e., a relevant data structure is copied from the client's address space to the server's address space, then manipulated at the server site, and finally copied back to the client's address space.

Although most RPC implementations are synchronous (i.e., the client suspends execution until the server has fulfilled and acknowledged the requested service), asynchronous RPC implementations are possible. An asynchronous RPC (see also asynchronous message exchange, p. 13) complicates the call-by-copy/restore scheme because some threads of control at the nonblocked client site during this time lapse may have accessed and updated the copied data structure. Due to the asynchrony, consistency becomes a real issue. We will discuss asynchronous RPCs in Sect. 1.5.3.

RPC and OSI. Remote procedure calls provide an ideal layer to implement distributed applications based on the client-server model. In the following, we will discuss this RPC layer in terms of the ISO reference model for an open systems interconnection (OSI).

The request-answer protocol, as introduced in Sect. 1.3.3, can be assigned to OSI-layer 5, also called the session layer. An RPC realizes a transparent view of data and data structures. Therefore, we can assign RPCs to OSI-layer 6, also called presentation layer. On top of the presentation layer resides the application layer (OSI-layer 7) to which we can assign the client-server model. We have already discussed some of the protocols that fit into OSI-layer 4, also called the transport layer, namely the transport protocols UDP and TCP.

Table 1.3 summarizes this layering.

Table 1.3. RPC and OSI

OSI-layer 7	(application layer)	client-server model
OSI-layer 6	(presentation layer)	RPC
OSI-layer 5	(session layer)	message exchange e.g., request-answer protocol
OSI-layer 4	(transport layer)	transport protocols e.g., TCP, UDP, or OSI TP4

Structure of RPC messages. In this section we will describe RPCs from the inside. We will see how the beauty and the main success of RPCs are achieved, namely due to the fact that neither the client nor the server assume that the procedure call is performed over a network rather than locally. Our description draws upon Sun's RPC protocol (Corbin 1991).

Code fragment (Structure of an RPC request message).

```
typedef operation = struct    /* Defines the requested service operation. */
    int ProgramNumber;
    int VersionNumber;
    int ProcedureNumber;

typedef source = struct
    struct reference =
        string Host;
        string UserName;
        string UserGroup;
                              /* Here we mean the name of the user who owns the
                                 client program, and the group this user belongs
                                 to – user groups are defined along the lines of the
                                 Unix pendants.                                  */
        key Verifier;         /* DES-authentication based on the encryption of
                                 the current time.                               */

typedef request = struct
    int Identifier;           /* The identifier created by the client will be used to
                                 map answers to the corresponding request, and to
                                 detect duplicates.                              */
    int Version;              /* Identifies the version of the RPC protocol used –
                                 a server may support different protocol versions
                                 at the same time.                               */
    operation RequestedServiceOperation;
    source Client;            /* Specifies the client.                           */
    list of unspecified ParameterList;
                              /* Arguments for the remote service operation.     */
```

Service operations may or may not be successful. This is independent of failures in lower layers which are handled elsewhere. We must therefore distinguish between two kinds of answers, one for the successful and one for the unsuccessful case. A success depends on the used RPC library and on the requested service operation. The server checks whether the request violates the specified RPC protocol. If the request as such can be accepted by the server, but the parameter list contains faulty arguments, the requested service operation cannot be fulfilled and the result is an error message. To accommodate both cases, the structure of an answer looks as follows:

Code fragment (Structure of an RPC answer message).

```
typedef answer = struct
   int Identifier;
   status AnswerStatus;
   source Server;             /* This is used to authenticate the server – only the
                                 field verifier is set.                           */
   list of unspecified ResultList;
                              /* The result list may contain the status of the exe-
                                 cuted service operation.                         */
```

Distributed applications based on remote procedure calls. We now examine what is needed to implement distributed applications based on remote procedure calls. Let us briefly look at the standard (local) case first. Let a local application consist of the source files client.c, server.c, and the corresponding header file ms.h. Then, in a traditional Unix environment, we would build the application by compiling both sources (using the header file) and linking them into a main program. Figure 1.22 illustrates this approach.

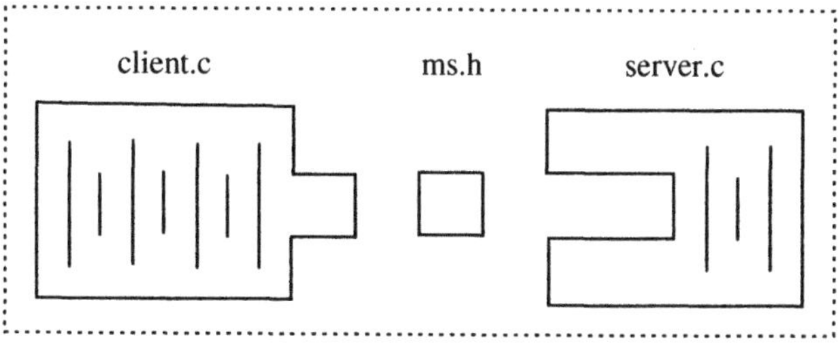

Fig. 1.22. Building of a traditional application

Obviously, a distributed application needs additional code to support the necessary communication facilities between clients and servers. In order to isolate the communication idiosyncrasy of RPCs and to make the network interfaces transparent to the application programmer, so-called stubs are introduced. Figure 1.23 shows the usage of stubs within a distributed application.

For the application program, an RPC appears local. The stub at the client site (client stub) contains a proxy definition for each (remote) service operation provided by a set of servers. A proxy definition contains the operation definition only (e.g., types and number of parameters); the executable code of the operation resides completely at the server. The stub at the server site (server stub) contains a proxy invocation of the service operation implemented locally.

Both stubs also convert the argument values of the parameters and the results from and to their local representation formats. For these internal and external representation swaps, the stubs use data conversion procedures and

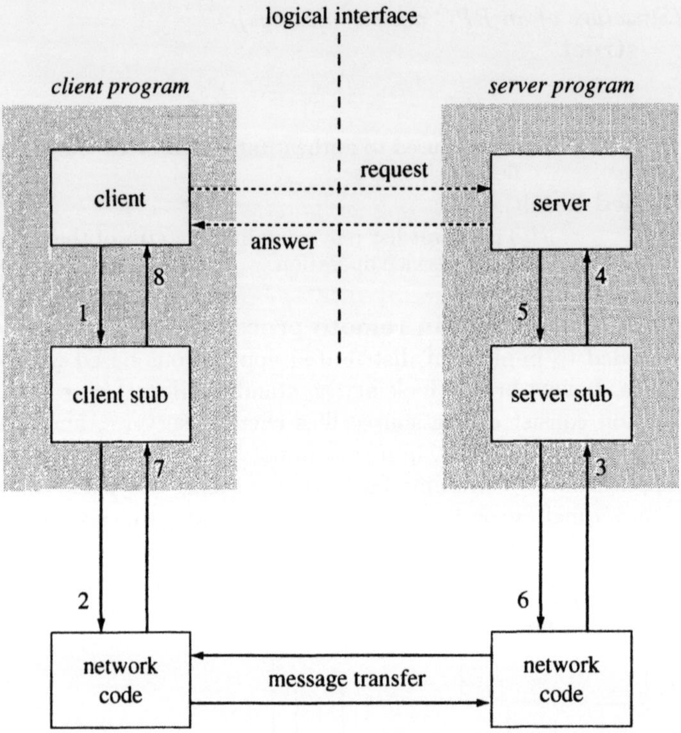

Fig. 1.23. Usage of stubs within a distributed application

filter functions. In this context, the client stub is responsible for specifying the requested service operation, for assigning the call to the correct server, and for preparing the parameters in the transmission format. Moreover, the client stub also handles answers sent to the client, i.e., it decodes the result values and provides them in the format understood by the client application.

The server stub, on the other hand, is responsible for decoding the argument values sent as part of the request, for finding the call address of the corresponding service operation (e.g., through a table lookup), and for calling the service operation with parameters set in the correct local format. Moreover, the server stub also handles the answer provided by the service operation (i.e., it prepares the result values in the transmission format, checks for the correct client address, and ships the answer). Routing of messages and retransmissions of lost messages are out of the scope of the stub functionality. These issues are handled in the lower layers.

A manual implementation of stubs and of their interfaces to the network is quite error-prone. Therefore, the interfaces between clients and servers should be coded automatically when a declarative specification is given. A so-called RPC generator (Corbin 1991, Lyons 1991) supports the application programmer in this task. In Fig. 1.24, let the file ms.idl contain the specification for the client and server interfaces.

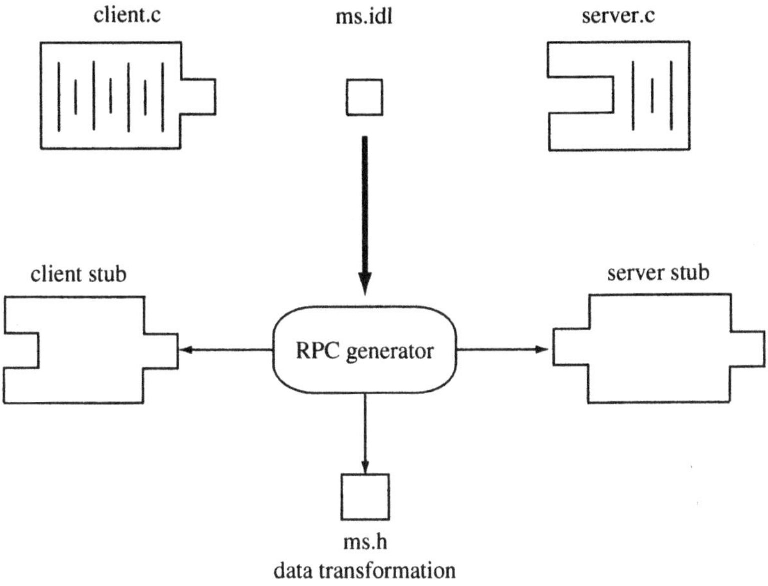

Fig. 1.24. RPC generator

Specifications for the client and server interfaces as required by the RPC generator are easier to create and to adapt and are, therefore, less error-prone than manual coding of the full interface codes. An RPC generator dramatically reduces the effort needed to implement and maintain a distributed application. Figures 1.25 and 1.26 illustrate the building and the internal structure of a distributed application created using an RPC generator.

RPC language. Let us now look at the declarative language used to specify the interfaces between clients and servers. Examples of such languages include NIDL by Hewlett Packard (Lyons 1991) and RPCL by Sun (Corbin 1991). The interface specifications coded with RPC languages such as NIDL or RPCL allow the RPC generator to create stubs and filters automatically.

Among other things, an RPC language applies attributes to identify the version of the RPC protocol and to find out the fixed port number used to communicate with the server subsystem. If the client knows the fixed port number, it can use the number to open a communication with the server subsystem without having to involve a so-called mediator, also known as a broker subsystem. If two or more server subsystems running on the same server share the same port number, port conflicts may occur. A way out of this dilemma is to assign separate fixed port numbers to the different service

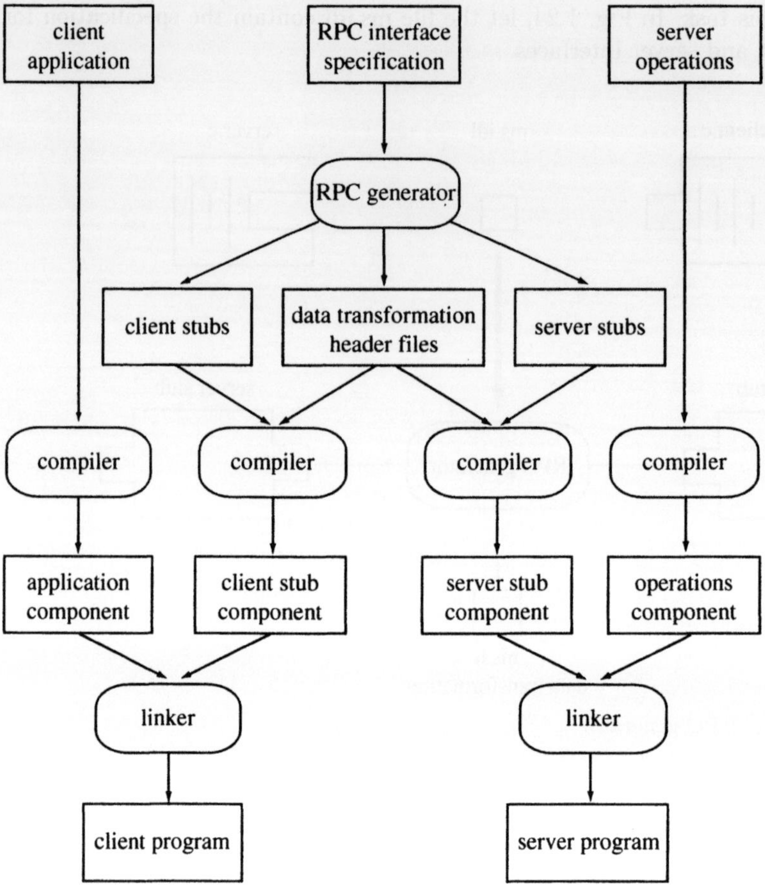

Fig. 1.25. Building of a distributed application using an RPC generator

operations provided by the afflicted server subsystems. Another possibility takes advantage of the flexibility offered by a broker subsystem. In analogy to a name service, servers register their port numbers at the broker subsystem where potential clients can ask for a particular port number on demand. This kind of dynamic mediation via broker subsystems is highly flexible. Dynamic adaptations of port numbers can easily be achieved. Broker subsystems and their services offered will also play an important role when we discuss agent-based CSCW applications in Chapter 9.

Phases of RPC-based distributed application. The entire process of building an application based on remote procedure calls can be split into three phases, namely realization, binding, and execution.

In the phase realization, all modules – i.e., the building blocks for the application at the client and the server site – are programmed as if they were linked into a single program. Using the specification of the client and server

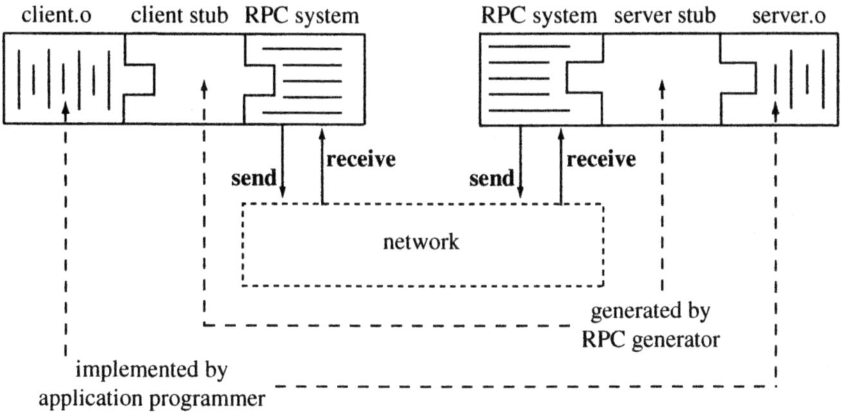

Fig. 1.26. Internal structure of a distributed application created using an RPC generator

interfaces, data filters as well as the stubs for client and server are generated automatically. Then, both client and server programs are created.

In the phase binding, the mapping of both programs is achieved. Note, however, that the binding phase has nothing to do with the linker as described earlier in Fig. 1.25. Here, we simply mean binding of the components of the distributed application, e.g., the assignment of the client to a server program. The server makes its operations public (i.e., it exports its interface). In turn, the client imports this server interface. This assignment of the client to a server by means of exporting and importing interfaces (essentially, assigning the server address) is known as binding. Remember that a server address, or more precisely, the address of the service operation of a server subsystem, may be expressed as a host address and a port number. To simplify the description, in the following we shall simply speak of a server address.

Binding can be static, semistatic, or dynamic.

- Static binding takes place when the client program is generated. In this case, the server address is hard-coded within the client program. Migrating servers or servers that have to change their address for some other reason require a new generation of the client program to update the server address. Static binding is simple but less flexible than the other types of binding.
- When semistatic binding is utilized, the client determines the server address during the initialization of the client execution. The server address remains unchanged within the client code for the whole life span of the client process. As in the case of static binding, problems are caused by migrating servers or servers that have to change their address for some other reason. A restart of the client program is necessary in these cases. But how do clients determine the server address in the first place? Again, a name service or a brokering service is the answer. A client either explicitly

requests the server address from a name service, or it charges a broker with the task of providing the server address. The broker subsystem may then use, for instance, a name service itself to get the requested server address. In other words, the broker subsystem implicitly acts as a mediator between a client, a server, and as in the description above, a name server.
- The most flexible case is dynamic binding. Here, the server address is determined immediately before an RPC is performed. As in the case of semistatic binding, name or brokering services can be exploited. Migrating servers or servers that have to change their address for some other reason do not harm the client. During the life span of the client, server addresses may be bound several times without influencing the correct behavior of the client.

In the phase execution (i.e., when requesting service operations), stubs provide a call semantics based on structured communication between two peer processes. Moreover, data representations for parameters and result arguments are homogenized.

1.5.2 Mediation and brokering

The following discussion assumes a distributed application based on the client-server model which uses an RPC mechanism to implement the interaction between the components. As we have seen already, a broker subsystem implicitly acts as a mediator between a client and a server, and possibly other server subsystems. Well-known frameworks establishing broker subsystems are NCA (Lyons 1991) and ODP. In ODP the broker subsystem is also called a trading system (see Sect. 1.7.3).

Figure 1.27 illustrates how a broker subsystem can be embedded into a client-server interaction.

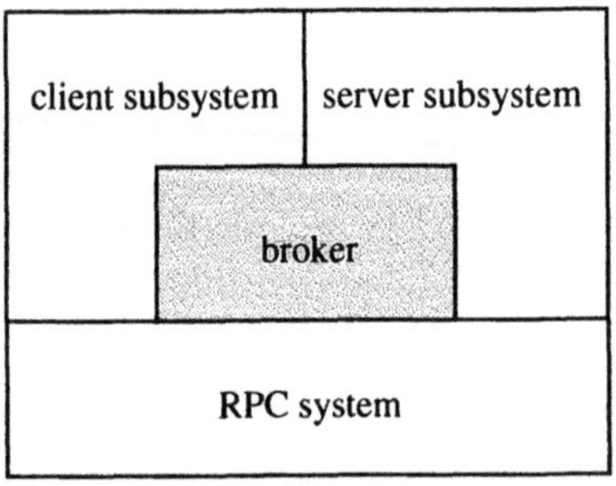

Fig. 1.27. Embedding a broker subsystem into a client-server interaction

A distributed system may contain multiple broker subsystems where each individual broker subsystems manages a particular domain. To achieve the task a broker has been charged with (e.g., localizing a server address), communication among several broker subsystems could be necessary. In this case, we get a quite complicated scheme of interaction. Figure 1.28 shows how a set of broker subsystems manage the export of server and the import of client interfaces.

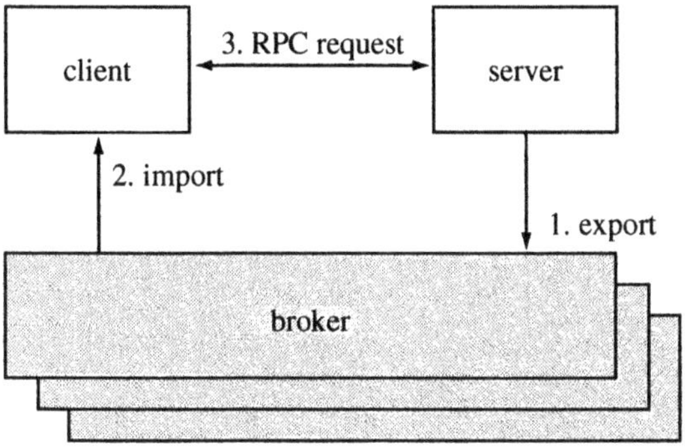

Fig. 1.28. Export and import via broker subsystems

When the broker subsystem has provided the server address to the client, client and selected server can communicate directly through remote procedure calls. This situation is depicted in Step 3 of Fig. 1.28. Alternatively, client and server may not communicate directly. Instead, they may interact through the mediation of the broker subsystem or through a sequence of broker subsystems where appropriate (i.e., the client sends the request to the broker subsystem, and the broker subsystems transmits the request to the selected server, then waits for the answer from the server, and finally, ships the result to the requesting client).

Until recently, in most of the available implementations of broker subsystems, managing export interfaces simply meant managing server addresses via so-called white pages. Essentially, this was a bookkeeping of names. Other more interesting attributes such as behavioral or functional attributes, or quality and cost of the services provided played a minor role. Of true benefit to any broker subsystem would be services managed in so-called yellow pages. For today's world wide web which is mostly driven by e-commerce activities, this kind of improvement in the brokerage quality is becoming increasingly in demand.

1.5.3 Asynchronous RPC

Most RPC protocols are synchronous, i.e., client and server are synchronized and their execution becomes sequentialized. When we look back at the producer-consumer interaction (see Sect. 1.3.4) where a producer does not expect results from the consumer,[7] we see a method of interaction which is

---

[7] This is why this style of interaction is also called fire-and-forget interaction.

particularly easy to achieve with asynchronous RPCs. If we want to generalize this to the full request-answer protocol where a client obviously expects an answer message, we have to solve the problem of asynchrony. This becomes even more complicated when the server sends the results in portions, wrapped up in several answer messages. To cover this situation in an asynchronous RPC, the portions are stored for further usage in an appropriate data structure. In the distributed operating system of Cronus, this data structure is called Futures (Dean et al. 1987). Figure 1.29 illustrates the usage of Futures in an asynchronous RPC.

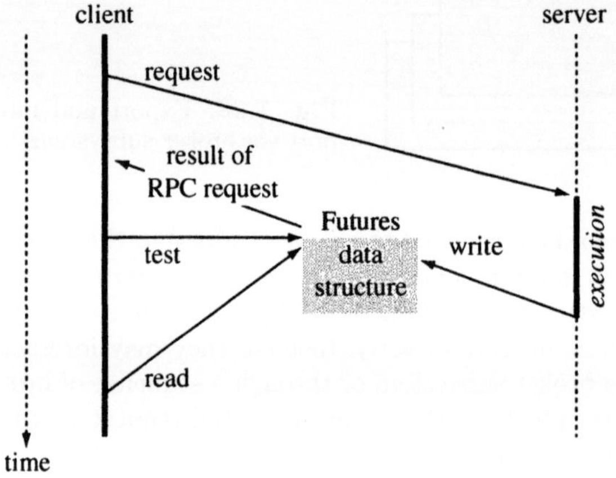

Fig. 1.29. Usage of Futures in an asynchronous RPC

In an asynchronous RPC, the process of providing a result starts with the creation of an empty Futures data structure.

Valid operations on Futures are **test**, **read**, and **write**. With the operation **test**, the client checks whether results of the request have already been inserted into the Futures data structure. Testing exists with and without busy-waiting. With the operation **write**, the server subsystem implicitly (i.e., through the underlying RPC system) inserts the results into the Futures data structure. With the operation **read**, the client reads the results from the Futures data structure. Reading can have two forms, one where a **read** reads the whole data structure (i.e., all results of the request), and one where only portions of the results are read individually. The latter form is interesting when server subsystems provide partial answers only. When implementing the Futures as a cyclic buffer, we could even imagine that server subsystems inserts data continuously into this data structure, i.e., server subsystems provide answer streams. Answer streams are particularly appropriate when results provided by a server are time-dependent and continuously changing. Consider, for instance, a server subsystem that provides the latest stock exchange rates, the current temperature, etc. This approach is quite popular for filtering agents which are discussed elsewhere (Chapter 9).

A set of Futures is called FutureSet. This data structure can store the results of multiple parallel asynchronous RPCs. FutureSet supports the same operations as Futures (i.e., **test**, **read**, and **write**). In FutureSet, result arguments or result elements can be read individually and in any order. Depending on the client's needs, testing can be applied to any Future.

Synchronous vs. asynchronous RPC. A comparison of synchronous and asynchronous remote procedure calls reveals an advantage for the synchronous case as far as better comprehensibility, simpler semantics, simplified failure notifications, and omission of data structures for buffering (e.g., Futures or FutureSet) are concerned. Better comprehensibility for the application programmer follows from the fact that a (synchronous) RPC can be seen as a smooth generalization of the local procedure call. Simpler semantics and simplified failure notifications follows from the blocking of the client until the server subsystem answers, either successfully or unsuccessfully. In any case, the client is prepared to receive the answer at any time, and ready to process the embedded results (or the embedded failure notification) appropriately. In contrast to an asynchronous RPC where several requests can be submitted in a row, in the synchronous case there is at most a single pending request. This simplifies failure notification. Complicated mapping of failure notifications to sent requests is needless. In contrast to an asynchronous RPC in the synchronous case we do not need to answer the following question. After having processed the failure, should we continue the client process right after the code position where the failed request was sent, or at the code position where the client was interrupted when notified of the failure? In a synchronous RPC, both code positions coincide. Since clients have no need to buffer data (as said above, there is at most a single pending request), a data structure for buffering can be omitted in the synchronous case.

The asynchronous RPC is advantageous as far as increased throughput and potential parallelism of client and server are concerned. An asynchronous RPC is, furthermore, a more powerful programming instrument. For instance, we can easily emulate synchronous RPCs through asynchronous RPCs.

1.5.4 Failure semantics of remote procedure calls

Let us now look in more detail at the failure semantics of remote procedure calls. The following failures may impair correct processing of an RPC:

- If the target server machine is unavailable – either because the server no longer exists, has crashed, or simply because the network is congested – then this type of failure will be handled in the transport protocol. Alternatively, the application programmer may have provided an exception handler for this case. The disadvantage is that some programming languages (e.g., Pascal) have no adequate language constructs for coding such an exception handler. Furthermore, implementing exception handlers may destroy the transparency of an RPC when compared with that of a the local procedure call.

- Another rather harmless failure occurs when the requested service operation is no longer supported by the target server subsystem. This failure can be handled through the RPC runtime system. Since nothing is executed, inconsistent states cannot turn up. A possible solution is to charge a broker subsystem to find other alternative interfaces for the requested service operation.
- A more uncomfortable failure may occur when either the client or the server machine crash while processing an RPC.
  If the server machine crashes before the request can be handled, the behavior from the client's point of view is identical to the case where the selected server subsystem is unavailable (see above). If the server machine crashes while the relevant server subsystem is in the middle of processing a request for a service operation, the situation becomes more problematic. Here we have to distinguish between a crash (i) before the server subsystem has produced some results (and, possibly, some side-effects), and a crash (ii) after the server subsystem has produced some results (and, possibly, some side-effects), but still before these results could be sent to the requesting client. In the latter case, the RPC system should detect this failure and notify the client about it, whereas in the former case, a repeatedly sent request could be a solution. If a timeout at the client site occurs, the request is sent once more. However, the requested service operation should be either idempotent, or the duplicated request should somehow be identifiable at the server site.
  If the client machine crashes after the request for a service operation has been sent, the server subsystem processes an orphan request. Ideally, the server should neither waste processing time for this orphan request nor send results to a crashed client machine. In practice, however, the server will detect the break down of the client through a timeout while waiting for the acknowledgement of the sent results. When the client machine recovers, the client could either try to cancel the pending request (here, it needs some information about the status of the sent request on stable storage), or reincarnate itself – a even more difficult undertaking. A more practical approach is to equip each request with an expiration date. If the server subsystem is not able to contact the client before the processed request expires, it may forget about the results delivery and may redo all side-effects.
- Finally, failure may occur due to message losses. The request message as well as the answer message can be lost. In both cases, timers can provide an adequate solution to handle these failures. In the first case (loss of the request message) a timeout at the client site triggers a repeatedly sent request. Since nothing has happened at the server site, this case is innocuous. In the second case (loss of the answer message), a timeout at the client site

triggers again a repeatedly sent request. But this time, the server subsystem has already processed this request. If the requested service operation is not idempotent, then problems arise when the duplicated request is not detected and ignored. Some solutions to this problem were already discussed in the context of the exactly-once semantics in Sect. 1.3.3.

1.6 Object-Oriented Distributed Systems

The central motivations for the intensified utilization of object-oriented programming include the increased complexity of software systems, and at the same time, the increased wish for reusability of the software modules. Since distributed systems are extremely complex (e.g., due to inherent concurrency), object-orientation presents itself as an ideal programming methodology for distributed applications.

Another important aspect is encapsulation of data and operations. Objects are a means for better structuring of data and operations as well as for providing a uniform technique for operation invocation based on message-passing. The latter facilitates the splitting into and the distribution of the components of a distributed application. Each component may then consist of a set of objects that communicate with each other through message-passing.

Object-orientation has so far played a minor role in programming distributed applications (at least until the mid 1990's – we will see exceptions to that in later chapters). The major application classes where we could find successful impacts of object-oriented programming include distributed operating systems, and distributed runtime systems including an object-oriented programming language. Well known examples for the first class are Amoeba (Tanenbaum et al. 1991) and Apertos (Yokote 1992). In the second class we find, among others, Argus (Liskov 1988), Emerald (Raj et al. 1991), and Linda (Gelernter 1985). The Java idea could revolutionize the design, the programming, and most importantly, the acceptance of ubiquitous distributed applications in the years to come. This is especially true for CSCW applications. Today, groupware based on the Java idea may considerably improve the ad hoc building of user communities, and may help to form user groups and project teams across organizational boundaries.

1.6.1 Definitions

In the relevant literature, we find terms such as object, class, method, and inheritance. In the following, we will discuss and define these terms in more detail.

Definition 1.6.1 (Object). *An object represents an individual identifiable entity that either exists in the real world or is only abstractly defined. In any case, the object plays a well-defined role in the problem area in question.*

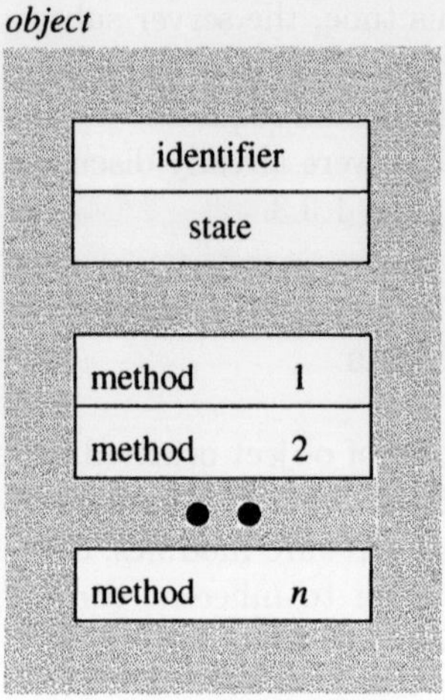

Fig. 1.30. Structure of an object

Figure 1.30 illustrates the structure of an object. It consists of an identifier, a state, and a behavior. The behavior of an object specifies how an object behaves, and how it reacts with regard to state transitions and requests from other objects. The behavior is fully defined through the set of methods provided by the object. Methods can be compared to procedures or service operations the object is able to provide.

The property that allows us to distinguish one particular object from another is called the object identity. The identifier of an object can take one of the following forms: An approach initializes the identifier once and for all, i.e., the object gets a unique identifier assigned that will not change during the entire life span of the object. Another approach makes use of the storage address where the object resides. Problematic is an object migration because this leads to a dynamic change of the identifier. It is by far more comfortable to let the user assign names to objects (logical identifier), and to let the system internally concatenate a physical identifier (e.g., host address and port number) in order to make the identifier unique across the network.

The state of an object contains the private data the object manages.

Definition 1.6.2 (Class). *A class is a set of objects that share a common structure and a common behavior.*

In all modern object-oriented languages, objects are instances of one or several classes. Typically, classes already exist during the time of compilation whereas objects are created, manipulated, and deleted at runtime. Figure 1.31 depicts the relationship between object and class.

Due to the construction of a class hierarchy, specialized (sub)classes may inherit data structures and methods from one or many of the (super)classes. The class hierarchy may also support polymorphism. Starting point here is an object variable of a more general class. An object of a more specialized

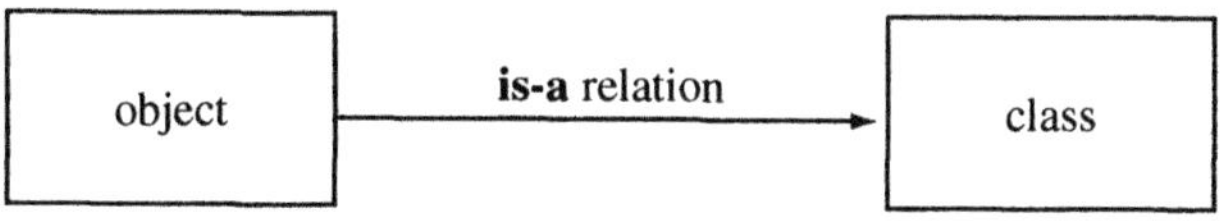

Fig. 1.31. Relationship between object and class

class may get assigned to this object variable. The object variable contains policies or procedures to check for class and type conformity.

Figure 1.32 shows an example of a class hierarchy.

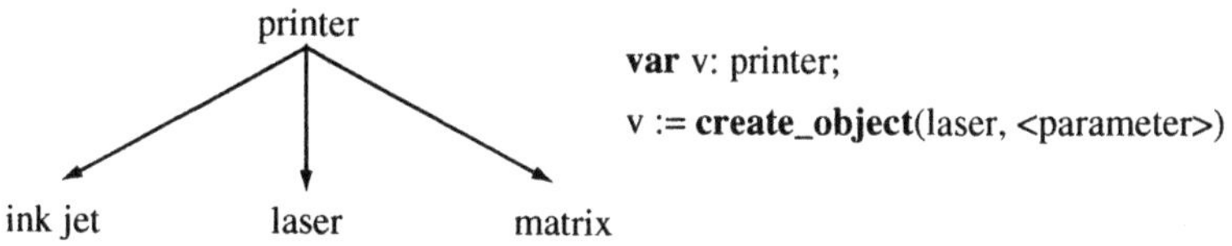

Fig. 1.32. Example of a class hierarchy

In the example, v is an object variable of the general class *printer*. After assigning the object variable v to an object of the more specialized class *laser*, the behavior of v is determined through this specialized class.

Methods are not directly called but indirectly requested through messages (in analogy to requests for service operations as introduced in the client-server model). The corresponding message contains the relevant object identifier, a selector for the requested method (in most cases, selectors are realized as method names), and the needed parameters for the requested method. The invoked method may not only access locally defined, private data of the method but also all private data the relevant object manages.

Objects are elementary entities for distribution that reside on logical nodes within the network. They represent the building blocks of a distributed application based on the object-oriented paradigm. Within a logical node, objects may communicate over shared memory. As depicted in Fig. 1.33, the communication of objects residing on different logical nodes – distributed among several physical nodes - makes use of a transport-oriented protocol.

1.6.2 Object distribution

An application that allows for object distribution has some interesting properties: Firstly, objects must be referenced and localized using a so-called object directory. Obviously, the object directory could be managed by a broker subsystem that helps in referencing and localizing objects. Secondly, the execution of methods depends heavily on the distribution of objects. This distribution-dependence implies that method calls should be passed (possibly, over a network) to the relevant objects transparently. Again, we distinguish

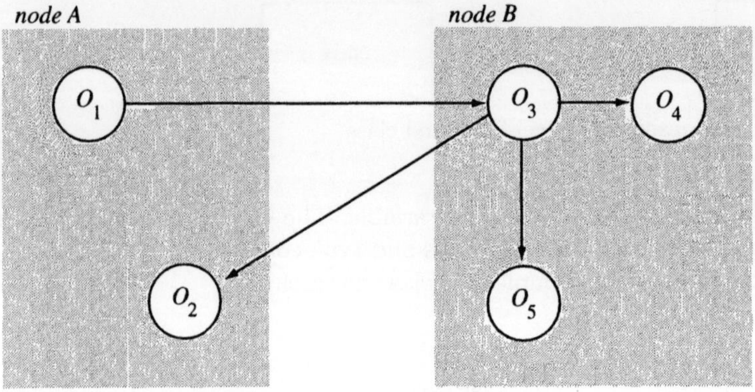

Fig. 1.33. Structuring of objects in logical nodes

synchronous and asynchronous method calls. The synchronous method call supports a sequentialized flow of control spanning several distributed nodes.

Referencing and localizing of migrating objects is an issue. In this case, the need for a broker subsystem managing the dynamically changing entries of the object directory is evident.

One of the strengths of the object-oriented approach lies in the uniformity of the communication among objects. Local and remote method calls have the same semantics. In contrast to that, recall the RPC discussion where the call semantics *exactly-once* in the case of the local procedure call differed quite a bit from the call semantics *at-least-once* in the case of the remote procedure call. Furthermore, we remember the problem of parameter-passing schemes such as call-by-reference.

Appropriate systems and language support exist. For instance, at Washington University, Raj et al. (1991) designed with Emerald a highly integrated object-oriented language concept that supports distribution of objects.

1.6.3 Object mobility

Object mobility refers to the migration of objects from one logical node in the distributed system to another. Migration can be static or dynamic. In the static case objects migrate, or better, are assigned statically during the initialization phase, to selected logical nodes within the distributed system. This is also called static allocation. We will discuss relevant selection criteria in Sect. 1.7.4. In the dynamic case, also called dynamic allocation, objects may migrate during the execution phase of the distributed application. We will discuss so-called mobile CORBA objects in Sect. 9.2 where we also introduce IBM's Aglet Workbench.

Another aspect of object mobility concentrates on the execution state of the migrating object. Here, objects can be seen as active or passive entities. A passive object is either a simple data object or an object that is not active while migrating (i.e., during the transition the object does not execute any method). Migration can be achieved through a simple copying of the object (including its private data) from one logical node in the distributed system to another. An active object, on the other hand, may execute some methods while migrating. Simple copying of the object together with its private data is not sufficient here. Rather, the stack segments of the methods that are executed during the transition phase have to migrate as well. Migrating an active object becomes even more complicated if the object invokes methods of other objects that remain in place and do not migrate with the invoking object. Figure 1.34 illustrates such a situation.

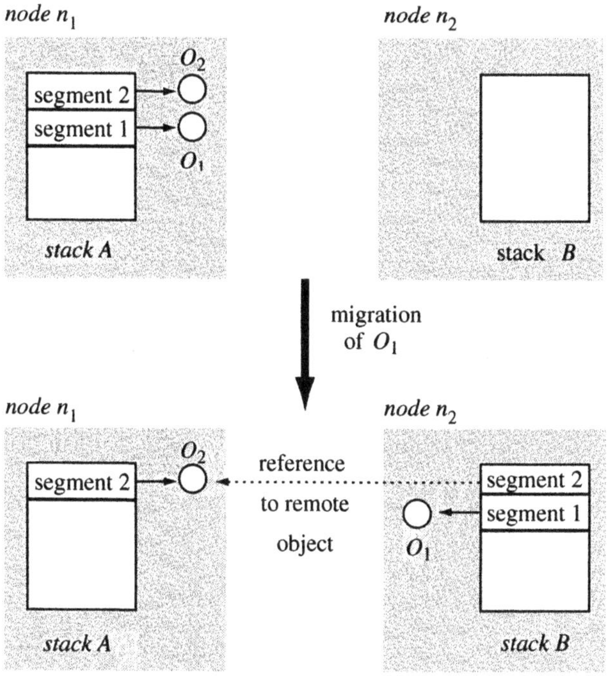

Fig. 1.34. Object migration

The stack segments of the methods that are currently processed by the transient object O_1 will also migrate from node n_1 to node n_2. In this complex scenario it is not sufficient to relocate all relevant stack segments belonging to object O_1. In addition to that, all stack segments – including the ones that do not even belong to object O_1 – must also be relocated provided that they are stacked above the migrating segments. In the example given in Fig. 1.34, it is necessary to copy segment 2 from stack A to stack B. Afterwards, segment 2 exists on node n_1 as well as on node n_2. Both nodes now reference object O_2. On node n_1 this reference is local whereas on node n_2 this reference is remote.

Let us now assume that object O_1 migrates to another logical node, and some object O_i then attempts to invoke a method of object O_1. It could happen that object O_1 now resides on another physical node that is no longer known to object O_i. In this case, object O_i has to localize the new location of object O_1 somehow. Localizing objects should not be the task of the application programmer, instead, the system should transparently manage the relocation. We have already seen some ways to achieve this relocation transparency using object servers, object directories, and broker subsystems.

Possibilities for object localization.

1. A simple possibility of localizing objects is provided if the location of an object is hard-coded in its identifier. However, this possibility does not work properly for mobile objects. After a migration, the object identifier may point to the wrong location.
2. Another possibility that is robust against mobile objects is provided if the location of an object is managed at a central site, say, an object server. However, an object server may become a bottleneck and may cause problems as far as availability is concerned. A crashed object server may lead to a standstill of the entire distributed system.
3. Cache broadcast of object locations is another possibility. Here, every node manages a cache where the locations of recently used objects are stored. If the location of a needed object is not stored within the cache, or if the cached location of a needed object turns out to be outdated, the object broadcasts a request in which it asks for the (new) location of the needed object. Upon reception of an answer, the object updates its cache and proceeds as usual.
4. Forward-addressing is yet another possibility. If an object migrates from one logical node in the distributed system to another, it leaves behind a reference to its new location. There is no immediate notification of the new location to all objects with references to the relocated object. These objects discover the new object location when trying to contact the object at the old location. Using the forward address left behind, they can then easily manage to switch to forwarding their requests to the new object location. If objects migrate more often, we get a forward-addressing chain. Following the chain could make the first access to the current location of a very mobile object quite expensive, and, since many intermediate nodes might be involved, could decrease the availability. If the forward-addressing chain is broken for some reason (due to crashing of some of the intermediate nodes with forward addresses for example), a broadcasting scheme similar to the one described above could be used to bypass the crashed nodes. Such a scheme has been implemented in Emerald (Raj et al. 1991).

   A forward address always contains the host address and a timestamp. If there exist more than one forward address for an object (e.g., multiple forward addresses for the same object are returned after a broadcast request), the valid forward address is the one with the latest timestamp.

5. Finally, a possibility is given by immediate notification of the new location to all objects with references to the relocated object. In order to make this immediate update scheme work properly, backward references must be stored (i.e., every object knows about all other objects that have references to it). Objects that reference a relocated object maintain a so-called proxy object where they maintain the new location of relocated object.
   Migration of a relocated object back to its previous location while maintaining proxy objects leads to double bookkeeping. This is especially unsatisfactory when there are no accesses to the mobile object at its relocated location. The additional work of maintaining proxy objects would in this case have been wasted. In this scenario, we would certainly prefer possibilities that localize an object only when it is really needed.

Mobile objects seem to have some similarities with mobile processes. Table 1.4 points out the main differences between object and process migration (Mühlhäuser and Schill 1992).

Table 1.4. Differences between object and process migration

	Object migration	Process migration
Layer	application layer	operating system layer
Node	logical node	physical node
Granularity	object and segments of active methods, i.e., fine-granular	process and data of the whole address space, i.e., coarse-granular
Motivation	joining together of communicating objects	load balancing

In contrast to what we have seen in the discussion of the remote procedure call, communicating objects may pass parameters not only as values but also as references to other objects. To avoid repeatedly sent requests to remotely referenced objects, these parameter objects migrate to the calling object. But what happens to the relocated parameter objects once they are no longer needed by the calling object? There are two implementation choices, called call-by-move and call-by-visit. The two alternatives are depicted in Figs. 1.35 and 1.36, respectively.

The alternative *call-by-move* lets the migrated parameter object remain at the location of the calling object, while the alternative *call-by-visit* migrates the parameter object back to its original location once the call comes to an end.

The difficulties of a migrating parameter object concern the question of whether or not the migration makes it necessary to relocate the object's class,

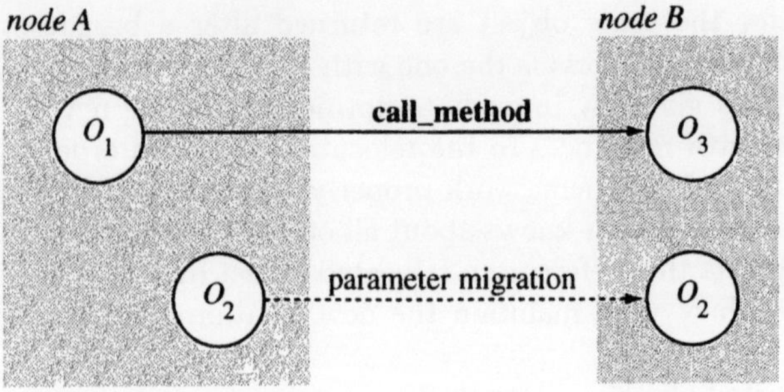

Fig. 1.35. Call-by-move

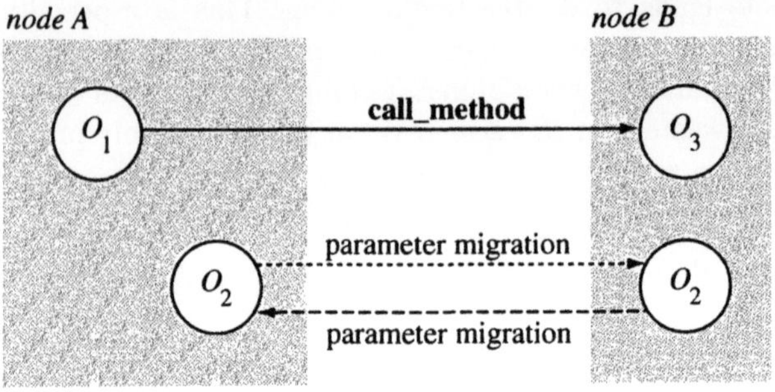

Fig. 1.36. Call-by-visit

and whether or not the new location is equipped in such a way as to allow for the execution of all needed methods. In general, there are dependencies from the class library (concerning the hierarchy of inheritance), from the runtime system, and from hardware properties. Given all that, it could also be necessary to relocate semantics information (in addition to the syntactical description).

1.6.4 Common Object Request Broker Architecture (CORBA)

As we have already seen in a previous discussion (see Sect. 1.5.2), brokers can improve the efficiency of a distributed system based on remote procedure calls. An example was the efficient way to register server ports at a broker subsystem where clients could then easily request relevant ports on demand. Dynamic changes were managed by the broker subsystem without involving the client's application. For a client, updates of server ports could be achieved fully transparently. The same advantages are also welcome in an object-oriented system.

A so-called Object Request Broker (ORB) is a mediator that provides (i) a transparent request interface for clients willing to invoke some object methods, and (ii) a transparent answer interface that ships answers provided by the called object to the requesting object. An ORB hereby supports (and integrates) heterogeneous distributed applications on different object-oriented system platforms.

The goal of the Object Management Group (OMG), – where a wide range of IT companies participate[8] – is the design of a common (implementation-independent) ORB architecture. The same goal is also pursued by X/Open within its Common Applications Environments (X/Open CAE). X/Open is an independent, worldwide acting organization for open systems that is supported by almost all big IT vendors.

Both organizations propose with CORBA an architecture that defines a generic and quite flexible framework for different ORB implementations (OMG 1995). Among others, the following choices for the ORB implementations are supported:

- *ORB is a resident component of the client and the object implementations.* The client stubs utilize either a location transparent interprocess communication (IPC) mechanism, or directly access a name service to get in touch with the desired objects.
- *ORB is a server.* In this case, all client and object implementations communicate with a central ORB server. From the point of view of the (distributed) operating system, the ORB server can be as simple as a process with which an IPC is possible. Letting the ORB be a central server leads to the already known problems (e.g., possible bottleneck and decreased availability).
- *ORB is a library function.* For lightweight objects with a shared object description, the object implementation could be stored in a library. In this case, the stubs are identical with the current object methods. This approach assumes that a client has sufficient access rights to access the relevant object data, i.e., clients are seen as trustworthy, especially in a distributed, heterogeneous, and open environment. The latter aggravates the level of acceptance of this approach dramatically.
- *ORB is a service of the (distributed) operating system.* There are several good reasons to choose this alternative: Object references can be managed safely (i.e., no counterfeiting). This improves performance by avoiding permanent authentication for each request. Another performance improvement can be achieved through the knowledge of location and structure of clients as well as of object implementations. Consider, for instance, the case where client and object implementations share the same host. Here, expensive marshalling and unmarshalling while passing parameters from client to object implementations, and vice versa, can be avoided.

Communication and semantics. In CORBA the interfaces of the distributed objects are described in a so-called interface definition language (IDL). Using the IDLs, an IDL-compiler (see RPC generator) generates the client stub (used for marshalling purposes) and the corresponding server site skeleton (used for unmarshalling purposes). The client stub is implemented in

[8] Founding members were DEC, HP, HyperDesk, NCR, Object Design und SunSoft.

the client's language while the server site's skeleton is produced in the language of the server subsystem. Language transparency is provided. CORBA-compatible programming languages include C, C++, Cobol, and recently, also Java. The IDL-compiler for the latter makes heavy use of Java's remote method invocation (RMI) and nicely combines with CORBA's internet inter-ORB-protocol (IIOP). Using RMI and IIOP, Java programmers are now able to interact smoothly with non-Java objects. Most of the time communication between objects is synchronous.

Besides synchronous communication, CORBA also supports a so-called deferred synchronous communication. This type of communication is closely related to an asynchronous RPC. The predefined semantics for a successful call is the exactly-once semantics. For an unsuccessful call "at-most-once" is guaranteed. Apart from that, CORBA utilizes a call semantics called "best-effort." In a communication with this semantics no result is expected, and therefore, no synchronization of clients is needed.

The desired type of semantics for a given communication between the client and the object implementations is coded as part of the request specification.

Context object. In many cases it is not very comfortable to specify every minute detail necessary for a desired request. Therefore, CORBA provides the notion of a context object where environmental parameters could be stored. Constants and parameters that are used multiple times are stored at and made available through the context object. A repeated passing of information that remains unchanged can be dropped.

CORBA as industry standard. In the meantime, many development platforms are completely based on CORBA, or at least provide a CORBA-compliant realization. Among others, we know

- Distributed Objects Everywhere (DOE) by SunSoft, Inc.
- Distributed System Object Model (DSOM) by IBM
- Inter-Language Unification (ILU) by Xerox PARC
- OpenDoc by Component Integration Lab. (founded by Apple, IBM, Novell, Oracle, Sun, Taligent, Wordperfect, and Xerox)
- Orbix by IONA Technologies, Ltd.
- XShell by ExpertSoft, Inc.

Table 1.5 shows the hierarchical embedding of CORBA within three well-known distributed application environments.

Before we return to our main topic of distributed applications, let us briefly discuss two basic approaches in the context of object-oriented programming, namely Linda's tuple space and Linear Objects. For the sake of conciseness, we will omit a discussion of other similar models. At the end of the chapter, the interested reader will find relevant references for further reading about the other models.

Table 1.5. Distributed application environments and CORBA

	Microsoft	OpenDoc	Unix
Scripting language	Visual Basic	Open Scripting Architecture (OSA) e.g., AppleScript, HyperTalk, Tcl/Tk	e.g., Tcl/Tk
Application communication protocol	OLE	AppleEvents, OLE	e.g., ToolTalk
Object model (CORBA)	COM (also DEC)	SOM/DSOM (IBM)	DOE (SunSoft)
Basis communication model	OSF/DCE	RPC	Sun RPC

Linda's tuple space and Linear Objects are just two approaches out of a rich set of similar ones. Among others, we know

- ActorSpace (Agha and Callsen 1993)
- Chemical Abstract Machine (CHAM) (Berry and Boudol 1990)
- Gamma (Banâtre and Métayer 1990)
- Swarm (Roman and Cunningham 1990)
- Unity (Chandy and Misra 1988)

1.6.5 Tuple space

The so-called tuple space was invented by Gelernter (1985) as an object-oriented approach to managing distributed data. It was specially designed for Linda language.

Tuple space consists of a set of tuples that could be interpreted as lists of typed fields. For instance, the list ('Linda',3) represents such a tuple of two fields. The first field 'Linda' is of type **string**, the second of type **int**.

Processes may manipulate tuples by means of three atomic operations: **out**, **read**, and **in**. The operation **out** creates a new tuple in the tuple space, **read** simply reads a tuple while **in** reads and simultaneously removes a tuple from the tuple space.

All accesses to tuples are associative, i.e., **read** (**in**) reads (and removes) the tuple that matches with a given pattern. For example, the operation

$$\textbf{in}(\text{'order'}, ?i, ?j)$$

reads the 3-ary tuple whose first field matches the string 'order', and whose second and third fields are of the type of the given variables i and j. If such a matching tuple exists, the tuple will be removed and at the same time the variables i and j will be instantiated with the corresponding entries found in this matching tuple. If more than one tuple matches, the operation **in** selects one of them, randomly. If no match can be found in the tuple space, the operation **in** is suspended (same for **read**). If later, an operation **out** creates a matching tuple, the operation **in** resumes and the tuple access will be carried out. **in** and **read** are synchronous operations in the tuple space.

Apart from the three operations introduced so far, the tuple space also supports the operation **eval** which spawns a new process, and the asynchronous pendants to **in** and **read**, namely **inp** and **readp**. If no matching tuple exists, the operations **inp** and **readp** are not blocked but return an error message.

In the following a simple example shows how the client-server style of communication could be programmed in the tuple space model.

Code fragment (Client site).

```
constant int ClientId;                  /* This is a unique identifier.     */
list of unspecified ParameterList;      /* Arguments for the service
                                           operation.                       */
list of unspecified ResultList;
  ⋮
provide arguments for the service call and compose ParameterList;
out('Request', ClientId, ParameterList);
in('Answer', ClientId, ?ResultList);
process results;
```

The following code fragment represents the server loop (see p. 22).

Code fragment (Server site).

```
int ClientId;
list of unspecified ParameterList;      /* Arguments for the service
                                           operation.                       */
list of unspecified ResultList;
  ⋮
while (true) do
   in('Request', ?ClientId, ?ParameterList);
   calculate results and compose ResultList;
   out('Answer', ClientId, ResultList);
```

1.6.6 Linear Objects

Linear Objects, LO for short, are tightly-related to the tuple space model described in the previous section.

Linear Objects propose a rule-based language, especially designed for coordination purposes in open distributed systems (Andreoli et al. 1992, Andreoli and Pareschi 1991). The language is an excellent choice if the goal is to rapidly prototype a distributed system based on the notion of interacting, autonomous, and heterogeneous agents.

In contrast to traditional programming languages, Linear Objects is a pure coordination language, i.e., it is mainly concerned with event communication of distributed agents. Traditional procedural activities (e.g., manipulations of data structures, arithmetic calculations) are handled in agent-local procedures that are out of the scope of Linear Objects. Today, such a language fits into middleware.

A LO-system consists of a set of concurrent agents. The state of each agent is given by a token pool (see tuple space in Sect. 1.6.5). A LO-program contains rules that manipulate the tokens, and thereby, may change the state of the agents. Figure 1.37 describes the syntax of LO-rules.

<table>
<tr><td><rule></td><td>=</td><td><trigger> <bcast> ‘<>-’ <body></td></tr>
<tr><td><trigger></td><td>=</td><td><token></td></tr>
<tr><td></td><td>|</td><td><token> ‘@’ <trigger></td></tr>
<tr><td><bcast></td><td>=</td><td><></td></tr>
<tr><td></td><td>|</td><td><bcast> ‘@ ^’ <token></td></tr>
<tr><td><body></td><td>=</td><td><token></td></tr>
<tr><td></td><td>|</td><td><body> ‘@’ <body></td></tr>
<tr><td></td><td>|</td><td><body> ‘&’ <body></td></tr>
<tr><td></td><td>|</td><td>‘#t’</td></tr>
<tr><td></td><td>|</td><td>‘#b’</td></tr>
</table>

Fig. 1.37. Syntax of LO-rules

In a rule, *<token>* is a tuple of a given arity containing some variable names. The tuple is prefixed with a predicate name.

A *<rule>* of the form

$$p(X) \ @ \ q(X,Y) \ @ \ \hat{}r(Y) \ <>\text{-} \ <\!\mathit{body}\!>$$

allows a state transition within agents that possess the specified *<trigger>*. The given rule triggers (i.e., fires) if the token pool of an agent contains the two tokens $p(a)$ and $q(a, b)$. The corresponding state transition in such an agent leads to the removal of both tokens from the local token pool. Simultaneously, a token $r(b)$ is broadcast to all other existing agents, i.e., the token $r(b)$ is atomically added to the token pools of all other existing agents in the system. Finally, all tokens of the right hand side (*<body>*) instantiate the variable X with value a, and Y with value b.[9]

A right hand side *<body>* of the form

$$s(a) \ @ \ t(a,b) \ \& \ u(b)$$

is executed as follows: The operator ‘&’ creates an agent clone. Into the state (i.e., into the token pool) of the cloned agent, the tokens $s(a)$ and $t(a,b)$ are added. The original agent (i.e., the agent where the rule in question was fired) gets the token $u(b)$ added to its state.

[9] As in Prolog, we denote variables with a starting uppercase letter, and atomic values with a lowercase.

These complicated state transitions are exemplified in Fig. 1.38 for a rule of the form:

$$p(a) \ @ \ q(a,b) \ @ \ \hat{\ }r(b) \ \texttt{<>-} \ s(a) \ @ \ t(a,b) \ \& \ u(b)$$

Tokens that are involved in the state transitions are printed bold face.

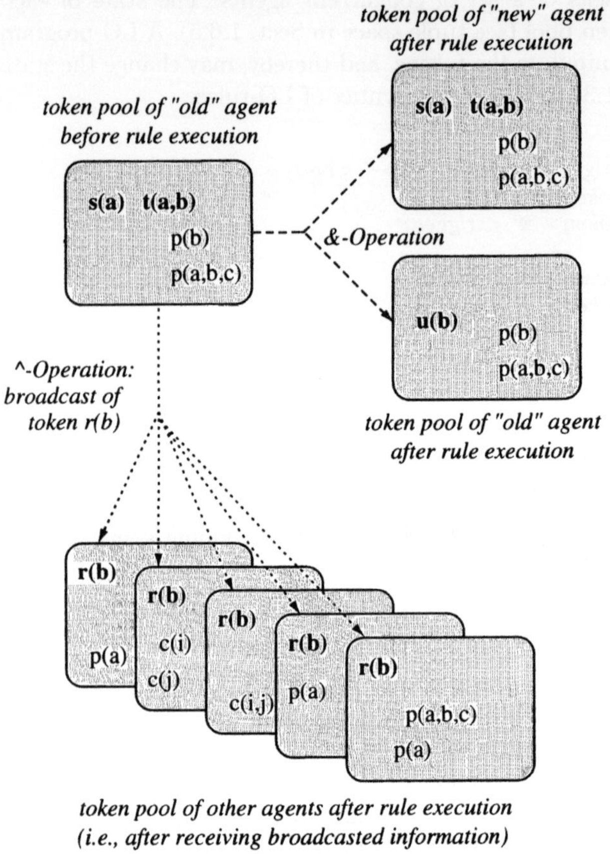

Fig. 1.38. Illustration of state transitions in LO

If the operator '&' is missing on the right hand side of a rule, no agent clone is created. In this case, all tokens on the right hand side (of course, after bound variables have been instantiated) are simply added to the agent's token pool. The right hand side could be as simple as '#t' or '#b'. A '#t' kills the agent whereas '#b' represents the empty operation. The effect of the latter "degenerated" rule is simply the removal of the token on the left hand side.

In sum, the right hand side of a rule determines whether new agents are cloned dynamically or are terminated. Moreover, it allows for local incremental state modifications of an agent.

The entire state transition is an atomic transaction. This transaction property has been heavily exploited in prototyping various applications (Borghoff et al. 1996a).

With Linear Objects, the client-server style of communication using time-outs can be implemented in a straight-forward manner. In the following implementation, client and server are heavyweight processes that may run on different machines. Message exchange is achieved via broadcast, the standard messaging mechanism of Linear Objects. The given rules are skeletons of a complete program. For the sake of clarity, we do without carrying along all the identifiers needed for a tight binding of client and server. Furthermore, we do not include the management of timestamps needed to detect obsolete requests for service operations.

Code fragment (Initialization).

```
main
   <>- client(someUniqueID) & server.
```

Code fragment (Client site).

```
client(ClientId)
   @ provide arguments for the service call and compose ParameterList
   @ ^request(ClientId, ParameterList)
   <>- clientclock(ClientId, SomeTimeSpan)
   & client(ClientId, suspended).
                              /* The client composes the arguments for the ser-
                                 vice call, sends the request, and suspends execu-
                                 tion. Simultaneously, a client clone, prefixed with
                                 clientclock, is created.                        */

client(ClientId, suspended)
   @ answer(ClientId, ResultList)
   @ process results
   <>- client(ClientId).      /* When receiving the answer from the server, the
                                 suspended client resumes, and processes the re-
                                 ceived results.                                 */

client(ClientId, suspended)
   @ timeout(ClientId)
   @ start timeout handler
   <>- client(ClientId).      /* The suspended client gets a timeout from its agent
                                 clone clientclock.                              */

clientclock(ClientId, SomeTimeSpan)
   @ wait(SomeTimeSpan)
   @ ^timeout(ClientId)
   <>- #t.                    /* The agent clone clientclock waits the agreed upon
                                 time span, sends a timeout, and terminates.     */
```

Again, the following code fragment represents the server loop (see p. 22).

Code fragment (Server site).

```
server
    @ request(ClientId, ParameterList)
    @ calculate results and compose ResultList
    @ ^answer(ClientId, ResultList)
    <>- server.          /* In each loop, the server receives a request, calcu-
                            lates the results, and broadcasts the correspond-
                            ing answer.                                     */
```

We could also implement client and server as lightweight processes sharing the same address space, or more precicely, the same token pool. Message exchange is realized via shared tokens. In this case the implementation becomes simpler:

Code fragment (Initialization).

```
main
    <>- client(someUniqueID) @ server.
```

Code fragment (Client site).

```
client(ClientId)
    @ provide arguments for the service call and compose ParameterList
    <>- clientclock(ClientId, SomeTimeSpan)
    @ request(ClientId, ParameterList)
    @ client(ClientId, suspended).
                         /* The client composes the arguments for the ser-
                            vice call, puts the request in the token pool, and
                            suspends execution. Simultaneously, a lightweight
                            client clone, prefixed with clientclock, is created.
                            */

client(ClientId, suspended)
    @ answer(ClientId, ResultList)
    @ process results
    <>- client(ClientId).  /* When finding the answer token in the pool, the
                            suspended client resumes and processes the re-
                            sults.                                          */

client(ClientId, suspended)
    @ timeout(ClientId)
    @ start timeout handler
    <>- client(ClientId).  /* The suspended client finds the timeout token in
                            the pool.                                       */

clientclock(ClientId, SomeTimeSpan)
    @ wait(SomeTimeSpan)
    <>- timeout(ClientId).  /* The agent clone clientclock waits the agreed upon
                             time span, puts a timeout token into the pool, and
                             implicitly terminates.                         */
```

Code fragment (Server site).

```
server
   @ request(ClientId, ParameterList)
   @ calculate results and compose ResultList
   <>- answer(ClientId, ResultList)
   @ server.              /* In each loop, the server finds a request token in
                             the pool, calculates the results, and puts the cor-
                             responding answer into the token pool.          */
```

1.7 Distributed Applications

A distributed application is an application that consists of a set of cooperating, interacting functional units. Reasons to distribute these functional units are potential parallelism during the execution, fault tolerance, and inherent distribution of the application domain (e.g., CSCW applications where the users are geographically distributed, e-commerce including e-banking, or global supply chain management).

Definition 1.7.1 (Distributed application). *The term distributed application contains three aspects: Firstly, it means an application whose functionality is split into a set of cooperating, interacting functional units. Each functional unit has an internal state (data) and operations to manipulate the state. Secondly, these functional units can be assigned to different machines. A single machine, however, may host several functional units at the same time. Finally, the functional units communicate with each other through message exchanges, remote procedure calls, or simply, shared data structures.*

Consider a distributed application that consists of the functional units $A_1,\ldots,A_5$. The functional units may cooperate and interact as depicted in Fig. 1.39.

Interface specification. As we have mentioned in our discussion of the client-server model, interfaces help to establish well-defined points of interaction. Essentially, an interface specifies the operations provided by a functional unit. This specification includes the names and the functionality of the operations (i.e., needed parameters including arity and type), the results returned by the operation (i.e., arity and type of the results), side-effects, and where relevant dependencies among operations. As an example of side-effects and dependencies among operations, let us look at a **read** operation. As a side-effect, a **read** operation may increment the position in a file each time the operation is performed. A dependency of the **read** operation may exist with the operation **open**. Due to the need of a file descriptor, a **read** must not occur before a corresponding **open**.

Roughly, a distributed system can be interpreted as a three layered system, with a distributed application on top of a distributed virtual machine on top of a distributed computer system.

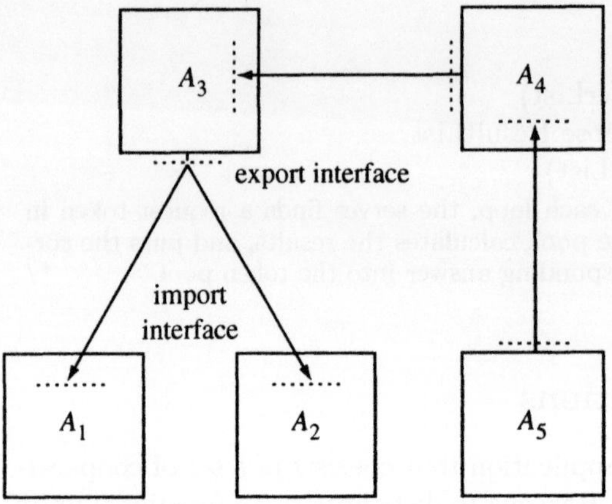

Fig. 1.39. Cooperation and interaction of functional units in a distributed application

In layer 1 (i.e., distributed computer system) we see a set of independent functional units (e.g., workstations) connected through a set of communication links. Layer 2 is a distributed virtual machine that could be seen as a distributed runtime or operating system. The tasks of this virtual machine include the management of the functional units used to implement the distributed application, and the coordination and communication among these units. Finally, in layer 3 we find the distributed application that consists, as mentioned previously, of a set of cooperating, interacting functional units.

Cooperating, interacting functional units might also be found in parallel programs. Is there an intrinsic difference between a distributed application and a parallel program? Although distributed applications might look similar to parallel programs at first glance, there are still some differences, as highlighted in Table 1.6.

Table 1.6. Distributed application vs. parallel program

	Distributed application	Parallel Program
Granularity	coarse	fine
Data space	private	shared
Failure handling	within the communication protocols	not considered

1.7.1 Group communication

Usually, the communication primitives known in operating systems are binary, i.e., an individual sender opens a communication path to a single selected receiver. These binary communication primitives also build the foundation for the discussed one-to-one communication (also known as point-to-point communication) in a client-server model based on remote procedure calls.

Many application areas such as CSCW, however, profit immensely if primitives for a group communication are supported properly. Other relevant application areas include fault-tolerant file services and replication-transparent file systems. In both cases, all communication to the "original", primary file server subsystem must also be propagated to the so-called stand-by file service or to the file replicas, respectively. In the first case, a standby file service takes over when the primary site crashes or becomes unavailable for some other reason (e.g., link failures, network partitioning), while in the second case the communication helps to maintain a consistent state among the file replicas.

Group communication is based on the composition of functional units (including users) within a group. The group is then seen as an abstraction that may mask the existence of the individual functional units. Consequently, a distributed application can now be interpreted as an application that consists of a set of cooperating, interacting groups. In an extreme case, a single group may represent an entire distributed application.

Addressing of groups. If groups cooperate and interact, we have to provide a way to help address the individual groups. There are mainly three types of group addressing: a unique group address, a comprehensive list of addresses of the group members, and the so-called predicate addressing.

- If a message is sent to a unique group address, the underlying runtime system will automatically propagate this message to all members of the group. For analogy compare with an email system where aliases (i.e., mailing lists) are provided. Sending an email message to a mailing list is as simple as sending it to an individual user. The email system transparently multicasts this message to all listed users.
- If a sender explicitly knows all addresses of the group members, it could directly multicast a message to all group members.
- A more elegant way of group addressing is provided by the so-called predicate addressing. Here, the message contains a predicate parameter that is evaluated at the receiving sites. If the predicate is **true**, the receiver accepts the message, otherwise it deletes the message. Broadcast could be the basis for this type of communication. Broadcast together with predicates, or more precisely, with pattern matching, was the basis for communication in the Linear Objects model (see Sect. 1.6.6).

The first two types of addressing are relevant for explicit groups where the members of the group are aware of each others existence. Both types allow direct cooperation and interaction among the members of a group. Predicate addressing, on the other hand, is especially interesting for implicit groups. For instance, consider the case where a message should be sent to just the subset of group members that have a given storage capacity currently available. Evaluation of the predicate at the receiving sites could itself be implicit (i.e., instead of sending the predicate as an explicit parameter, consider a broadcast message that is encoded in some way). Only receivers having the right key at the moment are able to decode and process the message. As a far-fetched example, compare this to a pay-TV broadcast which can only be viewed if a decoder or a prepaid chipcard has been purchased.

Possibilities for communication in a group. We have already mentioned several possibilities for communication within a group, namely unicast, multicast, and broadcast. Using unicast, a message is sent from a sender to a single receiver. Reaching all members of the group requires several unicast messages. Using multicast, the message is sent to a well-defined subset of group members. Very often, multicast is not supported directly in the message system. Rather, it is emulated in software (i.e., for the sender the message is transparently sent to all addressed group members using unicasts). A broadcast message is sent to all group members. In a local area network this is quite simple to achieve. In wide area networks, however, this causes problems. In contrast to a local area network where the nodes can be addressed easily due to the known network topology, in a wide area network it is nearly impossible to address all nodes over all possible links, to remove broadcast duplicates consistently, and most importantly, to react properly to dynamic changes in the network (e.g., new nodes, new subnets, disconnected hosts). Try to imagine an Internet broadcast.

Classification of groups. A group exists in two forms: open and closed. In the latter the members can cooperate and interact solely with each other using group communication facilities. In the case of an open group, other functional units – not belonging to the group – may send messages to the group as such (see Fig. 1.40). Sending messages explicitly to individual group members is allowed in both cases.

Apart from open and closed, we can distinguish groups with regard to their internal structure. In a uniform group, all functional units of the group are at the same level (i.e., each functional unit can in principle cooperate and interact with every other functional unit). A uniform group is ideal for collective decision making processes. The other case is the hierarchical group. Here, a so-called coordinator may guide the communication and make the decisions for the whole group. As with all of the centralized approaches which we have discussed so far a coordinator is a potential bottleneck and a high risk as far as availability is concerned.

Management of groups. A group manager provides methods for the creation and termination of groups. It also controls the dynamic insertion and deletion of group members (i.e., functional units including users). Moreover, it disseminates information concerning the internal states of groups.

Again, there are centralized group managers. A centralized group manager can be realized as an individual group server. This group server maintains a central database where it manages group information, such as participating members. Modern group managers are decentralized: there is no central group server. Here, a new member willing to participate in a particular group,

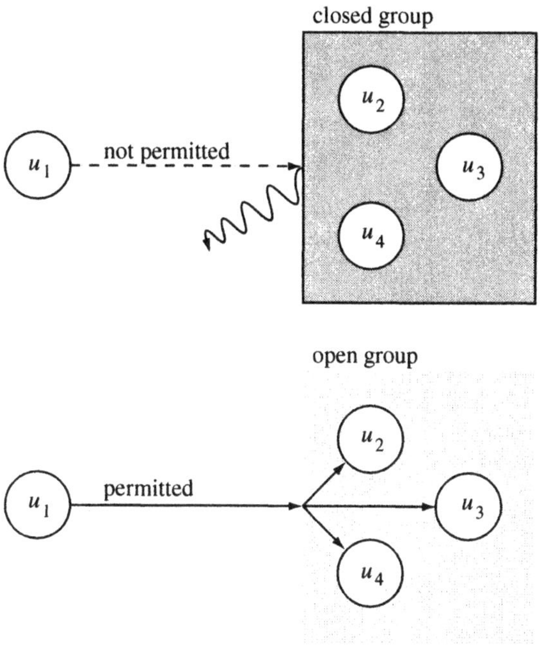

Fig. 1.40. Open vs. closed group with users u_1, .., u_4

sends a multicast (where he states his willingness to join the group) to all members of the group in question. Analogously, a member who wants to quit a group may send a multicast (where he states his intention to leave the group) to the remaining members of his group. Decisions about accepting these requests are made by the entire group. Besides the complexity of the involved protocols, problematic is also the synchronous character of the decision results. Accepting a new member implies that from this precise moment all messages sent to the group must also be propagated to the new member. Analogously, messages sent to the group should no longer be propagated to members that have already left the group.

Objectives of group communication. The main objective of all protocols for group communication is that all messages sent to the group are to be propagated to all group members. In order to guarantee consistent states among the group members, another objective of equally high importance is that all these propagated messages are to reach the group member in exactly the same sequence. Otherwise, the system could evolve nondeterministically, resulting in incompatible states for different members of the same group.

In an ideal world, all messages could be delivered without delay in the same sequence in which they were sent to the group as a whole. In a distributed system this is unachievable. In the best of all worlds, we can reach a sequence of message propagation and delivery that is either synchronous (at least in theory), loosely-synchronous, or virtually-synchronous.

In a synchronous system where we would like to assume a system-wide global time, message propagation and delivery could orient itself at the sending time. Although in the literature we see attempts to provide system-wide global time, or more precisely, system-wide agreement on the maximum distance between the local times, a full synchrony is difficult, if not impossible to achieve.

A loosely-synchronous system provides a consistent time ordering. A system-wide global (absolute) time does not exist here. Instead, the system chooses a "first" message in the case where a sender S_1 and a sender S_2 send their messages M_1 and M_2, respectively, at almost the same point in time. Without loss of generality let the chosen first message be M_2. Both messages are now delivered to all group members in the sequence M_2, M_1.

The most sophisticated way to propagate and deliver messages is provided in a virtually-synchronous system. Here, the causal dependencies between two events (i.e., the events of sending and of receiving a message) are considered.[10] If two messages are causally dependent upon each other, message propagation and delivery must maintain the necessary sequence. For concurrent messages without causal dependencies upon each other, the system does not retain any sequence nor does it guarantee any order at all. As an example, the Isis system by Birman (1993) supports this kind of group communication.

Virtually-synchronous systems. The determination of a correct sequence during message propagation and delivery is based on the relation *before* (in symbols: $\longrightarrow$). Using the relation, a partial ordering of events within a group of distributed members can be achieved. Among events considered are both the sending and the receiving of a message. If we follow Lamport (1978b), the relation *before* is defined by the following rules:

1. Events of an individual group member are ordered along the relation *before* (i.e., if e_1 and e_2 are two events of a particular group member and e_1 happened before e_2 then: $e_1 \longrightarrow e_2$).
2. Sending comes before receiving (i.e., if e_1 is a sending event of a particular group member and e_2 is the corresponding receiving event of another group member then $e_1 \longrightarrow e_2$).
3. The relation *before* is transitive (i.e., if $e_1 \longrightarrow e_2$ and $e_2 \longrightarrow e_3$ then $e_1 \longrightarrow e_3$).

Concurrent events are unordered, i.e., it holds: $\neg(e_1 \longrightarrow e_2)$ as well as $\neg(e_2 \longrightarrow e_1)$.

In a virtually-synchronous system the causal dependencies of the events define a *before*-relation on the set of group messages. These dependencies are managed in so-called status vectors. Let a relevant group have n members. Each group member u_j, $j \in 1, \ldots, n$, has a unique identifier, maintains a status vector s_j, and belongs to a particular application. The status vector

[10] Two events e_1 and e_2 are said to be causally dependent if the behavior of e_2 is influenced by the existence of e_1.

s_j is a n-dimensional vector. Its i-th component (i.e., $s_j(i)$), indicates how many messages sent by a group member u_i have already been propagated and delivered to the application of group member u_j in the correct sequence. It is important to notice that the status vector s_j specifies the local view of u_j only.

If a group member u_j multicasts a message M to the group, u_j increments the value stored in the j-th component of its status vector: $s_j(j) := s_j(j)+1$. This increment determines the next message in correct sequence. The sent multicast message M carries the modified status vector s_j as a parameter.

Upon reception of a message M sent by a group member u_i, a receiving group member u_j compares its own local view (represented by s_j) with the local view of the sender of the message (represented by s_i and shipped as a parameter of the message M). In order to decide about a delivery of message M to the u_j's application, the comparison by u_j checks the following conditions:

Condition 1: $s_j(i) = s_i(i) - 1$ (i.e., all previous messages sent by group member u_i have already been propagated and delivered to group member u_j in the correct sequence).

Condition 2: $\forall k \in 1, \ldots, n : k \neq i \wedge s_i(k) \leq s_j(k)$ (i.e., before sending its message M, group member u_i has not received any other group messages that group member u_j is not aware of).

If, upon reception of message M, both conditions are true then group member u_j delivers this message to its corresponding application. Simultaneously, u_j updates its local view to $s_j(i) := s_i(i)$. If conditions are not true due to delayed message propagations, group member u_j postpones message delivery for M until both conditions become true.

When groups are created, all status vectors are initialized as 0. Figure 1.41 gives an example of the above described technique.

Sending events are characterized through message identifiers and their corresponding status vectors. In the example, group member u_1 has to postpone the delivery of message M_3 because Condition 2 is false (see dotted line). The messages M_4 and M_5 are concurrent (i.e., there is no causal dependency between the two). From the point of view of group member u_3, both conditions are true for both concurrent messages.

As the discussion of operation transformations in Sect. 4.8 will show, the same technique can also be applied to control the concurrency in a group editor supporting joint authoring of a shared document by several users.

1.7.2 Design of distributed applications

In traditional, nondistributed applications, procedures or modules help to structure functionality and data structures. Components of the application use procedures or modules to encapsulate algorithms that logically belong

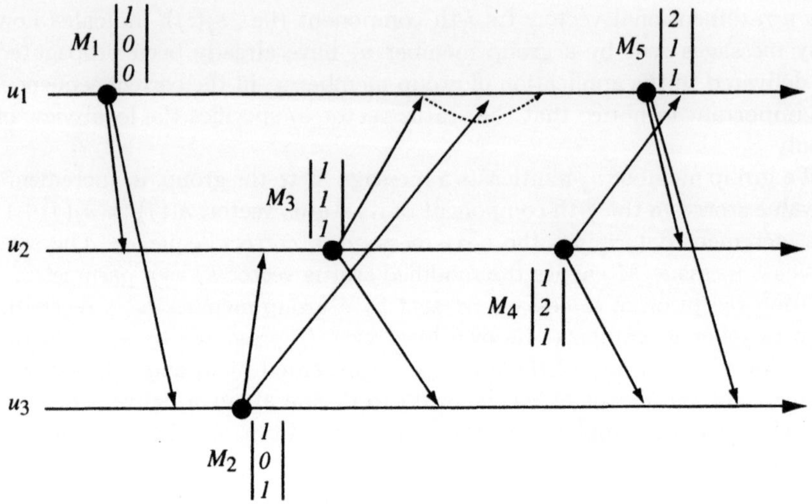

Fig. 1.41. Ordering of messages in a virtually-synchronous system

together. This encapsulation may also solve reusability issues. The binding of all components into a complete software system is purely static. Software engineering of distributed applications, on the other hand, raises interesting issues (Corbin 1991): Which functionality is provided locally and which remotely? How can an application localize and make use of a remotely provided service? What should happen if a client cannot contact the localized server subsystem? What should happen if clients and servers face communication failures? What kind of security mechanisms are provided? Is authentication an issue? Obviously, this is just a small subset of issues a designer of a distributed application has to tackle.

In the 1980's and early 1990's solutions to many of these issues were proposed. The distributed system Athena is a good example of a system that has focused on, among other things, the security issue. Athena (Balkovich et al. 1985) argues that there are no trustworthy client workstations. Every user of a workstation could login as the superuser and try to become superuser on other machines, as well. For this reason, Athena introduces the concept of authentication servers (e.g., Kerberos) which authenticate users before they are allowed to access network-wide services. In addition, messages are sent in encrypted form over the network.

A question not raised so far concerns the homogeneity of a distributed application and its possibilities for staying independent (e.g., independent of computer architectures, of operations systems, and of network idiosyncrasy such as packet size of messages, addressing methods, or timeout handling). Moreover, independence from IT vendors and software versions is of importance. Last but not least, there is the issue of testing and debugging a distributed application. This is a complex undertaking because delays in the network due to the load or the chosen routing may cause transient and intermittent failures that are extremely difficult to detect. In many cases the components of the distributed application are tested and debugged in isolation. The distributed application is often insufficiently tested in integration. Beta-users or worse end customers test the integrated distributed application in their final setting, write bug reports, and get patches and updates from the vendors in turn.

In the following we will look at some of these issues in more detail.

External data representation. One way to get the desired independence from hardware characteristics while exchanging messages can be provided by an external data representation which is independent of any individual method of representing data. Clients and servers exchange messages (e.g., while performing an RPC). The request arguments and the result values delivered as answers have to be coded in some way. The so-called marshalling prepares the argument list that is sent to the server subsystem, while a corresponding unmarshalling extracts these arguments at the server site.

In a homogeneous environment (i.e., same hardware and software) data representation is identical on all machines. In a heterogeneous environment, the typical case nowadays where personal computers, workstations, and mainframes form the hardware basis of the distributed system and where a rich set of different vendor software is installed, different data representations exist. For example, processors of different vendors may represent words in different ways. However, the differences are not limited to byte sequences and their interpretation but also encompass entire data structures. This makes it necessary to transform data from one format to another while passing information within the distributed application. Again, there is a design choice of whether the needed data transformations are performed at a central site or fully decentralized. The centralized case has all the disadvantages already mentioned. In practice this choice plays no important role. Therefore, we will concentrate on the decentralized case. Here, all nodes are able to transform data from one format to another. In principle, there are three variants:

1. The message is sent in a form so as to be understood at the receiving site (i.e., the sender has to transform the data representation into the target format). The receiver can then directly work on this data representation. In analogy, a German would write his letter to an American friend in English while the American would then answer in German.
2. The message is simply sent in the source format (i.e., the representation of the sender). There is no additional transformation work for the sender. Consequently, the data representation has to be transformed into the target format at the receiving site.
   In analogy, a German would write his letter to an American friend in German while the American would then answer in English.
3. The message is sent in a network-wide unique standard representation (i.e., the sender has to transform the data into this agreed upon format).

The receiver then has to retransform this data representation into its local format.
In analogy, both the German and the American would write their letters in, for example, Esperanto.

If new system components are dynamically added to the distributed system, the first variant faces problems of maintenance. A mechanism is needed that propagates the data representations of these new system components to all existing system components. At the same time, the mechanism has to ensure that the existing system components are aware of the new data representations. Without further support, the second variant would face similar problems. Therefore, in the OSF/DCE realization of this variant (Foundation 1992), all messages carry a format description as an additional parameter. The strength of the first two variants is that, at most, only one transformation of the data representation is needed. This transformation, if needed at all is either performed by the sender (first variant) or by the receiver (second variant).

In analogy, two American friends would write their letters in English. No translations are needed.

But what happens in the third variant? To take our analogy even further, as a worst case scenario, two Americans would first translate their English letters into Esperanto and then back into English. Still, there are very prominent realizations of this variant, for example, Sun's external data representation (XDR). Although, as in the above illustrated worst case scenario, there are two transformations instead of none, this variant has its advantages. If new system components are dynamically added to the distributed system, the new system components simply have to "learn" about the network-wide unique standard representation (to stress our analogy for a last time, to join the penfriends, a newcomer only needs a simple knowledge of Esperanto).

Steps in the design of a distributed application. Designing a distributed application is a 7-step approach:

1. The repositories of the application data are identified. The major goal of this step is to find an allocation of the application data (in repositories) that reflects the inherent distribution of the data. Ideally, data should be stored near the location where they are needed. This is also called resource allocation. We will come back to this issue in Sect. 1.7.4.
2. Data are assigned to individual modules. This is a fundamental step of any software engineering approach.
3. The module interface is defined. It contains a minimal set of constants, data types and functions together with their functionality (i.e., number and type of the parameters plus the result type).[11]

[11] **module**-specifications would be given in languages such as Haskell or Modula, in other languages such as Ada a particular **package** would be specified.

4. A network interface is defined (e.g., RPC-based) for all remotely available operations.
5. Each module is classified as client or server as far as its network interfaces are concerned. Thus, some modules may be classified as client and server at the same time.
6. Servers are registered. The method in which servers are to be made available to other functional units is determined.
7. A strategy for the binding process of client and server subsystems is defined. It is decided here whether the binding process is static or dynamic, and whether binding is to take place just during the initialization phase or for every call.

Integration of network management functionality into a distributed application. Looking at distributed applications from another angle we see that a distributed application falls apart into an application part and a communication part. Given a declarative specification, the communication part can be created by an RPC-generator automatically. However, there is more management functionality needed as far as communication is concerned: Networks become more complex and more heterogeneous almost every day. Thus, additional integration of sophisticated functionality for network and system management is a must. Consequently, there are already serious proposals of methods for integrating management functions into distributed applications which help to supervise and control the distributed system as a whole (Hegering and Abeck 1994).

Failure handling in distributed applications. Failures occurring in a local application are either handled through a programmer-defined exception-handling routine or ignored. While in the first case the exception handler may either stop the application in a controlled manner or continue in an adequately modified way, ignoring a failure leads in most cases to a crash. The operating system will then clean up the environment (i.e., open files will be closed, allocated address space will be freed, and all locked resources will be unlocked, etc.).

In contrast to a local application, in a distributed application there exist a variety of additional failure types such as communication link failures, crashes of machines hosting individual subsystems of the distributed application, failure-prone RPC-interfaces, or bugs in the distributed subsystems themselves. Failures of the communication link include broken "wires", bridges, routers, and faulty broker subsystems as well as faulty RPC-runtime systems, locally and remotely. The crash of individual subsystems may not necessarily lead to a crash of the entire distributed application. Standby subsystems, as described earlier, may take over the tasks of the crashed subsystems. Installed redundancy (like replicated services) may help to tolerate such crashes of individual subsystems to a certain degree. This failure transparency is one of the strengths of a distributed system.

Obviously, the needed mechanisms to manage the redundancy in the system (e.g., the protocols to access replicated server subsystems) and the programmer-defined exception handlers become more complex. In the last two decades, a rich set of such mechanisms has been proposed (prominent examples include the family of fault-tolerant protocols for replicated file services which we will discuss in some detail in Chap. 5). Furthermore, relevant supporting services are now at every programmer's disposal. The so-called RPC-info (Corbin 1991), for instance, is a service that checks and lists the states of all registered servers in the distributed system. Moreover, clients may request the idempotent service operation called **rpc_are_you_there** to verify a server subsystem's state. An answer to such a request implies that the server subsystem in question is still available and may accept forthcoming requests.

Development platforms for distributed applications. Distributed applications like CSCW applications are rarely built on top of the bare transport layer. The complexity and the risk of failures is too high. Rather, programmers of such applications work on top of more or less sophisticated development platforms. This is especially useful since distributed applications are typically built by a group of programmers. Gurus who design, implement and test an entire distributed application may exist, but they are the exception. Therefore, a motivation to use these development platforms comes from insights of the software engineering community. Programming-in-the-large may help to design, implement and test applications built by a group of programmers. For example, it could support the cooperation among a team of interface designers where temporal dependencies exit, it could look after operational aspects that play a role when machines and links may crash (here, for instance, support for an optimal allocation and relocation of subsystems is relevant), and it could give support as far as maintenance issues are concerned. The latter is of some importance because a distributed application has to maintain a rich set of (external) interfaces of heterogeneous subsystems. At the same time, there is a need for a full integration of these subsystems into different target environments (i.e., different computer architectures, different runtime systems, and various versions of different operating systems).

When a group of programmers has the task to build a distributed application, in addition to distributed code management there is also the need for distributed file services. For a distributed application there is also a need for tools that help to model concurrency (e.g., based on Petri nets), partial failures, message delays, etc.

Within OSI a framework has been specified that should facilitate the development of distributed applications. Special attention has been given to the specification of external interfaces and to the overall behavior of the system.

1.7.3 Distributed applications in ODP

The Open Distributed Processing (ODP) (Bowen 1991) has been introduced by ISO with the goal of defining a reference model that integrates a wide range of standards for distributed systems.

Among others, ODP should help to solve the consistency problem. The starting point for this endeavor is a heterogeneous distributed system where in addition to the interfaces specifications based upon the OSI reference model, global properties of the system are specified. Unfortunately due to the system's evolution and the need for possible future integration of various applications it has become impossible to create a common standard that fits all different systems. Consider, for instance, management information systems that rely on information from office communication systems, or CIM systems[12] that interact with CAD systems.[13]

ODP can be distinguished from the pure RPC-level in the following sense: ODP sees the distribution as the initial position. An RPC, on the other hand, can be seen as an extension of an existing language construct developed for local applications. Consequently, an RPC may see the distribution as a special (extreme) case. Moreover, the relationships between data and procedures accessing the data are not described within an RPC.

For standardization purposes, ODP identifies four different types of interfaces:

1. A programming interface specifies calls to well-defined functions (e.g., data base queries).
2. A human-computer interface specifies the user interfaces.
3. A communication interface defines a specification compliant to the OSI reference model.
4. An interface for external (physical) storage media specifies the modes of information exchange.

The ODP reference model is composed of a descriptive model, a prescriptive model, a user model, and a model for semantics and architecture.

While the descriptive model contains definitions of the concepts and the analytical framework as well as normalized descriptions of distributed systems, the prescriptive model specifies the characteristics that are needed to call a distributed system open. The term *open* reflects the situation of almost all distributed systems (i.e., multihardware, multivendor systems). The user model contains the descriptions of the ODP environment from the user's perspective. Finally, the model for semantics and architecture relates the concepts of the descriptive model with standard techniques for a formal specification. This leads to a uniform interpretation of the descriptive model.

[12] Computer Integrated Manufacturing.
[13] Computer Aided Design.

Viewpoints in ODP. ODP tries to reduce the inherent complexity of a distributed system by means of introducing five different viewpoints. Each of them focuses on a particular level of abstraction of the distributed system. The viewpoints are:

1. Enterprise viewpoint
2. Information viewpoint
3. Computation viewpoint
4. Engineering viewpoint
5. Technology viewpoint

The appropriate viewpoint is chosen while designing a distributed system. Unfortunately, the computation viewpoint dominates the other four (i.e., it is most frequently chosen). The computation viewpoint is the designers' favorite viewpoint for some reason, whereas enterprise and information viewpoints are often seen as subordinate (below we will explain why). There is some truth in the saying "If your only tool is a hammer than every problem looks like a nail." We can express here the necessity of an appropriately composed design team. Essentially, an interdisciplinary background of the team members is as important here as it is for CSCW in general. We will come back to this issue when we discuss roles, skills and competencies of team members in the next chapter.

The decisions of an inappropriately composed design team may cause great difficulties and prohibit a smooth integration of a distributed system in an organization. Ideally, we would like to start with the viewpoint that is most appropriate for the organization in question, and would then regard other viewpoints while the system evolves.

After this short digression let us come back to a detailed description of the different viewpoints:

1. *Enterprise viewpoint:* This viewpoint focuses on the activities (and aspects of their execution) that optimally pursue the objectives of the target organization. It pays special attention to the goals that the distributed system should reach within the organization.
   The system requirements refer to the aforementioned activities and also reflect the mutual dependency between the distributed system used by an organization and that organization. The system is always measured against the benefit the organization derives from its usage. Thus, the designers have to analyze the organizational structures, the information infrastructures and, most importantly, policies and nonformal procedures the organization follows.
   The designers have to keep in mind that the end users (besides being sponsors and enablers) of this viewpoint will be members of upper management. In their function, they "contemplate" and view the organization as a whole. For them, this viewpoint must answer questions of the kind: Where and how is information managed and processed? Is access secure

and reliable? How can we get timely, decision-relevant information? Is knowledge management enabled? Where is value added and how do we compare to the competition? Some of these questions can only be answered if the information viewpoint has also been considered.

2. *Information viewpoint:* This viewpoint focuses on aspects of the structure, the control of and the access to information that is needed for the key activities of the organization. It identifies information objects and describes the methods for manipulating and managing these objects.
   As a consequence, the system requirements mainly focus on how to encapsulate data into objects and what functional units are needed to manipulate and manage the objects. Whether the manipulation and management is automatically or manually performed is of no importance here; subsystems are seen as black boxes only. At this level of abstraction, the system specification is functional rather than algorithmical.
   Typical end users of this viewpoint are system analysts, system designers themselves, as well as, (upper-level) managers and data modelers of the information.
3. *Computation viewpoint:* This viewpoint concentrates on aspects of the logical distribution of data and subsystems. Physical distribution is not considered at this level of abstraction.
   The system requirements refer to cooperating subsystems that as a whole realize the overall system functionality. Structuring and composition of functional units allows the definition of (abstract) data types. The application is then modeled as a set of computational objects that interact in a predefined way. There is no distinction between objects that manage information and objects that manipulate information.
   End users of this viewpoint are mainly application programmers. Since application programmers have tended to dominate design teams, it becomes clear why the computation viewpoint has been the designers' favorite viewpoint.
4. *Engineering viewpoint:* This viewpoint looks after the support of the distributed applications as far as the physical system environment is concerned. Among others, aspects are: physical distribution of data and subsystems (also called allocation; see Sect. 1.7.4), heterogeneity of systems components, and quality of service. The latter subsumes system attributes like performance, reliability, availability, and where needed, response time for real-time applications. Section 3.2 discusses some of these attributes in detail.
   The requirements for the engineering viewpoint have to resist against the mapping of the distributed application to the underlying infrastructure (i.e., the system configuration). Thus, the requirements may include the desired levels of transparency (e.g., location, access, migration, replication, and concurrency transparency). Furthermore, using an object-oriented approach, another level of transparency may be of interest: the

so-called liveness transparency. This level of transparency masks the fact that objects are activated and deactivated due to some allocation mechanism.
Main users of this viewpoint are system programmers and network specialists.

5. *Technology viewpoint:* This viewpoint considers the appearance of the different physical and technical subsystems.
In this viewpoint, the requirements focus on technological aspects and real-world components. Real-world components include the hardware platforms (including peripheral devices as well as network constituents such as multiplexing units, bridges, routers, etc.) and corresponding software artifacts like the operating systems.
The main users of this viewpoint are network and computer support teams.

Figure 1.42 shows the connections between the last three viewpoints (i.e., computation, engineering and technology viewpoints). The components of the engineering viewpoint are instances of application-specific functional units. Several functional units might be mapped into a single component. The transparency layer provides the desired levels of transparency while the system kernel contains the basic functionality the distributed system should provide. The basic functionality includes communication facilities, local process execution and resource management.

1.7.4 Resource allocation

Resource management is a basic functionality of a distributed system. It may contain functions to assign resources to logical nodes (according to some criteria), either statically or dynamically. In both cases the main objective is to allocate resources near the logical node where the resources are needed. Fault-tolerance might also be an objective of the system. In this case, resources will be replicated and allocated to different (physical) nodes.

In the remainder of this section, we will use the term resource as a synonym for file and distributed system as a synonym for distributed file system. However, most of the discussion can easily be generalized and adapted to other types of resources.

If the system is distributed across a wide area network, the chosen file allocation strategy has a high impact on performance, and, if files are replicated, may increase the availability of the entire distributed file system. It is obvious that performance degrades if clients have to access remote file server subsystems over low-bandwidth links. It is also clear that there is a tradeoff between performance and availability. A **read** operation on a file is performed rapidly if the file is stored locally, or at least within the same local area network. The same is true for **write**. Replicating the file can increase the availability because the crash of a file server in charge of an individual replica

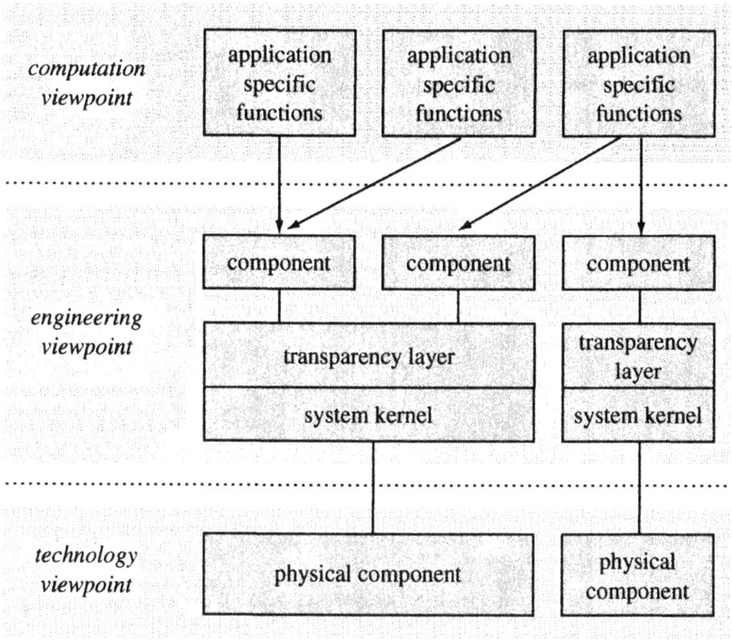

Fig. 1.42. Connection of the computation, engineering and technology viewpoints

does not prohibit accesses to the remaining replicas. Protocols supporting the desired replication transparency usually provide some sort of consistency and concurrency control as well.

A simple protocol, known as write-all-read-any, would allow each **read**-client to access the file from the most appropriate file server subsystem. Most appropriate could mean in this context: the nearest file server subsystem, or the file server subsystem up and running when needed. To guarantee consistency, a **write**-client, in turn, has to update all replicas (i.e., it must successfully write at all server subsystems responsible for the replicated, logical file). It should be clear that this requires some sort of two-phase locking policy, possibly within a transactional scheme. Section. 5.2.3 will discuss this protocol in more detail.

The more replicas which exist the more unlikely is a successful write operation. In any case, more replicas usually also means more performance loss, at least for writers, not to mention storage space considerations. The simple protocol write-all-read-any already gives some motivation for the fact that we need a good compromise between the number and allocation of replicas with regard to access modes, performance and desired availability: The higher the number of replicas the higher the availability of the logical file, at least for readers, and the higher the secondary storage needs.

Taking all this into account, how should this compromise look? What we need is an optimization that determines (i) the optimal number of replicas, and (ii) the optimal allocation of these replicas. Since access patterns, current load and other relevant parameters change over time, this so-called optimal file allocation should be modified, dynamically.

Definition 1.7.2 (Static vs. dynamic file allocation).
File allocation means the assignment of files and their replicas to physical nodes. It is part of the engineering viewpoint of ODP.

The allocation can be static, i.e., the files and their replicas are assigned once, or dynamic (the file allocation is modified when optimization parameters dynamically change).

Ideally, we would like to modify the optimal file allocation immediately after relevant optimization parameters have changed. Unfortunately, besides the amount of time needed to get and evaluate these optimization parameters, calculating the optimum takes a considerable length of time. Moreover, changing the file allocation is not an easy task. Files have to be relocated, and if in the new optimal file allocation the number of replicas has to change as well, new replicas must be created or existing replicas must be deleted. All that should happen while clients access these files.

The problem of finding an optimal file allocation, in the literature also known as file assignment problem (FAP), has been the focus of attention for many years.

Origins of the file assignment problem. The first FAP-isomorphic approaches originated in the 1960's (Cooper 1963, Efroymson and Ray 1966, Feldman 1966). Then, the main focus was mathematical models to calculate optimal locations for factories and warehouses (Ramamoorthy and Wah 1983). Optimization meant minimal transport costs.

First isolated approach. The paper by Chu (1969) proposed the first isolated approach to the file assignment problem. Chu developed a linear optimization model which considered a purely static allocation of files and their replicas to nodes within a fully-connected computer network. Optimization meant minimal storage and communication costs. His model used two constraints: average access time (it should not fall below a given threshold), and secondary storage space (this was a tough issue at the time of his proposal). The second constraint was found to be fundamental and was used in almost all later proposals.

Chu's proposal can be formalized as follows: Find an index set $I = \{n : 1 \leq n \leq |N| \wedge Y_n = 1\}$ that optimally solves the stated problem. Thereby, let N be the set of all nodes within the fully-connected computer network and let $Y_n = 1$, if node n gets a file replica assigned, (0, otherwise).

A few years later, Chu (1973) refined his approach. He developed a procedure that calculated the number of replicas according to some availability requirements. This number of replicas was then fed into his previous proposal as a constant. Overall, his allocation remained static.

Reformulation of the file assignment problem. The approaches for FAP were influenced by financial objectives. Optimal allocation always meant assignment at minimal costs. Examples include Chu (1969, 1973), Mahmoud and Riordon (1976) as well as Irani and Khabbaz (1979).

Starting with the declining prices in microelectronics, the original file assignment problem was reformulated: the main emphasis became optimization of the system's performance. At the same time, the underlying optimization model was enriched with more realistic assumptions like: accesses to files are initiated by processes, and these accesses can be of mode **read** or **write**.

The first assumption led to more complex communication models because the communication between users and their processes (input/output behavior) as well as between these processes and the file server subsystems have to be considered (Coffman et al. 1981, Laning and Leonard 1983). In this context, Akoka (1980) stated the so-called return flow of information (from server subsystem to client to end user) but did not fully integrate its consequences in a dynamic model. If processes were modeled then the execution location of processes and possible restrictions for this execution on particular nodes in the network became an issue.

The second assumption made the modeling of replication more difficult. This is why the early optimization models mostly applied the simple protocol write-all-read-any for consistency and concurrency control (Casey 1972, Sumita and Sheng 1988).

Table 1.7 compares the most influential proposals for the file assignment problem.

Table 1.7. Comparison of FAP approaches

Criteria	Akoka 1980	Casey 1972	Chu 1969	Chu 1973, Laning 1983	Levin 1975	Mahmoud 1976
Number of replicas	variable	variable	fixed	variable	variable	variable
Read/write distinction	yes					
Access protocol	write-all-read-any					
Access via process	yes	no	no	no	yes	no
Execution location of processes	local	not considered			local	not considered
Execution restriction of processes	yes	not considered			yes	not considered
Allocation	static	static	static	static	dynamic	static
Storage space considered	yes					
Availability considered	no	no	no	yes	no	yes
Input/output behavior	yes	no	no	no	no	yes

FAP is an NP-complete problem (i.e., as we said before, calculating the optimum file allocation may take a considerable length of time, even for small problem sizes). There is no known algorithm that works in polynomial time. The high complexity forces those searching for solutions to dynamic file allocation either to look at too simplified, unrealistic models or to consider specific subproblems only (Gavish and Pirkul 1986, Pattipati and Wolf 1990).

1.7.5 History of highly influential distributed systems

This section overviews important, highly influential distributed systems (see Fig. 1.43).

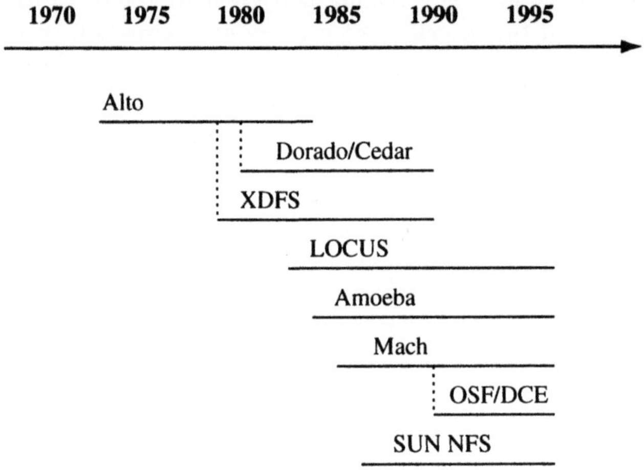

Fig. 1.43. History of important distributed systems

In the 1970's at the Xerox Palo Alto Research Center (known as Xerox PARC), Thacher et al. (1979) designed and constructed with Alto a machine that can be seen as the origin of today's personal computers and workstations.[14] It was mainly used for demonstration purposes of interactive single-user applications.

Alto was considerably innovative for its time: It had a high resolution display, a mouse, a 2.5 MB hard disk, a microprogrammable processor for halftone graphics manipulations, and an Ethernet adapter. The utilized 3 MHz research Ethernet was a predecessor of the later 10 MHz variant.

Experimental applications for the Alto included graphic games (e.g., Maze), programming language environments for Interlisp, Smalltalk and

[14] It took some years for the Apple II, Commodore's C64 and, certainly, the I8088-based IBM PC to bring about the great marketing success of personal computers, and for the DEC MicroVax and later models from Apollo, Hewlett Packard and Sun to penetrate the workstation market.

Mesa[15], and office applications. For the latter the focus was on document editors, document management tools, message systems and graphical user interfaces.

Later at Xerox PARC, Sturgis et al. (1980) developed the so-called Xerox Distributed File System (XDFS). XDFS was distributed across a set of server subsystems (see Sect. 1.4). Clients were enabled to request service operations over the Xerox internet. Communication between clients and the XDFS server subsystems was asynchronous. Every XDFS file had a file name and a unique identifier (UID) that allowed the clients to directly access the files. Identifiers were simple integers generated while creating a file. Since catalogs for a structuring of the file name space were not provided, a separate directory server was installed. File accesses were managed as transactions by each file server. Hence, the applications had to manage the operation logs themselves when accesses to multiple files on several file servers were needed. The additional burden for the application programmers and the risks of error-prone behavior of the applications are evident.

Successor of Alto was Dorado, at the time of the development an extremely powerful machine. Dorado was based on the ECL technology and could be compared to a Vax-780. Cooling and noise was an issue for the Dorado development team. Therefore, they developed a long connection cable that allowed them to place the machine up to several hundred meters away from the end user displays. The programming language environment was tailored for Cedar (Swinehart et al. 1986), an extension of Mesa with some Interlisp functionality. As an example, automatic garbage collection was added. Furthermore, Cedar supported joint group work of geographically distributed programmers. Remote debugging and configuration management functions were provided. The researchers had several questions in mind for this very early groupware: Which files belong to what configuration? Where are these files (hints to file servers)? Where are the files copied to if new versions are created?

At the University of California in Los Angeles (UCLA), Popek and Walker (1985) designed the location transparent distributed operating system Locus. For the end user Locus presented itself as a large Unix system where client and server subsystems ran on connected machines. Files were stored with system-wide unique names. For reasons of availability files could be replicated. Moreover, Locus allowed remote process execution on client demand.

At the University of Amsterdam, The Netherlands, Tanenbaum et al. (1991) developed Amoeba first as an experimental testbed for distributed system studies then as a commercial product. Amoeba is characterized through its hybrid architecture consisting of workstations, a processor pool and ter-

[15] Mesa was an Ada-like programming language.

minals where a small operating system kernel[16] provides interprocess communication among (heavy and lightweight) processes organized in clusters. Client and server subsystems communicate over remote procedure calls, or where appropriate (e.g., lightweight processes), over shared virtual memory. Access to system resources is managed via capabilities describing the clients rights, e.g., the right to **read** or **write** a file. For security reasons capabilities are encrypted.

At the Carnegie-Mellon University, Acetta et al. (1986) developed Mach. It is also characterized through its small kernel, called microkernel. Mach is especially suitable for multiprocessor applications or applications designed for a distributed system.

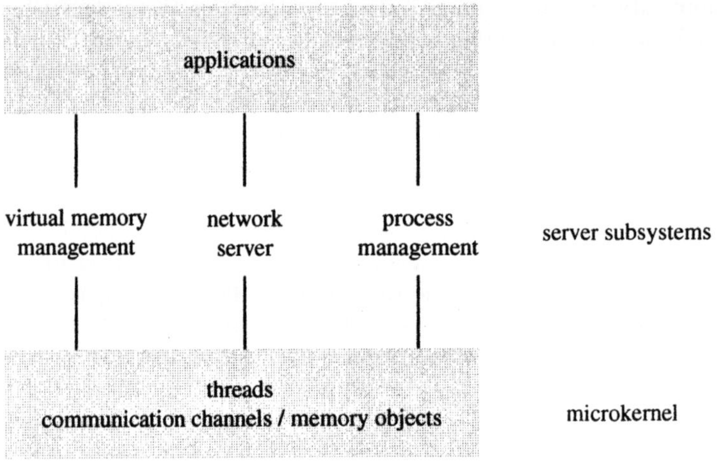

Fig. 1.44. Structure of a microkernel

Figure 1.44 shows how a process (a task) defines an execution environment that provides secured access to system resources such as virtual memory and communication channels. Again, a set of lightweight processes enables fine-grained execution distribution. Shared usage of memory space is based on the so-called copy-on-write principle (Nelson and Ousterhout 1988), i.e., the corresponding memory space is copied when writing. As illustrated in Fig. 1.45 processes communicate through communication channels, called ports. In the example, process 1 may send its message to a process 2 through port number 47.

A port can be realized as a message queue to which multiple senders may send messages. A single receiver process per queue (i.e., per port number) is in charge of the arriving messages. Mach also supports communication

[16] Tanenbaum brought this idea of a small system kernel where many operating system services are realized – outside of the kernel – as user processes to an extreme in his educational operating system Minix.

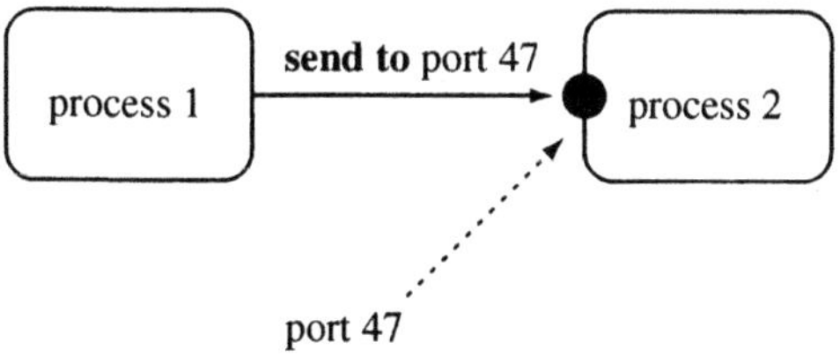

Fig. 1.45. Process communication through ports

through so-called network servers (see Fig. 1.46). Network servers act as local representatives for processes that run on remote machines. For the calling processes these network servers are fully transparent.

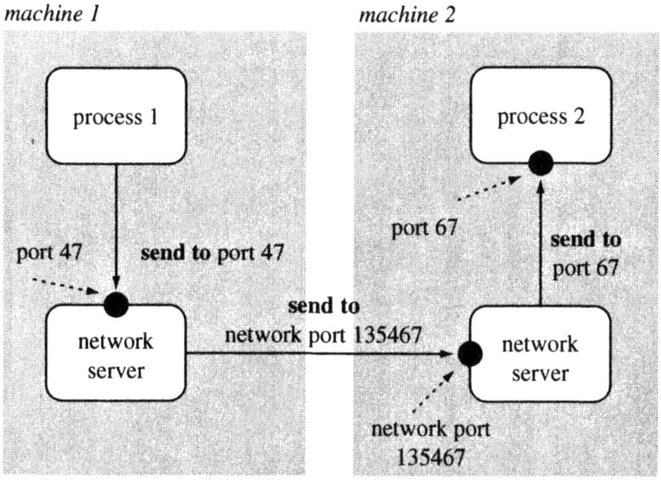

Fig. 1.46. Network servers in Mach

The Open Software Foundation (OSF) takes Mach as its basis for a standardized operating system version for Unix. In addition, OSF defines with the Distributed Computing Environment (DCE) (Foundation 1992) a set of system components that provide a coherent development platform as well as an execution environment for applications targeted to heterogeneous distributed systems. The main features in DCE include the client-server paradigm, RPC and information sharing. Figure 1.47 depicts the architecture behind DCE.

A well-known networking extension to Unix and other operating systems is obtained through Sun's Network File System (NFS).

NFS supports RPC-based, transparent remote access to files stored under conventional operating systems. Therefore, file catalogs are exported (by server subsystems) and mounted (by the client machines). Figure 1.48 illustrates the mounting mechanism for the local as well as the remote case.

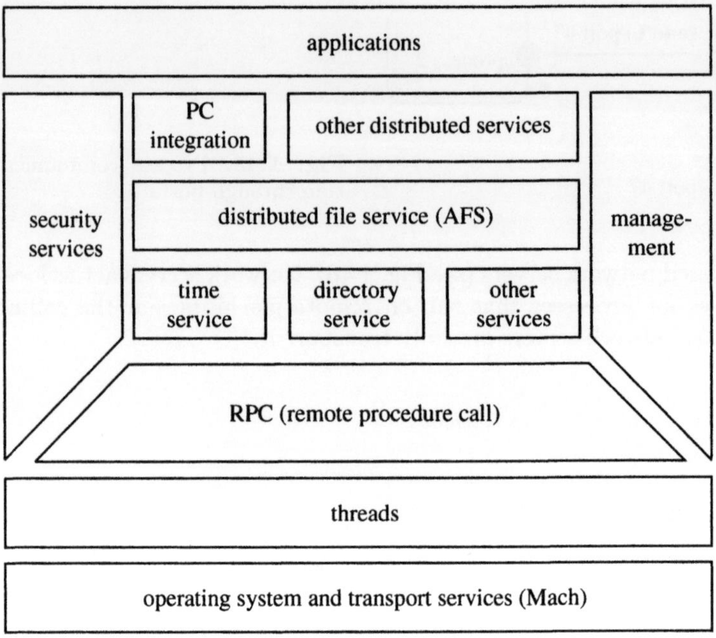

Fig. 1.47. DCE architecture

Files ready for export are enumerated in "/etc/exports" of the corresponding exporting server subsystem. A so-called *v-node* (consisting of host identifier, file system identifier and *i-node number*) is a unique identifier for files managed under NFS.

NFS is a stateless file server subsystem, i.e., a server subsystem does not store state information about its clients and their activities (see also Sect. 1.19). NFS manages a system-internal file cache.

1.7.6 Caching

As shown in Fig. 1.49 there is a single file cache per system, not per program. Consequently, changes made by program 1 are seen by program 2 immediately after a **fflush** has been performed (both run on system 1). However, for program 3 these changes are hidden until the data have been transferred to system 3. This weakness can partly be avoided if one of the following cache coherence protocols is used (see below).

Code fragment (Reading a cached data block). In the following code fragment we assume that the needed data block is stored in the cache.

function read(file f, block k): block;
  if (file f is local) **then return** k-th block
  else /* File f is remotely located. */
    if ($t_{last\_read\_of\_k} < (t_{now} - w)$)

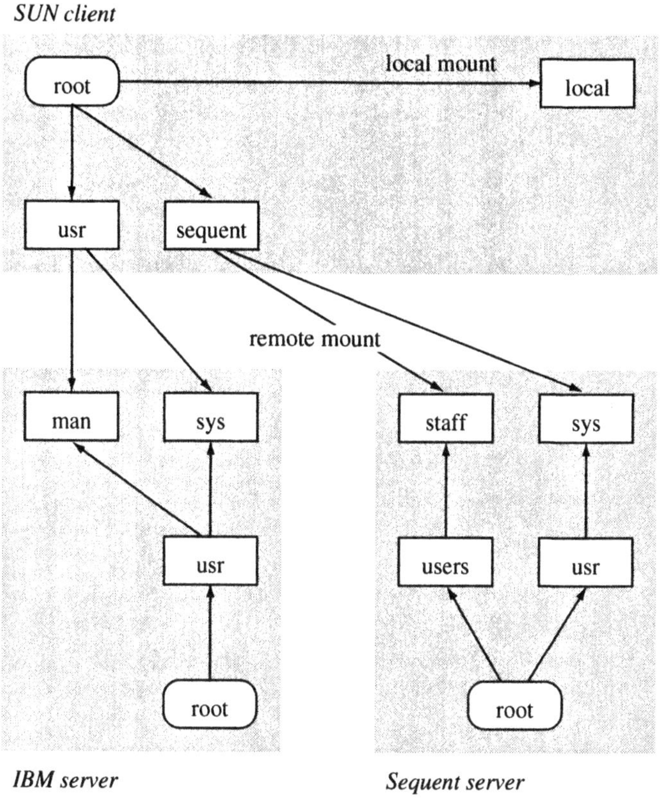

Fig. 1.48. Export and mount of file catalogs

/* If the last **read** was performed more than w seconds before, check the validity of the cache entry; t_{now} be the actual time. */

then request latest modification time $t_{modRemote}(k)$;
if $(t_{modRemote}(k) = t_{modLocal}(k))$ **then return** k-th block
else fetch the block from the remote location; **return** k-th block

As with all approaches which introduce redundancy into the system in order to increase performance (e.g., file replication schemes), caching must also address the issue of consistency. What should happen when cache entries managed at different hosts become outdated with regard to the original file? Some applications do not deal with this issue. Your favorite Web browser application might be an example. For other applications cache coherence is of more importance. In any case, for distributed file systems appropriate cache coherence protocols could mean success or failure in acceptance and market penetration.

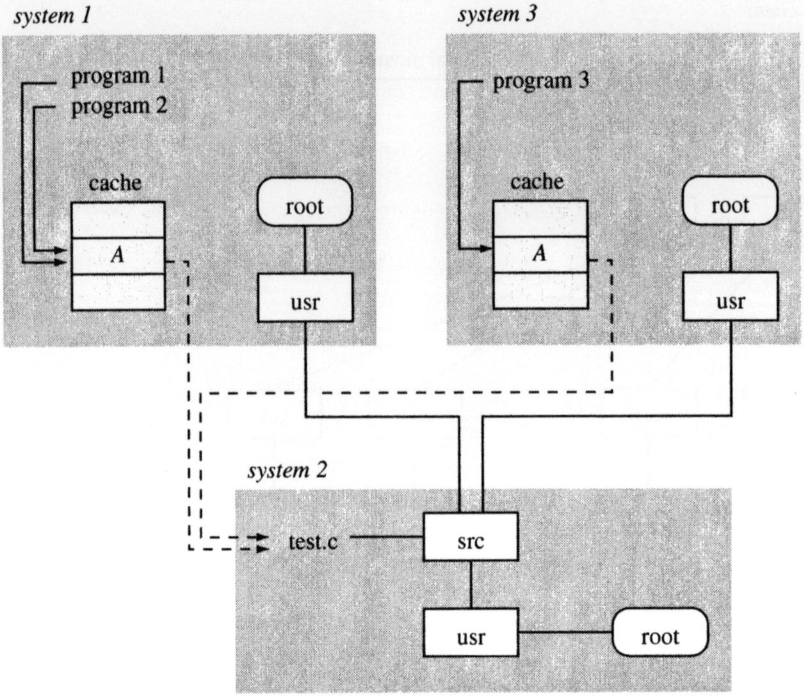

Fig. 1.49. Usage of a system-internal cache

In principle there are two basic protocols to guarantee cache coherence:

1. *Write-invalidate:* In this approach the protocol guarantees the following invariant:
   – there is no cache at all, or
   – all caches are used read-only, or
   – there is exactly one cache used for writing.
   To guarantee this invariant, a **write** to the cache leads to an invalidation of all other caches in existence. This is easy to achieve in a multiprocessor system because the invalidation transaction can be realized as an atomic broadcast over the shared bus system. In a distributed system where a shared bus system does not exist, atomic invalidation is more tricky (see below).
2. *Write-update:* In this approach multiple caches may be used for writing. However, every **write** to a cache has to be propagated to all other caches in existence. In a multiprocessor system this can again be realized as an atomic broadcast over the shared bus system.

In a distributed system to achieve a cache invalidation or a write-update, message exchanges are needed between the cache possessing nodes. Therefore, another level of indirection is introduced, the so-called directory entries.

A directory entry maintains the addresses of all nodes that possess a cache entry for relevant data blocks. A node willing to update a cache entry looks up the directory entries, and gets in (bilateral) contact with the nodes that possess a cache entry for the relevant data block in order to (1) invalidate or (2) update their cache entries.

1.8 Further Reading

This first chapter could not describe all aspects of distributed systems. Relevant books on distributed systems include the books by Coulouris et al. (1994), Goscinski (1991), Maekawa et al. (1987), Mullender (1993) and Tanenbaum (1992).

Tay and Ananda (1990) give an excellent introduction to the aspect of remote procedure calls. Ananda et al. (1992) surveys asynchronous remote procedure calls.

Tanenbaum (1996) gives a nice introduction to the ISO OSI reference model. Stalling (1998) discusses security aspects of distributed systems while Hegering and Abeck (1994) focus on network management aspects.

Orfali et al. (1996) summarize CORBA. They also relate CORBA with OLE and OpenDoc. Andreoli et al. (1996b) give a collection of articles on the subject of coordination language (e.g., Gamma, Linear Objects).

Ibaraki and Katoh (1988) describe algorithmic approaches for resource allocation problems. Using a uniform notation to compare the different approaches for the file assignment problem, the papers by Dowdy and Foster (1982) and Wah (1984) represent the most comprehensive surveys on the subject.

Pong and Dubois (1997) discuss verification techniques for cache coherence protocols. Lilja (1993) illustrates cache coherence issues in the light of large-scale shared-memory multiprocessor systems.

2. Computer-Supported Cooperative Work

Contemporary literature is overflowing with technical terms defining various aspects of computer-supported cooperative work. In the following chapter, we will introduce these terms and discuss them with respect to practical teamwork support. In addition to demonstrating typical usage scenarios and their characteristics, we will also present several classification models, in particular time space taxonomy. When dealing with so-called application level classification, we will discuss message systems, group editors, electronic meeting rooms, conferencing systems, shared information spaces, intelligent agents and coordination systems.

Furthermore, we will investigate factors which contribute to the success or failure of groupware systems. Research and experiments with computer-supported cooperative work in real environments will underlie this work. The results of these studies demonstrate the way in which groupware should be designed and CSCW concepts should be validated.

Moreover, we will give reasons for the overwhelming success of email, discuss the Portland experiment and introduce the commercial system Lotus Notes.

2.1 Introduction

The widespread use of personal computers with their associated networks has for some time led to attempts at not only using these resources for distributed data processing, but also for collaborative work. Terms, such as "Computer-Supported Cooperative Work" (CSCW for short), and "Groupware" have been introduced. The term "supported" refers to both very simple, uncoordinated access to shared data and to complex, synchronized modeling and provision of group-internal relationships and interactions (like group processes).

At the present time, the terms groupware and CSCW have become very fashionable, just as "Artificial Intelligence" (AI for short) was in the late 1970's and early 1980's. Use of the term AI due to its ambiguity caused misunderstandings or undue expectations from the industrial sector which scientific research was in no position to live up to. This problem should be avoided with groupware and CSCW, which is why this chapter will pay special attention to precision and formality where terminology is concerned. While CSCW includes the universal scientific research field, groupware deals with the respective practical system solutions of collaborative work.

Networks are having a major impact on the evolution and changes of the way in which users collaborate to perform common tasks. System examples supporting collaboration are, among others, message systems (email), news groups and distributed file systems. All these examples open up new ways of cooperation, albeit exclusively asynchronous ones. There are also so-called talk programs, which support interaction, but they are limited with respect to synchronously involved users and the degree of their interaction. More often than not, only two users are permitted and the interaction is restricted to the exchange of textual messages.[1] In this book, we discuss asynchronous and synchronous groupware which require significantly more interaction functionality.

As opposed to multiuser systems, such as distributed database systems or time-sharing operating systems, groupware systems send a notification whenever something is altered. This facilitates users' awareness of each other's existence and concurrent actions. The notification informs all users involved in a group session of modifications in their shared environment. If we take a look at conventional multiuser systems with respect to these notifications, the difference becomes obvious. If a user executes a certain task, such as inserting a new record into a distributed database system or generating a new process in a time-sharing operating system, then other users will not be informed. Instead they must initiate an explicit system query (database query or process listing) in order to be informed of the aforementioned activities. Active databases (Chakravarthy et al. 1992, Bussler and Jablonski 1994),

[1] The Unix program "talk" only allows transmission of text and is limited to two participants. Internet relay chat (IRC) or the chat environment ICQ are extensions of talk to groups.

which at present play an important role in database research, will in the future integrate notification mechanisms in a way most conductive to teamwork.

2.2 Background for Team Support

Experiences of larger organizations indicate three sectors which commonly cause the most serious problems: inefficiency in intraorganizational communication, restricted communication both intra- and interorganizational, and inadequate information management. Inefficiency refers to lost work caused through coordination problems, lack of memory, information overflow and incomplete information utilization and task analysis. Also, having too few people in charge of an organization may contribute to inefficiency since being those in charge being consulted will continually be overworked leaving other's work capacities underutilized.

Often, very limited areas of competence cause a restriction of communication channels within an organization: vertical communication along the organizational hierarchy dominates over horizontal communication on the same organizational level. Since this kind of infrastructure channels most of the communication through the supervisor, communication is often delayed due to the lag time inherent in funneling a large stream information through the narrow channel of a single individual. Moreover, information is sometimes lost because of unintended filtering.

Though in theory the requested information might be available, poor information management might make it difficult to localize this information; often, the end user is put in charge of arranging and filing the information. Inappropriate information management models and strategies might prevent later access to the filed information by other team members. These issues make the promotion and support of teams by computers advisable both for economical and technological reasons. On the one hand, computers are useful for adapting hierarchical organizational structures to technological innovations, on the other hand, they facilitate the integration of horizontal communication into the hierarchical organizational structure, thereby making it possible for employees in different departments of an organization to cooperate.

Teams are created on demand to solve specific problems and are dissolved after the work has been completed. The setup of goal-oriented, temporary teams can improve the efficiency of all employees and allows better utilization of the skilled work force. As seen in Japan, the precedence of teams over individual persons can greatly facilitate the achievement of such goals as shorter development times, faster information transfer, more efficient utilization of knowledge workers within the organization as well as decrease the amount of necessary administration. Since the entire team is responsible for both successes and failures, each and every team member is personally interested in the highest possible efficiency.

The last decades have brought substantial improvement in the communication domain including such media as telephones, telexes, computer networks (for example the Arpanet in the 1970's and now the Internet as its successor), and, most recently, videos. It must, however, be mentioned that the unchanneled use of some technologies, such as email and bulletin boards, has had some very negative effects: the flood of information remains incomprehensible to the individual user.

Example (Internet). At the beginning of the Internet boom in the early 1990's, there were approximately 200,000 computers attached to the network. At that time, Usenet, a bulletin board system for the Unix environment, served more than 37,000 organizations. A daily average of more than 20 MB of new text was created, which equals a yearly output of 7.25 GB. The integration of national networks into the global Internet and the evolution towards multimedia information has multiplied the amount of information being exchanged within the last few years. In July, 1998 the Internet consisted of more than 37 million computers.[2] Internet services like gopher and the world wide web (Obraczka et al. 1993) have especially contributed to the rapid growth of information exchange. For the year 1994, an estimated 12.5 terabytes per month was sent through the Internet (Nejmeh 1994). Between 1994 and 1998, the number again multiplied. Munich universities alone received and sent more than 5 terabytes in November 1998 via Internet.[3]

The use of CSCW, in combination with an organizational restructuring, results in more flexible and efficient organizations. Firstly, the flattening of hierarchies shortens information transfer routes which improves information flow and speeds up the decision-making processes. Secondly, the potential of communication and cooperation innovation offers additional synergetic effects with regard to the pluralistic competencies of team members. New market developments can be acknowledged faster and with more flexibility and efficiency.

The evolution of CSCW has been strongly influenced by a variety of technologies. Figure 2.1 depicts a selection of the most important technologies and their interdependencies. Current research and development mostly consider CSCW to be simply a part of office communication. Teamwork as it is practiced in industrial production has not yet had much impact on CSCW research.

2.3 Terminology

The field of collaborative work still lacks a standardized terminology. The terms "groupware" and "computer-supported cooperative work", however,

[2] http://www.nw.com/.

[3] http://www.lrz-muenchen.de/.

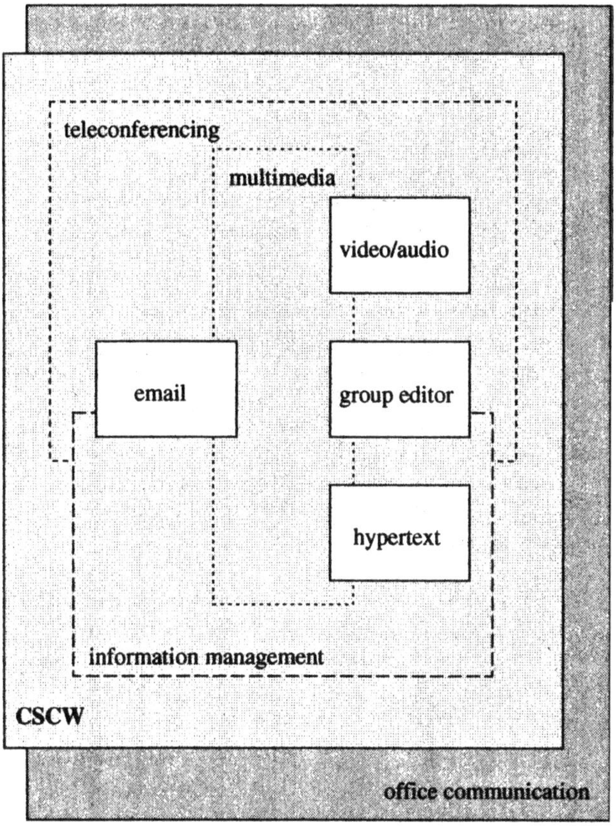

Fig. 2.1. Relationship of technologies within the context of CSCW

prevail. Besides these two, the following terms are also found; see also Johansen (1988) as well as Johansen et al. (1991):

- Technological Support for Work Group Collaboration
- Workgroup Computing
- Collaborative Computing
- Interpersonal Computing
- Computer Conferencing
- Computer-Mediated Communication
- Computer-Supported Groups
- Group Decision Support Systems
- Computer-Assisted Communication
- Augmented Knowledge Workshops
- Flexible Interactive Technologies for multiperson Tasks

The terms groupware and CSCW can be traced back to the early 1980's: Johnson-Lenz defined the term groupware, whereas CSCW was introduced by Greif and Cashman as the slogan for a small workshop with various participants from differing fields.[4] As mentioned above, CSCW refers to the theoretical foundations and methodologies for teamwork and its computer support. Wilson (1991) writes:

> "CSCW is a generic term which combines the understanding of the way people work in groups with the enabling technologies of computer networking, and associated hardware, software, services and techniques."

In contrast to this, groupware refers to software systems supporting teamwork and integrating theoretical foundations achieved by CSCW research. Johansen (1988) writes:

> "Groupware is a generic term for specialized computer aids that are designed for the use of collaborative work groups. Typically, these groups are small project-oriented teams that have important tasks and tight deadlines. Groupware can involve software, hardware, services and/or group process support."

Throughout this book we will use CSCW to refer to the theoretical foundations of computer-supported cooperative work and groupware to refer to software systems supporting cooperative work. In the late 1970's, industry had similar expectations with regard to Artificial Intelligence to those currently existing with regard to groupware. Since AI failed to deliver on these high expectations, a phase of frustration ensued. The CSCW community is attempting to prevent unrealistic expectations. This is why Winograd (1989) writes:

> "Groupware doesn't try to do magic. It doesn't get the work done for you, but lets you stay on top of the work. That is the real promise."

First and foremost, let us define the term "team": A number of people does not in and of itself constitute a team. Rather, certain characteristics must be added. Within a team, all members must be engaged in a common task and interact within a shared environment to perform it. In order to reach a common understanding, team members have to share and exchange information. Team members should also complement each other's talents. Problems with human resources often crop up when one attempts to form teams with a widespread range of relevant skills and competencies. An interdisciplinary background of team members is highly welcome, and in many cases an essential precondition for the team's achievements.[5] Knowledge about team membership as well as information about skills, competencies and roles of the other team members provides a high degree of group awareness (Rüdebusch

---

[4] The workshop took place in 1984 at Endicott House in Massachusetts, USA.

[5] Recall the discussion of selecting the appropriate viewpoint while designing an ODP-based distributed system.

and Mühlhäuser 1991). Last but not least, teamwork will only be efficient if communication and activities within the group are well-coordinated.

For practical reasons, the following discussion will primarily focus on small groups (i.e., groups containing less than one hundred participants), thus we exclude workshops and conferences. A group may be either constituted interdepartmentally (i.e., it is made up of members of one department within a single organization), or cross-departmentally (i.e., it is made up of members of different departments of a single organization). An example for the latter case is a strategic product planning team. Certainly, there may also be a third kind of group, namely interorganizational which means that, for example, a standardization committee consists of members from various organizations. These teams are supported by a choice of communication media between team members, dependent on the focus of the teamwork. It has to be decided individually whether to use telephone, telefax, telex, paper, face-to-face meetings, televideo conferencing, email, or shared databases.

We may also distinguish between electronic groups and electronically supported groups. In the former case group members communicate exclusively via computer; they might not even know each other personally. The latter group uses personal contact in addition to electronic communication (for instance via telephone or face-to-face meetings).

The field of CSCW deals with cooperation within groups and tries to develop innovative computer technologies supporting this kind of teamwork. In order to be both a success and widely accepted, the cooperation between such individuals as computer scientists, industrial psychologists and sociologists is inevitable. Basically, computer-supported cooperative work is not just an information management problem. It is rather an interdisciplinary application domain in which mechanisms and methodologies of computer science, telecommunications, information management (e.g., management information systems, MIS for short), sociology and organizational theory converge. At present, there is no official consent as to whether CSCW is actually a completely new research field or an all-encompassing "umbrella" for activities with similar goals in the aforementioned disciplines. Hughes et al. (1991) see CSCW as a new perspective in which computer support is designed and applied.

Computer-supported cooperative work also influences other areas, as the following aspects demonstrate: Since team members are often distributed with respect to space and time, we have to deal with the decentralization of data, control, and processing of tasks which results in distributed problem solving. Difficulties arise in distribution due to an effort to achieve a consistent global system state which requires the observation and manipulation of local parameters of all involved distributed system components. As far as communication is concerned, CSCW facilitates information transfer between distributed group members. This can only be achieved through an efficient utilization of the network bandwidth and a specification of appropriate communication protocols. Due to the use of different media to present and to convey information, the interaction between group members requires support for multimedia communication. CSCW aims at making distributed communication as efficient as face-to-face communication. For the involved people, the use of a computer as mediator in human-human interaction should be as inconspicuous as possible. The extension of user interfaces for use in groups enables multiuser applications. Finally, activities of AI are influenced by CSCW, because group activities can be automated by agents (v. Bechtolsheim 1993). The behavior of agents must be adapted to the group behavior, which itself is for the most part not static but may vary dynamically during the existence of the group. Both a heuristic and a learning approach may be used for contemplating the varying group behavior inside agents.

Furthermore, the influence of CSCW on sociology must not be ignored. Teamwork always involves people. This means that human behavior and the individual roles within the group must be examined closely. Also, effects of groupware systems on individual team members have to be analyzed. For example if a system stores an entire conversational history, some of the parties involved may not wish to have their comments recorded, reducing the system's effectiveness. Thus, computer support influences the behavior of individuals.

With all the above mentioned factors, a system for computer-supported cooperative work can be defined as follows:

Definition 2.3.1 (Ellis et al. 1991). *"Groupware are computer-based systems that support groups of people engaged in a common task (or goal) and that provide an interface to a shared environment."*

The emphasis is on common task and shared environment. Figure 2.2 shows the range for both dimensions (see also Ellis et al. 1991). Note that groupware systems are characterized by their high values for the common task and the shared environment. A software review system which assists a development group in the evaluation process of a software system is a typical example where group members focus on the same task. An email system provides hardly any shared environment, while an electronic classroom does so to a high degree.

In certain areas, a groupware system can be regarded as a logical extension of a single user system. A traditional text system, however, does not convert into a groupware system simply by allowing several users sequential reading or writing access to the same document. Firstly, in such a text system the activities of several users remain isolated (for example due to a transaction mechanism). Secondly users are mostly ignorant of others working on the same document at the same time (i.e., there is no group awareness). We can therefore specify as integral requirements of groupware that group members must not be isolated, that they must be informed explicitly about each others existence, and that modifications must be mutually reported. Displaying

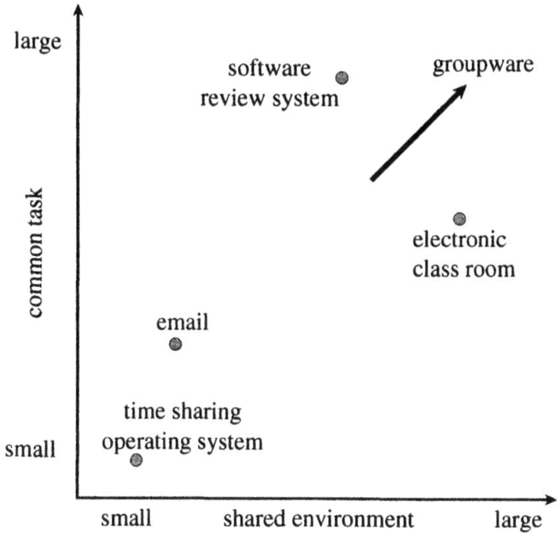

Fig. 2.2. Ranges for the dimension common task and shared environment

desktop images of all other users who work on the same document meet these demands to some extent.

2.4 CSCW in Practice – Scenarios

In the following sections, we will introduce a number of team situations using scenarios and their computer support. For a detailed discussion of more scenarios for CSCW applications, we refer the reader to Johansen (1988). Topics covered range from passive support by personal computers for recording meeting notes to active computer support by agents. For example, if a computer is involved as an active rival in a game, then its functionality replaces that of a human.

2.4.1 Support of face-to-face meetings

In a face-to-face meeting, participants are physically present in the same place at the same time and they may interact with or without technological support.

1. *Presentation support:* Team members often use face-to-face meetings for presentations. These presentations may be rather informal, or they may have quite a professional character. In the former case there is little preparation required and some notes on paper will suffice. Preparation for formal presentations utilizes a special document layout software which can be seen as a by-product of desktop publishing. Thus, computer support

is needed mostly in preparation of the formal meeting. Furthermore, presentation software is being increasingly used during informal and formal meetings for computer-supported presentation, as well. Meeting participants do not need any special computer knowledge. For computer-based presentations a laptop and LCD[6] projection equipment is required.

2. *Support for recording the meeting discussion:* In most meetings, the moderation and the minutes are done by one or several participants. The role of the facilitator is that of a chauffeur who is in charge of keeping the discussion running,[7] whereas the person doing the minutes focuses on content, using paper, blackboard and similar aids. The ideal situation would be one in which the information is typed directly into a personal computer and electronically projected onto the screen (see Fig. 2.3). In addition to instant availability of the typed information while the meeting is still under way, there is the added advantage of all participants getting a paper copy directly after the meeting has ended. Recording of the minutes at a later time might cause the loss of essential information which was produced during meeting discussions.

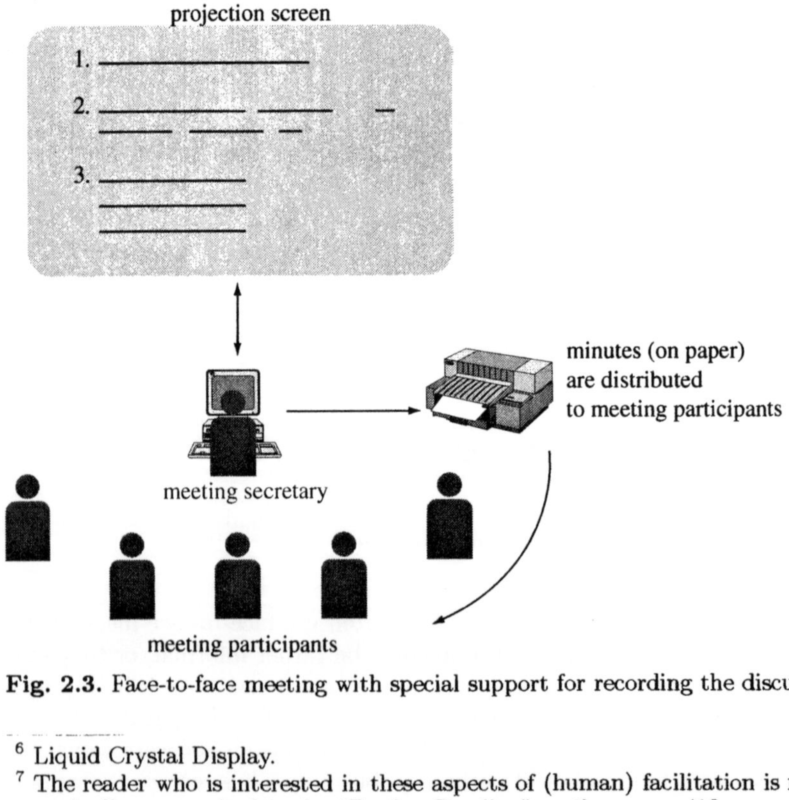

Fig. 2.3. Face-to-face meeting with special support for recording the discussion

[6] Liquid Crystal Display.

[7] The reader who is interested in these aspects of (human) facilitation is referred to the literature cited in the "Further Reading" section on p. 413.

This approach necessitates the meeting secretary to be familiar with the computer, whereas all other participants need have no specific computer knowledge. What is, however, indispensable is an appropriately equipped conference room.

3. *Computer-supported meetings:* An extended range of varieties for all group members is provided by a meeting in which all participants have their individual personal computers. The participants are grouped in a semicircle around a shared screen and work directly with their own computers, rather than indirectly through one person doing the minutes (see Fig. 2.4). Since all participants should still have the possibility of eye contact at all times, the personal computers must be integrated into the conference table.

Fig. 2.4. Face-to-face with direct computer support as practiced in the Ocean Lab at GMD

Information presented on the public electronic whiteboard originates from one or several personal computer screens. A special interface between the individual computers and the electronic whiteboard is required to control concurrent access to the shared environment. Each participant can choose between private work on his personal computer, projection of parts or of the entire information displayed on his computer screen onto the electronic whiteboard, or active participation in the discussion. The moderator may, if he so desires, have a special personal computer for determining which participant may access or alter public data displayed on the electronic whiteboard. The functionality of personal computers can change with conference rooms and meeting types: the system administrator can choose different systems or user interface configurations. There is no question that these kinds of meetings have significant advantages. However, it must be observed that few companies can afford the high equipment costs and most participants of company meetings are not yet sufficiently computer literate to justify the large investment in this type of equipment.

2.4.2 Support of distributed electronic meetings

In the category computer conferencing, the computer is an integral component. The participants are geographically dispersed.

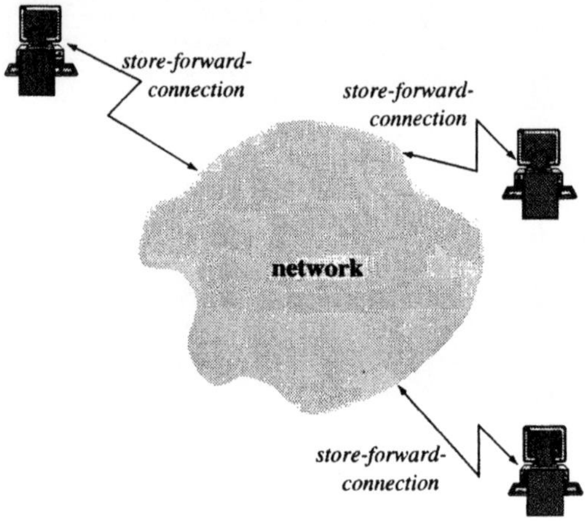

Fig. 2.5. Asynchronous computer-supported conference

1. *Asynchronous computer conferencing:* While email usually is a point-to-point connection between two individuals, asynchronous computer conferencing supports group communication with more than two users. In Fig. 2.5, three users are shown in conference via so-called store-forward connections. Group communication is a logical extension of traditional email systems.
   The required technology, for example for specifying groups as recipients of electronic messages or distribution lists, is already available. We expect to see a substantial increase in the number of email connections in the near future due to the rapid growth of the Internet.
2. *Shared screen and audio connection:* Each participant sits in his own environment (in his office, for example). Through both an audio connection (as in a telephone conference) and a data link[8], he can communicate and

[8] ISDN (Integrated Services Digital Network) transfers both information media (data and audio) via the same network.

interact with other participants. Each participant has a personal computer on his desk displaying identical information. Modifications on an individual screen are propagated to all other screens according to the WYSIWIS principle[9] (see Sect. 3.5.1).
Requirements for this kind of conference are the existence of computer networks connecting the individual personal computers, computer literacy of all participants, and network bandwidth which allows short or at least tolerable response times. In wide area networks, it will be hard to achieve reasonable response times, which will mostly necessitate information replication.

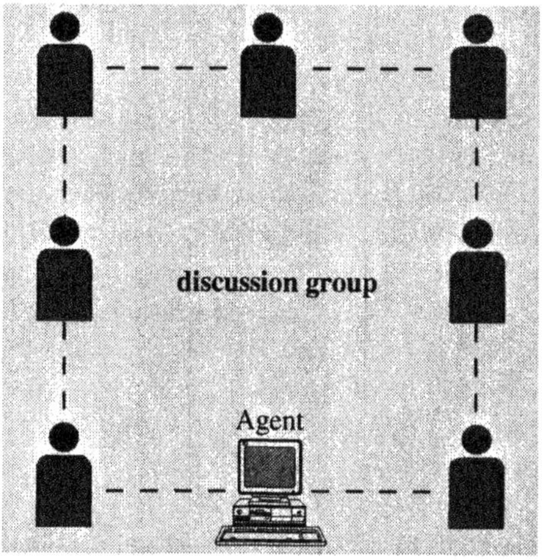

Fig. 2.6. Agent as meeting participant

3. *Agents as meeting participants:* An agent is a piece of software which participates in a group discussion as an active participant (see Fig. 2.6). The agent can have special functions, like recording the minutes, seeking information on demand or filtering relevant information. A meeting with an agent as a participant may take place as a face-to-face meeting, as a video conference or as an asynchronous group conference. However, this kind of meeting can result in complete observation by the agent, since every single activity of the participants, even negative activity such as passive participation can be monitored by the agent.
4. *VR conference:* In a VR[10] conference, participants meet indirectly in a 3D virtual reality. Each participant is represented by a so-called avatar, i.e., an animated synthetic person. If the real users are equipped with special hardware (e.g. data gloves and goggles) their avatars may interact accordingly. Research is going on to reproduce the user's facial

[9] WYSIWIS stands for What You See Is What I See.
[10] VR stands for Virtual Reality.

expressions on the avatar's face. This futurist approach is still in its infancy. Leading research organizations such as the Fraunhofer Institute in Germany, the Ishida Laboratory, Department of Information Science, Kyoto University, Japan,[11] and Fuji Pal in Palo Alto, USA, have already demonstrated encouraging prototypes.

Although we do not see an immediate impact of this technology upon standard business meetings, VR conferences could eventually enable meetings that would otherwise be impossible to set up: Examples might include meetings at locations that

- do not exist in reality,
- are too dangerous for human beings, or
- are out of reach or off-limits for most of the participants.

For the first case imagine a VR conference of architects that meet in an edifice that is not yet built and exists only in "silicon". They could argue about design and interior without having to put a single brick in place. For the second case consider meeting environments that could exist in reality but are too unhealthy etc. for the participants. A computerized representation of this environment might be sufficient for some experts to make up their minds about a certain issue (e.g., discuss nucleonics of a damaged power plant). In the third case, for instance, rooms of the Vatican or the White House otherwise closed to the public could be opened in virtual reality. Visitors, researchers and other interested people could then walk around in this virtual setting, share ideas and interact while discussing the surroundings. In another example, a jury could visit a digitized reproduction of a crime scene years after the incident without having to leave the courtroom.

Although some of the examples might seem far-fetched (at least presently), in the sense of CSCW all mentioned groups could eventually become valid electronically-supported or even electronic groups. They all fit the criteria of valid CSCW groups. The architects, the nuclear experts and the jury are all engaged in common tasks (designing a building, clearing away a danger zone, or bringing in a just verdict, respectively) and interact within a shared (virtual) environment to perform it.

2.4.3 Support in between meetings

1. *Project management systems:* These specialized software systems support teams when planning or coordinating tasks, or monitoring project progress. An example of this is the checking of milestones or the providing of an overview of the current project state (see Fig. 2.7). Team members contribute information for the creation and updating of the project plan, the execution of which the manager supervises. In the computer industry, these systems are already well established. Communication between

[11] http://www.lab7.kuis.kyoto-u.ac.jp/services/free-software/freewalk/

team members is asynchronous and happens via shared project data. The manager uses the system for supervising the project plan thereby achieving early problem detection.

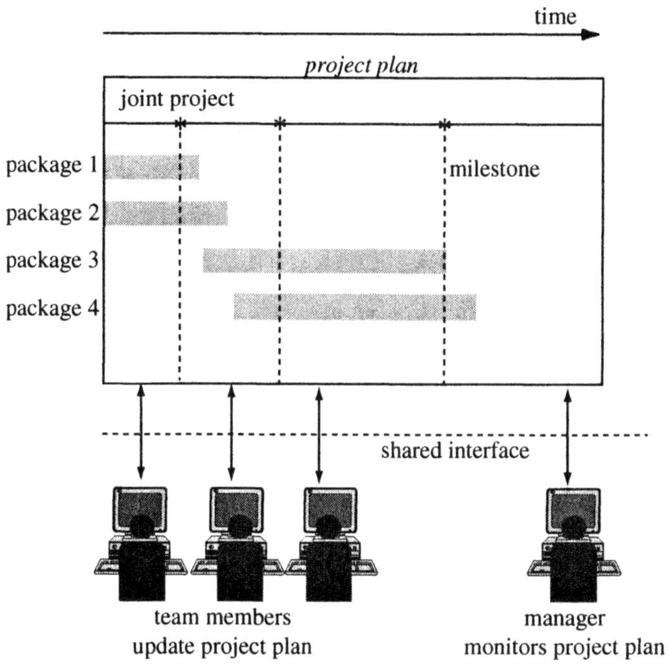

Fig. 2.7. Project management system

All team members are obliged to use the system, for example by entry of the time they plan to allocate to certain tasks or of the current time needed for execution of a task. This requires additional work for team members. However, if the information is also used for automatic generation of monthly time sheets of the team members, then both the manager and the individual team members can benefit from it.

2. *Calendar management for groups:* The system manages an electronic calendar for team members. Individual schedules are entered into the shared calendar. The calendar information facilitates the selection of suitable meeting times and the planning of project completion by allowing for vacation times of project members.
   All team members must enter their schedules, since otherwise a planning system based on calendar information is worthless. Data security must, however, be considered to avoid the danger of "Big Brother" control. Since the currently available electronic calendars have not yet quite substituted conventional paper calendars, schedules are often made twice, both on paper and electronically. Innovative developments for manage-

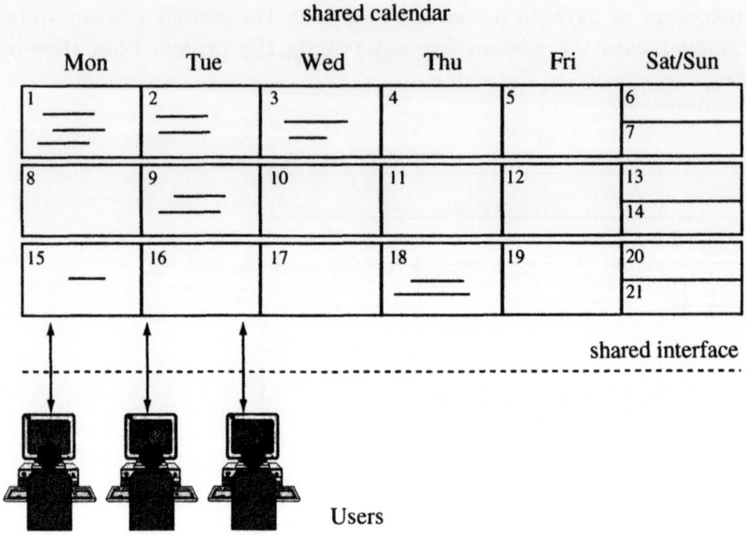

Fig. 2.8. Calendar management for groups

able and lightweight Palmtop computers indicate an optimistic future for electronic calendars.

3. *Joint/group authoring:* A number of distributed persons work on a shared document. Team members generate new sections, update information and include annotations. Group authoring aims at shorter document creation times and improved document quality. Rather than each team member writing a separate, complete section, all team members are in principle responsible for the entire document (see Fig. 2.9). This makes the document consistent in style and content.
   In the case of synchronous work on a shared document, modifications must be synchronized and serialized for the document to be consistent. We will deal with this problem in detail below (see Chap. 4–5).
4. *Spontaneous interaction – electronic hallway:* Modeling spontaneous meetings, as they often occur in office corridors or near the coffee machine, is quite important because information is often exchanged during these encounters. The electronic hallway utilizes various communication media, such as data, audio and video. An example for the electronic hallway is the Xerox video link between Portland, Oregon and Palo Alto, California (Olson and Bly 1991).
   At both locations there was a reserved room equipped with video, audio and computer devices. Lounges which resembled recreation rooms containing a coffee machine which is known to promote informal communication were linked together on a 24 hour basis. Persons could enter their room at any time to look and see whether there was, by any chance,

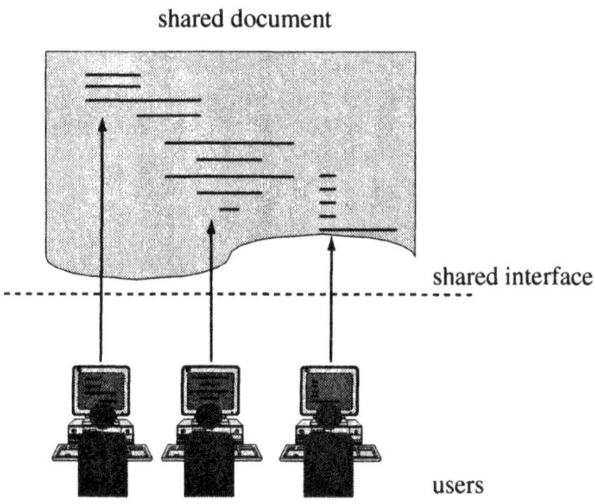

Fig. 2.9. Joint editing

somebody in the respective room at the other location eager to start informal communication.
The supporting technology is similar to video and computer conferencing. In case of the electronic hallway, however, the focus is on spontaneous, informal interaction.
In 1996, this idea was taken up by the Xerox research center in Grenoble, France. As in the Portland experiment, the focus was on spontaneous interaction in the electronic hallway, virtually linking two adjacent buildings of the laboratory. In order to make as many employees partial to it as possible (in particular amongst those who were less than enthusiastic about this kind of "constant ear in the background"), the video image alone was always on. Audio transfer needed to be explicitly switched on. This, however, was found to reduce spontaneity to some extent.

2.5 Application Domains and their Characteristics

In the following chapter, we briefly introduce a few examples of application domains and discuss their groupware related characteristics.

2.5.1 Software design and development

Groupware aims at allowing all parties involved in the design and development of software to cooperate both on macro and micro levels. As far as the macro level is concerned, this means that the department doing the analysis of the existing system and specifying the requirements of the future system and the technical department which is responsible for the technical realization, must cooperate. This results in a seamless interaction of the departments. As opposed to this, the micro level refers to the cooperation within groups (e.g., the group which designs, implements and tests a software module).

It is this latter field of software development which will be dealt with here in detail, since it appears to be the most practicable for groupware: Firstly, the information (such as program code) is already generated and managed electronically, and secondly, there is no rejection of technology amongst team members, since they are all adept at working with computers.

The main emphasis of cooperation in this application domain concerns information transfer, for example system requirement documents, source code, test data, etc. Both asynchronous and synchronous cooperation are common. The phases of the software process which may be supported by groupware are the following (see also Gibbs 1989a):

1. *Generation of the requirement catalogue:* The user can work with a system in order to generate ideas and decisions (Group Support System, GSS).
2. *Specification of a high level design:* This might be supported by a system for synchronous, distributed electronic meetings (computer conferencing).
3. *Specification of a detailed design:* Electronically supported face-to-face meetings may be applied during this phase (see also Sect. 2.4.1).
4. *Implementation:* The implementation of software modules can be supported by a group editor (i.e., several users can edit the same source code simultaneously).
5. *Documentation:* The documentation can also be produced by a group editor with special attention to the joint authoring of text and graphics.
6. *Installation:* The installation phase can be supported by a system for synchronous electronic meetings (desktop computer conferencing). Both salespeople of the software company and representatives of the customer organization (for example, future system administrators) may participate.

2.5.2 Teaching environment

In education and learning, a group typically consists of one educator and a number of students. Cooperation aims at the transfer of information and skills. Figure 2.10 depicts the information types transferred in teaching environments.

Typically, team members cooperate synchronously, for example via an electronic classroom (all participants are in the same room) or via a distributed electronic meeting for remote teaching. The latter case is also called virtual classroom or teleteaching. Thanks to the integration of functionality for the support of groups in information systems, teleteaching can also be applied asynchronously. An example for this is UniTeach 2000 by Paderborn University in Germany (Nastansky 1994) which provides a framework for achieving a virtual classroom based on Lotus Notes (Press 1992). All

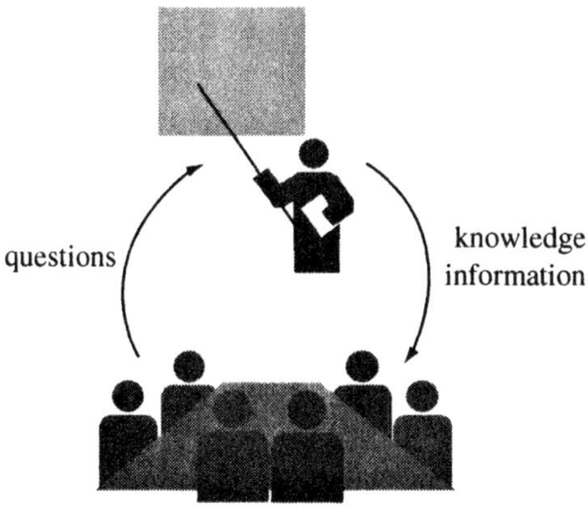

Fig. 2.10. Information transfer in teaching and learning

information concerning teaching (for example lecture notes or seminar papers), research and student administration are managed electronically and may be accessed from inside and outside of the university environment using a suitable computer network. Processed documents are forwarded automatically to the next recipient according to a workflow plan. For example, practical work by students is automatically forwarded to the educator for review. Since in most cases the curricula, even if it is adaptable to student's skills, is well-defined, the interaction and the communication flow within teaching environments is well-structured.

2.5.3 Telecooperation

Reichwald et al. (1998) define telecooperation as media-supported, cooperative work executed between individual employees, organizational units and organizations distributed across multiple locations. Telecooperation is often compared with approaches of software and consulting firms in the early 1960's: programmers and consultants were allowed to do their work at home. The potential of telecooperation overcomes the space and time limits and thus, it is often considered the silver lining at the horizon for necessary restructuring in industry and administration. As opposed to telecommunication whose perspective is limited to the technical infrastructure, telecooperation incorporates aspects of the human task performers. The division of labor when solving a team problem includes both the solution of the actual task and the necessary coordination. In Reichwald et al. (1998), telecooperation is differentiated according to the following three dimensions:

1. *Telework:* Structuring the distributed task execution and its preconditions.
2. *Telemanagement:* Coordination and administration of distributed task execution.
3. *Teleservices:* The resulting service, its market and its clients.

Telecooperation is viewed as a hopeful approach to reducing business traveling. In particular, it is predicted that an increase in telecommunications technology can replace a number of face-to-face meetings with video conferences. Reichwald et al. (1998), however, have found the use of media in management to be no substitute for business traveling. On the contrary: Frequent users of telecommunication technology are at the same time frequent business travelers. It has been observed that improved media usage greatly promotes the preference of face-to-face communication for trust building, which is exceptionally high when contact with new cooperation partners is initiated on the management level. Through telecooperation technology, managers can remain in contact with their co-workers even when traveling.

A well-known telecooperation project in Germany is POLIKom (Hoschka et al. 1993) which has been initiated in the wake of the decision by the German "Deutscher Bundestag" to substitute Bonn for Berlin as capital. This project aims at the development of a framework concept for the support of distributed environments. The project has several subprojects, among others the management of conferences, the coordination of distributed work and the joint document editing by a distributed team of authors.

2.5.4 Further examples for teamwork

To further illustrate the matter, let us give some more examples from various areas in everyday life:

- *Architectural design:* Groupware might allow several geographically dispersed architects (sometimes along with their clients) to work on the same design. Each participant can introduce his ideas and alterations which will immediately be visible to all parties concerned, since they are connected via computer or video conference, or, as mentioned before, via VR conference.
- *Shared design and manufacturing of an industrial product:* For the design of user interfaces, the so-called "Scandinavian approach" (participatory design) which promotes close cooperation between designers and end users enjoys widespread acceptance. This approach is easily adaptable to the design and manufacture of industrial products. After several employees have worked on the shared design of the future product, the technicians cooperate with the design group in order to complete the production. Cooperation between designers and technicians takes place during several electronic meetings, in the process of which the technicians are first made familiar with the design and then report on their experiences and the results of the ongoing production.
- *Cooperation of doctors:* Groupware is mostly unknown in the medical sector, even in those cases where a patient has to consult several specialists at different times. Although it may be desirable for doctors to be able to exchange their diagnoses without any problems and although technologies for electronic transfer of relevant information are available (such as data

transfer, telefax), the current exchange between specialist is still carried out through the patient himself. Groupware and electronic data transfer in these application domains must pay special attention to information losses since, for example, x-rayed images must not acquire additional shadows through the transfer mechanism.

2.6 Interpretation of CSCW

As already mentioned above, CSCW still suffers from nonuniform terminology, divergent goals and a lack of support in a wide range of areas. The different interpretation variants of CSCW already demonstrate this dilemma:

- *CSCW = Computer-supported teamwork:* This interpretation focuses on the team aspect. Investigations usually aim at research on and support of special group processes.
- *CSCW = Computer-supported cooperative work:* The main focus here is on the cooperative aspect which encompasses a wide range of interpretation possibilities. On the one end, cooperative work is interpreted as a form of teamwork under psychosocial criteria; on the other end of the scale, cooperation can also be viewed as planned interrelated work between several persons with identical aims but with no further assumptions made about the social relationships between the parties concerned.
- *CSCW = Computer support for organized activities:* The two aforementioned interpretations focus on computer support of several persons. Solving a task, however, usually calls for both cooperative *and* individual work elements. An interpretation of CSCW which totally disregards individual work can hardly be correct.

Even the term CSCW has been criticized (Greenberg 1991), since groupware systems do not use exclusively computer technology. Rather, they include audio and video technology, as well. Grudin (1991, 1994b) describes CSCW as converging between previous trends of development: Supportive systems for teamwork as a linked domain between two trends: Groupware systems may link single user applications with large scale systems for organizational support (see Fig. 2.11). Single user applications have been substantially influenced by research in human-computer interaction (Human Computer Interaction, HCI), whereas organizational systems can be traced back to developments in information systems (Management Information System, MIS). This overview highlights the independence of three separate development areas, although Grudin himself admits that activities of individual persons, groups and organizations are interwoven. More recently, a fourth development area has evolved due to the special attention paid to community support systems (Social Information System, SIS).

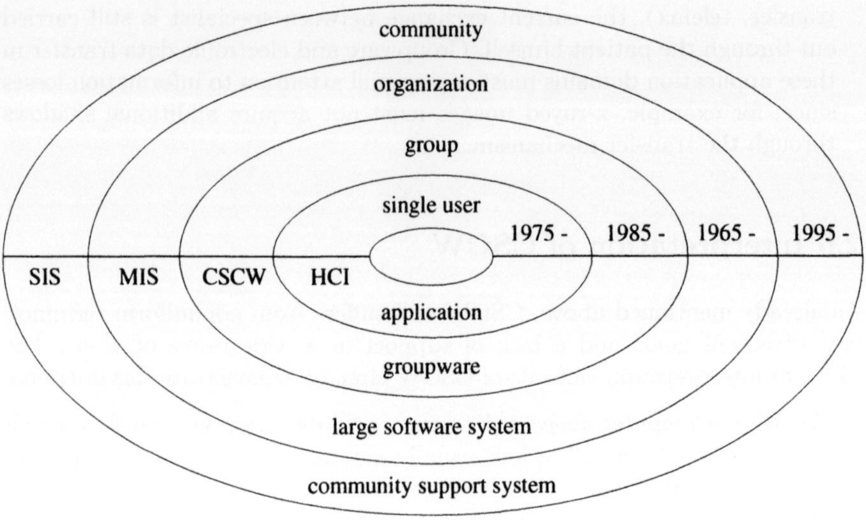

Fig. 2.11. CSCW in context of other research and development areas

In principle, an analysis of the acronym CSCW can be done in two different ways: Forward analysis and backward analysis. Forward analysis is mainly viewed as being composed exclusively of computer science aspects:

- *C:* The computer is the starting point.
- *S:* It is to be used as the supporting medium.
- *C:* Innovative technologies enable new supportive forms for cooperative activities.
- *W:* The task to be executed (which under the forward interpretation of CSCW has lower priority).

As opposed to this, the backward analysis starts with issues relevant to the organization and considers the influence of cooperation and computer support:

- *W:* Central issue of the area CSCW is the task itself.
- *C:* The execution of tasks, however, is in general done through division of labor which means that several partners cooperate.
- *S:* The problem solving process is to be supported.
- *C:* In particular, potential use of computer technology is to be considered and further developed.

Let us now analyze the term CSCW backwards by interpreting its individual morphemes in detail.

2.6.1 CSCW: Work

With regard to CSCW, work refers to the work system, its components and their interdependencies.

The work system consists of four components: task, organization, people and technology. The so-called Leavitt rhombus, as first introduced in 1958 (see Fig. 2.12) shows an illustration of the components. In an organization wishing to execute a task, humans work with a supporting technology. We will not elaborate on the individual components; the interested reader is referred to publications of organizational theory and industrial psychology. Groupware focuses on the technology component. The influence on other components, however, must not be left out of the considerations.

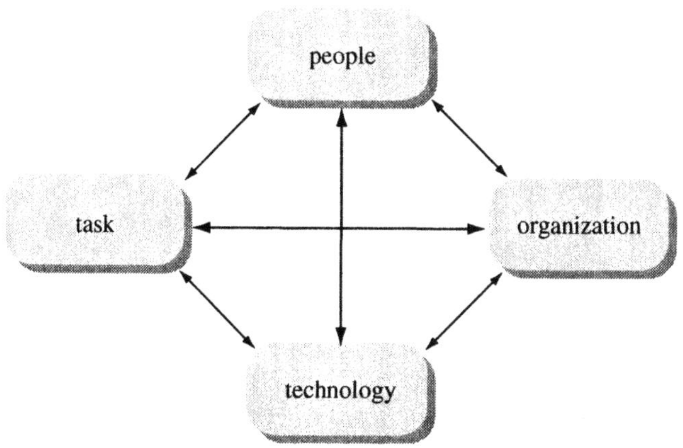

Fig. 2.12. How different aspects interrelate in CSCW (Leavitt rhombus)

The development of groupware systems must incorporate four perspectives: The design of a multiuser interface (people component) and the access control on information (organizational component) must be given the same amount of care as both granularity and storage of individual information objects (technology component) and possible parallelism of task execution (task component). Along with formal, structured interactions, sporadic, often loose social contact is to be considered just as important, since informal interaction can act as a pre-stage and thus, facilitate the actual work process.

2.6.2 CSCW: Cooperative Work

With different disciplines, the interpretation of the term cooperative work differs. One theory defines cooperative work as work processes where several persons are involved, whereas a second theory focuses on a special form of work without hierarchical structures and with a high degree of autonomy for the individual employee. The historical development of the importance and the usage of the term cooperative work is outlined in Bannon and Schmidt (1991).

Communication among team members is an important aspect of cooperative work. A closer look reveals that the term communication is interpreted differently in the various disciplines. In computer science, the common model is the one adapted in telecommunications by Shannon (1948). As opposed to this, linguistics usually defines the term on syntactic, semantic and pragmatic levels. The syntactic level focuses on the transfer of symbols, the semantic level on the meaning of these symbols and the pragmatic level on the intention of the sender and the effect of the message on the receiver.

Teamwork can be categorized according to the level of interaction between group members specifying the intensity of the information flow within the team (see also Bair 1989).

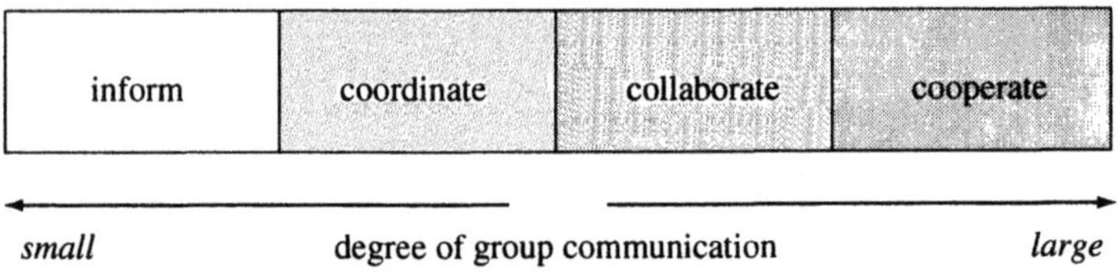

Fig. 2.13. Intensity of information flow within the team

As the intensity of communication increases, so does its computer support. The levels depicted in Fig. 2.13 will be discussed in more detail.

- Informing is at the lowest level of communication; computer systems in the early days were used this way. Sender and receiver have little contact, since – like when reading a book – information only flows in one direction. An example is a bulletin board where one person posts information while another person unknown to the author retrieves that information from the information base. This scenario is similar to books where author and reader rarely know each other.
- The next level – with an increased degree of communication – is that of coordination: Sender and receiver have direct contact with each other and coordinate both information and activities, for example by using shared resources.
- A further increase of the communication level leads to collaboration: Sender and receiver strive towards the same goal which is that of a team. The activity is shared. The interaction is, however, still sporadic.
- The highest level of communication occurs during cooperation between individuals, groups or organizations. In CSCW, the term is restricted by various characteristics. Common goals, a shared plan, or the processing of shared data that support and coordinate cooperation may be some of

them. On the cooperation level, the demand for face-to-face meetings as an integral part of teamwork has particular emphasis. Goals of the team have priority over personal goals. In general, decisions have to be based on group consensus. The result of such decisions is the responsibility of all team members. Regular and frequent interaction is combined with evaluation of the team as a whole. Besides cooperation, the social process has to contain all work modes, from rivalry and loose cooperation to tight cooperation.

The cooperative behavior of the individual team member is determined by his degree of interest and his level of cooperation. In the former case, the attitude towards individual goals is important, and the spectrum ranges from egoism to self-denial. The latter case is related to the attitude towards the team goals; the spectrum ranges from cooperation to hostility.

According to Piepenburg (1991), cooperation can be characterized along three dimensions. One aspect is to view the number of persons involved in a cooperative process. Bilateral cooperation (i.e., two persons involved) is thus opposed to multilateral cooperation where more than two persons are involved. Another dimension is the distinction between conjunct and disjunct cooperation, which focuses on how the goal is reached in a cooperative process. In the latter case the task is achieved if only one cooperative partner reached the goal while in the former case all involved parties must complete their jobs. A third aspect is the space and time distribution between parties involved, that is, between direct and indirect cooperation. Direct cooperation calls for interaction of parties at the same place, so that no technical cooperation media is needed as an intermediary. Indirect cooperation, on the other hand, includes all kinds of technology supported cooperation, enabling time and place independence.

2.6.3 CSCW: Supported Cooperative Work

System support for cooperative work deals with its impact and usability aspects. We differentiate between support on the content level and on the process level. The former support level emphasizes the information created and manipulated by the group, i.e. the specification of the structure of the shared information. The latter support level focuses on the information production process. Databases and knowledge bases, for instance, are characterized by a high content orientation. Email and conferencing systems emphasize, on the other hand, process support.

The process support can have different forms:

- *Compromising:* This aims at a compromise between differing opinions and suggestions. The best possible solution is derived from diverging viewpoints.
- *Structuring:* Special functions enable team members to structure their information appropriately.

- *Motivating:* The system provides a creative environment for the generation of ideas and opinions. Examples are decision support systems which support brainstorming techniques.
- *Controlling:* The system enforces rules for a well-structured group process, thus providing an atmosphere for harmonious groupware.

Task-oriented groupware systems covering the entire problem solving process should provide both a high degree of content and process support. It must be considered that group support as a whole might indeed diverge or even hinder individual activities of team members.

2.6.4 CSCW: Computer-Supported Cooperative Work

Role, function and impact of computers when supporting cooperative work can be those of an intruder, an initiator, or a service. As an intruder, the computer substitutes traditional support forms, such as flipcharts or group calendars. In the initiator role computers enable innovative communication relations, like the loose contact between individuals through email. These connections would in all probability be near or completely nonexistent if there were no email. Computers can provide innovative services which hitherto have not been available, such as browsing in worldwide distributed information systems.

Johansen (1991) described his vision for a possible role of groupware in the year 2000 in 6 scenarios titled as follows: Any Time/Any Place, Orchestrated Workflow, Virtual Team Rooms, Culture Bridging, Just-in-time Learning and Window to Anywhere. Dimensions of activities are the aspects integration, decentralization and flexibility. Groupware systems can initiate integration tendencies in temporal (Just-in-time Learning), spatial (Virtual Team Rooms), organizational (Orchestrated Workflow) and cultural (Culture Bridging) respects. By delegating responsibility and decision making rights to lower hierarchical levels (Any Time/Any Place and Window to Anywhere), they also help solve decentralizing tasks. Last but not least, experts also expect groupware to increase the flexibility of the problem solving process.

2.7 History of the Most Important CSCW Systems

Figure 2.14 shows the history of the development of the most important groupware systems and their predecessors. The time periods are only rough estimates. The dashed arrows represent influences of other systems. The development of Augment was completed in the late 1970's. Its influence on later systems, however, still exists (as seen in the dotted line). Note that the figure only shows a small sample of groupware systems; due to the rapid development in the field of CSCW there has been a proliferation of new innovative groupware systems, particularly in the last few years.

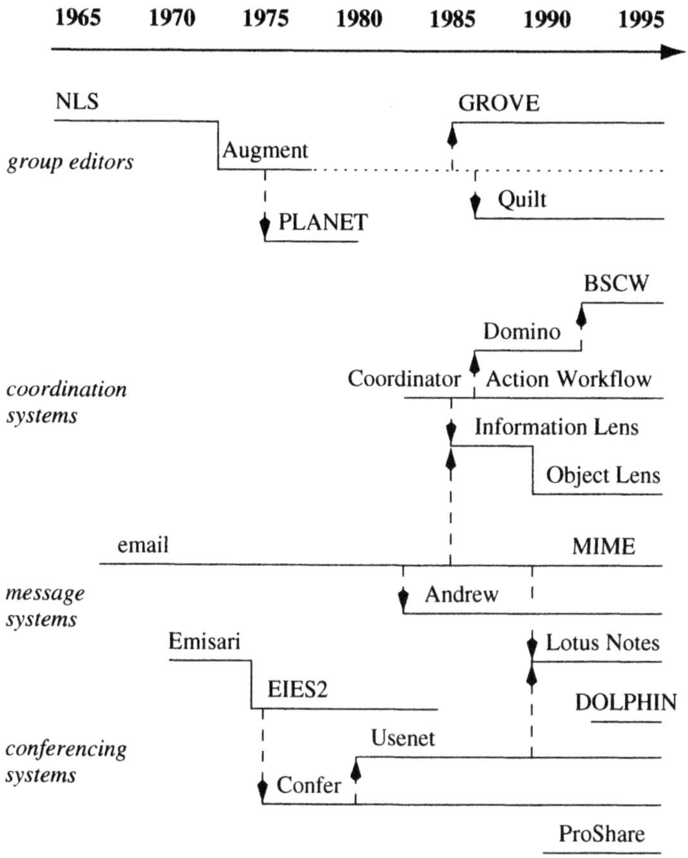

Fig. 2.14. History of important groupware systems

In the following section, we give a brief description of the systems mentioned, see also the book of Rapaport (1991). Later chapters will discuss some of the most important systems in more detail.

- The development of NLS (oN Line System) took place in the Augmentation Research Center (ARC) at Stanford Research Institute (SRI), USA, under Engelbart and English, beginning in the year 1963.
  NLS aimed at supporting and augmenting teamwork, not its automation. NLS includes the following functions:
  - asynchronous cooperation between geographically dispersed persons: only a single participant has writing access to a shared file, while several other people might have concurrent reading access,
  - generation, modification and reading of structured texts; structure and content are separated and stored in different files,
  - fast navigation within the information space,

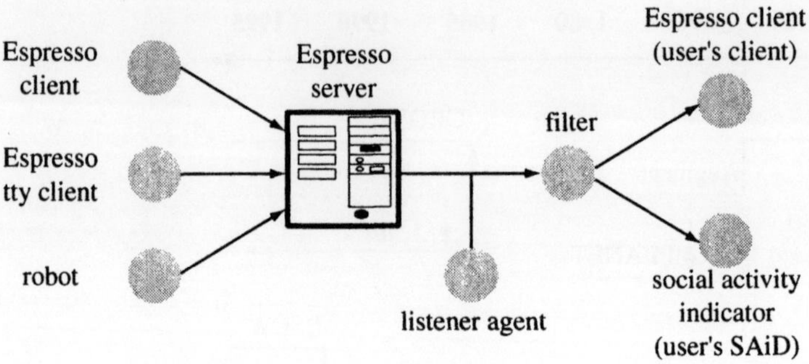

Fig. 2.15. Espresso application architecture (sample)

- definition of filters with regard to content and structure, thus enabling different views,[12]
- support of real-time cooperation: Several users may virtually link their terminals and thus work on shared screen displays (an earlier version restricted this approach to local environments, i.e. to a single shared computer, later versions, however, used the Arpanet for distributed shared screen displays).

NLS has had a major impact on the evolution of personal computers, especially in the areas: graphics-oriented user interfaces, screen-oriented editing, mouse-cursor control, hypertext structure of information with different nodes and links that may be interpreted in different ways, thus providing multiple views of the same information.

- Augment (Engelbart 1982) is the commercial version of NLS.
- Planet (PLAning NETwork, Rapaport 1991) allows synchronous communication between several participants. After its entry, a message is immediately displayed on the screens of all other participants. The system supports voting procedures (e.g., selecting a proposal by majority consensus).
- Espresso is built in the Cafe ConstructionKit (Ackerman and Starr 1996), and is a synchronous chat application. Espresso clients communicate with an Espresso server that routes the communication to the appropriate subscribers. Other services, such as listeners, filters, and visualization indicators, can also be placed on the message stream (see Fig. 2.15).
- Grove (GRoup Outline Viewing Editor, Ellis et al. 1991) is a group editor for synchronous, distributed computer conferences and allows joint editing of shared text objects. Grove's most common usage is for brainstorming and collecting ideas. It uses a special algorithm based on operation transformation for concurrency control. Section 4.8 will discuss this very interesting algorithm in more detail.

[12] This is similar to the outline mode of the screen-oriented Unix text editor Emacs. The outline mode is mostly used during brainstorming phases and it structures text into topics and subtopics. The screen display can be controlled by the user, for example subtopics may be hidden.

Grove uses a group window which shows the identical file segment to all concurrent group users, strictly following the WYSIWIS principle (see Sect. 3.5.1) Apart from the time delay during the propagation of modification operations across the network, the screen information remains identical on all displays. Synchronous scrolling is supported. The system supports different views of the document or portions of it. Grove distinguishes between:
 - *Public views:* Information is visible to all team members.
 - *Selected views:* Information is visible to a selected set of team members only.
 - *Private views:* Information is only available to one particular person.

The creation of a new view results in the popping up of a new group window on the screens of all involved group members.
- Quilt is a tool for joint document editing which Fish et al. (1988) and Leland et al. (1988) developed at Bell Communications Research in Morristown, USA. Quilt is based on a sociological analysis of the writing process. The system supports annotations, posting of information, notifications of changes in the document, as well as the shared use of information. It provides hypertext-like storage of text, annotations, an integrated computer conferencing system, automatic version management and a notification mechanism based on multimedia email.
  A Quilt document consists of the current basic document, revision information as well as textual and verbal annotations. The integration of existing editors is a basic concept of Quilt. Users almost exclusively work with their own editors. The placement of text and mouse cursors is a problem; annotations must be associated with their proper place in the document. Thus, a monitor process which is integrated between the user and editor interface updates transparently for the user a document copy and records any cursor movement. Quilt uses a notification mechanism in order to warn the individual user if he is about to alter a document part which is already being modified by another user.
- Coordinator (Flores et al. 1988) is a commercial product of Action Technologies. It controls asynchronous activities, using structured exchange of electronic messages between partners. The system is based on the conversation theory by Searle and Austin (Winograd and Flores 1986) and supports a number of predefined conversational structures (see Sect. 7.2.4). Based on these structures, message types are defined, a limited choice of which are available at the respective conversation states.
- Action Workflow (Medina-Mora et al. 1992) is a further development of Coordinator. Basic structure for specification of asynchronous activities is the workflow loop which consists of four phases and describes the interaction between a customer and a performer.
  During the initial phase (the proposal phase) customer and performer start contacting each other about what is to be achieved. The initial con-

tact might either happen at the instigation of the customer, i.e., he demands something from the performer, or else the performer offers a service. Throughout the second phase (the agreement phase) customer and performer come to terms as to what will be delivered; the successful completion of this phase results in a service contract between both parties. In the third phase (the performance phase) the required service is carried out, and the performer informs the customer of the results when the task is completed. In the final phase (the satisfaction phase) the customer reviews the delivered service and informs the performer of the acceptability of the work.

Each phase encompasses a set of conversational structures specifying possible alternatives for person's activities. Additional constraints describe customer's wishes and the context in which the task is to be performed. The workflow loop models the interaction between the two parties involved. More complex activities involving several parties can be constructed by a combination of workflow loops.

- Domino (Kreifelts et al. 1991), which is under construction at the German National Research Center for Information Technology (GMD), is a system for controlling office procedures (for example, vacation planning). Communication is based on email and the procedure model describing the sequence of interactions follows the Petri net principle. The procedure description consists of three parts:
  1. *Role declaration:* People are assigned roles based on the office procedure.
  2. *Documents:* All documents used during the office procedure.
  3. *Information flow:* The third part specifies the assignment of people to office activities and to documents used and created as part of their activity execution.

  For a detailed description of Domino see Sect. 7.2.5.
- BSCW (Basic Support for Cooperative Work, Bentley et al. 1995) is under construction at the GMD as part of the POLIKom project. This project involves the development of a framework for the support of a distributed government (see p. 106). BSCW supports shared workspaces in the world wide web where team members may file documents for shared use in a structured manner. In addition, it contains mechanisms for obtaining information on group composition, modifications of documents and current activities. BSCW has been in use since the mid-1995's and is continually being improved.
- Information Lens (Malone et al. 1987) has been developed by the Massachusetts Institute of Technology (MIT) and is a system for the generation, sending and management of semistructured messages for coordinating activities. Apart from free-text fields, semistructured messages also contain a number of predefined fields with fixed syntax. Examples of these fields are sender, expiration time and reference. The system allows intelligent filtering, processing and management of received email messages.

- Object Lens (Lai et al. 1988, Malone and Lai 1988) is an improved version of Information Lens. It uses objects to represent messages, activities, information or persons.
- Email systems have been developed as part of the Arpanet. Initially, they were only used for the exchange of textual information. Newer systems, like the Andrew email system, also allow the exchange of multimedia information.
- Andrew (Borenstein et al. 1988) is a project of Carnegie Mellon University. It contains a portable multimedia message and bulletin board system including text, graphics, calculation table and animations.
- MIME (Multipurpose Internet Mail Extension, Tanenbaum 1996) defines a standard for the transfer of multimedia information via the Internet. The message structure is extended by content types and coding rules for non-ASCII information. Along with coding binary information (for example base64) MIME also standardizes the transfer of images, audio and video.
- Emisari (Emergency Management Information and Reference System, Hiltz and Turoff 1978) is the origin of electronic conferencing systems. The system was developed under Murray Turroff in the early 1970's. It aimed at coordinating activities within the government through faster distribution and collection of time critical information. Support was provided for the following activities:
  - Creating a stream (notebooks) of textual information with new text being appended at the end of the stream; the text can be edited and read concurrently by several persons; the information is centrally administrated.
  - Structuring of text according to topics (so-called conferences).
  - Sending of emails to persons and groups; an association of email messages and notebook entries is possible. In this case, the email message contains the references to notebook entries.
- EIES2 (Rapaport 1991) is very similar to Emisari, with additional integration of private notebooks and group notebooks.
- Lotus Notes (Press 1992) was one of the first successful commercial groupware systems which had the required market maturity. It is a bulletin board system based on email and database applications supporting information transfer between users. Lotus Notes contains a special revision protocol for propagating concurrent modifications of shared data and for consistent updating of replicated information (see Sect. 2.9.8).
- Confer (Rapaport 1991) was developed at Michigan University. Initially, it was used for the distribution of proposals for the participants to vote upon. Later on, it was extended to include computer conferences which are structured according to topics.
- Usenet is probably the most widely accepted and used bulletin board system. It supports asynchronous discussions by explicit sending of textual messages. Discussion contributions are hierarchically structured and man-

aged according to topics. Usenet is available worldwide as an Internet application and thereby enables globally distributed discussions. In the year 1996, the Internet was comprised of approximately 80,000 networks serving between 30 and 50 million individual users. Further commercialization of Internet services will certainly cause another substantial increase in this number. Services of this kind rely on indexing/search systems, printing-on-demand services or digital libraries, like the Bibliotheca Universalis initiated by the G7 countries.
- The system Dolphin (Streitz et al. 1994) at GMD supports the preparation and holding of team meetings. Participants of a meeting are supplied with personal computers and a shared electronic whiteboard (like Xerox LiveBoard). For a discussion of the different roles in a Dolphin team meeting, see Haake and Streitz (1996). Shared documents can be manipulated synchronously and Sepia hypertext documents can be integrated.[13] Dolphin installations communicate via the TCP/IP protocol and are based on the ParcPlace-Digitalk VisualWorks.
- ProShare is a commercial desktop conferencing system by Intel Corporation. It integrates audio, video and application sharing. Communication links between participants are achieved through ISDN using point-to-point connections. An Internet version of ProShare based on the TCP/IP protocol has already been tested. Another important vendor of video conferencing equipment is PictureTel.

2.8 Groupware Classification

Groupware systems may be classified according to the common time space matrix, application domains, or the so-called 3C model. In addition, there is a quantitative, an organizational and a social taxonomy.

2.8.1 Time space taxonomy

Team members can be either in the same room or geographically dispersed. Depending on the distance, a hierarchy can be observed. The distribution may refer to different rooms on one corridor or different floors in the same building. In the case of team members not working in the same building, we must make a distinction between a distribution within the same town or between different towns, and, in extreme cases, even between different time zones around the globe. The degree of geographical distribution can influence the usage of a particular communication media, such as direct conversation, telephone or computer connections.

---

[13] Sepia is another system by GMD. The Sepia functionality has been integrated into its successor system Dolphin.

Just as team members may be distributed based on location, the same can be true based on time. Team members may either communicate synchronously (hence the name synchronous groupwork), or they may communicate asynchronously. These classifications are exemplified by direct meetings, telephone calls and real-time computer connections (e.g., *talk* in Unix) for synchronous teamwork with the "note on your desk", messages on the answering machine or electronic messages in the case of asynchronous teamwork (see also Table 2.1).

The two-dimensional taxonomy by space and time is the most common and most often used classification of groupware systems. However, it must be emphasized that this classification should not be seen as limiting or exclusive. Comprehensive groupware systems should meet the requirements of all four quadrants, thus only system components are assigned to individual categories.

Table 2.1. Groupware classification according to time and space (extended after Grudin 1994a)

Space/time	Same time (synchronous)	Different times (asynchronous)	
		predictable	unpredictable
Same place	face-to-face meeting	shift-work	blackboard
Different places (predictable)	video conference	email	joint editing of documents
Different places (unpredictable)	mobile phone conference	non-real-time computer conference	workflow management

Grudin (1994a) has further differentiated the distribution in time and space, through consideration of aspects of mobile communication. The category "different from" is additionally subcategorized into "different from, but predictable" and "different from, unpredictable". In Table 2.1, examples are given for all nine options. For instance, places and receivers are usually known when using email, which is not so for non-real-time computer conferences (for example, Usenet). The distribution in time follows similar patterns. Senders of an email expect the receiver to read the message within a certain period of time, whereas the execution of tasks by the responsible person is generally unpredictable.

2.8.2 Application level classification

Application classes are yet another taxonomy approach. Ellis et al. (1991) distinguish between message systems, group editors, electronic meeting rooms, computer conferencing, intelligent agents and coordination systems. The resulting application categories are, however, not exclusive. For example, in asynchronous conferencing systems there are often message systems integrated in order to allow asynchronous communication between team members.

Message systems. Textual messages can be exchanged asynchronously between team members. Modern systems can handle graphics, images, and even sound and video. The message management is facilitated by additional structural information, such as fields for "topic" or "group".

By integrating rules or scripts, the functionality of a message system can be substantially extended:

- *Rules:* Rules are receiver specific, i.e. they are defined by the receiver and not sent along with the message. Rules refer to fields within messages, for example sender, group, subject, and they may be used for automatic filtering and management of messages. The following code fragment[14] can serve as an example of a rule in message filing:

  Code fragment (Rule for message filing).

```
class message
    var sender, receiver, type, subject, content, ...
                        /* Only information in this header is sent via net-
                           work; operations (rules) of the class message are
                           local.                                         */
    public:
    void refile (var type);
void message::refile (var type)
    if (type = 'design order')
    then move message N to "Folder Design";
                        /* files the message N in the folder design      */
    else ...
```

  Example: Information Lens (Malone et al. 1987).

- *Scripts:* As opposed to rules, scripts are sender-specific; they are specified by the sender and sent along with the message. They will be executed in the receiver's environment on receipt. However, execution of an unknown, not trustworthy code in an individual environment is critical. The following script automatically returns a notification to the sender after the message has been read by the receiver:

  Code fragment (Script for automatic receipt notification).

```
class message
    var sender, recipient, group, ...
                        /* Both an instance of the class message and the im-
                           plementation of the operation report are sent via
                           network.                                       */
    public:
```

[14] For specification of the rule, we use a C++-like notation.

```
    void report ();
  void message::report()
    if (message N is read)
    then send(message Ack) to sender;
                        /* Creates a message of the type acknowledgement
                           and sends it back to the sender of message N; N
                           refers to the message in the context of which the
                           method report is executed.                    */
```

Example: Imail (Hogg 1985).

Group editors. Group editors[15] are very useful if several team members edit a shared document or do joint programming of a software system. The editor is aware of its multiusability in the sense of teamwork (instead of isolating the users from each other it integrates a special notification mechanism which informs the users of each others activities). Group editors are categorized according to the working modes into real-time editors and asynchronous editors. In the case of real-time editors, several users edit one object at the same time. The object is divided into several segments usually allowing only one write and several read accesses.

When editing asynchronously, as in the case of Mercury (Kaiser et al. 1987) a group editor for joint programming of large software systems, team members work at different times on the software modules. They are, however, notified automatically if activities of other team members occur. This is especially important if changes in one software module require modifications in other software modules. Another example of a group editor is Iris (Koch 1997) which supports both working modes.

Electronic meeting rooms. The ideal room for face-to-face meetings is equipped with computers. Since these computer systems are often used for the support of group decisions, they are also called group support systems (GSS).

GSS tools have been designed to help users in decision making and in the researching of unstructured problems. They facilitate brainstorming, the exploration of alternative information structures, the voting process and the decision analysis. For example if a team has to come to a decision and both the question itself and the decision making process are already agreed upon, then the procedure is as follows: Opinions, ideas, doubts and self assessment of the participants are collected by the GSS anonymously and then displayed to the group for assessment. In general, this sequence of questioning and evaluation leads to a decision. GSS supports an iterative decision making process, the decision itself is always one made by the entire team.
Example: GroupSystems of the University of Arizona (Valacich et al. 1991).

[15] Often also called distributed multiuser editors.

Conferencing systems. Conferencing systems cover a wide range of interaction between team members. They range from computer conferences to video and desktop conferences. There are four types of conferences:

1. *Non-real-time computer conferencing:* In a non-real-time computer conference, team members confer asynchronously via personal computers. Communication is based on the sending and the receiving of email messages suitably structured, sorted and managed by system support. All participants will have their computers in their offices. The lack of interactive contact between participants can cause time loss when questions and misunderstandings are to be clarified. The example of Usenet illustrates this.
2. *Real-time computer conferencing:* In the case of synchronous computer conferencing, the so-called real-time computer conferencing, persons are distributed across several meeting rooms. The use of electronic equipment in meeting rooms, including personal computers, is indispensable. All participants must be able to operate a computer. Attempts at providing the software necessary for this kind of conference are well under way. They are based either on the use of single-user applications (input and output are controlled via a special multiplexing component) or collaboration-aware group applications. The second approach provides more flexibility and functionality with regard to the support of parallel work and ergonomic multiuser interfaces. In both cases, communication between team members is often limited to data transfer without any additional audio and video link. An example is the system Cognoter (Tatar et al. 1991).
3. *Teleconferencing:* Teleconferencing uses telecommunication technology for interaction support between team members. Between meeting rooms, there is an audio link and sometimes – for the transfer of gestures – also a video connection. Unlike real-time computer conferencing, shared data are not manipulated jointly and concurrently. Only joint viewing of data is possible. The system can be exemplified by the Xerox video link between Portland, Oregon and Palo Alto, California (Olson and Bly 1991).
4. *Desktop conferencing:* A combination of the last two types results in desktop conferencing. In addition to audio and video connections, desktop conferencing uses personal computers which support shared applications, thus enabling joint manipulation of common electronic information. The video images are integrated into a screen window. The major focus lies on the integration of the work environments of the geographically dispersed group members rather than on the display of the videos of the group members on the screen. For communication between audio, video and data, a multimedia network is used, such as for instance at MMConf (Crowley et al. 1990) and Rapport (Ahuja et al. 1988). In the teleconferencing system MASSIVE (Greenhalgh and Benford 1995) the

live videos are replaced by avatars. Each participant is represented by an avatar which may move within the 3D virtual space. Depending on orientation and distance avatars may interact with each other and exchange information, such as text messages.

Shared information spaces. Processing and consistent management of shared information are central aspects of all teamwork. For shared information spaces, system-oriented management of group documents is the central issue. This allows persistent storage of data and provides suitable access mechanisms. If communication between team members takes place exclusively via shared documents in the information space, then it is called implicit communication (see Sect. 1.3.1). It is typically asynchronous. Depending on the access mechanism selected by the users we distinguish between the following operation modes:

1. *Separate responsibility:* Each team member is exclusively responsible for a certain part of the group document. The individual parts are independently processed.
2. *Mutual exclusive access:* Only one team member has access to a shared group document at any given time. This is either guaranteed by mutual agreement or through a system component using a technical protocol, like locks, to exclude concurrent access.
3. *Alternate versions:* Each team member develops his own version of the group document. Later, all versions must be integrated in order to get a consistent version, which reflects the manipulation of all team members. In general, the merge cannot be done fully automatically; it requires manual intervention by the team members.
4. *Synchronous access:* Team members work at the same time in a tightly coupled mode on the shared group documents; they have the same view of the document (WYSIWIS principle[16]). Special mechanisms are required for concurrency control in order to keep documents consistent.
   These mechanisms for synchronous access will be dealt with below, see Chap. 4–5.

Important groupware systems of this application level category are special databases, e.g. Lotus Notes, and distributed hypertext systems such as BSCW. Due to the rapid evolution of the world wide web, the latter group has gained significantly in importance.

Intelligent agents. Computer programs may be actual meeting participants or play an active part in asynchronous collaborative work. These programs are often called intelligent agents. Computer games have been using agents for quite some time already: Whenever the number of human players dwindles down, agents are used as substitutes.

[16] WYSIWIS stands for What You See Is What I See.

Agents can serve as surrogates for human participants by appropriating their functions. These intelligent agents are assigned special tasks such as a moderator's position of monitoring and controlling a meeting. Liza (Gibbs 1989b) is one example of this kind of agent.

Workflow management/coordination systems. Coordination problems mainly arise with asynchronous activities. To coordinate the activities of team members necessary to achieve the common goal, there are four types of coordination systems, depending on the information to be modeled:

1. *Form-oriented systems:* A form-oriented system models the data flow within an organization. Take for instance a document which circulates among team members: whenever a participant has received the document, he performs the assigned task, signs the document off and forwards it on to the next team member (like an insurance case with different departments involved). The destination is specified by the procedural plan which is included in the document. The Electronic-Circulation-Folder system (ECF) is an example (Karbe et al. 1990).
2. *Procedure-oriented systems:* This category models functions and procedures within an organization, like the software development process which consists of the phases specification, design, implementation and evaluation/verification. Team member's activities are predefined in a procedure description and then combined into a procedure plan. Thus, a procedure consists of several steps to be executed by individual team members if the global goal is to be reached. A single step consists of the receipt, processing and sending of information units. An example of this kind of coordination system is Domino (Kreifelts et al. 1991).
3. *Conversation-oriented systems:* This system type models the interactions between team members and the resulting actions as they occur as part of activity coordination. Cooperation is based on the exchange of verbal speech acts (conversation). For example, if a person requires something from another person, then this other person will promise to perform the required task. The speech acts will in general be mapped to electronic messages exchanged between conversation partners. To implement different interaction patterns, the respective message types are specified and used according to the state of interaction. The underlying conversation model is discussed below in Sect. 7.2. An example of a conversation-oriented system is Coordinator (Flores et al. 1988).
4. *Communication structure-oriented systems:* If complex communication structures are to be modeled within an organization then the systems should be communication-oriented. The communication structure encompasses both the organizational structure and the roles of the people within the organization. The roles and their social and organizational relationships determine the structure. For example, if a shared document is edited, the communicational behavior of team members depends on their respective roles (like author, reviewer, editor). The goal of this system

type is the provision of a basic, commonly accepted component for generating communicative processes. These processes are specified by the description of dependencies amongst roles, message objects, rules and operations. For an example, see Amigo (Pankoke-Babatz 1989).

2.8.3 Classification according to the 3C model

In general, groupware is "C-oriented" in one way or another. Depending on the intensity of cooperation within a group, we can distinguish between communication, coordination and cooperation. Communication focuses on the mutual understanding of persons through information exchange. Coordination aims at finding the best way in which to arrange task-oriented activities and the allocation of resources in the best possible order, whereas the additional requirement of common goals makes cooperation the most demanding of the three (see Sect. 2.6.2).

Teufel et al. (1995) classify groupware systems as to the degree of support they give to these three basic phenomena. The system types of the application level classification can thus be positioned in a triangle (see Fig. 2.16, as derived from Teufel et al. 1995).

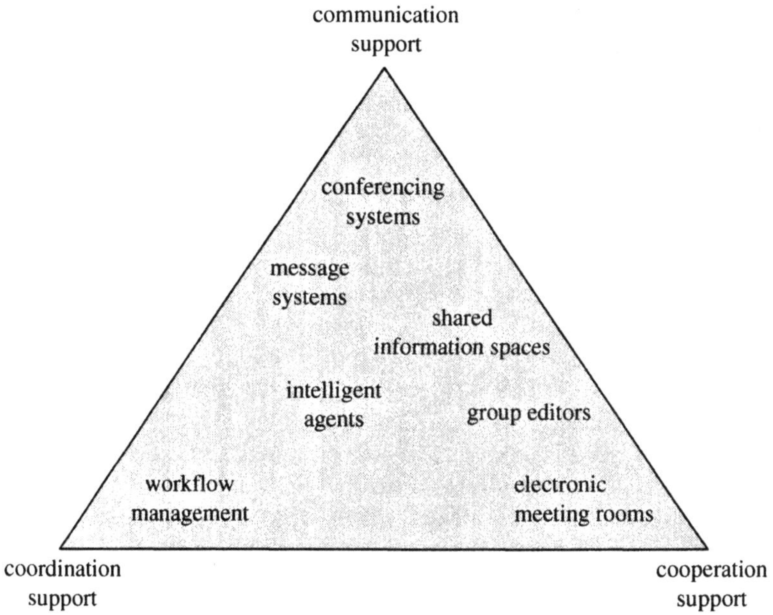

Fig. 2.16. Classification according to support functions

2.8.4 More classification models

In addition to the three methods of categorizing groupware systems (space and time, application-oriented functional classes, and the 3C model), there are also a quantitative, an organizational and a social taxonomy.

Quantitative classification focuses on the team size, social classification distinguishes between formal and informal communication within the group, and organizational classification asks whether meetings are face-to-face or electronic, with geographically dispersed participants.

2.9 Design of Groupware

In this section we will discuss the question of which criteria influence the design of groupware and what effect electronic support has on teamwork; see also Grudin (1988, 1990). Apart from email, we will give special consideration to computer conferencing systems and the commercial groupware system Lotus Notes. Some of the results presented are based on empirical studies and experiments conducted with existing groupware systems in actual university and commercial environments.

2.9.1 Possible aspects

An analysis of the technological side alone is not sufficient if we want to identify the impact of computer-supported teamwork on the individual team member, or on the organization as a whole. Sociological and psychological aspects, too, must be considered.

The sociological aspect deals with the effects of computer support on the position and evaluation of team members. As opposed to face-to-face meetings, where usually the team structure and position of team members is clear, the role differentiation is often not apparent in computer conferences (Turoff and Hiltz 1982). Groupware facilitates the assignment of responsibilities and the recording of the decision making process.

The psychological aspect primarily deals with the consequences on the individual behavior. Studies have shown that computer support tends to focus the attention on the actual task, reducing social interaction between participants (Applegate et al. 1986). In some experiments, however, this focusing did not reduce the time needed for decision-making, since participants often had differing opinions and were not prepared to compromise, regardless of the social pressure exerted by other team members. Computer support apparently encouraged participants to be more insistent on their arguments and less willing to reach a quick consensus.

For coordination of interactions between team members, 7 issues are important with regard to behavior. Implications for the provision of functionality can be derived from the respective behavior desired. For example, on the technical side, the speaking permission implies a suitable floor control mechanism for coordination of team members' activities, especially if activities are synchronous. Table 2.2 lists the behavioral issues in relation to their implications for technical implementation in groupware systems.

Table 2.2. Questions to be answered when coordinating team activities

Behavioral issues	Implementation issues
Who speaks during interaction?	responsibility for creating data, audio or video information
What is being said?	syntax, semantics, pragmatics of information
Who is being spoken to?	1-to-1, 1-to-many or 1-to-all communication
When does someone speak?	floor control, role of people
How long and how often does interaction occur?	simultaneous communication, bandwidth of communication
What is the medium used during interaction?	multimedia
What method is used for decision making?	voting, negotiate

Seamlessness. Another important aspect for CSCW is that of seamlessness. Its significance was first discovered during the development of the Colab system (Stefik et al. 1987b), where seamlessness stood for the seamless transition between individual work and teamwork. Ishii and Miyake (1991) extended the notion of seamlessness and defined it as unobtrusive integration of any noticeable system aspect into the surrounding context. We can distinguish between several types of seamlessness:

- *Communication media:* Seamlessness of communication media requires an integration of various media types, such as text, graphics, audio and video. However, traditional multimedia technology is not sufficient, since seamless transitions between digital and analog media, such as gestures and mimicry, may also be required. The system ClearBoard (Ishii et al. 1992) tries to avoid any kind of media inconsistency. Apart from shared drawing, the working environment allows the users to interact via gestures, eye contact and mimicry.
- *Working mode:* There is a seamless transition between individual work and teamwork. Various levels of teamwork are possible, dependent upon the intensity of the cooperation.
- *Phases of the group process:* A group process passes through several phases (see Fig. 3.2, p. 149) during which synchronous and asynchronous cooperation can take place, alternatively. There should be a seamless transition between the phases of the group process life cycle.

- *Technology:* Seamlessness with respect to technology is that of unified interfaces between heterogeneous systems. CORBA represents an attempt to standardize the communication and cooperation between distributed objects (see Sect. 1.6.4). The inconsistency resulting from switching between work with and work without computer support, however, must also be reduced.
- *Time:* Teams often undergo substantial changes as far as their memberships are concerned. Some members may join later, while others may leave the team during its existence. The team history should provide sufficient means to inform latecomers on the current state of the team. For those who had to leave the team early, access to subsequent team decisions and artifacts (such as team documents) should be possible.

2.9.2 Criteria for the acceptance of groupware systems

The groupware system must be accepted by all team members. Usually, team members have different preferences (for text processing systems etc.), different backgrounds and different experiences.

The different team roles as well as the dynamic assignment of roles to team members must be supported by the groupware system. Social and political factors must be considered, as well as group dynamics.

The group behavior when groupware systems are used must be studied with great care. These studies are time-consuming and expensive, since the number of team members involved may be quite large and it can take a long time to determine the behavioral patterns.

2.9.3 Why groupware systems sometimes fail

Often, there is a disparity between the person doing the work and the person benefiting from it. If only a few team members benefit from the groupware system, then it quite often results in a failure. For most participants, the system usage requires additional workload. The following examples illustrate the problem accurately (Grudin 1994b).

Example (Electronic Calendar). An electronic calendar for automatic planning of meetings is an advantage for the manager, since it makes it easier for him to arrange the appropriate time and agenda for such meetings. However, an automatic planning system makes it necessary for all team members to have their own private electronic calendars. The manager usually already has a private calendar irregardless of his involvement in a groupware system. For most of the other team members, however, maintaining a private calendar may mean a substantial increase in work.

Example (Email and audio). If email messages with audio information are used, it is easy for the sender of a message to generate the audio segments.

The receiver, on the other hand, must spend more effort in processing the audio segments. Since it is part of human nature to take in audio information slower than written information or images, a quick browsing over of audio information is not possible for the receiver.

Obstacles against the use of groupware can be socially or politically motivated. On the one hand, groupware systems may well violate social taboos, on the other hand, existing political and organizational structures may be challenged. Often, users of groupware systems are simply demotivated.

Example (Project management system). Let us assume that a project management system is used for the management of a software project. Every task is assigned to a person who is responsible for the daily report on his progress of the work in the project management system. As soon as the system detects a deadline problem with one task, the superior is automatically notified; the director, as well, gets a copy of this message. Many employees refuse to use this system, or else modify the time information so that no automatic alarm is raised, because they do not want to risk this kind of exposure.

Another problem groupware has to contend with is the lack of exception handling. Teamwork rarely consists of well-structured, completely predefined tasks, thus the specification of the group process by a set of fixed rules seems inappropriate. Teamwork is characterized by improvisation and exceptions from rules.

Another difficulty lies in evaluating groupware systems. Although individual groupware systems can be evaluated by elaborate procedures and observations, it is still hard to generalize results of these evaluations. Moreover, a laboratory situation which mirrors exactly the social, economical, organizational and motivational structure of the workplace is extremely hard to construe. Mostly, we have to rely on actual commercial environments in order to get information on groupware systems. Section 2.9.5 will deal with empirical research on this topic.

Grudin lists 8 challenges for developers of groupware, all of which he has scrutinized as to their relevance for the development of single-user applications and management information systems (Grudin 1994b):

1. Disparity between cost and benefit of groupware systems (i.e., who has to do the work and who benefits from it).
2. Critical mass of users for economical usage of groupware systems.
3. Violation of social taboos and challenge to organizational structures.
4. Support for exception handling.
5. Complexity of the user interface after integrating CSCW functionality in addition to application-oriented functionality.
6. Problems in evaluating and analyzing CSCW systems.
7. Lack of experience in design of multiuser applications.
8. Problems with introducing groupware systems in organizations.

Grudin is positive that all these challenges have to be considered during the design and development process of a successful and suitable groupware system.

Success of email. The following section analyses the success of email with regard to the compliance with the aforementioned requirements.

Both sender and receiver have approximately the same workload: It takes a bit longer for the sender to type the message; the receiver has little problem reading the message at his convenience. Since the sender is the one who mainly benefits by email, he will be willing to do slightly more work.

Email is conversation-oriented and easily compatible with our common office practice.

Email is asynchronous, informal and unstructured by nature (i.e., exceptions are easy to model).

We can conclude that the success of email in practice speaks for itself. Ever since the 1970's, both universities and commercial enterprises have made intensive use of email, so that an evaluation was possible under various conditions.

2.9.4 Benefits and risks of groupware

Tables 2.3 and 2.4 list benefits and risks of groupware, structuring them according to respective groupware components and roles (see also Wilson 1991). The groupware components are: communication support, shared workspaces, shared information, coordination support and electronic support of face-to-face meetings. For the distinction of team roles, we have chosen the office environment and distinguish between manager, expert and secretary.

2.9.5 Development methodology of groupware systems

In comparison with traditional single-user systems, the design and implementation of groupware systems is very complex, since both application-oriented and CSCW-oriented functionality have to be considered. For example, the user interface must provide for parallel, concurrent work by several team members. Also, it may sometimes be desirable to have a communication link between team members in order to increase group awareness. Another problem may be that during the group life cycle individuals may change their roles. Thus, the system has to support individual persons working on the common tasks, as well as to take into account their different and possibly altering roles during the group process. For instance, a team member can be both (co-)author and reviewer during the creation of a shared document.

Besides technological aspects, social and psychological aspects have to be considered for the design of groupware. Bock and Marca (1995) note that groupware systems are by nature sociotechnical, since they contain both technical and social components.

Table 2.3. Benefits and risks of groupware support

CSCW-Component	Benefit of groupware	Risk of groupware
Communication support	interaction within the team is facilitated and the work is not hindered by problems due to traveling	costs limit access to a certain group of people; the private sphere may be violated
Shared workspace	cooperation with geographically dispersed people in real-time	lack of standards restricts usage to similar or compatible systems
Shared information	shared team knowledge may facilitate the coordination of activities; the organization presents a coordinated view to the outside	security risk of shared information with respect to outsiders; sheer volume of information makes access difficult
Workflow management	efficient information flow improves coordination of activities	fixed working procedures and poor support of adhoc situations
Electronic support of face-to-face meetings	meetings are more productive, relevant information can be displayed interactively to all team members	expensive equipment may not sufficiently be exploited; handling requires special training

Table 2.4. Benefits and risks for different team roles

Team role	Benefits of groupware	Risks of groupware
Manager	faster communication with colleagues and management; manager can access relevant information, even during meetings; workflow management systems improve progress control	poorer performers may feel excluded and at a disadvantage; reduction of face-to-face meetings if manager relies too much on communication systems
Expert	communication with colleagues is facilitated; expert's advice is easier to get; improved creativity and innovation	time required for communication cannot be used for other tasks; communication with partners outside of the organization increases the risk that sensitive information might leak
Secretary	schedules are facilitated; less paper is wasted and less time is spent trying to "run after" people	if not all parties are using groupware, work may have to be done twice (within the groupware system and without).

The validation of CSCW concepts is fundamental to the further development of this innovative research area. Validation takes place either by systematic analysis of teamwork and the respective behavior of team members, or by using groupware prototypes in real environments and observing the interaction during the usage of the prototypes. Tang (1991) suggests an iterative process (see Fig. 2.17).

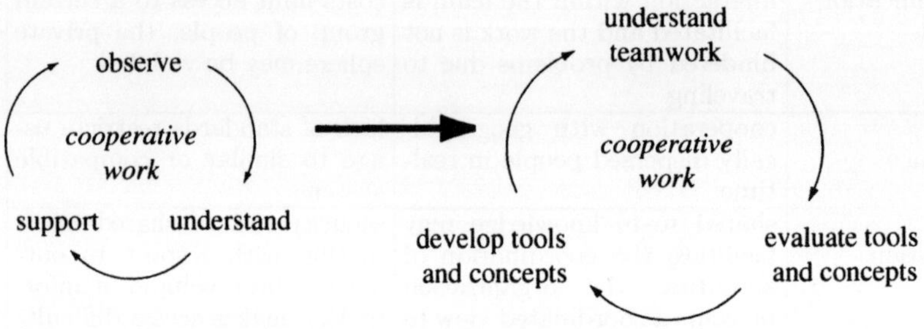

Fig. 2.17. Process for validation of CSCW concepts

This approach observes, understands and supports cooperative work. In order to support cooperative work sufficiently, the current state must first be observed and understood. The use of supportive mechanisms can change the behavior of cooperative work. Krcmar (1991) transfers this approach to the conception of groupware, identifying the following three basic phases:

1. Understanding must be achieved for both teamwork and for its supportive tasks.
2. Concepts and prototypes of groupware systems have to be developed and continually extended.
3. The concepts and prototypes must be evaluated in the context of teamwork.

There is no predefined sequence for the phases, for example it may make sense to first develop the prototypes and then evaluate them during actual usage in order to gain knowledge about basic characteristics of teamwork. One of the reasons for this approach is that using tools also has effects on the cooperation within the team, and thus it alters the interaction between the team members. Moreover, it will often be necessary to progress through these phases more than once. Dourish (1995) calls this a *cycle of design*.

Tang (1991) has used this validation process at Xerox PARC for analyzing teams working on collaborative design of user interfaces. Teams consisted of three to five persons. All interactions of team members during face-to-face meetings were recorded on video and later analyzed. The following conclusions and requirements for the functionality of synchronous groupware systems were determined:

- People use gestures to convey important information. In the context of the shared working environment, all team members should, therefore, be aware of other team members' gestures. With ClearBoard Ishii et al. (1992) describe a special experimental environment based on video communication

which meets this requirement for geographically dispersed team members. In addition, it provides seamless integration between individual and shared workspaces.
- The simple recording of a result is not sufficient. The entire process during which an artifact (like a design drawing) has been created and later used contains substantial information.
- Concurrent access to the shared working environment and the shared group documents are important for the success of teamwork.
- It is desirable for team members to have a shared view of group documents. This facilitates the semantic interpretation and promotes creativity.

Empirical research. Eveland and Bikson (1988) compared a conventional group without computer support and one with electronic support. Both groups had the same goals. The infrastructure of the electronically supported group contained a network of personal computers including email and common office software, for example supporting asynchronous computer conferencing. As opposed to the conventional team lacking computer support, the electronically supported team developed a team structure in which individual members felt far more involved in the teamwork, since they were more frequently in contact with each other. In addition, team members appreciated working according to their own work schedules. The electronic medium did not replace traditional communication media, but introduced innovative types of communication not accessible to the conventional team.

Investigating groupware from the perspective of groupware designers and that of organizations applying groupware, Bullen and Bennet (1991) have questioned employees in 25 organizations on the use of groupware. Designers determine the functionality and interfaces of groupware systems:

- The most commonly used groupware tool is email, even if the systems also support other functions, like group calendars.
- Linking email messages facilitates access to and management of information.
- Isolated tools are an impediment to productivity.

Organizations applying groupware consider aspects necessary to the planning and installation of groupware systems within their organization. Among these aspects are social and technical impact, cost-benefit analysis for the individual employee, and the modification of work processes in order to achieve the best possible productivity improvement with the groupware system.

Streitz et al. (1997) explored the influence of computer support on the decision making process and solution quality in face-to-face meetings. The following three situations were investigated:

- *WS situation:* Team members had their own personal computers, linked through a network. There was no shared electronic whiteboard.

- *(WS+LB) situation:* In addition to the personal computers as described in the WS situation, all team members had access to a shared electronic whiteboard. The interactive electronic whiteboard was capable of both input via pencil-based interface and output.
- *LB situation:* Team members had only the electronic whiteboard. Along with paper, it served as the workspace for the development and the recording of ideas, thereby becoming the medium for focusing teamwork.

The groupware system used was the cooperative hypermedia system Dolphin (see Sect. 2.7). Each meeting lasted four hours and was recorded on video tapes in full length. Review of the recordings and evaluation of group documents showed that the (WS+LB) situation had produced more and higher-quality ideas than both other situations. Although the LB situation had increased cooperative work Streitz et al. (1997) still found that an ideal mixture of individual and cooperative work resulted in the highest-quality final product.

2.9.6 Methods for studying groups

The above examples on empirical research show that there are numerous methods for studying group behavior. All of them have inherent advantages and disadvantages. For example, a questionnaire can focus on the individual situation of a person; there is, however, no guarantee that the persons questioned will answer truthfully.

Questionnaires on work procedures in order to determine the requirements for workflow management systems revealed the following: employees often described their activities more as they wished the work to be done rather than as it was actually carried out. A workflow management system based on such questionnaires alone would therefore not be suitable for real situations.

According to McGrath (1993), all empirical research methods suffer from the dilemma of having inherent shortcomings, as well as certain advantages. McGrath formulates the following hypothesis:

1. All methods allow conclusions, yet all methods have limited scope.
2. All methods have errors, yet all methods are useful.
3. Various errors of different methods can be corrected by successively applying several methods.
4. Different methods should be combined so that one method's shortcomings can be corrected by another method's advantage.

It is therefore advisable to use several methods which complement each other in order to examine teamwork. This is the only way of getting reliable results useful for the groupware design and of confronting the above mentioned challenges successfully.

Classification of methods. The study of teamwork encompasses three basic questions:

(A) Who are the actors? This question aims at generalizing the results on types of actors.
(B) Which behavior is to be examined? A study is supposed to provide data on activities as accurately as possible.
(C) Which is the current and realistic context of teamwork?

Although it is desirable to achieve a solution through all three questions by one examination method, reality has proved this to be impossible. Measurements increasing the accuracy of data on behavior often influence the situation to be examined, thereby making it more artificial. McGrath (1993) classified the methods along two dimensions: the general validity and the influence of the study on the results. As Fig. 2.18 shows, any strategy focusing on one of the three above listed questions is far from ideal with respect to the two remaining aspects. Maximum values are represented by letters (A), (B) or (C).

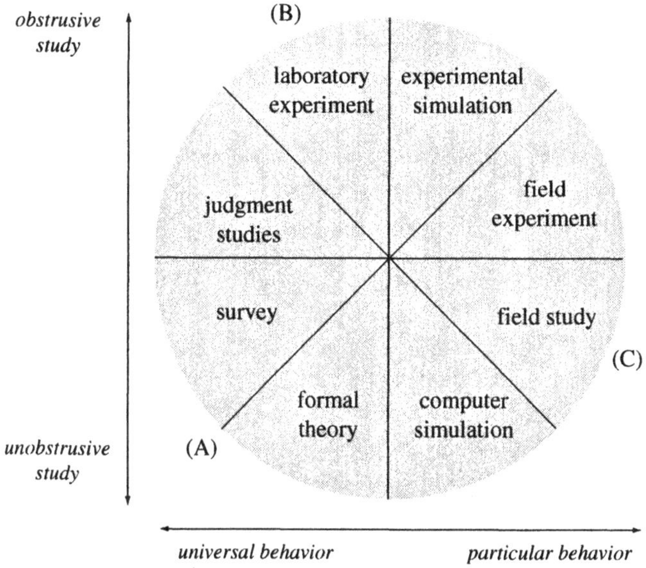

Fig. 2.18. Classification of methods after McGrath

Field studies are observations on actual work groups which do not modify the group context in any way. Ethnographic methods[17] are preferred approaches for field studies, since they provide results both on real work prac-

[17] Ethnographics originated in social studies and was first used for studying ethnic groups.

tices and on social structures at the work place, tools and technologies used and views of team members. Ethnographic researchers participate for some time in the group process by merely listening, never impeding it. Observations are documented either in written form or as video and audio recordings. Sources of problems are the duration of observation and review of collected material; imagine the number of video recordings if a team was accompanied during several weeks. Field studies have a high accuracy with respect to authenticity of the situation.

Field experiments are similar to field studies, except that the research experts actively influence the group process and alter certain conditions in order to achieve information on their effects.

Laboratory experiments are attempts at creating a group environment in which the research expert controls all external conditions in order to explore specific questions. Laboratory experiments are suitable for exactly determining behavioral patterns.

An experimental simulation is a laboratory study exactly mirroring a real-life situation or system. It is "artificial" in that it has been created for research only and persons under observation solve contrived instead of naturally occurring tasks.

Surveys aim at collecting information from several actors on the same issues. In general, the choice of persons to be questioned is based on certain criteria. Judgement studies explore issues by questioning a limited number of persons. Surveys are highly generalizable (A), however, the accuracy of measurement for behavior (B) is low.

The last two methods mentioned are highly theoretical and nonempirical. The formal theory is based on group modeling in which work habits of groups are analyzed. Computer simulations model a real system. Compared with formal theories, computer simulations tell more about the context. They are, however, less generalizable, since they only refer to one specific system.

We can conclude: Field studies are more realistic (C), but have less generalizability (A) and accuracy (B). Laboratory experiments maximize measurement accuracy (B), losing in generalizability (A) and being less realistic (C). Surveys and formal theories have a high degree of generalization (A) but are least reliable with respect to accuracy (B) and real-life authenticity (C).

2.9.7 The Portland experiment

Between 1985 and 1988, Xerox PARC had laboratories both in Palo Alto, California and Portland, Oregon. To approximate field experiment conditions, members of several groups were distributed between the two places. The work at both places aimed at emphasizing interpersonal computing in a distributed environment (Olson and Bly 1991, Bly et al. 1993). Interpersonal computing refers to the support of people communicating through computers while working on a common project. Figure 2.19 depicts the infrastructure of the communication links, and Fig. 2.20 gives an outline of the historical development of the technological support.

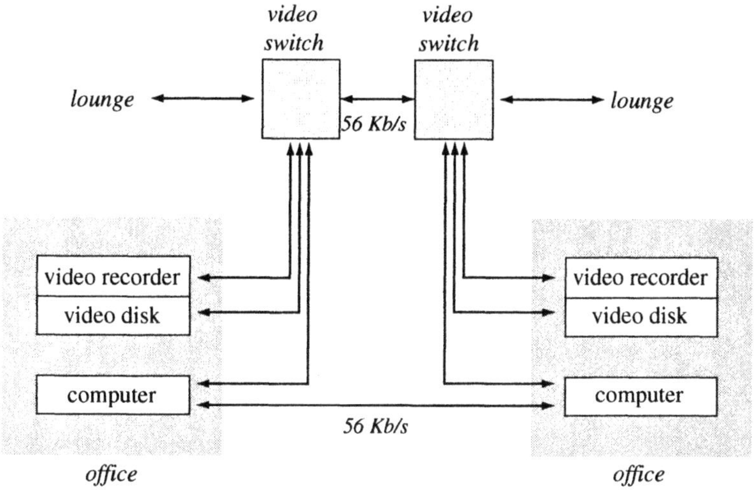

Fig. 2.19. Infrastructure of the Portland experiment

The distributed groups focused on three project areas. In addition to developing an infrastructure for shared software project environments, design methodology and media spaces (see electronic hallway, p. 102) were explored. The first project area resulted in the development of a common architecture for organizing the shared use of heterogeneous on-line information sources. During the experiment, a shared object-oriented database was implemented, the so-called object server. The design methodologies were centered around the work processes of a team of designers, in particular the representation of the design process through electronic media. Communication and cooperation between team members in distributed laboratories depended on the use of multiple media, e.g. computer data, video and audio.

Experiences gained throughout the experiment were evaluated according to four different aspects:

1. *Cooperation:* The aspect of cooperation within a work group focused on a special application domain, the cooperative design between the distributed locations. Other cooperative activities, like joint programming, were seen as interesting research areas too, but were never explored and investigated in detail. Due to the focus on one application domain, the tools developed were specialized and customized for that domain.
2. *Innovative tools:* Special emphasis was given to the development of innovative tools. An attempt was made at supporting two physically separated environments in such a way as to make them behave as a single environment. Researchers became eventually frustrated at their inability to

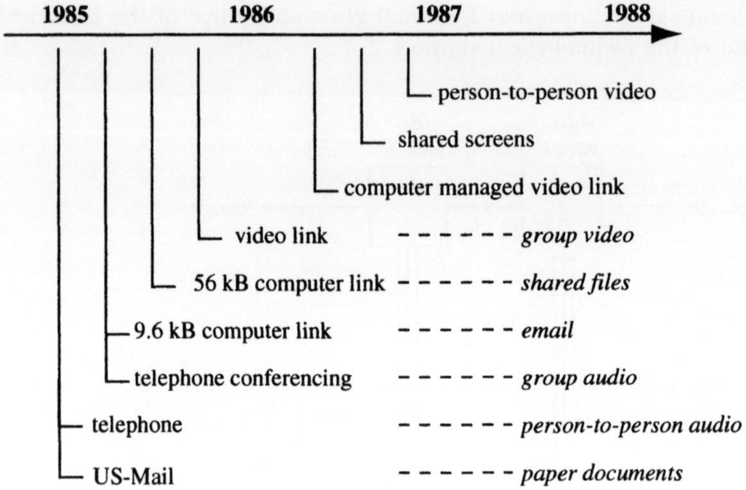

Fig. 2.20. Historical development of technology support

achieve this goal. Video conferencing was never able to completely replace face-to-face interaction. A necessity for a shared workspace remained. Further, improvement of the efficiency of reciprocal dependencies did not receive adequate consideration. For the best possible usage of resources in both places, coordination between these places was necessary; this usage of resources, however, caused a mutual dependency. Improved access to shared data can increase the capacity for mutual dependency. For this purpose, a shared object server has been designed and realized.

3. *Organization:* A third issue was the type of organization for both laboratories. A study analyzed how each individual team member saw his own role within the group, how he identified himself with this role and how he behaved with respect to this role. The alternatives of authoritarian vs. democratic, negotiation-oriented behavior were investigated. Results can be summarized under the motto: "Palo Alto is where the decisions are made". This meant that extended connections, such as broadband computer, audio and video connections could not replace an actual physical presence in Palo Alto, since this was where important decisions were made.
   Video cameras in the private offices enabled flexible borderlines between private and public workspaces. Team members accepted ethically used video cameras, where notice was given as soon as an office was monitored by a remote video camera.
4. *Management:* Management was quite satisfied with the decentralized control of the work processes and task execution. In the case of telecommuting a liberal management style must transfer some of the control mechanisms to the employee himself. Those employees not at the same place as

the manager were evaluated less subjectively and intuitively, and more according to their actual performance.

2.9.8 Lotus Notes

In this chapter, we introduce Lotus Notes which is one of the few groupware systems that has gained wide market acceptance and a significant installation base.

Success criteria. The success of Lotus Notes is based on the observation that teamwork calls for various, highly flexible communication forms, all of which should be easy to learn by persons involved in the group process and applicable in a way familiar to team members. In addition, the system must easily adapt to common security demands and work habits. Technical perfection, with respect to concurrency control or synchronization are less significant for the group process.

Another aspect of success is the fact that a number of highly respected firms (IBM, Novell, etc.) already have Lotus Notes in their portfolios, and that big enterprises like Kodak or federal agencies already use Lotus Notes as their management system for shared documents. Andersen Consulting uses Lotus Notes successfully as the basis for its knowledge management effort. These factors are highly beneficent to the system.

Short overview of the system. Lotus Notes is a bulletin board system based on email and database applications for users who, in general, are not continually connected via a communication channel. Based on the client-server model, it creates a communication platform on which several users can cooperate as a team. For the types of cooperation, three models can be distinguished:

1. *Send Model:* The send model promotes a form of communication based on email where, for example, team members can send predefined forms for ratification or a memo for evaluation to their supervisor. Circulation folders, too, belong to this model. The current state of a circulating folder is recorded in status documents which are sent to the initiator at regular intervals.
2. *Shared Model:* In this model, team members communicate indirectly through a common Notes database. They are aware of the database, know their own role in the work process, and the functions relevant to them within the database application. For example, in this model requests are no longer sent to the recipients. Instead, they are filed to the respective request database by the sender. Potential recipients regularly inform themselves on whether or not new requests have been sent. Further work on the request may either be an answer to the applicant or the follow through on a request after the work on it has been completed.

3. *Mixed Models:* For some applications, a combination of both models is advantageous. For example, the send model may be used for initiating a process (like email request to an employee); afterwards, the shared model is used to continue and complete the procedure (e.g. the responsible party files the required information in a database for other team members to evaluate).

The shared model is based on Notes database applications. If the Notes database is distributed via a communication network (LAN, WAN), then the database entries can be replicated. Modifications in the database are propagated to all accessible replicas. For the propagation, Lotus Notes does not apply locking mechanisms or time-intensive synchronization processes. The goal is for all replicas to be "as far as possible synchronized at regular intervals".

Many Notes applications can well afford this procedure, since often the databases are just used for filing information. Replacing information and strict consistency demands (in which case a lack of total synchronization is undesirable) are mostly avoided. Instead, new entries are simply added.

In the case of several team members making modifications in different replicas of the same shared document and the application wishing to be notified of conflicting entries, then a so-called revision protocol must be applied. Lotus Notes generates a revision protocol for all documents recording all modifications. If the server receives modified copies of the same document, then the respective revision protocols are checked and compared with each other. The strategy of determining the new current version is relatively simple: The copy which has, according to the revision protocol, been modified most often is declared the new original document. All other (also modified document copies) are marked as "reply documents" and saved in the Notes database. The marked documents make it easy for the users to find conflicts and to subsequently try to resolve inconsistencies manually. This might require additional communication within the team. Lotus Notes promotes system acceptance by incorporating functions found to be indispensable in the business world: Access rights on databases to control access to documents, classified information may be encrypted and electronic signatures may validate documents. User identification takes place according to the standardized, hierarchical X.500 naming syntax.

The user interface which is quite similar across heterogeneous computer platforms and the aforementioned system characteristics have helped to make Lotus Notes widely accepted and applied in many fields of computer-supported cooperative work.

2.10 Further Reading

Groupwork, especially common pitfalls, cooperation and antisocial behavior in a group are discussed by Cohen and Goodlad (1994).

Textbooks on computer-supported cooperative work have only recently been published (for example in German Teufel et al. 1995). Note also that there are some anthologies by Baecker (1993), Diaper and Sanger (1993), Greif (1988) and Marca and Bock (1992) giving a collection of articles on the subject.

The book by Jessup and Valacich (1993) contains many important works in the field of group support systems. The books by Johansen (1988, 1991) view CSCW under organizational aspects. Groupware as an enabler for knowledge management is presented by Smith (1999). In Igbaria and Tan (1998), the focus lies on telecooperation and its influence on future enterprise structures. Besides a management-oriented CSCW perspective Coleman and Khanna (1995) provide a number of practical examples. The book by Hazemi et al. (1998) discusses the relationship of CSCW and the future development of digital universities.

For an extended bibliography on CSCW, see the electronic version on the web server http://www.telekooperation.de/cscw/.

Part II

Basic Concepts of Computer-Supported Cooperative Work

3. Concepts of Asynchronous and Synchronous Cooperation

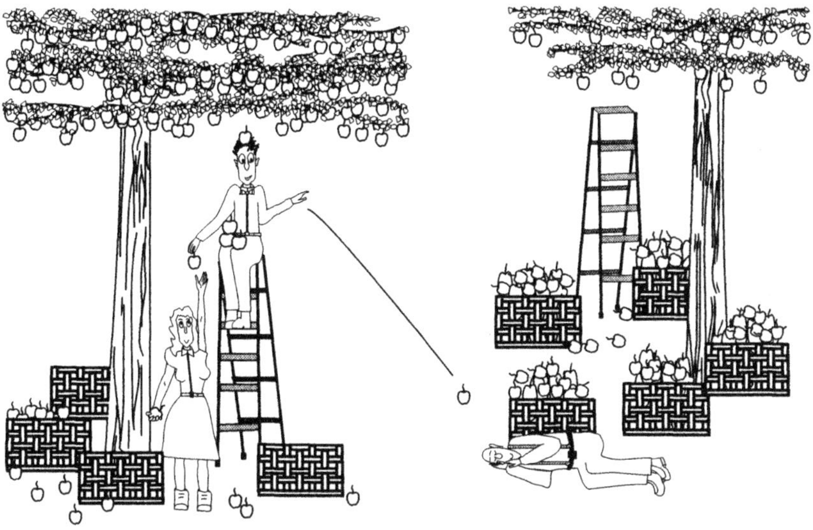

The group process is a fundamental CSCW concept which specifies the goals and structure of the team as well as the progress of the cooperation between team members. We will discuss the centralized, distributed nonreplicated and distributed replicated group process models.

After an introduction to a general cluster model, we will explain strategies for distributing information within and between clusters. Special attention will be given to possible structures of asynchronous team interaction, exemplified by the linear Emisari model, the comb model and the Parti tree model.

The management of a shared context is a further basic CSCW aspect we will deal with, focusing on the WYSIWIS (what you see is what I see) concept and the support of group awareness.

Possible architectures of groupware systems will conclude the chapter. Issues are window sharing, conferencing components and conference managers, as well as collaboration aware systems.

3.1 Group Processes

Cooperation within a team is typically both a repeated alternation between asynchronous and synchronous cooperation and a process during which subgroups constitute themselves for solving individual subproblems. This process is similar to the modularization of software systems. Usually, the group project initiation happens synchronously, for example during a face-to-face meeting. The project can, however, be completed both synchronously and asynchronously. A seminar can exemplify the alternation between the different cooperation modes, as seen in Fig. 3.1.

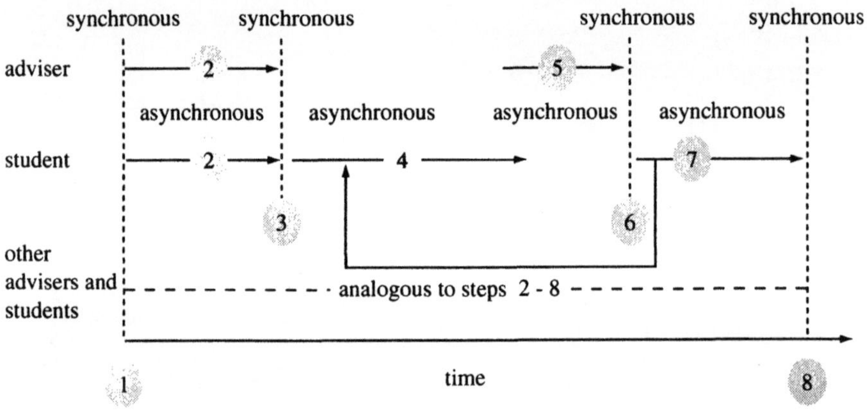

We can sum up as follows:

1. Introduction of topics and assignments during a face-to-face meeting;
2. Adviser and student read separately about the topic;
3. Adviser and student discuss open issues;
4. Student works on the paper (ith iteration);
5. Adviser reads the paper (ith iteration);
6. Adviser and student discuss the paper (ith iteration);
7. Student produces the final version of the paper;
8. Student presents the paper in front of the entire class.

Fig. 3.1. Cooperation exemplified by a seminar paper

Tasks and activities which are performed as part of a CSCW application can be interpreted as a process. A suitable process model can both increase the comprehension of groupwork and serve as a basis to specify different degrees of computer support, including automation of the entire process.

Definition 3.1.1 (Group process). *A group process is the specification of information, activities and characteristics of an electronically supported team, including the context for the group interaction.*

Groupwork has an initial and a final state, the latter of which represents the result of the groupwork.

A group process usually consists of a static and a dynamic part. The former describes the team and its environment for performing the activities, the latter specifies the progress of the groupwork and its respective state. Since the structure of a team can undergo significant changes during the group existence (people may leave or join the team), the term "static" must not be interpreted too strictly. It refers to information being fairly constant.

Group processes consist of the following components: goals, organization, protocol and environment of the group make up the static part of group processes, while shared documents, group activities, the current group state and group sessions specify the dynamic part. The following describes these components in more detail:

- *Group goals:* Group goals describe the global goals to be achieved by a predefined team. Individual goals can differ from group goals, for example the group goal may be the authoring of a technical description of a product, while an individual team member may only wish more information on the product itself. Group goals have priority over individual goals.
- *Group organization:* This component describes team members according to profiles (their skills and competencies), and their position within the team and the organization in which the team is embedded. The roles of team members within the group may depend on their role within the organization. It may also change dynamically as the groupwork progresses. During a group session we can distinguish between active and passive participants. The former are actively contributing to the progress of the group session (manipulating shared documents), while the latter are just observing the operations of the other team members.
- *Group protocol:* The group protocol describes the way in which team members cooperate and communicate with each other. This component has special importance in the case of synchronous cooperation, for example in group sessions, where special floor-passing schemes are used to synchronize and control concurrent interactions. We will describe these schemes in detail in Sect. 4.6.

  If a protocol is based on hardware or software approaches, then it is called technical. Technical protocols have the following characteristics: better support of those participants who are not yet quite familiar with the way the group interacts, an obligation for a certain behavior by the participants, well-defined structure and possible restrictions of interactions. A typical example of a technical protocol is the specification of document access rights which are automatically checked by the system when a team member attempts to access the document.

  As opposed to technical protocols, a social protocol can be, and mostly is, controlled by team members. Besides the social role of people within a team or organization, the interaction specified by the social protocol can also be influenced by individual characteristics or cultural background.

Conventions for "polite interruption" or "drawing attention by show of hands" are examples.
The social protocol usually helps to determine who will speak during a session. This procedure again can be divided into an informal and formal approach: While in the first case each participant can feel free to speak according to predefined rules, in the second case a moderator is in charge. The social protocol, too, has certain characteristics. It may encourage participants to interact according to their own style if the groupware system is flexible enough. However, if individual persons tend to dominate the interaction, the social protocol can be unfair and inefficient. Lastly, an interaction may be totally unstructured and chaotic.

- *Group environment:* Another component of the group process is the group environment. Among other factors, it is determined by the context of the groupwork, such as the hardware and software systems, room equipment and room layout.
- *Group documents:* Group documents belong to the dynamic part of the group process; they store information and relate it to the group process. Examples are documents which have been used or created during a group process, such as minutes of meetings, design documents etc.
- *Group activities:* Activities taking place during a group process can have temporal or causal dependencies upon each other. Since activities often take place in unexpected situations or with insufficient information, it is generally impossible to list all potential situations on initialization of a group process. Thus, the system must include the option for defining new group activities or redefining/deleting of existing activities based on progress of the groupwork. In other words, the group activities must be dynamically adaptable to new situations. For groupwork, the slogan: "exceptions are the rule" holds true.
- *Group sessions:* A group session is performed as part of a group activity. It can be both synchronous and asynchronous, and it may include the participation of one, several or all team members. Within a group session the participants execute a variety of operations. For example, during a group session aimed at creating a document, the choice is between operations such as insert, delete, replace and copy.
- *Group state:* This component describes the current state of groupwork and it changes according to the execution of group activities. The group state changes quite frequently as the groupwork progresses.

The group process is a dynamic entity passing through several stages during the group life cycle. Teams are not constituted at random and the cooperation progress is not linear (see Step 6 in Fig. 3.1). Rather, both the team and cooperation develop step-by-step and are sometimes even deteriorating with time. After Drexler and Sibbet (see respective sections under Johansen et al. 1991) all groups develop from a creation to a consolidation phase (see Fig. 3.2). Each of the seven phases branches into two directions:

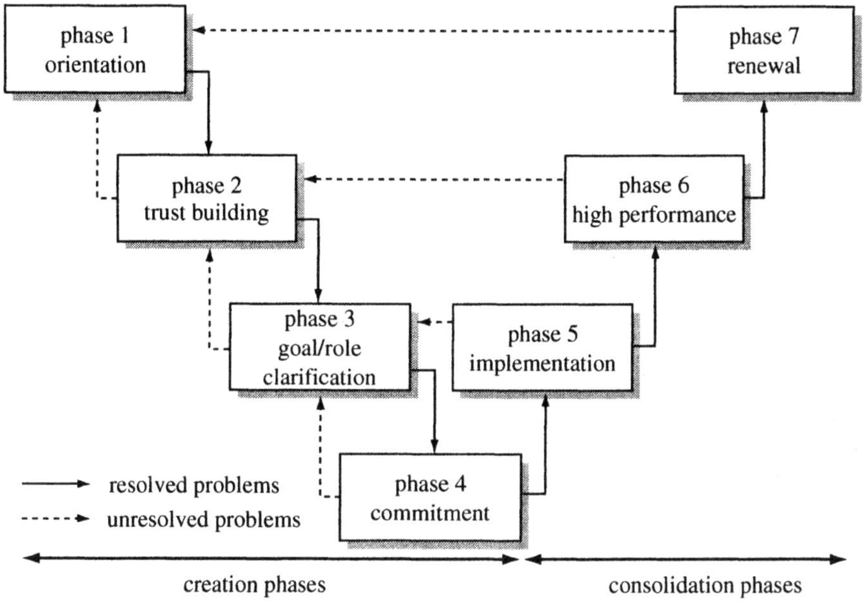

Fig. 3.2. Group process model after Drexler/Sibbet

Option a): If all problems have been solved in a given phase, then the team advances to the next phase. Option b): If problems have remained unsolved, then the team returns to an earlier phase. During the creation phases groups will only have to return to the preceding phase. However, in case of the team having been in a consolidation phase, then it will have to return to another phase of the same level, for example from phase 5 to phase 3.

Creation phases.

1. *Orientation:* This phase represents the beginning of the group process. The team members discuss the overall goal of the group and ask the following questions: "Why is this team to be created?" and "What is the purpose of the team?" The orientation occurs from the viewpoint of the individual team member.
2. *Trust building*: Next, the integration of individual persons into the group process is of interest: "What is expected of me?", "Who are my direct contacts?", "What amount of work am I expected to do?" Trust building leads to an open atmosphere and mutual respect. Disorientation or uneasiness of team members requires backtracking to the previous phase.
3. *Goal/role clarification*: During this phase the goals and tasks of a group are defined. Discrepancies among team members with respect to expectations, views and knowledge can result in conflicts. However, progress can only be made after goals and tasks have been agreed upon.

4. *Commitment:* The procedure for achieving the group goals is outlined; among other things, decisions are made with respect to problem structure and the assignment of resources. All team members must agree to support that procedure. Unresolved dependencies and responsibilities may require the return to phase 3.

Consolidation phases.

5. *Implementation:* After team members have agreed upon a problem, individual tasks are assigned to people. Temporal and causal dependencies during task execution must be taken into consideration. Conflicts between tasks and confusion of team members could result in backtracking to the goal/role clarification phase.
6. *High performance:* When methods and procedures are defined, it is no longer necessary for the team to convene to discuss and determine each and every step. Instead, activities occur intuitively and flexibly.
7. *Renewal:* The high performance phase is only of limited duration. As time goes by, team members become less motivated, the group structure changes and the question arises: "Why go on?".

The structuring of a group process into phases and their interdependencies helps us pinpoint the potential of groupware to support the tasks of the individual steps. According to Johansen et al. (1991) the first two phases require direct contact (e.g., face-to-face) between team members. Synchronous conferencing systems or electronic meeting rooms also seem adequate. Activities within the goal/role clarification phase may well be supported by a mixture of synchronous and asynchronous groupware. For mutual understanding, fast communication is indispensable. During the phases of commitment, implementation and high performance, the focus is on the determined and agreed upon group activities. For cooperation, coordination systems and information spaces are useful while for communication, email will often suffice. During the last phase of the group process, the renewal phase, direct contact between team members will often be necessary.

3.1.1 Group process models

According to Rapaport (1991) we distinguish between three types of group processes:

1. the centralized group process model;
2. the distributed, nonreplicated group process model;
3. the distributed, replicated group process model.

Centralized group process model. The information associated with a group process is stored and managed at a central location as shown in Fig. 3.3. Different group processes are isolated from each other by application software.

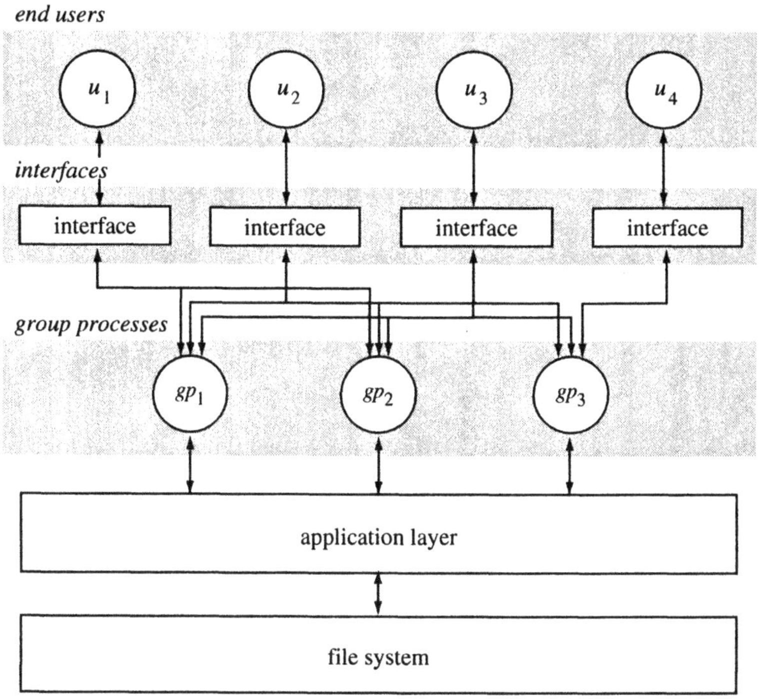

Fig. 3.3. Centralized group process model

This model does not require private information storage. All team members read the same version, which means that there are no differing copies. The history of the group process is recorded and archived. If the group composition changes dynamically with time, new team members can inform themselves and update their knowledge about the group process by reading the archived information.

Distributed, nonreplicated group process model. The distributed, nonreplicated group process model is depicted in Fig. 3.4. The nodes shown in the model can be either personal computers, servers or local clusters. Units of distribution are complete group processes. There is only one original version of group information which is stored at the local node managing the group process. Nodes are assigned by the system administrator. For team members, remote access is transparent, i.e., access to local and remote group processes (group documents) is identical. The system is access and location transparent.

Distributed, replicated group process model. Figure 3.5 outlines a distributed, replicated group process model. Again, nodes may be personal computers, servers or local clusters. As opposed to the nonreplicated group process, the processes are distributed and replicated in this model. Informa-

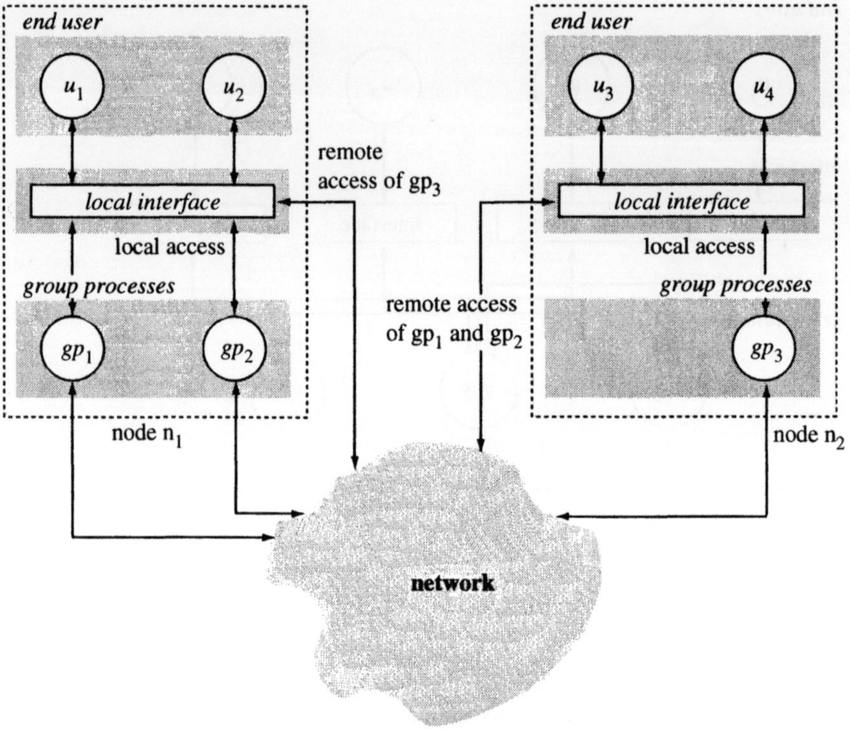

Fig. 3.4. Distributed, nonreplicated group process model

tion units of the group process, are distributed and replicated, per relevant node and not per team member.

For individual team members, the distribution is transparent (see Sect. 1.2), i.e., the work mode is the same as that for the centralized model. In addition to access and location transparency, the model also offers replication transparency. User operating and control information are forwarded to all nodes managing part of a replicated group process. Thus, the information of the replicated group process is kept consistent.

Replication has two advantages: Information availability is improved for a variety of error situations (e.g., a system crash of a node), and response times are shorter.

3.1.2 Group communication

Group communication can be structured according to the type of information distribution and according to the direction of the information flow.

In the former case, there are three possible models (see Table 3.1). Information either flows from one team member to several (one-to-many communication) or vice versa (many-to-one communication), from several team mem-

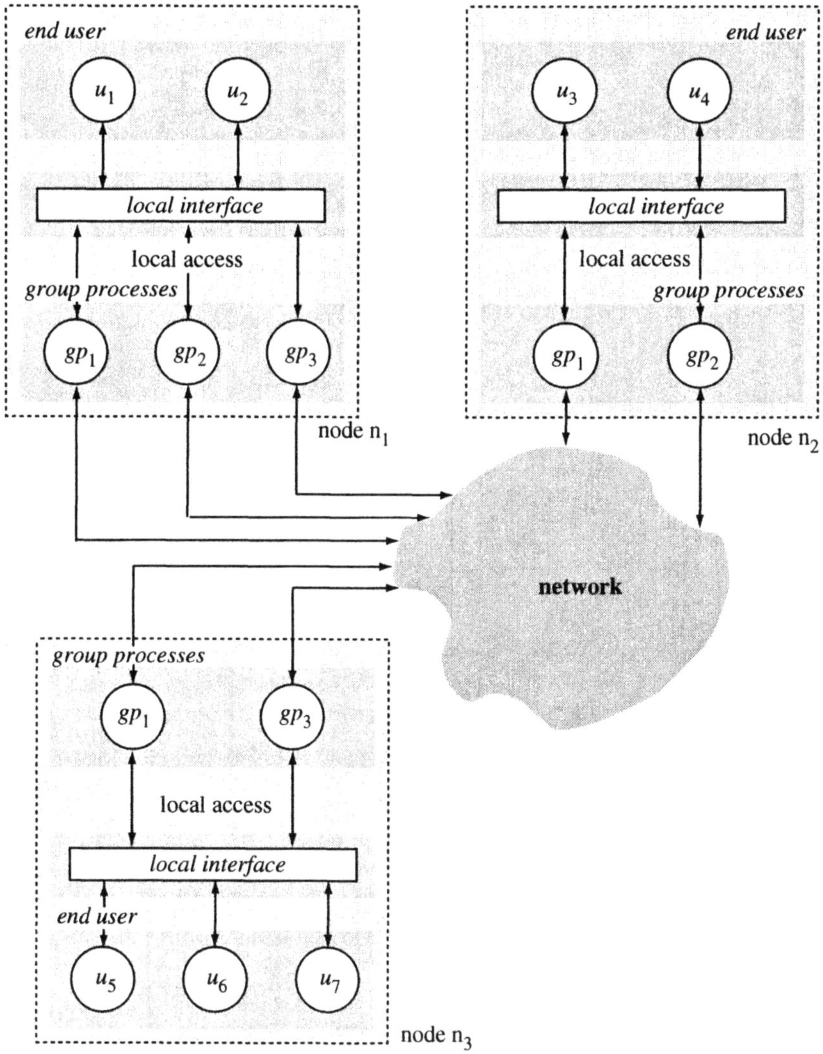

Fig. 3.5. Distributed, replicated group process model

bers to several others (many-to-many communication), or between two team members (one-to-one communication). An example of the first case is that of assignments by the project supervisor to the project members, whereas the second case is exemplified by project members convening amongst themselves. A dialogue between two project supervisors is one-to-one communication.

The second classification of group communication is based on the direction of the information flow. The unidirectional information flow we daily experience, for example, in newspapers and radio implies no interaction, whereas bidirectional information flow always requires interaction between team members.

Table 3.1. Classification of group communication

information flow	one-to-one	one-to-many	many-to-one	many-to-many
	distribution type			
	synchronous			
unidirectional	instruction	speech	report	demonstration
bidirectional	dialogue	teaching	vote	conferencing
	asynchronous			
unidirectional	notification	announcement	status report	circulation
bidirectional	exchange of letters	distance teaching	agent communication with 2-phase-commit protocol	bulletin board

Communication links must take the network structure and the transport mechanism into consideration.

- *Transmission via a designated control unit:* Let $|N|$ be the number of nodes. If the transmission of information occurs via control unit n_{CU}, then there are $|N|-1$ links, provided the control unit n_{CU} itself belongs to the group (see Fig. 3.6).

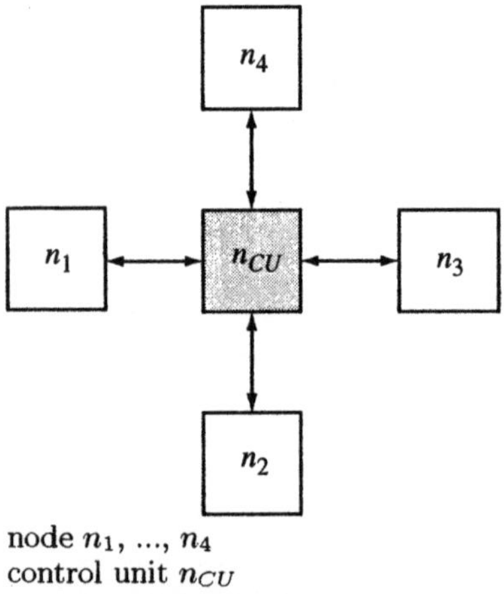

Fig. 3.6. Transmission of information via a designated control unit

- *Direct communication:* In the case of direct communication between all nodes (see Fig. 3.7), $\frac{|N|\times(|N|-1)}{2}$ connections are necessary, resulting in a complexity of $O(|N|^2)$. By applying multicast communication, the system performance can be improved.

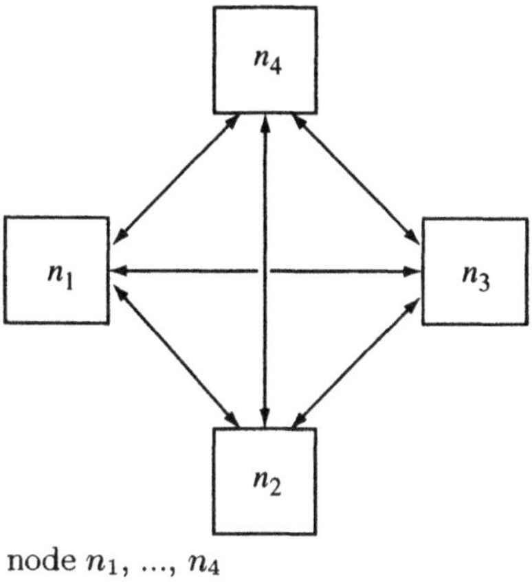

Fig. 3.7. Direct communication

3.1.3 Concurrency control

Shared usage and exchange of information is an integral part of every group process. In order to keep information consistent, concurrency control is essential. Figure 3.8 illustrates the problem using the example of a group editor where user u_1 wants to delete a sentence while user u_2 inserts a new word.

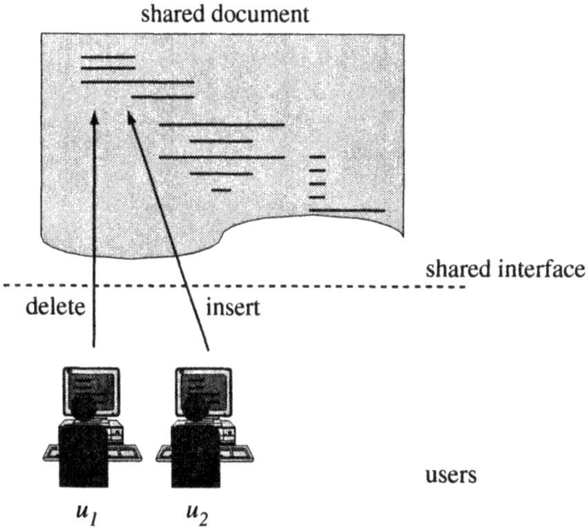

Fig. 3.8. Example: group editor

A strict interpretation of consistency can be achieved by requiring intermediate states to remain identical for all team members during a group session. For a loose interpretation of consistency, identical final states at the end of a group session will suffice. During the progress of the group session participating team members may have different intermediate states.

Among the aspects of concurrency are:

- *Responsiveness:* Interactions such as team brainstorming are mainly conducted synchronously. Groupware systems supporting synchronous groupwork must, therefore, have the following characteristics:
  1. Short response times: The time required for input to be displayed on the user's screen must be short.
  2. Short notification times: The time required for input to be propagated to all other team members must be short. Notification time is, however, also dependent upon the network infrastructure and the current network load.
- *Group interface:* Concurrency control should avoid a display of "very" out-of-date information on the users' screens. The WYSIWIS principle or a relaxed form of it should be applied (see Sect. 3.5.1).
  Sometimes it is, however, desired for less than completely current information to be displayed. In this case, the user has to be informed that the information he is reading is out-of-date; for example, using a different font or color.

  Example. The user desires a quick overview of the information without going into details. Constant updating of the screen would be both an impediment and too time consuming.

- *Wide area distribution:* Transmission times are longer in a WAN, which influences notification times. Since communication errors are common in WANs, flexible protocols are necessary for concurrency control.
- *Replication of information:* Short response times can be achieved by replicating the data at the user's location. The local availability of data for read access is increased. Replicated information must, however, be kept consistent.
  There are two alternatives:
  1. Sending the entire display (including the modifications)
  2. Propagation of the operations, which then are executed in the receiving environments. Applications must act identically on all nodes, i.e., they must be independent of the execution environment (for example, independent of the current load of an individual machine).
- *Robustness:* Recovery after machine crash or communication error must be provided. Likewise, a recovery is required after operations by users, for example reconfiguration of the concurrency control algorithm after a new member joined the team.
- *Notification:* In order to make users aware of concurrent operations, concurrency control must include notification mechanisms in the case of conflicting changes.

For example, the Gordion-System (Yeh et al. 1987) defines the following notification variants:

Definition 3.1.2 (Immediate notification). *An immediate notification informs the user about all conflicts. Conflicts of this kind refer to access of hard locked data objects or access of data objects for which a new version is currently being created.*

Definition 3.1.3 (Delayed notification). *A delayed notification informs the user no sooner than the conflicting activity is about to be completed (soft locked).*

The consistency problem cannot be solved by the aforementioned notification mechanisms. In most cases systems are not able to resolve conflicts because of missing semantics of the operation or of the user intention. The following will discuss two possible concurrency control schemes. A more detailed discussion will follow in Chapters 4–5.

1. *Detection of dependencies:* The system discovers conflicting operations using timestamps. A timestamp may consist of the pair (author, time) and is generated with each execution of an operation. Detected conflicts are resolved manually. For each operation, the current timestamp must be specified in addition to the information unit.

   Example. Let u_1, u_2 and u_3 be users and T a text block.
   Situation a): Text block T has timestamp $S(T) = (u_1, t_0)$, i.e., at the time t_0 the user u_1 has executed an operation on T successfully.
   Situation b): At time $t_1 > t_0$, the user u_2 executes operation OP on T: Let $OP(T, (u_1, t_0))$ be the operation. OP is accepted because the current timestamp has been specified; for the new timestamp, we have $S(T) = (u_2, t_1)$.
   Situation c): At time $t_2 > t_1$, user u_3 executes the operation OP' on T: Let $OP'(T, (u_1, t_0))$. OP' will be rejected, because the timestamp specified in operation OP' does not match the current timestamp $S(T) = (u_2, t_1)$. User u_3 must resolve the conflict manually.

   The algorithm for the execution of an operation OP with timestamp S is as follows:

   Code fragment (Operation execution with timestamp).
   if (S = timestamp in database) **then**
       execute operation OP;
       generate new timestamp;
   else create conflict;

   This concurrency control scheme has the following characteristics:
   - no synchronization necessary;
   - brief response times;
   - manual user intervention is required;
   - for replicated and distributed data storage, clock synchronization is necessary.

2. *Reversible execution:* Operations are immediately executed. However, the system retains information for each executed operation in order to undo its effects if a conflict arises with another operation on a remote machine. A conflict is defined as concurrent operations on shared information causing different information states for different operation sequences. A global time may be used to define an ordering of the operations.

   Example. Let operations $OP_1(T, t_1)$ and $OP_2(T, t_2)$ be two conflicting concurrent operations on a text block T. If $t_1 < t_2$, then the effect of OP_2 on text block T is reversed.

   The approach has the following characteristics:
   - short response times;
   - disadvantage: First, the effect of an operation is displayed on the screen and then later it disappears after a conflict has been detected.

3.1.4 Roles of group members

The role of the individual group member is an important aspect of the design of CSCW applications. The example of a project manager who is at the same time a fellow worker illustrates the fact that one team member can have several roles at the same time.

Roles help to structure interactions between team members and define functionalities and access rights on group documents. There are two aspects of a role concept:

1. The role defines the social function of an individual with regard to the group process, to the group organization and to other team members. In particular, the roles are often based on the skills, competencies and knowledge of the team members.
2. A role defines rights and duties within the group process. It specifies the access control of information units (like read and write access) and activities to be performed by individual team members.

Roles can be categorized formally or informally. In the first case, the distinction tends to be a bureaucratic one, whereas the second alternative can improve creativity and spontaneity. It can, however, also lead to chaotic situations.

3.2 Cluster Model

In the following section, we will introduce a cluster model for networked computers generalizing existing approaches.

We assume different average transmission rates of communication links between nodes (e.g., personal computers) and we introduce communication nodes, the so-called routers to handle message transfers between subnets. The routers are characterized by their transfer rates and reliabilities.

Our cluster model includes a set of nodes N with varying reliability values $rel\_node(n)$, $n \in N$. Reliability is measured over a period of time and represents the ratio between the times the nodes are up and running and the total time the nodes are connected to the network. The availability of nodes refers to the correct behavior of hardware and software. The marginal difference between hardware and software failure characteristics is neglected. Robust architecture and high fault tolerance of current computer systems allow us to set a reliability value of approximately 1.

3.2.1 Direct point-to-point connection

We assume network configuration and topology, in particular the direct point-to-point connections between pairs of computers $(n_i, n_j) \in N \times N$ are known in advance. It is not necessary for all computer pairs to have a direct point-to-point connection. We define $directlink(n_i, n_j)$ to be true iff $n_i = n_j$ or n_i and n_j belong to the same LAN. All direct point-to-point connections are characterized by the following two features:

1. *Average transmission rate:* The average transmission rate is hardware dependent and it is measured in blocks per second. It describes the bandwidth of the direct point-to-point connection.
2. *Reliability:* Reliability is hardware dependent, and also sensitive to external influence. External influences are, for instance, temperature or electromagnetic fields. Rather than taking these influences into consideration, we will assume that the reliability of a direct point-to-point connection is known at all times.

In the following, we will define some of the parameters of the cluster model.

Average transmission rate. Our definition of a direct point-to-point connection includes an internal communication link (i.e., $directlink(n, n)$). Internal communication links allow data exchange between main memory and secondary storage. The average transmission rate over internal communication links is modeled the same way as that for the average transmission rate of communication links between two directly connected nodes. The values of both communication links are of the same order of magnitude for a LAN environment.

Definition 3.2.1 (Average transmission rate, point-to-point). *The average transmission rate of a direct point-to-point connection is defined as*

$$rate\_direct\_link(n_i, n_j) = \begin{cases} 0, & \textit{if } \neg directlink(n_i, n_j) \\ \textit{average transmission rate(blocks/sec)}, & \textit{else} \end{cases}$$

Reliability. The internal communication link between main memory and secondary storage is extremely reliable. Let the reliability be 1. We assume that the reliability of all external communication links (i.e., *direct-link*(n_i, n_j), $n_i \neq n_j$) is less than 1. In general, precise reliability values cannot be determined and they may even change over time.

Definition 3.2.2 (Reliability, point-to-point).
The reliability of a direct point-to-point connection is defined as

$$rel\_direct\_link_t(n_i, n_j) = \begin{cases} 1, \text{ if } n_i = n_j \\ 0, \text{ if } \neg directlink(n_i, n_j) \\ \text{reliability at time } t, \text{ else} \end{cases}$$

3.2.2 Indirect communication links

Let us assume that all nodes $n \in N$ can communicate with each other. This means that there is a communication link (direct or indirect) for all pairs $(n_i, n_j) \in N \times N$ between n_i and n_j. Then we have $link(n_i, n_j)$ if *direct-link*(n_i, n_j) or if $\exists n_k \in N, n_k \neq n_j : directlink(n_i, n_k) \wedge link(n_k, n_j)$. Thus, the link relation is the transitive closure of direct point-to-point connections.

Let n_k be a node in the communication link between n_i and n_j, with $n_k \neq n_i, n_k \neq n_j$. The node n_k is called a router or a switching computer. The communication link between n_i and n_j is either a direct point-to-point connection or a sequence of direct point-to-point connections over the routers.

The difference between routers and the other nodes (called hosts) within the cluster is their additional task of establishing direct point-to-point connections between two nodes and of transmitting messages. It is assumed that there is exactly one communication link between two nodes n_i and n_j, i.e., there is exactly one direct point-to-point connection or exactly one possible sequence of direct point-to-point connections over the respective routers between n_i and n_j. If there are several communication paths between two nodes, then the one with the highest average transmission rate is selected. All messages between these two nodes are transmitted across the selected communication path. This approach conforms with routing algorithms which usually select the communication link with the highest bandwidth. Other path selection criteria, such as cost, security or reliability, will not be dealt with in this chapter. This simplified cluster model allows a load specification for direct point-to-point connections without using stochastic distribution or routing strategies. This enables the evaluation of communication traffic in terms of transmitted message blocks between nodes, and in particular the determination of the load of individual direct point-to-point connections and routers. This simplification reduces the complexity involved in determining the reliability value of the communication link. In our model, the combinatorial analysis of all possible communication paths is not necessary. The following section will define parameters for the description of indirect communication links.

Average transmission time. In the following we will consider average transmission times, rather than average transmission rates. The average transmission time of an indirect communication link depends on the average transmission rate and the current load. The current load can be derived from the number of link users and the amount of data transferred across the link. Increasing either value results in higher average transmission times. Message blocks arriving at a router are entered into a queue before they are processed and transferred to the next communication link. Thus the average processing time of a router is the sum total of the average waiting time of blocks in the queue and the average block transfer time itself.

Determining the average transmission time of an indirect communication link can be complex since the communication path between the nodes n_i and n_j might encompass a large number of routers and links. For the following discussion we assume a communication path between the nodes n_i and n_j as depicted in Fig. 3.9.

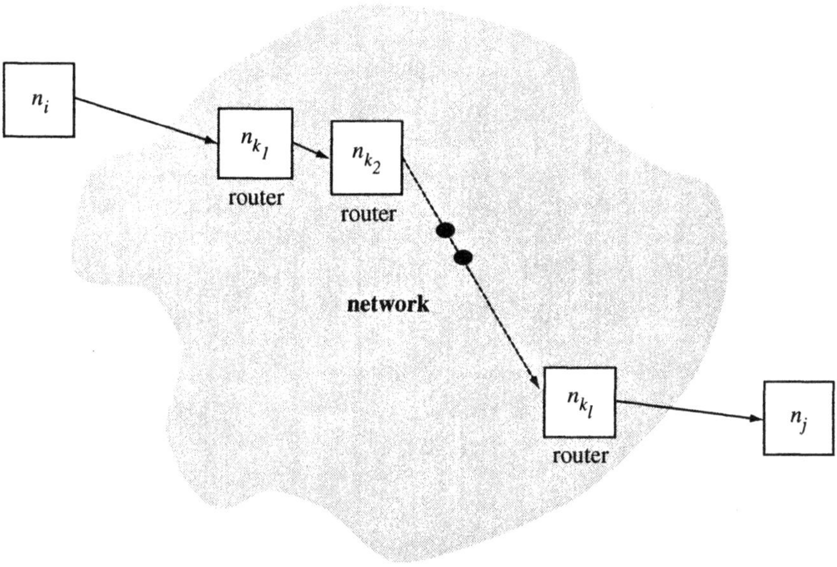

Fig. 3.9. Communication path between nodes n_i and n_j

The average transmission time of a block to be transferred from n_i to n_j is the sum total of the average transmission times for the transfer of the block across the direct point-to-point connections and the average processing times at the routers. For the average transmission times of a communication link, waiting times might also be present when several message blocks are to be transmitted across the same communication link. Thus, our model includes queues for routers and direct point-to-point links. All waiting times are added to the transmission and processing times in the following manner:

- $T_{n_i,n_{k_1}}$: average transmission time of a block between n_i and the first router n_{k_1}.
- $P_{n_{k_1}}$: average processing time of the block at the first router n_{k_1}.
- $T_{n_{k_1},n_{k_2}}$: average transmission time of the block between the routers n_{k_1} and the second n_{k_2}.
- $P_{n_{k_2}}$: average processing time of the block at the second router n_{k_2}.

$\vdots$

- $P_{n_{k_l}}$: average processing time of the block at the last router n_{k_l}.
- $T_{n_{k_l},n_j}$: average processing time of the block between the last router n_{k_l} and n_j.

Definition 3.2.3 (Transmission time, communication link).
For the average transmission time of a communication link, we distinguish between two alternatives:

1. *For the nodes n_i and n_j, there exists a direct point-to-point connection, i.e., $directlink(n_i, n_j)$. Then:*

$$time\_link_t(n_i, n_j) = T_{n_i,n_j}$$

2. *The nodes n_i and n_j, are connected via an indirect communication link. Both nodes communicate via a sequence of l routers $n_{k_1} \ldots n_{k_l}$. We have: $directlink(n_i, n_{k_1}) \wedge directlink(n_{k_l}, n_j) \wedge \forall \xi \in \{2, \ldots, l\},\ l \geq 2:$ $directlink(n_{k_{\xi-1}}, n_{k_\xi})$.*
For the average transmission time of the communication link, we have:

$$time\_link_t(n_i, n_j) = T_{n_i,n_{k_1}} + P_{n_{k_1}} + \\ + \sum_{\xi=2}^{l} \left(T_{n_{k_{\xi-1}},n_{k_\xi}} + P_{n_{k_\xi}} \right) + T_{n_{k_l},n_j}$$

For $l = 1$ we have $time\_link_t(n_i, n_j) = T_{n_i,n_{k_1}} + P_{n_{k_1}} + T_{n_{k_1},n_j}$

Reliability. The reliability of communication links is the combination of the reliability values of all direct point-to-point connections and the involved routers. All values are multiplied to determine the reliability value of the complete communication link.

This approach is realistic because a block can only be transmitted correctly via a communication link if all communication components of the connection, process and transfer the block correctly. We assume that all reliability values are independent.

Definition 3.2.4 (Reliability, communication link).
The reliability of a communication link is defined as

$$rel\_link_t(n_i, n_j) = \begin{cases} rel\_direct\_link_t(n_i, n_j) \times rel\_node_t(n_j), \\ \text{if } directlink(n_i, n_j) \\ \\ rel\_direct\_link_t(n_i, n_k) \times rel\_node_t(n_k) \times \\ \quad \times rel\_link_t(n_k, n_j), \\ \text{if } directlink(n_i, n_k) \wedge link(n_k, n_j) \end{cases}$$

$rel\_node_t(n_k)$ specifies the reliability of the router n_k, whereas the value $rel\_direct\_link_t(n_i, n_k)$ is the reliability for the direct point-to-point link between n_i and n_k. Both values are time dependent; thus, the definition includes the parameter t to specify the time at which the reliability value has been determined.

3.3 Strategies for the Distribution of Information Units

The following section will discuss information distribution within teams. We will investigate the case of one participant defining an information unit associated with a group process and sending it as a message to all nodes of the group process.

In the nonreplicated group process model (regardless of centralized or distributed architecture, see Sect. 3.1.1) the message is simply sent to the local node of the group process.

The following will deal with the distribution according to the distributed, replicated group process model (see Sect. 3.1.1), which requires a far more detailed approach; see also Rapaport (1991).

3.3.1 Direct point-to-point connection

We assume that the group process is distributed and replicated across the nodes n_1, n_2, n_3 and n_4 (see Fig. 3.10). The node n_1 is the first to receive the message.

All nodes managing a replica of the group process are connected and a copy of the current message is sent to each of them.

This strategy is only advisable for a small number of group process replicas. Increasing the number of replicas results in a large number of required point-to-point connections.

3.3.2 Cluster hierarchy

A cluster consists of a set of components and a router which controls the information flow between the components as well as to the parent cluster.

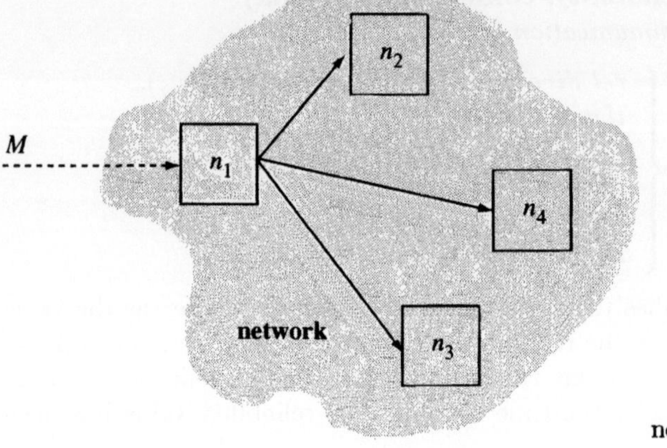

node n_1, ..., n_4

Fig. 3.10. Group process for direct point-to-point connection

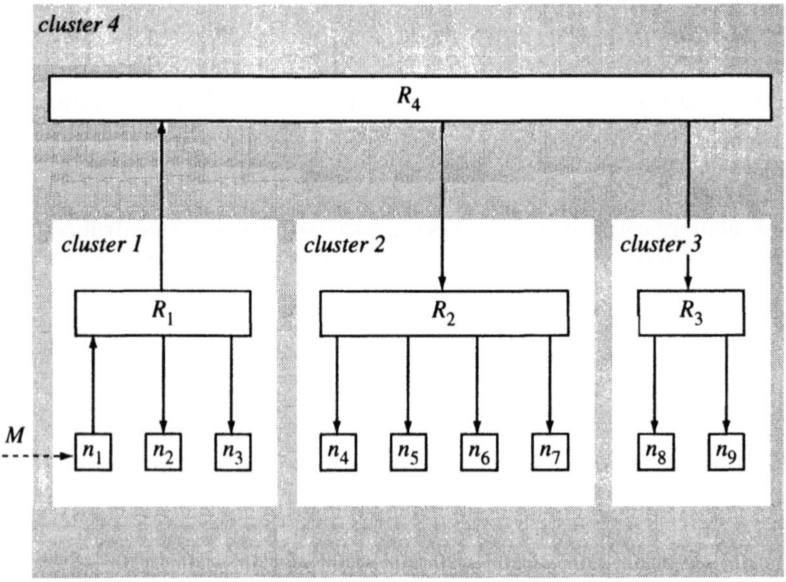

router R_1, ..., R_4
node n_1, ..., n_9

Fig. 3.11. Group process for cluster hierarchies

Components may be either subclusters or nodes. Figure 3.11 illustrates the information flow within a cluster hierarchy.

For the example in Fig. 3.11 we assume that the group process is distributed across the nodes n_i, $i \in \{1, \ldots, 9\}$ and the routers R_j, $j \in \{1, \ldots, 3\}$. Messages are distributed within the cluster via routers, for example using point-to-point connections. Let the node n_1 be the first node to receive message M. First, the message is sent to the local cluster router R_1 via node n_1 for distribution within cluster 1. In addition, the message is forwarded to the router R_4 in order to enable propagation to the clusters 2 and 3. Because the router R_4 of cluster 4 is not part of the group process it acts only as a message distributor.

Code fragment (Message distribution).

```
void router::distribution (message M)
                    /* Code fragment for router R of cluster C; this
                       refers to router R                         */
   nlist = { all nodes in C } \ { this, entry node };
                    /* For cluster 1 nlist consists of {n2, n3}; this is R1
                       and n1 is entry node; entry node and this can be
                       identical                                  */
   for all n ∈ nlist do send(message M) to n;
   if ((this has parent cluster) and
                (M has not been received by parent cluster))
   then send(message M) to parent-node of this;
                    /* Parent node is the router of the parent cluster */
```

Within a cluster broadcast flooding might be used to distribute messages to all nodes of the group process (see Sect. 3.3.3.) This approach is especially interesting if nodes of the cluster are connected via a broadcast medium, such as the Ethernet.

The strict hierarchical message propagation and distribution within clusters avoids duplication. The message is either sent directly from the parent node to the child node or vice versa. There is no direct communication between routers of clusters having no parent-child relationship with each other, i.e., there is no direct communication between R_1 and R_2.

3.3.3 Broadcast flooding

In broadcast flooding each node propagates the message to all its neighboring nodes (Fig. 3.12). Each individual node n decides whether a message is used locally (i.e., node n checks if the message is for a local group process) or just buffered for the transmission to the neighboring node.

The message propagation may be initiated in two ways. Either the message is immediately forwarded to all neighboring nodes or else a node polls its neighbors at frequent intervals to discover if any messages have arrived for it.

Redundant communication paths might provide a certain degree of fault tolerance since despite node or link failures messages can be propagated to all nodes of the group process. For example, a message can reach node n_4 regardless of the failures of node n_3 or one of the two links L_{13} or L_{34}. If the failure of only one node or one link results in a breakdown of a communication

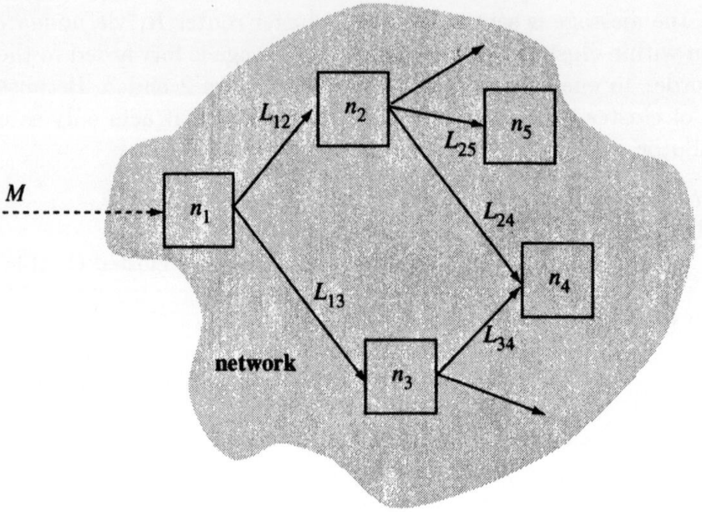

node n_1, ..., n_5
link L_{12}, ..., L_{34}

Fig. 3.12. Group process in broadcast flooding

link between nodes n_i and n_j, then n_i and n_j are called weakly connected, i.e., the connection between n_i and n_j contains one or several single points of failure. An example of a weak connection is the pair (n_1, n_5), since the failure of either n_2 or L_{25} is sufficient to disconnect n_1 and n_5. If there is no single point of failure between a pair of nodes, then we call them strongly connected, for example the nodes n_1 and n_4.

Example (Usenet). In the Usenet, single points of failure are scarce, since there are many redundant connections.

Duplicate detection. The main problems of broadcast flooding are the network overflow and duplicate detection. The former is solved by each node storing information on the messages already received and forwarded. If a message is received for the second time, it is not propagated to the neighboring nodes.

Duplicates are detected as follows:

1. either the receiver has a list of all received messages with unique message identifiers (like a combination of node address, timestamp and internal counter), or
2. the sender concatenates the message with a list of those nodes that have already received the message. This second approach reduces the number of duplicates without totally eliminating them, which means that the receiver has to handle the remaining message duplicates, for example as shown in the first alternative.

Code fragment (Duplicate detection).

nlist = set of neighboring nodes to n;

/* Node n has received message M and respective list ML from its neighbor n_L; ML is the list of all nodes that have already seen this instance of M; $n_L \in ML$ */

$ML' = ML + \{n\}$;
for all $n_j \in$ nlist **do**
  if $(n_j \in ML)$ **then continue**;
  else send(message M, list ML') **to** n_j;

3.3.4 Routing

Routing is a variant of direct point-to-point connections. A message is sent along a path between two nodes with routers as part of the path (for example when a message is sent from n_i to n_j, as seen in Fig. 3.9).

The path can be determined either automatically or manually by the user. In the first case, all nodes have a routing table to determine a path. The problem of updating the table can be solved by periodically exchanging routing information between nodes within the network. In the context of computer networks, a number of methods for automatic routing have been developed (see Tanenbaum 1996). In the case of the manual approach the user has to determine the path towards the destination node.

For scalability transparency node names are not globally unique. Local uniqueness will suffice. Only direct neighbors have unique names. This facilitates the integration of nodes into the network without having to coordinate with all existing nodes. It suffices to notify the new neighbors.

3.4 Structures of Asynchronous Group Interaction

During the existence of an asynchronous group process, team members repeatedly exchange information, such as newly created or modified group documents. We can distinguish three general models for the management of information distributed within the group:

1. the linear model;
2. the comb model;
3. the branch model.

3.4.1 Linear model (Emisari)

As Fig. 3.13 shows, communication is strictly sequential in the linear model. There is always an information unit M_1 preceding the next information unit

M_2. New information is simply appended to the already existing information. M_i can be either an answer to M_j, $j \in \{1, \ldots, i-1\}$ or the initiation of a new topic. All information units are structured according to their time of entry. A filtering mechanism can extract the information according to the topic.

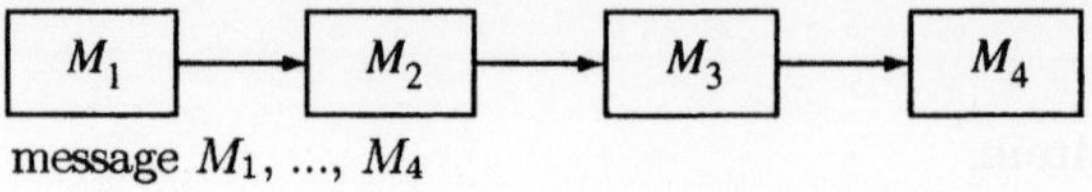

Fig. 3.13. Linear model (Emisari)

New team members can easily inform themselves on the historical process and sequence of interaction. The linear model contains both the results of the groupwork and the process through which these results were developed.

3.4.2 Comb model (Confer, Usenet)

As is shown in Fig. 3.14, the comb model structures the information of the group process into a set of subtopics (e.g., T_1, T_2, T_3). Each subtopic implies the goal and the expected information, and within subtopics, the information exchange proceeds linearly.

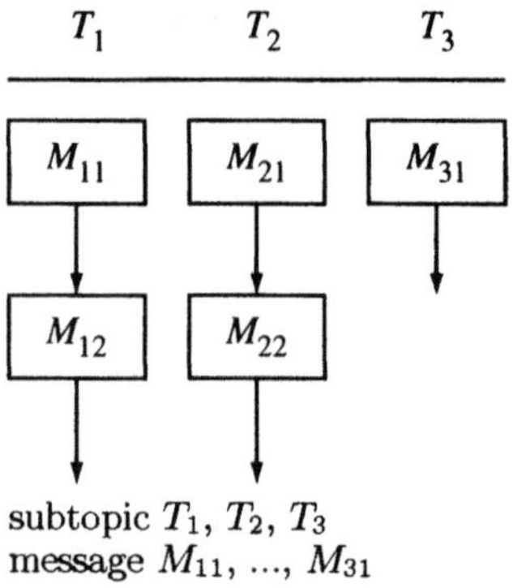

Fig. 3.14. Comb model (Confer, Usenet)

With respect to its subtopics, the entire group process has a comb structure. A comb tooth represents the progress of the discussion with respect to an individual subtopic. The comb model does not support shared information between several subtopics. Thus, hypertext navigation between subtopics is not possible. However, information units of several subtopics may be linked using textual references. These references are not clickable links in the hypertext sense. If an information unit is explicitly desired to be part of several subtopics, then it must be copied respectively. The major advantages of this model are the excellent structuring of the group process information, the easy navigation and the simple information access by new team members.

Although all team members can initiate new subtopics, the actual setup of the necessary infrastructure is restricted to a few privileged members in order to control the information flood. In general, a new comb tooth is only established after a positive vote of most of team members.

Example (Usenet). Usenet is a well-known system which follows the comb model paradigm. It allows a multilevel, hierarchical structuring of topics. Let *WS* be a group process representing a discussion on workstations:
WS.SUN information on SUN workstations;
WS.HP information on HP workstations;
WS.IBM information on IBM workstations.
WS.SUN may furthermore be subdivided into:
WS.SUN.General general information on SUN workstations;
WS.SUN.OS information on the SUN operating system;
WS.SUN.SUNview information on the SUN window system.

3.4.3 Branch model (Parti)

The branch model is based on one main topic from which several subtopics may be derived.

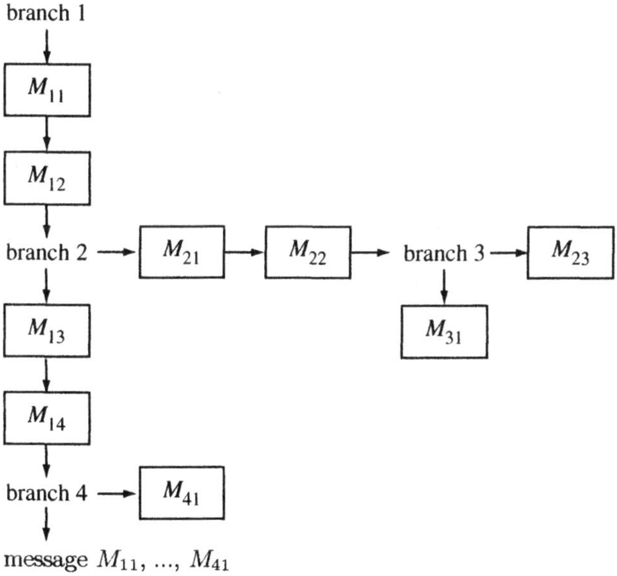

Fig. 3.15. Branch model (Parti)

Branch 1 in Fig. 3.15 is the root for communication within the group process. Each initiation of a new subtopic generates a new branch and can take place at any time. New branches are recorded and integrated into the originating branch. As opposed to the comb model, the branch model is far more flexible, since normally all participants can start new branches. The structure of the information space resulting from this model can be compared to that of a hypertext information space (see Sect. 6.3).

As with the comb model, the sequence within a branch is always linear; the branches equal the subtopics of the comb model. Since finding subtopics is no longer quite as easy as in the comb model, a special query language should be provided for navigational support.

The system Parti developed at Stockholm university (Rapaport 1991) provides a special function for reorganization of branches. For example, branches can be removed at one place and inserted at another. Branches can be concatenated and it is also possible to disconnect a branch A, which creates a new group process with the root A.

3.5 Management of Shared Context

When designing CSCW applications, it is important to provide a multiuser interface which presents the shared objects and the progress of the joint work. The system should represent the shared context of group sessions. For face-to-face meetings, whiteboards have traditionally served as tools for providing this shared context. They are used to focus the meeting as well as to record the meeting progress.

Traditional tools have the following disadvantages:

- The space on the whiteboard is limited.
- It is difficult to restructure information on a whiteboard. Often, information must be deleted and rewritten elsewhere.
- Handwriting can be illegible.
- Meeting room and whiteboard are often shared by several groups at different times. This may often result in the following question at the beginning of the meeting: "Can we wipe the whiteboard?".
- If several meetings are necessary at different times during groupwork, the intermediate results must be saved on other media.

Groupware systems are gradually replacing traditional whiteboards. They represent the shared context of a team meeting. Ellis et al. (1991) define the shared context of group sessions as a set of objects, which are jointly viewed and manipulated by the participants. The set of objects defines the shared workspace. The representation of a shared context refers to the joint processing of information and includes the following aspects:

- Effective cooperation requires a shared view of the jointly manipulated objects.

- Each individual user should be aware of his fellow workers efforts (i.e., he should know who is currently participating in the group process and what their contribution is).

It is essential that a collaboration-aware user interface represents both the shared objects and the team dynamics. In the example of meeting environments, computers and projection screens replace whiteboard and blackboard. Each participant has his own desktop computer and shared information is displayed on all screens.

The design of shared context is very important for synchronous cooperation. In CSCW applications, "synchronous" means that the users cooperate simultaneously and are aware of this. Activities on shared data are immediately propagated to all participating users to achieve real-time behavior (all other users can view the effects within predefined time limits). Time limits are determined by communication technology (transmission times) and group protocol restrictions (the time it takes to converge replicated data to a consistent state).

Synchronous (real-time) groupware is characterized by the following requirements:

- *Short response times:* Modifications should immediately be visible to the person who initiated the modification.
- *Short notification times:* Modifications should be propagated as quickly as possible to all other group session participants. For synchronous groupware, the requirement is often that the notification time should be close to the response time, (i.e., due to high interaction and interest, all participants should be able to view the operation results at the same time as the initiating person). For distributed group processes, this requirement is constrained by the communication media which is used.
- *Flexibility of group sessions:* It should be possible for participants to come and go at any time during an ongoing group session.
- *Access conflicts:* Participants often manipulate a shared group document. In order to maintain document consistency, schemes for concurrency control are necessary (see Chapters 4–5).
- *Group interaction often does not follow a predefined plan:* This means that a priori specification as to which information will be accessed is often impossible.
- *The group process is often distributed:* It cannot be assumed that all participants work on the same machine or within the same local network.
- *External communication channels:* Participants are often linked by an additional external channel (apart from the computer connection), for example via audio or video connections. These channels can be useful for synchronizing activities of team members and thereby preventing access conflicts.

3.5.1 The concept WYSIWIS

The first approach in the direction of a shared context is the so-called "WYSIWIS" concept, which aims at a consistent presentation of shared information to all participants. WYSIWIS is the acronym for *what you see is what I see* (Stefik et al. 1987a) and often it is used with synchronous groupware.

Example (WYSIWIS). Each participant opens a window on his screen and the same section of a file is shown to them all. All participants have the impression that they are reading and manipulating the same information. It is possible to highlight the information units that other participants are working upon and to track the progress of their activities.

WYSIWIS in its most strict form, means that all participants have exactly the same context. Only public windows are used and the whole information is presented to all participants using the same view. Thus, the screens of all session participants display the identical information. Team members are thus able to specify certain objects by referring to their position via an audio channel.

Modifications of screen information require certain conventions, since without such conventions the following problems may arise:

- *Scroll-War:* One participant wants to read displayed information. At the same time, another participant starts scrolling and thereby altering the information currently displayed. Between the two participants, a Scroll-War breaks out.
- *Window-War:* One participant wants to read information currently displayed. At the same time, another participant pops up a new window which covers part or all of the previous screen information. Between the two participants, a Window-War breaks out.

Announcements concerning screen changes via another communication channel, such as audio, is indispensable but at the same time tedious. For many cooperative situations relaxed forms of WYSIWIS may be more appropriate because they allow for more individual work by the participants.

3.5.2 Relaxed forms of WYSIWIS

Strict WYSIWIS can be modified as follows:

1. Structuring of the workspace into private and public areas.
2. Personalized screen layout and views.
3. Time divergence with respect to the states of shared objects.

Separation of workspaces. Some of the problems of strict WYSIWIS may be avoided by dividing the workspace into private and public areas. In general, each workspace area is represented by a separate window on the screen.

Public workspaces meet the requirement of a shared context; the information is available to all team members for viewing and manipulation. The public workspace, which in the strict form of WYSIWIS fills the entire screen space, is limited to one or several windows. These windows can be called group windows, since the team as a whole uses them.

Each participant can have his own private workspace which is represented by private windows on the screen. These private windows provide an environment similar to the one common in single-user applications; these windows are invisible to other participants. An example for the separation between private and public workspaces is the calendar system RTCAL (Greif and Sarin 1987). The public windows display information on the state of appointed scheduling and are visible and available to all participants, while the private windows present information accessible only to the individual user, like details on scheduled meetings.

Private windows can also be used in face-to-face meetings in order to prepare ideas and contributions. However, a seamless transition from private to public workspace must be guaranteed at all times, which means that it must be possible to copy information between public and private windows (e.g., using the drag-and-drop approach). Experiences of Stefik et al. (1987b) with the Colab-System (developed at Xerox PARC) show that private windows tend to draw the attention of other participants, even to frustrate participants, since they cannot see private information. For example, if one person works privately, other participants might ask the following question using the audio channel: "Would you mind copying your private information to a public window?" or "What are you typing".

Cursor display. Strict WYSIWIS includes the display of both the shared objects and the cursors of all participants. If we assume that a team has ten members, it is easy to see that the display of all cursors in a group window would cause nothing but confusion. All cursors displayed should therefore be marked (for example by an identifier) or personalized using different colors.

A relaxed form of WYSIWIS would display only the private cursor of the respective user. Cursors of other participants would only become visible on explicit demand. Users can determine whether or not they wish to export their cursor position and whether or not they wish to import other participants' cursors.

Example (Selective cursor display). Assuming that person B wants to point out one particular section of the displayed information to all other participants. He would invoke the function *Propagate_Cursor()*.

The command *Show_Cursor(B)* enables other participants to display the propagated cursor on their local screen.

Management of screen layout. Window-Wars can be avoided through personalized screen layout. Each participant can determine where he wishes to position his windows on his screen. Because of the individual screen layout propagated cursors of other participants must be window-related, rather than screen-related. Additional communication using the audio channel such as "look at the upper right" can, however, be confusing.

Management of displayed information. Another looser form of WYSIWIS is the support of different views. A view is the full or partial visual representation of the shared context.

The following are examples of different views of the shared context:

- Identical information is presented in different ways. For instance, a set of values can be represented as a diagram in one view and as a table in another view.
- The users display different parts of the shared context.
  Regardless of the selected representation, participants can view and manipulate parts independently of each other. Each user can scroll at his own convenience throughout the shared context.
  However, screen-related annotations referring to context content are not possible. For example, if participant B (on his display with his cursor) points to a part of the shared context, then another participant (by invoking the command *Show_Cursor(B)*) might see B's cursor pointing to a totally different part. Thus, propagated cursors are position dependent; they must refer to a logical position within the shared context.

Time divergence. Time divergence during synchronization of shared objects' current state is another relaxed form of WYSIWIS. The shared context is synchronized after a certain time delay. Participants may see different versions of the objects on their display. For example, Dourish (1998) employs a model of multiple simultaneous streams of activity over shared data instead of creating a single thread of control. The system Prospero handles the divergence between these streams and provides mechanisms to construct consistent information out of diverging streams.

In general, time divergence may be either initiated explicitly by a user or implicitly by the system. In the former case, object alterations are first only locally visible. The user must propagate his modification explicitly (e.g., by invoking a command), thus making his changes visible to all other participants. In the latter case, the system delays for longer time periods the propagation of modification operations to other participants. The notification times increase.

Coupling of user interfaces. The discussion of the WYSIWIS concept illustrates the different coupling levels that exist when team members view and manipulate the shared context. Strict WYSIWIS supports a tight coupling of user interfaces on the presentation level. Each participant views the same object, using identical views. On the next coupling level, the object level, team members view the same objects, but different representations or different parts of them. If team members access a shared workspace but manipulate different objects, we speak of loosely coupled user interfaces.

3.5.3 Telepointing

Although relaxed forms of WYSIWIS facilitate private, undisturbed work, they reduce group awareness. In order to improve the communication between team members many groupware systems support telepointers which are used exclusively for pointing to shared information in public windows. As soon as a telepointer is moved on one display, it will do so on all other displays, as well. A telepointer is a special cursor which is not used as a private cursor for editing information in private or public windows. In general, only one person at a time may use the telepointer, and thus it must be managed like a mutually exclusive resource. The screen representation of a telepointer differs from that of private cursors. Some systems display the telepointer in addition to the private cursor of the user. Note that the telepointer is characterized by the logical position of the information in the shared context rather than by its physical position on the screen display (i.e., if a participant points the telepointer to a specific word, then the other participants should see it at the same word, no matter where that word happens to be positioned on their screen).

3.5.4 Group awareness

The emphasis of recent research within CSCW has been to provide awareness-oriented groupware systems where users coordinate their work based on the knowledge of what other team members are doing or have done (Schlichter et al. 1998). Dourish and Bly (1992) define group awareness as follows: "as an understanding of the activities of others which provides a context for your own activity." The advantages of an improved group awareness are:

1. It encourages spontaneous, informal communication, for instance video conferences or phone calls, since team members are better informed about the current activities and workload of their partners. For example, if one partner is not too busy, then other team members are more likely to contact him because they assume that he will not mind being interrupted in his work.
2. Improved awareness also keeps team members better informed about the current state of team activities. This contributes to their ability to make conscious decisions.

Particularly unstructured business processes whose activities cannot be described in advance (see Sect. 7.1.4) require a high degree of awareness information.

Example (PlaceWare). As Fig. 3.16 shows, PlaceWare[1] provides group awareness while a user browses in the world wide web. It supports collaborative queries incorporating contributions of different experts; see also Grasso et al. (1998).

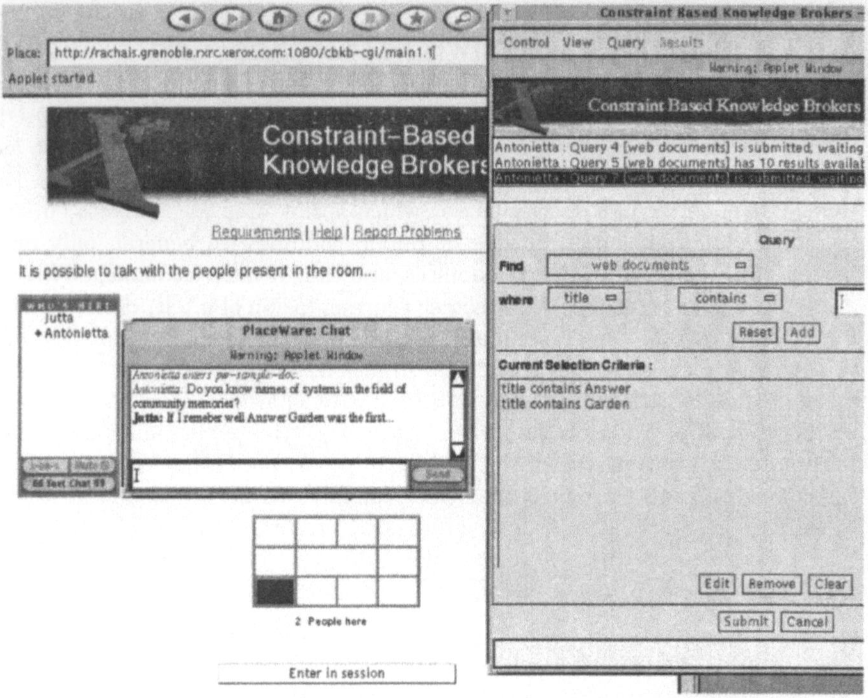

The window *Who's here* displays names of available experts to the user (here Antonietta) who can start a dialogue with them via the window PlaceWare Chat. The result of the dialogue (here between Antonietta and Jutta) can directly influence the query specification, as illustrated by "Answer Garden".

Fig. 3.16. Group awareness through PlaceWare

Greenberg et al. (1996) distinguish between various types of group awareness:

– *Informal awareness:* This refers to general knowledge about team members, such as who is currently in a room with you or how far is the distance between team members and myself.

[1] http://www.placeware.com
For alternative platforms, the reader is referred to MetaWeb (Trevor et al. 1997) by the GMD and Habanero by the NCSA (http://www.ncsa.uiuc.edu/SDG/Software/Habanero/).

- *Group-structural awareness:* Apart from information on group membership, this category also includes knowledge about roles and responsibilities of fellow team members, especially their role and position within the group process.
- *Social awareness:* This kind of information specifies knowledge about the social group context (How interested is a team member in the group process? What is his emotional state? What are his special abilities? etc.).
- *Workspace awareness:* This refers to up-to-date knowledge about access and modifications of group documents in the shared workspace by other team members. It provides information about another team member's interaction with a shared workspace.

Group awareness supports the orientation within the group process and, thus, it facilitates the structuring and planning of team activities. Usually, events triggered by activities are used to develop group awareness information. Fuchs et al. (1995) distinguish between two orthogonal criteria for categorizing events in order to identify group awareness modes. Synchronous group awareness concerns current events, while asynchronous group awareness refers to what happened in the past. The second criterion refers to the focus of the group members within the shared context. In the case of tight coupling, team members have a shared focus (they work on the same artifact). As opposed to this, team members have no shared focus in the case of loose coupling. Working on different artifacts does not, however, exclude their interest in what is happening or has happened at other places within the shared workspace. Table 3.2 shows the four group awareness modes derived from these orthogonal criteria.

Table 3.2. Group awareness modes (adapted from Fuchs et al. 1995)

	synchronous	asynchronous
tightly coupled	what is currently happening in the actual scope of the work?	what changes have occurred in the actual scope of the work since the last access?
loosely coupled	what is currently happening anywhere else in the shared workspace?	which important events have taken place in the workspace since the last access?

Groupware systems must handle the various modes differently. Group awareness information must be presented less persistently in the case of loose coupling than in tight coupling, since closely cooperating persons usually have greater interest in events concerning their own individual work. In the latter case, popup menus may well be an adequate means for presenting awareness information, while unobtrusive coloring of icons or output of status information in the command line might suffice in the former case.

3.6 Groupware Architectures

The requirement of support for synchronous and asynchronous group cooperation, and the joint manipulation of sometimes distributed objects, implies applications that supply the group with suitable multiuser interfaces and ample forms of cooperation.

The central design issue is the question of whether or not a brandnew collaboration-aware system with explicit group support has to be developed or whether the extension of existing single-user applications would suffice. Collaboration-aware systems are distributed applications whose components are distributed across several nodes. These components exchange messages in order to achieve a consistent state of all shared objects on all nodes. As opposed to this, there are groupware systems aimed at a shared use of existing single-user applications. This means that the application itself is not collaboration-aware. All input/output of participants must be filtered and sequentialized in order to interact with the single-user application. The advantage of this approach is that readily available single-user applications can be included in groupware environments, which reduces the time required for system design and implementation as well as the time required by team members to get familiar with the application. There is, however, a disadvantage; supported teamwork tends to become less flexible. For example, there is almost no concurrency control integrated into single-user applications.

Another aspect of groupware architecture is the question of the group process being distributed and/or replicated. Some of the following groupware architectures are particularly suitable for the integration of traditional systems. In the following we distinguish between centralized and replicated architectures.

3.6.1 Centralized architectures

Centralized architectures have only one application instance on a selected node. All entries of geographically dispersed users must be forwarded to this application. Prior to this, they must be serialized and filtered. Output is propagated to all participants of a group session and displayed on their respective screens. Centralized architectures are particularly suitable to the integration of single-user applications. There is no need for modification because concurrent input of several users is serialized by a special component.

Window Sharing. Figure 3.17 shows a simple centralized architecture using a network window system (for instance X-Windows).

There is a distinction between the application (client of the window system) and the user interface (server of the window system). In addition to handling input/output, the user interface includes management of screen information. There is only one instance of the application, which is located on a selected node.

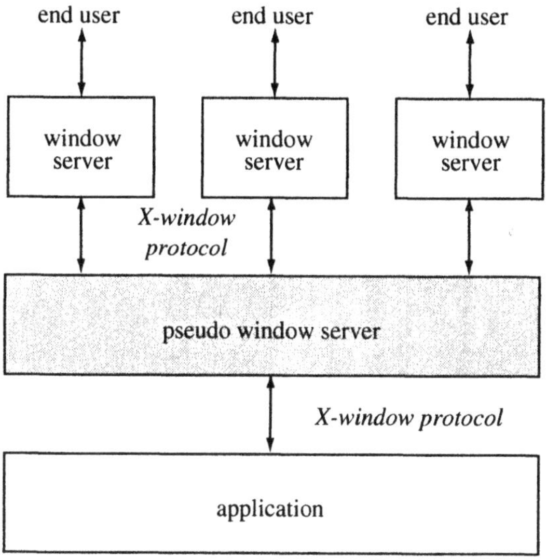

Fig. 3.17. Example for the use of a network window system

The pseudo window server serializes the concurrent input of the users, i.e., the association of input to the window server which has generated the input event. Also, it propagates all output to the window servers of individual users. Thus, simultaneous output of information on several screens is possible.

Existing applications are easily integrated, since no single-user applications have to be modified. Parallel, competing input by several users must, however, be coordinated via other communication media (such as an audio channel), since otherwise Scroll-Wars or Window-Wars might result.

Conferencing component. For this architecture the application is subdivided into the two components of presentation and execution (Fig. 3.18). The integration of a conferencing component extends the application to support synchronous group sessions.

As opposed to the shared window approach, the protocol between components is application specific (i.e., it contains semantic information important for the application). The respective presentation components are replicated per user. The presentation component is responsible for input/output of the shared application. The conferencing component is not replicated and coordinates concurrent input/output. Unlike replicated architectures, no consistency problems arise, since there is only one application instance manipulating shared group artifacts. The only problem with this architecture is the bottleneck of the conferencing component.

Information sharing. One form of centralized architecture often used in shared information spaces is that of centralized, integrated information management (see Sect. 1.3.1). Although each team member has his own application instance, the exchange of operations and group documents is not via

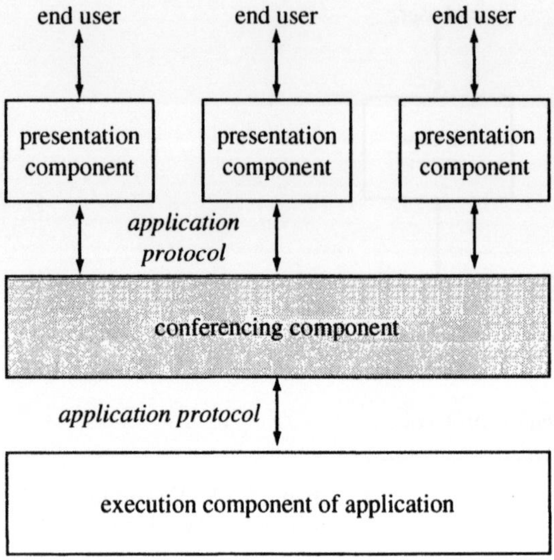

Fig. 3.18. Example of the embedding of a conferencing component

application instances. Rather, it is conducted indirectly, via the shared information space. This architecture is only suitable for asynchronous cooperation because indirect communication does not generally occur in real-time. Typical examples are the world wide web and Lotus Notes.

3.6.2 Replicated architectures

Replicated architectures assume that a replica of the application exists on all user nodes. Input by users must be distributed to all application replicas, where they are locally serialized and then processed by the local application copy. Output is only locally propagated and thus does not cause any network load.

Conference manager. Figure 3.19 shows a replicated architecture which includes a conferencing manager and the use of conferencing interfaces. Since the application is replicated per user, parallel work of participants is possible. However, this requires flexible synchronization mechanisms.

The conferencing interface handles the input/output of the shared application, which makes it similar to the presentation component of the aforementioned approach. The individual conferencing interface accepts the input of the respective user and forwards it to both the other conferencing interfaces and the local replica of the shared application. The local replica executes relevant functions and forwards possible output to the local conferencing interface for subsequent forwarding to the individual user. There is no forwarding of output to other conferencing interfaces.

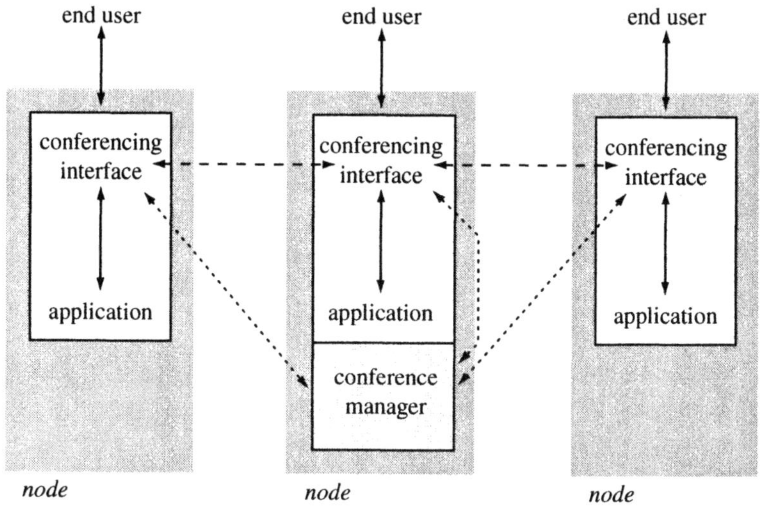

Fig. 3.19. Example for the embedding of a conference manager

In order to achieve identical output data on all nodes, the application replicas must be deterministic. They must not be environmentally dependent. For example, the load of a node should not influence the application behavior.

The conference manager is not replicated and runs on a selected node. It serves as the coordinator of the group session performing tasks such as session management, floor control, concurrency control and other synchronization functions. For example, the conferencing manager coordinates and structures the read and write access to shared information of synchronous applications. For more details the reader is referred to the Sect. 4.6 in this book.

Collaboration-aware conferencing systems. Collaboration-aware conferencing systems have been specifically designed and implemented. They do not integrate already existing single-user applications. Screen management, as well as synchronization and concurrency control are integral parts of the application (Fig. 3.20).

Characteristics of replicated architectures. Replication of applications improves response times, since the operation is locally executed while at the same time the operation specifications are propagated via the network. Output is only local, which reduces the network load.

The following problems may arise with replicated architectures:

- *Different initial states of the application replicas:* At the beginning of a group session, individual application replicas often start out from different initial states. Required files are only available on one node and must be copied to the other participating nodes. Conflicts may arise, for example if an application replica is ready to process user input while other replicas are

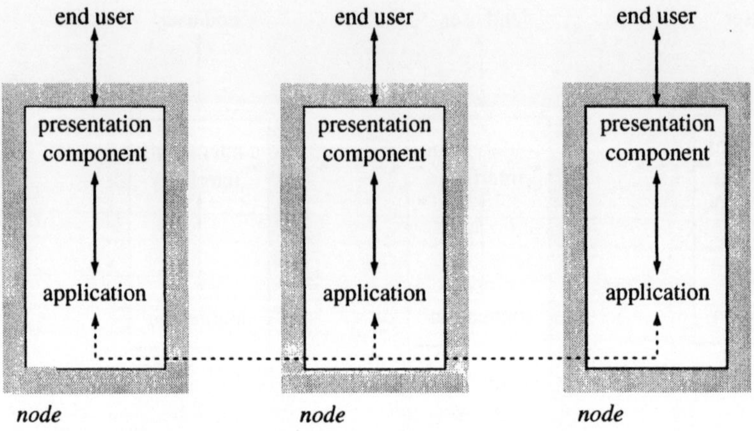

Fig. 3.20. Example for collaboration-aware conferencing systems

still in their initialization phase. This problem can be solved by delaying the processing until all application replicas are ready.

- *Deterministic behavior:* Provided that the initial state and input sequence have been identical, the application replicas should generate the same output sequence and terminate at the same final state. Neither environment nor temporal parameters should influence the application behavior.
- *Identical state:* It may sometimes be difficult to keep all application replicas identical. A number of applications allow the user to customize and adapt the local application instance according to his individual taste. For example, the user may refine his own menus and define key combinations for commands, which creates different application versions.
- *Ordering of input events:* Consistency often requires all replicas of an application to obtain equivalent input in the identical sequence. This can be achieved through the use of input sequence numbers and floor passing by the conference manager.
- *Session membership:* Often, group sessions have no static behavior with respect to group membership. During a group session, members may leave while new participants may join. In the latter case, it is necessary to initiate a new application replica for the latecomer. Past events may have to be replayed or the current state of an already existing application replica must be forwarded to the new participant.

3.7 Further Reading

The interested reader is referred to the books by Rapaport (1991) and Pankoke-Babatz (1989), in addition to the surveys by Baecker (1993) and Marca and Bock (1992), where you will find relevant articles on the concepts mentioned in this chapter. The book by Conen and Neumann (1998) discusses various coordination aspects for collaborative applications.

4. Concurrency Control

Concurrent access to shared information is a central problem of computer-supported cooperative work. The following chapter will introduce schemes and protocols for concurrency control of existing groupware which maintain consistent information despite simultaneous access by several geographically dispersed persons.

Besides optimistic concurrency control, we will investigate pessimistic approaches with both centralized and decentralized control. The discussion of decentralized control will focus on floor-passing, as well as transactions and operation transformations, the latter of which will be exemplified by the group editor Grove.

4.1 Introduction

The concurrent manipulation of shared information is an integral part of all group processes. Thus, groupware needs some sort of concurrency control in order to keep the information consistent. In the context of database systems consistency has already been explored extensively (for example permitting only one write access at a time or supporting atomicity, i.e., either all of the operations of a transaction are executed or none of them). For groupware, however, the term consistency must be redefined.

CSCW applications with few consistency constraints might allow concurrent modifications of the same group document by several users. Rather than only one modification being successful, all modifications should be reflected in the group document. In order to make conscious decisions for one's activities the groupware system must provide information about the activities of other group members (e.g., by sending notifications to all group members if the group document is modified). Other possible approaches are the creation of different document versions, as used in the system Xanadu (Nelson 1981) or revision protocols as provided by Lotus Notes (see Sect. 2.9.8).

Groupware with high consistency requirements for shared information synchronize concurrent write operations by applying special concurrency control protocols. The following subsections will introduce the reader to approaches with different levels of consistency support.

4.1.1 Motivation

In order to achieve short response times in a distributed environment it is often necessary to replicate the shared documents of a group process (i.e., participants of a group process have a local copy of the shared data). Response times decrease, since data are found "closeby". This is particularly beneficial in cases of read accesses. However, replication has some negative effects on write operations. In general, response times increase because there is additional work required to execute multicopy update operations.

Furthermore failure situations may occur which may be especially difficult to handle for distributed group processes. We distinguish between the following two basic failure types:

1. Individual computers may crash, which means that all group processes running on these computers are terminated. The local group documents are no longer available, neither for reading nor for writing.
2. Communication links may break down due to noisy links or temporary failure of communication components.

Definition 4.1.1 (Partitioning). *A computer network is called partitioned if there are two or more disjunct sets of sites (e.g. computers) with the following characteristics: Sites of different sets cannot communicate with each* *other. Each of the disjunct sets is called a partition. Partitioning is caused by interrupted communication links or failed communication components.*

Partitionings caused by interrupted communication links are difficult to handle, since sites of one partition usually cannot determine whether the sites of the other partition have crashed or whether the link to these sites has been disconnected. For distributed, replicated group process models with high consistency demands on shared data, it must be guaranteed that write operations are only allowed in one partition at a time. Thus, complex concurrency control protocols are necessary.

4.1.2 Classification of concurrency control approaches

Basically, there are two types of approaches for concurrency control: the optimistic one and the pessimistic one.

1. With optimistic concurrency control, there is no guarantee that the shared data are consistent at all times. Rather, it allows access to inconsistent data,[1] which may be useful for special applications (Davidson 1984).
2. For groupware with high consistency requirements, the usage of optimistic concurrency control is not appropriate. Instead, pessimistic concurrency control should be applied using either centralized or decentralized control. For decentralized control, we further distinguish between schemes with and without voting.

Figure 4.1 gives an overview of the aforementioned concurrency control classification.

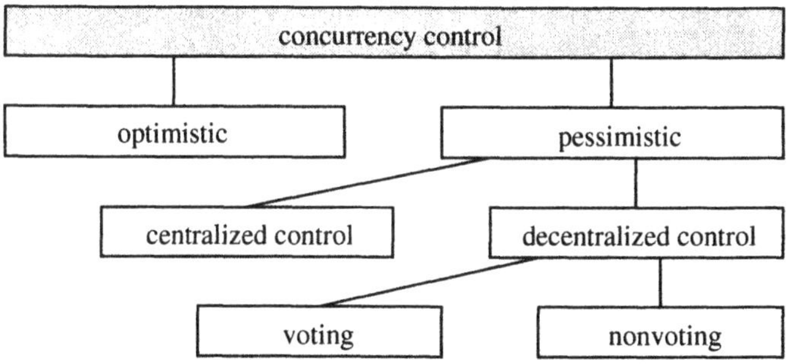

Fig. 4.1. Classification of concurrency control: Overview

[1] The term optimistic concurrency control (OCC) is also commonly used by the database community where it guarantees consistency in the context of transactions. So-called certifiers or optimistic schedulers first try to execute the transactions concurrently. As soon as nonserializable transactions occur, certain transactions are subsequently terminated.

Voting schemes solve the concurrency control problem through negotiations and voting among sites in order to obtain a coordinated decision. Among other things, they aim at a global agreement between the sites which is both "democratic" and achievable by using decentralized control. It is not necessary for all sites to participate in the voting process. The use of majorities instead of unanimous decisions of all sites facilitates the process of keeping the replicated group documents consistent (Nicol et al. 1988a, 1988b).

On the other hand, schemes without voting solve the concurrency problem without negotiations between sites. The control decision, e.g., permitting write access or providing a global order for modification operations, is made by a selected and authorized site.

The following sections will introduce concurrency control concepts of existing groupware. For our discussion we assume that group documents are structured according to the hypertext concept consisting of nodes and links. The content of the group documents is distributed among the various nodes of the hypertext network.

4.2 Optimistic Concurrency Control

Optimistic concurrency control does not constrain the activities of the user. He can manipulate the content of a node or create new nodes at any time. As soon as he leaves the manipulated or newly created node, it is stored in the group database. The optimistic scheme enables high efficiency, since multiple users may modify different nodes simultaneously. Distribution of text across several small nodes makes concurrent access of the same node less likely, but still, conflicts may arise in certain cases.

Example (Optimistic concurrency control in KMS). The Knowledge Management System (KMS) supports optimistic concurrency control (Akscyn et al. 1988). The KMS database is distributed across several machines and the physical storage is transparent for the user. The size of the manipulation unit is restricted to a screen page representing a node (a so-called KMS-frame) in the hypertext network. Users can only modify one node at a time. If a user tries to store a modified node, the system checks if in the meantime (i.e., between entering the node and the store operation) activities of other users have already modified that node. In the case of conflicting activities, the system warns the user and creates a new node saving his modifications. Subsequently, the user can merge his modifications with the current state of the original node, thus, creating a new version of the original node.

4.3 Centralized Control

Before describing pessimistic concurrency control with decentralized control in detail, we will discuss two classes of centralized control schemes: control unit and token-passing (see Fig. 4.2).

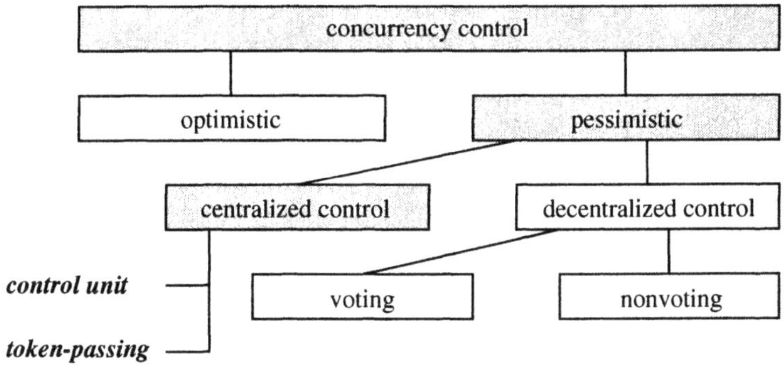

Fig. 4.2. Classification of concurrency control: Centralized control

4.3.1 Control unit

The control unit is a centralized system component serializing and synchronizing all (write) operations. Alsberg and Day (1976) describe an example of this kind of approach for pessimistic concurrency control, the so-called standby- or primary-site approach. Despite the replication of a file and the assignment of replicas to different sites, only a single selected site is "primarily responsible" for the file. File access is only possible in the partition where this primary-site is located. If the selected site breaks down, access to the file becomes either impossible or another primary-site is chosen. The selection process of the new primary-site is by no means trivial, since only one active primary-site is allowed at any given time. Thus, the selection process may only be triggered if the current primary-site fails; the unavailability of the current primary-site due to a network partitioning is not sufficient for the selection of a new primary-site. Besides, the old primary-site must not be reactivated after repair.

Concurrency control with a centralized control unit is easy to implement. However, the selection process for a new primary-site, when the previous one fails, is very important in order to increase the availability of replicated information. Liskov (1993) proposed the lazy-replication approach to further improve availability.

Example (Central locking server of MULE). The group editor Mule (Pendergast and Vogel 1990) stores its data in a completely replicated form (every site has a replica). Local read access is very fast. Write operations require the transfer of the modified data and a lock request to a central locking server. This server is responsible for lock assignment, the update of all replicas, the lock release and, above all, the synchronization of operations necessary to maintain consistency.

Example (Coordination unit in rIBIS). The real-time issued-based information system (rIBIS) is an extension of gIBIS (Rein and Ellis 1991) and it supports both loose and tight coupling of group members. In the case of loose coupling user operations are executed immediately locally and propagated to the other participants with a time delay. It can take considerable time for all changes to be made available to all users. Concurrency control in the loosely coupled mode is based on a simple locking mechanism. During modification the information unit (in general, a hypertext node) remains locked. The lock is released only after the modified information unit is saved; this results in a low degree of simultaneous work. In the case of tight coupling all modifications are immediately propagated to all other users, thus applying the WYSIWIS principle: All users of rIBIS send their modification requests to the central coordinator, where upon the coordinator transmits the requests to all other participants by broadcast message. Concurrent requests are synchronized by the coordinator.

Example (Coordinator in GroupSystems). The system GroupSystems, developed by Nunamaker et al. (1991) at Arizona University, also uses a centralized coordinator. Users can read the shared information directly. Modifications, however, must be initiated via the coordinator.

There is an apparent problem with all approaches using a centralized control unit: the control unit represents a performance bottleneck in the system and a single point of failure. If the control unit is disconnected or fails, then all modification operations are prevented. Distributed groupware tries to avoid any centralized coordination unit and replaces it by a decentralized control scheme.

There is yet another scheme for control units, namely implicit floor-passing with a centralized coordination unit (the so-called facilitator). For systematic reasons, we will postpone the discussion of this approach until floor-passing has been dealt with (see Sect. 4.6.2).

4.3.2 Token-passing

Token-passing is derived from the standby approach. Rather than making a specific site responsible for a file, this scheme introduces a token traveling the network between sites managing a replica (Minoura and Wiederhold 1982). There is one token for each replicated file. The site currently owning the token has the same rights as the central control unit. This means that it serializes and synchronizes all access to the replicated file within its domain, which is to say, a centralized control decision is made.

The token is forwarded along a virtual ring on the network sites; the virtual ring is predefined in most cases. Changes of the ring structure are only necessary if new sites are added to the system or if existing sites are removed from it. However, it is often very difficult to define the appropriate virtual ring, especially in wide area networks. Large virtual rings have extensive token roundtrip times and thus, reduce simultaneous work.

Since there exist only one token per file, synchronization is assured. Only a single site can access the file. All sites receive the token within a predefined time determined by the token roundtrip time and the token-holding time. During the token-holding time the site may access and manipulate the file. Problems arise if

- sites and/or communication links break down. If this happens the virtual ring must be reconfigured dynamically.
- token losses occur: A token is lost if the site currently holding the token crashes or the propagation of the token to the next site of the virtual ring is unsuccessful. Thus, a new token must be generated. However, the virtual ring may contain only one token per file in order for the concurrency control scheme to function properly.

In addition to their simplicity the major advantage of token-passing schemes is their fairness. Every site of the virtual ring receives the token within a certain time interval. However, all token-passing schemes remain somehow "undemocratic". Voting schemes which are described in more detail in the next chapter give all sites an equally fair chance to access replicated files, at any given time.

4.4 Decentralized Control: Overview

The following sections will expand on a variety of pessimistic schemes for decentralized control which do not employ voting. In particular, we will deal with simple locking schemes, floor-passing, transactions, and operation transformations (Fig. 4.3). Further examples are presented in Sect. 5.3.

4.5 Simple Locking Schemes

Locking mechanisms must cope with the following three issues:

1. Additional effort is necessary to request and obtain a lock. If the lock cannot be granted immediately waiting times occur.

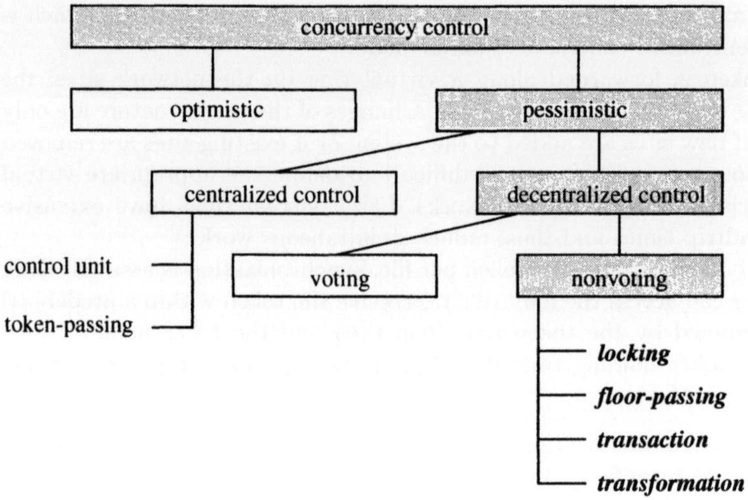

Fig. 4.3. Classification of concurrency control: Decentralized control and nonvoting scheme

2. The locking granularity has a major influence on the achievable degree of concurrency. It has to be determined whether only a character, an entire sentence, a paragraph or even the whole document is to be locked. A fine locking granularity interferes less with the user's actions, however it requires more system overhead because repeated lock requests and lock release commands must be triggered.
3. Finally, the conditions for initiating a lock request must be identified. For example, is the movement of the cursor into an information unit already sufficient to request the lock for that information unit or must the user invoke a special command?

Example (Locking in ZOG). Robertson et al. (1981) proceed as follows in the hypertext system ZOG: As soon as a user selects and enters a node, this node is locked. After the user leaves the node the lock is immediately released. Each node of the hypertext network contains a segment of the entire document. In practice, this locking scheme caused unnecessary restrictions on reading accesses which resulted in the usage of an optimistic approach for KMS, the commercial successor of ZOG.

The specification of access rights provides another implicit locking scheme for nodes. If every node is stored in a separate file, the read, modification and navigation rights can easily be specified by setting the file access bits appropriately. A node can be locked by removing the read permission of the associated file for other users. This locking scheme is not universally applicable since the owner has exclusive locking rights. The following sections will discuss universal locking schemes.

The moment at which a lock is to be released is another important issue. For example, the user may be required to invoke explicitly a release command. If the user fails to do so, the information unit is not accessible to any other user even if the user who locked the information unit has already finished his operations. In this case either other users must notify the lock holder of their intentions (e.g., via email) or the system administrator must remove the lock forcefully. Tickle locks provide another approach.

Definition 4.5.1 (Tickle lock). *Tickle locks are only maintained as long as the application (or the user) holding the lock is active. As soon as the application (or the user) becomes idle for a certain period of time, the lock is released and thus the information unit becomes available to other users.*

Definition 4.5.2 (Probabilistic lock). *The probabilistic lock is an optional lock with an automatic timeout. The application tries to set the lock. If the lock request is not granted before the timeout, then the application (or the user) has to decide whether or not it (he) wants to continue without the lock. Inconsistencies are consciously accepted. If the lock is granted before the timeout it will be assigned for a fixed time interval before being released again.*

Probabilistic locks are very similar to tickle locks, yet there are some differences: If the site holding the tickle lock has crashed or the communication link to the site is interrupted, then the lock will not be released until the site is restarted or the communication break resolved. With probabilistic locks, on the other hand, several applications may simultaneously hold a lock to the same information unit due to communication delays or system failures. This situation is tolerable if it does not happen too often and if mechanisms are provided for detecting inconsistencies. For example, after detecting the conflict the system might create for each lock holder a different version which may then be merged into a single version by manual user intervention.

Example (Locking with notification in MultimETH). The group editor in the system MultimETH (Lubich and Plattner 1990) uses hierarchically structured documents. Each document is logically organized as a tree with each node containing parts of the document, for instance title, summary or individual sections. If a user intends to modify a document part, then he applies for a reservation by sending a lock request. Nodes are the smallest units which may be locked. Users can extend this access granularity by locking an entire subtree. However, this can only be successful if all nodes within the subtree are unlocked. As soon as the lock is granted, both the user requesting the write access and all other users are notified. Note, however, that reading access does not require explicit reservation which sometimes may result in the reading of out-of-date information. An update of the information occurs after the write access has been successfully completed and the local replica has been notified.

Example (Locking with cache in Shared Books). The system Shared Books (Lewis and Hodges 1988) has been integrated into ViewPoint, a distributed office system of Xerox Corporation. It improves system efficiency by local caching and it supports simultaneous modification of a document by several users. The current version of the document is propagated according to the WYSIWIS principle (see also Sect. 3.5.1). Each user may open a window which displays the current state of the document. The state information encompasses the description, the structure, the locking states and version numbers of text units, the time stamps of current versions as well as comments. In order to improve system performance, state windows are not immediately updated after a change notification has been received; the change is buffered and the update is delayed until the next operation is invoked (demand updating). However, operations cannot be initiated with old state information, since the system always updates and displays the current state first. This may result in modified operations. Locks on individual text units are explicitly set and released, which makes concurrency control easy. The assignment of locks follows the FCFS (First-Come-First-Served) principle and locks have no time limit. The starvation of other users caused by the unavailability of locks is not prevented. Tickle locks as in CES (Greif et al. 1986) are not part of the concept. There is only one possibility of preventing starvation: the sending of a message to the user who currently holds the lock. An email system has been integrated for this purpose. The document management system is location transparent (the user need not know where individual text units are stored). In general, the text units will be stored on a central server. Shared Books localizes and controls the data transfer between users and the server independently. On request, entire text units can be cached locally. This kind of caching is widely accepted in distributed file systems; see for example the Andrew File System AFS (Satyanarayanan 1990) or Sprite (Nelson et al. 1988). After invoking an explicit store request, the cached text unit is written back to the server, the version number is incremented and the lock is released. Now the new version is accessible to all users.

4.6 Floor-passing Schemes

Floor-passing schemes alternate the access permission among participants of the group process. Locking schemes are not necessary because only one user is in control at any given time and thus, only he has access permission to the shared information. A distinction is made between explicit and implicit schemes and those with, versus those without time limits. The implicit schemes are subdivided into those with a centralized coordination unit and those with distributed coordination.

In the following section, we will discuss different schemes and illustrate graphically the associated coordination flow (see Fig. 4.4–4.6). The figures depict a situation with three users u_1, u_2 and u_3 with u_1 being the first in control. Next, let u_2 be in control and eventually u_3. The necessary coordination messages are numbered according to their sequence of occurrence. If one number is associated with several messages, then these are part of a single multicast or broadcast message. A continuous line symbolizes a floor transfer while a dashed line represents a floor release. The request message in the case of an implicit floor-passing scheme with distributed coordination, is depicted by a dotted line.

4.6.1 Explicit floor-passing scheme

In the explicit floor-passing scheme the current floor owner passes actively the floor to another requesting user (user u_1), who currently is in control. He hands the floor on to user u_2, who again passes it on to user u_3.

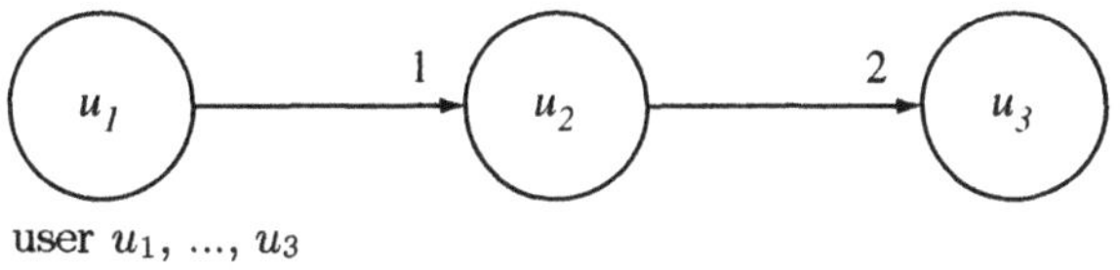

Fig. 4.4. Flow of coordination information for the explicit floor-passing scheme

Example (Explicit floor-passing in Augment).
Engelbart (1982) developed one of the first systems, the Augment system, using explicit floor-passing for concurrency control. Shared screen sessions allow all users to collaborate via a common communication medium. The control is explicitly passed on by the individual session participants. If participants leave or join a session, the system recognizes this and informs all remaining or already present participants. Participants who have left the session will no longer be considered for floor transfers, whereas new members become potential control recipients.

4.6.2 Implicit floor-passing with coordination unit

As opposed to explicit floor-passing schemes where the users themselves perform the floor management, the system is in control for the implicit scheme. This increases the "fairness" of the scheme, since concurrency control is no longer the affair of an individual, potentially egoistic user, but transferred to an "unbiased" software component, a centralized coordination unit (see Fig. 4.5). The specification of upper time limits may avoid extensive floor possession. If the current floor owner remains inactive for a certain length of time, the system can deprive him of the floor and pass it on to another user. This approach is similar to that of tickle locks.

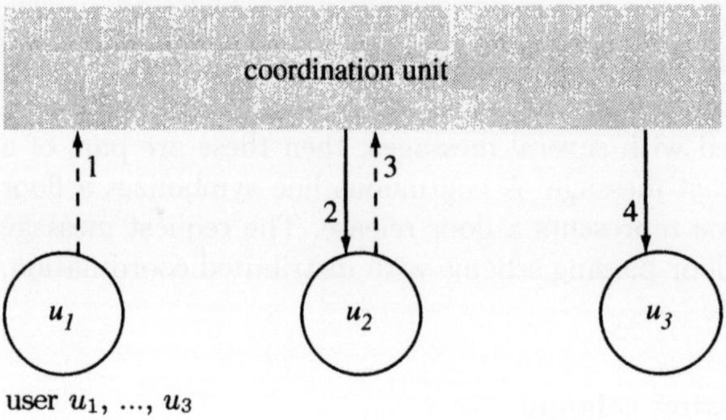

Fig. 4.5. Flow of coordination information for the implicit floor-passing scheme using a coordination unit

The concurrency control of a variety of groupware systems is based on implicit floor-passing with a centralized coordination unit. Often, in addition to synchronizing among the users, the coordination unit also controls data access. The tasks to be performed depend strongly on the respective application and the chosen data storage mechanism.

The disadvantage of the coordination unit is the same as with all mechanisms using centralized control units: If the coordination unit is not available (it crashed or the connection is interrupted), then all data access is prevented.

Example (Floor control and Isis-broadcast in DistEdit).
The group editor DistEdit (Knister and Prakash 1990) stores its data fully replicated which enables high availability for local read operations. Write access is controlled via the atomic Isis broadcast protocol by Birman (1993). This kind of concurrency control, and above all its high availability and performance characteristics will be discussed at length in Sect. 5.2.3 when the write-all-read-any scheme is introduced. At any given time, only one user can change the data. All other users of the system are limited to read access, which in practice reduces the usability for collaborative work. The first user accessing the data gets the floor. After control has been returned by the floor-holding user another user can request the floor and thus, he can gain write access. In contrast to the system rIBIS (Rein and Ellis 1991) DistEdit does not include any time limit for floor ownership.

4.6.3 Implicit floor-passing with distributed coordination

Some implicit mechanisms apply distributed negotiation in the context of floor-passing. A user requiring control for his activity (to modify the group document), sends a request to all other sites involved in the groupwork. The current floor-holding site checks as to whether or not control can be released (Fig. 4.6).

To guarantee fairness, the check for the possibility of a floor transfer should be performed by the system. Two possible factors might prevent immediate floor transfer: First the remote site might refuse to give up control.

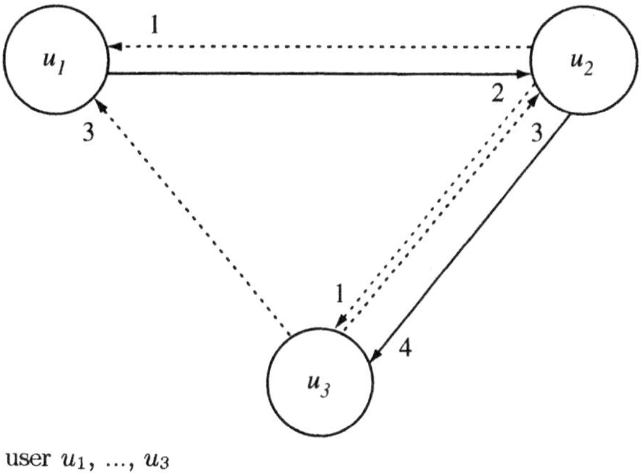

Fig. 4.6. Flow of coordination information for implicit floor-passing with distributed coordination

The second is caused by a special communication situation. In general, the floor is a token which is exchanged via message transfer between sites. If the floor-passing request is broadcasted exactly at the same time as the token is being transmitted through the network, then there is no current floor-holding site which is able to transfer control. The request must be repeated at a later time. This mechanism was, for example, used by Crowley et al. (1990) in their system MMConf.

4.7 Transactions

A conservative approach to pessimistic concurrency control is based on transactions (Barghouti and Kaiser 1991). According to Greif and Sarin (1987), this approach is applicable to groupwork situations in which transactions are extremely short and conflicts between concurrent operations may be resolved very quickly. However, this approach is not feasible for applications with long transactions. For example, if a complete editing session were to be defined as a single transaction extending for several hours then other group members would not be able to perform any modification operation on the shared group document during that time period. Additionally, during long transactions the probability of computer crashes or network partitionings increases. Since in many cases it is not possible to determine whether or not a transaction has been completed correctly or aborted, the locks set by a transaction cannot be released. Furthermore, for some collaborative work situations it may make sense to permit concurrent operations of different group members on the shared information, even if these operations cannot be serialized.

Example (Experiences with large software projects, Bancilhon et al. 1985). Large software projects are often divided into smaller subprojects each of which is managed and accomplished by a group of developers. Subprojects themselves consist of a set of subtasks which are usually performed by several collaborating developers, thus requiring schemes to manage concurrent access in order to maintain consistent data (e.g., source code or design specifications).

In order to improve efficiency and to increase parallel work, large software projects often apply optimistic concurrency control in combination with transactions: Instead of locking parts of the shared group documents, there is a test at the end of each transaction. If the test does not detect a conflict, then the transaction is correctly completed, otherwise it is aborted. In the latter case the user must then decide if he wants to do manual correction of inconsistencies.

Transaction mechanisms are typically used for asynchronous groupwork (team members work at different times on different parts of the shared group document). Often, it is not even necessary to propagate modifications immediately to all other group members. However, the goal should be to avoid any inconsistency in the few exceptional cases where several team members perform concurrent operations on the same part of a group document.

There are a variety of groupware systems which apply transactional concurrency control (e.g., CES which we will discuss in more detail in the following subsections).

Granularity in CES. In CES (Collaborative Editing System), a group editor developed by Greif et al. (1986) at MIT (Massachusetts Institute of Technology, Cambridge, USA), each document contains a structural description and several text units. Structural modifications are independent of textual modifications. Text units are arbitrary in size (sometimes many Kbytes) and are characterized by a unique identifier, a version list and a locking state. The locking granularity ranges from individual text units up to the file level. Besides editing operations traditionally available in group editors CES also provides functions for creating and manipulating structured documents.

Various users can manipulate a document simultaneously. This goes for both the document structure and the actual document text. In order to increase the availability, the document structure is replicated on all relevant sites. As opposed to this, there is exactly one user responsible for each text unit. Each user stores the text units he has generated locally. Thus, the text of the complete document is distributed across the sites of all team members.

Concurrency control in CES. CES has been implemented in Argus which means that concurrency control in CES is based on mechanisms supported by Argus, such as logging the individual steps of atomic transactions, status reports on document accesses, handling of the 2-phase commit problem during multicopy write accesses to the document structure, and the management of locks and versions. Before discussing CES in more detail, we give a short description of Argus; the reader is also referred to the works by Liskov (1988) and Liskov et al. (1987).

Argus is both a programming language for distributed applications and a distributed system. In our discussion, we will focus on its use as a programming language. Argus supplies two new language constituents: guardians and actions. Guardians are responsible for certain resources (in CES, the resources are text units). They are implemented as a set of procedures which are invoked using RPCs. They tolerate computer crashes since all relevant data are stored in stable storage and thus retrievable after recovery.

Actions are atomic transactions which may be nested. They mask error and concurrency problems. A 2-phase commit protocol provides atomicity for nested actions. A locking scheme serializes the actions in order to provide synchronization. After computer crashes, recovery retrieves a consistent state from stable storage.

In the following section we will describe concurrency control for read and write access in CES. Each user can read any text unit at any time. For each text unit, there is a stack of all consistent text versions ordered according to their age. The topmost stack element contains the current version of the respective text unit as shown on display. If another user modifies the text unit which is being read, then the reader will view the old but consistent version. After the write access has been finished, a new stack element is generated and shown to the reader. CES tries to minimize the processing time to display the new version.

If several users try to modify the same text unit, then CES locks it for exactly one user. The user holding the lock may successfully modify the text unit while others must wait for the lock to be released. Extended locking times are avoided by using tickle locks. If the user does not invoke any editing operation on the locked text unit for a considerable length of time the lock is automatically withdrawn by the system and may be assigned to another user.

Both screen and screen buffer are held in a single abstract object, the so-called display object which is realized as a guardian. Each user views his own modifications immediately on his screen. Due to version management, modifications of other users are only displayed after the associated atomic transaction has been completed successfully.

Integration of existing database systems. Many transaction-based systems are implemented on top of existing database systems. Examples of this approach are the following:

- Orion (Banerjee et al. 1987), a centralized database system, stores all information on Quilt documents. The central storage as well as the used transaction mechanisms reduces the applicability in wide-area networks.[2]
- gIBIS (Conklin and Begeman 1988) is based on the relational database system UNIFY, which supports locking on the record level, transaction

[2] The same is true for CoAuthor (Hahn et al. 1991) with MULTOS and Prep (Neuwirth et al. 1990), all of which use a database for data storage.

management, reliable data storage and an efficient access mechanism. Unfortunately, the database system does not provide any notification mechanism. Thus, a separate layer, the so-called notification layer has been incorporated on top of the database interface. Significant database modifications are discovered by this layer, upon which respective notifications are generated and propagated to the other users of the group.

- Intermedia (Meyrowitz 1986) supports concurrent access within a LAN and it uses Sun NFS for transparent, distributed document access. The usage of the relational database system INGRES, along with a transaction mechanism guarantees data consistency.
- Neptune (Delisle and Schwartz 1986), developed by the Tektronix laboratories stores hypertext documents on a central database server which group members access via the local network. A write access to the database server is handled by a transaction management. If a transaction has to be aborted Neptune restores a consistent state. Both the transaction management and the consistent recovery are implemented by the abstract hypertext machine (see Sect. 6.3.3).

Private contexts. Empirical studies of Neptune showed that collaboration on identical document parts occurs rather seldom. Parallel work on different document segments has proved to be more efficient. Each user creates a private view (the so-called context). Within the context, he works locally and without external influence by other users' operations. As soon as a context is finished, it is released and visible to others. A **merge** operation transmits the context and incorporates it into the hypertext document.

In Neptune the **merge** operation is more powerful than simple copying mechanisms. The version history contains context and structural information. The context information allows version tracking along the context structure; the structural information also guarantees that all annotations and attributes of an incorporated context are included. It is sometimes advantageous to assign individual hypertext nodes simultaneously to different contexts. Because contexts are disjunct, Neptune allows links between contexts in order to support this feature.

After a new context has been incorporated into the hypertext document, a consistent version history can be created either by copying or by specifying a link to the version history of the original node. Copying has the advantage of making the different contexts more independent of each other (at the cost of increased storage space). In the case of links all versions must be kept available as long as a reference from a context to this version history continues to exist. This is why the copying mechanism has been chosen for Neptune.

4.8 Operation Transformation

Operation transformation schemes synchronize access to small units, such as individual words or characters, which is why they are often used for tightly coupled, synchronous groupwork. These schemes propagate immediately any modifications within the group, thus enabling the group to interact based upon the WYSIWIS principle. Time consuming transaction mechanisms are useless for synchronous groupwork. Strict serialization of operations has to be abandoned in favor of a more "optimistic" concurrency control scheme.

Before discussing one of the operation transformation schemes in more detail, the following will introduce some of the basic features.

4.8.1 Sites

Let G be a group process and gs a synchronous, distributed group session within G with $n > 1$ participants. gs is modeled as the pair (S, O). S is the set of sites. There is exactly one site $s \in S$ per participant of gs. In general, s will run on one machine, for example a personal computer. It is possible that several sites $s \in S$ run on the same machine. Let O be a set of parameterized operators which are available as part of the group session gs. The execution of an operator in combination with the specification of parameters is called operation.

Definition 4.8.1 (Site). *Each site $s \in S$ is made up of the triple (site process, site object, site identifier) with:*

- *site identifier is a unique identifier for the site participating in gs.*
- *site object is a passive data object, for example a group document manipulated during gs by read and write operations. Each site has a complete replica of the shared data object.*
- *site process provides three basic functions:*
  1. *Generation of operations according to the specification of the user to whom s has been assigned. For every operation specification the site process creates an operation request which is then propagated to all other sites of gs.*
  2. *Receiving of operation requests from other sites.*
  3. *Execution of operation requests which may have been generated locally or received from remote sites.*

The following discussion assumes that a text processing system is used in the context of gs, i.e., the site object of s is a string of characters.

Examples for operators.
O_1 = **insert**[X; Φ]: The character X is inserted at position Φ.
O_2 = **delete**[Φ]: The character at position Φ is deleted.

Operations are instances of operators. Each operation modifies the state of the site object.

*Example (**insert**).* Assume o = **insert**['x'; 3]. The execution of o on the string 'abc' defines the following result: o('abc') = 'abxc'.

Basic definitions. If two concurrent operations are to be executed on the same data object, then the so-called precedence property defines the execution ordering of the operations for all sites of gs (i.e., if an operation o_1 has precedence over an operation o_2, o_1 has precedence over o_2 on all site objects within the system). A group session gs is idle if all operation requests have been distributed to all sites of gs and executed on all site objects.

Despite the immediate propagation of operation requests the objects of all sites are not identical at all times due to the transmission delays within the network. However, the goal of the operation transformation scheme must be for all replicas to converge to the identical state after all operation requests have been executed. The so-called convergence property requires all site objects to be identical when the group session is idle.

Definition 4.8.2 (Correctness of operation transformation).
The operation transformation is called correct if the precedence and the convergence properties are satisfied.

Correctness of group sessions. The goal is to find an operation transformation scheme for concurrency control that meets the demand of correctness. One possibility is the definition of a total ordering on all operations of the group session. A total order, as proposed by Lamport (1978b) has two disadvantages:

- Increased response times due to the propagation delay within the network.
- If the user initiates an operation request, then the user interface remains locked until the operation request is processed at all sites. Otherwise subsequent operation requests could refer to the state of the local site object which might be different from the state of other site objects.

4.8.2 Group Outline Viewing Editor (Grove)

Grove is a group editor designed by Ellis et al. (1991) at MCC (Microelectronics and Computer Technology Corporation) in Austin, Texas, USA supporting tightly coupled groupwork. Thus, it features short response times and a high level of concurrency for the parallel work within the group session. The document is replicated at all sites in order to increase availability and to reduce access times.

Concurrency control in Grove is based on the operation transformation scheme, i.e., for two operations o_1 and o_2 the following property must be true ($o_1\prime$ and $o_2\prime$ are the transformed operations of o_1 and o_2):

$$o_2\prime \circ o_1 = o_1\prime \circ o_2 \qquad (4.1)$$

$o_2\prime$ applied to o_1 results in the same site object as $o_1\prime$ applied to o_2.

In the following, we will show under which conditions these kinds of transformations can be applied. We define a partial order on the operations by assigning priorities. The Grove algorithm which operates on the partial order of operations has the following characteristics: Local operations are executed immediately, locks are unnecessary and the algorithm is robust as far as computer crashes are concerned. Access granularity is a single character resulting in a simple realization of the transformation algorithm.

We assume the following:

- The number of sites involved is constant (we define it as N).
- All messages are received exactly once (exactly-once semantics) without any errors (see also p. 17 and Fig. 1.10).
- All messages are triggered explicitly by user interaction.

Grove guarantees document consistency, regardless of the type and sequence of operations. Semantical conflicts are not detected. The algorithm for concurrency control in Grove works as follows: After an operation has been initiated by a site, it is executed locally. A priority is defined for the operation. The priority is based on both the site identifier and on past operations at the character position of the string. All the relevant information is combined into an operation request which is propagated to the other sites. They queue the received operation requests according to their priorities and check if concurrent operations have taken place in the mean time. If this is the case and the concurrent operation has lower priority than the received one, a transformation might become necessary. Grove assumes that only insert and delete operations can lead to possible conflicts. Thus, a transformation matrix T is defined which incorporates transformation rules for the four combinations of insert and delete operations meeting the requirement of the Equation (4.1). The following expands on this.[3]

Transformation matrix. Let $gs = (S, O)$ be a group session and T an $(m \times m)$ transformation matrix of gs, with $m = |O|$. Let o_i, o_j be operations with priorities p_i and p_j. Then let O_u and O_v with $u, v \in \{1, \ldots, m\}$ be the respective operators associated with o_i and o_j. Suppose T includes the two transformation rules

$$o_{i'} = T_{uv}(o_i, o_j, p_i, p_j) \text{ for } o_i \rightarrow o_{i'} \text{ according to } o_j \tag{4.2}$$

and

$$o_{j'} = T_{vu}(o_j, o_i, p_j, p_i) \text{ for } o_j \rightarrow o_{j'} \text{ according to } o_i \tag{4.3}$$

meeting the requirement $o_{j'} \circ o_i = o_{i'} \circ o_j$. In the Case (4.2) there is a transformation T_{uv} which depends on the operation o_j transforming the operation o_i into another operation $o_{i'}$. The same is true, respectively, for Case (4.3).

[3] For a detailed description of transformation rules, including precedence and convergence property, the reader is referred to Ellis and Gibbs (1989).

Example (Transformation matrix). We assume the transformation matrix T for **insert** and **delete** operators of the two sites s_i and s_j:

$$\begin{bmatrix} (\mathbf{insert}|X_i;\Phi_i|,\ \mathbf{insert}|X_j;\Phi_j|,\ p_i,p_j) & (\mathbf{insert}|X_i;\Phi_i|,\ \mathbf{delete}|\Phi_j|,\ p_i,p_j) \\ (\mathbf{delete}|\Phi_i|,\ \mathbf{insert}|X_j;\Phi_j|,\ p_i,p_j) & (\mathbf{delete}|\Phi_i|,\ \mathbf{delete}|\Phi_j|,\ p_i,p_j) \end{bmatrix}$$

Example (Implementation of transformation matrix). We assume that o_i is the original operation which is transformed by the transformation matrix T into a new operation $o_i\prime$.

1. Implementation of T_{11} (**insert**$[X_i;\Phi_i]$, **insert**$[X_j;\Phi_j]$, p_i,p_j):
   if $(\Phi_i < \Phi_j)$ **then** $o_i\prime :=$ **insert**$[X_i;\Phi_i]$;
   else if $(\Phi_i > \Phi_j)$ **then** $o_i\prime :=$ **insert**$[X_i;\Phi_i+1]$;
   else if $(X_i = X_j)$ **then** $o_i\prime := \emptyset$;
   /* If positions and arguments of both operations are identical, then $o_i\prime$ is set to be the empty operation; otherwise the same operation would be executed twice, which is why one of the two operations is ignored). */
   else if $(p_i > p_j)$ **then** $o_i\prime :=$ **insert**$[X_i;\Phi_i+1]$;
   else $o_i\prime :=$ **insert**$[X_i;\Phi_i]$;
2. Implementation of T_{12} (**insert**$[X_i;\Phi_i]$, **delete**$[\Phi_j]$, p_i,p_j):
   if $(\Phi_i < \Phi_j)$ **then** $o_i\prime :=$ **insert**$[X_i;\Phi_i]$;
   else $o_i\prime :=$ **insert**$[X_i;\Phi_i-1]$;
3. Implementation of T_{21} (**delete**$[\Phi_i]$, **insert**$[X_j;\Phi_j]$, p_i,p_j):
   if $(\Phi_i < \Phi_j)$ **then** $o_i\prime :=$ **delete**$[\Phi_i]$;
   else $o_i\prime :=$ **delete**$[\Phi_i+1]$;
4. Implementation of T_{22} (**delete**$[\Phi_i]$, **delete**$[\Phi_j]$, p_i,p_j):
   if $(\Phi_i < \Phi_j)$ **then** $o_i\prime :=$ **delete**$[\Phi_i]$;
   else if $(\Phi_i > \Phi_j)$ **then** $o_i\prime :=$ **delete**$[\Phi_i-1]$;
   else $o_i\prime := \emptyset$;

Example (Concurrent operations, see also Fig. 4.7). We assume that the string 'abcd' is the shared object of the sites s_1 and s_2.

Also, let us assume that $o_1 =$ **insert**['x';3] and $o_2 =$ **insert**['y';4].

If no operation transformation would take place the result after executing both operations depends on the execution sequence:

$$o_1 \circ o_2(\text{'abcd'}) = o_1(\text{'abcyd'}) = \text{'abxcyd'} \tag{4.4}$$

and

$$o_2 \circ o_1(\text{'abcd'}) = o_2(\text{'abxcd'}) = \text{'abxycd'} \tag{4.5}$$

Applying the aforementioned transformation rules we get the transformed operations $o_1\prime =$ **insert**['x';3] und $o_2\prime =$ **insert**['y';5]:

$$o_1\prime \circ o_2(\text{'abcd'}) = o_1\prime(\text{'abcyd'}) = \text{'abxcyd'} \tag{4.6}$$

and

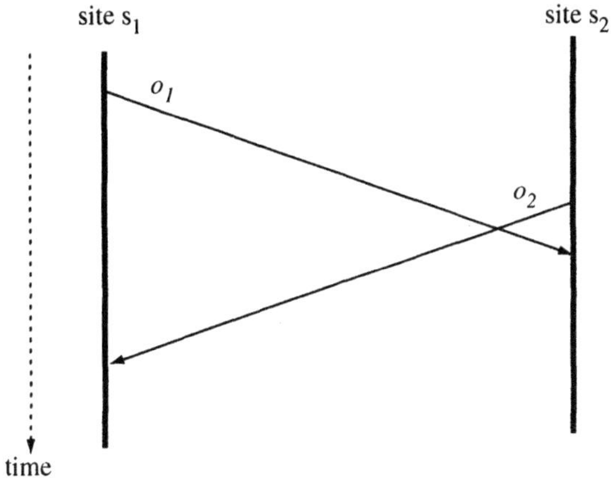

Fig. 4.7. Example of concurrent operations

$$o_2\prime \circ o_1(\text{`abcd'}) = o_2\prime(\text{`abxcd'}) = \text{`abxcyd'} \tag{4.7}$$

Thus, we have: $o_1\prime \circ o_2(\text{`abcd'}) = o_2\prime \circ o_1(\text{`abcd'})$.

Figure 4.8 depicts the execution of the Grove algorithm at site s_i. The following data structures are used:

- *State vector:* The state vector of a site s_j is an N-dimensional vector. The ith component of the vector specifies how many operations initiated by site s_i have already been received and processed by site s_j. Focusing on the two status vectors sv_i and sv_j we define:
  1. $sv_i = sv_j$, if both states vectors are identical, i.e., the corresponding components of both vectors have the same value.
  2. $sv_i < sv_j$, if each component of sv_i is smaller or equal to the respective component in sv_j and if at least one component of sv_i is smaller than the corresponding component of sv_j.
  3. $sv_i > sv_j$, if at least one component of sv_i is bigger than the corresponding component of sv_j.
- *Operation request:* An operation request is defined by a tuple $< i, sv_i, o, p >$, with i as the identifier of the initiating site, sv_i as its state vector, o the requested operation and p the priority of that operation.
- *Request queue:* Local and received operation requests are managed in a queue until they are scheduled for processing. Q_i is the request queue of site s_i.
- *Operation log:* This data structure lists all operation requests which have been successfully processed at site s_i. The operation log of site s_i is called L_i.

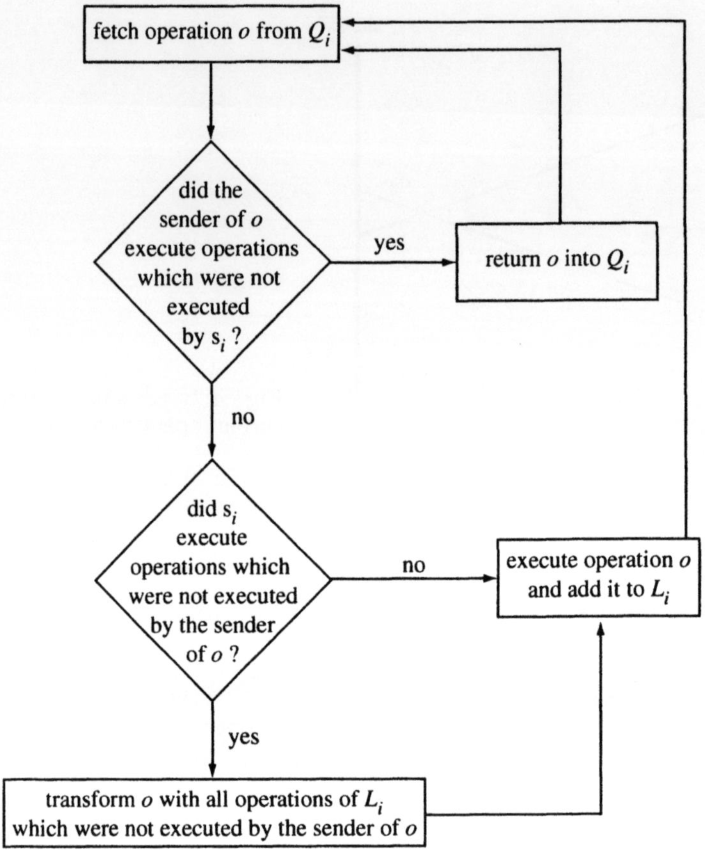

Fig. 4.8. The Grove algorithm

4.8.3 The Grove algorithm: distributed Operational Transformation (dOPT)

Code fragment (Grove algorithm).

```
main:
   initialize()
   while not abort do
      if there exists a local user operation o then generate-request(o)
      else receive-request()
      execute-request()

initialize():
   Q_i := ∅;
   L_i := ∅;
```

$sv_i :=< 0, \ldots, 0 >;$

generate-request(o):
accept local user operation o, compute its priority p, specify the request and enter it into the request queue, i.e., $Q_i := Q_i + < i, sv_i, o, p >$;
propagate $< i, sv_i, o, p >$ to all other sites;

receive-request():
receive $< j, sv_j, o_j, p_j >$ from other sites;
$Q_i := Q_i + < j, sv_j, o_j, p_j >$;

execute-request():
for all entries $< j, sv_j, o_j, p_j > \in Q_i$ (with $sv_j \leq sv_i$) **do**
$Q_i := Q_i - < j, sv_j, o_j, p_j >$;
if ($sv_j < sv_i$) **then**
$< k, sv_k, o_k, p_k > :=$ latest entry in L_i, with $sv_k \leq sv_j$
(or $\emptyset$, otherwise);
while ($< k, sv_k, o_k, p_k > \neq \emptyset$ **and** $o_j \neq \emptyset$) **do**
if (kth component of $sv_j \leq k$th component of sv_k) **then**
$u :=$ index of $o_j \in O_u$ (i.e., o_j is an instance of O_u);
$v :=$ index of $o_k \in O_v$ (i.e., o_k is an instance of O_v);
execute transformation , i.e.,
$o_j := T_{uv}(o_j, o_k, p_j, p_k)$;
$< k, sv_k, o_k, p_k > :=$ next entry of L_i (or $\emptyset$);
execute operation o_j;
$L_i := L_i + < j, sv_i, o_j, p_j >$;
$sv_i := sv_i$ with jth component incremented by 1;

Besides the restrictive assumptions (constant number of sites, error-free exchange of operation requests, etc.) there is another drawback to this transformation algorithm: Since all processed operation requests are recorded, the operation log grows continually and quickly due to the fine granularity of concurrency control (recall that the granularity is a single character). For operation transformations and for priority computation there is the potential that the entire log must be checked. This is why Grove enforces once per minute the processing of all pending operation requests; new operation requests are not accepted during that time period. According to the designers, the medium length of these time periods is about ten seconds which might impair the editing operations of the users. After all pending operation requests have been processed at all sites the operations logs are reset to zero and new operation requests are accepted.

4.8.4 Correctness of the Grove algorithm

The proof of correctness for the Grove algorithm will only be outlined in its basic elements. Assume that $r =< j, sv_j, o, p >$ is the operation request sent from s_j to s_i. For each inserted character X of the site object, a position counter Ψ is defined. During a group session, X can be shifted to the left or right within the string. The position counter Ψ of X is then defined as the net value of all shifts of X. Shifts can be initiated either explicitly (i.e., operation transformations) or implicitly by inserting or deleting other symbols.

Basic idea of the correctness proof. Ellis and Gibbs (1989) prove the following:

A) The algorithm determines the same value for the position counter Ψ of a character X for all sequences of operations (consistency).
B) If operation o_i takes place before operation o_j (both having the same insert position Φ), then the position counter of X_i (the character inserted by o_i) must be bigger than the one associated with X_j (the character inserted by o_j) due to the temporal ordering of the two operations.

Proof.

A) Operations executed during a group session can arrive at a passive site (i.e., the site does not create any new operation requests locally) in an arbitrary order. Each sequence of operations can be derived from another sequence by reordering the operations; however, reordering might change the required operation transformation. It is shown that all correctness requirements are satisfied despite reordering of operations.
We assume that the operations $o_i =$ **insert**$[X_i; \Phi]$ and $o_j =$ **insert**$[X_j; \Phi]$ are concurrent (i.e., there is no temporal ordering for o_i and o_j): Further we assume that Ψ_i and Ψ_j are position counters of the characters X_i and X_j. With respect to the priorities we assume: $p_i < p_j$ (i.e., Grove assumes the execution order o_i before o_j).
Viewpoint of the operation o_i:
   1. Let o_i be executed before o_j. Prior to the execution of o_i the operation log is checked and the position counter Ψ_i with initial value Φ might be replaced by a new value Φ_i (if a transformation is necessary).
   If later o_j is executed, then character X_j is inserted before character X_i. Character X_i is implicitly shifted to the right. For the position counter of X_i, we get: $\Psi_i = \Phi_i + 1$.
   2. Assume that the operation o_j is executed before o_i. At the processing of o_i the operation log is checked and the prior execution of o_j discovered. The operation o_i is transformed and we get $\Psi_i = \Phi_i + 1$ for the position counter of X_i.
Viewpoint of operation o_j:
   1. Assume that the execution of o_j precedes that of o_i and let Φ_j be the value of the position counter Ψ_j after execution: Later, during

the processing of operation o_i, the operation log is checked. Since the priority $p_i < p_j$, Ψ_j is not incremented which means that it retains the value Φ_j. The character X_i is inserted after X_j.

2. The execution of o_i takes place before o_j. During processing of o_j the prior execution of o_i is detected in the operation log. However, since the priority is $p_i < p_j$ there will be no transformation of o_j with respect to o_i. The position counter Ψ_j remains on Φ_j. Consequently, the character X_i is positioned behind the character X_j.

B) The correctness is derived through the method in which the priorities are computed.

4.9 Further Reading

For more information on the issues discussed in this chapter, the reader is referred to Goscinski (1991).

The book by Helal et al. (1996) gives a good introduction to data, process and object replication.

A formal analysis of concurrent systems is given by Milner (1995). Roscoe (1997) describes concurrent systems based on CSP (Communicating Sequential Processes).

Based on state models, Mageel and Kramer (1999) present a modern approach to concurrency in the development of control systems. Their excellent textbook gives a sound introduction to the theory of concurrency as well as practical guidelines for the design of concurrent programs using UML and Java.

5. Replication and Concurrency Control

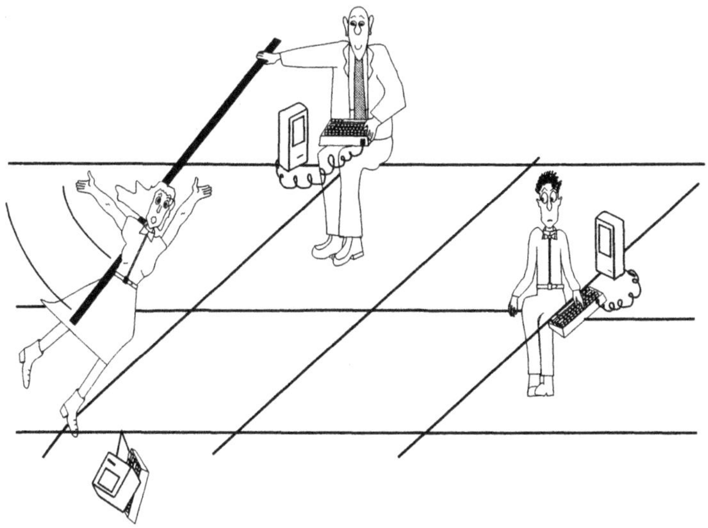

This chapter introduces schemes for replication and concurrency control that were originally developed in the context of distributed file systems but which could become prevalent in synchronous groupware, as well.

A central focus of attention is voting schemes such as majority consensus (with and without primary site), weighted voting, write-all-read-any (also known as read-one-write-all, ROWA for short), voting with witnesses (including volatile witnesses, and with and without leading minority), available-copy, dynamic voting (with update sites cardinality and linear ordering, respectively), voting-class, multidimensional voting, and hierarchical voting schemes, especially the hierarchical quorum consensus and tree quorum. In addition we discuss the coding scheme and the grid protocol.

For each scheme we analyze its availability.

5.1 Introduction

The previous chapter has shown that a variety of tried and tested approaches for concurrency control exist in CSCW. The most modern approaches have been proposed for distributed file systems. Due to the well-known disadvantages of centralization, most of these schemes work with decentralized control like all the voting schemes. To get a better understanding of their readiness for use in CSCW, we discuss in some detail how voting schemes work, what strengths and weaknesses they share, and, most importantly, what benefit they bring with regard to consistency issues.

Since we have to deal with a large variety of voting schemes, we have developed a catalog of criteria. Among other things, we examined whether or not network partitioning can be tolerated, and what kind of availability improvements can be achieved.

Replication and network partitioning. While designing groupware with a distributed and replicated model for the group process, important aspects to consider include performance, consistency of the replicated group documents in the case of network partitioning, and the degree of document access concurrency.

Replication of shared data of a group process may reduce the performance of a CSCW application. Mainly for updates performance decreases because writing becomes more expensive the more physical replicas (of a logical data unit, say file) have to be held consistent. Another influencing performance parameter is the chosen access granularity. Here we have to deal with a series of tradeoffs.

If we choose as granularity big data units such as entire files, accesses lead to message exchanges of high data volume with an obvious impact upon peak loads of the network. If we choose very fine-grained data units (a small number of bytes), accesses cause many individual message exchanges with a high risk of overloading the network due to the involved overhead. On the other hand, the bigger the granularity of the data units the higher the probability that concurrent accesses to the logical data unit interfere with each other. Since in many cases the designers of a CSCW system with a distributed and replicated model for the group process do not allow diverging versions of replicas of the group documents, concurrent accesses have to be synchronized. The required locking (and blocking) phases can decrease performance, as well. The compromise between a small number of messages with high data volume and a high number of messages with small data volume on the one hand, and the legitimate request to reduce the probability of interfering concurrent accesses to the logical data unit on the other hand, often leads to the option of having a data block (of some kilobytes) as access granularity. Since we do not measure performance quantitatively, we just use the simple term data block without giving a concrete block size. We are interested in examining issues such as: what is the degree of concurrency while accessing these data blocks? How can we guarantee consistency of replicated data blocks in the presence of computer crashes, link failures, and worse, network partitioning. In principle, data blocks can be as simple as a fraction of a group document (stored in a data block managed by the underlying distributed file system), or a buffer or a cache item in main memory (see, for instance, the code fragment for reading of a cached data block in Chap. 1, p. 82).

In groupware based on a centralized or a distributed and nonreplicated model for the group process, a single node (e.g., a workstation) is responsible for the consistency of a shared data block. Here, consistency is easy to guarantee with the help of well-known locking techniques. The situation becomes more complicated in a groupware system based on a distributed and replicated model for the group process where several nodes are responsible for the consistency of their individual physical replicas of shared logical data blocks. The additional problem areas can be summarized as follows:

1. The replication management requires additional programming effort in order to provide replication transparency. Replication transparency means that a user – in spite of replicated data – sees a logical single-copy image of the data only. Without replication transparency, user applications would be too difficult to write and too failure-prone as far as the consistency of the replicated data is concerned. Therefore, replication management is embedded into the underlying groupware system, and in most cases, replication transparency is provided.
2. In most cases, mutual consistency among all physical replicas of a logical data block is a requirement.
3. Due to physical factors such as time delays in message exchanges between nodes possessing a replica, it cannot be guaranteed that all replicas of the same logical data block will be identical at all times. Rather, the goal of all replication and concurrency schemes is for all replicas of the same logical data block to converge after an update into a mutually consistent state.[1] During the convergence phase, successful accesses to the potentially inconsistent logical data block must be prohibited.

Locking state of a data block. In the following we assume that locks are set on the level of physical data blocks. The locking state describes whether a physical data block is read or write locked, or whether there is no lock at all. A read locked data block prohibits any concurrent access, be it a read or a write access. A write locked data block prohibits concurrent write accesses but allows read accesses. The setting of locks on the level of data blocks implies that accesses only interfere with each other when accessing the same logical data block. Accesses to different logical data blocks can be carried out in parallel. This improves performance.

[1] As we will see in later discussions that does not necessarily imply that all replicas of the same logical data block have to be identical in this mutually consistent state.

Concurrent accesses to different logical data blocks may lead to deadlocks through a cyclic blocking while trying to set desired locks. We do not discuss this issue here. The interested reader is referred to Brachman and Chanson (1989) who propose a solution to this problem.

Version number of a data block. Every (physical) data block has a version number. In the most simple case, this version number is an integer counter which is incremented after each successful update of the data block.

Version numbers could also be implemented with time stamps of the last successful update to the data block. Since clock synchronization can be an issue here, we shall not ascribe to this variant.

Let the data structure for a data block contain the block number, the locking state, the version number, and the data themselves (see Fig. 5.1).

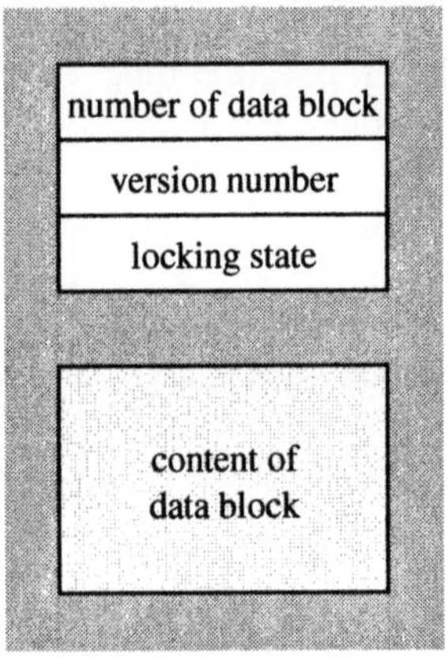

data block

Fig. 5.1. Data structure for a data block

As we will see, using the version numbers, readers can inform themselves of the most up-to-date (physical) data block while writers can detect and avoid "outdated" update requests.

Example (Use of version numbers). Let us consider the situation depicted in Fig. 5.2: Nodes n_1, n_2 and n_3 possess the relevant replicas of a data block with block number k. Node n_1 has the physical data block with version number 5 and data content 'XX' , while the nodes n_2 and n_3 both have their physical data blocks with version number 6 and data content 'YY'. The locking state is in this example irrelevant.

A reader of data block k transparently requests the data block in question from all three nodes.[2] Comparing the version numbers of the received data

[2] For our purposes, this level of abstraction is sufficient. In a more realistic and more efficient setting, a reader would probably first transparently request the version numbers of the data block in question from all (or a majority) of replica

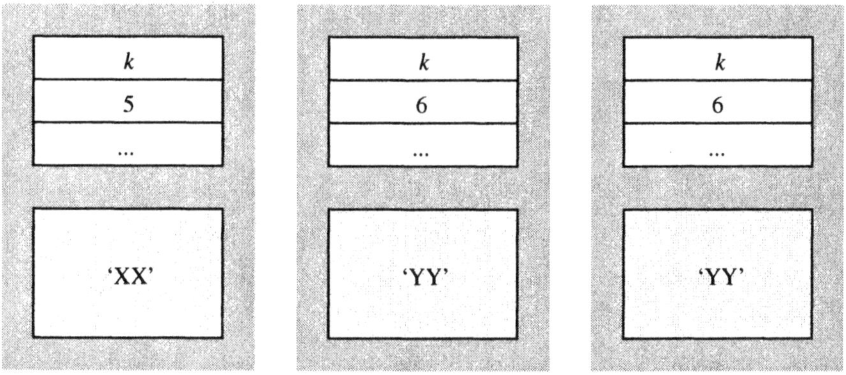

data block k at node n_1 *data block k at node n_2* *data block k at node n_3*

Fig. 5.2. Use of version numbers: situation before reading the data block

blocks, the reader can detect that 'YY' is the most up-to-date data content. If we assume that the logical data block is said to be consistent if a majority of nodes possesses an up-to-date physical data block (this assumption will play an important role in the remainder of this chapter), the reader can also determine that 'YY' is the most up-to-date data content, even if only two of the three nodes have answered the read request.

Let us now assume that the reader becomes a writer. He updates the data content to 'ZZ', increments the version number to 7 and (transparently) requests an update of this new data block at the three nodes which possess the (physical) replicas of the desired data block. Let node n_3 be crashed or otherwise made unavailable to the writer. Under the majority assumption made above, we get the situation depicted in Fig. 5.3.

Again, the logical data block is consistent because a majority of nodes possess an up-to-date physical data block. Any subsequent reader will get 'ZZ' as the most up-to-date data block, even if only two of the three nodes have answered the read request. No problem exists if one of these two nodes is the formerly crashed and now recovered node n_3. In any case, the other answering node is either n_1 or n_2; each of them will answer with an up-to-date physical data block.

If later, another writer tries to update this data block with a version number 7, both nodes n_1 and n_2 will detect and prohibit this outdated update.

Although we have neglected some important aspects of the involved protocols such as "How does a reader or a writer know what the current majority is?", or related to that "How does a reader or a writer know about and address the replica possessing nodes?", this simple example has already demonstrated how helpful a version number is and how dangerous incorrect handling of

possessing nodes, and would then request the data content from one of the responding nodes with the most up-to-date data block.

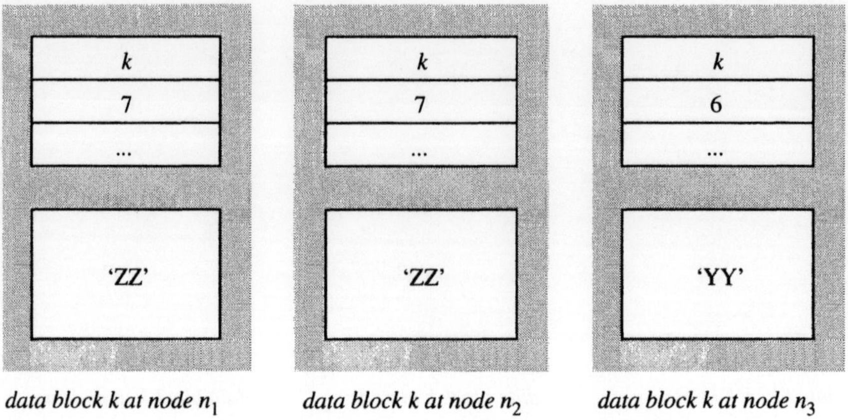

Fig. 5.3. Use of version numbers: situation after updating the data block

version numbers can be. In order to avoid chaotic situations in a groupware system, concurrency control – especially for the replicated model – is fully embedded in the data block access protocols. Chapter 1 has discussed some of the possibilities for identifying and addressing server subsystems (address lists, mediation and brokering etc.). Knowing about the server subsystems (here: the replica possessing nodes) may then allow simple calculation of the current majority. In our further discussions we will see examples where this scheme is more complicated (for instance, when we have to deal with dynamically changing majorities or with relocated replicas).

It is beyond the scope of this introduction to discuss the higher layer where transactions are managed. It is obvious that accessing a replicated data block can only be carried out correctly when a transactional multiphase commit protocol is followed. Especially for updates, atomicity is needed. The interested reader is referred to the relevant (distributed) data base literature at the end of the chapter.

Catalog of criteria. We could evaluate the different replication and concurrency schemes on various criteria. The main reason to use groupware based on a distributed and replicated model for the group process is an increased availability of the group's data. We shall, therefore, analyze the different schemes with regard to availability and discuss whether and to what degree the schemes tolerate network partitioning.

Availability analysis. The availability A of a node (or a physical data block replica stored at a node) is defined as the limit $\lim_{t\to\infty}$ of the probability function $p(t)$. Here, $p(t)$ is the probability that a given node (or a physical data block replica stored at a given node) is available for an access at time t (i.e., the node is up and running and can be contacted over the network without problems). Thus, we define

$$A = \lim_{t\to\infty} p(t) \tag{5.1}$$

Let node failure and repair rates be independent events and exponentially distributed. Both simulation studies, by Carroll and Long (1989) as well as Long and Pâris (1988) where the availability of voting schemes were analyzed, show that the obtainable availability is only marginally influenced by nonexponentially distributed failure and repair rates.

Definition 5.1.1 (Failure rate). *The probability that a node is usable for access during a time interval of length t be $e^{-\lambda t}$ where λ denotes the failure rate.*

Definition 5.1.2 (Repair rate). *The probability that a node recovers and becomes usable for access again in less than t time units be $1 - e^{-\mu t}$ where μ denotes the repair rate.*

With the quotient $\rho = \frac{\lambda}{\mu}$ we measure the expected amount of time where a given node is not usable for accesses. The probability $p(t)$ that a given node (or a physical data block replica stored at a given node) is usable for an access at time t can easily be expressed by ρ as well as by λ and μ. Since we assume a time-invariant Markovian property for λ and μ we drop the index t:

$$p = \frac{1}{1+\rho} = \frac{\mu}{\lambda + \mu} \tag{5.2}$$

$$\rho = \frac{\lambda}{\mu} = \frac{1}{p} - 1 \tag{5.3}$$

To further simplify our discussion, let us assume that all nodes share the same behavior (i.e., their failure and repair rates, respectively, are identical).[3]

As a result of these simplifications we get a uniform formula of the availability for all schemes differentiated in read and write accesses where the formula's main parameter is the degree of replication (i.e., the number n of physical replicas of the data blocks). For instance, $A^r_{\mathrm{WARA}}(n)$ denotes the availability for read accesses under the write-all-read-any scheme with n replicas. Analogously, $A^w_{\mathrm{WARA}}(n)$ denotes the corresponding availability for write accesses. For some of the schemes (e.g., the majority consensus (MC) scheme), read and write have the same availability. In this case we simple write $A_{\mathrm{MC}}(n)$.

The availability can be understood as a value for measuring whether a read or a write access to a data block is successful (as seen from the outside). If we want to model also the fact that a read or write access to a data block is successful for a particular node in the network then we must multiply the given availability with the probability for this node to successfully perform the request (i.e., the node must be up and running and able to contact the

[3] For some of the schemes that we will discuss (for instance, weighted voting and both hierarchical voting schemes), this assumption will mask potential advantages because these schemes may exploit exactly these different node behaviors.

relevant subsystems). In most of the following cases we give the availability without considering a particular accessing node.

Nonreplicated case. The availability analysis for the nonreplicated case is simple and can be seen as a reference case: the data block is available if the node possessing the data block is usable for accesses. Thus we get

$$A_{\mathrm{NR}} = A_{\mathrm{NR}}(1) = p = \frac{1}{1+\rho} \tag{5.4}$$

In the following charts of the availability analysis, the nonreplicated case is plotted with a dotted line. In these charts we will vary the quotient ρ from 0 to 0.5. The smallest value, $\rho = 0$, characterizes nodes that do not crash and are available for accesses at all times. The highest value, $\rho = 0.5$, characterizes nodes that, on the average, crash once per hour and need half an hour for repair (reliable network links provided).

5.2 Voting Schemes

Voting schemes provide pessimistic concurrency control. There is a trade-off between the overhead for the voting protocols and the obtainable (high) availability. Therefore, voting schemes are especially useful if the access granularity is coarse, i.e., data blocks of at least some kilobytes. The origins of the voting schemes can be found in distributed file and data base systems; see, for instance, Cosmos (Walpole et al. 1990), Eden (Almes et al. 1985), VAXclusters (Kronenberg et al. 1986). Although we see great opportunities, in groupware systems only very few implementations are known so far; see, for instance, Iris (Borghoff and Teege 1993b).

We start our discussion of voting schemes with the variants emphasized in Fig. 5.4.

Terms and definitions. Accessing a (replicated) data block involves a set N of responsible nodes. That a node is responsible for a data block access is not directly related to the fact that this node has a replica of the data block in question (in most cases it will indeed have a replica but the reverse could also be true, as we will see). Rather, all nodes in N possess the right to vote for a data block.

Definition 5.2.1 (Votum and Quorum). *The votum for a desired access to a logical data block is defined as the sum of votes from the set of nodes that have voted for the desired access, i.e., the sum of votes from the set of nodes that could have been reached over the network, that are up and running at the time of the access, and that have no lock on their local physical data block replica and no other objection (e.g., denial of access due to insufficient access rights) that would prohibit the desired access.*

The obtained votum is called successful if the sum of votes from the set of nodes that have voted for the desired access is equal to or greater than a

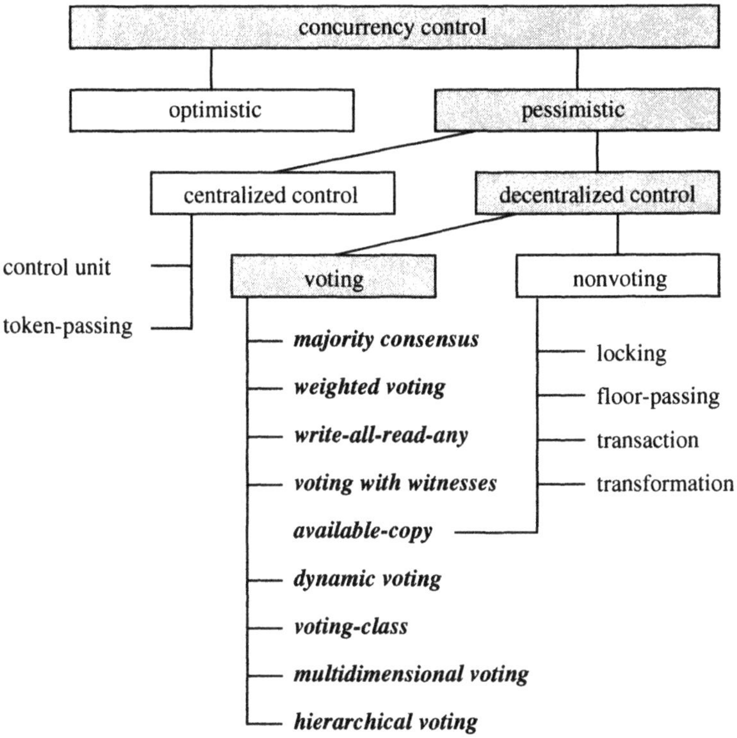

The available-copy scheme is discussed here for reasons of completeness. It is not a voting scheme in the purist sense because the voting phase is omitted. Therefore, it has been classified as a nonvoting scheme with decentralized control.

Fig. 5.4. Classification of concurrency control approaches: voting schemes

lower bound QU. This lower boundary is called a quorum. With a successful votum the desired access can be fulfilled in principle. We say "in principle" because nodes that have voted for the desired access could become unavailable – due to a node crash or some link failures – at the time when the access to the data block should be performed. Recall that updates to replicated data blocks follow a transactional multiphase commit protocol where the collection of votes falls into the first phase, also called the prepare-to-commit phase.

The choice of the quorum QU must support the multiple-reader-single-writer strategy and must guarantee that among the nodes that have allowed the access there is at least one node with the most up-to-date physical replica of the desired logical data block.

In addition, the procedure for obtaining a successful votum has to fulfill the following:

1. In the presence of network partitioning, the procedure must prohibit diverging parallel "consistencies" within the partitions.

2. In the presence of link failures and node crashes, the procedure should be fault-tolerant (i.e., it should allow a restricted continuation of accesses as long as the consistency of the logical data blocks is unharmed).

After a short discussion of some of the most important replication and concurrency control schemes, we evaluate their availability. To simplify the evaluation we start with the assumption that links are fully reliable, i.e., there is no network partitioning – although most of the schemes would tolerate failures of this kind to some extent. The only considered failures are node crashes. Crashed nodes immediately start their repair phase. Repair processes at different crashed nodes run in parallel. Moreover, we assume that the repair processes try to update the out-of-date data blocks of the crashed nodes. These attempts cannot always be successful. It could happen that no node with a needed up-to-date data block is available at the time of the repair.

5.2.1 Majority consensus

For a replicated data base, Thomas (1979) developed a scheme based on majority consensus (MC).

Main idea. Thomas gives each node that possesses a replica a right to vote. In his majority consensus scheme, a votum is successful if at least a majority of nodes with a right to vote have voted for the desired access.

For the lower boundary, the quorum QU, we can thus formulate:

$$QU = \begin{cases} \frac{n}{2} + 1 & \text{, if } n \text{ is even} \\ \frac{n+1}{2} & \text{, if } n \text{ is odd} \end{cases} \tag{5.5}$$

Example (Fully connected network). Consider the fully connected network depicted in Fig. 5.5. Let the nodes $n_1, \ldots, n_4$ possess a replica of all data blocks. Obviously, a successful votum needs at least three votes (i.e., $QU = 3$).

Coterie. Garcia-Molina and Barbara (1984) introduce the term coterie. They define a coterie[4] as the minimal sets of nodes that can support a successful access to the replicated data blocks.

Definition 5.2.2 (Coterie). *A set C of node sets is called a coterie if the following three conditions are true:*

1. *Empty set condition: If c_i is a node set in C then c_i is not empty.*
2. *Intersection condition: If c_i and c_j are node sets in C then their intersection is not empty, i.e., both node sets c_i and c_j have at least one node in common.*

[4] Coterie is a French word meaning a "clique" or a close circle of friends who share a common interest. Here the common interest can be interpreted as the interest of supporting successful accesses to replicated data blocks.

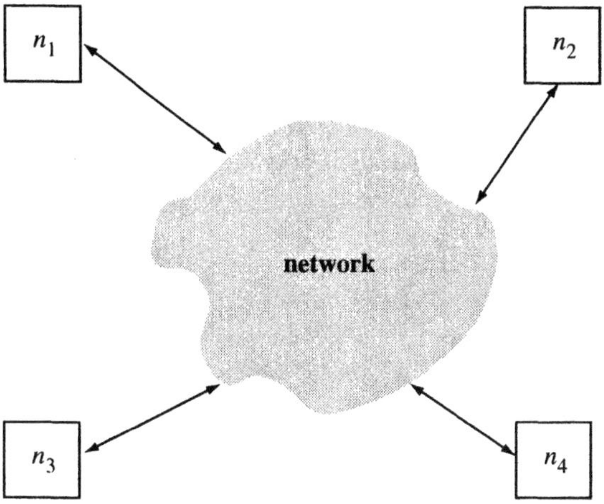

Fig. 5.5. Fully connected network

3. *Minimality condition: There are no node set pairs c_i and c_j in C such that $c_i \subset c_j$.*

As we will see in the next example, the intersection condition prohibits conflicting accesses to the same data block whereas the minimality condition avoids the handling of redundant information in a coterie.

Example (Coterie). Let us consider again the situation as depicted in Fig. 5.5. Here, we can define the following coterie C_1:

$$C_1 = \left\{ \begin{array}{l} \{n_1, n_2, n_3\}, \{n_1, n_2, n_4\}, \\ \{n_1, n_3, n_4\}, \{n_2, n_3, n_4\} \end{array} \right\} \tag{5.6}$$

Each coterie element in C_1 is a set of three nodes (i.e., a majority). Node sets that contain a coterie element like $\{n_1, n_2, n_3, n_4\}$ are trivially a majority, too. Due to the minimality condition, such supersets are not stored in a coterie.

If the coterie is known at each accessing node, the coterie can be used to determine whether a successful votum has been obtained. Instead of counting the number of nodes that have voted for the access, the accessing node could check whether the nodes that have voted for the access build a set that is an element or a superset of a coterie element. In this case a successful votum is obtained. The desired access can be performed.

Nodes that are not a member of any coterie element are not considered for the votum. Likewise, a right to vote can be given to a particular node by simply adding this node to a coterie element.

This approach of defining a coterie is helpful for a variety of voting schemes and provides the main motivation for the development of the multidimensional voting scheme that we will discuss in Sect. 5.2.8.

Availability. We calculate the availability with the help of a state diagram and the knowledge of the probability of the system being in one of the possible states. Knowing the voting scheme's characteristics (i.e., votum and quorum), we can decide whether a state represents a situation where a successful votum could be obtained (in principle) or not. The availability is then given as the sum of the probabilities of all states where such a successful votum could be obtained.

In the following state diagrams we always emphasize states that represent a situation where a successful votum can be obtained by gray circles.

Figure 5.6 shows the state diagram of the majority consensus scheme. We denote with Z_i, $i \in \{0, \ldots, n\}$, a state where i nodes with a right to vote are available.

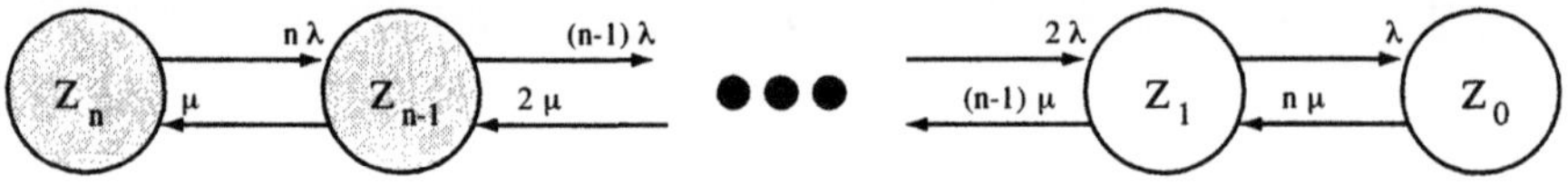

failure rate λ
repair rate μ

Fig. 5.6. State diagram of the majority consensus scheme

Due to the equilibrium we can formulate the following n equations for the $n+1$ states:

(1) $n\lambda Z_n = \mu Z_{n-1}$
(2) $(n-1)\lambda Z_{n-1} = 2\mu Z_{n-2}$
(3) $(n-2)\lambda Z_{n-2} = 3\mu Z_{n-3}$
$\vdots$
(n) $\lambda Z_1 = n\mu Z_0$

Since we deal with probabilities, we can add another equation:

(n+1) $Z_0 + Z_1 + \ldots + Z_n = 1$.

Fortunately, we now have $n+1$ linear-independent equations with $n+1$ variables. Immediately, we get:

$$A_{\mathrm{MC}}(n) = \sum_{j=\lfloor \frac{n}{2} \rfloor + 1}^{n} \binom{n}{j} p^j (1-p)^{n-j} = \sum_{j=\lfloor \frac{n}{2} \rfloor + 1}^{n} \binom{n}{j} \frac{\rho^{n-j}}{(1+\rho)^n} \quad (5.7)$$

Figure 5.7 plots the availability of the majority consensus scheme for different values of n. We can detect that the availability of the majority consensus scheme for an even n is lower than the corresponding availability for the odd $n' = n-1$.

We can improve the situation as follows.

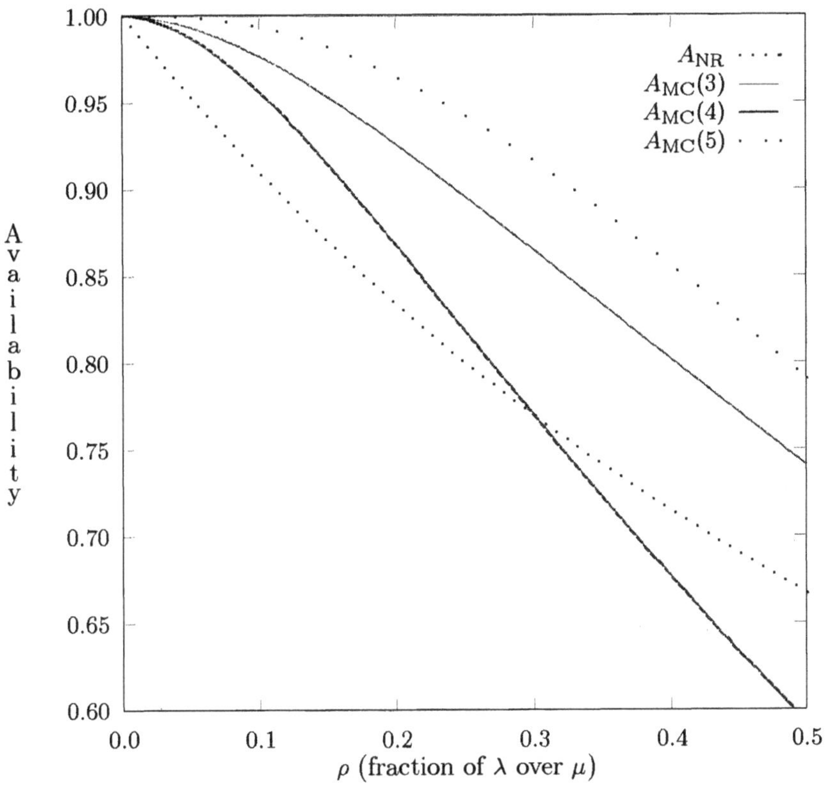

Fig. 5.7. Availability of the majority consensus scheme

Majority consensus with primary site. Majority consensus with primary site works just like the standard scheme, except that it helps to "break the tie" when the votum is obtained from exactly half of the nodes with a right to vote. The final ballot is given by a preselected node (with a right to vote), the so-called primary site.

The votum is successful

1. if at least a majority of nodes with a right to vote have voted for the desired access (as in the standard majority consensus scheme), or
2. if exactly half of the nodes with a right to vote have voted for the desired access and the primary site is one of these voters.

Obviously we only need to preselect a primary site if the number of nodes with a right to vote is even. For an odd number, there is no improvement as far as the availability is concerned.

The network partition that contains the nodes (with or without the primary site) which help to obtain a successful votum is also called the quorum partition.

Availability. For an even n, the availability of the majority consensus scheme with primary site is increased, compared to the standard scheme without a primary site, by the following factor of the binomial distribution:

$$\frac{1}{2}\binom{n}{\frac{n}{2}}\frac{\rho^{\frac{n}{2}}}{(1+\rho)^n} \tag{5.8}$$

In sum, we get for an even n:

$$A_{\mathrm{MCPS}}(n) = \sum_{j=\frac{n}{2}+1}^{n}\binom{n}{j}\frac{\rho^{n-j}}{(1+\rho)^n} + \binom{n}{\frac{n}{2}}\frac{\rho^{\frac{n}{2}}}{2(1+\rho)^n} \tag{5.9}$$

From Equation (5.9) we can derive:

$$A_{\mathrm{MCPS}}(2k) = A_{\mathrm{MC}}(2k-1) \tag{5.10}$$

The availability of the majority consensus scheme with primary site and an even number of nodes with a right to vote is equal to the availability of the standard majority consensus scheme and the next smaller odd number of nodes with a right to vote. For reasons of availability and simplicity of the voting protocol, we might prefer an odd number of nodes with a right to vote. However, the optimal file allocation (see Sect. 1.7.4) may force us to install an even number of replicas, and, consequently, an even number of nodes with a right to vote.

An improvement in flexibility can be reached with the weighted voting scheme that is discussed next.

5.2.2 Weighted voting

Gifford (1979) improved the majority consensus scheme by giving each relevant node not only a right to vote but also a weight for its vote. The weights can be different for the individual nodes with a right to vote. With weighted voting, we now can favor nodes and even install nodes with zero-votes.

In the following let $w(n)$ be the weight of the vote of node n with:

$$w(n) \in \{0, 1, 2, \ldots\}, \ \forall n \in N \tag{5.11}$$

Let the sum of all these weights be W defined as:

$$W = \sum_{n \in N} w(n) \tag{5.12}$$

The majority consensus scheme did not distinguish between a read and a write access. With the weighted voting scheme, we are now able to easily tell a lower boundary for read accesses, called a read quorum, from a lower boundary for write accesses, called a write quorum. For a read access, the obtained votum is successful if the sum of weights of votes from the set of nodes that have voted for a desired read access is equal to or greater than the read quorum QU_r. For a write access, the obtained votum is successful if the corresponding write quorum QU_w has been reached.

The read quorum QU_r and the write quorum QU_w can be different but have to meet the following two conditions:

$$QU_r + QU_w > W \tag{5.13}$$

$$2 \times QU_w > W \tag{5.14}$$

Both conditions support the multiple-reader-single-writer strategy and guarantee consistency among the replicated data blocks. If we choose the same read and write quorum, we get:

$$QU_r = QU_w = \begin{cases} \frac{W}{2} + 1 & \text{, if } W \text{ is even} \\ \frac{W+1}{2} & \text{, if } W \text{ is odd} \end{cases} \tag{5.15}$$

The weigthed voting scheme has several advantages:

1. *Zero-votes:* If we store a replica at a node but give this node a weight for its vote of zero then we install so-called weak representatives or temporary copies. These nodes change neither the read quorum nor the write quorum. Therefore, we can dynamically add or remove replicas at weak representatives without influencing the overall voting behavior. Still, these temporary copies can participate in any votum with the consequence of improving the performance – especially for read accesses – if an up-to-date "nearby" weak representative can satisfy the desired read access.
   If nodes are less reliable than others, we can give them zero-votes, or, at most, votes with a small weight. If these nodes crash then the loss of weight is small, and the probability of obtaining a successful votum with the remaining nodes might still be high. We can also directly favor particular nodes in the network and give them a right to vote with a high weight. In an extreme case, we could configure the scheme for a CSCW application in such a way that the group leader's node has to participate in any successful votum. Consequently, his local physical replica would always be up-to-date and could be seen as a "reference replica" for backups of the group documents.
2. *Freedom of choice for the read quorum and the write quorum:* As we mentioned earlier, read quorum and write quorum may differ as long as they meet the two stated conditions. This gives a freedom of choice for the configuration of the system. For instance, we would choose a small read quorum (in an extreme case, we could choose $QU_r = 1$) if data blocks are more often read than updated. On the other hand, if updates are the preferred access mode, then we can go as low as $\frac{W}{2} + 1$ (if W is even) or $\frac{W+1}{2}$ (if W is odd) for the write quorum.
   It is beyond the scope of this book to look into optimal quorum sizes. The interested reader is referred to the literature at the end of the chapter.

3. *Odd W:* As we have seen in the discussion of the majority consensus scheme, we prefer odd numbers while voting. It is also advantageous if the sum of all weights W is odd. The weighted voting scheme can bring this about without touching the number of physical replicas, as shown in the next example.

Example (Odd sum of all weights). Again, a replica is stored at the nodes $n_1, \ldots, n_4$. If we give each node a vote with weight 1 and use the same quorum for read and write accesses then every successful votum needs three votes. Consequently, we get the coterie C_1 (see Equation 5.6), again.

If we now increase the weight of the vote of node n_1 to 2, we get $W = 5$. Obviously, each successful votum still needs three votes (i.e., all node sets in C_1 still reach a successful votum).

The vote by node n_1 and another node n_i, $i = 2, \ldots, 4$, are, however, now sufficient to obtain a successful votum.

We get the following improved coterie:

$$C_2 = \Big\{\{n_1, n_2\}, \{n_1, n_3\}, \{n_1, n_4\}, \{n_2, n_3, n_4\}\Big\} \tag{5.16}$$

There is no disadvantage to increasing the weight of node n_1 to 2. Rather, the availability (i.e., the probability of obtaining a successful votum), has been increased. Performance can thus also be improved (Ahamad and Ammar 1989).

5.2.3 Write-all-read-any

Without loss of generality, let the weight of each vote be 1.

Write-all-read-any (WARA), also known as read-one-write-all (ROWA) can be seen as an extreme case of weighted voting:

- $QU_r = 1$
- $QU_w = n$

If read accesses dominate and network links are highly reliable (see Sect. 3.2 for more details) then write-all-read-any is an appropriate scheme for replication and concurrency control (Gelenbe 1985).

Availability. For the availability of write-all-read-any we have to distinguish between the availability for read and write accesses:

$$A^r_{\text{WARA}}(n) = 1 - (1-p)^n = 1 - \left(\frac{\rho}{(1+\rho)}\right)^n \tag{5.17}$$

$$A^w_{\text{WARA}}(n) = p^n = \frac{1}{(1+\rho)^n} \tag{5.18}$$

Figure 5.8 plots the availability of the write-all-read-any scheme for different values of n.

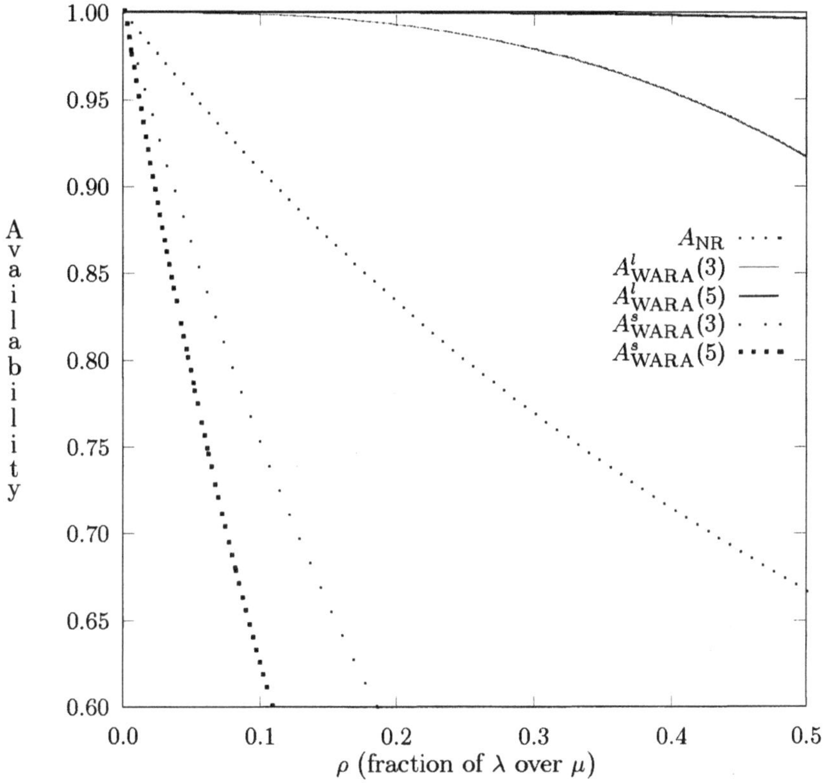

Fig. 5.8. Availability of the write-all-read-any scheme

5.2.4 Voting with witnesses

Pâris (1990) enriched the weighted voting scheme by introducing so-called witnesses.

Main idea. A witness is a node with a right to vote that does not possess a replica of the data blocks it is voting upon. Instead, a witness just knows the minimal information needed for the voting process (i.e., the locking state and the version number of the data block it is voting for, as well as the weight of its vote).

Obviously, a witness needs less storage space than a node that possesses a full replica. Since a witness has no data content, "real" accesses to the data block of a witness cannot be carried out. What is, therefore the advantage?

As far as availability is concerned, a witness can bring almost the same improvements as a node that possesses a full replica. Let us look at the following example.

Example (Voting with a witness). Consider the situation of Fig. 5.9: Here, the nodes n_1 and n_2 have a full replica of data block k. Node n_1 has this data block with version number 5 and content ‘XX’ whereas node n_2 has the same data block with version number 6 and content ‘YY’. Node n_3 is a witness. It just knows that data block k has version number 6. It knows nothing about the content of the data block.

For this example, let the weight of the votes for each of the three nodes be 1, and let the read and the write quorum be identical (i.e., 2).

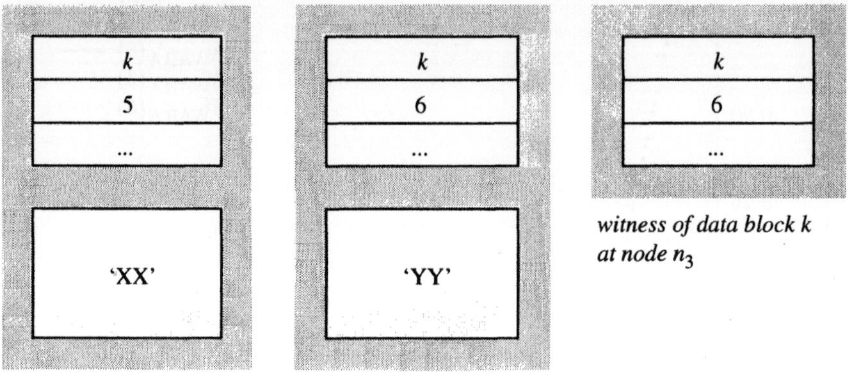

witness of data block k at node n_3

data block k at node n_1 *data block k at node n_2*

Fig. 5.9. Use of a witness

A votum is successful if

- all three nodes or
- the witness and node n_2 or
- the nodes n_1 and n_2

vote for the desired access. The up-to-date data content ‘YY’ can be identified. In the case of a read access, the data block is, of course read from node n_2.

As previously stated a witness can bring about almost the same degree of improvement as a node possessing a full replica. This becomes evident when we look at the following situation after collecting the votes for a read access. Imagine that only node n_1 and the witness have voted for the desired read access (assume node n_2 to be unavailable). Although the votum could be seen as successfully obtained (the read quorum has been reached), the accessing site can only detect that version number 5 is obsolete. Accessing the data block content is not possible.

In other words, the read quorum is sufficient to support the multiple-reader-single-writer strategy and to guarantee that among the nodes that have allowed the access there is at least one node with the most up-to-date version number of the physical replica of the desired logical data block. The read quorum is not sufficient to guarantee that among the nodes that have allowed the access there is at least one node with the most up-to-date data block content. What we would need – besides a sufficient quorum – is a necessary quorum that would help to guarantee a successful access once the votum has been obtained. We will come back to that in Sect. 5.3.1.

Witnesses "tip the scales" as we have seen in our example. It is not realistic, however, to replace many nodes containing full replicas with witnesses. If this were attempted, the availability for read accesses would drop dramatically. If storage space is an issue, better schemes exist. We will discuss one of them in Sect. 5.3.1.

Availability. At first glance voting with witnesses looks like weighted voting. The situation becomes different in quorum partitions where the witness is the only node with an up-to-date version number of a data block in question. In this situation a successful update can be allowed for write accesses since the accessing site is aware of the up-to-date version number, for write accesses we can allow a successful update in this situation. Thus, the availability for write accesses is as high as that for the standard weighted voting scheme.

As mentioned earlier, we cannot perform a read access here. Consequently, the availability for read accesses is lower than the corresponding availability for the standard weighted voting scheme.

Let $A_{\mathrm{WIT}}(n-m,m)$ denote the availability of voting with witnesses where m witnesses and $n-m$ full replicas have been installed. It is rather complicated to give a closed formula for $A_{\mathrm{WIT}}(n-m,m)$. Therefore, we limit ourselves to the special case $A_{\mathrm{WIT}}(2,1)$ where two full replicas and a single witness have been installed. To compute the availability, we want to solve a system of equations (similar to the one of majority consensus) that we derive from a state diagram.

Jajodia and Mutchler (1987b) propose a notation for the different states, namely "Z_{axb}" where a and b are integer variables and x is a character variable.

The variable a indicates how many nodes with a full replica are available, i.e., a may take the values 0 (neither of the two nodes with a full replica is available), 1 (one of the two nodes with a full replica is available), or 2 (both nodes with a full replica are available).

The variable b indicates whether the witness is available ($b = 1$) or not ($b = 0$).

The variable x describes the state of the version numbers of the two nodes with a full replica: $x = S$ indicating that both full replicas have the same version number, $x = D$ indicating that their version numbers are different, and, finally, $x = X$ indicating that their version numbers are different and that only the obsolete full replica is available.

In Fig. 5.10, the state Z_{2S1} denotes the situation where both full replicas and the witness are available. A crash of the witness leads to state Z_{2S0}.

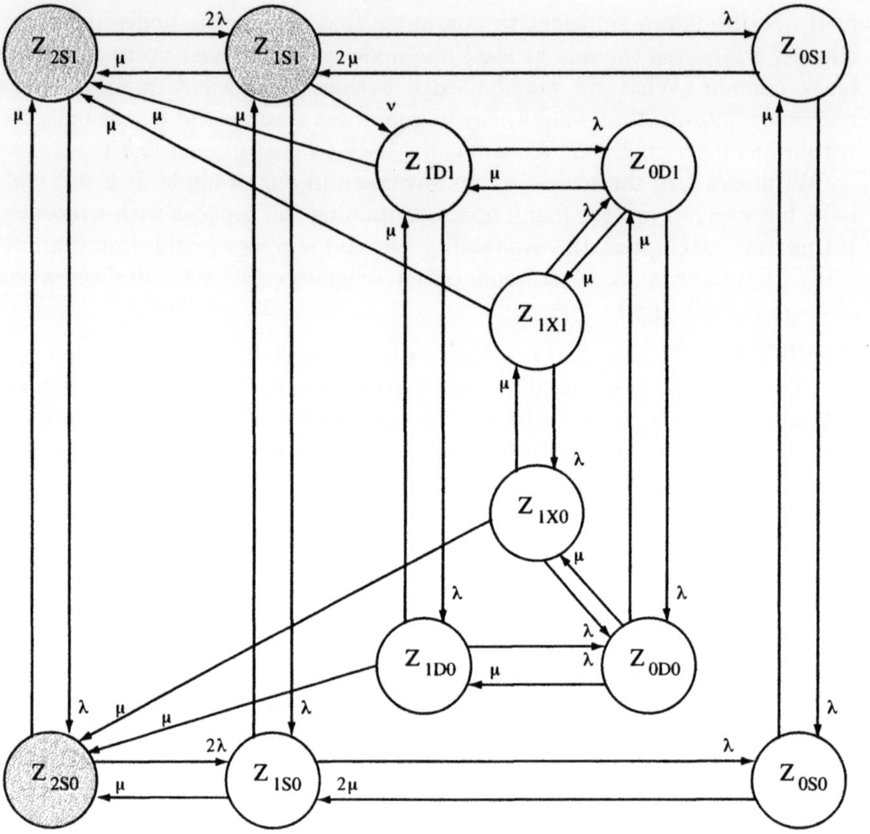

failure rate λ
repair rate μ
update rate ν

Fig. 5.10. State diagram of the voting scheme with two full replicas and a witness

The crash of a node with a full replica before the witness recovers leads to state Z_{1S0}. The logical data blocks are no longer available here. A successful votum cannot be obtained. The crash of the second node with a full replica then leads to state Z_{0S0}.

The recovery of the witness in state Z_{1S0} leads to state Z_{1S1} whereas the recovery of a crashed node with a full replica leads to state Z_{2S0}.

If in state Z_{2S1} one of the nodes with the full replica crashes state Z_{1S1} is reached. A successful update leads to state Z_{1D1} with the update rate ν. In this state, a recovery of the crashed node (including a repair update) brings the system to its initial state Z_{2S1} whereas another crash leads either to Z_{1D0}

(crash of the witness) or Z_{0D1} (crash of the second node with a full replica), respectively. In both states, a successful votum cannot be obtained.

In state Z_{0D1}, a recovery of a crashed node with a full replica leads back to state Z_{1D1}, if the replica is up-to-date, or back to state Z_{1X1}, if the replica is obsolete.

From this state diagram we can extract a system of equations. The state transition from Z_{1S1} to Z_{1D1} is marked with ν, the update rate. Let ψ be defined as $\frac{\nu}{\mu}$. Furthermore, let p_{axb} denote the probability that the system is in state Z_{axb}.

With this we are able to formulate the availability of this scheme:

$$\begin{aligned} A_{\mathrm{WIT}_{\psi}}(2,1) &= p_{2S1} + p_{2S0} + p_{1S1} + p_{1D1} = \\ &= \frac{7\rho^3 + 18\rho^2 + 15\rho + 3}{3(\rho+1)^5} \\ &+ \frac{4\rho^5 + 18\rho^4 + 30\rho^3 + 18\rho^2}{3(2\rho^2 + \psi(3\rho+6) + 6\rho + 6)(\rho+1)^5} \end{aligned} \tag{5.19}$$

With $\psi \to \infty$ we get the limit:

$$A_{\mathrm{WIT}_{\to\infty}}(2,1) = \frac{7\rho^3 + 18\rho^2 + 15\rho + 3}{3(\rho+1)^5} \tag{5.20}$$

Figure 5.11 plots the availability of the voting scheme with two full replicas and a witness for different values of ψ. The chart shows that with increasing ψ the availability decreases. This is because an increased update rate increases the probability of the state transition from state Z_{1S1} to state Z_{1D1} with the consequence of a quicker arrival at unavailable states.

Voting with volatile witnesses. Since a witness knows only the minimal information needed for the voting process, witnesses easily fit into main memory. This is especially useful for diskless nodes. These witnesses are called volatile because a node crash destroys relevant state information kept by the witness for voting purposes (such as locking states and version numbers). After the node has recovered, the possibly reinstalled volatile witness is said to be in a state of temporary amnesia. It might have regained the knowledge of its right to vote with a given weight but it remains ignorant of the current locking states and version numbers of data blocks upon which it has a right to vote.

Let us now construct the state diagram for a voting scheme with two full replicas and a volatile witness. In contrast to the state diagram of the voting scheme with two full replicas and a standard witness, we get a slightly modified state diagram including two new states, namely Z_{1A} and Z_{0A}. These states represent situations where the volatile witness has been reinstalled after a crash but is still in a state of temporary amnesia. The volatile witness remains in this state until the next update is successfully performed (until

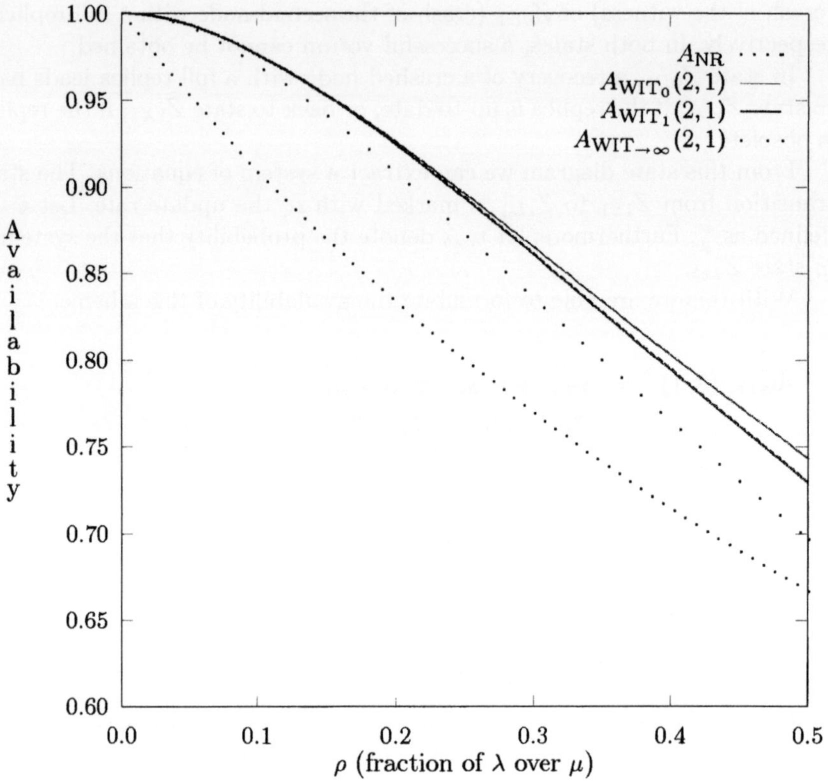

Fig. 5.11. Availability of the voting scheme with two full replicas and a witness

a successful votum has been obtained without its participation). In our setting this means that both nodes with full replicas must become available. Again, an update will then propagate the up-to-date state information to the volatile witness. The volatile witness leaves the state of temporary amnesia and becomes a proper volatile witness again (one which may participate in any forthcoming votum).

In addition, in the state diagram we can merge several states because they are marked with the same failure and repair transitions: The states Z_{1S0}, Z_{1D0} and Z_{1X0} are merged into the combined state Z_{1SDX0}. Moreover, the states Z_{0S0} and Z_{0D0} are merged into the combined state Z_{0SD0}.

Figure 5.12 shows the resulting state diagram of the voting scheme with two full replicas and a volatile witness.

Availability. The availability of the voting scheme with two full replicas and a volatile witness $A_{\mathrm{VWIT}_\psi}(2,1)$ is defined as:

$$A_{\mathrm{VWIT}_\psi}(2,1) \quad = \quad p_{2S1} + p_{2S0} + p_{1S1} + p_{1D1}$$

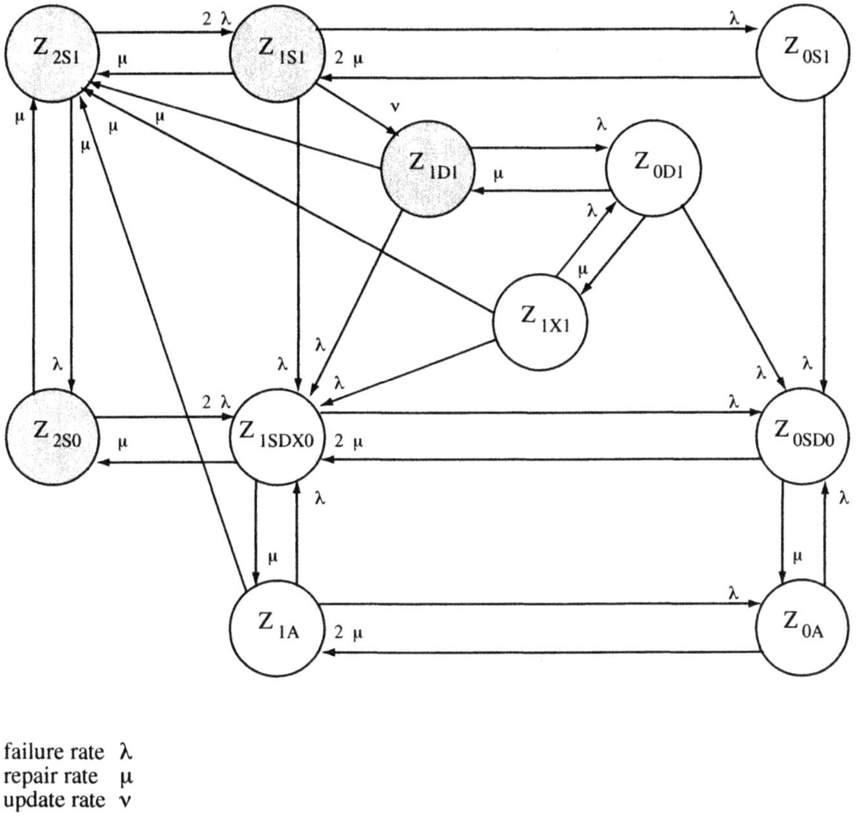

Fig. 5.12. State diagram of the voting scheme with two full replicas and a volatile witness

$$= \frac{4\rho^3 + 12\rho^2 + 11\rho + 2}{4\rho^5 + 16\rho^4 + 27\rho^3 + 24\rho^2 + 11\rho + 2} + \frac{2\rho^2}{(2\rho^2 + \psi(\rho+2) + 3\rho + 2)(2\rho^4 + 7\rho^3 + 9\rho^2 + 5\rho + 1)} \tag{5.21}$$

With $\psi \to \infty$ we get the limit:

$$A_{\text{VWIT}_{\to\infty}}(2,1) = \frac{4\rho^3 + 12\rho^2 + 11\rho + 2}{4\rho^5 + 16\rho^4 + 27\rho^3 + 24\rho^2 + 11\rho + 2} \tag{5.22}$$

To better compare our findings, Fig. 5.13 plots the availability of a voting scheme with

1. three full replicas,
2. two full replicas and a (standard) witness, and
3. two full replicas and a volatile witness.

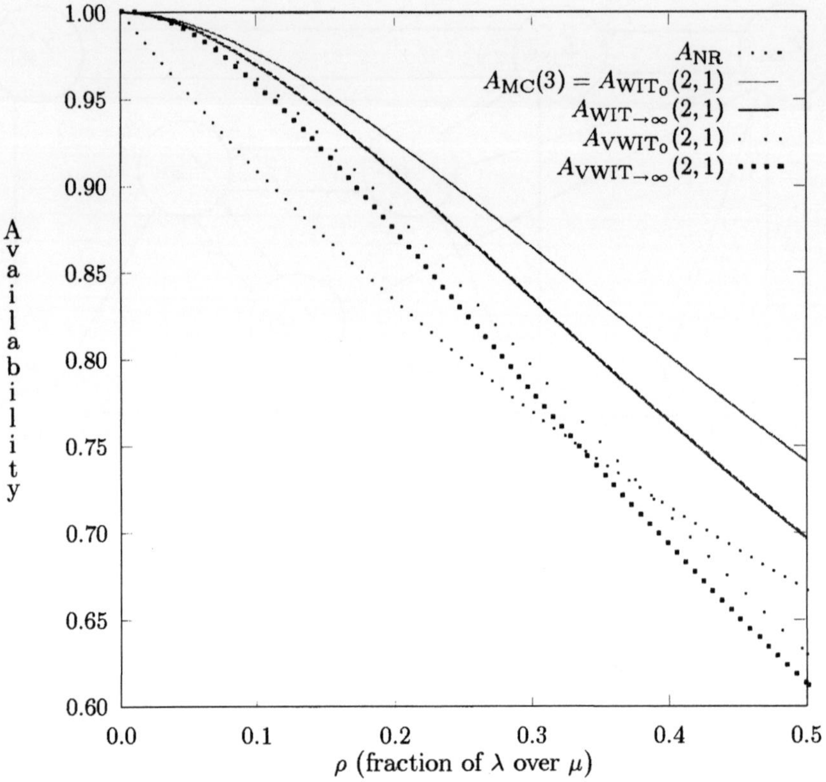

Fig. 5.13. Availability of the voting scheme with two full replicas and a volatile witness

Voting with witnesses and leading minority. The voting variants with witnesses discussed so far were too restrictive as far as the check of an obtained votum is concerned. Since each successful votum requires that at least one node with an up-to-date full replica votes for the desired access, we do not harm consistency if we treat the set of all nodes with an up-to-date full replica as if this set would possess the totality of all votes needed to obtain a successful votum. In the remainder of this section we call such a set a leading minority after the definition given by its inventor J. Pâris (1990). His implementation of a voting scheme with witnesses and leading minority requires each node with a full replica to carry – besides locking states and version numbers – an additional state variable, called update full replica cardinality.[5]

The update full replica cardinality maintains the number of nodes with an up-to-date full replica. The collection of a successful votum is heavily

[5] The term update full replica cardinality is used analogously to the term update sites cardinality which will be introduced on p. 249.

dependent upon the maximum value of the update full replica cardinality that was received while votes were being collected. In order to determine whether the accessing node belongs to the quorum partition (i.e., whether or not a desired access can be performed or not), the following algorithm is applied. Without loss of generality, assume that nodes with a full replica as well as witnesses have a vote with weight 1:

1. The accessing node (or better, the subsystem that transparently manages the desired access) extracts from the given vote the version numbers of all available nodes (nodes with a full replica and witnesses).
2. The accessing node extracts from the given vote the update full replica cardinalities of all available nodes with a full replica.
3. Let vn_{max} be the maximal version number obtained by the accessing node.
   The accessing node constructs two sets:
   a) Let NF_{max} be the set of available nodes with a full replica and version number vn_{max}.
   b) Let NW_{max} be the set of available witnesses with version number vn_{max}.
4. Furthermore, let rc_{max} be the maximal update full replica cardinality obtained by the accessing node.
5. The votum is successful if
   - the needed quorum QU has been reached and at least one node with an up-to-date full replica participates in the votum, i.e.: $|NF_{max} \cup NW_{max}| \geq QU$ and $NF_{max} \neq \emptyset$.
   - the needed quorum QU has not been reached but all nodes with an up-to-date full replica (a leading minority!) participate in the votum, i.e.: $|NF_{max} \cup NW_{max}| < QU$ and $|NF_{max}| = rc_{max}$.

   Otherwise, the votum is not successful (the accessing node does not belong to the quorum partition).

Availability. If a votum is successful (if a leading minority votes for the desired access) then availability is increased compared to the other voting schemes with witnesses. In an extreme case, a single node with an up-to-date full replica could make up a successful votum.

In the following we consider a voting scheme with

1. two full replicas and a (standard) witness and leading minority, and
2. two full replicas and a volatile witness and leading minority.

In the case of two full replicas and a (standard) witness, the introduction of a leading minority leads to the state diagram of Fig. 5.14. It is especially interesting to note that Z_{1D0} has become an additional available state.

For the availability we get:

$$A_{\mathrm{WITLM}_\psi}(2,1) = A_{\mathrm{WIT}_\psi}(2,1) + p_{1D0}$$

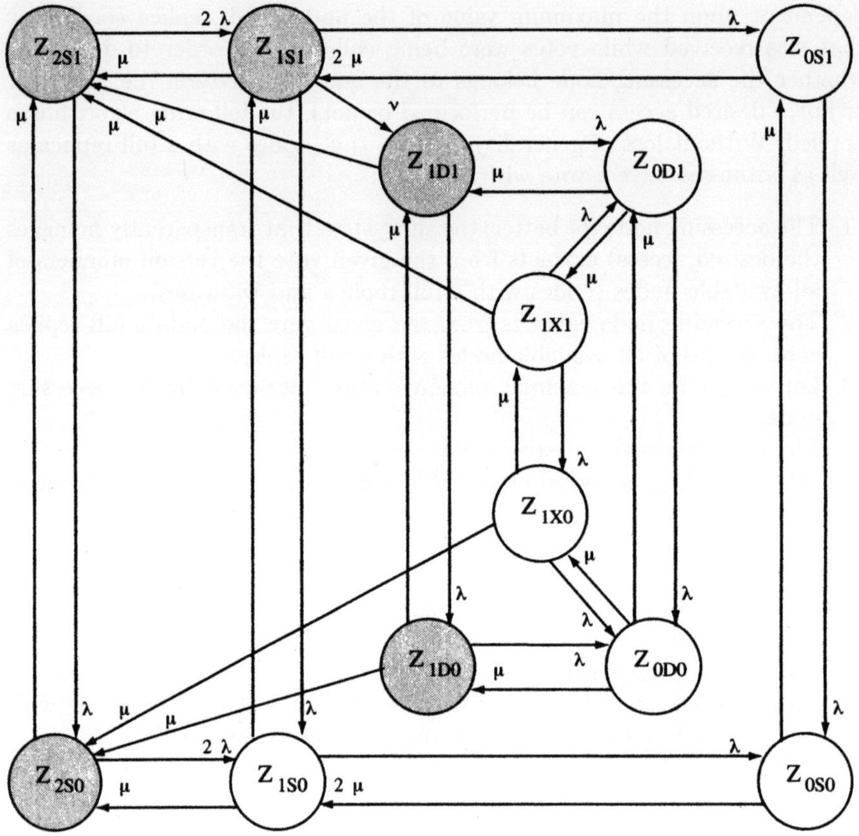

failure rate λ
repair rate μ
update rate ν

Fig. 5.14. State diagram of the voting scheme with two full replicas and a witness and leading minority

$$= \frac{2\rho^3 + 9\rho^2 + 12\rho + 3}{3(\rho+1)^4} - \frac{4\rho^5 + 12\rho^4 + 12\rho^3}{3(2\rho^2 + \psi(3\rho+6) + 6\rho + 6)(\rho+1)^4} \quad (5.23)$$

With $\psi \to \infty$ we get the limit:

$$A_{\text{WITLM}_{\to\infty}}(2,1) = \frac{2\rho^3 + 9\rho^2 + 12\rho + 3}{3(\rho+1)^4} \quad (5.24)$$

In the case of two full replicas and a volatile witness, the introduction of a leading minority leads to the state diagram of Fig. 5.15.

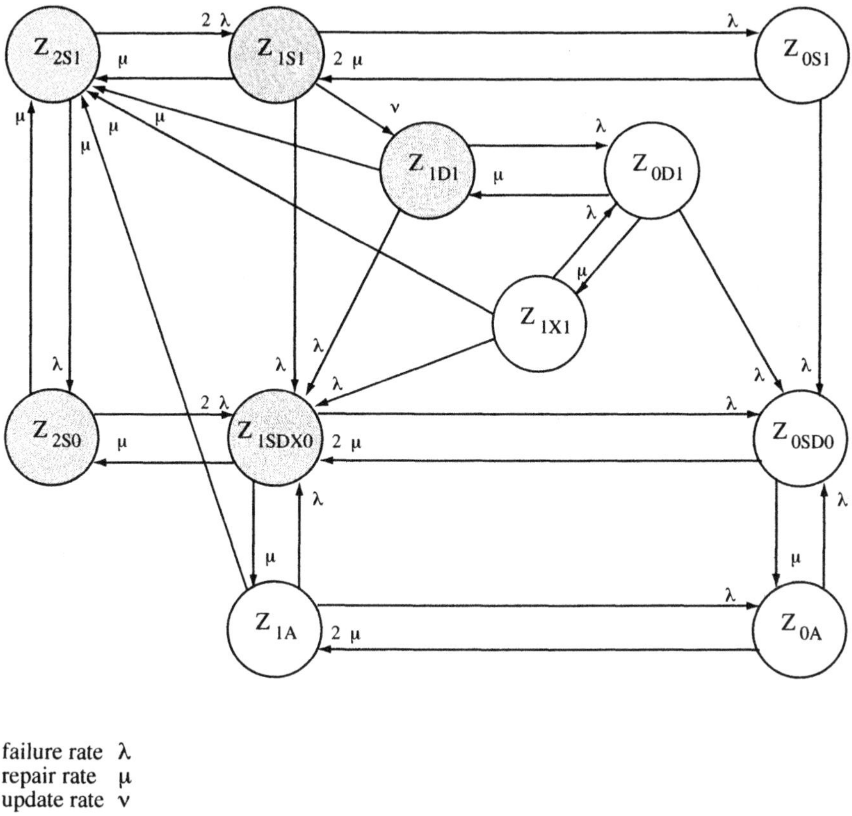

Fig. 5.15. State diagram of the voting scheme with two full replicas and a volatile witness and leading minority

Since state Z_{1D0} and, therefore, the combined state Z_{1SDX0} has become an additional available state, the reinstalled volatile witness spends less time on the average in the state of temporary amnesia.

For the availability we get:

$$A_{\mathrm{VWITLM}_{\psi}}(2,1) = \frac{2\rho^2+4\rho+1}{(\rho+1)^4} - \frac{2\rho^4+5\rho^3+2\rho^2}{(2\rho^2+\psi(\rho+2)+3\rho+2)(\rho+1)^4} \tag{5.25}$$

With $\psi \to \infty$ we get the limit:

$$A_{\mathrm{VWITLM}_{\to\infty}}(2,1) = \frac{2\rho^2+4\rho+1}{(\rho+1)^4} \tag{5.26}$$

To better compare our findings, Fig. 5.16 plots the availability of a voting scheme with

1. three full replicas,
2. two full replicas and a (standard) witness and leading minority, and
3. two full replicas and a volatile witness and leading minority.

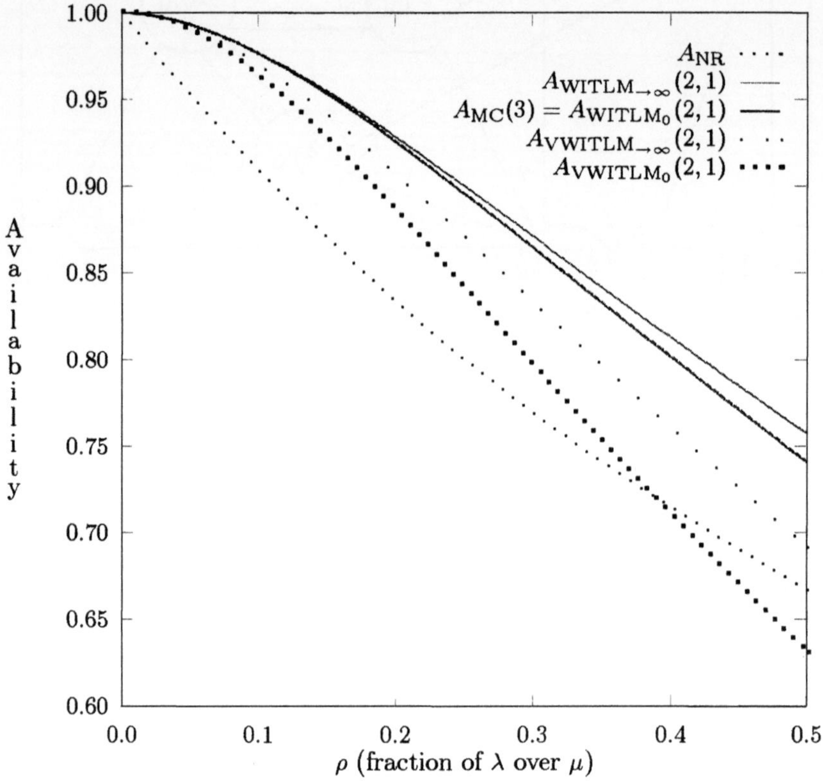

Fig. 5.16. Availability of the voting scheme with two full replicas and a volatile witness and leading minority

Additional remarks. In contrast to $A_{WIT_\psi}(2,1)$ and $A_{VWIT_\psi}(2,1)$ that are both decreasing functions in ρ and ψ, $A_{WITLM_\psi}(2,1)$ and $A_{VWITLM_\psi}(2,1)$ are decreasing functions in ρ but increasing functions in ψ. In this case, a logical data block that gets updated quite frequently has a higher availability than a data block that is rarely modified. This observation justifies periodically generated "dummy" write accesses.

A quite surprising result of voting with witnesses is the following (see Fig. 5.16): Paradoxically, for every $\psi > 0$, the availability $A_{WITLM_\psi}(2,1)$ of a voting scheme with two full replicas and a witness and leading minority is higher than the availability $A_{MC}(3)$ of the majority consensus scheme with three full replicas. This is because a leading minority is a dynamic set. Its cardinality varies over time. As we have seen before, in an extreme situation a single node with an up-to-date full replica is sufficient to obtain a successful votum. On the other hand, for a successful votum in the majority consensus scheme, a rigid majority of at least two nodes must vote for the desired access.

Ghosts and bystanders. Similar to the idea of witnesses are ghosts (v. Renesse and Tanenbaum 1988) and bystanders (Pâris 1989). In contrast to witnesses that are preinstalled, ghosts and bystanders temporarily take over voting responsibilities when nodes with full replicas crash. As with witnesses, they do not store data contents. Consequently, "real" accesses to the data blocks of a ghost or a bystander cannot be carried out. To avoid situations where the given read quorum is no longer sufficient for successful accesses, ghosts and bystanders are not allowed to vote for read accesses.

5.2.5 Available-copy

The available-copy scheme has been designed for decentralized concurrency control (Bernstein and Goodman 1984, Bernstein et al. 1987).

Although the available-copy scheme is not a voting scheme in the purist sense, we shall nevertheless use the terminology introduced for voting schemes.

Main idea. A votum for a read access is successful if at least one of the nodes with a replica votes for the desired access. As a consequence, the read availability is quite high. Correspondingly, in a successful votum for a write access all nodes with a replica should participate. This would match exactly the characteristics of write-all-read-any. However, the available-copy scheme allows a votum for a write access to be successful if all *available* nodes with a replica vote for the desired access.

Without loss of generality, let the weight of each vote be 1. In our notation we can state:

- $QU_r = 1$
- $1 \leq QU_w \leq n$

Since QU_w might be smaller than n, this strategy causes problems when network partitions occur. Multiple divergent versions of the same logical data block might be the result. Read accesses could return obsolete data blocks.

Therefore, the available-copy scheme makes the following assumptions:

- There are no network partitions. If a node is unavailable, it is crashed.
- While a repaired node recovers it does not vote for accesses until all data blocks of the local physical replica are once again up-to-date.
  For details of the relevant recovery protocols the interested reader is referred to the literature at the end of the chapter.

Availability. For the availability of the available-copy scheme we immediately get as approximation:

$$A_{\mathrm{AC}}(n) = \sum_{j=1}^{n} \binom{n}{j} p^j (1-p)^{n-j} = \sum_{j=1}^{n} \binom{n}{j} \frac{\rho^{n-j}}{(1+\rho)^n} \tag{5.27}$$

Why is this an approximation? Consider the admittedly extreme situation where all nodes with a replica have crashed. A later access might not be successful although some of the crashed nodes may have meanwhile been repaired (but not fully recovered due to the problem of not being able to update their local replica).

In the following sections we will discuss solutions to this problem, namely the naive available-copy scheme as well as the available-copy scheme with was-available set.

Naive available-copy scheme. In the above mentioned extreme situation where all nodes with a replica have crashed, the naive available-copy scheme (NAC) waits until all these nodes are once again repaired. The recovery process is then able to update all obsolete data blocks at all nodes (here, we could imagine a voting scheme to detect which nodes have up-to-date data blocks and which do not).

Figure 5.17 shows the resulting state diagram. Again, available states are emphasized with gray circles.

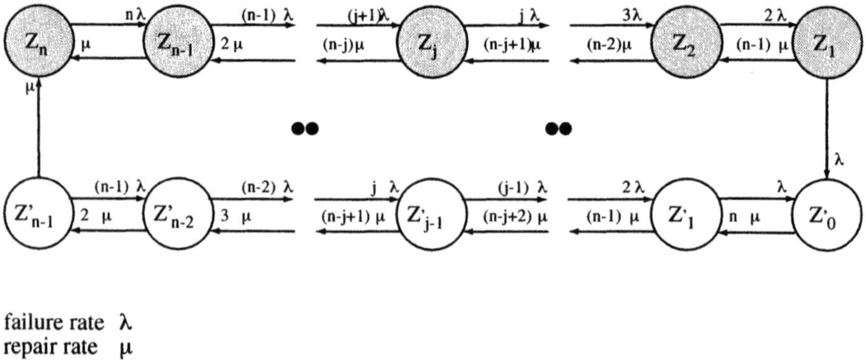

Fig. 5.17. State diagram of the naive available-copy scheme

The state diagram has $2n$ states. The states $Z_1, \ldots, Z_n$ represent situations where $1, \ldots, n$ replicas are available. The states $Z'_0, \ldots, Z'_{n-1}$ represent situations where all nodes had been crashed and $0, \ldots, n-1$ nodes have already been repaired.

From the state diagram we get for the probabilities p_j and p'_j (i.e., for the system states Z_j and Z'_j, respectively) the following three equations, for $k = 2, \ldots, n$:

$$\begin{aligned} k\lambda p_k &= (n-k+1)\mu p_{k-1} + \lambda p_1 && (5.28)\\ k\mu p'_{n-k} &= (n-k+1)\lambda p'_{n-k+1} + \mu p'_{n-1} && (5.29)\\ \lambda p_1 &= \mu p'_{n-1} && (5.30) \end{aligned}$$

From Equation (5.28) we get:

$$p_k = \sum_{j=1}^{k} \frac{(n-j)!(j-1)!}{(n-k)!k!} \rho^{j-k} p_1 \tag{5.31}$$

Analogously, from Equation (5.29) we get:

$$p'_{n-k} = \sum_{j=1}^{k} \frac{(n-j)!(j-1)!}{(n-k)!k!} \rho^{k-j} p'_{n-1} \tag{5.32}$$

Since the sum of all probabilities must be 1, we get:

$$p_1 = \frac{1}{B(n;\rho) + \rho B(n;\frac{1}{\rho})} \tag{5.33}$$

where

$$B(n;\rho) = \sum_{k=1}^{n}\sum_{j=1}^{k} \frac{(n-j)!(j-1)!}{(n-k)!k!} \rho^{j-k} \tag{5.34}$$

A logical data block is available in the states $Z_1, \ldots, Z_n$. If p_j be the probability that the system is in state Z_j then we can calculate the availability for the naive available-copy scheme:

$$A_{\mathrm{NAC}}(n) = \sum_{k=1}^{n} p_k = \frac{B(n;\rho)}{B(n;\rho) + \rho B(n;\frac{1}{\rho})} \tag{5.35}$$

Thus for $n = 2$, 3 and 4 we get (see Fig. 5.18):

$$A_{\mathrm{NAC}}(2) = \frac{1+3\rho}{(1+\rho)^3} \tag{5.36}$$

$$A_{\mathrm{NAC}}(3) = \frac{2+7\rho+11\rho^2}{(1+\rho)^3(2+\rho+2\rho^2)} \tag{5.37}$$

$$A_{\mathrm{NAC}}(4) = \frac{3+13\rho+23\rho^2+25\rho^3}{(1+\rho)^5(3-2\rho+3\rho^2)} \tag{5.38}$$

Available-copy scheme with was-available set. Besides this naive approach, we also know another more sophisticated variation, the so-called available-copy scheme with was-available set (WAC).

The available-copy scheme with was-available set tries to detect which nodes with a replica crashed last. Therefore, each node with a replica maintains a data structure where the nodes that have participated in the last

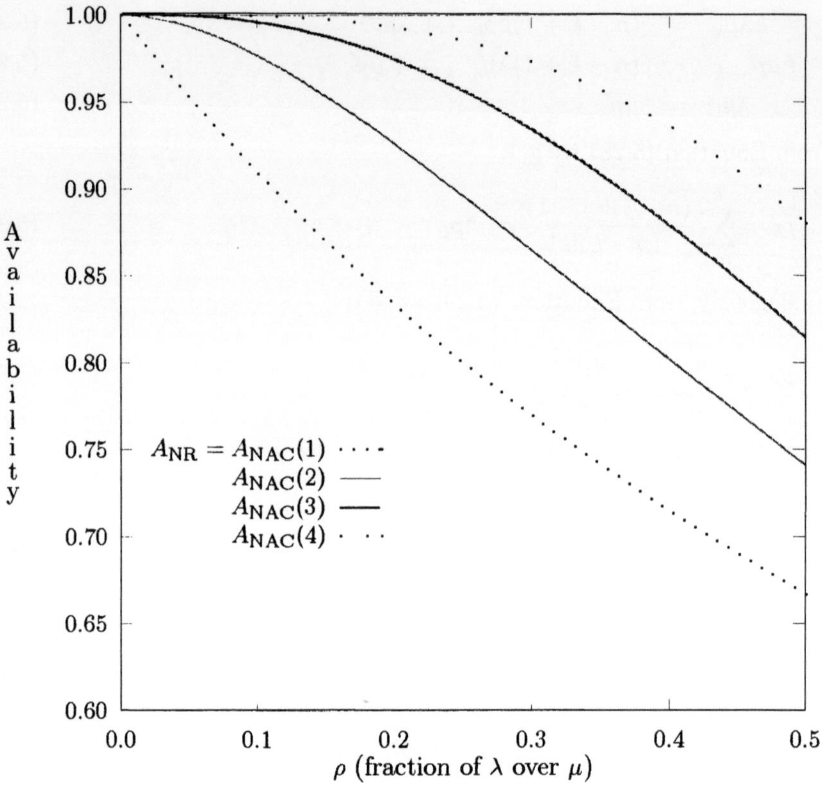

Fig. 5.18. Availability of the naive available-copy scheme

successful update are kept. Carroll et al. (1987) called this data structure "was-available set."

The maintenance of a was-available set improves the recovery process after the extreme situation where all nodes with a replica have crashed. While a repaired node recovers it can easily detect whether it has the up-to-date data blocks itself, or, if not, from which other node it could fetch the up-to-date data blocks. A simple check of the locally stored was-available set would be sufficient.

Recovered nodes with the relevant up-to-date data block or nodes that have updated their obsolete relevant data block can immediately vote for desired access. This improves performance and availability since it is not necessary to wait until all crashed nodes have been repaired.

Figure 5.19 shows the state diagram of the available-copy scheme with was-available set. We use the same notation as for the naive available-copy scheme.

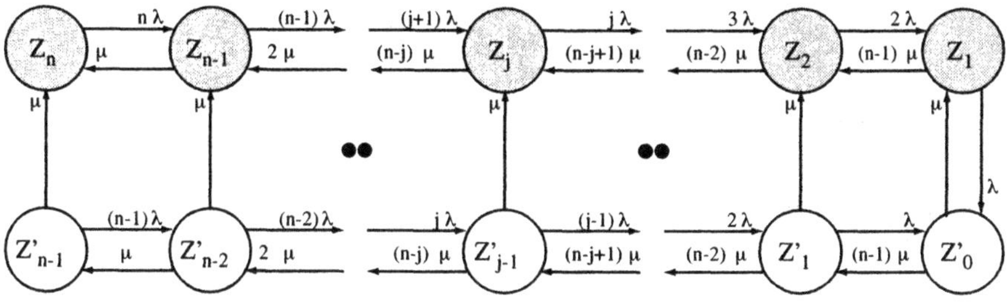

failure rate λ
repair rate μ

Fig. 5.19. State diagram of the available-copy scheme with was-available set

If all nodes mentioned in the was-available set are available, we get additional repair transitions from the states $Z'_0, \ldots, Z'_{n-2}$ to the states $Z_0, \ldots, Z_{n-2}$, respectively.

Hence, we get

$$\mu(p'_{n-1} + p'_{n-2} + \cdots + p'_1 + p'_0) = \lambda p_1 \tag{5.39}$$

and

$$p_1 + p'_1 = \frac{n\rho^{n-1}}{(1+\rho)^n} \tag{5.40}$$

This gives us an upper boundary for the probability of being in a state where the logical data block is unavailable:

$$p'_{n-1} + p'_{n-2} + \cdots + p'_1 + p'_0 < \frac{n\rho^n}{(1+\rho)^n} \tag{5.41}$$

For the availability of the available-copy scheme with was-available set we can deduct:

$$A_{\mathrm{WAC}}(n) = 1 - (p'_{n-1} + p'_{n-2} + \cdots + p'_1 + p'_0) < 1 - \frac{n\rho^n}{(1+\rho)^n} \tag{5.42}$$

A closed formula for an arbitrary n is difficult to calculate. Therefore, we follow Long and Pâris (1987) and just state the results for $n = 2, 3$ and 4 (see Fig. 5.20):

$$A_{\mathrm{WAC}}(2) = \frac{1 + 3\rho + \rho^2}{(1+\rho)^3} \tag{5.43}$$

$$A_{\mathrm{WAC}}(3) = \frac{2 + 9\rho + 17\rho^2 + 11\rho^3 + 2\rho^4}{(1+\rho)^3(2 + 3\rho + 2\rho^2)} \tag{5.44}$$

$$A_{\mathrm{WAC}}(4) = \frac{6 + 37\rho + 99\rho^2 + 152\rho^3 + 124\rho^4 + 47\rho^5 + 6\rho^6}{(1+\rho)^4(6 + 13\rho + 11\rho^2 + 6\rho^3)} \tag{5.45}$$

With the results obtained so far, we can prove the following theorem:

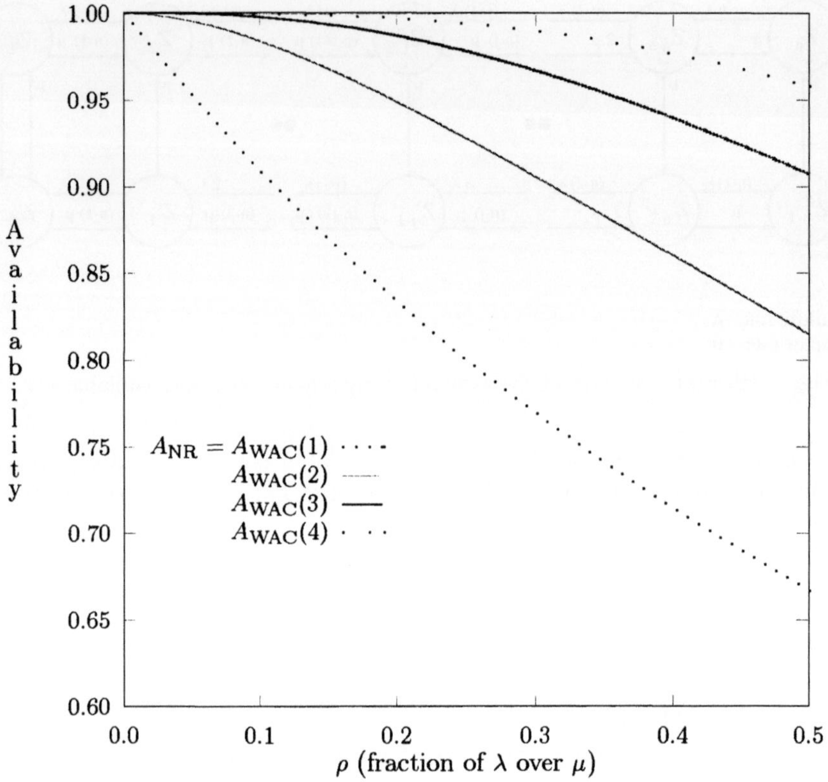

Fig. 5.20. Availability of the available-copy scheme with was-available set

Theorem 5.2.1. *As long as the quotient ρ of the failure and repair rate is smaller than or equal to 1, the availability $A_{WAC}(n)$ of the available-copy scheme with was-available set for a logical data block composed of n physical replicas ($n > 1$) is higher than the availability $A_{MCPS}(2n)$ of the majority consensus scheme with primary site for a logical data block composed of 2n physical replicas:*

$$A_{WAC}(n) > A_{MCPS}(2n), \text{ if } \rho \leq 1. \tag{5.46}$$

Proof. From equation (5.10) we already know that $A_{\mathrm{MC}}(2n-1) = A_{\mathrm{MCPS}}(2n)$. Thus it is sufficient to prove that $A_{\mathrm{WAC}}(n) > A_{\mathrm{MC}}(2n-1)$, for $\rho \leq 1$.

1. Through the comparison of the results from equations (5.7), (5.43) and (5.44) we also know that $A_{\mathrm{WAC}}(2) > A_{\mathrm{MC}}(3)$ and $A_{\mathrm{WAC}}(3) > A_{\mathrm{MC}}(5)$, respectively.
2. For $n \geq 4$ we can relate the lower boundary for $A_{\mathrm{WAC}}(n)$ from equation (5.42) with the upper boundary for $A_{\mathrm{MC}}(2n-1)$:

$$A_{\mathrm{MC}}(2n-1) < 1 - \frac{\binom{2n-1}{n}\rho^n}{(1+\rho)^{2n-1}} \tag{5.47}$$

A sufficient condition for $A_{\mathrm{WAC}}(n) > A_{\mathrm{MC}}(2n-1)$ would be:

$$\frac{\binom{2n-1}{n}}{n} > (1+\rho)^{n-1} \tag{5.48}$$

This equation holds true for $n \geq 4$ and every $\rho \leq 1$.

In sum we can formulate the following equations:

1. For $\rho \leq 1$ we get: $A_{\mathrm{WAC}}(n) > A_{\mathrm{MCPS}}(2n) = A_{\mathrm{MC}}(2n-1)$.
2. For $n > 1$ and every ρ we get: $A_{\mathrm{WAC}}(n) > A_{\mathrm{NAC}}(n)$.
3. Moreover, for $n > 2$ we get: $A_{\mathrm{NAC}}(n) > A_{\mathrm{MC}}(2n-1)$, if $\rho < 1$.
   However, we get: $A_{\mathrm{NAC}}(n) < A_{\mathrm{MC}}(2n-1)$, if $\rho > 1$.
   Likewise, for $n = 2$: $A_{\mathrm{NAC}}(2) = A_{\mathrm{MC}}(3)$

These results make the available-copy scheme with was-available set an ideal candidate for replication and concurrency control in a network where we can exclude network partitioning.

For instance, replicated group workspaces that are distributed over reliable local area networks could profit from an available-copy scheme with was-available set. Some group members could have a local replica of the workspace on their laptops. If they disconnect their machine from the network, the scheme would treat them as crashed. Once they reconnect, a "recovery" process could reinstall the latest up-to-date data blocks of the workspace. Although this is extremely useful for mobile workers, the remaining nodes in the network do not benefit from this. A disconnected machine (like a crashed one) could decrease availability. Especially under voting schemes, the loss of the votes of a disconnected (or crashed) machine reduces the probability of obtaining a successful votum. The so-called dynamic voting scheme is a way out of this dilemma.

5.2.6 Dynamic voting

Main idea. Davĉev and Burkhard (1985) modified the static assignment of weights to nodes with a right to vote through dynamic voting. Under the dynamic voting scheme, nodes with a right to vote get their individual weights for their votes dynamically assigned. Consequently, the quorum becomes dynamic too.

The advantage of this scheme becomes evident if we study the voting behavior while the network is partitioned, while several mobile workers have disconnected their machine from the network, or while several nodes have crashed.

Let the remaining nodes (in the quorum partition) still have enough votes to obtain a successful votum. However, the probability of obtaining a successful votum is lower than before because some of the nodes with a right to vote lie outside of the quorum partition, having been disconnected or crashed. Let us focus on the case where the network is partitioned. In the cases of disconnected or crashed nodes the discussion is analogous.

If we now assume that the network partitioning lasts for quite some time, the lower probability of obtaining a successful votum might not be tolerable. What we would like to achieve is an increased availability even if the network remains partitioned (Barbara et al. 1986). Therefore, the weights of the votes (of the nodes with a right to vote) within the quorum partition are dynamically reassigned. This reassignment has two objectives: Firstly, it tries to increase the probability of obtaining a successful votum, while the network is partitioned. Secondly, it has to guarantee consistency of the replicated data blocks. All that under the assumption that the end of the network partitioning (analogously, the recovery of crashed nodes or the reconnection of disconnected nodes) cannot be predicted.

Let us illustrate the dynamic voting scheme with our example again.

Example (Dynamic voting). Let n_1 have a right to vote with weight 2 and let the other three nodes have a right to vote with weight 1 (i.e., $W = 5$). Moreover, let the quorum for read and write be the same (i.e., $QU = 3$).

Consider the following situation where the network is partitioned in such a way that node n_1 lies in Partition 1 whereas the nodes n_2, n_3 and n_4 lie in Partition 2 (see Fig. 5.21).

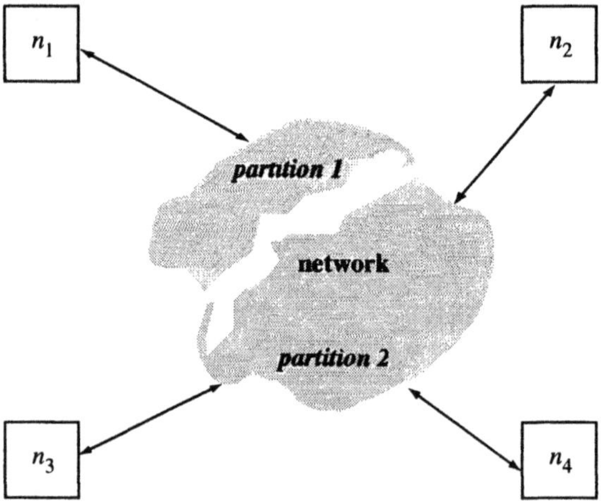

Fig. 5.21. Partitioned network

Partition 2 is the quorum partition because it contains three nodes with a right to vote with weight 1. A successful votum can be obtained if all three nodes vote for a desired access. While the network remains partitioned, we have the following coterie:

$$C_3 = \left\{ \{n_2, n_3, n_4\} \right\} . \tag{5.49}$$

A further partitioning of the quorum partition (Partition 2) would prohibit any accesses. Therefore, after the next successful update, the nodes n_2, n_3 and n_4 dynamically are assigned a new weight of 5 for their votes. The weight of the vote of node n_1 is still 2. Since the sum of all weights W is now 17, the quorum QU for read and write accesses is 9. Consequently, two nodes of the quorum partition are sufficient to obtain a successful votum. We get the following coterie:

$$C_4 = \left\{ \{n_2, n_3\}, \{n_2, n_4\}, \{n_3, n_4\} \right\} . \tag{5.50}$$

The availability has been improved while the network remains partitioned. The coterie C_4 also shows that a further partitioning of the quorum partition would produce another quorum partition and not prohibit any further accesses. With the two nodes of the new quorum partition, an accessing site could obtain a successful votum.

The dynamic assignment of a new weight of 5 to the nodes of the quorum partition is not arbitrary. There are two strategies:

1. *Group consensus:* The nodes with a right to vote within the quorum partition decide together on a method of reassigning the weights of their votes. Therefore, they proclaim a node coordinator. This coordinator calculates appropriate new weights and communicates its decision to the other nodes. The reassignment is, of course, transactional.
2. *Autonomous decision:* Nodes believing that they belong to a quorum partition autonomously decide on the new weights of their votes. It should be clear that before they can vote with the new weights, a majority of nodes must accept the new weights. This reassignment is also transactional.

Still we have not answered the question of how the new weight of 5 is determined for the nodes of the quorum partition. Barbara et al. (1989) demonstrate methods for calculating these new weights:

- Variant $[1 * 2w(n)]$:
  If a node n with a vote of weight $w(n)$ is no longer part of a quorum partition (in our example, this node is n_1 with a vote with weight $w(n_1) = 2$) then *one* of the remaining nodes within the quorum partition increases the weight of its vote by $2w(n)$. This reassignment is reversed as soon as the node n joins the quorum partition, either because the network partitions reunite, because the crashed node n has been repaired and recovers, or because the disconnected node n has once again been reconnected to the network.
- Variants $[N * 2w(n)]$, $[N * w(n)]$ and $[N * \lceil \frac{2w(n)}{N} \rceil]$:
  In principle, these variants work as the variant $[1 * 2w(n)]$. The only difference is – that after a node n with a vote of weight $w(n)$ is no longer part of a quorum partition – *all* remaining nodes within the quorum partition increase the weight of their votes by $2w(n)$, $w(n)$ or $\lceil \frac{2w(n)}{N} \rceil$, respectively.

A simulation study by Borghoff and Obermaier (1991) has quantitatively analyzed the different variants. The best results as far as availability is concerned were provided by the variants $[1*2w(n)]$ and $[N*2w(n)]$. In the variant $[1*2w(n)]$ an accumulation of weights in an individual node could be detected. If this node "leaves" the quorum partition the probability of reaching a successful votum decreases dramatically. In this respect, the variant $[N*2w(r)]$ benefits because of its equal distribution of vote reassignments.

Dynamic voting also has certain weaknesses. Consider the following scenario:

Example (Weaknesses of dynamic voting). Let us look at a situation where $n = 100$ nodes each with their respective replica have been installed. Without loss of generality, assume that nodes with a replica have a vote with weight 1, i.e., $W = 100$ and $QU = 51$ (let read and write accesses have the same quorum again).

Let a first network partitioning occur that splits the nodes with a replica into a partition 1 with 51 and a partition 2 with 49 nodes. Obviously, partition 1 is the quorum partition. Here, accesses are still possible. The dynamic reassignment of weights to nodes within this quorum partition might lead to the toleration of another network partitioning.

Let another network partitioning occur that splits the quorum partition into a partition 3 with 26 and a partition 4 with 25 nodes. The dynamic voting scheme ensures that everything runs smoothly. Weights are increased in the new quorum partition (partition 3). A further partitioning might then be tolerated.

If we take this scenario to its extreme, we get smaller and smaller quorum partitions, with 14, 8, 5, 3, 2, and, finally, a single node. The dynamic voting scheme allows accesses only in the current quorum partition. It could happen that an overwhelming majority of nodes (in an extreme case, 99 nodes with a right to vote but possibly with outdated data block versions) cannot obtain a successful votum because a minority (in the extreme case, a single node with the only up-to-date replica) possess the dominating "over"-weighted vote.

The scenario of our rather artificial example reflects a general phenomenon of injustice due to partial favoring of "minorities." We have already seen an example of this under voting with (volatile) witnesses and leading minority. There we could accept this injustice with regard to the (volatile) witnesses because they do not possess a full replica and have only been installed to improve availability. However, as we have seen, for the dynamic voting scheme, we could hardly accept such a situation because the injustice concerns nodes with full replicas.

In a nutshell, there is a tradeoff between increased availability within the quorum partition and the fairness of reuniting (minority)partitions. In Sect. 5.2.7 we will discuss a solution to this problem. In detail we will show how reuniting (minority)partitions could facilitate the successful obtaining of a votum without harming the overall consistency.

Dynamic voting with update sites cardinality. Jajodia and Mutchler (1987a) have proposed an interesting variant of the dynamic voting scheme.

In this variant, the weights of the votes are not really reassigned to the nodes within the quorum partition. Rather, an algorithm is proposed that helps the nodes to detect whether or not they belong to a quorum partition. Therefore, each node maintains an additional data structure, called update sites cardinality.

The update sites cardinality contains the number of nodes that successfully participated in the last update.[6]

The collection of a successful votum is heavily dependent upon the maximal value of the update sites cardinality that has been received while votes are collected. In order to determine whether or not the accessing node belongs to the quorum partition (i.e., whether a desired access can be performed or not), the following algorithm is applied. Without loss of generality, assume that all nodes with a right to vote have a vote with weight 1:

1. The accessing node (or better, the subsystem that transparently manages the desired access) extracts from the received votes the version numbers as well as the update sites cardinalities.
2. Let vn_{max} be the maximal version number obtained by the accessing node.
   The accessing node constructs the set NF_{max} (the set of available nodes with a replica and version number vn_{max}).
3. Let sc_{max} be the maximal update sites cardinalities of all nodes in NF_{max}.
4. The votum is successful if $|NF_{max}| > \frac{sc_{max}}{2}$.
   Otherwise, the votum is not successful (i.e., the accessing node does not belong to the quorum partition).

This improves the standard dynamic voting scheme since it no longer requires the propagation of the dynamically readjusted quorum to nodes joining the quorum partition.

Example (Dynamic voting with update sites cardinality). Let the five nodes n_1, n_2, n_3, n_4, and n_5 possess a replica. In the beginning all five nodes are part of a single partition. The data block in question is updated nine times. Thus we get the following situation.

[6] In contrast to the voting scheme with (volatile) witnesses and leading minority where we have introduced a data structure, called update full replica cardinality (see p. 234ff), the update sites cardinality is maintained at all nodes with a right to vote. There are no (volatile) witnesses.

	n_1	n_2	n_3	n_4	n_5
vn:	9	9	9	9	9
sc:	5	5	5	5	5

Now, let an accessing node try to update the data block. Let only the nodes n_1, n_2 and n_3 vote for the desired write access. By performing the algorithm described above, the accessing node understands that it belongs to the quorum partition. The update can be performed. This leads to the following situation:

	n_1	n_2	n_3	n_4	n_5
vn:	10	10	10	9	9
sc:	3	3	3	5	5

Let the accessing node try to update the data block once more and let only nodes n_1 and n_3 vote for the desired write access this time. By performing the above algorithm again, the accessing node detects that it still belongs to the quorum partition. The nodes n_1 and n_3 represent a majority of nodes with the up-to-date data block. The update can be performed leading to the following situation:

	n_1	n_2	n_3	n_4	n_5
vn:	11	10	11	9	9
sc:	2	3	2	5	5

Now, let the nodes n_4 and n_5 reunite with the partition $\{n_1, n_3\}$. Thus we get:

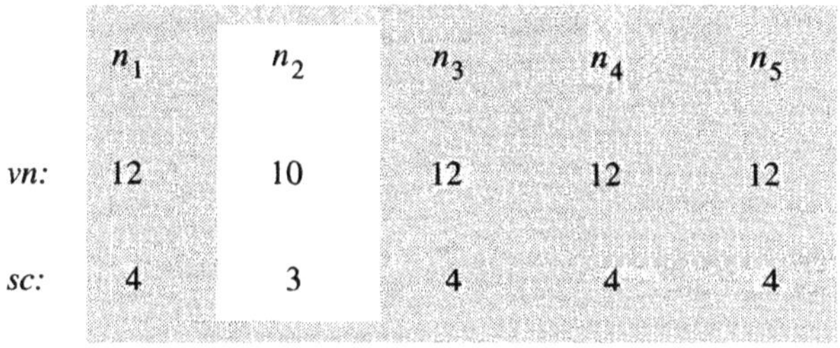

Figure 5.22 shows the state diagram of the dynamic voting scheme with update sites cardinality. States are tripels of the form (X, Y, Z) where

- the variable Y denotes the update sites cardinality of the nodes with an up-to-date replica,
- the variable X denotes the number of the available nodes with an update sites cardinality equal to Y, and
- the variable Z is the number of the available nodes with an update sites cardinality different from Y.

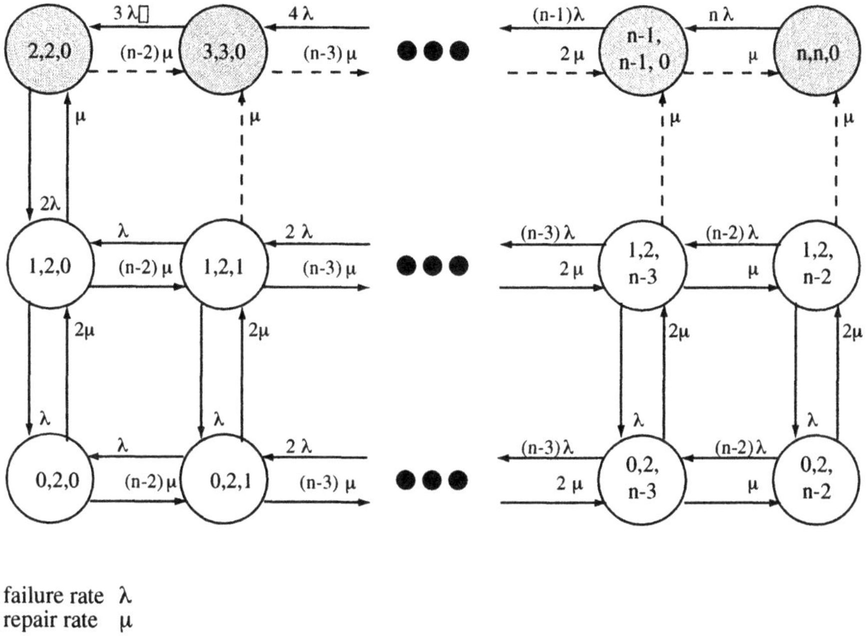

Fig. 5.22. State diagram of the dynamic voting scheme with update sites cardinality

Let us look at the states and their transitions in more detail. In the first row, we find states where at least two nodes with an up-to-date replica are available. Therefore, the states $(2, 2, 0)$, $(3, 3, 0)$, ..., $(n, n, 0)$ represent available states (emphasized with gray circles again).

The transitions between the states of the first row are simple. For instance, in state$(n, n, 0)$ – where all nodes with a right to vote are available and possess an up-to-date replica – the unavailability of a node (due to a crash, a disconnection from the network, or a network partitioning) leads to state $(n-1, n-1, 0)$. Properly speaking, the state would be $(n-1, n, 0)$. However, since updates can be performed in available states (and the state $(n-1, n, 0)$ is an available state), we denote such states as if an update has already occurred, i.e., $(n-1, n-1, 0)$.

If the unavailable node becomes once again available (due to a repair process, a reconnection to the network, or a reunification of the network partitions) then we assume that its possibly outdated data blocks become updated. This is possible because this available state allows successful read accesses. Thus, we immediately get a transition to the initial state $(n, n, 0)$.

We find analogous transitions in the entire first row where we assume this sort of forced update after a node becomes available again. Without this assumption, we would otherwise have to introduce – as in Fig. 5.10 – ν-transitions where ν denotes the update rate. Figure 5.22 plots transitions where a forced update occurs with dashed arrows.

Interesting is state $(2, 2, 0)$. The unavailability of one of the remaining two nodes leads to the state $(1, 2, 0)$ in the second row. In all states of the second row, only a single up-to-date replica is available. Hence, all states of the second row are unavailable states. No successful votum can be obtained here.

If in state $(1, 2, 0)$ a node becomes once again available, we must distinguish whether this node possesses an up-to-date replica or not.

- If this node possesses an up-to-date replica (in this situation there is only one node with this property) then we reach state $(2, 2, 0)$ with a μ-transition.

  There is no need for a forced update since data accesses were not possible in the meantime.
- If this node possesses an obsolete replica (in this situation there are $n-2$ nodes with this property) then we reach state $(1, 2, 1)$.

We remain in the second row as long as the node with the needed up-to-date replica remains unavailable. Eventually, this node becomes again available. This leads then immediately from the current unavailable state in the second row to the corresponding available state, above in the first row.

The transitions from the states $(1, 2, i)$ in the second row to the states $(i+2, i+2, 0)$ in the first row, $0 < i \leq n-2$, are plotted with dashed arrows, i.e., there are forced updates for all available nodes (there are i of them) with obsolete replicas.

The states of the third row represent states with the following characteristics:

- There is no node available with an up-to-date replica.
- If a node with an up-to-date replica becomes once again available, we reach the corresponding state above, in the second row.
- If a node with an obsolete replica becomes unavailable, we reach the next state left, in the same (i.e., third) row.
- If a node with an obsolete replica becomes once again available, we reach the next state right, in the same (i.e., third) row.

Availability. In order to simplify the notation, we denote the states of the first row (from left to right) with $A_0, A_1, \ldots, A_{n-2}$. Analogously, the states of the second and third row are denoted as $B_0, B_1, \ldots, B_{n-2}$ and $C_0, C_1, \ldots, C_{n-2}$, respectively. Furthermore, let A_i, B_i and C_i represent the probability that the system is in the corresponding states.

The availability of the dynamic voting scheme with update sites cardinality is given as the sum of the probabilities that the system is in an available state, i.e.:

$$A_{\mathrm{DVU}}(n) = \sum_{i=0}^{n-2} \frac{i+2}{n} A_i \tag{5.51}$$

The term $\frac{i+2}{n}$ should reflect the fact that the accessing node has been one of the $i+2$ nodes that are in state A_i. As usual, the individual probabilities can be calculated with the help of a system of equations derived from the state diagram. Let us start with the states plotted on the left side of the diagram:

$$[2\lambda + (n-2)\mu]\, A_0 = 3\lambda A_1 + \mu B_0 \tag{5.52}$$

$$[\lambda + (n-1)\mu]\, B_0 = \lambda B_1 + 2\mu C_0 + 2\lambda A_0 \tag{5.53}$$

$$n\mu C_0 = \lambda C_1 + \lambda B_0 \tag{5.54}$$

For the remaining states of the first row we get $(k = 1, 2, \ldots n-2)$:

$$\begin{aligned} [(k+2)\lambda + (n-k-2)\mu]\, A_k &= \\ = \quad (k+3)\lambda A_{k+1} + (n-k-1)\mu A_{k-1} + \mu B_k & \end{aligned} \tag{5.55}$$

Then, for the remaining states of the second row we get $(k = 1, 2, \ldots n-2)$:

$$\begin{aligned} [(k+1)\lambda + (n-k-1)\mu]\, B_k &= \\ = \quad (k+1)\lambda B_{k+1} + (n-k-1)\mu B_{k-1} + 2\mu C_k & \end{aligned} \tag{5.56}$$

Finally, for the remaining states of the third row we get $(k = 1, 2, \ldots n-2)$:

$$[k\lambda + (n-k)\mu]\, C_k = (k+1)\lambda C_{k+1} + (n-k-1)\mu C_{k-1} + \lambda B_k \tag{5.57}$$

If we define $A_{n-1} = B_{n-1} = C_{n-1} = 0$ and add the equation that the sum of all probabilities equals 1, then we get a solvable system of linear equations.

Jajodia and Mutchler (1987b) show that the availability of the dynamic voting scheme with update sites cardinality, for particular values of ρ is higher than the availability of the majority consensus scheme with primary site. In detail, they found the following interesting results:

$$A_{\mathrm{DVU}}(4) > A_{\mathrm{MCPS}}(4), \text{ if } \rho < 1. \tag{5.58}$$

$$A_{\mathrm{DVU}}(5) > A_{\mathrm{MCPS}}(5), \text{ if } \rho \leq 0.76. \tag{5.59}$$

$$A_{\mathrm{DVU}}(n) > A_{\mathrm{MCPS}}(n), \text{ for all } n \geq 6 \text{ and } \rho < 1. \tag{5.60}$$

Dynamic voting with linear ordering. The dynamic voting scheme with linear ordering tries to improve the situation that among the available nodes only two nodes exist with an up-to-date replica. Under the dynamic voting scheme with update sites cardinality, a further network partitioning could result in a situation where a successful votum can no longer be obtained. What we need is a sort of "primary site" that tells us which of the partitions can still act as a quorum partition (i.e., allow successful accesses). Unfortunately, this "primary site" cannot be selected in advance. In contrast to the majority consensus scheme where the a priori introduction of a primary site helped to "break the tie" when the votum was obtained from exactly half of the nodes with a right to vote, under the dynamic voting schemes a "primary site" must be determined dynamically.

Therefore, we introduce a linear ordering (according to some >-relation) among the nodes with a replica. Let $n_1 > n_2 > n_3 > \ldots$.

A votum is successful if

- a majority of nodes with an up-to-date replica vote for the desired access, or
- exactly half of the nodes with an up-to-date replica vote for the desired access, among which there is a distinguished site n_{ds} with an up-to-date replica where $n_{ds} > n_i$, for all other nodes n_i that have voted for the desired access.[7]

In order to detect whether the distinguished site n_{ds} participates in the obtained votum, every node with a replica stores – besides version number and update sites cardinality – an additional data structure, called a distinguished site.

The distinguished site contains the largest node with regard to the ordering that successfully participated in the last update. With the knowledge of the distinguished site, an accessing node can easily detect whether or not it belongs to the quorum partition (i.e., whether or not a desired access can be performed). The following algorithm is applied. Without loss of generality, assume once more that all nodes with a right to vote have a vote with weight 1:

[7] The distinguished site n_{ds} can be interpreted as a dynamically determined "primary site."

1. The accessing node (or better, the subsystem that transparently manages the desired access) extracts from the received votes the version numbers, the update sites cardinalities as well as the distinguished sites.
2. Let vn_{max} be the maximal version number obtained by the accessing node.
   The accessing node constructs the set NF_{max}, i.e., the set of available nodes with a replica and version number vn_{max}.
3. Let sc_{max} be the maximal update sites cardinalities of all nodes in NF_{max}.
4. The votum is successful if
   - $|NF_{max}| > \frac{sc_{max}}{2}$, or
   - $|NF_{max}| = \frac{sc_{max}}{2}$ and there is a distinguished site $n_{ds} \in NF_{max}$ for which the distinguished sites known at all other nodes in NF_{max} are identical to n_{ds}.

   Otherwise, the votum is not successful, i.e., the accessing node does not belong to the quorum partition.

Let us illustrate the algorithm by an example.

Example (Dynamic voting with linear ordering). Let the nodes n_1, n_2, n_3, n_4, and n_5 possess a replica and let their linear ordering be: $n_1 > n_2 > n_3 > n_4 > n_5$. In the beginning all five nodes are part of a single partition. The data block in question is updated nine times. Thus we get the following situation. The symbol * denotes a wildcard (the value is not relevant).

	n_1	n_2	n_3	n_4	n_5
vn:	9	9	9	9	9
sc:	5	5	5	5	5
ds:	*	*	*	*	*

Now, let an accessing node try to update the data block. Let only the nodes n_1, n_2 and n_3 vote for the desired write access. By performing the algorithm described above, the accessing node understands that it belongs to the quorum partition. The update can be performed. This leads to the following situation:

	n_1	n_2	n_3	n_4	n_5
vn:	10	10	10	9	9
sc:	3	3	3	5	5
ds:	*	*	*	*	*

Let the accessing node try to update the data block once more and let only nodes n_1 and n_3 vote for the desired write access this time. By performing the above algorithm again, the accessing node detects that it still belongs to the quorum partition. The nodes n_1 and n_3 represent a majority of nodes with the up-to-date data block. The update can be performed. Since the number of nodes within the quorum partition is even, the distinguished site has to be updated as well. The new distinguished site is n_1 because $n_1 > n_3$ with regard to the chosen ordering:

	n_1	n_2	n_3	n_4	n_5
vn:	11	10	11	9	9
sc:	2	3	2	5	5
ds:	n_1	*	n_1	*	*

Up to this point, the behavior is identical to that with dynamic voting and update site cardinality.

Let four more updates occur at nodes n_1 and n_3 before they are separated due to another network partitioning. This leads to the following situation:

	n_1	n_2	n_3	n_4	n_5
vn:	15	10	15	9	9
sc:	2	3	2	5	5
ds:	n_1	*	n_1	*	*

Now we have a situation where the node n_1 represents the quorum partition (i.e., with the vote of node n_1 alone an accessing node can obtain a successful votum). Assume another successful update at node n_1 before the nodes n_1, n_4 and n_5 reunite.

Furthermore, we assume forced updates at the nodes n_4 and n_5 after the reunification. Let us consider the needed steps for this forced update at node n_4 (for n_5, analogously):

First of all, node n_4 checks whether it has become a member of a quorum partition. Therefore, node n_4 performs a read access. From the obtained votes it extracts the maximal version number vn_{max} and constructs the set NF_{max}, i.e., the set of available nodes with a replica and version number vn_{max}.

- If node n_4 detects that it is a member of the quorum partition (by performing the algorithm described above) and that it possesses an up-to-date replica (i.e., its local physical replica has version number vn_{max}) then everything is fine and no additional steps are needed.
- If node n_4 detects that it is indeed a member of the quorum partition but possesses an obsolete replica (i.e., its local physical replica has a version number smaller than vn_{max}) then it has to update its local replica with the help of the nodes in NF_{max}. A successful (forced) update requires the following additional steps:
  The version numbers and the update sites cardinalities of node n_4 as well as of all nodes in NF_{max} are updated, i.e., $\forall n_i \in NF_{max} \cup \{n_4\}$:
  $vn_{n_i} = vn_{max} + 1$, and $sc_{n_i} = |NF_{max}| + 1$,.
  If $|NF_{max}| + 1$ is even then the distinguished sites have to be updated as well: The new distinguished site is the largest node $n_{ds} \in NF_{max} \cup \{n_4\}$ with regard to the chosen ordering (in our example, $n_{ds} = n_1$).
- If node n_4 detects that it is not a member of the quorum partition then its local replica cannot be updated at this time.

If after a successful forced update of the nodes n_4 and n_5 the node n_1 "leaves" the quorum partition, the two remaining nodes (n_4 and n_5) represent the new quorum partition.

If node n_3 joins this new quorum partition it can also participate (after a forced update) in any successful votum although it has not been reunited with node n_1. This is the main difference with regard to the dynamic voting scheme with update site cardinality where a split of the nodes n_1 and n_3 would prohibit any further successful votum, at least until both nodes are eventually reunited.

Jajodia and Mutchler (1987b) showed that the availability of the dynamic voting scheme with linear ordering can be calculated by solving a system of linear equations which can be extracted from the state diagram depicted in Fig. 5.23.

As for the dynamic voting scheme with update site cardinality, states are triples of the form (X, Y, Z) where

- the variable Y denotes the update sites cardinality of the nodes with an up-to-date replica,
- the variable X denotes the number of the available nodes with an update sites cardinality equal to Y, and
- the variable Z is the number of the available nodes with an update sites cardinality different from Y.

Transitions where forced updates occur are plotted with dashed arrows.

Initially the system is in $(n, n, 0)$ where n nodes with an up-to-date replica are available.

The transitions between the states $(2, 2, 0)$ and $(n, n, 0)$ within the second row reflect failures and repairs of at most $n-2$ nodes. As soon as state $(2, 2, 0)$ is reached, we must deal with the following situation:

- In state $(2, 2, 0)$, a failure of the smaller node with regard to the chosen ordering leads to the state $(1, 1, 0)$. This state is an available state (like all states of the second row). In state $(1, 1, 0)$ the quorum partition contains a single node.
  In state $(1, 1, 0)$, the failure of the last remaining node leads to state $(0, 1, 0)$ in the first row. All states of the first row are unavailable. For instance, the state $(0, 1, 2)$ reflects a situation where two nodes from the nonquorum partition have been repaired.
- In state $(2, 2, 0)$, a failure of the greater node with regard to the chosen ordering leads to the state $(1, 2, 0)$. This state is an unavailable state (like all states of the third row).
  The third row contains all states where the greater of the two nodes of the quorum partition has failed and the smaller node is still available. State transitions within the third row reflect failures and repairs of the other $n - 2$ nodes.

The forth row contains all states where both nodes of the quorum partition have failed. State transitions within the forth row reflect failures and repairs of the other $n-2$ nodes. In the forth row, the most crucial transitions are the

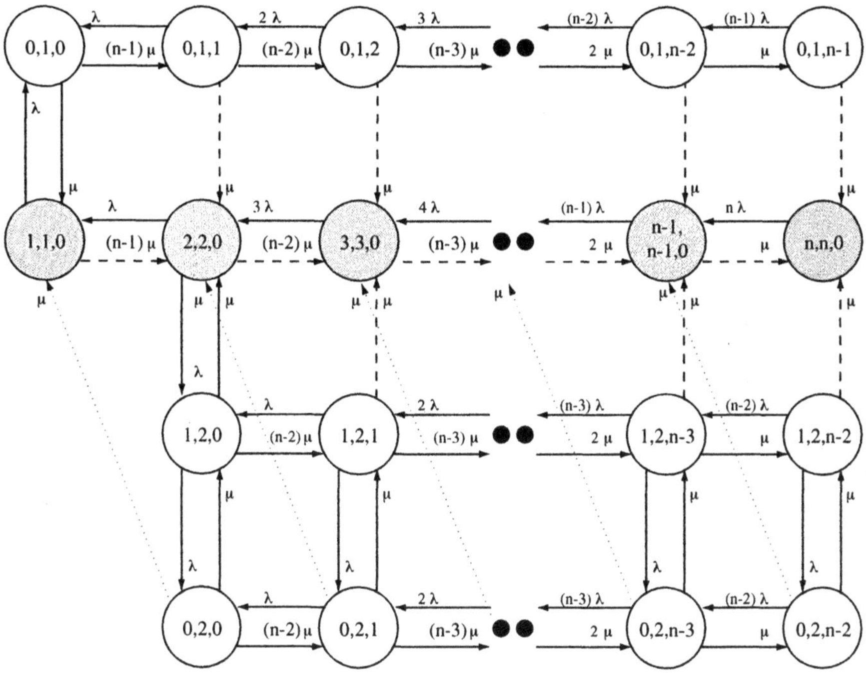

failure rate λ
repair rate μ

Fig. 5.23. State diagram of the dynamic voting scheme with linear ordering

dashed transitions to the second row (i.e., from an unavailable to an available state) when the greater node has been repaired, and the transitions to the third row when the smaller node has been repaired.

Availability. As expected, Jajodia and Mutchler (1987b) show that the availability of the dynamic voting scheme with linear ordering is higher than the availability of the dynamic voting scheme with update sites cardinality:

$$A_{\mathrm{DVLIN}}(n) > A_{\mathrm{DVU}}(n) \tag{5.61}$$

5.2.7 Voting-class

The weakness of the dynamic voting scheme arises from the problem of reuniting (minority-)partitions which contain a majority of replicas but cannot participate in a successful votum because collectively they only possess a minority of votes.

This section will show how reuniting (minority-)partitions facilitates the successful obtaining of a votum without harming the overall consistency of the logical data blocks they are responsible for.

The first of all desired improvement of the fault tolerance within the quorum partition can lead to a dramatic reduction of the availability. Recall the scenario where a single node could possess the dominating "over"-weight for its vote. Therefore, Tang (1990) restricts the minimal size of a quorum partition. He shows that availability can be increased by not letting the size of the quorum partition fall below a certain threshold. Tang calls his dynamic voting scheme "voting-class".

The voting-class scheme redefines the term quorum partition. Informally speaking, under the voting-class scheme a quorum partition must not only possess a majority of votes but also its size must not fall below a given threshold L. This scheme tries to achieve the situation where reuniting (minority-) partitions can – if they possess at least an up-to-date replica – obtain a majority of votes.

Besides version numbers and locking states, every node with a right to vote maintains the update sites cardinalities (SC).[8]

Without loss of generality, we assume n replicas and let the weight of each vote be 1. Under the voting-class scheme, a votum is successful if one of the following two conditions are met (NF_{max} and sc_{max} are determined as under the dynamic voting scheme with update sites cardinality, p. 249ff., Steps 1–3. Let NF be the set of nodes that have voted for the desired access):

1. $|NF_{max}| > \frac{sc_{max}}{2} \wedge |NF| \geq L$.
   This condition prohibits quorum partitions that are too small.
2. $|NF| \geq \max\{\lfloor \frac{n}{2} \rfloor + 1 \ , \ n - L + 1\}$.
   This condition allows reuniting (minority)partitions that possess at least an up-to-date replica to obtain a majority of votes.
   Since $|NF| \geq \max\{\lfloor \frac{n}{2} \rfloor + 1 \ , \ n - L + 1\}$, in the set of nodes NF there is at least one node with an up-to-date replica. Due to Condition 1 we have at least L up-to-date replicas!

Otherwise, the votum is not successful, i.e., the accessing node does not belong to the quorum partition.

Both conditions clearly show the strong influence of the threshold L on a successful votum. L alone determines what is understood by a "too small" or a "moderate" quorum partition. Hence, it is worthwhile to look at L in more detail.

For $L = 1$ the voting-class scheme works just like the dynamic voting scheme introduced by Jajodia and Mutchler (1987a). As an extreme case, a single node may possess the majority of votes (more precisely, the weight of the vote of this single node is sufficient to obtain a successful votum). For $L \geq \lfloor \frac{n}{2} \rfloor + 1$ the voting-class scheme degenerates to the weighted voting scheme as proposed by Gifford (1979).

In order to improve the overall availability of the voting-class scheme compared to the (standard) dynamic voting scheme as well as the weighted

[8] Tang (1990) calls this data structure update group.

voting scheme, the system designer might vary the values for L between 1 and $\lfloor \frac{n}{2} \rfloor + 1$. The optimal value for L depends heavily on the network configuration and topology, characteristics of the nodes (failure rates, etc.) and the update rate ν.

Tang suggests that once during the design phase a solution to a stochastical model for all possible values of L should be obtained. One of the values for L that optimizes the availability for the estimated model parameters should be chosen. However, since the model parameters may change dynamically and are tailored to a particular network configuration and topology, the optimal value for L cannot be calculated statically and, worse, does not possess universal validity. This is the reason why we renounce a discussion of L-specific analyses of the availability; see Tang (1990) for details.

Summary. Equations (5.58)–(5.61) showed that the dynamic voting scheme with linear ordering brings about the best results as far as the availability is concerned.

Although, the voting-class scheme seems quite useful at first glance (because it avoids "too small" quorum partitions), the difficulties in calculating an optimal value for the threshold L hinder its practical usage in real-world settings.

5.2.8 Multidimensional voting

The multidimensional voting scheme provides an extreme flexibility as far as the assignment of weights to votes is concerned.

Main idea. Barbara and Garcia-Molina (1987), Tang and Natarajan (1993) as well as Tong and Kain (1988) argue that in some cases it is of interest to start with the definition of a coterie rather than with the assignment of weights to votes (to the nodes with a right to vote). The underlying motivation comes from Lamport (1978a).

So far we have assumed the opposite (i.e., we have given a weight to all nodes with a right to vote), have then defined the read quorum and the write quorum and, finally, have built the coterie. If we invert the approach we get the following task: Find the assignment of weights to votes (to the nodes with a right to vote) that corresponds to a predefined coterie. Unfortunately, the following theorem holds to be true.

Theorem 5.2.2. *There are coteries for which there is no corresponding assignment of weights to votes (to the nodes with a right to vote) where the weights are positive integer values.*

The proof is through a (counter)example by Garcia-Molina and Barbara (1985).

Example (Motivation for the multidimensional voting scheme). The following coterie has no corresponding assignment of weights to votes (to the nodes with a right to vote) where the weights are positive integer values.

$$C_5 = \left\{ \begin{array}{l} \{n_1, n_2\}, \{n_1, n_3, n_4\}, \{n_1, n_3, n_5\}, \{n_1, n_4, n_6\}, \\ \{n_1, n_5, n_6\}, \{n_2, n_3, n_6\}, \{n_2, n_4, n_5\} \end{array} \right\} \quad (5.62)$$

The definition of a coterie implies that (be QU the needed quorum):

$$w(n_1) + w(n_2) \geq QU \quad (5.63)$$

$$w(n_1) + w(n_3) + w(n_4) \geq QU \quad (5.64)$$

$$w(n_1) + w(n_3) + w(n_5) \geq QU \quad (5.65)$$

$$w(n_1) + w(n_4) + w(n_6) \geq QU \quad (5.66)$$

$$w(n_1) + w(n_5) + w(n_6) \geq QU \quad (5.67)$$

$$w(n_2) + w(n_3) + w(n_6) \geq QU \quad (5.68)$$

$$w(n_2) + w(n_4) + w(n_5) \geq QU \quad (5.69)$$

From inequations (5.63)–(5.69) we can deduct a contradiction: Since $\{n_2, n_4, n_5\} \in C_5$ but $\{n_1, n_4, n_5\} \notin C_5$ follows that $w(n_2)+w(n_4)+w(n_5) \geq QU$ as well as $w(n_1) + w(n_4) + w(n_5) < QU$. Thus, $w(n_2) > w(n_1)$. This together with inequation (5.64) implies that $w(n_2) + w(n_3) + w(n_4) \geq QU$. Consequently, $\{n_2, n_3, n_4\}$ should be an element of coterie C_5. This is not the case!

Cheung et al. (1989, 1990) introduce the multidimensional voting scheme and show that it provides a method for determining a corresponding assignment of weights to votes (to the nodes with a right to vote) for every coterie.

Quorum and votum of the multidimensional voting scheme (MD). As usual, every node with a right to vote gets a vote. The weight of these votes is given as a K-dimensional integer vector. Formally, the vote assignment is a matrix V where $V(n, k)$ represents the weight of the vote of a node n in its k-th dimension.

The quorum $QU = (qu_1, qu_2, \ldots, qu_K)$ is also a K-dimensional vector with $qu_k > 0$, $k = 1, 2, \ldots, K$.

In order to decide whether a votum is successful or not, we need an additional parameter l, $1 \leq l \leq K$. This parameter l indicates the number of dimensions for which a successful votum must be obtained. Obviously, for $l = 1$ and $K = 1$ the multidimensional voting scheme coincides with the weighted voting scheme as proposed by Gifford (1979).

The system designer has two independent levels at which to configure the voting process:

1. *Voting within a dimension:* At this level, the voting process is analogous to the "standard" voting scheme which was discussed earlier. The votum in a particular dimension k is successful if the sum of the votes (i.e., the weights of these votes in the k-th dimension of the vote vectors) from the set of nodes that have voted for a desired access is equal to or greater than the lower boundary qu_k.

2. *Voting across dimensions:* At this level, the votum is successful if in at least l dimensions a successful votum could be obtained according to Level 1.

As with all voting schemes discussed so far, read and write accesses are distinguished. A read quorum qu_{k_r} and a write quorum qu_{k_w} exist, for every dimension k, $1 \leq k \leq K$. They have to meet the following condition: $qu_{k_r} + qu_{k_w} > W_k$ where W_k is the sum of all weights of the votes in dimension k. This prevents a reader and a writer from simultaneously obtaining a successful votum with regard to the votes in dimension k.

It is not necessary to meet the other condition that we would have expected, i.e., $2 \times qu_{k_w} > W_k$. Voting across dimensions (Level 2) will deal with the problem of concurrent writers. Consequently, we know a value l_r for readers and a value l_w for writers. The choice of the values for l_r as well as for l_w must support the multiple-reader-single-writer strategy and must guarantee that among the nodes that have allowed the access there is at least one node with the most up-to-date physical replica of the desired logical data block. Thus, we have to meet the following two conditions:

$$l_r + l_w > K \text{ and } 2 \times l_w > K. \tag{5.70}$$

If we choose $l_r = 1$ then a read access is successful if a successful votum can be obtained in one of the dimensions. Analogously, a write access is only successful if a successful votum can be obtained in all K dimensions.

Cheung et al. (1990) furnished proof that for every coterie there exists a corresponding assignment of multidimensional weights to votes (to the nodes with a right to vote).

5.2.9 Hierarchical Voting

The main application area for Hierarchical Voting schemes is that of a network with an extremely high degree of replication (a large number n of replicas). If we assume $n = 100$ and apply the majority consensus scheme, every successful votum requires some 51 votes. This leads to a large amount of communication for the voting procedures. Is there a way to reduce the communication overhead when dealing with a large number of replicas?

Main idea. Nodes with a replica are logically organized in a tree structure of height h. The root of the tree is at height 0. All nodes with a replica sit within the leaves (at height h) of such a tree. Moreover, let the root have a_1 branches, and let each of these branches have in turn a_2 subbranches, etc. Consequently, we find a_h leaves for all subbranches at height $h-1$.

A votum for a read access is successful at a height i if at least QU_r^i (QU_w^i for a write access) nodes with a right to vote have voted for the desired access (without loss of generality, let the weight of each vote be 1). Again, the read quorum and the write quorum have to meet certain conditions:

$$QU_r^i + QU_w^i > a_i,\ \forall i = 1,\dots,h \tag{5.71}$$

and

$$2 \times QU_w^i > a_i,\ \forall i = 1,\dots,h \tag{5.72}$$

Both conditions support the multiple-reader-single-writer strategy and guarantee consistency among the replicated data blocks.

The following example illustrates how a Hierarchical Voting scheme reduces the communication overhead when dealing with a large number of replicas.

Example (Hierarchical Voting). Consider a degree of replication $n = 27$. The nodes with a replica (and a right to vote) can be organized in a tree of height 3 where $a_1 = a_2 = a_3 = 3$. If we give each node with a replica a vote of weight 1 and if we assume a majority consensus scheme then a successful votum for a read or a write access requires 14 votes.

Under the Hierarchical Voting scheme the situation is improved with regard to the minimal number of nodes that can support a successful votum. Here, a successful votum for a read or a write access requires 8 votes only.

Since $a_1 = 3$, at height 1 the quorum is 2. In each of the selected subbranches, the quorum is again 2 because $a_2 = 3$, for all subbranches at height 1. The same argument holds for height 2. The overall quorum is given by $2 \times 2 \times 2 = 8$.

Is there some weakness? Indeed, the logical structure bears a weakness. Although the Hierarchical Voting scheme needs fewer votes for a successful votum than other schemes, those votes, however, must be given by a precisely defined subset of nodes. In our example, for instance, the nodes that should vote must lie in the selected subbranches. For other schemes such a logical organization of nodes is irrelevant to the voting process.

Replication was introduced to improve the availability. The logical organization of the nodes and the restriction of which node may participate in a successful votum as mentioned before must not substantially reduce the potential availability. In the following, we will study two particular instances of Hierarchical Voting schemes and discuss their availability.

Hierarchical quorum consensus (HQC). Kumar (1990, 1991) proposed a Hierarchical Voting scheme where – as described above – the nodes with a replica sit in the leaves of a tree (at a height h only). Altogether such a tree then contains

$$n = \prod_{i=1}^{h} a_i \tag{5.73}$$

leaves or nodes with replicas, respectively.

Kumar (1990) proved the correctness of his scheme and developed an algorithm to collect the votes while traversing the tree. Network partitions are tolerated.

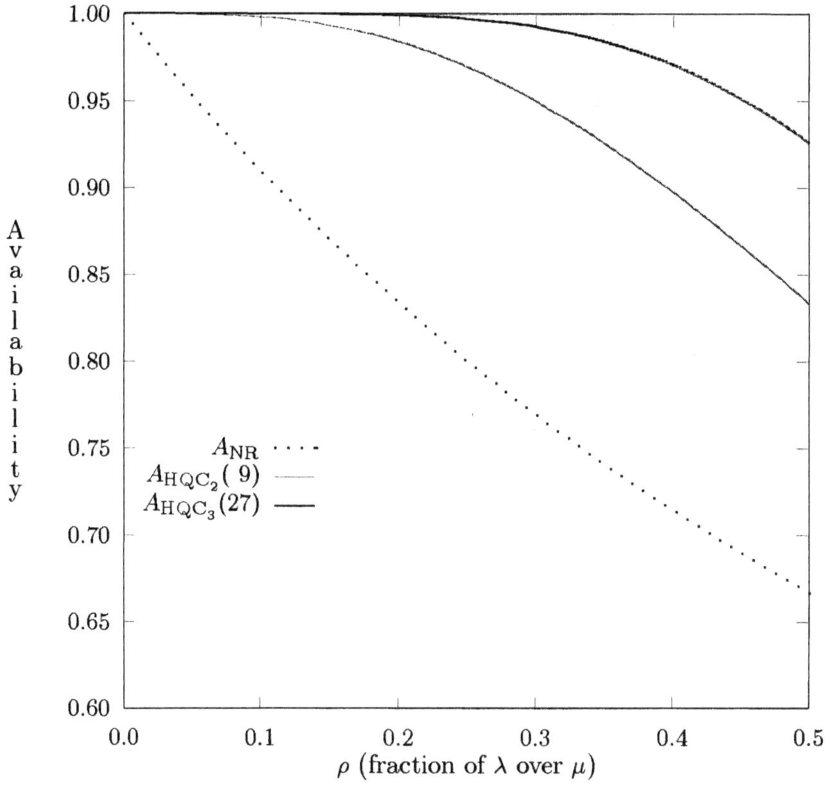

Fig. 5.24. Availability of the hierarchical quorum consensus scheme

Availability. We can express the availability of the hierarchical quorum consensus scheme A_{HQC_h} recursively: A_i denotes the availability at height i. Consequently, A_0 represents the availability of the root and, therefore, the availability of the whole scheme.

The availability at a height $i-1$ is given by the probability of obtaining a quorum QU_i among the a_i different subbranches. That means:

$$A_h = p = \frac{1}{1+\rho}$$

$$A_i = \sum_{j=QU_i}^{a_i} \binom{a_i}{j} {A_{i+1}}^j (1 - A_{i+1})^{a_i - j}$$

$$A_{\mathrm{HQC}_h}(n) = A_0 \tag{5.74}$$

We illustrate $A_{\mathrm{HQC}_h}(n)$ for $h = 2$ and $h = 3$ in Fig. 5.24. Here, we also assume that $a_i = 3$ at height i. Hence, we have 9 nodes with a replica for $h = 2$ and 27 for $h = 3$.

Tree quorum (TQ). Agrawal and Abbadi (1991) also use a logical tree organization for their Hierarchical Voting scheme. In their so-called tree quorum scheme the nodes with a replica (and a right to vote) are organized in the nodes (i.e., root, inner nodes and leaves) of a binary tree. Again, the root is at height 0. Let us furthermore assume that the binary tree is complete and full.

Altogether such a binary tree then contains

$$n = 2^{(h+1)} - 1 \tag{5.75}$$

nodes with a replica, respectively.

Availability. As before, we can express the availability of the tree quorum scheme A_{TQ_h} recursively. Since we deal with a binary tree, $a_i = 2, \forall i = 1, \ldots, h$. Let p_W denote the probability that the root of the binary tree or some (inner) root of a subtree is available. Moreover, let p_L and p_R denote the probability that the left or the right subtree, respectively, reach the needed quorum. Thus for height i we get:

$$\begin{aligned} A_i &= p_W \times p_L \times p_R + p_W \times (1 - p_L) \times p_R \\ &\quad + p_W \times p_L \times (1 - p_R) + (1 - p_W) \times p_L \times p_R \end{aligned} \tag{5.76}$$

Since $p_W = p$ and $p_R = p_L = A_{i+1}$ we immediately get:

$$\begin{aligned} A_i &= 2p(A_{i+1}(1 - A_{i+1})) + pA_{i+1}{}^2 + (1 - p)A_{i+1}{}^2 \\ &= 2pA_{i+1} + (1 - 2p)A_{i+1}{}^2 \end{aligned} \tag{5.77}$$

With ρ and the assumption $A_h = p = \frac{1}{1+\rho}$ for all leaves, we can now state the availability for the tree quorum scheme:

$$\begin{aligned} A_h &= p = \frac{1}{1+\rho} \\ A_i &= A_{i+1}{}^2 + \frac{2A_{i+1} - 2A_{i+1}{}^2}{1+\rho} \\ A_{\mathrm{TQ}_h}(n) &= A_0 \end{aligned} \tag{5.78}$$

Unfortunately this results in a nonlinear term A_{TQ_h}. Therefore we exemplify $A_{\mathrm{TQ}_h}(n)$ for $h = 2$ and $h = 3$ in Fig. 5.25.

5.3 Additional Schemes with Decentralized Control

Replication may provide the redundancy in a CSCW application needed for increased fault tolerance and improved availability of the group documents. Voting schemes allow fault-tolerant access to replicated group documents

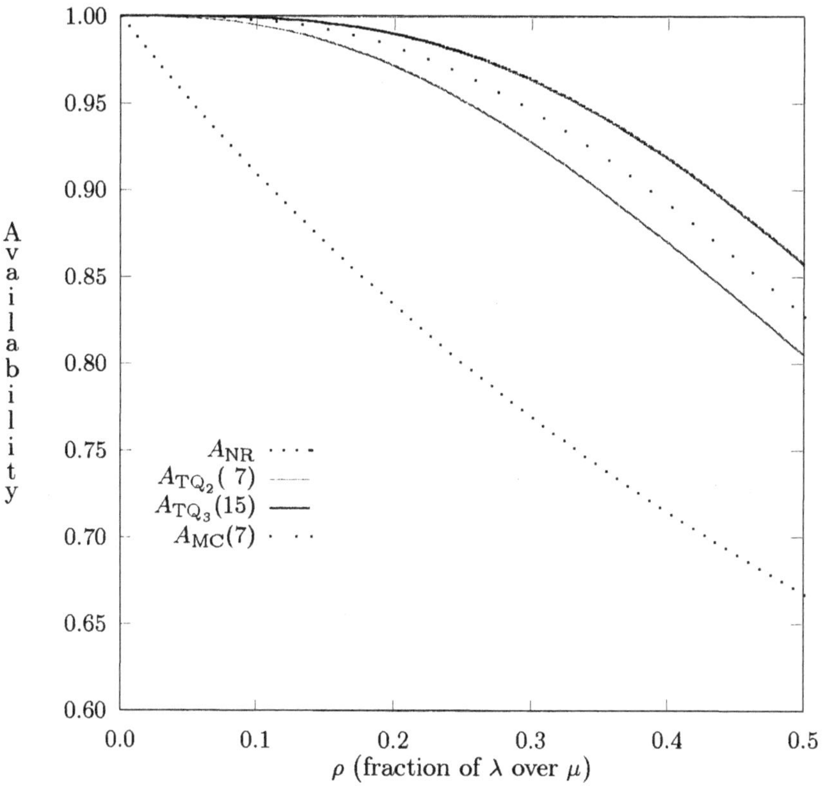

Fig. 5.25. Availability of the tree quorum scheme

while at the same time guaranteeing consistency. The last sections have introduced some of the most important variants of voting schemes.

In the next two sections, we will discuss two additional schemes for a pessimistic concurrency control with decentralized control that work without full-fledged voting, namely the coding scheme and the grid protocol (see Fig. 5.26).

5.3.1 Coding scheme

The coding scheme has been proposed by Agrawal and Jalote (1995). Besides synchronizing accesses to replicated data, the coding scheme attempts to achieve other more ambitious goals: firstly, a reduction of the needed storage space without limiting the advantages as far as the availability of the replicated data is concerned and, secondly, an increased data security.

We have already seen the reduction of the needed storage space as a subgoal when we discussed voting with witnesses in Sect. 5.2.4. There, storage space was saved through the introduction of nodes with a right to vote that do

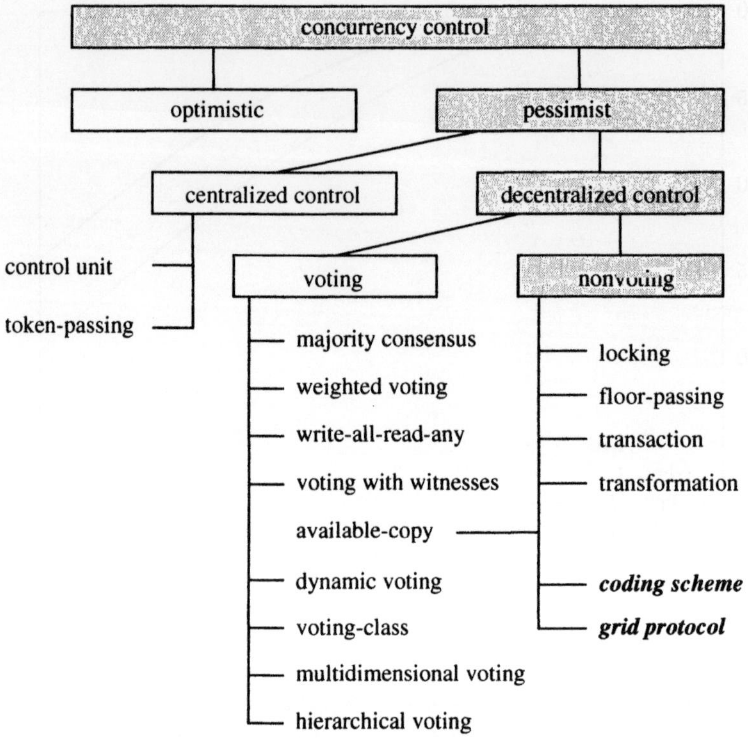

Fig. 5.26. Classification of concurrency control approaches: Additional schemes with decentralized control

not possess a full replica but store only the information needed for the voting process (locking states, version numbers, weight of the votes, etc.). Under the coding scheme storage space is saved through a distributed storage of data fragments. Data security is increased due to results by Rabin (1989) for a secure coding of these data fragments.

Main idea. A file[9] f is appropriately coded and split into N fragments of size $\frac{|f|}{M}$ in such a way that M arbitrary, pair-wise different fragments are sufficient to reconstruct the entire file f.

The parameters N and M are customizable as long as $N \geq M$ holds true. For the following discussion the coding theory is of no importance. The interested reader if referred to the relevant literature at the end of the chapter.

Each of the N file fragments is stored on a separate node. An accessing site (or more precisely, the subsystem managing the replication-transparent access to the fragments) has $\binom{N}{M}$ options to choose the M nodes from which

[9] In the following discussion we always argue for an entire file. Individual data blocks of the file are not distinguished. Instead we consider file fragments.

to reconstruct the entire file. This number of options heavily influences the availability of the coding scheme.

As a digression, let us briefly mention the security aspects: an (unauthorized) intruder has to access M different nodes (and break the individual coding algorithms) in order to read the file. This certainly increases data security. Under the voting schemes, on the other hand, where each node with a right to vote (except for the witnesses) always stores an entire replica of the file, an intruder has simply to break into one of these nodes to read the entire, possibly out-dated file (and break a single coding algorithm, if applicable).

Let us come back to the availability discussion. The redundancy that enables an accessing site to reconstruct the entire file out of M arbitrary, pairwise different fragments is just the basic concept of increasing availability. Obviously, a further improvement can be reached by replicating the individual fragments. The algorithms for synchronization become more complex. However, it is also the major attraction for this scheme.

If we assume a replication degree of n, with $n \geq N$, then n nodes get a fragment. For $n > N$, $n - N$ nodes get replicas of the fragments. In contrast to the voting schemes (except for voting with witnesses) where full replicas are stored, the overall storage space is reduced by a factor M. Each fragment is assigned a version number (similar to the one for data blocks as introduced for the voting schemes) that simply reflects successful updates. Again, without loss of generality assume that all nodes with a right to vote for a particular file fragment (or a replica of a file fragment) have a vote with weight 1. Additionally, let n be the given degree of replication and let QU_r as well as QU_w denote the read quorum and write quorum, respectively.

A new notion for the term quorum. If we look back to the discussion of the voting scheme, we see that there were values for a read quorum and values for a write quorum (that, of course, had to meet certain conditions). However, once appropriate values were found the quorum (for a read or a write access) was sufficient as well as necessary for obtaining a successful votum and for guaranteeing overall consistency.[10] Under the coding scheme we have to distinguish a minimally sufficient and a maximally necessary quorum.

A minimally sufficient quorum (for read or write accesses) is the minimal value for which the multiple-reader-single-writer strategy can be supported and for which the scheme can guarantee that among the nodes that have allowed accesses there is at least one node with the most up-to-date version number of an individual physical (file fragment) replica of the desired logical file (i.e., the accessing site can determine what the latest version number of the entire file is). However, this is not enough. The accessing site has to

[10] An exception to that is voting with witnesses: In the example of Fig. 5.9, p. 228, we have already learned to distinguish between a sufficient quorum that helps in the handling of conflicting accesses and that helps in the identification of up-to-date version numbers, as well as in the identification of necessary quorums that always guarantee the performance of desired accesses.

reconstruct the desired file out of M arbitrary, pair-wise different fragments. This is supported through a maximally necessary quorum.

A maximally necessary quorum (for read or write accesses) represents the worst-case (i.e., maximal) value for which an accessing site can be sure that nodes with M arbitrary, pair-wise different fragments participate in the obtained votum.

Let us give more formal definitions for these values:

Definition 5.3.1 (Minimal sufficient quorum). *The minimal sufficient read quorum QU_r^{ms} under the coding scheme is given as:*

$$QU_r^{ms} = \max(M\ ,\ QU_r). \tag{5.79}$$

Analogously, the minimal sufficient write quorum QU_r^{ms} under the coding scheme is given as: $QU_w^{ms} = \max(M\ ,\ QU_w)$. If a **write**-*operation updates at least κ file fragments, $\kappa \geq M$, we get more precisely:*

$$QU_w^{ms} = \max(\kappa\ ,\ QU_w). \tag{5.80}$$

Definition 5.3.2 (Maximal necessary quorum). *The maximal necessary read quorum QU_r^{mn} under the coding scheme is given as:*

$$QU_r^{mn} = n - \kappa + M. \tag{5.81}$$

Analogously, the maximal necessary write quorum QU_w^{mn} under the coding scheme is given as:

$$QU_w^{mn} = \max(QU_w\ ,\ n - N + \kappa). \tag{5.82}$$

File access. Firstly, let us consider a read access. The accessing site has to obtain at least QU_r^{ms} votes in order to guarantee mutual exclusion with regard to simultaneous write accesses. QU_r^{ms} votes are sufficient to determine the current version number (at least one of the nodes that have voted for the desired access possesses the current version number). Then, the accessing site checks whether at least M pair-wise different file fragments (with the current version number!) are participating in the votum. If this is the case, the accessing site is able to reconstruct the entire file out of M arbitrary, pair-wise different, up-to-date fragments. The read access is satisfied. Otherwise, the read quorum is not yet complete. From the above definition it is clear that no less than QU_r^{mn} votes have been successfully obtained, the read quorum is definitely obtained and the read access can be definitely satisfied.

The discussion of a write access is similar. Here, the accessing site has to obtain at least QU_w^{ms} votes in order to guarantee mutual exclusion with regard to simultaneous read or write accesses. A successful votum satisfying the write access requires at least κ votes because at least κ file fragments have to be updated. From the above definition it is clear that no less than QU_w^{mn} votes have been successfully obtained, the write quorum is definitely obtained and the write access can be definitely satisfied.

Example (Coding scheme). Consider a file that is split into ten fragments ($N = 10$) and coded in such a way that three arbitrary, pair-wise different fragments are sufficient to reconstruct the entire file ($M = 3$). Moreover, let the degree of replication be $n = 12$ (i.e., there are two additional replicas of some fragments). Without loss of generality assume again a situation where all nodes that possess a fragment have a vote with weight 1. Hence, read quorum and write quorum have to meet the following conditions (see (5.13), p. 225):

$$QU_r + QU_w > 12 \tag{5.83}$$

Therefore, let $QU_l = 4$ as well as $QU_s = 9$.

Under the coding scheme where $\kappa = 10$ (at least ten file fragments have to be updated) we immediately get:

$QU_r^{ms} = 4$, $QU_r^{mn} = 5$, $QU_w^{ms} = 10$ and $QU_w^{mn} = 12$.

These values are plausible: Even if 12 file fragments are updated each time (this is the maximum), a reader must at most fetch five file fragments. Only with five file fragments can a reader be sure of obtaining three pair-wise different file fragments from which to reconstruct the entire file. In the worst case, three of the five file fragments are identical ($n > N$).

Under the coding scheme where $\kappa = 7$ (i.e., at least seven file fragments have to be updated) we get slightly different values:

$QU_r^{ms} = 4$, $QU_r^{mn} = 8$, $QU_w^{ms} = 9$ and $QU_w^{mn} = 9$.

Here, for the sake of an increased write availability, the reading becomes more "difficult." This example also shows that there is a limit to the κ-values that favor writers. A further decrease of κ (i.e., below 7) makes the votum for a successful read access worse without improving the situation for a write access. This is because for all values of $\kappa \leq 7$, $QU_w^{ms} = QU_w^{mn} = 9$.

Availability. Figure 5.27 shows the state diagram for a coding scheme that makes use of an update sites cardinality (see Sect. 5.2.6). The figure shows a situation where the number of file fragments coincides with the degree of replication (i.e., $N = n$).

In analogy to the state diagrams of Sect. 5.2.6, each of the $(M+1) \times (n-M+1)$ states is denoted with (X, Y, Z) where

- the variable Y denotes the update sites cardinality of the nodes with an up-to-date replica,
- the variable X denotes the number of the available nodes with an update sites cardinality equal to Y, and
- the variable Z is the number of the available nodes with an update sites cardinality different from Y.

Now, let us look at the states in some detail. The states in the first row where at least M nodes with an up-to-date file fragment are available (i.e., the states $(M, M, 0)$, $(M+1, M+1, 0)$, ..., $(n, n, 0)$) , represent available states. The entire file can be reconstructed. The transitions between these

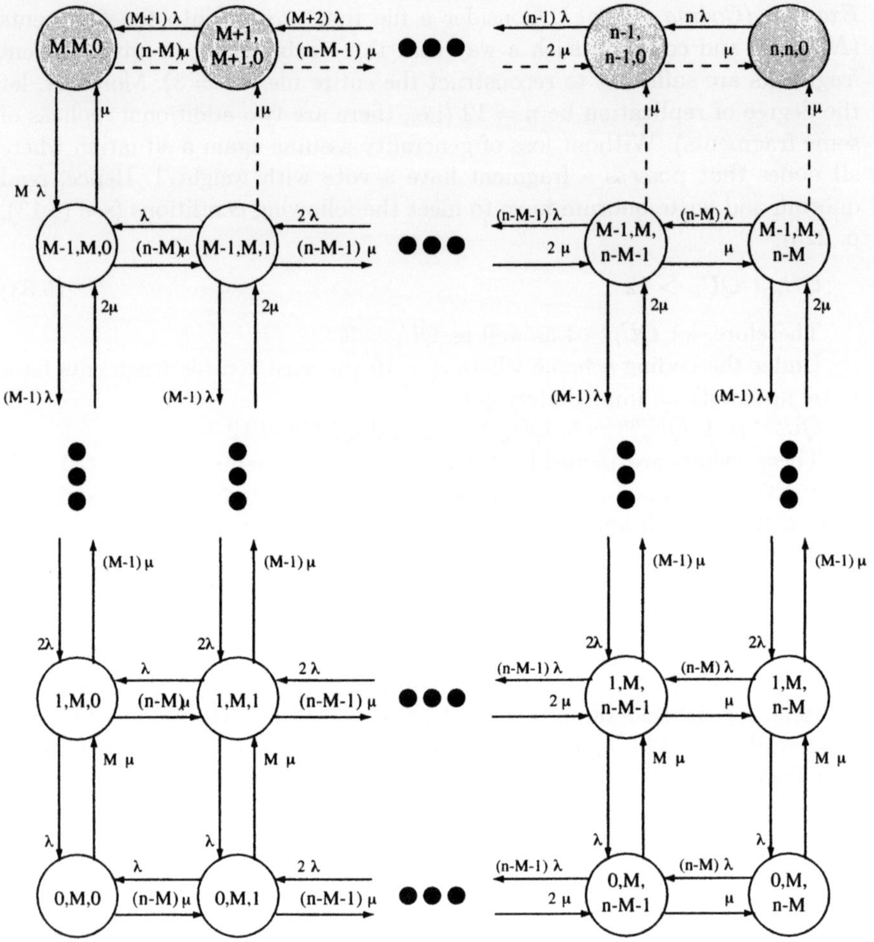

failure rate λ
repair rate μ

Fig. 5.27. State diagram of the coding scheme

states are simple. Consider, for instance, state $(n, n, 0)$ where all n nodes with an up-to-date file fragment are available. If one of the n nodes becomes unavailable, we reach state $(n-1, n-1, 0)$.[11] If the crashed node becomes once again available, we reach state $(n, n, 0)$ with a forced update. As before, transitions where a forced update occur are plotted with dashed arrows.

[11] In analogy to Sect. 5.2.6, all available states are denoted as if the next successful (e.g., forced) write access has already occurred.

State $(M, M, 0)$ is of some interest. If one of the remaining M nodes becomes unavailable, we reach state $(M-1, M, 0)$ in the second row. From $M-1$ file fragments, the entire file cannot be reconstructed, i.e., state $(M-1, M, 0)$ is an unavailable state.

If in the state $(M-1, M, 0)$ a crashed node becomes again available, we must distinguish whether or not this repaired node possesses an up-to-date file fragment.

- If the node in question possesses an up-to-date file fragment (in this situation there is only one such node), with μ we reach the available state $(M, M, 0)$ in the first row.
- If the node in question possesses an obsolete file fragment (in this situation there are $n-M$ such nodes), with $(n-M) \times \mu$ we reach the state $(M-1, M, 1)$. Although M nodes are available, the entire file cannot be reconstructed because one of the file fragments is out-of-date. Therefore, a successful forced update is not possible. Thus, state $(M-1, M, 1)$ is an unavailable state.

We remain in the second row as long as the node with the needed up-to-date file fragment does not become again available. If this, however, does happen, with μ we immediately reach the corresponding available state above, in the first row. An update is forced.

All the other states, i.e., the states in the third row (not plotted) down to the states in the last row ($(M+1)$-th row), share the following characteristic:

- If a node with an up-to-date file fragment becomes unavailable (third row down to the M-th row), we reach the corresponding unavailable state below.
  If a crashed node with an up-to-date file fragment once again becomes available (third row down to the $(M+1)$-th row), we reach the corresponding unavailable state above. Here, a successful forced update is not possible.
- If a node with an obsolete file fragment becomes unavailable, we reach another unavailable state, left in the same row.
  If a crashed node with an obsolete file fragment once again becomes available, we reach another unavailable state, right in the same row. Obviously, a successful forced update is also not possible.

If we look at the state diagram in more detail, we detect a similarity with the dynamic voting scheme: For $M = 2$ the proposed coding scheme corresponds to the dynamic voting scheme with update sites cardinality (see Fig. 5.22). We get the same results as far as the availability is concerned. The reduction of the storage space by a factor of 2, however, has to be paid for through an increased communication cost. For each access, the entire file has to be reconstructed from two fragments.

A particular analysis of the availability of the coding scheme for values $M > 2$ can be found in the seminal paper by Agrawal and Jalote (1995).

5.3.2 Grid protocol

The so-called grid protocol was proposed by Cheung et al. (1992). It provides, as the voting schemes, a means of synchronizing accesses to replicated data.

Main idea. In contrast to the voting schemes, the multiple-reader-single-writer strategy (and the guarantee that among the nodes that have allowed the access there is at least one node with the most up-to-date physical replica of the desired logical data block) is not supported by an appropriate read quorum and an appropriate write quorum but rather by a logical organization of nodes that possess the replicas. Let us briefly illustrate the idea behind this logical organization through an example.

Let 12 nodes with a replica be (logically) organized in a grid-like topology as depicted in Fig. 5.28.

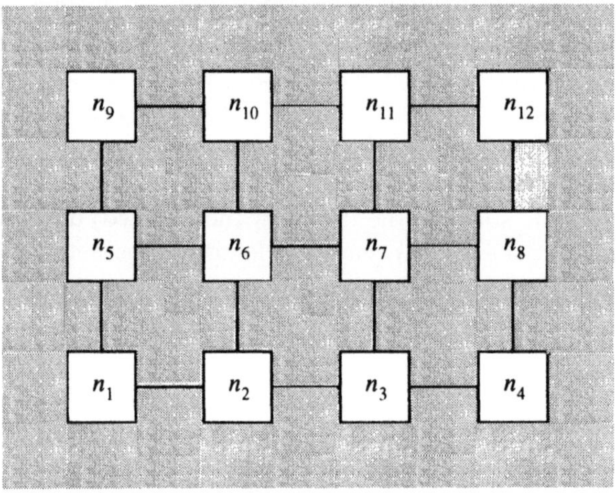

Fig. 5.28. Example of a grid-like topology

A reader or a writer, respectively, needs votes from a particular subset of nodes within the grid. But what does "particular subset" mean?

In order to reach a successful votum,

- a reader needs votes from at least one node in each column of the grid whereas
- a writer needs votes from at least one node in each column of the grid *and* votes from all nodes in at least one full column of the grid.

The grid protocol applies a two-phase commit protocol as well as multicast messaging for all nodes of a full row or a full column.

We denote the rows and columns of the grid with $1, 2, \ldots, R$ and $1, 2, \ldots, C$, respectively. Moreover, we define the operation **R_cast**$(r, (\textit{replyset}, N))$ as the sending of a multicast message $(\textit{replyset}, N)$ to all nodes of row r. Let

N be the request message and *replyset* the (sub)set of nodes in row r from which an answer is requested.

In analogy, we define the operation **C_cast**(c, (*replyset*, N)) as the sending of a multicast message (*replyset*, N) to all nodes of column c.

Definition 5.3.3 (C-cover). *A set of nodes G is called C-cover if each column of the logical grid has at least one node in common with G.*

Example (C-cover). In Fig. 5.28, the set of nodes $\{n_1, n_2, n_7, n_8\}$ is a C-cover.

The grid protocol also guarantees the consistency of the replicated data in the presence of link failures and network partitioning. Therefore, it applies the following strategy: A reader has to write-lock a C-cover while a writer besides read-locking a C-cover also has to read-lock all nodes of an entire column. The corresponding lock requests could be sent as a broadcast. However, since another goal of the grid protocol is some sort of load balancing among the nodes that have to process the request, these requests are sent as a multicast using the operations described above.

In order to reach a balanced load among the nodes that have to process the request, the accessing site first creates a random permutation Π_r of the row indices. This permutation is then used to determine the sequence in which (via a multicast) a C-cover is to be locked, either for a read or a write access.

For the following discussion, we consider the situation as depicted in Fig. 5.29. The nonconnected nodes within the grid are crashed or otherwise unavailable.

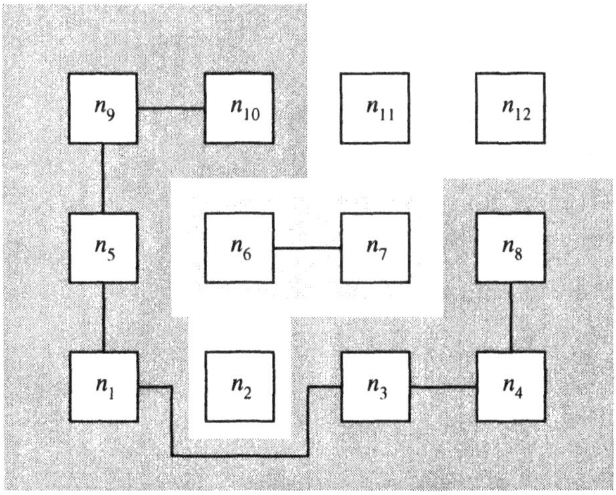

Fig. 5.29. Grid with crashed nodes

Read access. Let the created random permutation of the row indices be $\Pi_r = (3, 2, 1)$. Thus, the first attempt to lock a C-cover is initiated with the operation **R_cast**(3, ($\{n_1, n_2, n_3, n_4\}$, "**read** k **of** f")) where a read request for data block k of file f is multicast to the nodes n_1, n_2, n_3 and n_4. In the best of all possible worlds all four nodes would vote for the desired access. Unfortunately, if n_2 were to crash, only the nodes n_1, n_3 and n_4 would vote for the desired access and, therefore, set the requested lock. After a timeout, the next row (with regard to the created random permutation of the row indices Π_r) would be selected. The multicast **R_cast**(2, ($\{n_6\}$, "**read** k **of** f")) would be sent. Although this multicast would be sent to all nodes of the second row in the grid, only node n_6 would be asked to vote and to set a lock. Unfortunately, n_6 is also not available. After a timeout, the multicast **R_cast**(1, ($\{n_{10}\}$, "**read** k **of** f")) would be sent. Let node n_{10} vote for the desired access and set the lock. Thus, a C-cover would be reached. The data block k of file f would successfully be read.

Write access. First of all, the writer tries to lock a C-cover. This is done in an analogous fashion to that of the read access described above. Let us assume that the writer could lock the C-cover $\{n_1, n_3, n_4, n_{10}\}$.

Now, the accessing site creates a random permutation Π_c of the column indices. Let this permutation be $\Pi_c = (4, 1, 3, 2)$.[12]

Consequently, the first operation is **C_cast**(4, ($\{n_4, n_8, n_{12}\}$, "**write** k **of** f")). It is expected that all three nodes of this column will vote for the desired access and will set the requested lock. Assume that only nodes n_4 and n_8 vote for the desired access in time (i.e., before a timeout). Let the next multicast driven by the permutation Π_c, i.e., **C_cast**(1, ($\{n_1, n_5, n_9\}$, "**write** k **of** f")), achieve the desired goal where all nodes of this column vote for the desired access.

Now, a successful votum has been obtained because the nodes from a C-cover as well as all nodes from the first column have voted for the desired access. The update of data block k of file f can be performed successfully.[13]

Availability. As before, let R and C be the number of rows and columns, respectively. Moreover, let all nodes in the grid possess a replica of all data blocks of the file in question. Thus, the degree of replication is given by $n = R \times C$.

The probability that ξ nodes in an arbitrary column are available is given by $\binom{R}{\xi} p^{\xi} (1-p)^{R-\xi} C$.

[12] In the original proposal of the grid protocol, the permutation of the column indices is not fully random. Rather, the creation of the permutation considers which columns contain nodes that have been unavailable during the attempt to lock the C-cover. However, for simplicity we shall not consider this strategy here. The interested reader will find a discussion of the more complex strategy in the paper by Cheung et al. (1992).

[13] More precisely, we should say "in principle" because nodes that have voted for the desired access could have crashed in the meantime.

A column is said to be a C-cover candidate if at least one node in this column is available. The probability that a column is a C-cover candidate is given by $1 - (1-p)^R$.

Let $A^r_{\text{grid}}(R, C)$ denote the availability of a successful read access under the grid protocol, i.e., the probability with which a C-cover can be obtained for a read access (see Fig. 5.30):

$$A^r_{\text{grid}}(R, C) = \left(1 - (1-p)^R\right)^C \tag{5.84}$$

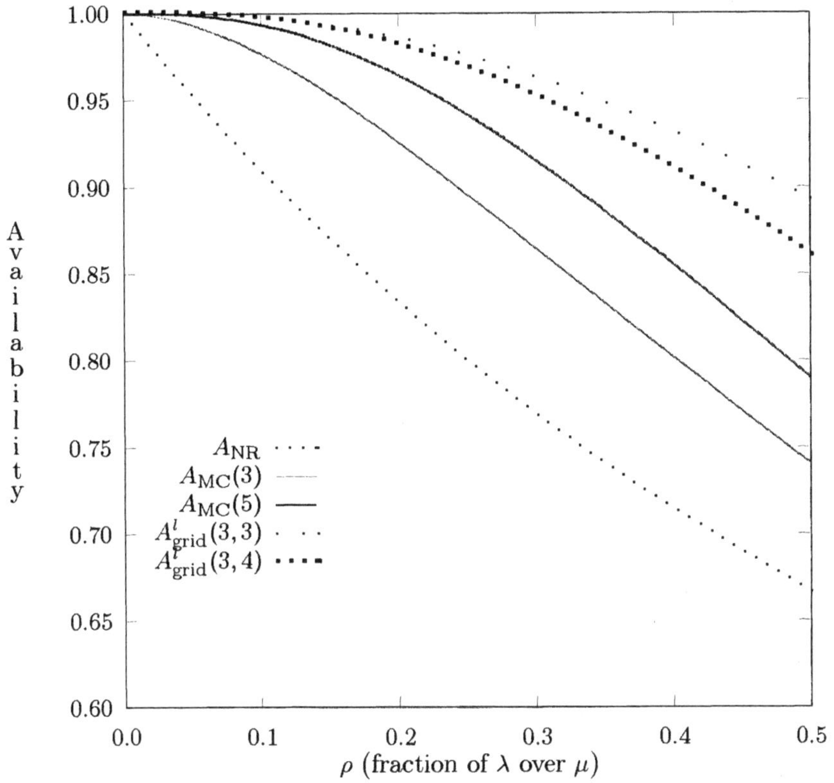

Fig. 5.30. Read availability of the grid protocol

A write access is successful if a C-cover and a complete column can be obtained. Let $A^w_{\text{grid}}(R, C)$ denote the availability of a successful write access under the grid protocol, i.e., the probability with which a C-cover and a complete column can be obtained for a write access under the assumption that the nodes of C columns have not yet been asked for their votes (using **C_cast**-operations). We can calculate $A^w_{\text{grid}}(R, C)$ by limiting ourselves to the number of nodes in the next (according to the created permutation) column that have not yet been asked for their votes.

If all R nodes are available, we immediately obtain a complete column. That is, we only need a C-cover in the remaining grid of size $(R \times (C-1))$. The probability for that is equal to $A^r_{\text{grid}}(R, C-1)$.

If only ξ, $0 < \xi < R$ nodes are available, this column is a candidate for a C-cover but, in the remaining $C-1$ columns, the accessing site still has to obtain a C-cover and a full column of available nodes.

The write access is not successful if all nodes in the next (according to the created permutation) column are unavailable. In this case, there is no way to obtain a C-cover.

In sum, we get:

$$A^w_{\text{grid}}(R,C) = p^R A^r_{\text{grid}}(R,C-1) + \textstyle\sum_{\xi=1}^{R-1} \binom{R}{\xi} p^\xi (1-p)^{R-\xi} A^w_{\text{grid}}(R,C-1).$$

If we further simplify the formula, we get:

$$A^w_{\text{grid}}(R,C) = p^R A^r_{\text{grid}}(R,C-1) + \left(1 - p^R - (1-p)^R\right) A^w_{\text{grid}}(R,C-1).$$

Since $A^w_{\text{grid}}(R,1) = p^R$ and $A^r_{\text{grid}}(R,0) = 1$, the availability of a successful write access under the grid protocol can be given without recursion by (see Fig. 5.31):

$$A^w_{\text{grid}}(R,C) = \left(1-(1-p)^R\right)^C - \left(1-p^R-(1-p)^R\right)^C \tag{5.85}$$

The first term is the already known availability of a successful read access (representing the need for a C-cover in a grid of size $(R \times C)$). The second term represents the probability of obtaining a C-cover but not a complete column of nodes which vote for the desired access.

Comparison to voting schemes. If the grid contains a single column only, the grid protocol coincides with write-all-read-any (see Sect. 5.2.3).

A comparison of the read and write availability of the grid protocol on the one hand and the voting schemes on the other hand reveals that the grid protocols needs a higher degree of replication to match the same availability as the voting schemes; see Fig. 5.31.

However, Cheung et al. (1992) show that load balancing through the multicast operations **R_cast** and **C_cast** justifies the increased degree of replication and leads to a uniform distribution of access requests, both for reading as well as for writing.

Voting schemes cannot balance the load for read and write accesses at the same time. If the read quorum is decreased, the write quorum has to be correspondingly increased: $QU_r + QU_w$ must be greater than the sum of the weights of all nodes with a right to vote.

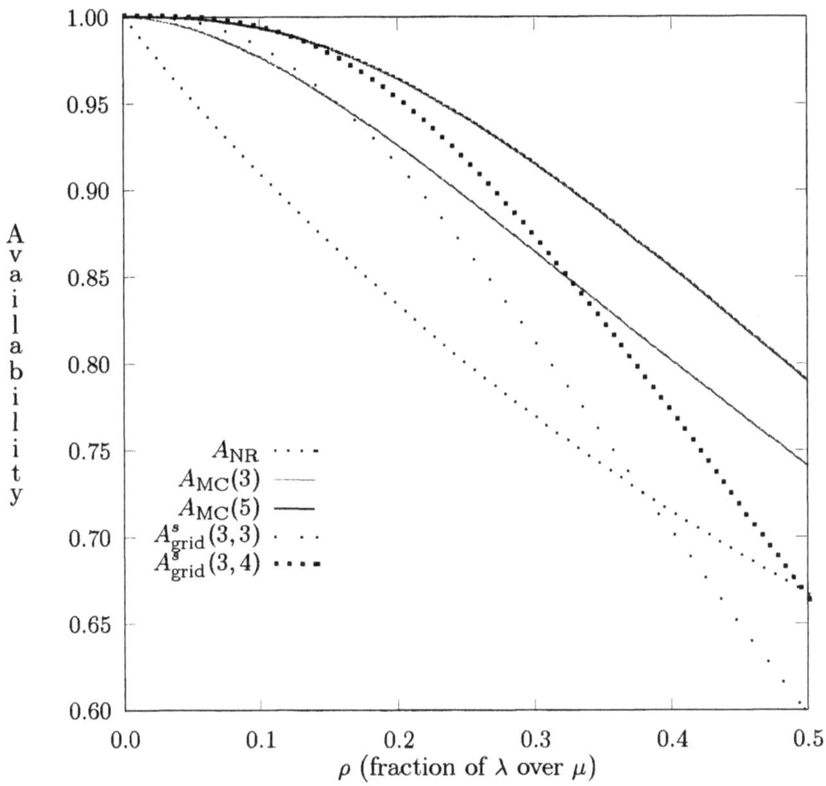

Fig. 5.31. Write availability of the grid protocol

5.4 Regeneration

An elegant way to adapt the degree of replication dynamically is provided by regeneration. The concept of regeneration was introduced by Pu et al. (1986). Regeneration increased the availability of a replicated file within the Eden system. Their regeneration protocol created new file replicas if existing replicas became unavailable. This was easy to achieve since Eden was used in networks where a partitioning of the network could not occur.

There is a certain relationship between regeneration and voting with witnesses, ghosts or bystanders. The probability of obtaining a successful votum under the regeneration protocol is similar to that of these voting schemes. However, the probability of a successful access is clearly higher under the regeneration protocol because witnesses, ghosts and bystanders – while having a right to vote – do not possess a full replica that could satisfy the desired access, especially for reading.

The regeneration protocol, on the other hand, allows successful reading (provided the needed votum could be obtained) as long as at least a single up-to-date replica is available. For writing the situation is slightly different. Here, writing is suspended in the case where the initial number of replicas could not be "regenerated." This might decrease the overall availability for write accesses. Still, the write availability can be further improved if the regeneration protocol is used as part of a weighted or dynamic voting scheme.

Long and Pâris (1990) introduce witnesses that can be regenerated. In this scheme, (volatile) witnesses are held in main memory and, when a machine hosting a witness crashes, these witnesses are regenerated. This is especially interesting for diskless machines.

Huang and Li (1989, 1990) propose a dynamic voting scheme with regeneration. In contrast to the standard regeneration protocol, the nodes with a replica store not only the latest data blocks but also a variety of versions of these data blocks. This can increase the availability even further.

Another voting scheme enhanced by a regeneration protocol has been developed by Adam and Tewari (1991). In contrast to the original variant by Pu, their scheme tolerates node crashes and network partitioning.

5.5 Further Reading

The book by Bernstein et al. (1987) gives a thorough introduction to concurrency control and recovery in (distributed) databases. Among others, the collection by Kumar (1995) presents a taxonomy of concurrency control mechanisms and introduces synchronization issues of long-lived computations. Atomic transactions are discussed in the book by Lynch et al. (1994). Replication techniques in distributed systems are covered in the book by Helal et al. (1996). The book on distributed operating systems by Goscinski (1991) contains a concise introduction to replication control schemes.

A theory of coteries for mutual exclusion in a distributed systems including a set of relevant algorithms is given by Ibaraki and Kameda (1993) as well as Neilsen and Mizuno (1992).

Bloch et al. (1987) describe an efficient application of weighted voting for replicated directories. Moser et al. (1990) have analyzed the strengths and weaknesses of several weighted voting algorithms. Kumar and Segev (1989) as well as Garcia-Molina and Barbara (1984) have developed algorithms to choose an appropriate read quorum and write quorum, respectively, according to certain optimality criteria.

The available-copy scheme and the relevant recovery protocols are discussed by Abbadi et al. (1985), Carroll et al. (1987) as well as Goodman et al. (1983).

Dynamic quorum adjustment while the network is partitioned is introduced by Herlihy (1987). Efficient dynamic voting algorithms are discussed by Pâris and Long (1988). Tang (1990) proposes the voting-class scheme.

The coding scheme has been proposed by Agrawal and Jalote (1995). Rabin (1989) discusses the underlying theoretical aspects of the coding scheme.

The grid protocol has been proposed by Cheung et al. (1992).

A "marriage" between a regeneration protocol and some voting schemes has been discussed by Long et al. (1989), Long and Pâris (1989) as well as Noe and Andreassian (1987).

Part III

Application Classes of Computer-Supported Cooperative Work

6. Communication Systems and Shared Information Spaces

The following chapter will first deal with asynchronous and synchronous message and communication systems. Asynchronous communication may be used in situations where people have a shared task but they do not work simultaneously on it. There are no real-time requirements. Examples of these groupware systems are information exchange, distance learning or bulletin boards. The architecture and functionality of a typical email system will be discussed. Further attention will be directed towards synchronous communication as exemplified by video conferences.

The second part of the chapter presents an information management approach to support the work on shared information in the context of workgroups. We will discuss an architecture for hypermedia systems, the hypertext abstract machine, and the Dexter reference model which facilitates the interoperability between different hypermedia systems. The navigation problem in large information spaces and hypertext-specific solutions are presented.

The IBIS method provides functions to systematically structure the problem solving information. Finally, we will present the information space of the Campiello system, a community support system for tourist applications.

6.1 Email Systems

For some people email is the only successful groupware system while others do not consider it as groupware at all. In the following we will briefly describe the functionality and architecture of the X.400 email standard.

Figure 6.1 depicts the architecture of an email system consisting of message transfer agents and user agents; see also Tanenbaum (1996).

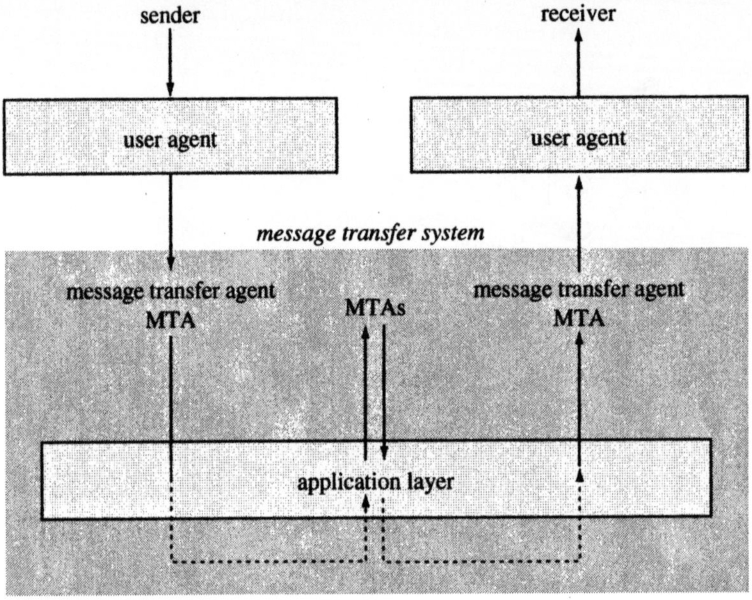

Fig. 6.1. Architecture of a typical email system

Email provides the following basic services:

1. *Composition:* This refers to the authoring process of creating new messages which may be replies to already received messages. In general, text editors are used for this process often incorporating special email support, e.g., automatic insertion of the recipient's address in the case of reply messages. Increasingly multimedia editors are used for the composition of so-called MIME (*Multipurpose Internet Mail Extension*) messages (Tanenbaum 1996).
2. *Transfer:* An email system provides mechanisms for message transfer between senders and receivers, and vice versa. Among other things, MIME standardizes the transfer of images, audio and video.
3. *Notification:* The sender is notified of the outcome of his message, for example if it could not be delivered within a certain time period. Modern

email systems also enable the sender to request an acknowledgement of the message reception.

4. *Conversion:* If the sender and receiver use different system platforms with different data formats, email systems convert messages. In the absence of MIME support ASCII text is often used as the common data format.
5. *Display:* The received messages are processed for representation on the receiver's screen. The processing depends on the local display characteristics and in the case of multimedia and MIME documents also on formatting information transmitted with the messages. External programs may be invoked by the email system to perform message formatting.
6. *Disposition:* Many email systems enable the user to specify actions, some are performed before a message is read and others are executed after a message has been displayed. Example actions are the deletion of the message or the archiving of the message in the message database.

6.1.1 Message transfer agent

The message transfer system consists of message transfer agents which relay messages from the originator to the receiver. For communication between the different message transfer agents, email systems require a computer network. Since email systems are generally based on the store-and-forward concept, they do not establish any end-to-end connection between the sending and the receiving node, as illustrated by the following code fragment:

Code fragment (store-and-forward system).

```
class messages_transfer_agent
    <class variables>
    public:
    void send(message N);
void messages_transfer_agent ::send(message N)
    if (N originates from the local user agent) then
        check for correctness;
        if (N is incorrect) then
            deny transmission and notify sender of N via local user agent;
            return
        else extend N by message identifier, sender address and timestamp;
    if (receiver of N is local) then
        store N in message buffer (mailbox) of receiver;
    else send(message N) to next message transfer agent;
                                /* store-and-forward; selection of the next message
                                   transfer agent depends on the receiver's address
                                   of message N                                  */
```

6.1.2 User agents

User agents handle the interaction with the users and communicate with the associated message transfer agents for sending and receiving of messages. Typically, a user agent is an independent program (sometimes called a mail reader) which is explicitly invoked by the user. The user interface is either graphics oriented or based on a traditional character oriented interface.

After a user agent is started it retrieves all newly arrived messages from the user's mailbox managed by the associated message transfer agent and incorporates them into the local message database of the user.

Example (Unix). In Unix the local message database is implemented via directories and files.

A message consists of two parts: the body and the header. The body captures the actual message content and is not interpreted by the message transfer system. It may contain different data formats or media (images, binary data or unstructured text). In general, message transfer agents possess only limited capability of converting between different types of media. The header consists of a number of fields whose values are entered in one of several ways: by the sending user manually, or by the user agent of the sender automatically, or else by the message transfer agents.

Example (Email message header). In order to avoid any malpractice the sender field of an email message is automatically specified by the email system (e.g., the value is derived from the login name). However, there might be a difference between the person who created the message and the person who is the actual sender of the message. For example, a secretary might send a message on behalf of his boss. The message header should include both names using the *From* field for the message creator and using the *Sender* field for the actual sender of the message.

Additional message header fields exist for the primary recipients of a message, i.e., the users to whom the message is sent (*To* field), as well as secondary recipients (*Cc* field). A secondary recipient is a person to whom an additional message copy is sent ("Carbon copy"). Moreover, there may be secret recipients (*Bc* field), i.e., they receive a message copy, yet are invisible to primary and secondary recipients ("Blind carbon copy").

Other message header fields are:

- *Message ID*, an automatically generated unique identifier for referencing a particular message later;
- *Date*, the time and date when the message was sent;
- *Reply-To*, the email address to which replies should be sent;
- *In-Reply-To*, the message is a reply to a previous message;
- *Subject*, short one line summary of the message content;

- *Expiration-Date*, the date and time when the message expires. For example, the announcement of a meeting becomes obsolete after the meeting has taken place;
- *References*, list of messages which are related to the current message. Reference messages are important for asynchronous computer conferencing.

6.1.3 Message envelope

During transfer within the network, messages are enclosed in an envelope (similar to conventional letters). Information on the envelope is only relevant to message transfer agents, and usually not visible to users. The message envelope consists of a number of fields. There are four categories:

1. address,
2. delivery,
3. conversion and
4. security.

For better understanding of the mechanism, some examples of these categories are listed below.

Example (Address). The category address usually contains the sender, recipient and alternative recipients' email addresses. If the address of the recipient has become invalid, the possibility of sending the message to an alternative recipient must be specified. These kinds of messages are often forwarded to the so-called postmaster.

Example (Delivery). This category determines the delivery priority (for example slow, normal or quick transfer within the network) and required actions on the receiving end. For example, it specifies whether or not an acknowledgement is automatically returned to the sender upon message delivery to the recipient.

The sender may even specify a desired delivery time. For example, in order to synchronize product announcements at all locations the message should be delivered at the same time to all addressed recipients.

Example (Conversion). Fields of this category typically define conversion permissions (i.e., whether or not the message content can be converted into another format at the receiving end). The sender may specify that conversion is only to be allowed if no information is thereby lost.

Example (Security). The security category typically contains fields for a sender signature (for example digital signature), a checksum of message content to detect transmission errors, a security classification (like top secret, secret, public). This category is especially important for PEM (*privacy enhanced mail*) (Kent 1993).

6.1.4 Email address

Currently, there are two major addressing schemes used in email systems for wide area networks: the domain addressing as used by the Internet and the OSI addressing scheme.

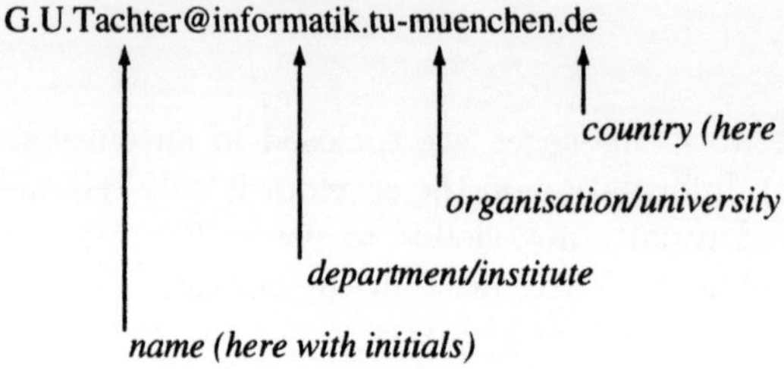

Fig. 6.2. Domain addressing scheme

In the former case, users are associated with domains which again may be subdivided into smaller entities (Fig. 6.2). The domain addressing scheme has a fixed structure and is easily adaptable for users accessing information via public or private organizations. Initially, it was assumed that this scheme would suffice for approximately one million users. The rapid development of the Internet surpassed these figure; for 1998 is was estimated that more than 50 million users have email addresses.

The OSI addressing scheme X.400 is closely related to domain addressing. It is based on the use of attributes (such as country, organization, department, name, telephone number, postal address) and includes an attribute inheritance hierarchy.

Example (Attribute inheritance and OSI addressing).
The attribute/value pair *organization* = *tu-muenchen* automatically implies the attribute/value pair *country* = *Germany*.

Example (Email address using OSI). The following attribute/value pairs specify the email address of Fig. 6.2 according to the OSI addressing scheme: *Name* = *G.U.Tachter*, *Department* = *Informatik*, *Organization* = *tu-muenchen* and *Country* = *Germany*.

6.1.5 Groupware characteristics of an email system

Email systems replicate messages in order to achieve many-to-many communication. Each site must store and update the address list of all group members, which might be a problem if the group composition changes frequently. Another problem is that newcomers to the group only receive those messages sent after they joined the group. Moreover, group discussion using email is only marginally structured. Each group member must arrange the local copies of the group messages in his own environment.

6.2 Video Conferencing

Besides economical and technological considerations, political aspects, such as the Gulf war, have strongly promoted a new form of communication: video conferencing. As opposed to email, video conferencing is a CSCW application type which supports explicit, synchronous, distributed communication between group members. It is used where personal contact is important but impeded by geographical distribution.

In principle, there are three categories of video conferences:

- video conferences held in special meeting rooms,
- video conferences supported by picture telephones, and
- computer-supported video conferences between offices, so-called desktop video conferences (see Sec. 2.8.2). ProShare by Intel Corporation is a commercially available system of this kind.

Video conferencing is often used as an additional communication channel to enhance group interaction. It should not be considered as a complete replacement of face-to-face interaction. Thus, we can distinguish between situations during groupwork requiring direct, physical contact (i.e., face-to-face meetings), and goals that might also be achieved through video conferencing. For example, if negotiations within the team require persuasion and getting acquainted with each other, then the personal contact and the awareness of peripheral information, such as the other person's mood, play an important role which suggests that a face-to-face meeting should be held. As opposed to this, information transfer and cooperative problem solving can easily be done via video conferencing. The increased connectivity via computer networks has opened up new application domains for video conferencing (e.g., teleteaching and interactive product presentation to a large, geographically dispersed group of people).

Business analysts expect a significant decline of business trips due to video conferencing. However, as some surveys show (Reichwald et al. 1998), the opposite may indeed happen. Conferencing systems allow managers to maintain contact with their departments even from remote locations and thus to inform themselves of the work's progress and problems. Business trips can be maintained for face-to-face meetings with those business partners the managers are less familiar with.

6.2.1 Aspects in the usage of video conferencing

In the following, we will give a brief overview of important aspects in the usage of video conferencing concentrating on telepresence, protection of private sphere, eye-to-eye contact, subconversations, the positioning of cameras and the size of video images.

Video conferences aim at providing the same high quality personal interaction for geographically dispersed people as that found in face-to-face meetings. The physical presence is replaced by the so called telepresence[1] providing the illusion that remote participants are present within the physical space of the local participant. Video enables an additional nonverbal communication channel, thus using gestures and mimicry to increase the information flow and information value. For example, a person listening may nod his head to indicate that he understood the verbal information, while bending forward often means that the listener is trying to understand something not yet clear to him. These expressions of understanding cannot be used in pure audio communication links; the speaker would have to demand explicit confirmation of the listener's comprehension of the conveyed information. Moreover, nodding one's head might anticipate the answer of the current verbal communication. Visual communication is extremely important during silence periods, since the reason for the silence is often obvious without any additional information. We can conclude that video is extremely helpful in situations which require a variety of communication channels to improve group interaction.

The protection of people's private sphere is especially important in situations where video cameras and microphones are permanently switched on and thus are sending continuous information about the local environment to all connected receivers. Aspects to be considered are the personal appearance and the private workspace. In order to avoid any secret monitoring situations many video conferencing systems are based on the concept of reciprocity (i.e., you cannot view a partner in his office without being seen by him).

Gaze awareness is another important aspect for the combination of verbal and nonverbal communication channels, especially for the transmission of vocal (loud or soft voice, pitch) or non vocal (gestures and mimicry) information. Small video images often cause a problem because speakers cannot be identified by their lip-movement, thus a formal approach is necessary. Floor-passing schemes (see Sect. 4.6) can help by alternating the permission to speak and by displaying the current speaker on the screen of the conference participants.

In face-to-face meetings, the speaker often seeks eye-contact with one or several listeners which is hard to achieve during desktop video conferencing. Firstly, computer screens are too small for the user to be able to identify small movements or gaze directions of remote partners, and secondly, the gaze direction often depends on where the video camera is positioned in relation to the video window on the screen. For example, if both are far apart, the user might look towards the video window and not into the video camera in order to achieve eye contact with his remote partner; however, to the remote partner it would appear as if the user was not looking at him. Users are usually unaware of the camera positioning and screen layout of the remote participants. The experimental teleconferencing system TELEPORT (Gibbs et al. 1999) incorporates innovative features to address the issues of

[1] Sometimes people use also the term copresence.

eye contact and gaze awareness. It uses full-wall display surfaces to reveal nuances of gestures and body language. Furthermore, it tracks the viewing position of the local participant to display remote participants on the wall display from the local participant's perspective.

It must also be decided how many cameras are to be used at each site. If only one camera is installed, it must be focused on the person, while the usage of multiple cameras allows the conveyance of additional information about the local environment and special characteristics of the conference room. Surveys have indicated that remote partners feel much more comfortable if they see their respective partners and their positions within their environments, rather than only seeing talking heads. However, this requires multiple video streams. If several geographically dispersed people participate in a video conference the limited screen size may not allow the display of all video streams.

During face-to-face discussions, the distance between participants plays an important role. In the context of video conferencing the size of the video image generally implies the perceived distance between the participants: desktop video conferencing uses small video images while in video conference rooms the oversized images of remote participants are projected onto large screens.

As opposed to face-to-face meetings, subconversations are more difficult to arrange during video conferencing, since generally verbal expressions are distributed to all participants. Modern desktop video conferencing systems allow the speaker to control the propagation of the audio stream originating from his site. He may either switch off the audio channel completely or select a subset of participants who are still able to receive his audio information while the remaining participants are disconnected from his audio stream. However, they may still receive the full video information. Usually the selection process is supported by a graphical user interface which allows a user to click on names or icons of the remote participants of a subconversation.

6.2.2 Conference management

A conference can be initiated either explicitly by invitation or announcement from the initiating person, or else by establishing a permanent communication channel. In the former case, we can distinguish between formally planned and ad hoc conferences. In the latter case, several group members may, for example, notice that they are working on the same group document. This information is provided as part of workspace awareness. This may lead to the initiation of a spontaneous video conference to discuss open issues and future activities.

If an initiator announces a conference, then the respective information is entered into the conference calendar, the content of which can be queried by all potential participants. It is their decision whether or not they wish to participate. This kind of conference initiation makes sense for open, dynamic groups with changing group membership; joining and leaving even during a conference are easy. An example is the MBone[2] tools (Macedonia and Brutzman 1994), which support video conferences in connection with a shared whiteboard across the Internet.

A permanently established communication channel implements media spaces, such as electronic hallways (see Sect. 4). These are especially useful for the initiation of spontaneous, informal interaction. However, the initiation process during which people contact each other requires a special protocol. Frequently, everyday items are used for the graphical representation of situations: a closed door, for example, means do not disturb, a slightly opened door indicates that the person inside is busy, but she might not mind being interrupted briefly, and if the door is completely open, then there is no restriction for prospective communication partners. However, it must be noted that the symbols may have different meanings in different cultural backgrounds, or no meaning at all to some ethnological groups. The system FreeWalk (Nakanishi et al. 1999) provides a shared 3D virtual space for casual meetings. Participants who are represented by 3D polygon pyramids having their live video mapped on to them may move freely within the virtual space (see Fig. 6.3). As a user approaches another pyramid the voice volume is adjusted to enable interaction with the participant represented by the pyramid.

Fig. 6.3. FreeWalk meeting environment

[2] Multicast Backbone

Besides the initiation of a conference, its termination must be given attention. Participants must be aware of who is allowed to close a conference (e.g., only the conference initiator or any conference participant).

6.3 Shared Information Spaces

An essential part of groupwork is the manipulation of common group documents as well as the communication via shared artifacts. Thus, shared information is used on the one hand as a communication medium to transfer knowledge and facts, and on the other hand as a means of formulating intermediate and final results of groupwork. Further, organizations may use an information management system to record the history of activities and their results to provide an organizational memory which allows the organization to learn from past mistakes.

Traditional text, like printed documents or computer files, are typically linear. There is a linear, sometimes hierarchical structure which defines the sequence for reading the text. Reference manuals and dictionaries are the exceptions. In the following, we will examine nonlinear structures, which seem to be more suited to the storage of shared information as created and used during groupwork. Hypertext is a typical example of a nonlinear method of structuring information. It supports nonlinear reading which means there is no predefined sequence for reading the information. Rather than defining a fixed reading sequence, a hypertext author incorporates a number of alternative paths through the entire information space.

Hypertext is particularly useful for managing the information created and used during groupwork. It is also ideal for applications such as electronic books, electronic libraries, on-line documentation, and software engineering organizing specification documents and source code. However, the basic node-link model of simple hypertext systems might often not suffice for representing and processing complex multimedia documents which are required by a variety of multimedia applications.

6.3.1 General definitions

Definition 6.3.1 (according to Nelson 1967, 1980).
"Hypertext is a combination of natural language text with the computer's capacity for interactive branching, or dynamic display ... of a nonlinear text ... which cannot be printed conveniently on a conventional page."

Hypertext provides a generic approach for the construction of nonlinear, computer-supported material; the user can display the material on his screen in a nonlinear manner. Figure 6.4 exemplifies the nonlinearity in a hypertext document (Nielsen 1990); see also Conklin (1987) and Kuhlen (1991).

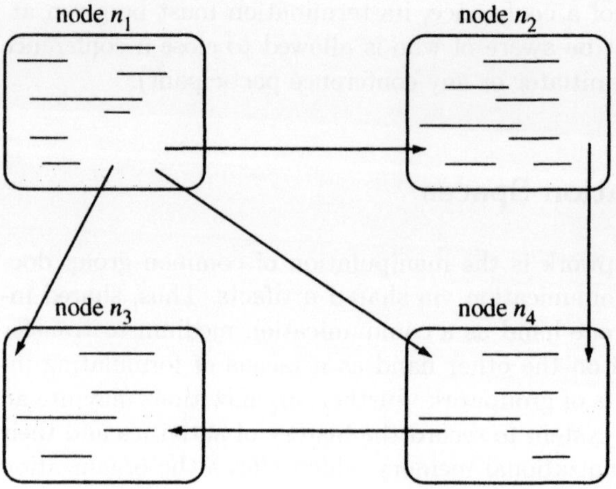

Fig. 6.4. Example of a nonlinear hypertext document

The term hypertext was coined by Ted Nelson in the 1960s to describe nonlinear books. Scientific publications often use the term hypertext to refer to nonlinear concepts, as well as the systems realizing these concepts.

Hypertext implies the following features:

- Heterogeneous information can be read and stored in a nonlinear form.
- In principle browsing and goal-oriented navigation through the information space are permitted.
- Heterogeneous data formats are supported. If the documents encompass multiple data formats, such as text, images, audio or video hypertext documents are often hypermedia documents.
- The content has priority over the representation on the screen or on paper.
- The entire information space is modularized into smaller information units which are interrelated.

Kuhlen (1991) investigated the importance of hypertext as a supplement to the traditional use of paper. The amount of available information doubles within short time periods. New storage media often with incompatible data formats are emerging. Information is increasingly distributed worldwide and calls for innovative means of overcoming these impediments. The success and often the survival in the competitive commercial world is conditioned by how fast high-quality information may be accessed. However, the creation and management of high-quality information must cost the same or less than information maintained through conventional means.

6.3.2 History of hypertext systems

Hypertext systems are computer-supported information systems. They represent and manage multimedia information through a network of nodes[3] defin-

[3] In some systems, nodes are also referred to as notecards or frames.

ing an information space. The information is subdivided into smaller units which are assigned to the nodes as their content. The relationship between nodes is specified by directed links. The users may navigate through the information space along the links.

Figure 6.5 depicts the historical development of some of the most influential hypertext systems. Dotted lines illustrate the mutual influence between systems. In the following, we will discuss some of these systems in more detail:

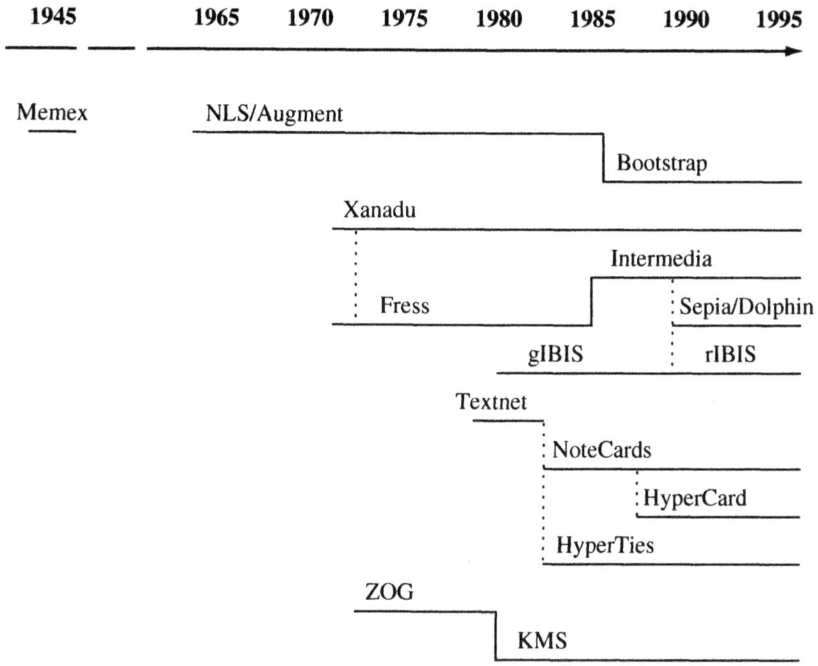

Fig. 6.5. Historical development of hypertext systems

Vannevar Bush[4] was far ahead of his time when he introduced in 1945 the system Memex. Memex should provide a system which allows users to store all types of information, such as books, notes, correspondence. An index facilitates fast information access. Bush had proposed a machine using microfilm and photographic cells. Although the idea of Memex was never realized and put into practice, it can be seen as the origin of all later developed hypertext systems (using computers instead of microfilms).

It took several years until a similar idea became reality: Between 1963 and 1968, Engelbart and English developed the system NLS which was modified in the early 1970s and marketed under the name Augment. The authors emphasized the tree structure of the textual information. The system allowed

[4] Vannevar Bush, scientific advisor of president Roosevelt.

the creation of cross-references between text units and the navigation across these links to quickly switch between different parts of the tree. Further, the nodes visited during navigation were recorded in a history list in order to allow backtracking.

One of the largest hypertext systems of its time with over 20,000 nodes was ZOG (Robertson et al. 1981) which was developed at Carnegie-Mellon-University in Pittsburgh. It was implemented for a distributed environment and it was used on the aircraft carrier USS Carl Vinson. Bush's Memex and ZOG (see also *Electronic Document System* (EDS), Feiner et al. 1982) store the navigational history in order to allow fast backtracking to previously read information. An important aspect of ZOG was the modeling of the textual information by the appropriate graphical structure.

Xanadu (Nelson 1981) supports a very flexible link management. An individual link consists of three parts. The first part points to the source node, the second part to the destination node, and the third part to a textual description describing the link type.

The idea for Xanadu was Ted Nelson's. Intending to design a system for the management of all the world's scientific works, he had the idea of developing a universal hypertext system that encompasses all that has ever been written. In order to avoid any replication, all information is to be stored only once. Thus, within a scientific paper, instead of numerous references to other scientific papers, the material referred to would be incorporated in the form of links. Xanadu also incorporates fee management mechanisms for handling situations when an author references the works of other authors. Some prototypes of the idea were implemented in the late 1960s; the first commercial implementation did not start until 1988.

NoteCards was developed at Xerox PARC by Halasz (1988; see also Halasz et al. 1987) as an experimental hypertext system allowing the creation of a semantic network of electronic cards. Cards represent here the nodes of the hypertext system. Four basic objects are provided:

1. *Cards* contain the user information, such as text or graphics. Each card has a title by which it can be referenced.
2. *Links* connect two cards, thus modeling a semantical relationship between them. The type of relationship is captured by the specification of the link type.
3. *Browsers* are special cards containing a visual representation of the semantic network or parts of it. They are used to structure the network in order to facilitate navigation. Modifications of a browser card have no consequence for the underlying network. Thus, users can easily experiment with different structural variations and compare the results.
4. Like browsers, *fileboxes* are special kinds of cards which are used for organizing extremely large card collections. NoteCards requires that each card is stored in at least one filebox. Additionally fileboxes may contain

other fileboxes, however, the set of fileboxes must constitute a direct, acyclic graph.

The primary application of NoteCards is the creation of a personal information database based on cards. It aims at supporting an individual user during the collection, categorization and interpretation of ideas. Since this is a typical single-user application, concurrency issues have been neglected for initial versions of NoteCards. Furthermore, NoteCards does not provide any version management. For each card and link there exists only one version; modification operations result in the replacement of the modified cards or links.

Although Intermedia (Meyrowitz 1986), too, only stores the current version of a node, it allows for the creation of additional versions under new names. Intermedia was developed by Andries van Dam at Brown University, Providence, Rhode Island as a hypertext system for multimedia documents. Being open for the integration of various applications (like text editor, graphics editor, etc.), it is supposed to help both teachers for organizing their lectures and students for learning and preparing for exams. Intermedia uses so-called web views to facilitate navigation in the information database. They are generated automatically from the hypertext structure within the database.

Sepia (Streitz et al. 1992, Haake and Wilson 1992) is a hypertext authoring system for the collaborative creation and manipulation of interrelated electronic documents. It was developed at the German National Research Center for Information Technology (GMD), Darmstadt, and it supports a seamless transition between asynchronous and synchronous cooperation. Sepia distinguishes between

- the disconnected work mode, where each author works independently on his own part of a hypertext document,
- the loosely coupled mode, where co-authors manipulate the same composite node, but have different views of that node, and
- the tightly coupled mode, where the co-authors have a shared view of the jointly manipulated composite node.

For persistent storage of hypertext documents, Sepia uses a database which is able to synchronize concurrent access by several authors.

Dolphin (Streitz et al. 1994) is the successor of Sepia at GMD and focuses on the cooperation aspect. Besides containing all Sepia functions, it provides electronic support for the preparation and execution of team meetings (see also p. 118).

Neptune (Delisle and Schwartz 1986) manages a linear version path for nodes and links. The partitioning mechanism "context" supports an independent version path generation for a given set of nodes. As opposed to NoteCards both Intermedia and Neptune allow concurrent access to hypertext documents.

Besides nodes and links, the system Textnet (Trigg and Weiser 1986) also supports *paths* which are structured node lists to enable linear browsing through the information. Textnet which was developed by Randy Trigg as part of a Ph.D. project at the University of Maryland does not include any version management and it allows only the access of one user at a time. Textnet can be considered as the predecessor of NoteCards and HyperTIES.

HyperTIES has been developed at the University of Maryland by Ben Shneiderman (1987). It is mainly used by museums to capture information about the exhibited artifacts. Touch screens provide easy information access and search functionality for museum visitors. References between hypertext nodes are automatically generated by interpreting text sequences, thus facilitating the task of the hypertext author.

Fress (*File Retrieval and Editing System*, Yankelovich and Meyrowitz 1985) was developed at Brown University under Andries van Dam. It includes basic functionality for document referencing and the navigation between documents.

HyperCard (Goodman 1987) has been developed for the Apple Macintosh. Information is organized in cards that can be displayed individually on the screen. Links between individual cards are achieved through buttons. It provides a scripting language to develop user programs for controlling the behavior of hypertext-based applications.

The *graphical Issue-Based Information System* (gIBIS, Conklin and Begeman 1988) is a multiuser hypertext system developed as part of the software technology program at the MCC in Austin, Texas. It integrates three different types of informational units: the problem, the position and the argument.

gIBIS is a collaboration-aware hypertext system for brainstorming and evaluating ideas in teams. An important aspect of gIBIS is the support of reliable multiuser capabilities, such as the concurrent but coordinated access to centralized data. Concurrency control handles the multiple update problem avoiding any data inconsistencies and incorporating automatic notification when significant changes have been made to the hypertext network (e.g., the creation of new nodes).

The Knowledge Management System (KMS, Akscyn et al. 1988), the commercial successor of ZOG (Robertson et al. 1981), applies optimistic concurrency control. KMS defines only one informational unit, the so-called frame which can be displayed completely on the screen. The creation of a new frame is facilitated by navigation to an empty informational unit.

The KMS database is distributed, a fact which is transparent to the user. In the database, WYSIWYG nodes are stored, which might contain text, graphics or images. The links between nodes are considered as elements of the nodes, which is an approach similar to that found in the systems NoteCards (Halasz 1988) and HyperCard (Goodman 1987). However, this approach is unlike systems such as Intermedia (Meyrowitz 1986) which represent nodes and links separately. The size of an informational unit is restricted to one page displayed on the screen. Users can only work on one page at a time. Sun NFS is used for distributed node access. There is one main file server which maintains the location information of all nodes. The location information itself is also stored in KMS nodes which enables their modification within the KMS application. All file servers managing part of the hypertext network get a local copy of the location information which is automatically updated. This replication increases availability of the location information within KMS. If the main file server cannot be accessed, the locally stored information is used for localizing nodes within the system.

Other well-known hypertext systems are Balsa (Brown and Sedgewick 1984), Document Examiner (Walker 1985), rIBIS (Rein and Ellis 1991) and WE (Smith 1986).

6.3.3 Architecture of hypertext systems

Hypertext abstract machine. According to Campbell and Goodman (1988), a hypertext system consists of three layers: database, hypertext abstract machine and presentation layer (see Fig. 6.6).

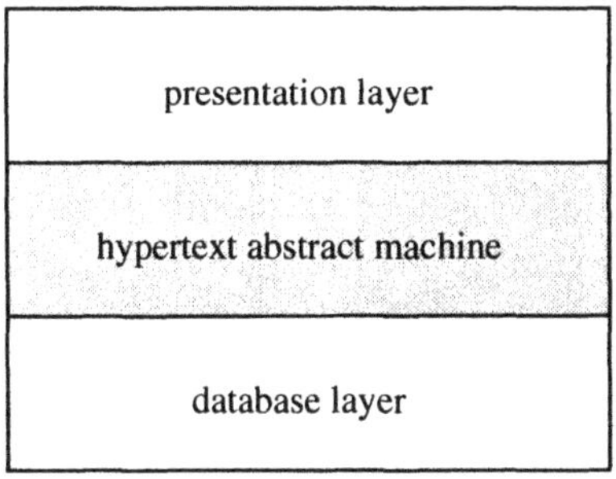

Fig. 6.6. Architecture of a hypertext system

1. *Database:* The database layer stores the hypertext information and handles typical database requirements, such as physical data storage, network access to shared data, and access to different storage media. The most important requirement for the database component of a hypertext system is the fast access to small information units. For this purpose, hypertext nodes are managed as data objects which makes object-oriented database systems an obvious choice for implementing the database layer. The semantics of nodes and links are not interpreted by the database layer.
2. *Hypertext abstract machine:* The hypertext abstract machine (HAM) models the basic characteristics of a hypertext system by specifying nodes (units of information) and links, as well as their attributes. The HAM layer defines an information network with links representing references

between multimedia-based information units. Standardization efforts of HAM deal with an exchange format to cross-reference or to exchange information between different hypertext systems. In the latter case the exchanged information must include the complete linking information.

3. *Presentation:* The presentation layer handles the user interface displaying nodes and links according to the information network structure and user specifications. Many systems associate nodes with respective windows on screen.

Nodes. According to the hypertext concept, the entire information is structured into small, logical informational units, the so-called nodes. Such a node is a basic constituent of hypertext. Other names for nodes are cards (e.g., in the case of HyperCard, Goodman 1987), units, documents (e.g., by Intermedia, Meyrowitz 1986) and frames (e.g., by KMS, Akscyn et al. 1988).

This modularization enables the author to refer to the same node multiple times and also to define several nodes as successors for the read process, thus representing several alternative pathways for the reader to follow. In the former case multiple references to a node reduce inconsistent and redundant replication of the same information. The latter case enables the reader, not the author, to choose the reading path through the information network.

A node consists of several components. One component is the node identifier which itself can be an information carrier (it can give a short description of the node content). The reader may use this identifier as a primary means to reference a node. Various attributes, such as owner or creator of the node, and node content are other node components. The descriptor component describes the node by a set of keywords which are crucial aids for the retrieval of nodes after a user query or the automatic generation of links between nodes, e.g., if two nodes contain the same keyword the hypertext system may automatically create a link between these two nodes. HyperTIES (Shneiderman 1987) is an example of automatic link generation, thus facilitating the effort of the hypertext author by reducing the need for manual link definition.

The last node component, the node summary, briefly summarizes the node content, giving the reader a clue as to whether or not it would be worth while to switch to a more detailed node content. In Fig. 6.7 the user would initially display the node n_1. If he selects the link L leading to node n_2 the hypertext system first displays the node summary of n_2. Based on that summary the user can decide whether or not he wishes to navigate along that link, and thus display the node content of n_2. This mechanism would be especially helpful in environments, such as the world wide web, where loading times of nodes may be extremely long.

According to the internal node structure we distinguish between typed nodes, semistructured nodes and composite nodes.

- Typed nodes determine the content type of a node, and thus the kind of content which may be stored in a node. For example, for each media type, such as text, graphics, video or audio we may choose a different node type.

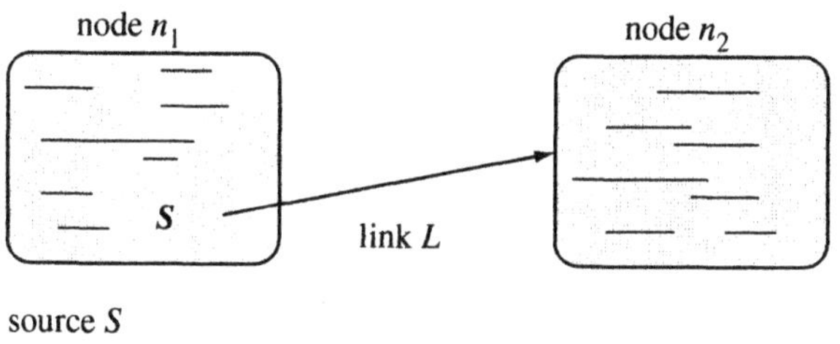

Fig. 6.7. Example for a link between two nodes

- Semistructured nodes determine the content structure of a node. Templates whose fields must be filled in by the user for each individual node define a generic node structure. For example, a hypertext system for decision making support may provide the following kinds of semistructured nodes: The "problem" gives a short description of the topic to be solved, whereas the nodes of type "alternative" contain the alternatives for solving the problem. "Analysis" evaluates the alternatives and "decision" formulates what was decided, including underlying arguments.
  The predefined internal content structure facilitates the design and implementation of agents to perform both computer-supported evaluation and computer-supported conclusion.
- Several nodes may be combined into a composite node, which is particularly useful if these nodes are part of a hierarchical structure. For example, the composite node "list" can be constructed out of the subnodes "list elements".
  A composite node is treated like an ordinary node. It has its own identifier and the user may modify node components. The subnodes of a composite node can be removed and reordered. Composite nodes are a suitable method for grouping a number of nodes according to certain criteria and for presenting them as one entity to the user. Often the internal structure of a composite node is irrelevant to certain applications.

Links. The second basic hypertext element is that of links. They represent relationships between nodes in the hypertext information space. These relationships between nodes of the hypertext information space constitute a hypertext network. The relation semantics are dependent both on the respective context within the information space and the interpretation by the reader. Authors of hypertext networks should be aware of this problem and assign specified semantics to individual links. The link L in Fig. 6.8 may allow multiple interpretations: n_2 is an example of n_1, n_1 is similar to n_2, n_2 is an argument for n_1.

A link is specified by a triple consisting of the source, one or several destinations, and the link attributes. Possible attributes are the creation time, the link type and the access permission.

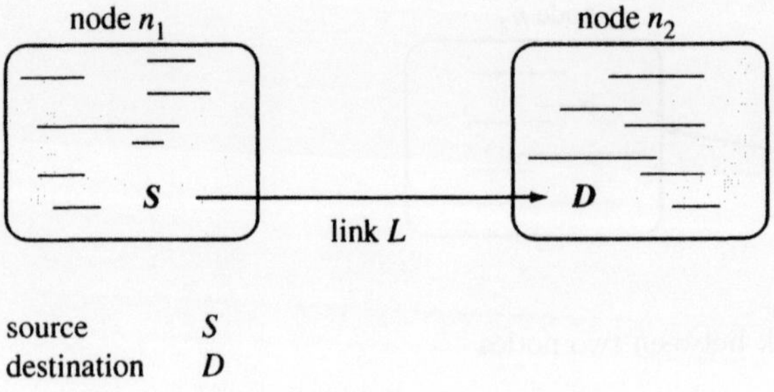

Fig. 6.8. Example of a link with one destination

The link L in Fig. 6.8 consisting of the source n_1 and the destination n_2 can be either uni- or bidirectional. In the first case, the link only works in the direction from n_1 to n_2, i.e., the user can only navigate from n_1 to n_2 (e.g., the world wide web), whereas bidirectional links also support the reverse navigation from n_2 to n_1, which is one of the assets of the commercial system Hyperwave.[5] Unidirectional links are easier to implement and to manage; however, they may cause difficulties during link maintenance when the link destination is deleted. Often systems allow dangling links with the link destination not being defined. During navigation links are checked as to their validity.

In general, there are three different methods for the placement of links within the source node:

1. The node content and the link specification are completely separate. The link source is not part of the actual node content, and thus is not associated with any node content element. The text or graphics of the node content is not interfered with by the link specification allowing for undisturbed reading by the user.
   This placement method is generally used for links which provide an organizational structuring of the hypertext information space. Typical organizational links which are often displayed as separate buttons are *goto-parent*, *goto-next-section* or *goto-next-chapter*. Menus containing the links emanating from the current node are other ways of implementing this placement method. These menus may be either displayed permanently or as popup windows upon user request.
2. Links are embedded in the node content. Elements of the node content which are link sources are emphasized using either typographic means (e.g., font changes, italics, underlining or borders) or cursor variations. In the latter case, the cursor assumes different representations, dependent on whether or not the mouse is pointing at a link source. Emphasized

[5] http://www.hyperwave.com

node elements are both link representations and information carriers for the node content.
This placement method is often used for the representation of referential links. The cursor representation may also depend on the respective link type. Figure 6.9 depicts the link types used by the Sepia system (e.g., the link types *so* for conclusions, *contradicts* for contradictions, *unless* for restrictions, and *reference* for cross-references. Sepia uses these link types to connect the following kinds of nodes: *claim*, *datum*, *rebuttal* or *statement*.

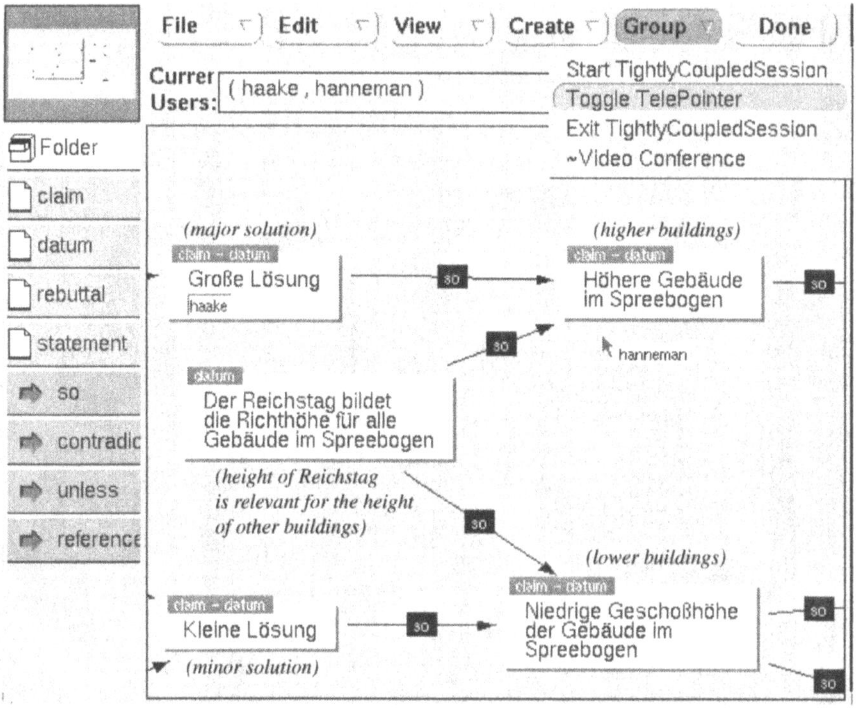

Fig. 6.9. Link types in Sepia (here as part of a Sepia supported argumentation network for the decision making process in the German House of Representatives on whether or not Berlin would replace Bonn as the German Capital. The English translation of the German node content is listed in parenthesis)

3. The link representations are embedded into general overviews. Examples for this placement method are the table of contents (see Fig. 6.10), a glossary or a clickable, graphical overview for browsing (see Fig. 6.11). The document glossary is by itself a hypertext node. Since an explicit manual specification by the author would be too time-consuming, the glossary is automatically generated by interpreting the content of all nodes. There is no explicit specification of the link source in the node

content, it is instead derived from the informational semantics of the node.

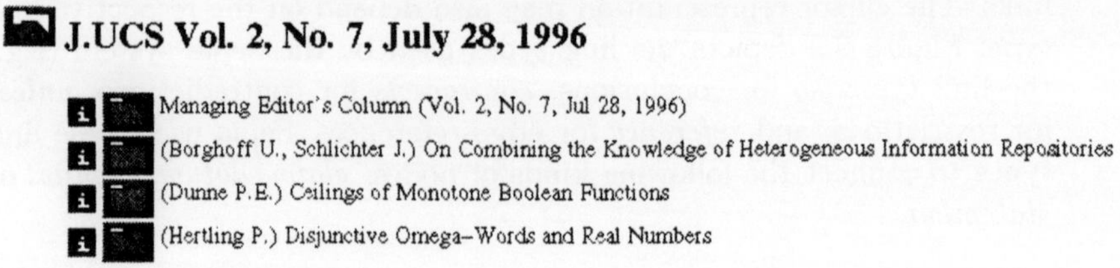

Fig. 6.10. Link placement using the table of content (here: for selecting individual articles in an electronic magazine)

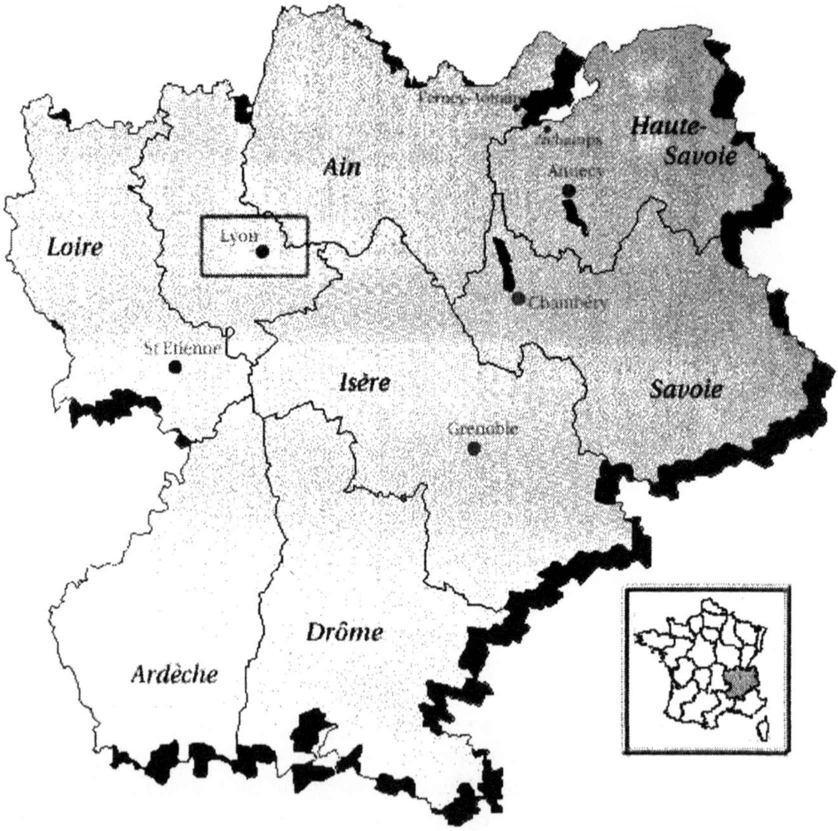

Fig. 6.11. Link placement using a graphical overview (here: Rhône-Alpes map)

Rather than predefining links by the author some hypertext systems support computed links which determine the link destination as the reader navigates along the link, which means that the computation of the link destination may depend on the reader's context. The context may include information about nodes visited in the past, the current time and the user profile.

Example (Tourist guide system). In a tourist guide system, links into the train schedule are calculated with respect to the current time. Only trains departing after the current time will be link destinations. Trains which have already left are neglected.

The link granularity is an important aspect for the design of hypertext systems. With respect to link source and link destination the following granularities are possible (Fig. 6.12):

1. *node* → *node*
2. *node content* → *node*
   Examples: HyperTIES (Shneiderman 1987) and HyperCard (Goodman 1987)
3. *node content* → *node content*
   Example: Intermedia (Meyrowitz 1986).

Links may be represented in textual form, graphically or by icons. For links pointing to nodes which are based on continuous media, such as audio and video, the so-called *micons* (moving icons) provide another point of reference; see also Steinmetz and Nahrstedt (1998). A micon may display in a small window only a trailer of the entire video film. If a link source is integrated into a continuous medium, the selection time of the link may be restricted to a subset of the video sequence. Only during that subset is the link active and displayed, and thus available for the user to initiate the navigation to another node.

6.3.4 Dexter reference model

The growing interest in hypertext has led to a variety of system developments. However, the information exchange on the layer of the hypertext abstract machine are very limited. The definition of the Dexter hypertext reference model is an attempt to specify an architecture for interoperability between different hypertext systems. It contains the most important abstractions of existing and future hypertext systems and is meant to provide the basis for the development of open hypertext systems which will hopefully support the exchange of network structures and node content between heterogeneous

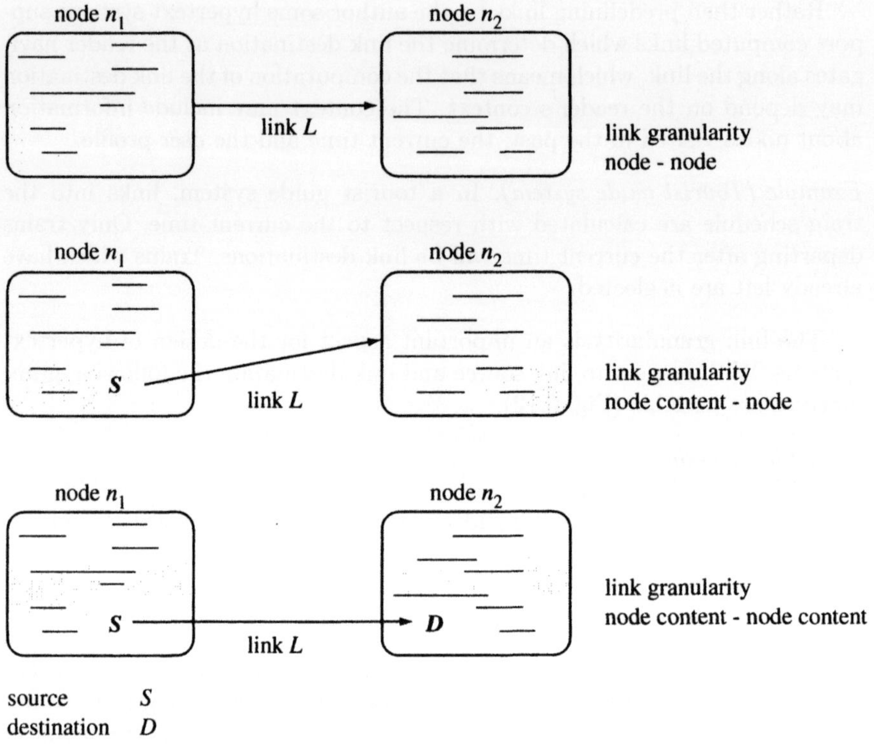

Fig. 6.12. Possible link granularities

systems.[6] Similar to Campbell and Goodman, the Dexter reference model (Halasz and Schwartz 1994) consists of three layers:

1. The runtime layer describes mechanisms of the human-computer interface. It displays nodes of the hypertext network, manages the user input, and initiates actions associated with these user events.
2. The storage layer, similar to the abstract hypertext machine, defines an abstract information space consisting of nodes and links.
3. The within-component layer describes content and the internal structure of hypertext nodes. This layer is not completely standardized in order to be able to integrate new media and future content types.

The storage layer is the central element of the Dexter reference model. It specifies a hypertext network consisting of a finite set of components: atomic and composite nodes as well as links. Links are components in and

[6] The name of this reference model stems from the motel "Dexter Inn" in Sunapee, New Hampshire, where a workshop of hypertext designers was held in October, 1988. The meeting aimed at reaching a consensus on terminology and semantics of basic hypertext systems.

of themselves rather than just being attributes of a node. Composite nodes represent a directed acyclic graph reflecting the hierarchical structure of the node. Each component, be it node or link, has a globally unique identifier.

Besides the hypertext network, the storage layer encompasses two special functions: the accessor function and the resolver function. The former allows access to components using their unique identifiers. In order to provide fast access the node identifier of the link destination can be embedded directly into the content of the source node. However, since this kind of link specification has too many restrictions and is difficult to maintain in the case of modifications, the Dexter reference model also provides a dynamic linking facility, the resolver function which calculates the destination nodes upon each link access. The resolver function interprets the link specification stored as attributes of the link component and the current access context to compute the actual destination nodes. The result of the resolver function are a set of identifiers which are interpreted by the accessor function to perform the link navigation.

Link specification. For many, hypertext system links on the node content level (i.e., source and destination of the link are elements within a node; see Fig. 6.12), pose a special problem. Changes within the destination node shift implicitly the destination point, thus requiring the adaptation of the link specification which requires the use of bidirectional links. For large hypertext system, such as the world wide web, this requirement is not realistic.

The Dexter reference model applies indirect addressing of link source and link destination to handle this link update problem. Each link is decomposed into "From" (the source) and "To" (the destination) anchors specifying the start and end points of a link. An anchor is defined within the respective nodes and consists of an identifier and a value referring to its position within the node content. If the node content is modified, only this value has to be adapted (i.e., a local change suffices to keep the link consistent). Link data structures contain only the identifiers of the anchors interpreted upon access by the resolver function for the computation of the current source and destination node positions. Figure 6.13 depicts the Dexter representation for links of the node content granularity as seen in Fig. 6.12.

For an extensive description of the Dexter reference model with possible extensions, the reader is referred to the special edition of the *Communications of the ACM* from February, 1994. First approaches for integrating collaborative work issues into the reference model are discussed by Groenbaek et al. (1994).

6.3.5 Navigation in hypertext networks

Orientation problem. The complexity of hypertext networks can cause a variety of problems. One of them is commonly referred to as "lost in hyperspace."

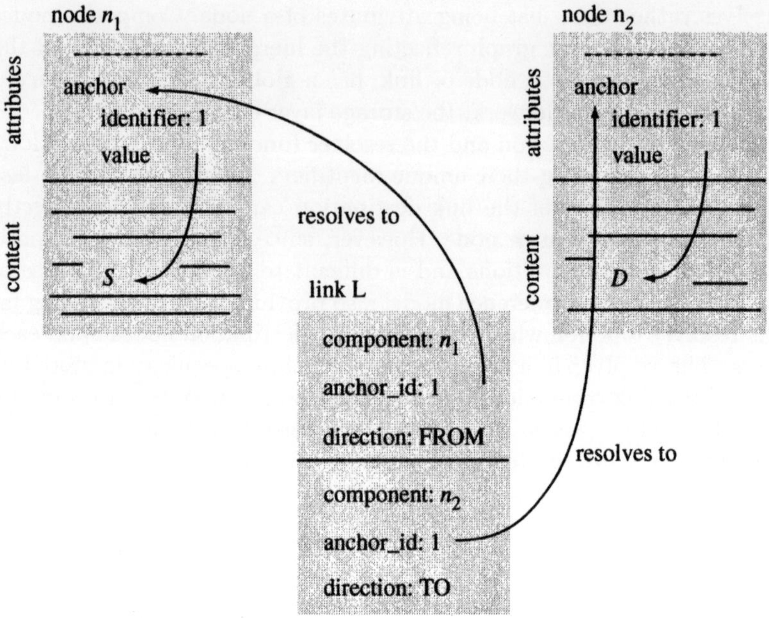

Fig. 6.13. Link representation in the Dexter reference model

During sequential reading (like reading a book), the reader finds it easy to maintain orientation. At any given time, the current "position" with respect to the entire document is known. In particular, the reader is always aware of how much he has already read and how much information (e.g., in number of pages) remains to be read. This latter aspect is usually unknown during non-linear reading of hypertext documents. The reader becomes disoriented and finds it difficult to keep focused. Hypertext browsers, fish-eye or thumbnail views and history management are generally insufficient to keep the reader oriented at all times.

Users often have difficulties in determining their current position within the hypertext network relative to the total amount of available information. Further, a user may be uncertain as to how to reach a specific hypertext node which he assumes must exist within the network. Both the best entry into the hypertext network and the best path to a specific node are difficult to determine. Optimal would be a path which is suitable both for the actual problem to be solved and the user profile. Another problem is the difficulty in finding what one has already seen (i.e., the reconstruction of those nodes of the hypertext network which have already been visited during the search process and the path in which they were reached).

If a user reaches a node which does not offer any alternatives for continuation he may decide to backtrack to one of the previous nodes. However, he may be doubtful as to which node may be the best one to backtrack to. Moreover, if a search has been carried out, there remains always the uncertainty of whether or not all relevant information stored in the hypertext network has really been accessed. Furthermore, it is difficult to estimate the amount of information still available which should be examined by the user when that user is looking from the closer context of the current node.

The aforementioned orientation problems are often caused by deficient concepts and insufficient modeling of the hypertext network. The "spaghetti syndrome" or the already described "lost in hyperspace" are similar to the usage of frequent **goto** commands in programs which may lead to inconceivable program code and unexpected program execution.

Conventional navigation mechanisms. The most commonly used conventional navigation mechanisms are direct entry, table of contents, glossaries, and queries.

In direct entry, a node is directly accessed by explicitly specifying its node identifier. The user may either type the identifier into a command window or select it from a menu. Typical examples are the explicit user specification of a URL or the selection of a web address from the bookmark entries.

Traditionally linear documents use the table of contents to provide an overview of the document, and thus to improve user orientation. It reflects the hierarchical structure of the hypertext document. Nodes listed in the table of contents may be accessed directly. Fish-eye and thumbnail views are a variation of this approach for hypertext systems. In the first case the context of the current node is displayed in great detail while the rest of the hypertext network structure is represented by a higher level of abstraction hiding most of the detail information. Fish-eye views dynamically adapt the table of contents depending on the current position in the hypertext network. Figure 6.14 exemplifies a typical thumbnail view of an electronic document.

Glossaries are collections of special terms and they facilitate the terminological orientation of the user in knowledge domains. A glossary entry may be used to directly access the appropriate nodes. Hypertext systems may dynamically adapt the glossary depending on the currently displayed node. For example, the glossary entries may be limited to terms used in the current node.

Queries in hypertext networks are similar to database queries. A query may either refer to the information content (e.g., a text pattern in the node content), or the information structure (e.g., the number or type of links emanating from a node). Selecting one of the entries in the result list enables the user to directly access the desired node. Figure 6.15 depicts a typical information query with the result items found by Alta Vista. Alta Vista is a search engine for the world wide web.

Hypertext specific navigation mechanisms. Navigation mechanisms especially designed for hypertext networks are graphical overviews, guided tours, backtracking and bookmarks. Figure 6.16 shows part of a guided tour available on the web server at Stanford University, Palo Alto, California.

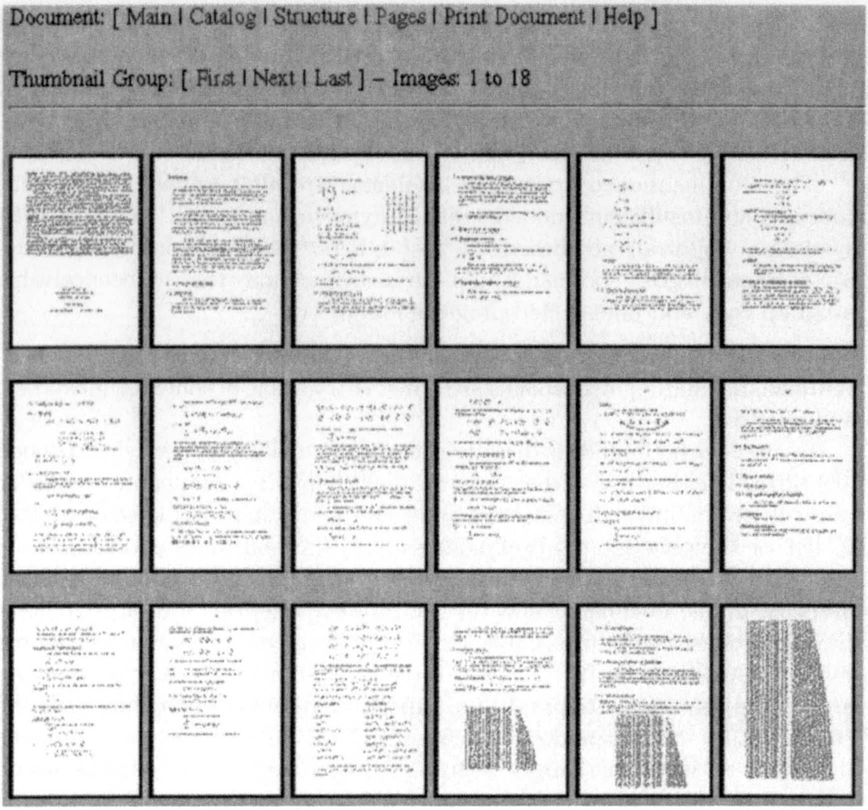

Fig. 6.14. Navigation using thumbnails

Graphical overviews are used for global orientation. They map the network or tree structure modeling the relationships between nodes of the hypertext information space onto a graphical representation which is then displayed on the screen. In the case of complex networks, it is often difficult to compute the appropriate screen representation. The user may zoom in from a coarse network representation to display more detailed information displaying individual nodes and links. Thus, zooming enables local orientation.

A possible variant for overcoming the obstacle of handling complex networks are web views of Intermedia (Meyrowitz 1986), as illustrated graphically in Fig. 6.17. A web view consists of three components: the current path, a map and a comment. The path records the access history during navigation to the current node, thereby providing the temporal context as to how the current node was reached. The map describes the links emanating from the current node. It informs the user about the local context, specifying the options for continuing from the current node.

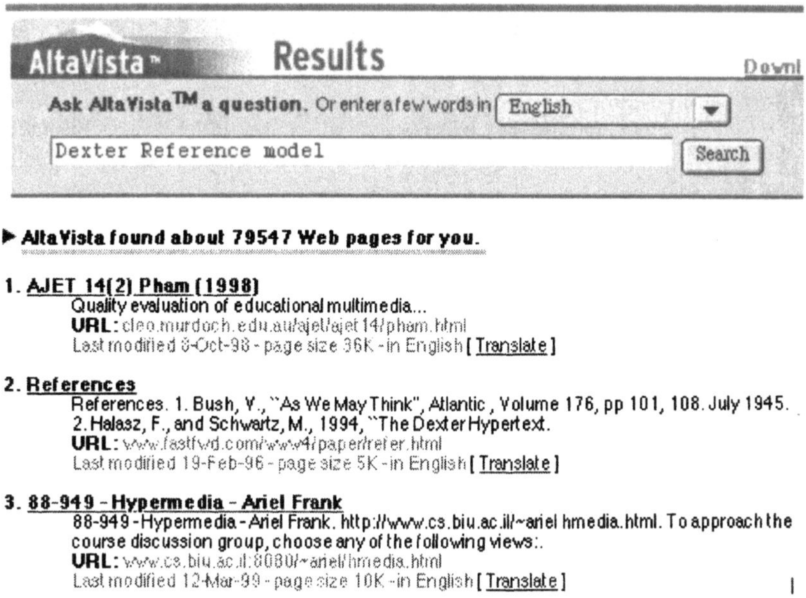
AltaVista
Results
Ask AltaVista™ a question. Or enter a few words in English
Dexter Reference model
Search
AltaVista found about 79547 Web pages for you.
1. AJET 14(2) Pham (1998)
Quality evaluation of educational multimedia...
URL: cleo.murdoch.edu.au/ajet/ajet14/pham.html
[Translate]
2. References
References. 1. Bush, V., "As We May Think", Atlantic, Volume 176, pp 101, 108. July 1945. 2. Halasz, F., and Schwartz, M., 1994, "The Dexter Hypertext.
URL: www.fastfvd.com/www4/paper/refer.html
Last modified 19-Feb-96 - page size 5K - in English [Translate]
3. 88-949 - Hypermedia - Ariel Frank
88-949 - Hypermedia - Ariel Frank. http://www.cs.biu.ac.il/~ariel hmedia.html. To approach the course discussion group, choose any of the following views:.
URL: www.cs.biu.ac.il:8080/~ariel/hmedia.html
Last modified 12-Mar-99 - page size 10K - in English [Translate]

Fig. 6.15. Navigation using queries (example: Alta Vista)

The author may predefine one or several paths through the information space for the reader to follow (so-called guided tours). This mechanism is a compromise between completely free navigation based on user interest and the retrieval of specific nodes identified through user queries.

We can distinguish between sequential, branching and conditional paths. In the first case, the nodes to be visited along the path are ordered by the author according to a thematic sequence, whereas branching paths offer the reader a choice between several options for continuing from certain nodes. For conditional paths, the system decides which part of the path should be followed. The decision may be based on a user's response or on previous user actions. Thus, the conditional paths are adapted to the temporal context of the reader. For example, the system may base its decision on the following issues: "How often did the reader visit this node in the past?" or "When did the reader last access the current node?"

The availability of a history list enables backtracking to one of the last n visited nodes. The selection of a node from a list corresponds to a **goto** to this node with the list entries either being identifiers of the nodes or retrospective overviews of the node layout. The latter approach is used by HyperCard (Goodman 1987) which creates iconic images of the visited nodes for the history list. The user may recognize nodes according to their general layout without distracting detail. However, the reader must have a visual memory.

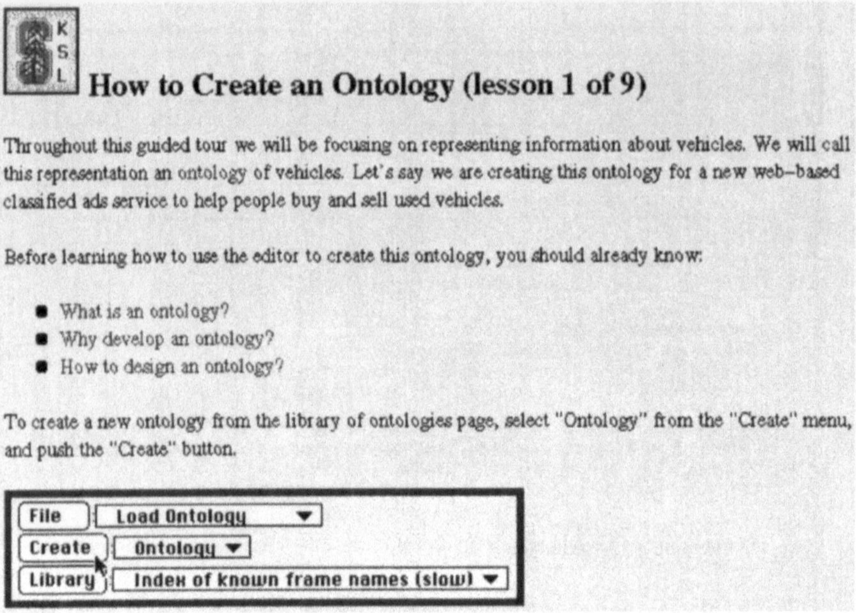
K
S
L
How to Create an Ontology (lesson 1 of 9)
Throughout this guided tour we will be focusing on representing information about vehicles. We will call this representation an ontology of vehicles. Let's say we are creating this ontology for a new web-based classified ads service to help people buy and sell used vehicles.
Before learning how to use the editor to create this ontology, you should already know:
What is an ontology?
Why develop an ontology?
How to design an ontology?
To create a new ontology from the library of ontologies page, select "Ontology" from the "Create" menu, and push the "Create" button.
File
Load Ontology
Create
Ontology
Library
Index of known frame names (slow)

Fig. 6.16. Part of a guided tour at Stanford University, Palo Alto, California for creating ontologies using Ontolingua.

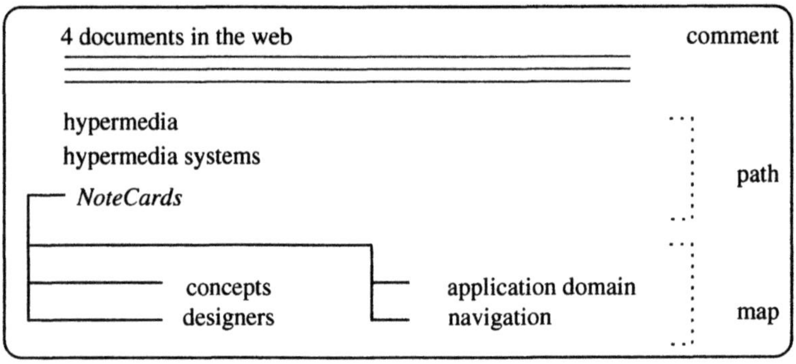

Fig. 6.17. Example of a web view

Bookmarks are a widespread mechanism to reduce the orientation problem in hypertext networks. If the user assumes that the currently visited node may be of interest at later times he inserts a reference to a node, i.e., the node identifier, into the bookmark list. The bookmark list is persistent and enables the user direct access to all nodes whose references are available as a bookmark.

6.3.6 Trellis model

Trellis is a formal model based on Petri nets for describing the logical structure of a hypertext network. Besides specifying the relationship between nodes it also defines the sequence in which the nodes are visited and how the individual node content is to be represented. For the formal definition of the Trellis model, the interested reader is referred to Stotts and Furuta (1989). Additionally, they discuss access control mechanisms and constructs for synchronized, simultaneous navigation along multiple hypertext paths. In the context of CSCW, the Trellis model has already been applied to describe coordination structures and group protocols (Furuta and Stotts 1994). The Petri net has been extended to incorporate the time aspect.

6.3.7 IBIS method

In the early 1970s, when investigating "wicked" problems, Rittel and Webber (1973) developed the so-called IBIS method for application domains such as planning, design and problem solving. IBIS stands for Issue-Based Information System.

First we compare possible characteristics of "tame" problems with those of "wicked" problems (Hashim 1991). Tame problems have well-constrained goals, are not unique, i.e., the same problem recurs, and problems may be precisely specified. Especially the latter characteristic allows for algorithmic solutions facilitating the usage of computers. As opposed to this, wicked problems are complex and rather vague in their descriptions. Due to changes in time, resources and context, the representation of a problem, too, is constantly subject to modifications and thereby imprecise. The solution of a wicked problem is unique and therefore not directly transferable, not even partially to other wicked problems. Wicked problems have no algorithmic solution, thus heuristics must be applied during the problem solving process.

The IBIS method was designed to support the problem solving process of wicked problems. It is based on the theory of argumentation applying a question-and-answer game to explore the problem and solution space. This game results in a number of potential solutions, their applicability, correctness and rationality which are discussed in the form of arguments and counter-arguments. During this process, which generally involves all group members assigned to solve the problem, all relevant aspects and possible positions, as well as arguments for and against these positions, are identified. The result of this problem solving process is an issue network of typed nodes and typed links. The typing limits the possible connections between nodes, and thus enables a clear and distinct arrangement of all issues.

Basic node types of IBIS are issue, position, and argument. However, for specific application domains additional node types may be defined. The issue represents the problem formulated as a question, while the position is the proposed solution for this problem. Finally, the argument contains one or several statements or facts supporting or contradicting the proposed solution. The available basic link types are graphically illustrated in Fig. 6.18.

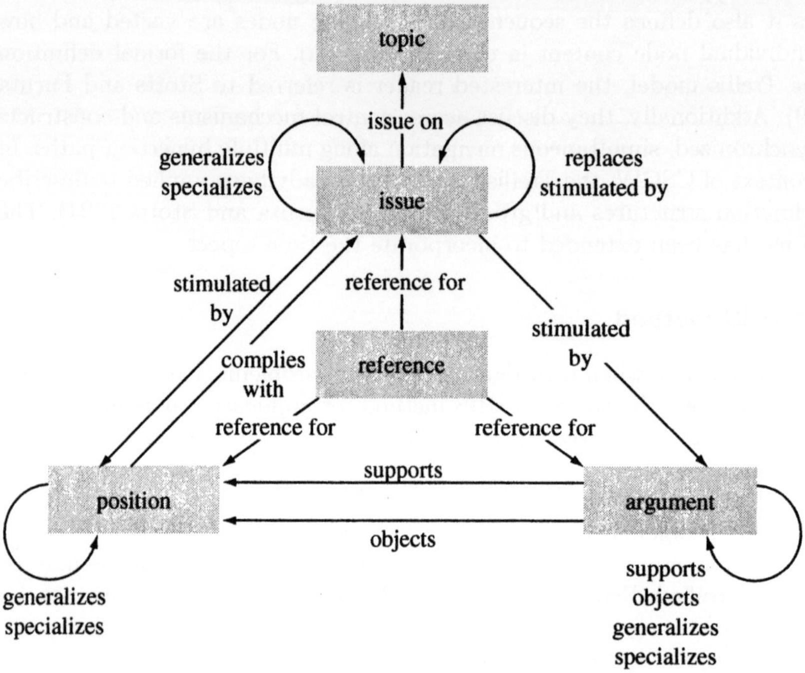

Fig. 6.18. Example of link types for the IBIS method, see also Fig. 6.9

References support positions, arguments and issues by referring to facts and events outside of the immediate problem domain. An issue network evolves step-by-step: First and foremost, the root of the network, the initial issue, is articulated. If necessary, it is refined or generalized. An issue is not simply a question with exactly one definite answer. Rather, it is a controversial question instigating supportive positions or counter arguments. Issues cannot be solved in terms of correct or incorrect answers. Positions specify alternative options of which one will be selected as the final solution for the initial issue. During the decision making process arguments for and against this position are evaluated and rated. Positions are chosen based on validity, relevance and importance of the respective arguments. Figure 6.19 gives an example of an issue network.

In conclusion we can identify three main features of the IBIS method:

1. Its hypertext structure enables the use of hypertext tools for information management and navigation within the issue network.

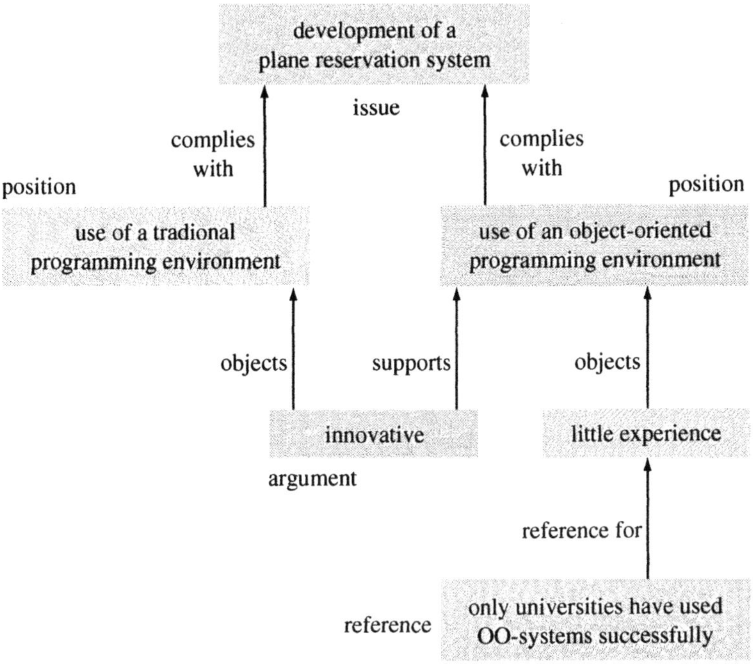

Fig. 6.19. Example of an issue network based on the IBIS method[7]

2. It records the development process by capturing the relationships between positions, arguments and references. Timestamps may be used to reflect the temporal evolution, as well.
3. It supports loose cooperation for exploring the problem and solution space. The cooperation is often asynchronous and the information may be distributed depending on the group composition and the application domain. In this case, the system must incorporate concurrency control schemes complicating the correct processing of replicated hypertext nodes.[8]

The IBIS method is an information management approach well suited to asynchronous cooperation supporting the decision making process of teams. On the basis of IBIS several hypertext systems have been developed, such as gIBIS (Conklin and Begeman 1988) and rIBIS (Rein and Ellis 1991). There

[7] The argumentation depicted in Figure 6.19 suggests that it was carried out in the 1980's, when Smalltalk was fashionable; programming of modern business applications increasingly apply object-oriented languages, such as C++ or Java.

[8] The concept of concurrency in hyperdocuments was first mentioned in the context of Augment (Engelbart 1982). Several persons may work on the same hyperdocument synchronously; the hyperdocument may be distributed among several computers.

have also been several proposals to adapt the method to special application domains by extending existing and defining new node and link types.

Example (WHAT, an IBIS adaptation). WHAT[9], a tool for argumentative writing of documents (Hashim 1991), combines two representation levels: one for capturing the writing process, and one for representing the document itself. The set of node types has been extended to include means for the specification of the document, such as the node types "main idea" or "pros and cons."

In the business world the use of the IBIS method has already led to hands on experiences. For example, Yakemovic and Conklin (1990) mention a two-year experiment using the IBIS method in a software development project. IBIS was mainly used for making design decisions more transparent and easier to follow. Software designers have pointed out that the resulting issue network did not only record the decision itself but also "why" this decision was reached. In the end, the project issue network contained over 8,000 nodes with approximately 2,200 issues. Observations during the experiment showed that the IBIS method addressed, above all, three cooperation aspects:

1. Support of decision making within the team,
2. Structuring the interaction between team members, and
3. Management of the group information.

6.3.8 Campiello – Information spaces and communities

The previous discussion considered information spaces as part of the environment supporting groupwork. They were used to file group documents and as a communication medium for the group members to interact with each other. The information spaces recorded all information created, manipulated and used during the group process. In the following we will introduce a current project which supports information exchange within communities applying the information space metaphor.

The term "community" has been defined in the literature in different ways; for example, Mynatt et al. (1997) sees a community as a "social grouping which exhibits in varying degrees: shared spatial relations, social conventions, a sense of membership and boundaries, and an ongoing rhythm of social interaction". Our understanding of community is a set of people who share something (e.g., a language, a network access) which distinguishes them clearly from the rest of the society. Examples for communities are all inhabitants of a town or all students listening to a lecture. The differences between communities and teams as defined in groupwork are the following:

---

[9] Writing with a Hypermedia-based Argumentative Tool

- In communities it is not necessary for all members to know each other personally or to interact on a personal basis. Direct interaction between community members are often purely accidental and not part of a group process.
- In general, communities do not have a common goal or task and thus, the interaction between community members is usually rather loose. Usually they do not work on shared artifacts (e.g., group documents); however, sporadic, spontaneous information exchange may still take place. Personal interests dominate over community interests.

Software focusing on the support of communities, so-called *community computing*[10] serves as a medium for initiating contact with unknown collaborators who have similar interests and preferences (e.g., students preparing for an exam) and as a means of exchanging information within the community. Even though the support systems for communities and teams have developed independently, there is no clear distinction. There is, rather, a seamless transition between groupware and community computing. In the example above, the students have the common goal of passing their exams. Examples for community computing are tools for identifying or localizing like-minded persons (e.g., ICQ[11]) or so-called community networks which specialize in mere information exchange.

The idea of community networks is also the basis of the Campiello project.[12] The focus of the project is cities with many tourist attractions. Empirical studies show that tourists have rarely any means of sharing their experiences with past, current and future tourists, and that the information exchange between tourists and local inhabitants is rather limited.

Therefore, Campiello aims at creating a "collaboration space" based on the information space already existing in some cities which enables people with shared interest to interact with each other or at least benefit from the knowledge and experiences of prior visitors. As opposed to earlier community network projects which have primarily aimed at creating a virtual collaboration space, Campiello focuses on the exploration of new user interfaces for integration of the system with city life itself.

Campiello information space. The information space encompasses information on places, events and organizations in the city. These information units may contain more general information on restaurants and museums,

---

[10] The term *communityware* which would fit perfectly as a counterpart to groupware is a trademark of Durand Communication Inc.

[11] http://www.icq.com/

[12] Campiello (Esprit LTR Project 25572) is being carried out between September 1997 and August 2000 by the following project partners: Department of Information Science Milano, Italy, Xerox Research Centre Europe, Grenoble, France, Domus Academy Milano, Italy, Multimedia Information Systems Laboratory Crete, FORTHnet Crete, and Municipality Chania (Greece).

but they may also include more temporary information on specific exhibitions in individual museums. Both official agencies, such as the cultural city department, and ordinary users can update and extend the information space.

Besides being allowed to extend the information space, all users are encouraged to provide comments and evaluations on existing information units (i.e., comments on places, events and organizations). The granularity of the annotations may cover a wide range (e.g., the user may comment on a museum as a whole, or he may submit his impressions and thoughts on individual exhibits). Comments can be read by all other people. Furthermore, the system may use collaborative filtering, to extract relevant information based on the evaluations of other users in order to generate appropriate recommendations. For example, it attempts to identify people with similar interest profiles; very positive evaluations of these people are then forwarded as recommendations to the querying user. For details on this issue and an example system, the reader is referred to Glance et al. (1998).

Collaborative filtering is facilitated by the hierarchical structure of the information space and the categorization of the stored information units. Examples for categories are "art museum", "art of the 18th century", or "eating Japanese". Moreover, individual information units may be connected with each other by typed links, such as "can be found in" or "is related to".

In Campiello information access is not restricted to browsing. Apart from browsing, a user can request recommendations to certain topics. In the latter case, the system will propose information units which might be of interest to the user.

Furthermore, Campiello offers a variety of other services, such as the identification and contact of "like-minded" people, communication with others, or being informed about other people's presence.

User interfaces. Besides the traditional web access Campiello explores new user interfaces for interaction with the information space. In the following we will present two new approaches the paper-based user interface and the so-called NewsWall (see Fig. 6.20).

- *Paper-based user interface*: Paper is an easily accessible, commonly accepted medium to capture and exchange information. People are quite familiar with it. Let us assume the following scenario:

  City restaurants and other sites lay out information cards containing brief descriptions of the site or the associated event. In many towns, this kind of visitor information is already available. The novelty of Campiello is that besides the more general information these cards also provide space for the visitor to express his own comments or to request additional information. Furthermore, the visitor may attach his personal identification number to personalize his submitted card. Filled-in forms are collected at various locations or can be submitted by Fax. Subsequently the system updates the user profile, returns the information material re-

Fig. 6.20. User interfaces in Campiello

quested by the user, and if necessary, creates new recommendations for other users with similar profiles.

- *NewsWall*: While the paper-based user interface made the system accessible at various locations within their respective towns, NewsWall attempts to make the system a meeting point for physical, rather than just virtual, contact.
  It is planned to set up large screens at one or several town locations displaying current news and user comments. The screen space is subdivided into smaller areas and assigned to the respective information categories. This enables better orientation and alerts persons sharing the same interest of each other's existence; since they stand in near proximity to each other looking at the same information category on the screen they may start to communicate with each other face-to-face.
  At NewsWall locations, the aforementioned paper cards can also be submitted. Immediately after scanning a paper card, the individual comments are displayed on the large screen.

The information space of Campiello uses a hypertext-like organization with hierarchically structured information categories. Based on this information space community support is provided enabling implicit communication between community members through annotations associated with the information units. Further differences between Campiello and conventional information spaces lies in the fact that the information access is recommendation-based, and the integration of innovative user interfaces connecting the virtual information space with the actual physical space. The interaction with the virtual information space occurs directly out of the physical space, though not always synchronously.

Although Campiello does not aim at supporting groupwork, the concepts and innovative aspects can certainly be applied in groupware environments benefiting from improved information exchange and the new user interface metaphors. It also provides functionality to better integrate working groups and interest groups.

6.3.9 Case studies: cooperative nature of information search activities

A number of case studies have studied the cooperative nature of information search activities. Notably, the case studies reported by O'Day and Jeffries (1993) as well as Twidale et al. (1995) provide insight into the forms of cooperation that can take place during a search process. Four basic modes of cooperation were identified: Firstly, sharing of results among members of a team or community. Secondly, self-initiated broadcast by one individual of interesting information encountered in search results. Thirdly, members of the team or community act as consultants, and, finally, archival of information judged potentially useful by group members into a group repository.

More evidence of cooperative aspects comes from the work of Crabtree et al. (1997) and Twidale et al. (1995) who have studied in depth the kinds of collaboration that can occur in either the physical or digital library. They have proposed a typology of the cooperative search activities that could benefit from computer support, constructed upon a foundation of the three main objects they identify as central to search activities: people, the search process and the search results. Specifically, they identify three main categories of computer support:

1. Services for identifying persons who could advise upon the search, possibly in a synchronous mode (as proposed by Hoppe and Zao 1994); for example, experts or users who have previously conducted a search on a similar topic.
2. Services for recommending, rating, annotating and creating bibliographies.
3. Services for supporting collaboration by appropriate enhancements of the representation of the search process, as is done, for example, in the Ariadne project (Twidale et al. 1997).

The first of the above studies refers to a work setting, the second to a library environment. Both show strong evidence of collaboration. Questions that remain are: How can the collaborative needs in different settings be further characterized in terms of the characteristics of the particular community of people? What further insights concerning information-related collaborative activities will result from a more in-depth study of the nature of the community? And, finally, how can various kinds of computer support be best adapted to suit the needs of different communities of people engaged in collaborative information activities?

To address these questions, Glance et al. (1999) have focused their research across two different communities: communities of practice in the workplace, and a community of users accessing common library facilities. These communities have different characteristics. Communities of practice in a workplace are stable. They consist of a closed group of people who know each other, execute well defined tasks, and usually collaborate for their work. Users accessing common library facilities have much less in common. They build somehow a community just because they use the same facilities, because they are at the same place at the same time. Collaboration between such people may emerge because they interact with each other. This collaboration consists essentially of sharing personal experience within the library.

Information search and information sharing engines enacted within the context of a community can provide improved support for these processes. For example, in some cases, a search may match well with one or more previous ones and the compiled results can be retrieved from the community memory. In other cases, some of the results of the new search may themselves match items in the community memory that have already been evaluated by members. In this case, collaborative filtering techniques can be used to predict the relative usefulness of the particular result for the persons conducting the search. Alternatively, the results returned by a search can be ranked against the community profile, which can itself be incrementally constructed on the basis of relevance feedback provided by members over time. In addition, searches that occur commonly within a community can be identified and automatically clustered to form FAQs. Finally, some search processes can be enacted as long-lived processes, with potentially different members of the community participating in refining the search and culling the results over time. Members can also be notified of ongoing searches that match their interests and expertise in a way that takes into account their history of participation in long-lived searches in the past.

The knowledge management system Agentware[13] of Autonomy, Inc., continuously monitors the activities of the user. While the user is editing a document with his favorite word processor, the system analyzes the document content and proactively generates links to related information in the shared information space (see Fig. 6.21).

These additional capabilities of information search and information sharing engines entail new forms of user interfaces to support such community activities. Ackerman and Palen (1996) advocate the treatment of people as first class objects in information systems, and the explicit consideration of the structure and the process of searches. One way of doing this is to use explicit social activity indicators, as in their Zephyr system.

The support of community activities such as collaborative help facilities are addressed in Answer Garden 2 (AG2), a system designed by Ackerman and McDonald (1996). AG2 consists of two separate underlying systems, the

[13] http://www.autonomy.com/

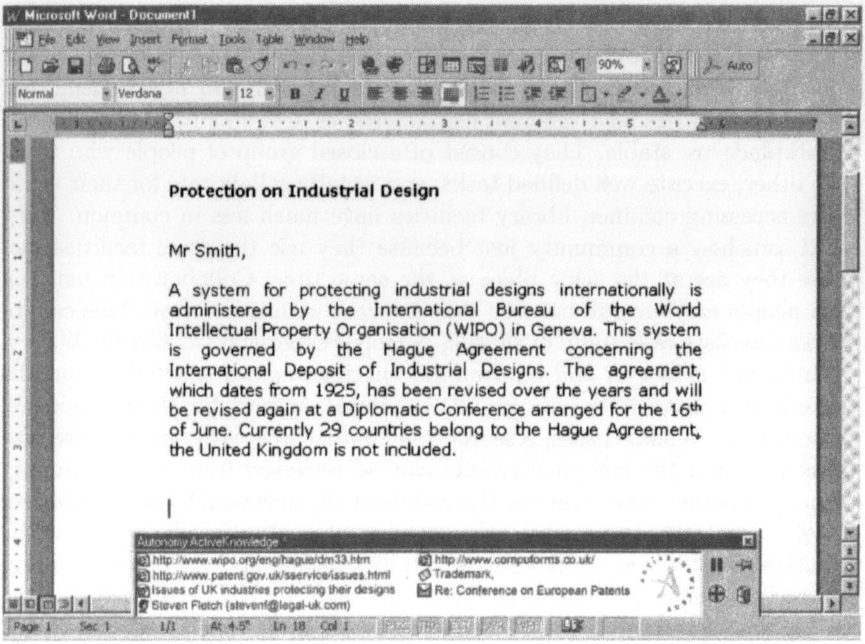

Fig. 6.21. The ActiveKnowledge component of Agentware

Cafe ConstructionKit and the Collaborative Refinery. Raw information comes into Collaborative Refinery through input filters. Collaborative Refinery also generates Web pages and handles user interaction. Collaborative help is provided by Cafe ConstructionKit communication facilities. Figure 6.22 shows the overall system architecture.

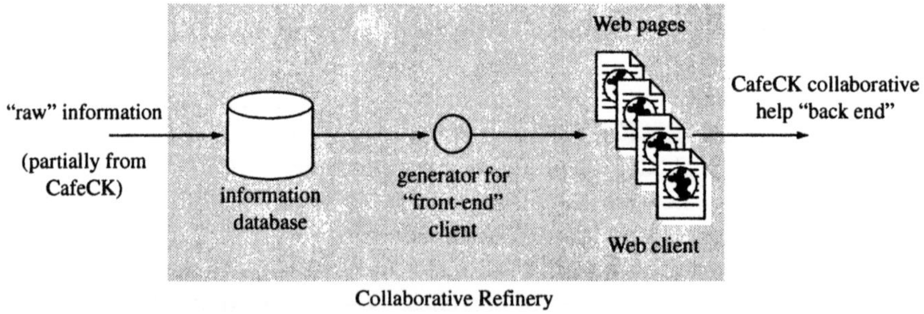

Fig. 6.22. Answer Garden 2 (AG2) architecture

6.4 Further Reading

The interested reader is referred to books by Rapaport (1991), Pankoke-Babatz (1989), and also by Baecker (1993) and Marca and Bock (1992). The latter two books contain collections of articles on communication support between group members. The April 1999 issue of *IEEE Multimedia* includes several articles on media spaces. Community computing is the central focus of the three books edited by Ishida (1998, 1999, 2000). The latter book concentrates especially on communities in digital cities.

Further reading on hypertext can be found in Lennon (1997) and Nielsen (1990), as well as the special edition on hypermedia from February 1994 of *Communications of the ACM*.

An early field study of the Answer Garden system – the predecessor of Answer Garden 2 (AG2) – is presented by Ackerman (1994).

Active collaborative filtering was introduced in Tapestry (Goldberg et al. 1992) and explored in a later system called Pointers (Maltz and Ehrlich 1995) (see also Beehive by Huberman and Kaminsky 1996). Among the earliest and best known automated collaborative systems are two that started as university research projects. Firefly (Shardanand and Maes 1995) is a movie and music recommendation system from MIT (Massachusetts Institute of Technology, Cambridge, USA); GroupLens (Resnick et al. 1994a) is another newsgroup recommendation system (inspired by Tapestry) from the University of Minnesota. A third system from Bellcore (http://www.bellcore.com)[14] is presented by Hill et al. (1995). Fab (Balabanovic and Shohan 1997) is a content-based, collaborative recommendation system for WWW pages, which is a project under the umbrella of the Stanford Digital Library Project. MyYahoo! is a personalized search engine from the makers of Yahoo[15] which uses Firefly technology. Other new enterprises offer similar services such as Each-to-Each[16] from DEC and Gustos[17].

[14] Since late 1997 owned by Science Applications Int'l Corp. (SAIC), Telcordia Technologies, New Jersey, USA.
[15] http://www.yahoo.com
[16] http://www.each.com
[17] http://www.gustos.com/index.htm

7. Workflow Management, Conversation and Coordination Systems

This chapter deals with workflow management systems coordinating and monitoring group activities by handling both causal and temporal interdependencies and the execution context. Informally, a workflow is the specification and the execution of a set of coordinated activities which represent a business process within a company or an organization.

After a brief introduction to some basic concepts of workflow management we discuss the functionality and a possible architecture of workflow management systems. Various coordination models, e.g., the customer-performer model, are discussed as well as the conversation model which is derived from linguistics. Based on the concept of a conversational network we present the conversation systems Coordinator and Domino, along with the activity management system Tacts.

Besides the standardization activities within the Workflow Management Coalition (WfMC), we will discuss adaptive workflows which handle exceptional situations in flexible ways.

7.1 Introduction

Since the late 1980's, the interest in workflow management has continually increased. In the past, system and solution vendors as well as market analysts have clearly dominated in this area, setting standards with respect to form and pace of development. Companies were looking for approaches for restructuring the organization in order to make the internal processes more efficient and economical and thus, the company more profitable and competitive. The use of information and communication technology, especially workflow management, was seen as a supporting tool for business process reengineering (in short BPR); see, for instance, Hammer and Champy (1995). Both workflow management and BPR view the organization of an enterprise from the economic perspective.

The growing interest in academic research in the domain of workflow management is illustrated by the growing number of papers which have begun appearing at scientific conferences. In the previous years the number of contributions from universities and research institutes on this topic was rather small.

Informally, a workflow is the specification and the execution of a set of coordinated activities representing a business process within a company or an organization. A workflow is an organization-wide task-sharing process typically involving a large number of people and software systems. Workflow examples are processes for handling orders or travel expenses, or the publishing of documents. By knowing the underlying business process and its structure a workflow management system can provide support in assigning activities to people (so-called actors), in allocating resources, and in monitoring the status of activity execution. Workflow management is therefore often used synonymously with administration and automation of business processes.

Workflow management improves the view of the shared task and it provides the basis for creating business process awareness for

- those people involved in the process: What are the open tasks on my to-do list?
- newcomers to the team: What is the underlying structure of the process?
- interested persons, such as managers: What is the current status of the workflow activities?
- workflow designers: Is the designed workflow used successfully? Can it be reused within another context?

Workflow management improves the mutual awareness of the common task and is thereby a means of enhancing group awareness (see Sect. 3.5.4).

Example (Document publishing). In many cases office work creates, manipulates and disseminates documents. The evolution of modern office technology enables people to author and publish documents more efficiently even using the world wide web for the dissemination of electronic documents. Document processing is a good example of a workflow consisting of several subtasks and involving multiple people in a variety of activities (see Fig. 7.1). The *publishing* process representing the top-level task consists of three activities: *authoring*, *reviewing* and *formatting*, each of which is assigned to a person for carrying it out, namely the *author*, the *reviewer* and the *editor*. During activity processing, the assigned person may access documents (represented by dashed lines in the figure) and, if necessary, use software systems (depicted by dotted lines), for example a word processor or a document formatting system. The solid arrows represent the dependencies between activities (e.g., *reviewing* is followed by another *authoring* activity). The small circle after the *authoring* activity models the decision of whether the process should continue with the *reviewing* or *formatting* activity. The decision depends on the result of the *authoring* activity. Figure 7.1 also illustrates that a sequence of activities may be executed repeatedly (e.g., the sequence *authoring* → *reviewing* may be traversed several times).

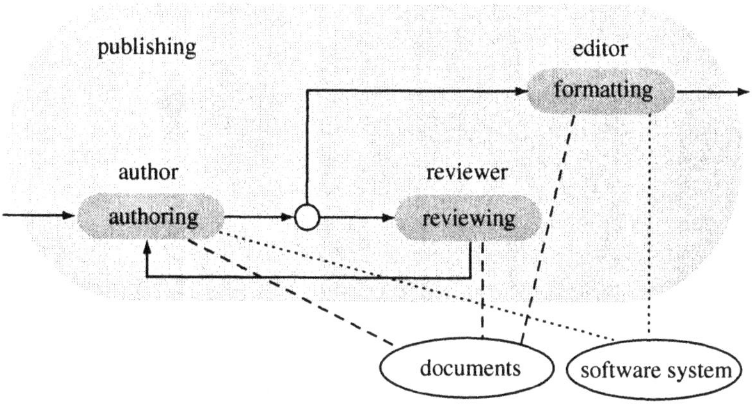

Fig. 7.1. Workflow: Document processing

Currently, business processes are often handled by the *tayloristic* approach.[1] Similar to working on an assembly line, the worker has to adhere to a strict division of labor; all activities are precisely specified in advance, and the assignment of people responsible for these activities is well-defined. Increased division of labor, however, often results in more communication between the involved people to clarify open issues. The individual person sees only his own activities and does not know how these fit into the overall

[1] Named after Frederick Taylor, who early in this century introduced the so-called *scientific management* concept. The underlying idea of this concept is the following: "The greatest production results when a worker is given a definite task to be performed at a definite time and in a definite manner."

business process. He is only responsible for his own activities and actions. Although this approach was extremely efficient earlier in this century, more and more people find it less desirable because due to their limited responsibility employees may become less motivated and thus, reduce their work efficiency.

Furthermore, surveys have shown that the actual processing time of many documents is far shorter than transportation and in-box waiting times. Quite often the information exchange between geographically dispersed departments requires documents to be converted and adapted to local work environments. Cases where electronic documents have been printed on paper and then retyped for the information system of another department are no exception. Usually, the seamless coordination is restricted to individual departments within large enterprises. Interdepartmental cooperation and coordination are scarce.

Companies hope that computer support can alleviate these deficits and thereby make business processes more efficient and cost-effective. Workflow management is seen as a means for modeling, automating and controlling business processes in the future.

7.1.1 The history of workflow management

The idea of workflow management can be traced back to a number of different sources. The most important and influential areas are certainly job scheduling of the manufacturing domain, office automation, software engineering, document processing, and more recently active databases, business process reengineering and CSCW. Early attempts of promoting workflow management in the context of office automation date back to the late 1970's. The first systems were Scoop introduced by Zismann (1977) and OfficeTalk-D by Ellis and Bernal (1982). These systems aimed at realizing a paperless office through computer supported automation of office tasks. However, these prototypes were not successful and the approach was not accepted in the commercial world. In addition to the rejection of the automation aspect for the office domain the necessary infrastructure was not in place at that time, the number of local and wide area networks were still rather small. People were convinced that office work included large portions of unstructured or weakly structured activities. Even though various office procedures are often similar, they are usually not identical. Thus, the complete specification of procedures results in inflexible workflows which are difficult to adapt to new and slightly different situations.

In the mid 1980's workstations and personal computers entered the office world. With tools such as word processors and spreadsheets several office activities became easier to perform or in some cases were even automated. After working initially in isolation soon the need for information exchange and information sharing emerged.[2] Now, readily available local and wide area networks provide the infrastructure necessary for distributed applications such as workflow management. Joosten et al. (1994) view workflow management "as an approach of information technology where the workflows are central." Examining implications of workflow management on business processes, they predict a reduction both of costs and time delays, which again will result in increased productivity and improved customer service.

Abbott and Sarin (1994) divided the evolution of workflow management systems into four generations. The first generation of systems had experimental character, resulting in proprietary applications with fixed implemented workflow definitions. Especially in document processing, some commercial systems have been developed and successfully introduced into companies. During the second generation, workflow management systems have been implemented as autonomous applications for usage in various domains. Script languages allowed the individual adaptation of workflow definitions. At the moment, we have the third generation, where workflow services may be invoked by external applications via special interfaces. Additionally, they provide graphical user interfaces which may be customized by the user for the specification and manipulation of workflows. Most prominently, functions for the simulation and analysis of workflows have gained in importance. However, external interfaces and data exchange formats are still proprietary. Future systems of the fourth generation should solve this deficiency: workflow services will then be fully and seamlessly integrated into the user's working environment. The workflow functionality will be embedded into other systems. Workflow services will exist as part of the middleware which may be accessed by different applications. Standardization of interfaces and data exchange formats are central issues to the future. The important role of the Workflow Management Coalition (WfMC) in this context will be discussed later in Sect. 7.6.2.

Due to its extensive influence on business reorganization, workflow management is seen as a promising technology with the possibility of high market growth rates in the future. According to estimates by BIS Forcast, the market for workflow management systems worldwide will grow from \$580 million in 1994 to over \$3000 million in 1999.

7.1.2 Terminology

As a recently evolved discipline, workflow management has not yet established a precise terminology. There exist a broad range of terms with similar meanings. In the following, we will adhere to the definitions by Abbott and Sarin (1994), Teufel et al. (1995) and Jablonski (1995) and will summarize the most important ones.

---

[2] Besides Lotus Notes (see Sect. 2.9.8), another prominent system supporting these needs is Microsoft Exchange; visit http://www.microsoft.com/exchange for more information on this product.

Definition 7.1.1 (Business process). *A business process is a collection of sequential and/or parallel activities necessary for the processing of economically relevant objects.*

Business processes occur in the context of an organization's structure and policy, and they are applied to achieve well-defined business objectives. They support interfaces to external market partners (e.g., to convey the results of a business process to the customer). In general, business processes are rigidly structured and have a high degree of recurrence. A company may encompass several business types each modeled by a separate business process.

Definition 7.1.2 (Business process reeingineering).
Business process reengineering is the complex, top-down reorganization of a company aiming at

- *a dramatic performance increase and*
- *a division of company activities into essential cross-functional, interdepartmental business processes.*

Business process reengineering is generally combined with the deployment of information and communication technology within the company. Applying the technology without modification and adaptation of the business processes usually will not result in the desired success. The following definitions of the terms workflow, workflow management and workflow management systems are derived from Teufel et al. (1995).

Definition 7.1.3 (Workflow). *A workflow is a finite set of sequential and/or parallel activities which are triggered by events. The activities have a defined start and completion. The terms procedure, process chain or business transaction are often used as synonyms for workflow.*

The activities have explicit and/or implicit relationships among themselves. Depending on the requirements and the context all or a subset of the activities may be executed in order to achieve a workflow objective. Coarse granular workflows are similar to business processes as they are known from business process reengineering while fine granular workflows refer to individual, personal tasks and activities performed as part of typical business processes.

Definition 7.1.4 (Workflow management). *Workflow management encompasses all the functions of modeling, specifying, simulating, analyzing, executing and monitoring a workflow.*

Definition 7.1.5 (Workflow management system). *A workflow management system (in the following abbreviated by WFM system) is a software system consisting of several tools supporting the tasks and functions of workflow management.*

McCarthy and Bluestein (1991) provide a very good characterization of WFM systems:

> "Workflow Management software is a proactive computer system which manages the flow of work among participants according to a defined procedure consisting of a number of tasks. It coordinates user and system participants, together with appropriate data resources which may be accessible directly by the system or off-line to achieve defined objectives by set deadlines. The coordination involves the passing of tasks from participant to participant in correct sequence ensuring that all fulfil their required contributions taking default actions when necessary."

A workflow must have a computer-internal representation which reflects the structure of work processes and activities, as well as their interdependencies with resources, such as consumed and produced data. This internal representation is interpreted by the WFM system in order to trigger the execution of activities and to monitor their progress.

A workflow management system is a particular kind of groupware intended to support groups of people involved in the execution of business processes. WFM systems are mainly used for coordinating spatially and temporally dispersed working groups and therefore belong to the category of coordination systems (see Fig. 2.16 on p. 125). People usually do not cooperate in real-time.

7.1.3 Goals, barriers and features

Companies hope to improve their business process quality and thus, to provide better customer services through workflow management. The usage of innovative information and communication technologies reduces the required execution times and cost. Transfer times of documents between people performing activities are shortened. A document management system[3] capable of handling all major data formats improves information access and thus, reduces time and resource requirements. Currently, many documents must be manually converted due to incompatible storage formats.

Coordinated forwarding of documents and tasks can optimize the information flow. All data required during workflow execution are associated with their related activities and automatically transferred to the persons currently working on these activities. This eliminates extensive search processes for information during activity execution.

Since all information and documents are available electronically, there are no media breaks. Incoming paper documents are scanned and interpreted by an OCR program[4].

[3] Among others, Documentum (http://www.documentum.com) and Open Text's Livelink (http://www.opentext.com/livelink) provide sophisticated workflow functionality as part of their products.

[4] Optical Character Recognition

In order to automate workflow execution WFM systems require a computerized specification of the workflow. Thus, workflow designers must analyze the business process and model it by a network of activities and their relationships, the necessary input data, the desired result data, and the specific criteria to indicate start and termination of the process. The workflow formalization makes the business process more comprehensible to both workflow designers and to actors responsible for activity execution.

Barriers. Along with its advantages, workflow management has a number of disadvantages which may cause some apprehension by the users. Since WFM systems provide monitoring facilities in order to determine the current state of workflow execution, many workers might feel that they are being electronically controlled. The supervisor could invoke at any time information about the work performance of an employee and display it on her screen (e.g., how much time has an employee already spent on his assigned task).

Managers, too, have complained about lack of functionality and flexibility which are necessary to support the different variants of business processes. It is feared that the formal specification of the workflow results in fixed and unchangeable business processes. Even if new situations occur companies might be very hesitant to adapt business processes and the associated workflows because of the required effort. One of the biggest problem, however, is the smooth introduction of a WFM system into a company and its seamless integration into the regular company activities. This usually requires a lot of extra effort and training of employees to utilize the full potential of the WFM system. Unlike single user applications where each user approaches the software according to his own philosophy, workflow management is a groupware solution which requires all group members to "play by the rules;" otherwise the WFM system might fail and not lead to the envisioned productivity improvement.

Features. Apart from the integration of legacy software, a WFM system must provide for access to already existing data and enable their use within workflow activities. Scalability is another important issue, since number and extent of supported processes cannot be predefined initially. A WFM system must grow as the company evolves and expands! Furthermore, a WFM system has to have a high degree of adaptability. Both the varying skills and desires of employees as well as changed tasks within the company require continuous adaptation of the workflows and the system supporting workflow execution.

There are many features that make up a WFM system. Marshak (1995b) has categorized them to the three R's (for *routes*, *rules* and *roles*) and three P's (for *processes*, *policies* and *practices*) of workflow management.

- *Routes:* Support of the flow of objects (e.g., documents, forms and activities between involved persons within an organization). A distinction is made between sequential, parallel and conditional paths.

- *Rules:* The business rules determine what information is to be routed and to whom. The rules must be represented explicitly in order to be interpretable by a WFM system.
- *Roles:* The responsibility to perform activities is assigned to roles rather than to specific people. For example, the reviewing activity in Fig. 7.1 may be assigned to the role department manager rather than to a Mr. G. U. Tachter. However, before an activity can actually be performed the associated role must be mapped to a specific person or software component. This mapping is often called role assignment. The use of roles makes the system more flexible in the case of organizational changes or exceptional situations (e.g., if the department manager is on sick leave his deputy might take over his role).
- *Processes:* Workflows automate business processes.
- *Policies:* The company policy is a formal written statement of how the business processes are handled. Examples are the vacation policy, travel expense policy or the hiring policy. The workflow rules are derived from these policies.
- *Practices:* While policies specify the formal ways of handling business processes, the practices represent the reality. They determine how the process really works. Practices evolve with the historical experience of the involved people (e.g., using unofficial office channels to communicate with relevant partners). Here we touch on another popular topic these days, namely knowledge management and the way it can best be exploited within an actual organization.

7.1.4 Taxonomy

Frequently used classification criteria for workflows are the structure of the modeled business process, the type of information flow between involved people (formal or informal), the kind of product which represents the result of the workflow, and the application domain (service industry, public administration, chemical industry, etc.).

Categorization according to the structure of the business process. In the context of BPR, organizations and their ongoing processes are analyzed with great care and in great detail; the results of the analysis are structured and repetitive business processes inherent to the organization. Examples are the handling of loan applications or sales order processing. These business processes are mapped onto workflows which are generally quite stable over long periods of time. We call these kinds of workflows *production workflows* and they are characterized by highly structured procedures and static information flows. They represent routine business processes whose structures and features are basically known in advance. Static, fixed structures facilitate a computer-supported automation of the workflow execution and its associated activities. Workflows of this kind are similar to parameterized process templates. As soon as a new process instance occurs (e.g., a new loan application is submitted by a customer), the process template is instantiated with the current parameters in order to create a representation for the new case. A suitable choice of parameters and their value ranges ensures a high degree of reusability.

At the opposite end of this categorization are *ad hoc workflows* which are characterized by flexible, often a priori unknown process structures. In this case, workflow management must adapt to changing situations and dynamically adjust its behavior. In general, it is not feasible to enumerate all possible situations and integrate alternatives into the workflow. Thus, ad hoc workflows cannot be specified in great detail in advance. The business processes of the advertising and media industry are typical examples of ad hoc workflows with tight time limits. For instance, the workflow for developing a market strategy depends on the product, the current market situation, the image of the company, and the potential customers.

Marshak (1995a) states: "a well-established workflow enables routine processing while an ad hoc workflow enables exception handling."

In between the two extremes (production workflow and ad hoc workflow), there is the *semistructured workflow*; Vossen and Becker (1996) also use the term administration workflow which has a well-defined, yet flexible process structure. Table 7.1 illustrates the characteristics of the three workflow categories.

Table 7.1. Comparison of workflow categories

	production workflow	semistructured workflow	ad hoc workflow
process	well-structured	partly prestructured	partly prestructured, yet subject to dynamic change
type of activity	describable in advance	partly describable in advance	indescribable in advance
relationship between activities	known in advance	partly known in advance	unknown in advance
information dependency between activities	may be planned in advance	may only be partially planned	planning is very incomplete
assignments and responsibilities	predefined in advance	only partially predefined	dynamically determined during execution of the workflow

Categorization according to the architectural model. Marshak (1995b) also classifies WFM systems with regard to the control and information flow. He distinguishes between three types:

- *Email-based model:* The information between activities and users is exchanged via electronic mail. This architecture model is appropriate for WFM systems realizing electronic circulation folders, i.e., document routing applications such as travel expense processing. It is easily scalable and can be extended for use in wide area networks. The control and information flow is described by a separate object or it may be attached to documents via attributes. Because documents migrate between private workspaces of the involved users it is difficult to determine exactly the current status of the workflow.
- *Shared database model:* The information of the workflow is stored in a shared database. When a user accesses a document stored in the database it is retrieved and copied into his local environment for manipulation. During that time other users may have only limited access to the document (e.g., only read access). Especially for wide area networks, a centralized shared database can cause some availability problems which is why it would make sense to replicate the database.[5] The current status of the workflow can be extracted from the database by interpreting the status of the documents stored in the database.
- *Client-server database model:* This model combines the benefits of the two aforementioned approaches. The workflow is monitored and controlled by one or several servers. Documents and activities are managed by servers, and users are notified of upcoming tasks. Section 7.5 introduces the architecture of a WFM system based on the client-server database model.

7.2 Conversation Model

Communication between people is usually based on sequences of words transferred either verbally or in writing. Other ways of communicating with each other, such as gestures and mimicry, will not be discussed here.

Human communication based on sets of morphemes copes with the following three aspects:

1. *Syntax:* The structure of a verbal or visible language expression specifies its syntax. Syntactical rules define the basic elements, such as letters or words and the way in which they can be combined (the grammar and sentence structure).
2. *Semantics:* The semantics defines the relationship between the syntactical structures of a language and the potential meaning of these structures.

[5] Taking into consideration the involved issues of concurrency control which were dealt with in earlier chapters.

3. *Pragmatics:* The effect of a communication on the speaker and the listeners is its pragmatics. The meaning of word sequences depends on personal knowledge and background.

Example (Pragmatics of a statement). Herbert says to his butler John, "It is cold in here." Literally spoken, this sentence represents information about the temperature in a room. However, the speaker's intent is that John should do something about it, such as turning up the heat.

Besides the pragmatics of a statement, there is also a pragmatic aspect with respect to an activity.

Example (Pragmatics of an activity). In his sketches on "Der Ritt über den Bodensee", Peter Handke uses the pragmatics of an activity as a stylistic means (translated from German):

> Somebody buttons up his jacket. "You are leaving?" - "No, I am only buttoning up my jacket". Another one hides his face behind his hands. "Are you crying?" - "No, I am just hiding my face behind my hands". Yet another clasps his arms before his chest. "Are you cold?" - "No, I am just clasping my arms in front of my chest".

Based on pragmatics, Austin (1962) and Searle (1969, 1979) developed a theory of speech acts.

7.2.1 Definition of speech act

Basic idea. The idea behind the speech act theory is the assumption that speaking means acting (speaking is a kind of action in itself). As opposed to traditional linguistic theories which focus on how words transport information, this theory emphasizes the activity.

Basically, the speech act theory deals with questions about the way in which utterances effect the future of speakers or listeners and which actions are caused by words. Thus, the speech act theory can be defined as follows:

Definition 7.2.1 (Speech act theory).
The speech act theory analyses speech as meaningful acts by communication partners in situations of shared activity.

Human communication is divided into a sequence of speech acts each of which is represented within the environment by a set of words, a so called verbal unit. A verbal unit can be a word, a sentence, a paragraph, or even an entire document. From this view emerge fundamental questions about the meaning of verbal units and which types of acts can be instigated by language (i.e. verbal units). In order to answer these questions we divide a speech act into three constituents: sentence content, category and presentation.

- *Sentence content:* The content of a sentence specifies the issue of communication (the subject, what the discussion is all about).
- *Category:* According to the speech act theory we can distinguish between five different category types:
  1. The assertive category is one in which a speaker asserts something to be true. Subsequent speech acts can serve to prove the truth of these assertions (e.g., by references).
  2. In directive category tries a speaker to make a listener do something, for instance by issuing a command or by asking a question like "Could you type that manual?".
  3. The commissive category is one in which the speaker makes a commitment via the speech act (i.e., he promises to do something, such as saying "I will type that manual").
  4. The declarative category defines a synergy between sentence content and reality. An example of this speech act category is "I hereby declare you husband and wife".
  5. The expressive category describes a current psychological state. An example for this would be "You did a good job".

  The categories 1, 4 and 5 refer to the past or present, whereas directives and commitments have implications for the future. The latter two differ only in the identity of the acting person. In the case of a commitment, the speaker will do something, in the case of a directive, it is the listener who is supposed to act. These five categories specify all the effects a speaker can have through verbal articulations.
  Speech acts are universal, that is, they are independent of culture and time. However, the actual transformation of different speech acts into a sequence of words depends on culture and language. For example, the Italian culture limits the term request to governmental directives, all other persons or organizations must use the term invite. In Japan, a request is never bluntly refused. Rather, a polite paraphrase is used. These examples lead us towards the third constituent of a speech act.
- *Presentation:* The presentation component specifies how verbal units of the speaker are presented to the listeners. Presentations can be polite, submissive or demanding. For example, the difference between the speech act "I hereby demand that you do what I told you to do" and the speech act "Should we go to the movies" is apparent.

The articulation of a verbal unit is often referred to as a locutional act. The intent behind a verbal unit is the illocutional act. The effect of the communication and the behavior of the listener result in a change of the current situation, which is called the perlocutional act.

7.2.2 Conversation networks

Winograd and Flores (1986) have investigated the structure of short conversations as they commonly occur within teamwork. The conversation between speaker and listener is formally described by a pattern of speech acts. Rather than trying to isolate recurring verbal utterances, this approach aims at isolating recurring categories of speech acts. Individual words constituting a speech act are of no interest for this formalization.

Speech acts are supposed to formalize human communication in order to enable computer support without requiring natural language understanding. It will suffice for the computer support to recognize the speech acts. Consequently, conversations can be viewed as a network of speech acts. There are some regularities with respect to links between speech acts, for instance, a directive usually precedes a commitment (Winograd 1988).

The conversation network can be interpreted as a state transition diagram; the nodes specify the conversation state while the arrows represent the speech acts.

Figure 7.2 depicts the state transition diagram for a "conversation for a action" network in which person A asks something of person B. The node 1 is the initial state, nodes 5, 7, 8 and 9 are possible final states.

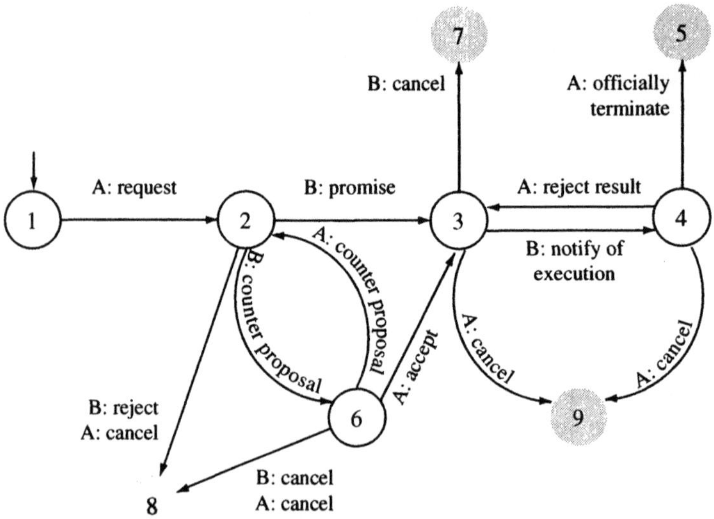

Fig. 7.2. Conversation network as a state transition diagram

A conversation network has the following features:

1. The conversation network defines for each state only a small set of applicable speech acts. The actual content of an utterance, however, is not

prescribed by the conversation network and may depend on the person and the context.
2. There are a number of final states in which the conversation partners do not expect any further acts.
3. All acts are linguistic, that is, they are expressed by verbal utterances between partners.
4. There are acts which are not expressed explicitly. For example, if B notifies A of having performed the request (transition from node 3 to node 4) and the solution offered by B is so outstanding that the transition from 4 to 5 is accepted by all partners, then the conversation is finished without official, explicit termination.
5. The conditions for a successful execution of a request depends on the interpretations of speaker and listeners. For example, if customer and performer have different opinions on the product to be manufactured by the performer, then a consensus will have to be negotiated through a sequence of speech acts.
6. The conversation network does not specify what a person should do or what consequences a speech act may have.

A group process can be viewed as a conversation consisting of several subconversations. Employees of an organization perform these kinds of subconversations in order to fulfill their duties within the team. As a result, we get a hierarchical network of conversations representing the group process.

If many people cooperate in one group the relationship between subconversations is often difficult to comprehend. Deficiencies in determining the necessary next steps and decisions, as well as miscalculations with respect to time schedules or the available resources are often the consequence.

The use of computer tools for coordinating group activities on the basis of speech acts may avoid these problems. An example for such a system is the Coordinator (Flores et al. 1988). Other important members of this system class are: Amigo (Danielsen et al. 1986), Chaos (de Cindio et al. 1988), Cosmos (Wilbur and Young 1988), Domino (Kreifelts et al. 1991), EuroCoOp (Hennessy et al. 1992), Object Lens (Lai et al. 1988), Strudel (Shepherd et al. 1990), Action Workflow (Medina-Mora et al. 1992) and Tacts (Teege 1993).

7.2.3 Conversation systems

The conversation paradigm is the basis for an entire class of cooperation and group support systems, especially in office environments. The spectrum of cooperation ranges between formal coordination systems (Domino) to informal systems for information exchange (Object Lens), as well as from user-specific, bilateral coordination systems (Coordinator) to application-specific models such as bulletin board systems (Amigo).

Conversation systems are cooperation systems based on the conceptual model of conversation. These systems map the conversation between people to the message exchange between actors. Both human users and intelligent computer programs, so-called agents, can be actors (see Chap. 9).

Example (TeamTalk). The graphical group conversation system TeamTalk by Trax Softworks, Inc., Culver City, CA, aims at improving communication within a group. As opposed to traditional email or bulletin board systems, TeamTalk does not record the sequence of a conversation as a set of individual messages, but as a homogeneous, well-defined document. For each conversation topic, a document is created. Topics can be hierarchically structured or contain additional information such as "private" or "public". As soon as a user joins a group conversation accessible to him, he is automatically notified of all modifications within the conversation document which occurred since his last document access. Moreover, thanks to the OLE support, even documents produced outside TeamTalk can be integrated into a conversation.

Conversation systems generally implement a conversation by a sequence of electronic messages exchanged between group participants. Communication takes place via an email system. Depending on the speech act categories respective message types are defined; thus there must be different message types for assertions, directives, etc. Within a group, the message exchange supporting the cooperation follows certain rules: Sending and receiving messages of a certain type changes the state of the sender and possibly also that of the recipient. Furthermore, subsequent messages or expectations for incoming messages are determined by the state of the respective actors.

Example (Tax office). Among others, possible message types exchanged between Internal Revenue Service and taxpayer are tax return, tax assessment and appeal to tax assessment.

The range of possible acts initiated by an actor is constrained by the type of the received message and his current state (the actor can only select a subset of possible message types to compose his answer). Note that only the message type is significant to the system, not the message content itself. The pattern of activities underlying a group process can thus be seen as a conversation game in which the messages represent possible moves and actors have certain roles with respect to cooperation. Using roles makes the definition of generic conversation networks more flexible, since actors are assigned to roles only at the instantiation of a specific conversation.

Group processes are often divided into phases. As the following example will illustrate, there is a well-defined cooperation pattern for each phase.

Example (Group process). Let us assume that a group process is divided into the following three phases: Brainstorming, idea evaluation and decision implementation. During the first phase, a "conversation for brainstorming" is applied in order to collect ideas for achieving the goal. Differences between means and goal, as well as between partial and complete solution are neglected. The focus of attention lies on causal relationships, ideas, possible results and problems to expect. Subsequently, during the "conversation for evaluation" the ideas are sorted and evaluated. The possible activities are explored and discussed in more detail. Finally, during "conversation for action" the selected activities are executed.

According to the aforementioned conversation patterns, respective conversation types can be defined.

Definition 7.2.2 (Conversation type). *A conversation type is the specification of a cooperation pattern based on the conversation model. Each conversation type consists of a set of message types, a set of actors and their respective states, and the conversation rules.*

Conversation rules describe the restrictions of message exchange depending on the current state of the respective actors (they determine which types of messages may be sent or may be expected to be received). If the rules are strict and extensive, then the conversation tends to be very formal; when the conversation rules specify few restrictions, the conversation tends to be informal and chatty.

7.2.4 The Coordinator

The Coordinator (Flores et al. 1988) is a system developed by Action Technologies and based on the conversation model. It is used for designing conversation networks within distributed systems and for monitoring their execution.

The Coordinator implements the generic conversation type of bilateral request handling. These kinds of conversations are made up of the following basic components: demand/commitment, offer/acceptance and announcement/confirmation. These pairs facilitate the implementation of conversation networks as well as the definition of competency, norms and rules for the organization (such as terminology and policies). The Coordinator is particularly useful in the following areas:

1. At initiation of a speech act the Coordinator creates an email-like message consisting of a structured part which contains the message type and an unstructured part which contains the content of the speech act in free text.
2. The Coordinator assists the user in monitoring the progress of the conversation during all phases up to the conversation end.
3. Time is a critical factor of speech acts. The Coordinator monitors the temporal dependencies between speech acts.
4. The conversation network is visually presented to the user.
5. The Coordinator initiates automatically certain acts specified by the user.
6. The Coordinator allows the integration of forms to be used for certain, recurring situations.

The system runs on standard hardware connected via a local or a wide area network. On each computer, the entire system is installed in order to interpret incoming messages and offer suitable replies according to conversation type and state. There is no central coordination unit controlling the group process. Exception handling is integrated into the conversation network. By categorizing all messages, the Coordinator forces the user to express himself clearly and thereby helps avoid misunderstandings.

7.2.5 The office procedure system Domino

The system Domino (Kreifelts et al. 1991) exemplifies the way in which the conversation model may be used to model office procedures. Examples of office procedures are the handling of insurance cases which circulate through different departments or the processing of a business trip application.

The underlying concept of Domino is based on the view that cooperation in the context of office procedures is a regulated information flow between certain units of an organization (e.g., people or departments). In practice, we can imagine electronic circulation folders, such as the system ECF (Karbe et al. 1990). A procedure system aims at handling and controlling the regular information exchange between the participants of the group process. With the exception of the Andrew message system, which is an early attempt to use active messages to control the information flow, email systems and computer conferences generally support a free uncontrolled information exchange. A procedure is a flow of documents between various actors who perform operations on these documents in order to achieve the procedure goal. However, the actors alone are responsible for the way in which they execute the procedural tasks.

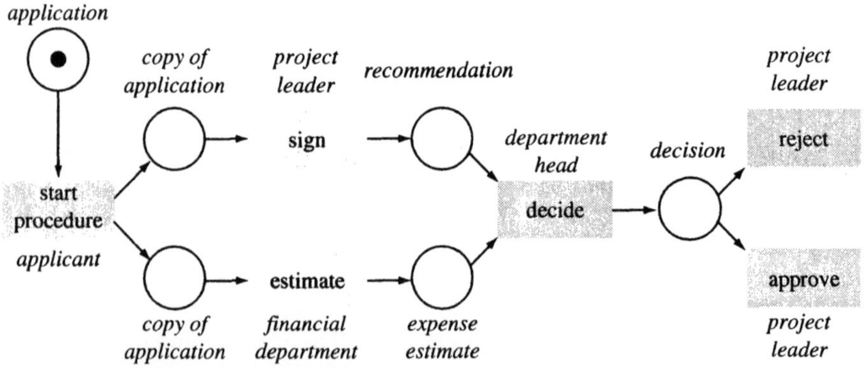

Fig. 7.3. Petri net for the procedure of a business trip application

A procedure can be modeled by a Petri net. Figure 7.3 depicts a Petri net for the procedure of a business trip application. Circles represent the procedure information ("circulating folder") while rectangles define activities to be performed by actors. The transition to activity *reject* or *approve* depends on the procedure information *decision*. For the specification of conversation rules Domino applies predicate/transition nets (Pr/T nets[6]). The actors (persons, programs or message channels) and their states become predicates, the activities become transitions. The Pr/T net describes the dynamic aspects of an asynchronous conversation. It contains the initial states of activities and considers subsequent states.

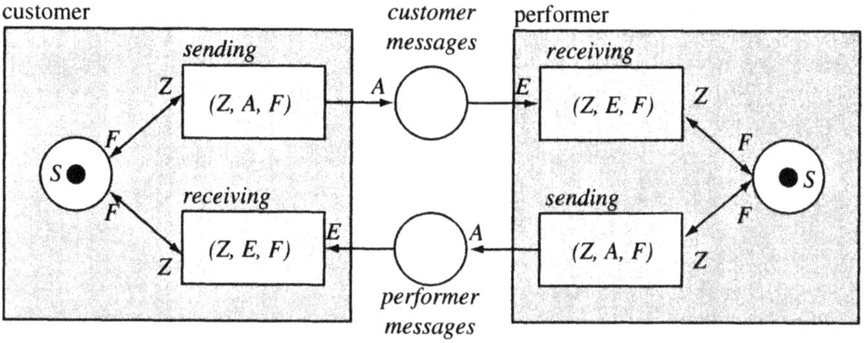

Fig. 7.4. Pr/T net representation of a bilateral conversation network

Figure 7.4 depicts a Pr/T net representing a bilateral conversation network. Each activity is specified by three components:

1. the state Z at the beginning of an activity;
2. the sent or received message (A is the sent message type and E the received message type);
3. the subsequent state F after the activity has been performed.

The initial state of the conversation network is represented by S. For example, if a customer wishes to send instructions to the performer, then the activity *sending* is triggered by the customer. In the above case S was the state at the beginning of the activity, the conversation rules specify *issued* as the subsequent state after the activity has been performed (see Table 7.2). The Pr/T net incorporates for each actor additional synchronization transitions (based on message channels) in order to model the asynchronous behavior of electronic message systems

A Pr/T net has the following features: First, it is connected and cycle-free. Second, each activity has at least one input and one – possibly fictional – output. Third, the procedure must not contain any deadlocks. Here we may apply deadlock detection algorithms developed in the field of Petri nets.

[6] Pr/T nets are extended Petri nets.

Table 7.2. Examples for conversation rules

predicate	state Z	input message type E	output message type A	subsequent state F
sending	S		order	issued
	issued		cancellation	cancelled
	performed		confirmation	confirmed
receiving	issued	rejection		rejected
	issued	completion		completed

Pr/T nets do not assume a global state; all states are local. Transitions between states represent the conversation rules which are implemented via tables. Table 7.2 shows the specification of rules for the customer in the aforementioned example. In practice, the granularity for message types and states are far more precise than the table would suggest, which is why this table should only be interpreted as a rough overview of possible rules.

Multilateral conversation. A multilateral conversation can be modeled by a set of bilateral conversations. A mediator or an autonomous group agent coordinates the interaction between the bilateral conversations of users u_1, u_2 and u_3 (Fig. 7.5).

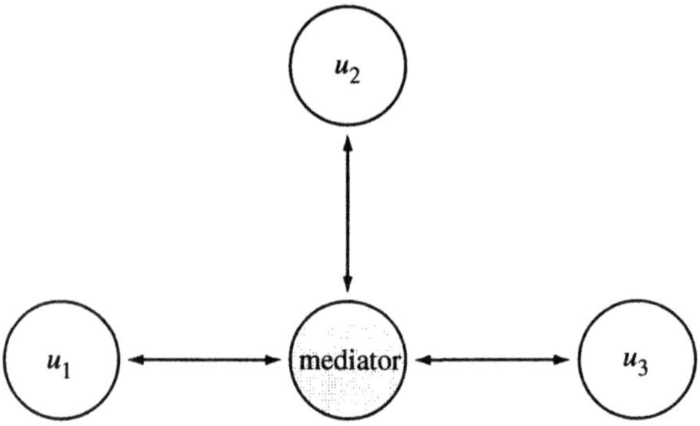

Fig. 7.5. Mediator-supported conversation

7.2.6 The activity management system Tacts

Tacts (Teege 1996) is an integrated activity management system. As opposed to systems like the Coordinator (Flores et al. 1988) or Domino (Kreifelts et al. 1991) Tacts is not based on collaborative activities. Instead, an arbitrary activity serves as the basic component, independent of the actor, cooperation situations, environment or possible contexts. Thus, the asynchronous interactions necessary for coordinating extensive group processes within Tacts can themselves be modeled as activities. Tacts supports the composition of simple activities in order to construct more complex activities. A group process with its coordination mechanism may be modeled as a complex activity. Tacts is an extensible framework providing a set of predefined mechanisms to construct group processes; however, the user may dynamically add new mechanisms in order to incorporate customized features. The framework even allows the combination of already existing group processes.

Tacts follows an object-oriented approach. Both activities and resources, such as documents, are represented explicitly as objects within the system. Object attributes and methods for dealing with objects are described in classes, which means that each kind of activity is specified by a class. Tacts supports multiple inheritance which allows quick construction of very similar activity types. Thus, it is possible to specify every single aspect of an activity by a separate class. Tacts provides a toolkit of activity types. The user may combine these aspects in different ways in order to tailor activities according to his needs.

The Tacts system provides three kinds of activity support:

1. *Structuring:* Tacts maintains the relationship between activities, their subactivities, the executing actor, and the context. The structure is used for accessing related parts of an activity and for determining the context in which the activity is executed. The structure may be predefined as part of an object class, thus predefining a certain activity type. However, the structure may also be manually specified by the user who can thus dynamically group his own activities according to his own preferences.
2. *History:* Tacts records information about the activity which is not already predefined by the activity type (e.g., the starting or completion times). The history may be used for determining how to proceed with an ongoing activity. Later after activity completion the history may be used to design activity types for similar activities, thus reusing the experience gained while executing the activity.
3. *Execution:* Last but not least, Tacts also supports activity execution either under system or user control. The system organizes the sequencing of substeps, the coordination among actors, and the processing of substeps. The execution is specified in the form of methods as part of classes. Examples for activities which may be automatically executed by Tacts are the printing of a document or the sending of an email. However, a letter only available on paper generally cannot be processed electronically. All Tacts can do in this case is to provide structure and history support.

States in Tacts. An important aspect of modeling an activity is the specification of all possible states, their potential sequence and the events triggering state transitions. The object-oriented mechanism in Tacts has been extended so as to provide each class with a pattern of possible states and state transitions.

Finite automatons are an obvious choice to formalize the state schemas. However, experience has shown that there are at least three reasons why they may be inadequate in Tacts. Firstly, the combination of independent behavioral aspects leads to an explosion in the numbers of states (Harel 1987). Moreover, a combination between finite automaton and inheritance causes problems known as inheritance anomaly (see Matsuoka et al. 1993). Lastly, a finite automaton does not support exception handling by the user. Some of these problems can be solved by using the Statechart formalism (Harel 1987), which is characterized by a hierarchical structure of states, so that each state can again contain an entire automaton. However, Statecharts do not support interactions between users, and they cannot be combined.

For these reasons, the HieraStates formalism has been specifically developed for use in Tacts (Teege 1996). It adapts the Statechart formalism, however, extending it to include direct interaction with the user, construction of complex schemas out of building blocks and support of exception handling. Rather than being atomic, state transitions can be interrupted and represent subactivities of their own. Figure 7.6 shows the graphical representation of a HieraStates diagram for a rather general activity predefined by Tacts.

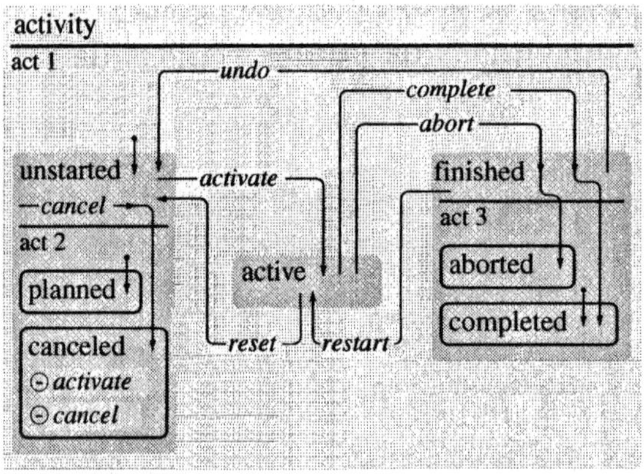

Fig. 7.6. Example for a HieraStates diagram

The topmost state hierarchy level *act 1* in Fig. 7.6 consists of the three states *unstarted*, *active* and *finished*. Here we discuss only the state *unstarted* and its transitions. For all other states and transitions similar statements are true. The complex state *unstarted* has assigned the state scheme *act 2* which consists of the states *planned* and *canceled*; the transitions *cancel* and *activate* may be applied. In state *planned*, both transitions are accepted, whereas they both are explicitly excluded for state *canceled* (i.e., transitions of complex states are inherited by substates, assuming that there are no local methods overwriting them). The execution of *cancel* leads to the new state *canceled* independent of whether the source state was *unstarted* or *planned*. The transition *activate* results in the new state *active* both for *unstarted* and *planned*. If the transitions *undo* or *reset* are triggered, the new state will be *unstarted* and thus, the substate *planned*. The state *planned* is the default state of the HierStates scheme *act 2* (represented by the arrow leading into *planned*, at the origin of which there is a dot). Respectively, *unstarted* is the default of *act 1*.

Transitions can be triggered by the user. In that case the system lists all transitions available in the current state and the user may select one of them. Furthermore, the explicitly specified automaton enables the system to provide help to the user as he attempts to identify possible paths from the current state to the desired final state.

Automatons may be applied to model conversation networks (as discussed earlier in Sect. 7.2.2). The activity represents the local view of the group process for the user according to his role. Transitions within the automaton correspond to speech acts which are related to transmission channels for propagating information. The user is either sender or recipient.

In Tacts state transitions can, however, also represent a variety of other activities (e.g., local single user activities). Thus, conversation networks can be extended to incorporate in addition to speech acts the activities triggered by these acts.

Furthermore, the user may also attach separately a subactivity described by an automaton to a state transition itself. On activating the transition, the subactivity is triggered and executed; only when it reaches its final state is the transition complete. This mechanism allows the construction of hierarchical conversations.

Another use of the automaton mechanism is office procedure modeling. Here, too, the entire procedure is hierarchically structured and may be mapped to a HieraStates diagram. Transitions within the automaton represent individual user activities and are typically executed by Tacts. In HieraStates, if a transition cannot be completed due to an exceptional situation, transitions starting in the next surrounding state are still applicable and may be invoked by the user to handle the situation. It is noteworthy to mention that the execution sequence predefined by the automaton is not obligatory. The user can always add new activities, skip activities, or else ignore the automaton altogether. This flexibility is especially important in the handling of exceptional situations.

Generally, a HieraStates diagram is associated with a single person. The automaton models only those parts of group activities which are local to that person. Thus, the automaton represents the participant's role in the overall group process. As an extension, Tacts also supports shared objects which allows the cooperation between group members via a shared information space. The group process itself may be modeled as a single object. Furthermore, Tacts provides mechanisms to support synchronous cooperation within the group.

Besides these general mechanisms which are implemented on top of an object-oriented environment Tacts supports a variety of classes which represent basic activity types. Examples are activities for sending and receiving email. Both can be used as components for the design of complex activities involving several communication steps, especially those that support coordination between several group members.

Documents in Tacts. Each activity has a context which is represented by a separate object. The context encompasses artifacts manipulated by the activity (documents), artifacts used for performing the activity (documents or tools), persons involved in the activity, and other information items (goals and policies). In Tacts, documents are the primary means of capturing arbitrary information. Since documents are represented as objects, all aforementioned mechanisms can be applied to them. Specifically, automatons are attached to documents modeling the state transitions during the document life cycle.

Further, a document may contain subobjects which represent either document parts or even activities which are applicable to the document. Thus, Tacts provides very flexible means to model the relationship between activities and documents. Documents may be either subobjects or parent objects of activities depending on the usage context. In Tacts, the information transmitted during a communication activity is always represented by a document. If the information exclusively serves the purpose of supporting the communication activity (e.g., as message content of an email), then the document is a subobject of the activity. As opposed to this, a document may be the parent object of a communication activity if the main user focus is on the document (e.g., the user is working on a book which he sends to his co-author for reviewing).

We conclude that Tacts is a framework for activity support. Rather than incorporating specific cooperation types, it offers mechanisms for modeling and implementing varieties of group processes using the object-oriented paradigm. Special emphasis is given to the integration of different work modes and the customization by the end user adapting the activities and their context to his own needs.

7.3 Coordination Models

Coordination between involved parties of a workflow is a basic requirement for successful execution of the workflow task. Informally, coordination is when several people harmonize within a working environment. In the words of Malone and Crowston (1994):

> "Coordination can be seen as the process of managing dependencies among activities."

Within a team, coordination is required for several reasons:

- to overcome geographic, temporal and knowledge distances between the group members,
- to convey the type and structure of a shared task, and

– to handle the complexity and intensity of interdependencies between group members and activities.

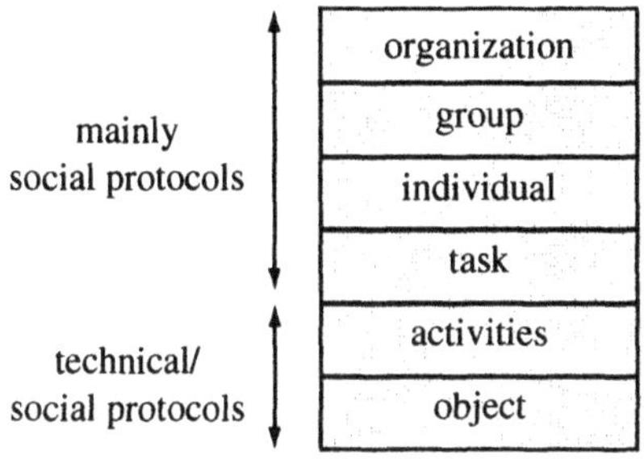

Fig. 7.7. Different coordination levels

Coordination takes place on different levels (see Fig. 7.7). The lower levels control access to the work environment (e.g., access to the shared information objects and the activities of the workflow). In general, the user can choose between technical and social protocols to perform coordination. Technical protocols are managed by the groupware system itself, whereas social protocols require interpersonal arrangements between the group members. In the latter case people are not constrained by the technical features and the provided functionality of the groupware system.

Higher coordination levels mainly apply social protocols to manage the interdependencies between the involved people. It is not possible yet to comprehensively model the complete work environment (including the organizational goals, policies and practices) which would be necessary to provide full system coordination. However, technical protocols can be used supportively (e.g., a WFM system to handle the information flow between the actors of the workflow or to support the assignment of activities).

The usage of technical protocols for resolving interpersonal conflicts has been repeatedly criticized. Condon (1993) wrote:

> "Systems to resolve interpersonal conflict will only translate it into conflict between the user and the computer system. Interpersonal conflict can sometimes be productive; human-computer conflict just leads to a frustrated cry: The computer won't let me."

Therefore, he proposes decentralized coordination for groupware systems distributing control among all participants. For example, if two participants attempt to modify an object concurrently, then the system recognizes the conflict and notifies the involved participants. However, the conflict resolution is left in the hands of the participants.

7.3.1 The coordination theory according to Malone

Malone and Crowston (1990, 1994) considered coordination to be a multidisciplinary research domain which, like CSCW, is based on interdisciplinary cooperation between such areas as computer science, organizational theory, psychology, and business administration. The above authors developed a coordination theory which may be applied to the design of organizations and coordination technology (i.e., the design of systems which support people in activity coordination) as well as the development of parallel and distributed systems.

The coordination theory formalizes dependencies between activities, and it provides a framework to analyze and evaluate different coordination approaches. According to Malone and Crowston, coordination can be divided into four basic components: goals, activities, actors and dependencies. One or several actors perform activities to achieve certain goals. Possible generic dependency types between activities are prerequisite constraints, shared resource and simultaneity. In the first case, an activity requires results of prior activities, in the second case, several activities use a shared resource, and the last type describes interdependencies between activities which are performed in parallel.

Table 7.3. Coordination components and the associated coordination processes

components of coordination	coordination processes
goals	goal identification
activities	mapping goals to activities, e.g., goal decomposition and activity planning
actors	assigning activities to actors, e.g., determine actors and assign activities
interdependencies	managing and handling dependencies, e.g., determine resource allocation, the sequencing and synchronization of activities

As listed in Table 7.3 associated with each component are basic coordination processes which may be characterized from different perspectives. Malone and Crowston (1992) describe them in terms of hierarchical levels of processes, each of which depends on the levels below it:

> "Coordination requires group decisions. In order to reach a decision accepted by the group, the group members must communicate in some form exchanging information about goals, activities and alternatives. The communication requires messages transmitted between the participants and the establishment of a common language in order to achieve a consistent perception of shared information objects."

Table 7.4 illustrates the four different perspectives together with the relevant components and coordination processes.

Table 7.4. Perspectives of coordination processes

perspective	components of coordination	coordination processes
coordination	goals, activities, actors, interdepencendies	goal identification, resource assignment, planning of activities, interdependency management
group decision	goals, actors, alternatives, evaluations, selections	proposing and evaluating alternatives, select an alternative (by authority, voting or consensus)
communication	sender, recipient, messages, shared languages	determining shared languages, determining communication paths (routing)
perception of shared objects	actors, objects	access to shared database, visualization of shared objects (e.g., based on WYSIWIS)

7.3.2 Customer-performer model

The customer-performer model is based on a conversation-oriented approach (see Sect. 7.2). A business process is interpreted as a sequence of customer-performer relationships. During the business process the roles of "customer" and "performer" may change (the performer of one relationship can become the customer of another relationship). However for each relationship, the customer and the performer must be well defined. The WFM system Action Workflow (Medina-Mora et al. 1992) uses the customer-performer model as a basic element for modeling workflows; it is referred to as a workflow loop.

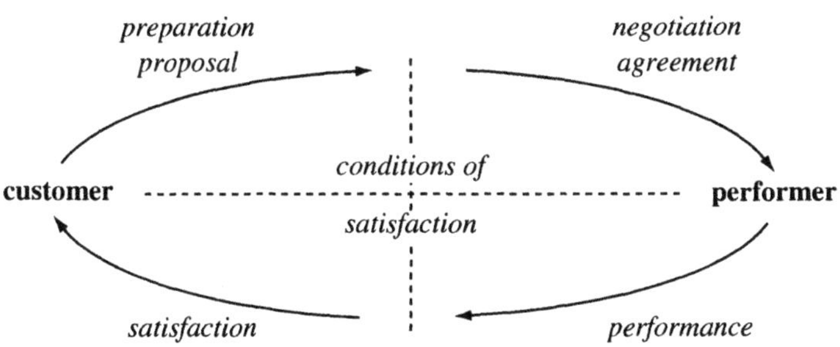

Fig. 7.8. Phases of the customer-performer model

A workflow loop incorporates all interactions between customer and performer. It consists of four generic phases (see Fig. 7.8). In each of the four phases speech acts are applied to specify activity alternatives of all involved parties:

- *Preparation/proposal*: During this phase, the first contact is established between the involved people. Both the customer and the performer can take the initiative. In the former case, the customer requests the completion of a service, consisting of one or several activities, from the performer, whereas in the second case the performer advertises a certain service. In both cases the service execution depends on the stated conditions of satisfaction.
- *Negotiation/agreement*: Customer and performer negotiate about what is expected of the performer. In this phase, particular emphasis lies on the bidirectional interaction between the persons involved. The result of this phase is a mutual agreement between the two parties on the conditions of satisfaction. The agreement is often only partially explicit and based on shared background and standard practices.
- *Performance*: The performer executes the activities associated with the requested service and subsequently informs the customer about the results. This phase can trigger additional customer-performer relationships, usually involving other parties.
- *Satisfaction*: The customer evaluates the service results according to the agreed conditions of satisfaction and informs the performer about the evaluation. Both positive and negative evaluations are possible. In the latter case, the service is not accepted as delivered, and further actions are required by the performer.

Besides the phases, each workflow loop incorporates the conditions for the service. They describe the requirements made by the customer and accepted by the performer (e.g., time restrictions or cost limits). At any phase these conditions may be renegotiated between customer and performer.

As opposed to traditional, product-oriented approaches, the customer-performer model is customer-oriented. Customer satisfaction, response time and customer requests are the main focus of attention.

Each individual workflow loop is again a workflow representing a task. In order to satisfy customers, it may be necessary to perform several subservices. Each phase within the loop can initiate further loops. These chained workflow loops allow for the realization of complex workflows incorporating more than two people (see Fig. 7.9).

7.4 Workflow Modeling

A workflow is a formally described business process which can be automated and monitored by a WFM system. Workflow modeling must include activities

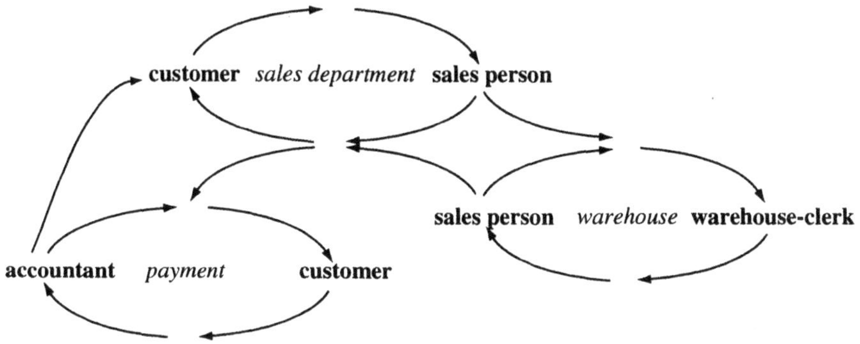

Fig. 7.9. Chain of workflow loops

("what task is to be performed"), actors ("who is supposed to perform the task"), dependencies ("when and under what conditions is the task to be performed"), reasons ("why is the task to be performed") and relationships between activities and actors.

7.4.1 Aspect-oriented workflow model

For each workflow, we can distinguish three different modeling areas:

1. *Procedures*: Modeling of activities and their execution order.
2. *Information*: Modeling of objects and documents created, processed and utilized within the workflow.
3. *Organization*: Modeling of actors, roles, responsibilities and permissions.

The semantics of a workflow are determined by the set of activities, each of which is specified by its operation, its structure, and its context. The operation description contains preconditions, input data, an action, output data and postconditions. The precondition serves as a trigger for the activity execution, while the postconditions may be used to trigger the execution of other activities. The context associates tools and information required for the execution of an activity.

Jablonski (1995) proposed modeling workflows according to aspects since they allow different perspectives of the information to be modeled and also consider incomplete business processes. New aspects can be added dynamically, even while the workflow is being executed.

Functional aspect. "What has to be done?"

The functional aspect defines the hierarchical structure of a workflow consisting of activities and subactivities. Activities are only described from the logical perspective and not with respect to their implementation. We distinguish between composite and basic activities. In the former case, the activity consists of a set of subactivities, whereas there is no further subdivision in the latter case. A basic activity is always related to an action performed by the associated actor (e.g., writing a letter or sending an email). Composite activities themselves may be interpreted as another workflow, albeit on another abstraction level. Consequently Jablonski proposed using the term workflow alone, rather than workflow *and* activity. Scientific works on the subject, however, often only refer to "top-level" activities as workflows, using the term activity for logical procedure steps within a workflow. This book conforms to the second view that is found in scientific works.

Operational aspect. "How is an activity implemented?"

This aspect specifies the way in which the functionality of a basic activity is achieved either by invoking software applications (automatically or triggered by the user) or by a human actor himself. In the latter case the user is in control. The user decides when an application should be used, usually outside of the WFM system, and which part of the functionality he will provide through manual work.

The operational aspect specifies an abstract interface between the WFM system and the applications associated with the activity, thus enabling a seamless data exchange. The abstract interface is independent of implementation details and implementation variants.

Behavioral aspect. "When and in what sequence are activities performed?"

This aspect deals with the control flow within the workflow determining the execution order of activities and their associated applications. Jablonski and Bussler (1996) distinguish between prescriptive and descriptive workflow control. The prescriptive specification contains constructs already commonly known from programming languages, such as sequence, loops, and conditional or parallel branching. Prescriptive flow control results in a concrete execution order while descriptive flow control merely describes possible processing classes. It specifies temporal and existential conditions for the activities. Jablonski and Bussler define the following constructs for the descriptive specification:

1. *Deadline*: $<(a, b)$
   The execution of a is limited by the start of b. The following rules apply:
   - a can be executed as long as b has not been executed.
   - b can be executed as long as a has not been started, or if a has already been completed.
   - neither a nor b are executed.

   This results in the following set of possible execution sequences: $\{$empty, a, b, $ab\}$.
2. *Delay*: $>(a, b)$
   The execution of a is delayed by b. The following rules apply:
   - a can only be executed if b has already been finished or if it is decided that b is never to be executed.
   - in principal b may be started at any time.

   Possible execution sequences are: $\{$empty, b, a, $ba\}$.

3. *Existence:* $\Longrightarrow (a, b)$
   The execution of b implies the execution of a:
   - a will only be executed if b has been executed prior to a or if b will be executed in the future.
   - if a is never executed, then the execution of b is optional.

   As possible execution sequences, we get the set: {empty, b, ba, ab}.

Informational aspect. "Which data are produced and consumed?"

The informational aspect describes the data produced and consumed by the workflow as well as the dataflow between its activities. Each activity has a parameterized interface listing its input/output data. Jablonski and Bussler distinguish between control and production data. Control data are internal to the workflow and are used to monitor workflow execution by the WFM system. Examples of control data are status information on activities, the execution history or other statistical information. Production data are data and documents which are produced or consumed during the execution of activities. Additionally the informational aspect specifies conversion routines in order to create the format necessary for local manipulation or to transfer data between activities.

Organizational aspect. "Who has to execute an activity?"

Workflows are embedded within organizations, and thus the execution of activities depends on the organizational context. The organization is the basic concept for the enactment of the organizational aspect. It models the employees as the organizational population and their roles. An actor is assigned to each activity, taking responsibility for its execution. Relationships between actors define the organizational structure. The actor can be represented by an individual person, a group of persons or a software system. Actors having the same set of knowledge, competencies, access rights with respect to activities and information, are combined to form actor types (so-called roles).

At activity creation a responsible role is assigned to the activity instead of actors enabling flexible reaction to organizational changes even after the workflow has started. Only when the activity is ready for execution, is an actor fitting the role assigned to the activity. The delayed assignment of an activity to an actor improves flexibility, allowing new situations within an organization to be more easily taken care of (e.g., handling a sudden illness of an employee). Organizational policies control the resolution of roles and thus the assignment of actors to activities. As soon as an activity has been assigned to an actor, he must be notified. This can either be achieved by an automatic entry into his to-do-list or by sending him email.

Causal aspect. "Why should the activity be executed?"

The causal aspect describes the reason for the execution of an activity. It allows the modeling of dependencies between activities not yet covered by the behavioral aspect. Examples are legal and company-specific elements of a workflow. The causal aspects also allow the specification of interworkflow relationships. For example, after a large order requiring additional personnel has been approved two workflows are initiated: a) the workflow processing the order, and b) the workflow hiring new people by the personnel department. If later the order is canceled, both workflows must be terminated.

Historical aspect. "What has been done in the past?"

This aspect records the execution history of an activity. It captures the steps and actions taken during the course of activity execution. It may also reflect all intermediate states between activity start and activity termination. The historical information may be used to improve the activity implementation.

Transactional aspect. "How are activities combined?"

This aspect models the activity execution with respect to atomicity and persistence by applying transactional characteristics.

Information Control Net (ICN). Ellis and Wainer (1994) add another aspect to the aforementioned ones by modeling the workflow goals explicitly and assigning them to the respective activities. This facilitates the modeling of unstructured activities, since they can now be combined under a shared goal without prior specification of all relationships. Even conflicting goals can be assigned, since conflicts are resolved during execution of the activities by determining a compromise according to the current situation.

An ICN graph consists of an organizational framework with goals, actors, resources, and a set of objects specifying activities and roles, as well as a mapping between the organizational framework and the objects. Figure 7.10 shows a workflow with goals. The goals are represented by small triangles. The dotted edges outline the effective range of the goals with respect to the activities concerned. Goals can be hierarchically structured, recursively splitting goals into subgoals.

7.4.2 Process grammar

In addition to special specification languages (Jablonski and Bussler 1996), Petri nets (see also Domino in Sect. 7.2.5) and state diagrams are alternatives for workflow modeling. Petri nets facilitate workflow simulations for analyzing and validating a previously defined workflow model. In Tacts (see Sect. 7.2.6), the modeling of the operational and behavioral aspects of activities is done by the HieraStates mechanism. Compared with Petri nets, they have the advantage of supporting specification changes even during workflow execution, which means that exceptional, a priori unknown situations can be handled dynamically.

Recently, research groups started to explore process grammars and constraints for workflow modeling and the specification of coordinated activities (Pentland 1994, Glance et al. 1996). Pentland developed a grammatical model supporting both the description of and the experimentation with workflows,

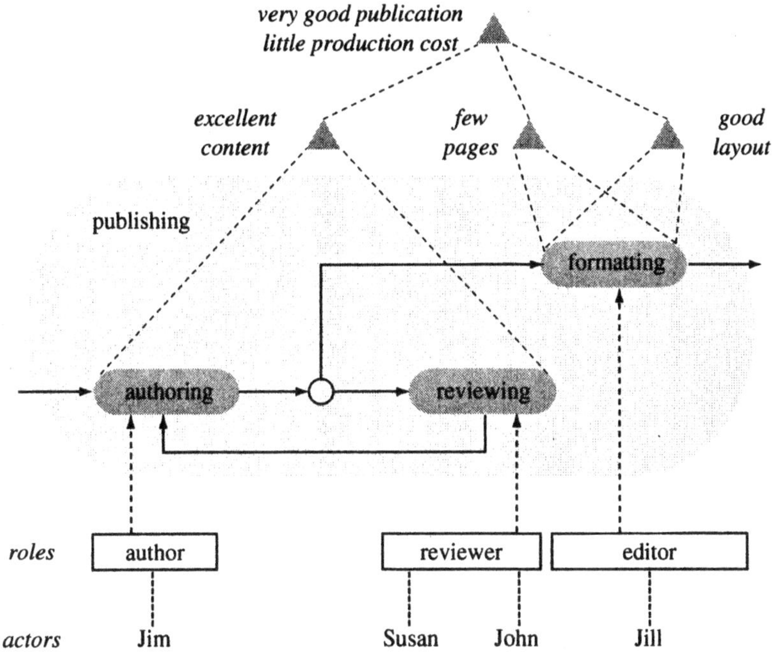

Fig. 7.10. Information Control Net for a document publishing workflow

and thereby business processes. The model contains a dictionary of basic activities and rules for the combination of activities in order to specify complex workflows. As opposed to Petri nets and the HieraStates mechanism, process grammars follow a declarative approach. Rather than an individual workflow, an entire class of workflows which is derived from the dictionary and the rules, is specified. Even during workflow execution the execution order may be changed dynamically by modifying the rules, thus, the WFM system is very flexible and unforeseeable exceptional situations can be treated efficiently. Moreover, the user can explicitly specify which situations should not occur. Process grammars can both model existing and familiar workflows and design new workflows (i.e., new business processes). The latter approach is being applied in a project by Malone et al. (1997) which involves the construction of a handbook for business processes. The handbook is being used to reorganize existing processes, to derive new processes, to analyze the organization itself and automatically generate software components supporting the processes.

7.5 Execution Environments for Workflows

After the modeling phase, workflow specifications may be instantiated and executed. Therefore, the execution and control component, the so-called workflow management engine, is central to a WFM system. Jablonski and Bussler (1996) proposed a workflow management architecture based on a client-server model. The workflow execution environment consisted of various servers, each modeling a different workflow aspect (see Fig. 7.11).

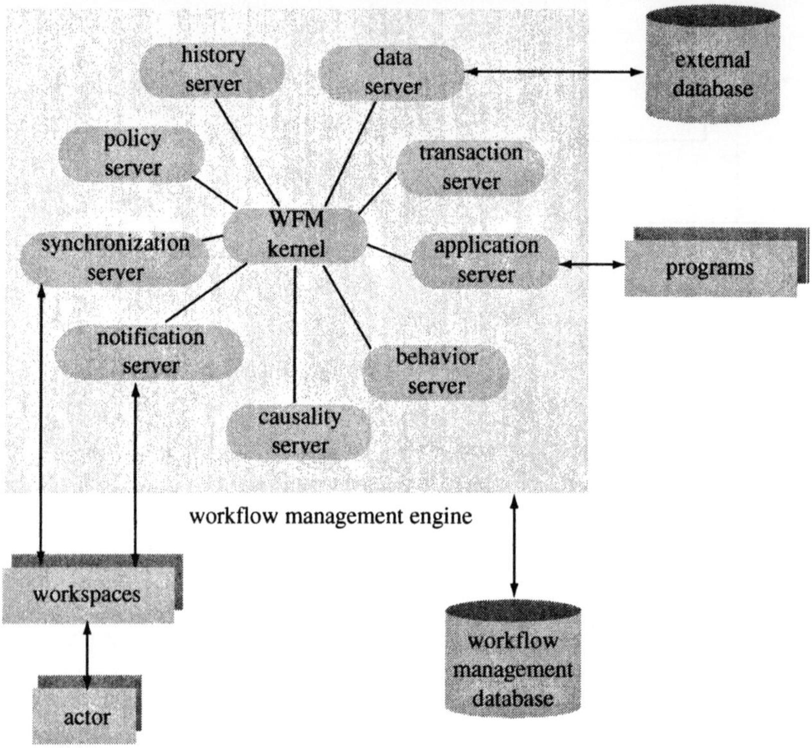

Fig. 7.11. Workflow management system architecture

The WFM kernel was the central module of this architecture; it dispatched tasks to the servers and controlled the workflow execution progress. Only the servers interpreted the aforementioned aspects of the workflow. Each server was responsible only for its individual aspect. The following list shows the servers included in the architecture:

- Application servers invoke external programs and supply them with parameters derived from the current activity. In addition to automated activities (i.e., activities assigned to a system process as the actor), a human

actor may use external programs to support his activity execution. In the latter case, the application server automatically starts the respective program and makes it available for user input.
- The behavior server implements the behavioral aspect of the activities. It discovers dependencies and determines the next activity according to the current execution state of the overall workflow.
- The data server implements the links to external data not managed by the WFM system. All other information, like workflow specification, control and production data administered by the WFM system are stored in the workflow database.
- The history server records the workflow execution.
- The causality server manages the causal information of activities. It examines the continued relevance of the reasons given for executing an activity and determines whether or not the workflow should be terminated due to external events or modifications.
- The policy server implements rules and organizational policies for assigning actors to roles. Work spaces in which the activity execution take place are assigned to individual actors.
- The notification server informs the actors about activity assignments. The system may either add a new entry to the actor's to-do list or send an electronic notification to him.
- The synchronization server coordinates the activities.
- The transaction server is responsible for the reliable and atomic execution of activities included in a single transaction. It monitors the persistent storage of transaction results in the case of a successful execution.

The research project Mobile at the University Erlangen-Nürnberg, Germany, aims at implementing this workflow management architecture (Jablonski 1994).

7.6 Further Developments

More and more companies view workflow management as the key technology for their business reorganization and future competitiveness.

During the WA-12 project Joosten et al. (1994) surveyed twelve companies from different application domains about their experiences with workflow management. Domains covered were industrial production, service industry, public administration and chamber of commerce. The results revealed that at present workflow management is mostly used for controlling the information flow within office environments. Prinz and Kolvenbach (1996) reported on the usage of workflow management in connection with the move of the German government from Bonn to Berlin.

A number of commercial WFM systems have already been successfully introduced into the business market. Example systems are FlowMark by IBM,

Action Workflow by Action Technologies, InConcert by a Xerox Corporation's spin-off and ProminanD by IABG. Marshak (1995b) discussed the most important systems in the workflow market at that time.

7.6.1 Problems and open issues

Although several commercial WFM systems have been successful in the marketplace, a number of issues have not yet been resolved and require further research and development. Business processes are often very complex, which makes a formal description using workflows and activities extremely complicated. Often, the "experts" have only a rather vague idea of how they perform their tasks in the daily routine which makes it difficult for analysts to capture relevant and complete information on the business process. Moreover, unstructured activities are hard to describe (e.g., a telephone conversation). For unstructured activities, the individual steps and the process structure cannot be determined beforehand. The unstructuredness refers to the activity type and the way in which necessary contextual information is embedded. The goal integration in ICN (Ellis and Wainer 1994) provides an approach for facilitating the modeling of unstructured activities.

Business processes involving people usually cannot be described completely a priori by a strict activity schedule. Depending on the current context and dynamically changing goals and work environments, exceptional situations may arise. These must be handled by a WMF system in order to control the continuation of the workflow execution. Thus, alternate paths for achieving the global goal must be provided or automatically generated as needed. A workflow breakdown caused by exceptional situations must be avoided. A WFM system should continue to provide support even if office workers do not adhere to the current workflow specification. Thus, it should be left to the informed office worker to decide whether an activity is really appropriate or not. Informed choices are a must!

Presently, WFM systems formalize the interactions between participants of a business process out of the perspective of the supporting technology (e.g., the exchange of electronic documents or the notification of users of their work assignments). However, informal communication between participants is an important aspect of office communication. Its support, for instance through videoconferencing, can improve exception handling without bureaucratic overhead and it contributes positively to the work environment by motivating the workers. The integration of workflow management and synchronous telecooperation (Schneider et al. 1996) is an approach towards that end. Conferences are integrated into the workflow as independent activities.

Many WFM systems treat the relationship between activity, role and actor in a very isolated way. Often, users only view those activities which they themselves perform and are responsible for, with no information on what goes on outside their own sphere. A global picture is missing!

7.6.2 Workflow Management Coalition (WfMC)

Currently available, commercial WFM systems still suffer from the problem of not being interoperable. Modeled workflow specifications and data cannot be exchanged automatically between different systems, instead requiring manual conversion of data and activity information.

In 1993 the Workflow Management Coalition (WfMC) was founded. It aims at improving the usage of workflow technology by trying to establish a general terminology and interoperability among individual systems. At present, WfMC incorporates more than 200 companies and organizations within its membership.

Besides the common terminology, a workflow reference model representing the basic architecture of a WFM system has been developed. It contains definitions of five interfaces to the workflow engine (see Fig. 7.12). In particular, it is expected that the standardization of interfaces will increase the interoperability between different WFM systems. In general, a WFM system contains one or several workflow enactment services, along with tools for workflow modeling as well as administration and monitoring of workflows.

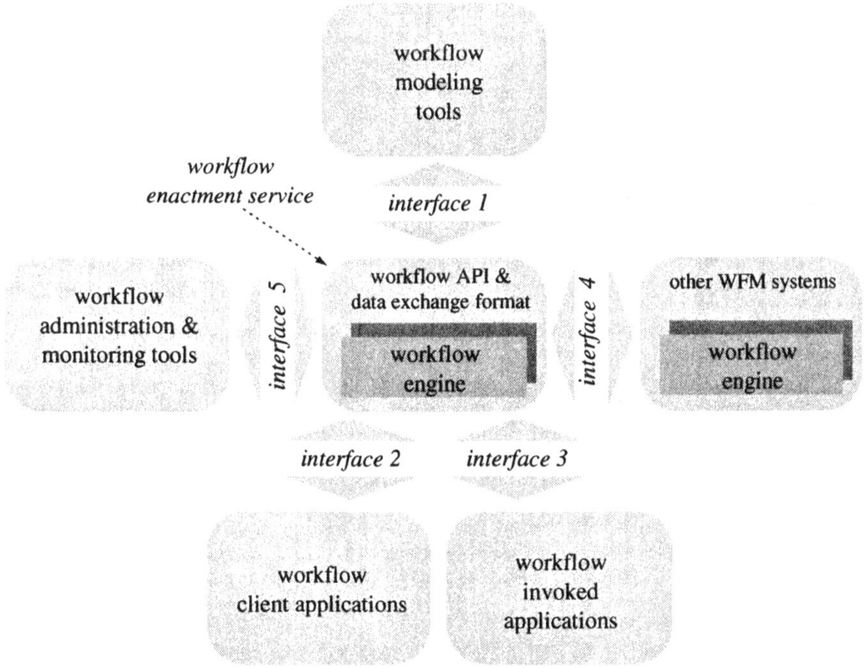

Fig. 7.12. Reference model of the workflow management coalition

Workflow modeling tools supporting the formal or semiformal specification of a workflow are connected with the workflow enactment service via *Interface 1.* Across the interface workflow descriptions are exchanged according to a common description language, the so-called Workflow Process Definition Language (WPDL). In addition to activities, the language allows the specification of preconditions for initiation and termination of the workflow, the usage of resources, data types, state transitions and procedural rules. Interface functions allow the conversion between internal representations of the workflow enactment service and the external representation in WPDL.

Interface 2 specifies arrangements for associating client applications with the WFM system although they still run independently of the WFM system and are usually controlled directly by the user. In particular, notifications to the user, such as those relating to an activity due for execution, are sent via this interface. The so-called Workflow Client Application Programming Interface contains functions for,

- establishing a connection to the workflow enactment service,
- controlling the workflow execution, and
- querying the workflow status.

Via *interface 3* the workflow enactment service may invoke directly external applications in order to perform certain automated activities requiring no interaction between system and end user.

Interface 4 standardizes the interaction between WFM systems by providing appropriate data structures and protocols. Thus, parts of a workflow can be transferred to other WFM systems for execution. The interface covers both synchronous and asynchronous calls.

Interface 5 standardizes the operation invocation and data transfer between workflow enactment service and the tools for administrating and monitoring workflow execution. Available operations are user management, resource control, queries of status information and process control of currently active workflows.

These interfaces are specified by several WfMC committees. Committee work was still under way in 2000.

7.6.3 Adaptive workflow

Execution schedules characterizing a workflow are frequently altered, thus requiring a specification language which allows a flexible adaptation of the workflow definition and even of workflow instantiations to dynamically changing situations. An example for the required flexibility is the common procedure of a business trip application. First, we implement the procedure represented as a Petri net in Fig. 7.3 in the programming language LO (see Sect. 1.6.6, p. 54ff.).

Code fragment (Business trip application).

workflow
<>- applicant @ project leader
@ department head @ financial department.
/* workflow initializes actors */

applicant /* start procedure */
@ start procedure by filling in a business trip application form
<>- applicant @ application(*business trip*) @ application(*business trip*).
/* applicant hands in two copies of business trip application */

project leader /* sign application */
@ application(*business trip*)
@ sign and approve application
<>- project leader @ application(*business trip, recommendation*).
/* project leader forwards signed business trip application including recommendation */

financial department /* estimate business trip cost */
@ application(*business trip*)
@ estimate costs
<>- financial department @ application(*business trip, estimated costs*).
/* financial department forwards business trip application including cost estimation */

department head /* decides on business trip application */
@ application(*business trip, recommendation*)
@ application(*business trip, estimated costs*)
@ decision on business trip application
<>- department head @ decision(*business trip, decision*).
/* department head forwards decision about business trip application */

project leader /* rejects business trip application */
@ decision(*business trip*, "deny")
@ inform applicant about denial
<>- project leader. /* procedure can be terminated at this point */

project leader /* approves business trip application */
@ decision(*business trip*, "approve")
@ inform applicant about approval
<>- project leader. /* further steps (such as booking of a flight, reservation of a hotel room, application for an advance, etc.) may be initiated. */

Frequently, business processes are modified in order to improve efficiency. Exceptional situations also often instigate modifications. For instance, in the above example, a decision must be made even if the department head is on sick leave, which means that the process has to be changed to delegate the decision making power to someone else. If there is an assistant department head who can decide in exceptional situations, then the workflow can be completed regardless of sickness.

In the case of improved efficiency, business processes are changed more substantially. Sequential steps may be divided into parallel streams of execution, some subprocedures may become obsolete. For example, if a project has a predefined financial budget and the project leader can decide within this budget, then the entire procedure is facilitated, as shown in Fig. 7.13.

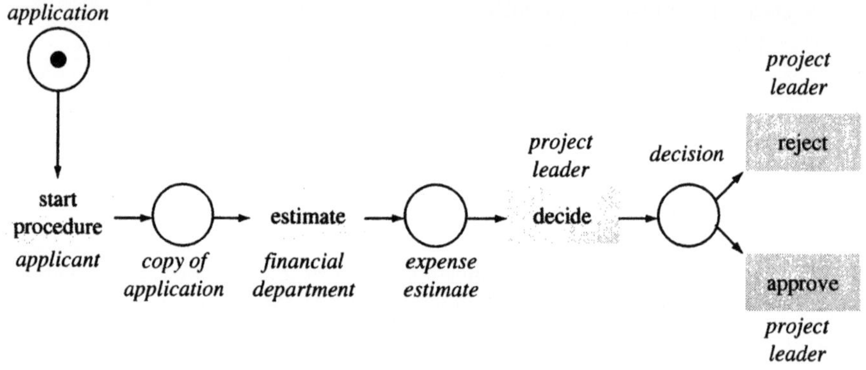

Fig. 7.13. Business trip application after changing the procedure

Again, we present an implementation in LO which integrates the scheduling changes.

Code fragment (Business trip application after scheduling changes).

```
workflow
    <>- applicant @ project leader @ financial department.
applicant                  /* start procedure                      */
    @ start procedure by filling in a business trip application form
    <>- applicant @ application(business trip).
financial department       /* estimate business trip cost          */
    @ application(business trip)
    @ estimate costs
    <>- financial department @ application(business trip, estimated costs).
```

```
project leader            /* decides on business trip application          */
    @ application(business trip, estimated costs)
    @ decision on business trip application
    <>- project leader @ decision(business trip, decision).
project leader            /* rejects business trip application             */
    @ decision(business trip, "deny")
    @ inform applicant about denial
    <>- project leader.
project leader            /* confirm                                       */
    @ decision(business trip, "approve")
    @ inform applicant about approval
    <>- project leader.
```

We conclude that it is desirable to dynamically change the activities and the structure of a workflow, even while it is being executed. Interrupting workflow execution during reimplementation of procedures can often not be tolerated because it is too time-consuming. Thus, we need dynamic adjustable procedures (i.e., dynamic "scheduling rules"). The rules of the workflow are parameterized with the execution schedules. This results in so-called meta-rules controlling the execution schedules and allowing dynamic modification.

Code fragment (Meta rules exemplified by the original execution schedule).

```
metarule (application)
    @ nextsteps(application, schedule_old)
    @ schedule_old = [ ]
    @ schedule(schedule_old,
            [[start_procedure(application)],
            [sign (application), costestimation(application)],
            [decide(application)]],
            schedule_new)
    <>- nextsteps(application, schedule_new).
metarule (application)
    @ nextsteps(application, schedule_old)
    @ schedule_old = [decide(application)]
    @ decision(business trip, "deny")
    @ schedule(schedule_old, [deny(application)], schedule_new)
    <>- nextsteps(application, schedule_new).
metarule(application)
    @ nextsteps(application, schedule_old)
    @ schedule_old = [decide(application)]
    @ decision(business trip, "approve")
    @ schedule(schedule_old, [approve(application)], schedule_new)
    <>- nextsteps(application, schedule_new).
```

nextsteps(*application*, [start_procedure(*application*)|*schedule_new*])
@ applicant
@ start procedure by filling in a business trip application form
<>- nextsteps(*application, schedule_new*)
@ applicant @ application(*business trip*) @ application(*business trip*).

⋮

nextsteps(*application*, [approved(*application*)|*schedule_new*])
@ project leader
@ decision(*business trip*, "approve")
@ inform applicant about approval
<>- nextsteps(*application, schedule_new*)
@ project leader.

The predicate **schedule**(*schedule_old, schedule_curr, schedule_new*) generates a new schedule *schedule_new* by appending the subschedule *schedule_curr* to the old schedule *schedule_old*. The aforementioned code fragment realizes the schedules as lists similar to Prolog. A list [[X,Y],[U,V],[Z]] represents a schedule in which the procedures X and Y run parallel, followed by the parallel processes U, V, and then Z. The expression [*beginning* | *remainder*] specifies a list the first element of which is *beginning*, whereas the remaining elements are represented by *remainder* (equivalent to the *tail* function in Prolog). For example, [approve(*application*)|*schedule_new*] defines a list whose first element is the activity approve(*application*).

The execution schedules are parameters of the meta rules and can easily be modified according to the rule pattern, even during workflow execution. The aforementioned meta rules are a simplified representation of an adaptive workflow. For a more detailed description, the reader is referred to Borghoff et al. (1997a).

7.6.4 Workflow life cycle

Similar to the development of large software systems, workflow design and development requires a methodology which guides the process from analyzing the original business process to the instantiation and usage of the modeled workflow. Traditional WFM systems apply an approach (Fig. 7.14) which is adapted from the waterfall model in software development.

The starting point of building a workflow is an in-depth business process analysis which isolates the characteristics and requirements of the examined business processes. During this phase, the most important activities, the production data, the structure of the involved organizational units and their roles in the business process, are identified at a high abstraction level. The output of this phase are requirements to be met by the workflow. If a business process should be reorganized, then the requirements must be adapted to

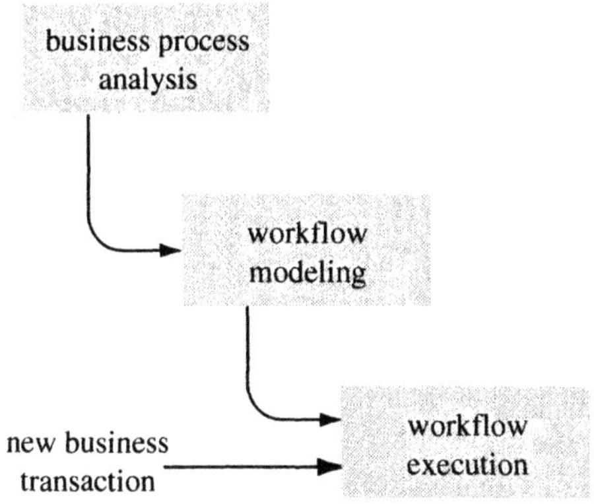

Fig. 7.14. Waterfall model of the workflow live cycle

the desired future procedures of the business process. Hammer and Champy (1995) discuss this phase in detail.

Based on the results of the analysis designers construct a parameterized workflow definition. Important in this phase are tools which enable the designer to simulate workflow execution visualizing workflow and activity behavior. Thus, the workflow designer can test alternative versions and evaluate them according to well-defined criteria, as well as determine the effects of modifications on the execution sequence, the production data, or the execution environment. The latter aspect is important for the interface between the WFM system and the accessible external applications. Changes to the execution environment might require modifications of the protocol and the data exchange formats. Simulation tools supply the workflow designer with an experimental environment for construction of a workflow model representing the business process under the given constraints. Examples for constraints are the functionality of the WFM system, the desired flexibility of the exception handling and the embedding of the workflow into the organizational infrastructure.

The result of the modeling phase is a parameterized workflow specification representing a specific business process. The designed workflow may contain different variants with respect to the execution sequence of activities (defining alternate paths through the workflow structure) which are selected depending on the actual parameter values. The integration of variants allows the designer to model and handle a priori known exceptions.

Each occurrence of a new business transaction entails the instantiation of the appropriate workflow specification with the actual parameter values. For example, for every new loan application a new workflow instance is generated. The workflow enactment service schedules the appropriate activities for the responsible actors or in cases of activities assigned to software tools it might even trigger them automatically. Several instances of the same workflow can be executed simultaneously by the WFM system.

Spiral model. In general, during the lifetime of an instance which was derived from a well-established workflow only minor modifications are performed, such as assigning a different actor to an activity. Also variations are a result of predefined rules and conditions that send the work flowing along alternate predefined paths. These modifications and variations remain local to a single workflow instance; they are restricted to parameters of activities, and to alternate predefined paths. The actual workflow model remains unchanged. If workflow failures cannot be handled locally, the workflow instance is often abandoned and the workflow is continued using traditional means, i.e., without workflow management system support. Workflow failures may provide valuable feedback to workflow designers for adjusting or even rebuilding the original workflow definition. However, the traditional waterfall model defines a sequential ordering of phases of the workflow life cycle without a well-established feedback to previous phases.

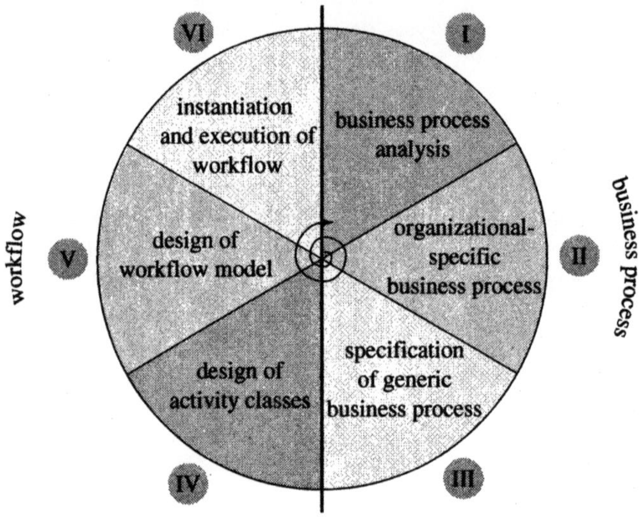

Fig. 7.15. Spiral model of the workflow life cycle

The spiral model (see Fig. 7.15) perceives workflow building as a continuous process in which business processes are evaluated and formally specified, workflow definitions are built, instantiated, executed and again evaluated. After a workflow execution, the cycle can be repeated. This avoids the setting into concrete of a business process after its analysis and the inhibition of any further improvement and evolution. Apart from distinguishing between business process (see I, II and III in Fig. 7.15) and workflow (see IV, V and VI) as already known from the waterfall model, the spiral model also makes a distinction between instances (see I and VI), organizational specific models (see II and V) and generic models (see III and IV). The three areas on the right of the spiral model are concerned with business processes from the organizational viewpoint. This is typically the viewpoint applied during business process reengineering. The three areas on the left are concerned with the mapping of business processes into workflows and their technical implementation.

The spiral model includes a distinction between generic models, specific models and instances. Generic models define generic business processes or parts of it which are independent of a specific organization. Examples are the generic approach of handling invoices or the production of publications. Malone et al. (1997) are currently developing a process handbook which specifies generic business processes. The phase "design of activity classes" is performed by a class designer who is effectively a sophisticated programmer knowing the internals of the activity class representations.

Dynamic refinement. The WFM system Regatta (Swenson et al. 1994) pursues a flexible approach for workflow construction alternating between building and execution phases. The execution order within a workflow can be modified by the user even after instantiation for an individual business transaction. Modifications are immediately effective and exceptional situations can be handled dynamically upon their occurrence. This approach avoids having to predefine all possible variants before workflow instantiation. Similar to Tacts, Regatta also supports the instantiation of incomplete workflows. As workflow execution proceeds undefined parts of the workflow are specified and additionally required activities are added. The amount of detail contained in the workflow depends on the time constraints. For example, activities which should be performed in the near future are specified in great detail while activities which should be performed much later are specified only in terms of milestones or subgoals. That means the workflow is not fully specified at the start of the execution and thus can react dynamically to goal and contextual changes.

We can distinguish between two basic types of refinement: vertical and horizontal refinement (see Fig. 7.16). Vertical refinement defines the hierarchical structure of a workflow with recursive decomposition of composite activities into subactivities. Complete vertical refinement creates an activity hierarchy where all leaves are basic activities. On the other hand, a horizontal refinement defines the causal and temporal activity dependencies on the same level of abstraction. In the case of incomplete workflows, a horizontal and vertical refinement must take place as the workflow execution progresses. In particular, activities executed in the near future must be described in detail. Paths to activities not yet fully described are represented by dotted arrows in Fig. 7.16.

Both refinement types provide the workflow designer and the end user with a means of controlling the degree of detail in the workflow specification before and during execution. The options range from a fully expanded workflow to a single, top-level workflow which is neither vertically nor hori-

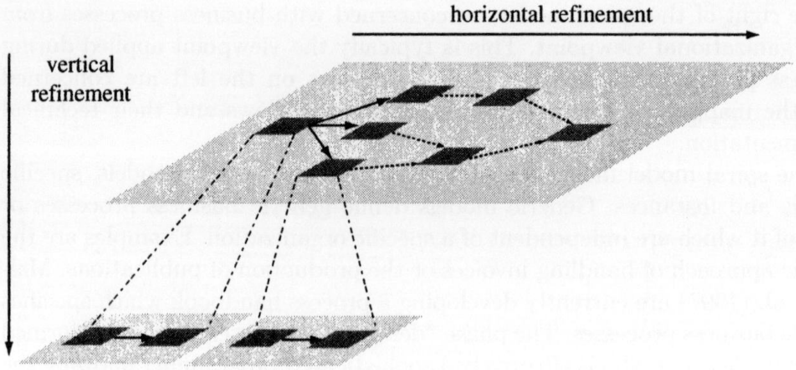

Fig. 7.16. Vertical and horizontal refinement

zontally expanded. In the latter case the workflow represents a single black box. Restricting vertical refinement leads to composite activities which are not recursively refined into their basic activities. Controlling the horizontal refinement provides the user with a mechanism for varying the amount of refinement over time. In other words, later activities of the overall workflow structure may become less refined than activities which occur in earlier stages of the workflow execution. As the workflow execution progresses these activities are refined as necessary and desired.

As the spiral model suggests, workflow instances already executed can be analyzed and evaluated, which allows a continuous adaptation of the workflow model for future executions. In particular, past experience can be utilized by the WFM system if a workflow is incomplete, thereby presenting the user with a choice of different variants for workflow continuation.

7.7 Further Reading

This chapter provided only a brief introduction to the field of workflow management. For more detailed information on this subject the reader is referred to the books of Vossen and Becker (1996), Jablonski et al. (1997) and Coleman and Khanna (1995).

Jackson and Twaddle (1997) and Chaffey (1998) discuss the implementation and reeenineering of business processes. The books by Khoshafian and Buckiewicz (1995) and Poyssick and Hannaford (1996) include in-depth case studies and practical examples on the subject.

The conversation theory is treated in detail by Winograd and Flores (1986). The book by Conen and Neumann (1998) provides more insights into coordination technology.

8. Workgroup Computing

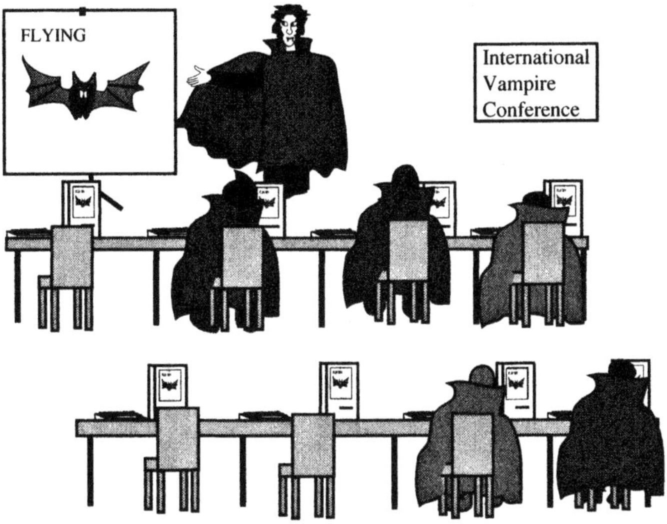

The following chapter deals with systems for workgroup computing focusing on the cooperation between people working in a team. Situations where several users synchronously perform a task obtain special attention, thus exploring the use of real-time applications. As an example for synchronous cooperation, we discuss architectural models for electronic meeting rooms.

Furthermore, we will investigate distributed document systems and we will provide an overview of existing group editors. Using the examples of Iris and DistEdit, we will introduce typical problem areas of group editors. The advantages of highly structured documents and logical document views for the handling of joint authoring scenarios and the management of shared documents will be demonstrated. Concepts for version and history management will be discussed. Finally, undo-operations in the context of group editors will be considered in detail.

8.1 Electronic Meeting Support

The previous chapters focused on situations in which group members were geographically distributed. The following sections will pay special attention to electronically supported face-to-face meetings. During these meetings, all participants are in the same room at the same time.

Depending on their position and role in the organization and the team, office workers spend a significant part of their time in meetings. Studies conducted by several institutions (such as the University of Arizona) developed a cost-benefit analysis of meetings held during group work (Nunamaker et al. 1991).

The following list gives a brief outline of the benefits of group meetings:

- *More information:* In general, a group as a whole generates more ideas than an individual person.
- *Synergy:* A group member uses an idea in a way that differs from that intended by the originator of the idea. Reasons may be differing background, knowledge or skills of the group members.
- *Better information exploitation:* An entire team is better at detecting inherent problems of a proposal than the individual person who introduced the idea.
- *Stimulation:* Working as part of a team can stimulate and encourage individuals to introduce new ideas. They may build upon already proposed ideas and develop them further.
- *Learning process:* Individual group members can learn from other participants and thereby improve their own knowledge.

However, as the following list shows, meetings are also costly, causing some problems:

- *Airtime fragmentation:* The group must partition the meeting time among all potential speakers.
- *Attenuation blocking:* Individual participants may be hesitant to contribute ideas, fearing that they lack originality, importance or relevance in the current context.
- *Concentration problem:* A participant draws all his attention to already proposed ideas, rather than generating new ideas (e.g., members concentrate on remembering comments).
- *Attention problem:* Closely connected with the concentration problem is the attention problem, which means that due to constant attention there is no time left for the participant to come up with new ideas of his own.
- *Lack of memory:* Participants often fail to remember because they lack focus on communication or on the current context. Ideas may be misinterpreted or completely missed.
- *Conformance pressure:* Politeness or fear of reprisals can keep a participant from criticizing others.

- *Evaluation apprehension:* Individuals withhold their ideas because they fear negative comments from others.
- *Passivity:* Instead of contributing, some participants rely on others to accomplish the common task; they perceive their input as being unnecessary.
- *Cognitive inertia:* In general, a discussion follows a certain train of thought. Participants refrain from introducing divergent opinions because they consider them to be irrelevant or not important in the current context. There is a close relationship between cognitive inertia and attenuation blocking.
- *Domination problem:* Some participants dominate throughout the meeting monopolizing the available group's time.
- *Information overload:* Information is generated and presented faster than the individual participant can process it.
- *Incompleteness:* Decision making is based on partial information due to incomplete access and use of generated ideas.

Apparently, the use of electronic support tools is necessary in order to improve efficiency and effectiveness of meetings. These tools (so-called electronic meeting system, EMS), aim at maintaining the benefits of meetings while at the same time reducing the meeting costs.[1]

An electronic meeting room usually consists of a conference table with integrated personal computers, and an electronic whiteboard visible to all participants. This electronic whiteboard can be interpreted as a large computer display for the group. Its role is similar to a conventional blackboard easily visible to all participants and serving as a shared working environment. However, electronic whiteboards are connected to the personal computers of the participants through a network. Thus, the information displayed on the whiteboard can be controlled electronically and information of one or several computers can be represented in large format on the whiteboard.

Examples of electronic meeting rooms are the collaborative management room at the University of Arizona (Nunamaker et al. 1991), the CATeam room at Hohenheim University (Lewe and Krcmar 1993) and the Ocean Lab at GMD (Mark et al. 1995). While the former two installations use GroupSystems as the software system to control group activities during meetings, the Ocean Lab has chosen the hypermedia system Dolphin. The latter system enables the structuring of the meeting information and documents according to the hypermedia paradigm (see Fig. 8.1).

A variety of studies and evaluations of actual face-to-face meetings held in electronic environments were already done. Petrovic (1992) used questionnaires to determine the requirements for electronic conference environments. Studies in the Ocean Lab and their results have already been discussed in Sect. 2.9.5.

[1] Already by 1991, IBM had installed more than 30 electronic meeting rooms worldwide, with more than 2,000 conferences being held with computer support.

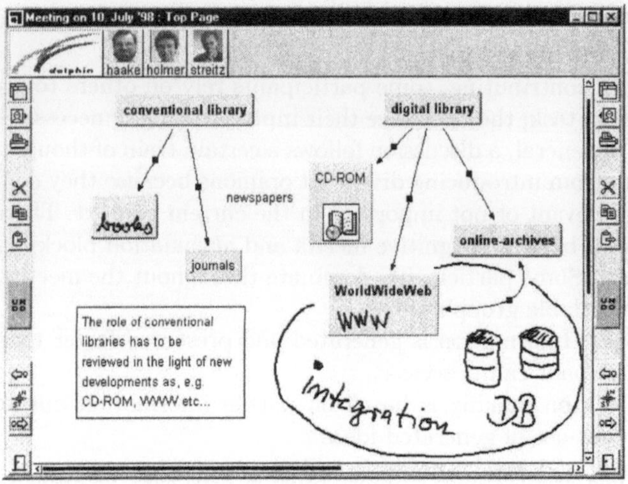

Fig. 8.1. Structuring of meeting information according to Dolphin

Example (LiveBoard). The Xerox LiveBoard (LiveWorks, Inc.) is a computer-supported electronic whiteboard with an integrated personal computer. Information displayed on the whiteboard, such as text and graphics, may be manipulated via keyboard, mouse or by using electronic markers. Both free-hand drawing and interactive "overpainting" of displayed information are possible. The system can thus be used as a local electronic whiteboard during face-to-face meetings. Information can be retrieved from local databases, interactively modified, and eventually stored.

The main advantage of the system, however, is the coupling of several LiveBoards via fast wide area networks (such as ISDN, ATM). They allow synchronous cooperation between geographically dispersed meeting participants according to the strict WYSIWIS principle. For example, sketches created on local LiveBoards are combined and integrated into a single shared meeting document which is displayed on each LiveBoard (all LiveBoards display the same information). Finally, the shared meeting document which may very well encompass several "whiteboard pages", can be saved at all locations for later local usage. An additional video window increases group awareness during the teleconference. Installations of this system via ATM have been successfully tested between French Universities in Paris, Grenoble, and Sophia Antipolis.[2]

8.1.1 Architectures for electronic meeting systems

Depending on the degree of computer support we distinguish between three basic architectural models for electronic meeting systems.

[2] Although the system was technically highly interesting, it was not commercially successful.

1. *Facilitator model:* In this model, the facilitator is the only user of a personal computer (see Fig. 8.2). All information created by him is displayed on a large electronic screen. Other meeting participants have no direct access to the electronic meeting support tools.

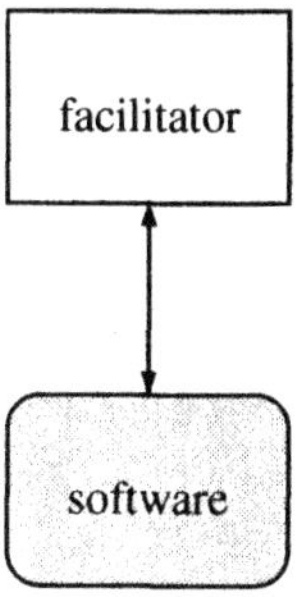

Fig. 8.2. Facilitator model

2. *Computer-supported model:* This model, too, specifies a designated user as the meeting facilitator. In addition, however, each meeting participant has his own personal computer. The facilitator coordinates the agenda, starts and terminates the meeting support software, and controls the meeting progress using floor control mechanisms. He supports meeting participants on all technical aspects of the electronic meeting system.
Users can work in parallel on their personal computers and by using application sharing or screen sharing mechanisms the local information is propagated to the personal computers of the other meeting participants. Besides his role as mediator of the meeting the facilitator may also be in charge of writing the minutes (see Fig. 8.3).

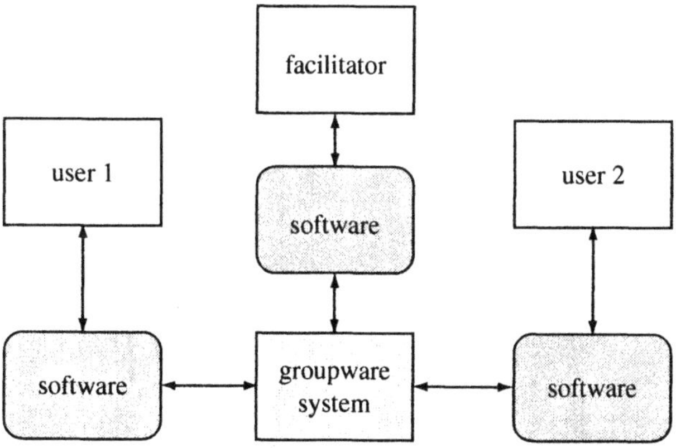

Fig. 8.3. Computer-supported model

3. *Interactive model:* This model is characterized by the lack of a designated person taking the role of the facilitator. All users can work synchronously

and modify group documents anonymously (e.g., by adding new ideas and proposals). Floor control and the coordination of the meeting progress are distributed among the meeting participants.

8.1.2 General characteristics of electronic meeting systems

An electronic meeting environment improves groupwork and team interaction by adding various advantages: Firstly, group members can work simultaneously with equal opportunity of participation for all. Antisocial behavior which decreases meeting productivity (by not giving others a chance to speak) is eliminated. Secondly, EMS supports the creation of a group database which records the meeting progress; the history of several meetings may be saved to provide an overview of the groupwork evolution. Additionally, EMS allows for larger meetings that can integrate a broader variety of ideas, opinions, knowledge and skills. Last but not least, EMS facilitates the access of external information and the utilization of it during the meeting.

The tools of electronic meeting environments influence the cost-benefit ratio of meetings. In particular with respect to the communication infrastructure, the meeting progress may be enhanced by parallel interpersonal communication using multimedia, by large network bandwidth and by representing the information in a way relevant to the user both on the screens of the personal computers and the public electronic whiteboards. The support of anonymous contributions is another important issue in order to decrease the evaluation apprehension. Research by Mantei (1989), however, has also shown that anonymity can lead to increased conflicts, since participants sometimes act more openly, directly, and occasionally even insulting.

In general, electronic meeting systems are characterized by a strong process orientation. Meetings are structured according to techniques and rules determining the interaction content and time schedule of the meeting progress, e.g., the meeting agenda.

Tatar et al. (1991) distinguish between three phases of a meeting for preparing a paper: During the first phase participants brainstorm collecting ideas; the second phase is used for organizing these ideas before they are evaluated in the third phase. Thus, the use of an electronic meeting system enables free information flow during the brainstorming phase. No evaluation whatsoever with respect to meaning, usefulness or validity of ideas is made. Ideas are added simultaneously by the meeting participants at any time; already posted ideas are not deleted, since this might be interpreted as implicit criticism. The organizing phase allows for grouping and linking of ideas. Removal of useless ideas is delayed until the last phase, during which the ideas are evaluated followed by a decision representing the final result of the meeting.

In Cognoter the main emphasis lies with the generation of as many ideas as possible, whereas Argnoter (Stefik et al. 1987b) aims more at evaluating and choosing proposals. The latter system also supports three phases with different functionality:

- *Proposal:* Proposals are made in the form of brief textual descriptions.
- *Arguments:* Reasons why a proposal has been accepted or rejected.
- *Evaluation:* Establishing criteria which are applied to evaluate the proposals.

These examples show that the structure of the meeting process depends on the respective group task. EMS provide special tools for supporting the individual phases performed during task solving. In order to use results of prior phases in subsequent phases, it is, however, necessary to seamlessly integrate these tools into a single environment.

Structuring the task allows the participants to better understand the meeting goals and provides a context for analyzing already available or newly developed information. The group performance is improved because losses due to incomplete information analysis are reduced. Along with methods to structure tasks, EMS provides the infrastructure necessary for task-oriented activities including tools to access external information sources. Furthermore, the electronic meeting environment enables the specification of rules and methods facilitating the analysis of task-related information.

Dennis (1994) carried out a number of studies observing larger groups (between ten and thirty participants) during their work in electronic meeting environments and later questioning them about their impressions. His investigations focused on the influence of the architectural model on the meeting process and the quality of the final meeting result. According to Dennis, 90% of all groups found the interactive model more effective and efficient than the facilitator model. Furthermore, he analyzed how simultaneous communication, anonymity and the usage of a group database changed the behavior of individual participants and that of the group as a whole. The advantages of electronic communication outweigh its disadvantages, although it was admitted that face-to-face communication between people supports a larger variety of media, such as gestures, mimicry and intonation, than electronic communication.

Figure 8.4 depicts a cost-benefit analysis of an EMS according to Nunamaker et al. (1991) who distinguish between process support and support to structure the meeting task. Meeting benefits are increased while most of the meetings costs are reduced, thus the group performance and meeting results improve.

8.1.3 Design alternatives for meeting rooms

The importance of the furniture and the layout of meeting rooms are often underestimated. Inadequate positioning of personal computers might impede eye-contact between participants and the view of the electronic whiteboard;

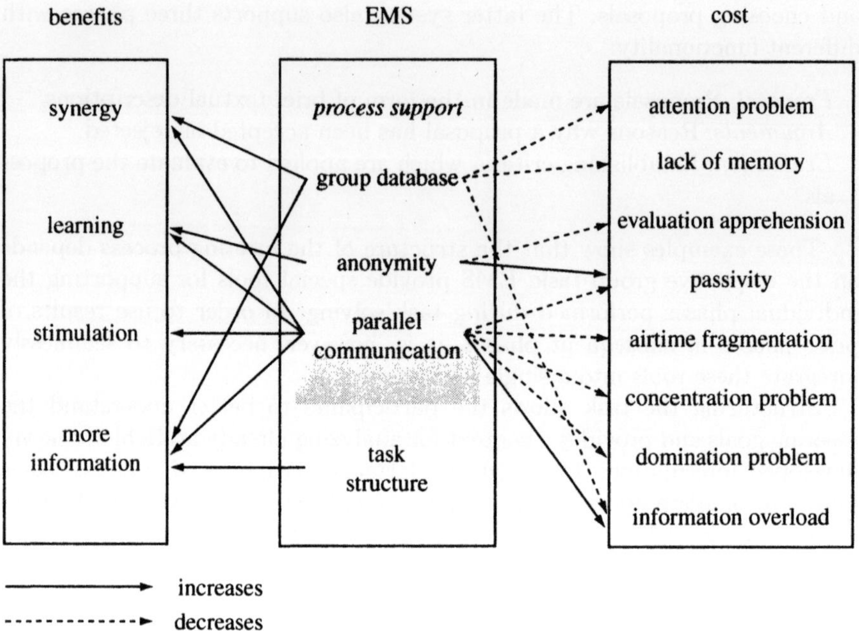

Fig. 8.4. Potential effects of an electronic meeting system

the integration of the personal computers into the conference table eliminates this problem.

The classic design alternatives of meeting rooms are the following:

- *Cathedral:* The so-called cathedral design as illustrated in Fig. 8.5 provides good view of all participants to the electronic whiteboard and eye-contact between all participants. Seating position at the conference table implies a hierarchy of meeting participants. Observations by Mantei (1989) in Capture Lab revealed that participants prefer sitting at the head of the table, since this place is considered the more powerful position; both the electronic whiteboard and the other participants are visible at the same time from that position.

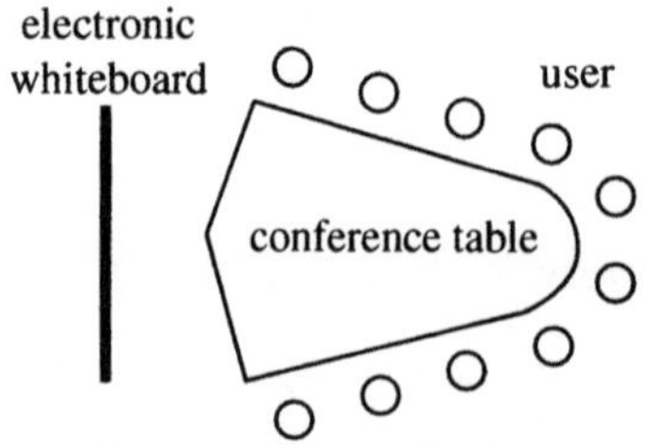

Fig. 8.5. Cathedral

– *Bistro:* As opposed to the cathedral design, the bistro arrangement consists of movable, small tables creating an informal work atmosphere (see Fig. 8.6). This meeting room design requires special attention to the network connectivity of the personal computers.

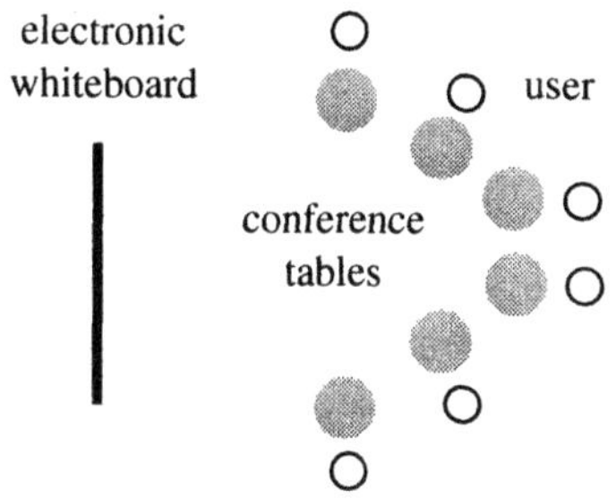

Fig. 8.6. Bistro

– *Classic Double:* The classic double (see Fig. 8.7) specifies a room layout suitable for negotiations between two opposing parties. It supports emergence of coalitions and good eye-contact between participants. The problem of unwanted hierarchies, as mentioned with the cathedral design, does not arise here. Two electronic whiteboards displaying identical information provide all participants with a good view of the public meeting documents.

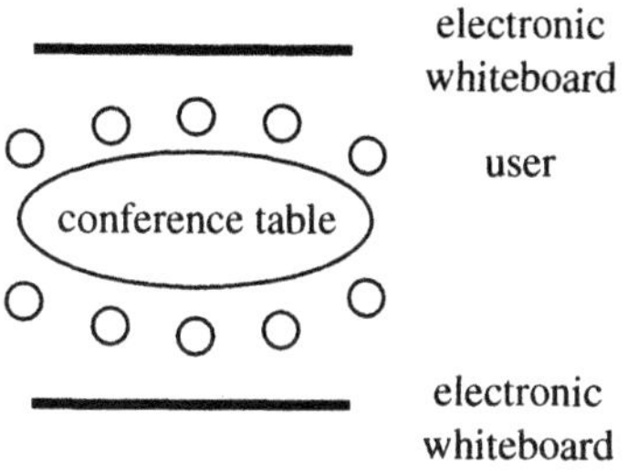

Fig. 8.7. Classic double

Ferwagner et al. (1991) discuss a number of other possible design alternatives for meeting rooms; for more detailed descriptions, the reader is referred to Lewe and Krcmar (1991, 1993).

Another concept developed by Streitz et al. (1998a) as part of the i-LAND project[3] at GMD in Darmstadt is far more visionary. It aims at realizing interactive landscapes to support the communication and cooperation between group members. The basic idea is the use of physical objects, like walls, chairs and tables which are extended by special functions to support

[3] http://www.darmstadt.gmd.de/ambiente

computer-supported interaction creating the impression of ubiquitous computing. Streitz et al. talk in this context of roomware. Components developed so far are:

- an interactive, electronic wall (called Dynawall),
- mobile and networked chairs with integrated interactive communication devices (called CommChairs), and
- an interactive table (called InteracTable).

Figure 8.8 gives an impression of the innovative work environment in the Ambiente laboratory, which has been developed as part of the i-LAND project.

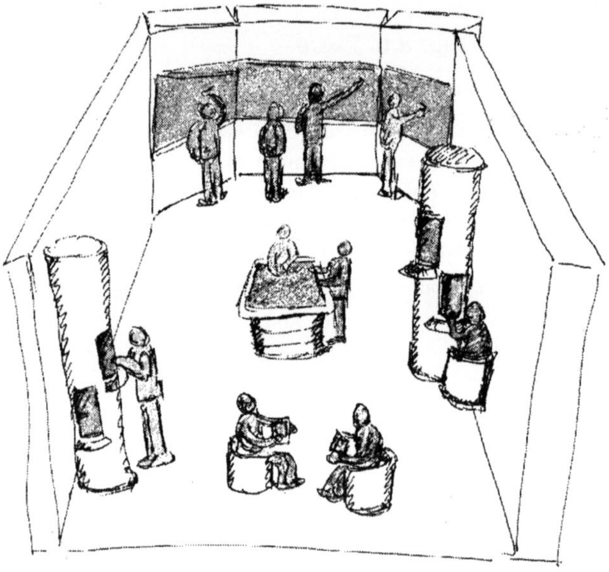

Fig. 8.8. Sketch of the work environment in the Ambiente laboratory

8.2 Distributed Document Systems

This section focuses on distributed document systems, in particular on group editors as they are used for joint document editing by a geographically dispersed group of authors. A document is a set of information units designed for human consumption. With the evolution of electronic office technology a new type of document has developed, the electronic document. Electronic documents are not restricted to text; they may also include other media types, such as graphics, images, scripts, and more recently even continuous media (audio and video). Electronic documents are generated electronically using word processors, graphics programs or other multimedia creation programs, distributed electronically across local and wide area networks, and filed electronically in file systems or databases. While this technology enables people to process documents more efficiently, it also creates new problems and challenges.

8.2.1 Cooperative document creation

From the outset, document processing has been one of the most important applications of personal computers. The goal of document processing is to create, manage and disseminate documents. Koch (1997) defines document processing as "an open-ended design task consisting of all activities necessary for creation of a document (electronic or paper-based version). The task is weakly structured and usually highly unstable, i.e., it must be adapted to the changing context, e.g., the work habits of new group members". The activities are executed either under the control of people or of software tools (e.g., a document formatter system). Document creation is an ongoing process which has no predefined end. The involved users decide themselves when document creation has been completed and an acceptable status has been reached. The lack of structure within document processing renders conventional workflow management systems worthless for this application.

Process model according to Flower and Hayes. Flower and Hayes (1981) interpret document creation as a problem solving process consisting of three basic components (see Fig. 8.9):

- Document creation can be divided into three phases: planning, creating and reviewing. During the planning phase, all information relevant to the document is collected and produced. A concept with regard to content, structure and representation of the document is developed. During the creation phase, this concept is applied to generate the actual document content, which is then reviewed and, if necessary, subsequently modified. In practice, these phases are not executed strictly sequentially. They may be performed in an arbitrary order depending on the behavior and wishes of the involved people. Transitions between the phases are possible at any time. Flower and Hayes integrated a coordination component into their model for controlling the transitions between phases. This component is not a software system, but it represents the actual decision by the author of when to, for example, stop brainstorming and start editing the document content. The initial phase of the document creation task, as well as the transitions between phases, is not predictable. It is subject to the author's decision alone.
- The long-term memory defines the author's personal knowledge which is to be used for document creation. It encompasses memorized knowledge and

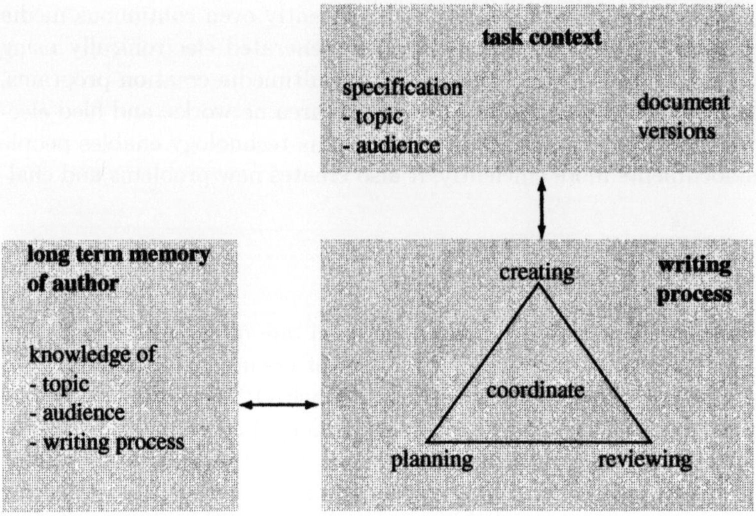

Fig. 8.9. Process model by Flower and Hayes

information stored on external media, such as books. Background knowledge on the topic, the group targeted for the reading of the document, and the intended document creation process are also parts of the long-term memory.

- The task context specifies all aspects of the document creation process not directly related to the author. It describes the author's work environment and specifies the topic and the intended audience, along with the document content already produced.

The process model by Flower and Hayes represents document creation as an interaction between the knowledge of the author and his intentions on the one side and the hitherto created document content on the other side. This model is based on the perspective of an individual person. Koch (1997) has extended this approach in order to model joint editing situations by multiple authors.

Cooperative document creation. Koch (1997) defines cooperative document creation as "joint editing of a document by multiple participants who all have the (sub)goal of creating the document. Since there are interdependencies between individual subdocuments, the activities of the authors influence each other. Thus, it is a prerequisite that communication and coordination between the authors takes place in order to reach the common goal". As opposed to the model by Flower and Hayes which only considers one author, the writing process was extended to incorporate mechanisms for the coordination between the co-authors. Thus, the isolated work of one author, including his tasks, can be linked to the isolated processes of his co-authors; the global writing process is, therefore, the union of all local writing processes (see Fig. 8.10). All people involved in cooperative document creation are considered authors, including reviewers and the editor. Besides coordination mechanisms, the local writing process again contains functionality to handle the phases of planning, creating, and reviewing. Again, the sequence of the phases is determined by the respective authors.

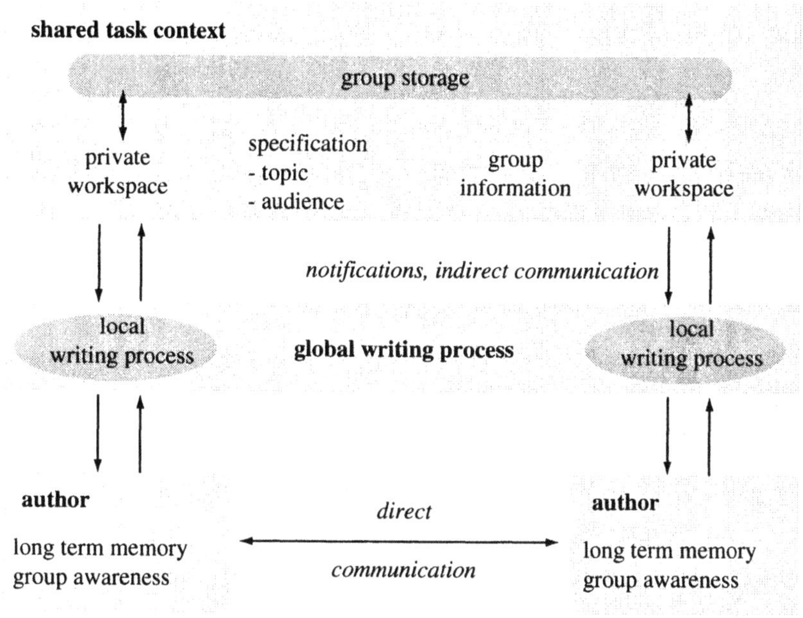

Fig. 8.10. Process model for cooperative document creation

Mutual coordination requires direct and indirect communication between the co-authors improving group awareness. Examples of direct communication are email and desktop conferencing, whereas indirect communication refers to notifications about changes of the document status and history information. Issues for coordination are the following:

- Which of the co-authors are currently active and which document part are they manipulating?
- What is the intent of their activities?
- What are the co-authors currently displaying on their screens?
- What are the possible effects of one author's activities on the activities of others?

According to the model for cooperative document creation (see Fig. 8.10) the task context is shared by all co-authors. Besides the private workspaces and the task description, the task context also includes information on the group membership and a group storage for the exchange of documents or parts of them. Logically the group storage is a centralized component which, however, may be implemented by a distributed and replicated architecture. Shared information spaces are appropriate groupware approaches to realize group storages.

Group editors. Joint document authoring by a group of co-authors is an important CSCW application which is why a variety of different group editors have been developed. Besides integrating functionality for document creation and distributed data storage, they also include functions for improving group awareness based on direct and indirect communication between co-authors. In general, group editors support a high degree of concurrency which requires special locking mechanisms and writing operations. An important issue is the locking granularity. Often, locking of entire data blocks is not an appropriate solution because it obstructs parallel work. Furthermore, it requires special notification mechanisms and policies to keep co-authors up-to-date on each other's activities (e.g., by sending notification messages after document changes or by simply updating the screen display according to the WYSIWIS principle).

All traditional single user editors and group editors pursue a layered approach distinguishing between a user interface layer and an access layer (Teege and Koch 1994); see also Fig. 8.11.

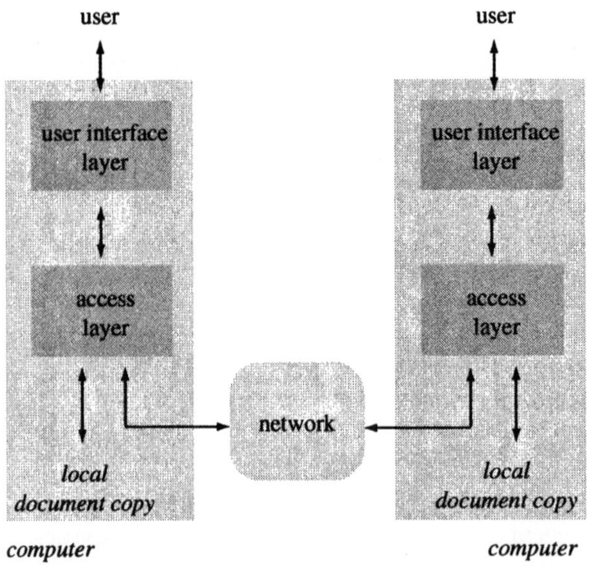

Fig. 8.11. Layers of a distributed group editor

The user interface layer accepts user input and updates the screen representation of the document. The access layer handles access requests to locally or remotely stored data (i.e., document data as well as the shared task context). Access requests are generated either by the local user interface layer or the access layers of remote group editors.

8.2.2 Group editors – overview

ForComment (Opper 1988), Quilt (Fish et al. 1988) and partially also the Collaborative Editing System (CES) (Koszarek et al. 1990) belong to the category of asynchronous group editors. The systems distinguish between authors and reviewers. While the author creates the document, reviewers comment on it asynchronously. A variety of group editors support both, synchronous and asynchronous cooperative situations. The following discussion will focus on concurrent accesses of arbitrary document parts.

Among the systems in which group editing functionality plays a major part are CoAuthor (Hahn et al. 1991), Collaborative Annotator (Koszarek et al. 1990), Group Outline Viewing Editor (Grove) (Ellis et al. 1991), Iris (Koch 1997), Mercury (Kaiser et al. 1987), Mace (Newman-Wolfe and Pelimuhandiram 1991), MMConf (Crowley et al. 1990), MMM (Bier and Freeman 1991), Mule (Pendergast and Vogel 1990), MultimETH (Lubich and Plattner 1990), Prep (Neuwirth et al. 1990) and Shared Books (Lewis and Hodges 1988).

Table 8.1 summarizes important group editors based on data management aspects, such as data storage, replication and concurrency control.

8.2.3 The group editor Iris

The group editor Iris was developed at the computer science department of Munich Technical University, Munich, Germany. The first prototype explored the usage of dynamic voting schemes for concurrency control. However, the communication overhead for synchronization of concurrent accesses limited the performance of the system in wide area and mobile networks; thus, the system was reimplemented based on Java and with optimistic concurrency control. The new architecture is especially important for mobile networks where no permanent network connections exist between active group editor instances.

Features of Iris. The group editor Iris is based on distributed control and with replicated data storage. It has the following characteristics:

- Iris manipulates structured documents. Besides the document content, the system captures the document structure description. As in CES and MultimETH the structure may be modified independently from its respective content.
- Full replication of the document during a joint document editing session, i.e., each active user gets dynamically a full replica of the document. Thus, the degree of replication varies dynamically and equals the number of active users.

Table 8.1. Data management in important group editors

system	data storage	replication	concurrency control
Augment	local	no	explicit floor passing (during teleconferencing)
Balsa	distributed	complete	implicit floor passing
CES	distributed	partial (only the structural description is replicated)	transactions (tickle locks)
DistEdit	distributed	complete	write-all-read-any, floor passing
EDS	local	no	optimistic
Fress	local	no	optimistic
gIBIS	centralized	no	transactions
Grove	distributed	complete	transformations based on priorities and semantics of operations
Intermedia	centralized	no	transactions
Iris	distributed	complete	optimistic
KMS	distributed	partial (only location information is replicated)	optimistic
Mace	centralized	no (only local text block caching)	centralized editor server
MMM	centralized	no	simple locking
Mule	distributed	complete	centralized lock server
MultimETH	centralized	no	simple locking
Neptune	centralized	no	transactions
NoteCards	local	no	simple locking
Prep	centralized	no	transactions
Quilt	centralized	no	transactions
rIBIS	distributed	complete	implicit floor passing during strictly coupled mode, simple locking during loosely coupled mode (centralized facilitator coordinates message exchange)
Shared Books	centralized	no (only local text block caching)	simple locking
ZOG	distributed	no	simple locking

- Users can join and leave a joint document editing session arbitrarily; all session participants are notified of session membership changes.
- Concurrent read and write access to all document parts in order to enhance parallel work of all co-authors.
- Optimistic concurrency control generating alternate versions when access conflicts arise. In addition to conflict detection, Iris also provides functions for conflict solving during the merge of alternate versions.
- Special service for distributing group awareness information between co-authors. Information refers both to current and past document modifica-

tions, the availability of co-authors and the state of their computers which they are currently using or which they have used in the past. Based on this service co-authors may use a social protocol to detect and handle conflicting operations.
- Integration of synchronous and asynchronous communication.
- Support of a group editing framework which integrates external tools for document content processing (tools for manipulating text, graphics, or images).
- Flexible configuration of the user interface layer based on author requirements and cooperation mode.

8.2.4 DistEdit

DistEdit which was developed by Knister and Prakash (1990) is a framework for creating synchronous group editors based on existing (single-user) editors. It was developed at the University of Michigan, Ann Arbor, USA. Using DistEdit the editors GNU Emacs and MicroEmacs have been extended to incorporate multiuser capabilities. The resulting group editors support synchronous work with one writer at a time, multiple readers and data replication at all involved sites. The user, however, has the impression that the document has been created and manipulated by a single editor instance. A generated group editor tolerates late arrivals to or early departures from an editing session, as well as computer crashes without interrupting an ongoing editing session.

Master and observer. With respect to concurrency control DistEdit distinguishes between master and observer:

- Modifications of the shared document can only be initiated by the master.
- Only nonmodifying operations, such as cursor movements, can be carried out by an observer.
- The master is determined by a floor passing scheme: A user passes on the master status by a special control command, thereby becoming an observer. The next observer initiating a floor request becomes the new master.
- The write-all-read-any scheme is used (see Sect. 5.2.3) to update the replicated data.
- DistEdit applies a loose form of WYSIWIS. Although the data available at all sites are identical, users may select different sections to be displayed on their screens.
- The additional functionality for the multiuser capability requires only minimal changes to existing single-user editors.[4]

[4] For the adaptation of GNU Emacs only 6 lines of source code were changed and 9 lines were added. MicroEmacs required 10 additional lines of code and 12 lines were modified. Furthermore, additional source code for transformation of editor commands was required (approximately 60 to 300 lines of code).

Basic functionality of DistEdit. There are three functions for manipulating text: **delete_string**, **insert_string** and **replace_string**. These three functions suffice for expressing all modification operations required by an editing system. However, only the user who has the master status may invoke these functions.

The function which propagates the master's current cursor position may be applied to automatically synchronize the cursor position of the observers with that of the master. However, observers can decouple themselves from the master and browse through the document at their own convenience.

Functions for floor release and floor request have been introduced for relinquishing or requesting the master status.

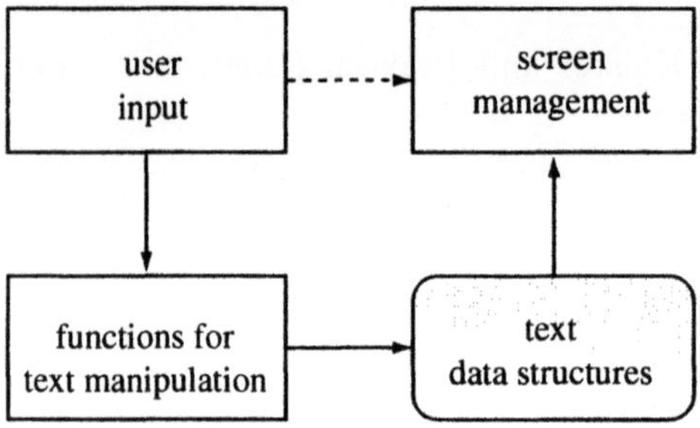

Fig. 8.12. Architecture of a single-user editor

Figure 8.12 depicts the architecture of a general single-user editor. User input is captured by the user interface and propagated to functions for text manipulation. Modified data structures are interpreted by the screen management in order to update the screen representation. Furthermore, there is a flow of control information between the user interface and the screen management component. Figure 8.13 depicts the architecture of a group editor based on the DistEdit framework.

The stub routines (see p. 33ff.) are basically proxies providing generic text manipulation routines which are mapped to the respective manipulation routines of the local text editor. Communication between group editor instances is based on Isis (Birman 1993) enabling safe data transfer. Editor functions may sometimes have to be renamed in order to avoid nomenclature conflicts with stub routines.

8.2.5 User interface layer of a group editor

The user interface layer is typically a family of specialized editors rather than a single editor application. Each application supports one or more media types. In the simplest case there is a specific application for each medium type. The user interface layer contains functions to display document related information on the screen and to handle user input. In the former case it

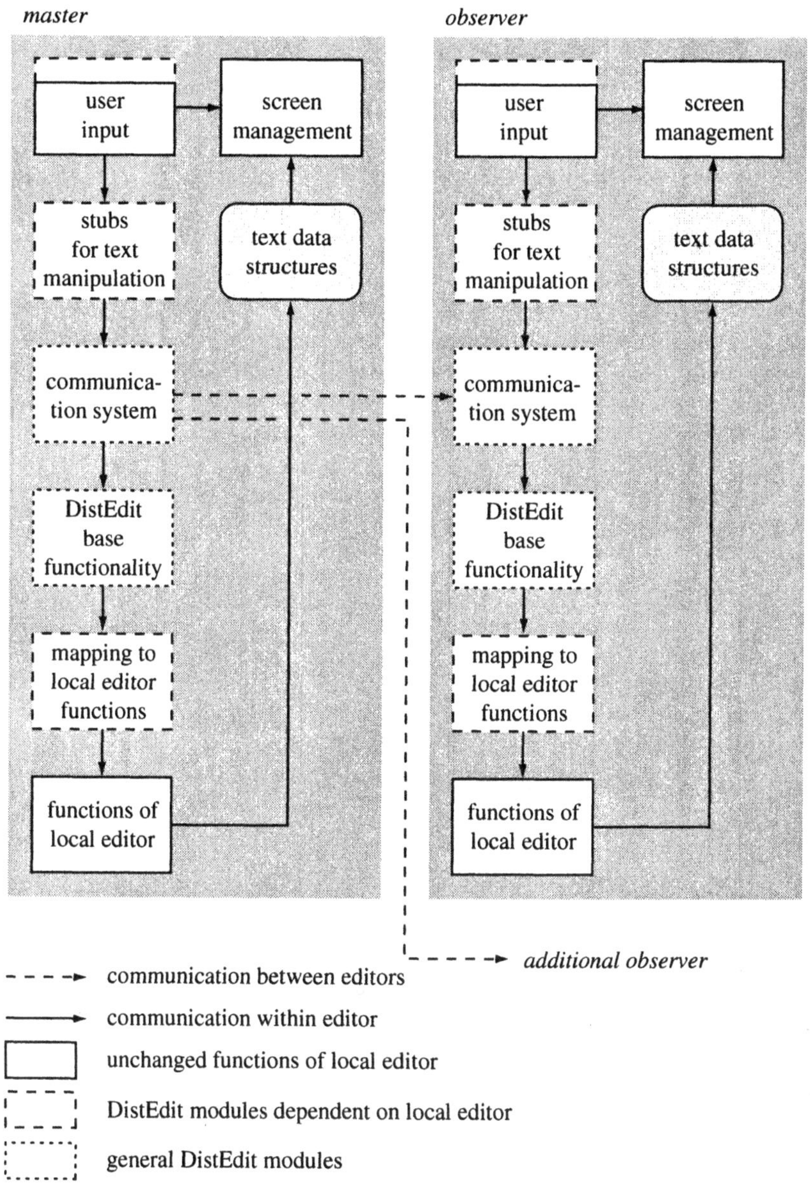

Fig. 8.13. Architecture of the DistEdit group editor

generates the appropriate representation of the document content, the document structure and the document creation process (e.g., which co-authors are currently active and which document parts they are modifying). In the latter case it invokes editing operations based on the user input. The results of an operation are interpreted to update the screen display, and furthermore, they are passed to the access layer to propagate document changes to other group editor instances participating in the joint editing session.

However, there is also information flow from the access layer to the user interface layer. For example, it notifies the user interface layer if the locking status or the content of a locally displayed document part has been modified by another group editor instance. Furthermore, group membership changes are propagated to the user interface layer. Thus, it is also responsible for displaying group awareness information.

Awareness is very important for successful collaboration in joint editing. An author needs to be notified of current and past events related to the shared document. In the former case the user is informed of currently active co-authors and of their current scope of work. Thus, the user can determine, if his operation might influence the actions of his co-authors and vice versa. In the latter case document modifications are recorded in a history list. The user may inspect this list to determine if anything of interest has occurred to the shared document (e.g., when and how has the document content and structure changed).

Co-authors usually work independently on separate parts of the document. Therefore, a variety of group editors support so-called private workspaces within the document. A private workspace is a document part available for full editing functionality to its owner, and for limited document access to all other co-authors (e.g., only read access). Rather than supporting the strict WYSIWIS paradigm during synchronous cooperation these systems support only a loose form of user interface coupling; thus, Mace (Newman-Wolfe and Pelimuhandiram 1991) uses the term WYSIWIMS (*what you see is what I may see*).

As soon as documents become more complex, simple content editing systems are not sufficient anymore. Content must be accompanied by structural information in order to facilitate the overview of the document creation process for all involved authors. Private workspaces are usually mapped to structural elements of the shared document. The granularity of private workspaces defines the degree of parallel work by multiple co-authors.

Example 8.2.1 (Mercury). The program editor Mercury (Kaiser et al. 1987) uses a notification mechanism for controlling interrelationships between structural elements. If a user changes a module interface (a module represents a structural unit within a program source), then all other users importing that module are informed about the changed module interface. A document editor might apply a similar approach. If the definition of a term is modified all other users are notified to determine whether usage of the term conforms with the changed definition.

A suitable screen representation of the dynamically changing document is an important aspect of synchronous group editor design and one major functionality of the user interface layer. Since screen updates are no longer exclusively caused by the local user's input, the user interface layer must provide a means for the user to differentiate between locally initiated changes and changes requested by remote sites. The identical display of both types of changes might be quite confusing to the user. The following techniques are feasible:

- A simple technique would associate attributes with text sections currently being manipulated by others (e.g., displaying the attribute value *locked by "username"*).
- Another technique would highlight text sections currently being processed by other users (e.g., using inverted color). Rather than inverting just single characters the highlighting usually encompasses the entire structural element in which the remote user is currently active.
- Modifications of other users are displayed "considerably slower" in order to distinguish them from one's own manipulations. The cloudburst model shows on the display a slowly dissolving cloud above text sections altered by other group members.
  Different color coding is an alternative. The text section which has been manipulated by a user would initially be displayed in a different color slowly changing into the regular text color as the modification ages (color-fading).

Besides the distinction between local and remote changes of document content or document structure it might also be helpful to provide information about the modification frequency. Text sections may be displayed according to the absolute number of modifications or to the time passed since the last modification. The aging process of document changes may be animated by color variations (e.g., frequently or just recently changed parts are displayed in red while others which have been modified very seldom or a long time ago are displayed in blue representing a stable state of that document part). If required, the absolute number of modifications can be displayed numerically. Repeated changes of the document structure might indicate an inadequate document design.

Notification messages also play a significant role when text patterns are to be globally replaced throughout the entire document. Within a group editor, it can not be assumed that all areas containing the pattern are unlocked and thus, all patterns are replaced by the new pattern. The principle of private workspaces prohibits any modifications by other group members except the user who owns the private workspace. Instead, the user initiating a global substitution is informed of his chances of successfully replacing all instances of the pattern. A variation is the so called pending substitution, where the user is notified at session end that not all patterns have been replaced as desired. He can then decide to repeat the substitution at a later time. It is also feasible to notify users holding locks that a substitution request is pending. They may then accept or reject the request. This approach improves group awareness while still supporting the principle of private workspaces.

8.2.6 Access layer of a group editor

The access layer of single user editors is generally quite small. It is responsible for data exchange with the local persistent storage and the management of cached information to improve system performance. In group editors with replicated data and distributed control the access layer is rather complex having a variety of tasks.

Every document access initiated by the user interface layer is controlled by the access layer. It synchronizes concurrent access operations of the group members (e.g., setting and releasing locks, sending notification messages), and manages the consistency of local document copies. The choice of access granularity influences both the size of the private workspace and the degree of parallel work by the co-authors. The following discusses various aspects of selecting the appropriate access granularity:

- *Computer specific granularity: block.* File systems often structure files into blocks of fixed length; a block has typically the size of several Kbytes. Since documents are generally stored in files, it seems appropriate to select a block as the access granularity. This would facilitate the usage of access mechanisms developed as part of distributed file systems.
  However, this approach does not conform with the idea of a distributed document system. Fixed sized file blocks do not correlate with semantic units of a document (e.g., a paragraph or a section). Thus, blocks are not adequate for these kinds of systems.
- *Editor specific granularity: character, word, sentence.* Although characters, words and sentences are semantic units within a document the experiences with Grove render a very fine granularity, such as a character or a word undesirable, since it requires complex schemes for handling conflicting operations of the group members in order to keep the document consistent (Ellis et al. 1990). The choice of a sentence as access granularity seems acceptable. However, with respect to the user perception of a private workspace it is still too restricted.
- *Granularity: paragraph.* In this case, a paragraph is the access and locking unit (only complete paragraphs are read, locked or updated). Version numbers are maintained on the paragraph level. The paragraph structure is integrated into the structural description of the document ensuring a correlation between processing units and logical document units. A paragraph defines both, semantically interrelated information and an adequate sized private workspace. Furthermore, the restriction to paragraphs may facilitate the close cooperation among co-authors.
- *User selected granularity.* Another alternative is to allow the user to specify the access granularity according to his own needs and intention since he knows best what would be the right size of the private workspace and the desired degree of cooperation with the co-authors. Mace (Newman-Wolfe and Pelimuhandiram 1991) is an example of a system supporting

flexible access granularity. The private workspace is defined by specifying a begin and an end marker. However, switching between workspaces is rather complicated impeding document editing considerably. The following option eliminates this deficiency.

- *Flexible granularity within the document structure.* The separation of access granularity and document structure as proposed by Mace has considerable disadvantages. Document editing always occurs within the structural boundaries of the document (e.g., a section, a subsection, a table or an image). Thus, it seems quite natural to use by default the smallest structural unit encompassing the current editing location as the access granularity. For example, if a user changes a table entry the table itself might be automatically selected as the access unit. Thus, the access granularity implicitly depends on the document structure not requiring any inconvenient marking of workspace boundaries. If the user desires a larger private workspace than provided by default, he may select the encompassing structural unit according to the structural hierarchy of the document.
  The Iris group editor applies this approach to flexibly define the size of the access units. The user navigates within the document structure; applying an open command at a document node specifies the subtree as the access unit; the appropriate document content editor is automatically invoked and the document content defined by the subtree is loaded.

Another important issue of the access layer which has significant influence on the degree of document replication is the ratio between the numbers of read and write operations. Applications with a very large number of read operations compared with write accesses imply an architecture with fully replicated documents, whereas applications with a majority of write accesses seem better served with a central, nonreplicated data storage, at least with respect to the performance of write operations. CSCW applications for distributed document editing belong to the first category. As Pendergast and Vogel (1990) have noticed, users of a joint editing team spend more time browsing through the document and reading portions of it than creating new entries. Based on this observation Schlichter and Borghoff (1992) proposed a replicated document architecture with a decentralized scheme for concurrency control.

Voting schemes. Cooperative work often results in a high degree of concurrency. Since read access is prevalent both in hypertext/hypermedia systems and distributed document systems, the replication of shared data seems appropriate in order to achieve high performance for local access. Concurrent operations on replicated, distributed data may be controlled by voting schemes (see Sect. 5.2). However, due to the high coordination overhead they are not appropriate for groups of collaborating users working in a tightly coupled mode.

Transaction and transformation schemes. According to Rodden and Blair (1991), traditional transaction schemes are not usable for synchronous groupware especially in the context of replicated shared data; they are just not efficient enough. Applying voting schemes within multiphase commit protocols, as described by Borghoff (1990), would make things even worse. Thus, several proposals have been made to support more flexible serialization constraints.

- Skarra (1988) modifies the strict serialization requirements for groupware by introducing so-called transaction groups. A transaction group provides coordinated access to shared data for collaborating users; serialization within the transaction group is replaced by access rules based on the semantics of the respective application and its operations.
- Another approach improving the performance of transaction schemes is that of Pu and Leff (1991). Their epsilon serialization (ESR) supports mutual data consistency in asynchronous cooperation modes. ESR permits read access to inconsistent data, yet it guarantees the convergence of replicated data into a consistent state. While read transactions may be invoked in an arbitrary order write transactions must be handled by the system according to a well-defined sequence (e.g., using the ordered-update method).
- Others proposed similar approaches to support a more flexible handling of concurrent operations: Harrison et al. (1990) with the so-called coordination consistency, Wiederhold and Qian (1987, 1990) with potentially inconsistent updates, Sheth and Rusinkiewicz (1990) with eventual/lagging inconsistency, and Barbara and Garcia-Molina (1990) with controlled inconsistency. Kawell et al. (1988) propose the one-way pull model which initially executes all modifications locally and then propagates them asynchronously using a special migration mechanism.

As opposed to voting schemes, transformation schemes (see Sect. 4.8) operate on smaller units, such as individual words or characters resulting in groupware applications with fine access granularity. Similar to the transaction group approach, they require knowledge of the operation semantics, as well as of the user-defined transformation rules. Thus, the fine access granularity is achieved at the cost of universal usage.

Optimistic concurrency control. While pessimistic schemes ensure the consistency of document replicas before an access operation is processed, optimistic concurrency control schemes focus on fast system performance and high availability of documents at low costs. Access operations are immediately processed on the local data and they are propagated to all other replicas at remote sites. Since operations are not strictly sequentialized inconsistencies between replicas may occur. However, the selection of a fine access granularity reduces the probability of access conflicts.

A distinction can be made between read-write conflicts and write-write conflicts. In the former case, the main problem is that the reader may have to contend with an outdated copy of the document. The latter case causes divergent document copies. Each write-write conflict results in a new branch within the version tree (see Sect. 8.2.11). In general, the merge process of different versions requires manual intervention by the involved users in order to create a shared consistent document version. Therefore, mechanisms for conflict detection and conflict resolution are very important for optimistic concurrency control.

8.2.7 Architecture of a distributed group editor

As soon as documents become more complex, pure outline-oriented group editors, such as Grove or toolkits for simple text editing, such as DistEdit become unsuitable. Document content information must be accompanied by structural information which can be used to define logical positions and regions of a document (Borghoff and Teege 1993a, 1993b). The logical document structure provides the basis for the handling of group awareness which notifies a user of the location in the document that his co-authors are currently working on or did work on in the past, e.g., "what is my current position in the document relative to my co-authors and what are other users currently doing?"

CES was one of the first group editors to distinguish between textual and structural information. In a multimedia environment it is even more important to separate the structure from the content. Only a media-independent structure can support a common media-independent functionality for coordination of collaborative editing operations. However, there must be seamless transitions between the different content editors and the document structure editor. The latter should be based on standards for specifying logical units of the document structure, and it should support multiple logical views of the document.

The following discusses various issues which are relevant to the design of a multimedia-based group editor covering the principal architecture, basic operations for structure editing as well as version and history management for both, content and structure.

Figure. 8.14 depicts a layered architecture of a general group editor framework for manipulating the structure and the content of multimedia documents. The operation layer contains components for content and structure editing, explicit user coordination, dynamic user profiling and further services relevant for joint editing applications. The data layer stores and manages the content and structure of documents, history information as well as static user profiles.

Data layer

- *Content information:* This component stores the actual document content including formatting information such as layout markup. The content of a multimedia document may consist of text, bitmaps, vector graphics, audio and video sequences.

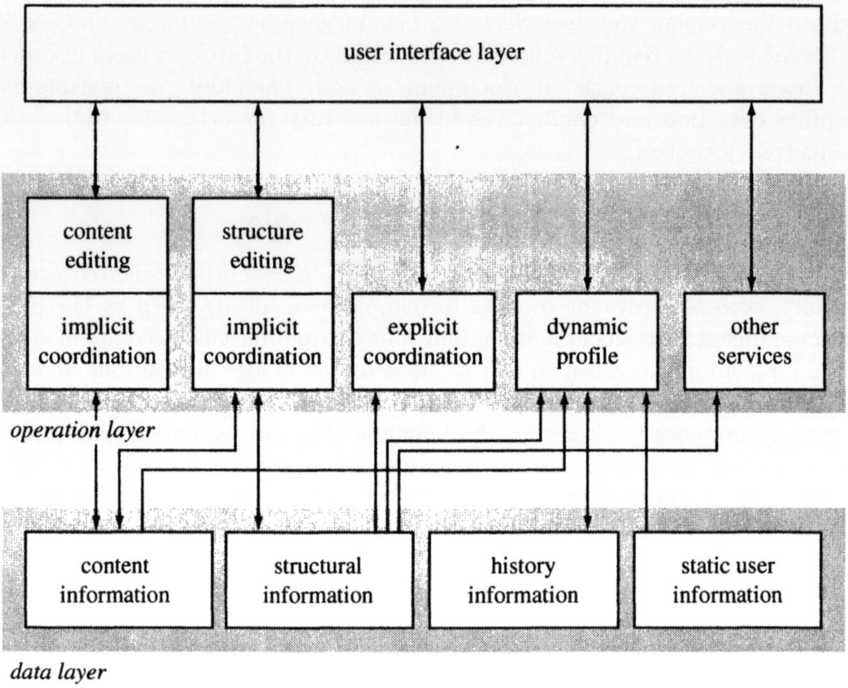

Fig. 8.14. Architecture for a group editor framework

- *Structural information:* The structural information contains the "explicit" document structure as the user perceives and manipulates it. It is mainly used by the group editor framework to provide users with a compact view of other users' activities within the shared document. Furthermore both, the content information and the structural information have an "implicit" structure which is only visible to the group editor for coordinating updates of the document. For the implicit structure a sequence of individually lockable document units is sufficient. However, the explicit structure should be multilevel based (e.g., a document structure consisting of chapters, sections, subsections, footnotes, figures and tables) to allow different logical document views of different granularity. Moreover, it should be possible to associate content information with the respective structural elements. Please note that we do not mean here any media dependent layout views; on this topic, the interested reader is referred to Appelt (1989).
  The explicit structure is utilized in three principal ways:
  - to notify users about operations which the other group members performed on the document.
  - to coordinate all operations in order to achieve a consistent document.
  - to support operations of a single user, such as positioning and navigation.

- *History information:* The history information contains previous document versions, as well as operations of users who have already left the joint editing session. Thus, it enables active users to distinguish between past modifications of the current editing session and "historic" work on the document (i.e., operations performed during previous editing sessions).
- *Static user information:* The system maintains for each user some profile information covering phone numbers, email address and bitmap photographs. Furthermore, it may include predefined text patterns which are sent automatically as notification messages to other group members (e.g., "please, unlock this section").

Operation layer

- *Content editing:* This component encompasses the functionality of a media dependent content editor; thus, it is equivalent to the functionality of a single-user editor.
  For reasons of simplicity, the following discussion will concentrate on text editors. However, most statements are similarly true for editors of other media types (e.g., bitmap editors or editors of animation sequences).
- *Structure editing:* In general, the document structure evolves during the existence of the document. Thus, analogous to the content editing functionality the editor framework must also support the manipulation of the media independent document structure.
  Typical operations are:
  - to define new structural units,
  - to delete existing structural units,
  - to move existing structural units.

  These and other structural operations will be dealt with separately below.
- *Implicit coordination:* Both components, content and structure editing must coordinate concurrent updates. This is achieved by implicit coordination which is performed by the individual editors.
- *Explicit coordination:* Besides the implicit coordination which is transparent to the users there is also a separate component providing explicit coordination at the user level. The user may explicitly lock a document part, request the unlocking of a part or even request (e.g., via email) that another user work on a document part. The locks managed by this component may be either "soft" or "hard". While soft locks are only shown to other users, hard locks guarantee exclusive access to the locked document area; they are enforced by the editor framework.
- *Dynamic profile:* The dynamic profile contains functions notifying users about the activities of the other group members (e.g., joining the editing session, locking or changing a document part). This component uses the logic document structure as a basis for showing which document parts are concerned with respect to locking or updating operations.

- *Other services:* The document structure can also be used for purposes other than coordination aspects. Among them are the positioning of the cursor at the beginning or end of a document part.

In summary the editor framework specified by the layered architecture in Fig. 8.14 supports the following functionality in addition to the typical single-user editor functions:

- *Explicit and implicit coordination of concurrent work:* Implicit coordination supports concurrent editing along the entire structure. Explicit coordination supports locking of document parts and provides communication mechanisms for all group members to coordinate their common task using social protocols.
- *Version control and history management:* Version control and history management are closely related to the document structure. The granularity for versioning are nodes of the document structure. History management captures the evolution of a document and it may be utilized to display the times at which the document was changed, and the group member who initiated the modification.
- *Information about current activities:* The dynamic profile component provides an overview of current activities related to the shared document. This information which is essential for short-term coordination helps group members to observe what is happening in the immediate "neighborhood" of their own work focus.

However, opening full access to the activity information of all group members might evoke some privacy concerns especially in hierarchically organized teams where group members have different roles and access rights. Thus, the dynamic profile should be extended by a so-called ask-and-grant mechanism or other mechanisms that limit access to specific user information.

Example (Iris). Iris is a modular group editing framework providing a replicated data storage and event service at the access layer and a set of tools at the user interface layer. The user may flexibly configure these tools and link tools in order to allow automatic propagation of information between them (see Fig. 8.15). Among other things Iris provides tools for navigation within documents, for editing structure and content of documents, and for filtering and representing group awareness information. Special wrapper components enable the integration of external applications, such as desktop conferencing systems or word processors. The major task of the event service is the propagation of group awareness information between active group editor instances. However, the decision of which information is to be presented to the user in what form is made by the user interface layer.

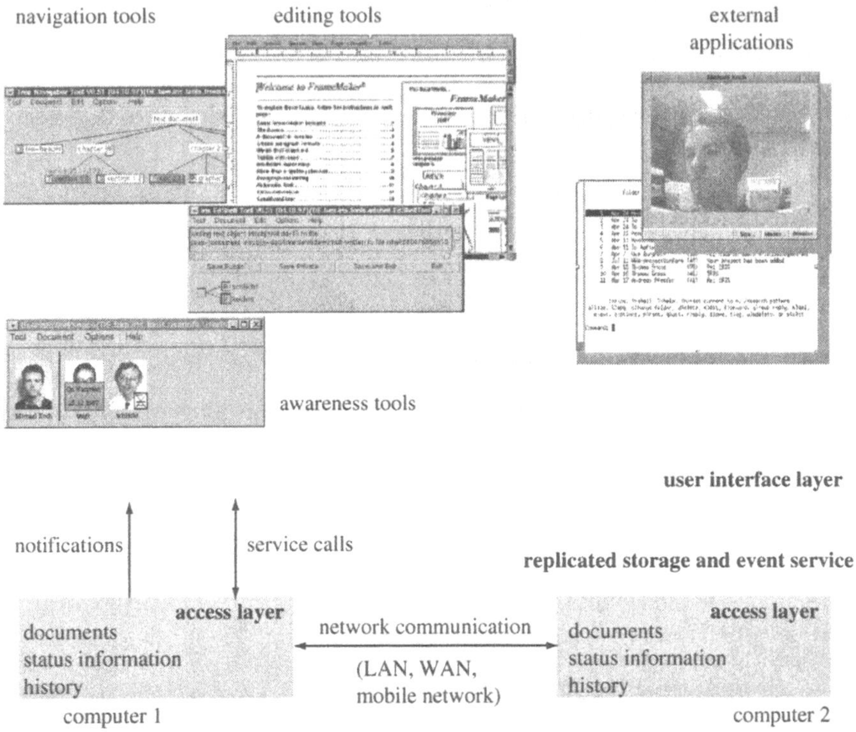

Fig. 8.15. Architecture of the group editor environment Iris

8.2.8 Document structure

As opposed to simple single-user editors, the use of a logical document structure in collaborative group editors is essential in order to precisely capture and manage information about users' activities. Since large documents are usually stored in several files, the logical document structure must extend across file boundaries.

Electronic document standards, like the "Office Document Architecture" (ODA) (ISO 1988), the "Standard Generalized Markup Language" (SGML) (ISO 1986), and more recently the "eXtended Markup Language" (XML) provide an appropriate means for specifying rich logical document structures. For approaches using and discussions focusing on ODA, the reader is referred to Cole and Brown (1991), Lubich and Plattner (1990), Nelson et al. (1991), Rosenberg et al. (1991) and Spiceley (1991).

SGML defines a syntax used to exchange document structures without providing an explicit definition of the semantics of such structures. Consequently, SGML-based systems require additional agreements between the involved sites. ODA, on the other hand, defines additionally schemes to describe data structures as well as rules for the document layout using standardized semantics.

The following description uses the specific logical structure of ODA as an example for a logical document structure. It forms a tree of four different types of objects:

1. The logical root of the document (i.e., the root of the tree).
2. The content portions which are contiguous parts of the document content.
3. The basic logical objects which contain only content portions as subnodes.
4. The composite logical objects are inner tree nodes containing basic or composite logical nodes rather than any content portions.

Each tree object has a number. The sequence of numbers on the path from the logical document root to the object uniquely identifies the object; it is called the object identifier. Each object which is not a content portion may also have a user visible name. The user visible name can be any string, such as "function model" or "chapter 1". Figure 8.16 exemplifies an excerpt of the logical structure of a project documentation using the ODA standard. The unique sequence of digits "31020" which is highlighted by gray coloring identifies the object "chapter 1".

In general, names are defined and modified by users. Yet, they may also be generated automatically. For the children of a node a sequential order is defined which may differ from the numbers of the object identifiers. Note that this induces a sequential order on the set of all content portions.

Most importantly, a content portion makes an ideal candidate for an update unit; content portions are the granularity for implicit coordination (i.e., for locking and notification). Content portions which are manipulated by media dependent content editors are stored separate from the document structure. First and foremost, a content portion belongs to exactly one logical object.

The explicit document structure is media independent and it consists of only the logical tree without content portions. This approach allows a high degree of flexibility: A node of the document structure can describe a single text paragraph, a declaration of a variable in a program source code, an audio sequence, an entire document, or even a set of documents.

8.2.9 Logical views of the document structure

The explicit structure is presented to the user in the form of one or more logical structure views. A logical view depicts one structure object in an iconic way. The object may be the logical root, or a basic or composite logical object, but never a content portion. For the following discussion we use nested rectangles to represent structural objects on the screen. Furthermore, the icon of an object may display one or more of the following items: the

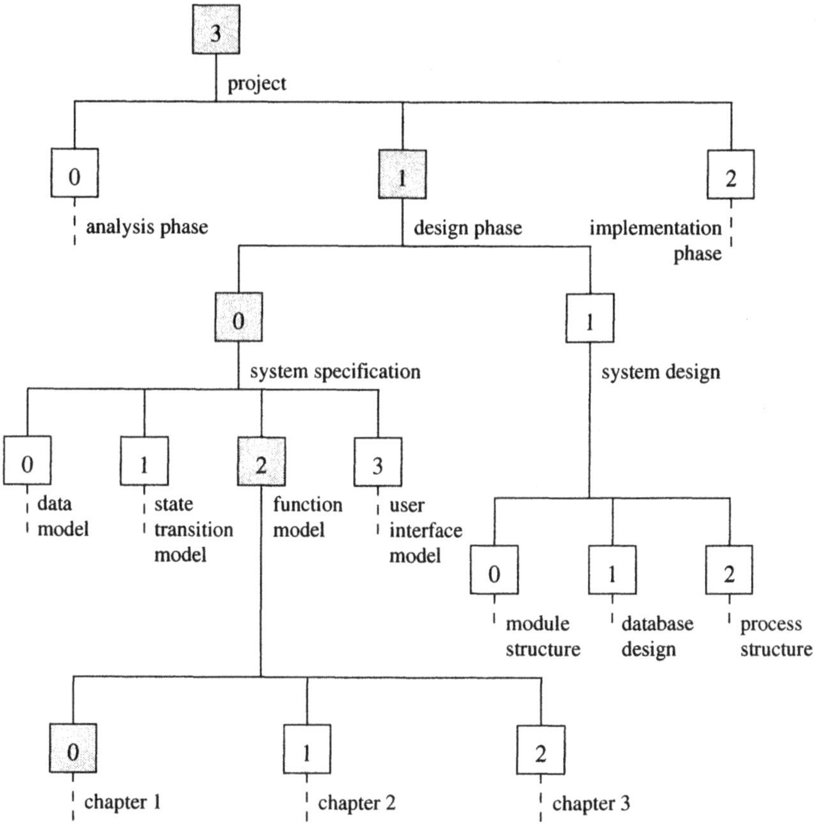

Fig. 8.16. Excerpt of the logical structure of a project documentation

identifying number, the user-defined name, and in the case of a composite logical object the sequence of iconic representations of all subnodes according to their sequential order. Note, the logical view does not display any part of the document content. Thus, it is independent of the content types used in multimedia documents. Figure 8.17 depicts two possible logical views of the node "design phase" from the document structure of Fig. 8.16.

A logical view may display either the current state of the document structure or the structure of an obsolete version (along with the, possibly also obsolete, corresponding version of the content portions). It may provide a view of the entire document or of a certain part of it. Logical views are used to manipulate the structure, and to navigate through the multimedia document, thereby alleviating the problem of getting lost in hyperspace as mentioned in Sect. 6.3.5.

The editor framework uses logical views as the user interface for handling input and output events. In order to facilitate this feature, the content editors must have access to a standard interface of the logical views. This interface

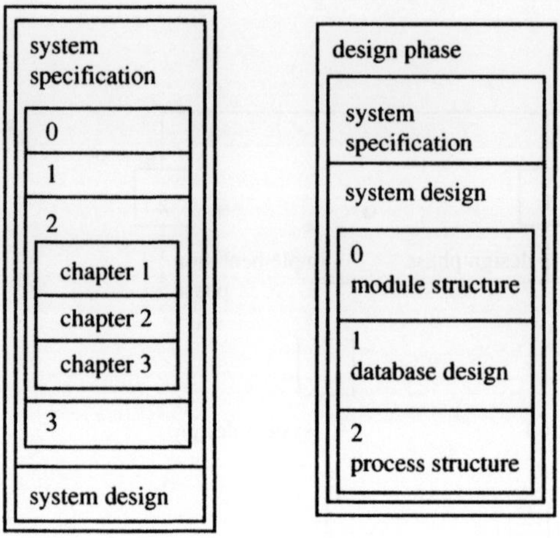

Fig. 8.17. Two logical views of the node "design phase"

allows a reaction to input events via a logical view and several functions for output via a structure view. Supported types of input events are the following:

- The selection of one or several objects according to their iconic representation.
- The selection of a position between objects (e.g., to insert a new content part).
- The selection of an object's user name or an object's identifier.

Among the supported types of output events are:

- Highlighting of an iconified object by shadowing or coloring. Other graphical approaches are discussed in detail by Hill et al. (1992).
- Pointing at an iconified object.
- In the case in which the object is not locked: displaying the name of the user who created or last modified the object.
  In the case in which the object is locked: displaying the name of the user who initiated the lock request along with the duration of the locking.

8.2.10 Structure editor

The operation interface of the structure editor is independent of the particular attributes of the content portions, especially independent of their concrete media. The media-dependent content editors for manipulating the content portions may be activated in uniform ways as subactivities.

Access coordination for structural information. As mentioned above, content editing uses content portions as access units. All content portions are independent of each other and may be locked separately. The manipulation of structural information and of content portions must be coordinated. Since structure editing may change any object in the tree structure it is appropriate to define any node of the tree as an access unit.

However, there is a fundamental difference between content portions and structural nodes. Since a structural node may be part of an encompassing composite node, the access units cannot be viewed or locked separately. The locking scheme must be extended to prevent locking of a node whenever a subnode is already locked. Furthermore, because content portions are treated as part of their corresponding basic logical objects locking of a structural node may even fail if any of the subordinate content portions are already locked. However, the extended locking scheme can use the same strategies and the same synchronization mechanisms as content editing (e.g., using version numbers and implicit coordination).

Structure browsing. An important part of the interaction with logical views is their interactive creation and configuration. After the editor framework is invoked on a document, the system automatically creates a logical view of the root of the document structure. It does not necessarily display all subnodes in detail. The user may configure a logical view as follows: For the selected object, he may choose between the user defined name or the internal object index. Moreover, he can determine whether each subnode should be displayed or not. Thus, a logical view may be configured to show some parts in detail while hiding other parts.

Furthermore, new views can be created by selecting an object depicted by an existing logical view. Unless this object is the document root, the new view only displays and gives access to a part of the document. Thus, the user can maintain several different views in parallel (e.g., an overall view of the document and a detailed view of that part he is currently manipulating).

At any time a logical view may be closed. By closing the last view of the document, the user terminates his editing session for that document.

Structure editing. There are five basic operations for manipulating the document structure. All of them may be invoked via a logical view (i.e., by selecting or dragging objects in the view). The operations are:

- *insert:* A new logical object is created as a subnode of the selected object. If the selected object was a basic logical object, it is changed into a composite logical object. However, this is only possible if no content portion has been assigned to the object. Subsequently, the user can specify the user visible name for the new object.
- *delete:* The selected object is deleted, along with all subobjects.
- *move:* The selected object is removed from its current parent object and added as new child to another object. As for the insert operation, the target object must not be a basic logical object with a defined content portion.
- *copy:* A copy of the selected object is added to another (or even the same parent) object. The copy has the same name, however, a new index number is created. The copying process involves all subobjects of the tree defined

by the selected object. As for the insert operation, the target object must not be a basic logical object with a defined content portion.
- *rename:* The user changes the user visible name of a selected object.

These basic operations may be combined to define more complex operations (e.g., replace). All structure editing operations implicitly lock the involved structure nodes using the chosen concurrency control scheme. Changes caused by the operations are propagated to all sites to update the logical views, thus providing a WYSIWIS behavior.

Activating content dependent editors. The last kind of operations initiated via logical views is the invocation of content dependent operators on user selected structural objects. The logical view remains associated with the operator until the operator is terminated. We can distinguish between two types of operators: content browsers which allow only viewing operations and content editors necessary to manipulate the document content. The reason for this distinction is that a multimedia document may encompass numerous content types. However, a content editor supports usually only operations for a single media type, thus an editor displays only an isolated portion of the document. In general, content browsers interpret a larger number of media types allowing the user to display a content portion as well as the surrounding portions even if they are of different types.

This concept allows a variety of content dependent operators. Simple operators handle only one content type. Other more complex operators might support interactive editing of various content types, such as text, bitmaps and video clips. By providing new and more sophisticated operators the editing framework may be incrementally extended to handle more kinds of content and to offer more manipulation functions to the user.

8.2.11 Versioning/history management

Versioning is based on two principles:

- *Implicit versioning:* Each change of a document part results in the creation of a new version for this part.
- *Hierarchical versioning:* Each change of a part implies a version change of the parent part.

The versioning of content portions is implemented by the content editors assigned to the respective content type. In particular, they define the update granularity and they manage the version history. Each content portion has its own version history independent of other content portions, thus enabling a high degree of flexibility.

The versioning of structural nodes is implemented by the content independent structure editor. Each of the basic operations described in Sect. 8.2.10 is interpreted as a structural change. This results in a fine-grained version history. Each version is characterized by a set of attributes (e.g., creation time and the name of the user who is responsible for the change). The user may even assign a name to a version which facilitates the version lookup in the version history.

In order to provide more flexibility during joint document editing the concept of a version list, as provided by Neptune (Delisle and Schwartz 1986) may be extended to support version trees. These enable the authors to manipulate even an old version which serves then as the source for a new version branch. The change operation may be a structure or a content operation. Version trees are very helpful if diverging versions of document parts (variants) are needed for certain applications. For example, there may be two alternate versions of the same document part: a summary and a detailed content. The Prep editor (Neuwirth et al. 1990) uses version trees to implement the concept of revision by versioning.

The user interface enabling access to old document versions is also a logical view of the document structure. Each logical view has a control panel to select the version it should display. This function supports both the associative access to versions via their attributes (such as the last version created by the user), and the step-by-step retrieval through the version history. A logical view is always in one of the following states: it either displays the current document version or an old, consistent version. In the former case, a document change which creates a new version results in an update of the logical view (i.e., the view keeps track of all changes and always shows the current version). In the second case, the view always shows the version the user has selected.

Fig. 8.18 shows a version tree with its attributes. It reflects the following scenario.

Example (Scenario). In the empty document, a new logical object is first inserted by Uwe. Subsequently, he inserts another logical object, changes the user visible name of a selected object and then deletes a logical object. All resulting versions are attributed (i.e., the creator's name, the creation time and the version name). For example, Uwe created version 7.0 on December 24th, 1999 at 12:04 p.m. by deleting a logical object. Later, on January 1st, 2000, at 08:58 a.m., Gunnar inserted a new logical object into the old version, hence creating version 1.1. A new version branch was added to the version tree.

8.3 Undo in Distributed Group Editors

Undo is an important feature of most text editing systems. Systems often only support a global undo which resets the last operation. In distributed group editors with many co-authors working in parallel, this does not suffice, since users often wish to undo their own last operation, yet this need not be the last operation in a global sense.

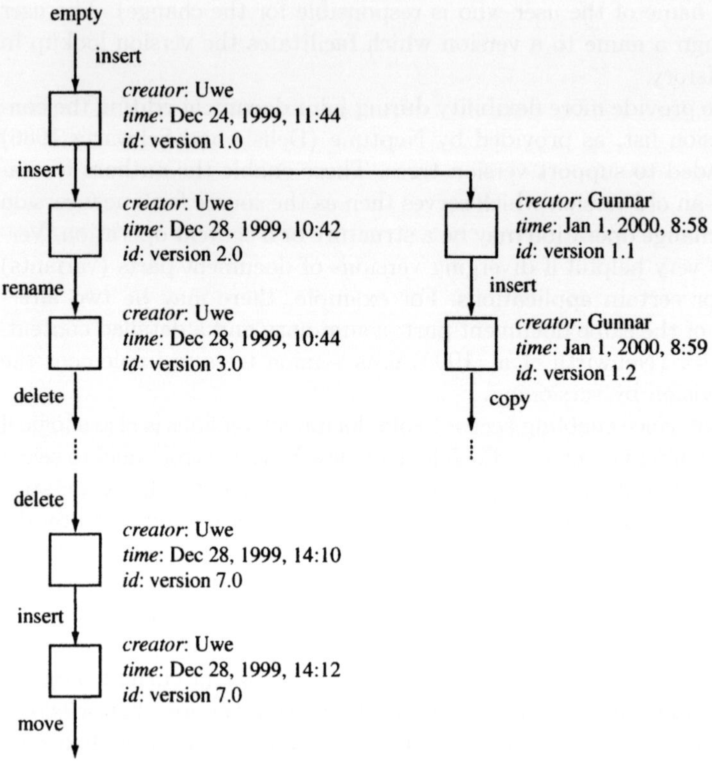

Fig. 8.18. Version tree of a distributed document

Compared with a single-user undo, the following three issues are important in distributed collaborative applications:

1. to select the operation to be undone
2. to determine how to undo the operation
3. to detect and resolve conflicts among the operations of different users

It often makes no sense to undo a user's operation without also at the same time undoing the related operations of remote co-authors' as well. In this case, interdependencies between different operations must be analyzed.

8.3.1 Basic concepts

No matter how functionally extensive the supported undo operation is, there is a need to integrate history management into the editor framework. The history contains the sequence of the last n operations which changed the document state. The operations are stored chronologically as they were executed.

In order to undo operations they must be reversible (i.e., for each operation o there must exist an inverse operation $\mathbf{inverse}(o) = \bar{o}$ for undoing the effect of o). For a text editor, the inverse operation of **insert** is **delete**. If an operation does not have an inverse operation a so-called cancellation operation is needed. However, for the following discussion we assume that all operations are reversible.

Typically, the inverse operation depends on the document state prior to the execution of the original operation. Let us, for example, assume that the operation $o =$ **delete**[Φ] deletes the character at position Φ of a text document. Subsequently, the inverse operation $\bar{o}$ will require information as to which character has been deleted. Thus, the history records the operation itself as well as the deleted character, e.g., **delete**[X; Φ] with X being the deleted character.

8.3.2 Simple undo

The single user editors GNU Emacs or Microsoft Word support the reversal of a sequence of operations. Rather than simply undoing an operation, the respective inverse operation is carried out and appended to the end of the history list. Thus, inverse operations are treated like regular operations. In particular, inverse operations can be reversed by the same mechanism (i.e., the inverse of the inverse operation is appended to the history list).

This approach enables the user to navigate along the document history. Conflicts within the single-user environment do not occur since all operations of the single user are recorded.

8.3.3 Selective undo according to Prakash and Knister

Like simple undo, the selective undo approach which was developed by Prakash and Knister (1992) treats inverse operations as ordinary operations and appends them to the history list after they have been invoked. However, the user may select the operation to be undone via attributes (e.g., the user name, the document region which was affected by the operation, or time when the operation was executed). Selective undo provides the flexibility necessary to support multiple co-authors in a group editing environment. The following discusses some of the issues related to selective undo.

Let us assume that the operation selection is based on the attribute "user name" and that the history contains the following entries ($o_j^{B_i}$ is the j-th operation carried out by user B_i):

$$o_1^{B_1} - o_1^{B_2} - o_2^{B_1} - o_2^{B_2} - o_1^{B_3}$$

If user B_1 wants to reverse the effect of his last operation, then the simple undo approach would first have to undo $o_1^{B_3}$ and then $o_2^{B_2}$ before the user could invoke the inverse operation of $o_2^{B_1}$. Selective undo, on the other hand, first checks whether or not the relevant document region has been relocated and whether or not the inverse operation would cause any conflicts with other already executed operations; this is similar to the Grove algorithm (see Sect. 4.8.2). Only after all conflicts have been resolved and adjustments with respect to the relocation have been performed, can the inverse operation $\overline{o_2^{B_1}}$ be invoked and then appended to the history list.

Example (conflict free relocation). Let us assume, the document consists of the character string 'abcd' and the following operations will be performed sequentially:

$o_2^{B_1}$ = **insert**['x'; 4],
$o_2^{B_2}$ = **insert**['y'; 1]
and
$o_1^{B_3}$ = **insert**['z'; 1].

The three operations change the document to the string 'zyabcxd'. Since the last two operations change the position of the characters within the string the inverse operation of $o_2^{B_1}$ is not **delete**[4], but $\overline{o_2^{B_1}}$ = **delete**[6].[5]

However, reversing an arbitrary operation is not always possible even after the inverse operation has been adjusted to reflect all position changes of later operations. In that case, a conflict arises which must be handled differently.

Example (Conflict within a text editor). Let

$o_2^{B_1}$ = **insert**['x'; 4],
$o_2^{B_2}$ = **insert**['y'; 1]
and
$o_1^{B_3}$ = **deletedocument**.

From the semantics point of view, the inverse operation $\overline{o_2^{B_1}}$ does not make sense in a deleted document. This conflict can only be solved by executing $\overline{o_1^{B_3}}$.

Example (Conflict in a graphic editor). Let

$o_1^{B_1}$ = **drawcircle**(x, y, *radius*, *circleId*)
and
$o_1^{B_2}$ = **changeradius**(*circleId*, *newradius*).

The operation $o_1^{B_1}$ draws a circle at position (x,y) with radius *radius* and assigning the identifier *circleId*. $o_1^{B_2}$ modifies the radius of the circle *circleId*.[6] Here, too, there is a dependency between the two operations, since $o_1^{B_2}$ does not make sense unless $o_1^{B_1}$ has been executed previously.

The examples illustrate that an operation can only be undone if all conflicting operations have previously been undone.

---

[5] The history list records the operation **delete**['x'; 6].

[6] **changeradius**(*circleId*, *newradius*, *oldradius*) is stored in order to make the inverse operation feasible.

The function **conflicts**(o_1,o_2) returns the result **true** if the operations o_1 and o_2 are in conflict with each other; otherwise it returns **false**. In addition, we need the function **transpose**(o_1,o_2) = ($o_2\prime$,$o_1\prime$), which satisfies the following constraints if there are no conflicts, i.e., **conflicts**(o_1,o_2) = **false**:

1. The execution of $o_2\prime$ prior to $o_1\prime$ entails the same document state as the execution sequence o_1 prior to o_2.
2. $o_2\prime$ is the operation which would have been applied to the document rather than o_2 if o_1 had not been executed before o_2.

Example (**transpose** *for* **insert/delete** *operations).*
The function **transpose** is closely related to the transformation matrix of the operation transformation supported by the Grove group editor (see p. 204).

The function **transpose**(**insert**[X_1; Φ_1], **delete**[X_2; Φ_2]) returns one of the following results:

1. (**delete**[X_2; $\Phi_2 - 1$], **insert**[X_1; Φ_1]), if $\Phi_1 < \Phi_2$;
2. undefined if $\Phi_1 = \Phi_2$ (conflict!);
3. (**delete**[X_2; Φ_2], **insert**[X_1; $\Phi_1 - 1$]), if $\Phi_1 > \Phi_2$.

The following example illustrates the general characteristics and the procedural steps of the selective undo mechanism.

Example (selective undo). Suppose the history list contains the entries

$o_1 - o_2 - o_3$

and we want to undo the operation o_1. If **conflicts**(o_1,o_2) returns **true**, then the undo fails. If there is no conflict between o_1 and o_2, then these operations are transposed, i.e., they are possibly modified to reflect position changes followed by an exchange within the history list.[7]

Now the history list records

$o_2\prime - o_1\prime - o_3$,

with ($o_2\prime$,$o_1\prime$) = **transpose**(o_1,o_2).

If **conflicts**($o_1\prime$,o_3) returns **true**, then the undo operation fails. Otherwise we get the following history list:

$o_2\prime - o_3\prime - o_1\prime\prime$,

with

($o_3\prime$,$o_1\prime\prime$) = **transpose**($o_1\prime$,o_3).

After **transpose** has been performed twice the desired operation is at the end of the history list. The inverse operation $\overline{o_1\prime\prime}$ can be executed, i.e., the history list records

$o_1 - o_2 - o_3 - \overline{o_1\prime\prime}$.

This is correct, since

$o_1 - o_2 - o_3 = o_2\prime - o_3\prime - o_1\prime\prime$

[7] Note, that the listed history entries are only used to illustrate the intermediate steps of the mechanism. In fact, if the history list contained the sequence $o_1 - o_2 - o_3$ before the undo operation, it would contain $o_1 - o_2 - o_3 - \overline{o_1\prime\prime}$ immediately after the successful undo.

and thus

$o_1 - o_2 - o_3 - \overline{o_1}'' = o_2' - o_3'$.

The execution of $\overline{o_1}''$ at the end of the original history list causes the same document state as if o_1 had never been executed. This means that the undo operation was successful.

The algorithm is correct, yet it has a major drawback: As the following example will illustrate, it cannot handle earlier undo operations.

Example (Problem with earlier undo operations). Suppose the history list contains the operations

$o_1 - o_2 - o_3$.

While o_1 and o_2 are in conflict with each other, there are no conflicts between o_1 and o_3 as well as between o_2 and o_3.

If the user wants to undo both operations o_1 and o_2, then first operation o_2 is undone which results in the following history list:

$o_1 - o_2 - o_3 - \overline{o_2}'$.

Subsequent attempts of undoing the operation o_1 will fail because o_1 and o_2 are in conflict which means that the algorithm cannot append the transposed inverse operation of o_1 to the history list. However, logically this should be possible because operation o_2 has just been undone.

8.3.4 Selective undo (extended version)

We need a more robust conflict detection mechanism in order to cope with earlier undo operations. Pointers in the history list record which operations have already corresponding undo operations. These pointers are called do-undo-pointers. The history list of the aforementioned example looks then as follows:

$$o_1 - \underbrace{o_2 - o_3 - \overline{o_2}'}_{\textit{do-undo-pointer}}.$$

If the user intends to undo the operation o_i, the system first creates a temporary work list copying o_i and all operations of the history list which occurred after o_i. Subsequently, the operation o_i is moved to the end of the work list using the **transpose** function. Prior to each individual exchange in the work list, neighboring operations are checked to determine if they are in conflict with each other.

If a conflict is detected with an operation that has already been undone (i.e., logically there is not really a conflict), then the two operations linked by the do-undo-pointer are removed from the work list. The procedural steps of this removal will be discussed in the following example.

Example (selective undo). Suppose the history list records the sequence

$o_1 - o_2 - o_3 - o_4$

with only the operations o_2 and o_3 in conflict. If operation o_3 is undone, the following history list emerges:

$$o_1 - o_2 - \underbrace{o_3 - o_4 - \overline{o_3'}}_{\textit{do-undo-pointer}}.$$

If the user wants to undo the operation o_2, a work list is created consisting of the sublist starting from o_2. Since o_2 and o_3 are in conflict with each other both operations, o_3 and $\overline{o_3'}$ are removed from the work list. Thus, the work list contains only the entries $o_2 - o_4'$ with $(o_4', o_3') =$ **transpose**(o_3, o_4).

Unless there is a conflict between o_2 and o_4', the operations o_2 and o_4' are transposed to o_4'' and o_2'. Even if there has been no conflict between o_2 and o_4 there may exist one between o_2 and o_4' (i.e., the transposition of operations may cause conflicts between the resulting transposed operations). An example is the modification of the position counter Φ in the aforementioned **insert-delete** transposition within a text editor.

After all transpositions have been performed and the operation o_2 is at the end of the work list, the inverse operation $\overline{o_2'}$ is executed and appended to the original history list. The undo of the operation o_2 is successful and the new history list encompasses the following information

$$o_1 - \underbrace{o_2 - \underbrace{o_3 - o_4 - \overline{o_3'}}_{\textit{do-undo-pointer}} - \overline{o_2'}}_{\textit{do-undo-pointer}}.$$

The removal of two operations linked through the do-undo-pointer (for example of $o_2, \overline{o_2'}$) works as follows: Operation o_2 is transposed and moved until it is a direct neighbor of $\overline{o_2'}$ within the work list. Since both operations together represent the identity operation, they can be removed from the work list without any problems. o_2 does not conflict with any other operation between o_2 and $\overline{o_2'}$ as long as none of these intermediate operations has been undone in a previous step; otherwise it would have been already impossible to undo o_2. In case, an intermediate operation has been previously undone (in our example the operation o_3) it is first together with its corresponding inverse operation ($\overline{o_3'}$) removed from the work list before further transposition of o_2 takes place. Thus, undo is a recursive process.

8.4 Further Reading

Introductions to workgroup computing are given by the books of Baecker (1993), Marca and Bock (1992).

The development of effective groups using a skilled facilitator is presented by Schwarz (1994). This book provides ground rules and a basic set of principles for governing group interaction (i.e., what to say to a group and when to say it, in order to keep the group as a whole on track and moving towards its goal). A similar approach is taken by Zimmerman and Evans (1992). Rees and Holt (1998) also focus on the facilitator's role in an efficient work group. Among others, they discuss the responsibilities of a facilitator, his verbal (what to say, and when to say it) and nonverbal (what to do) techniques, and the methods and tools a facilitator might exploit such as brainstorming, affinity, fishbone, or matrix diagrams as well as multivoting schemes. How to create group synergy is discussed by Hunter et al. (1995, 1999). Their books help to augment the training of "first-time" facilitators by providing many practical exercises. Masterful facilitation is the topic of the book by Kiser (1998).

Aspects of distributed document systems and collaborative writing are discussed at great length by Koch (1995), Rada (1996), Santos (1995) and Sharples (1993).

Design alternatives for meeting rooms are discussed by Ferwagner et al. (1991). Practical advice on setting up a meeting room are given by Putz (1998). Streitz et al. (1998b) present various issues and features of electronic meeting rooms.

9. Multiagent Systems

This chapter discusses various aspects of multiagent systems applied for intelligent coordination of agent-based computer-supported cooperation as required in groupwork.

After an initial classification and description of the most important features of agents, we will introduce aspects for modeling distributed multiagent systems and the cooperation between agents.

We will explore three basic approaches for distributed problem solving: the contract net protocol which is based on the exchange of semistructured messages, an agent-based information brokerage, and distributed meeting scheduling. The second approach is exemplified by an actual implementation, the Constraint-Based Knowledge Brokers (CBKB).

Finally we will discuss the actor model by Hewitt.

9.1 Introduction

Agent-based systems are used in a variety of application classes, e.g., in expert systems, in robotics, in computer-supported cooperative work, and in systems for information gathering which support the planned retrieval and collection of information stored in distributed locations (Wayner 1994). Groupware agents may support meeting scheduling (Sen and Durfee 1991a), or else have a central role in workflow management coordinating the information flow between activities as well as between the applications and their respective users.

A central question for the effective deployment of agent-based systems is the following: How can intelligent agents best be designed and customized to meet users' individual needs? Successful steps have been made in the context of linguistic frameworks for multiagent systems, such as Actors (Agha 1986) or agent-oriented programming (AOP, Shoham 1993) as well as in the context of multiagent architectures, e.g., the ones proposed by Bratman et al. (1988), Brooks (1991) and Kaelbling and Rosenschein (1990). In all these cases the agents are assumed to be situated in a flexible environment which they can modify while pursuing their own goals. The goals range from collecting physical items (for robotic agents), or solving scientific mathematical problems (for software agents in massively parallel multiprocessor architectures), to highly interactive types of activities (for dynamic agent families).

The way in which agents communicate and exchange knowledge has been well investigated. The Knowledge-Sharing Effort of ARPA[1] has developed an agent communication language (ACL) in order to standardize the different approaches for agent languages; see also the works of Neches et al. (1991) and Finin et al. (1994).

ACL consists of three parts: A vocabulary (e.g., Ontolingua), a knowledge interchange format (short KIF) and a knowledge query and manipulation language (short KQML).

The underlying idea of the Knowledge-Sharing Effort is based on the definition of agent ontologies. Multiagent systems need a shared view of the environment they model, and of the knowledge they acquire and exchange (e.g., the semantics of objects, the relations between objects, etc). A common ontology classifies an explicit specification of these ontological agreements between multiagent systems. This specification is an unbiased description of the used concepts and relationships between objects and facilitates the knowledge exchange between multiagent systems. As part of the Knowledge-Sharing Effort ontologies for different application domains were developed. They are specified using KIF and definitions provided by the vocabulary in

[1] ARPA stands for the Advanced Research Projects Agency. In addition to ARPA, AFOSR (Air Force Office of Scientific Research), NRI (the Corporation for National Research Initiative) and NSF (National Science Foundation) – all US-based – support the attempt to develop an infrastructure for multiagent systems to communicate and exchange knowledge.

Ontolingua. Each ontology defines the class members, methods and objects for a specific application domain, as well as a description for an unambiguous, context-independent interpretation of these constituents.

The knowledge exchange format suitable for ontology coding is a prefix version of the predicate logic calculus with certain extensions. However, we will not expand on this. KIF contains a large number of logic operators for the representation of quantifying expressions, negations, disjunction and rules. The following example which uses KIF language constructs demonstrates that the area of *table1* is larger than that of *table2*.

Example (KIF).
(>(×(length *table1*) (width *table1*)) (×(length *table2*) (width *table2*)))

KQML – the third component of ACL – defines the actions available for agent communication. So-called performatives enable – besides the pure communication of speech constituents, e.g., the above statement about two tables – the expression of an attitude concerning the content of the linguistic units. For example, the communication might be a request (**evaluate, ask, ask-if, ask-about, ask-one, ask-all** etc.) or an answer to a request (**tell, reply, sorry** etc.).

Performatives are a kind of speech act. In the following example, performatives are printed in bold.

Example (KQML communication performatives). An agent *A* requests from a "share agent" the current price for IBM shares. Language and vocabulary are agreed upon in advance.

(**ask**
:sender *A*
:content (share value *IBM ?price*)
:recipient *share agent*
:reply_to *IBM share*
:language *LProlog*
:vocabulary *New-York-Stock-Exchange-TICKS*)

The answer to the request looks as follows:

(**tell**
:sender *share agent*
:content (share value *IBM 96.625*)
:recipient *A*
:in_reply_to *IBM share*
:language *LProlog*
:ontologie *New-York-Stock-Exchange-TICKS*)

Apart from communication performatives, there are also performatives to define cooperation protocols within multiagent systems. For example, the construct **advertise** allows an agent to publicly announce which KQML requests it is capable of handling.

Example (KQML cooperation performative). During the initialization phase the share agent of the previous example could have made the following announcement, e.g., by broadcasting the message to other agents of the system:
(**advertise**
:sender *share agent*
:content (share value *?share ?price*)
:language *LProlog*
:ontology *New-York-Stock-Exchange-TICKS*)

Furthermore, an agent environment may encompass designated agents with special functionality and services (e.g., facilitators, mediators or brokers). Figure 9.1 depicts the agent F which mediates services between the requesting agent A and the providing share agent S. In Sect. 9.6.2 we will describe in more detail another information brokerage service.

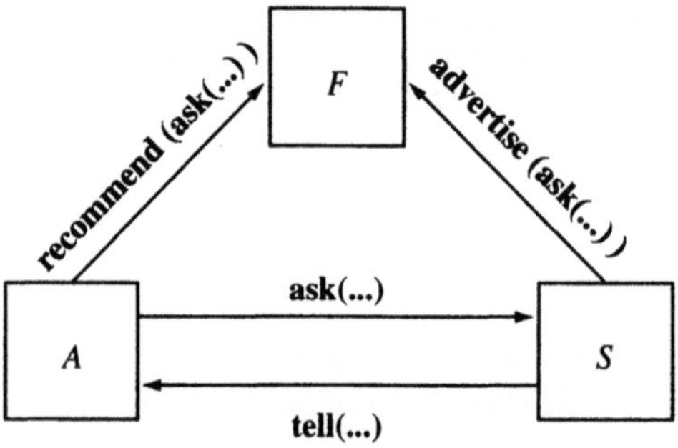

The agent A queries the facilitator F using the **recommend** performative in order to determine which agents might handle certain performatives, in our case **ask**. Potential agents (e.g., the share agent S), will have registered earlier with F. After the names of potential agents have been returned by F the agent A may select one agent and initiate a direct contact using the communication performatives presented above.

Fig. 9.1. Cooperation protocol in KQML

9.2 Characteristics and Classification

In previous sections we frequently used the term agent. We even formulated the method in which agents communicate and exchange knowledge. However, we have not yet provided a definition. Since scientific works on agents often vary in their use of the term, it is not easy to define it. Instead of attempting to provide a generic definition of the term agent we will proceed to list some of the more important features of agents.

Wooldridge and Jennings (1995) give a detailed, although not complete classification of different agent characteristics. In the following, we will discuss some important features of agents which have significant impact on agent-supported groupwork. It must be emphasized that not all agent implementations incorporate all features. Rather, these characteristics illustrate potential frameworks for agent-based applications.

Autonomy. Agents can act without the user's intervention. Being autonomous, they have total control over their activities. They have both an internal state and knowledge about their own actions. This knowledge is either explicitly specified or it can be provided implicitly through information on how and where to obtain the relevant knowledge. Thus, the agents have enough knowledge about the problem domain and the contextual constraints to interpret received messages and react appropriately. During execution, the user has no direct control over the agent's behavior (i.e., he may not directly access and manipulate rules which determine the agent's behavior).

Semiautonomous agents only carry out routine tasks for the user. Exceptional request or situations are referred to the user who handles them personally. The behavior of semiautonomous agents is directly controlled by the user who has read and write access to the rules which specify the agent's behavior.

Social ability. As with humans, agents are able to interact with other agents. This communication may be either implicit or explicit. In the latter case, multiagent systems use structured messages to convey information between agents (e.g., in Actors or AOP which even applies speech acts). Explicit communication will be discussed in more detail in the context of the contract net protocol (see Sect. 9.5). In the implicit case, agents communicate through the impacts their actions have on the so-called world state.[2]

Example (ICQ). The system ICQ (pronounced I seek you[3]) is an agent-based system for finding and contacting people of a previously registered group. Among persons who are currently connected to the Internet using Internet services online, ICQ initiates a connection through which they can exchange messages and files, initiate an IRC session (internet relay chat), or start multiuser computer games.

Social competence of agents which naturally consists of more than just the ability to communicate in some way or another, will not be expanded any further in this overview. Instead, we will turn to other agent features.

Reactivity, proactiveness and reflectivity. Agents are reactive, that is, they react to contextual and environmental changes, such as the receipt of a message or of user's activities.

Agents can be proactive in that they may initiate certain goal-oriented behavior. By querying system parameters or sending messages, they can again instigate the reaction of other agents.

[2] Following the definition by the entomologist P. Grassé in 1959, these agents are called stygmergic (or stigmergic).

[3] http://www.Mirabilis.com

Agents are called reflective if they can monitor their own behavior (i.e., their own execution plans), and modify it in case of environmental changes.

Passive and active agents, user agents. The two characteristics, reactivity and proactivity enable the distinction between passive and active agents. Passive agents act under direct user control. The user explicitly triggers the execution of agent functions (e.g., sorting and filing of electronic messages in the user's mailbox). Unlike passive agents, active agents react to environmental changes or incoming messages, such as requests for information or the execution of functions, autonomously or semiautonomously. Thus, an (active or passive) agent is a self-contained functional unit (e.g., a software module).

Agents which substitute for a user when performing tasks, and which are capable of performing interactive dialogues with the user are often called user agents. As illustrated in Fig. 9.2, user agents observe and imitate user behavior in order to provide the best service for executing routine tasks.

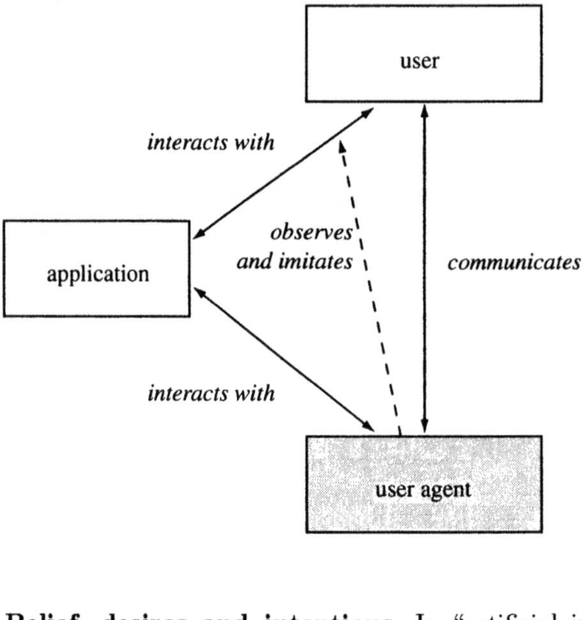

Fig. 9.2. Embedding of a user agent

Belief, desires and intentions. In "artificial intelligence", agents have even been assigned human characteristics. Besides knowledge, an agent also possesses beliefs, desires and intentions. For this BDI architecture, substantial language support has already been developed. Since we will not further expand on this, the reader is referred to the AI literature cited at the end of this chapter.[4]

[4] Note that agents applying KIF and KQML constructs are able to communicate beliefs, desires and intentions.

Mobility. Agents can be mobile. Innovative agent platforms for mobile agents have been developed using Java (especially remote method invocation), Tcl (especially the **send** command), Telescript (respectively Tabriz AgentWare) and the IBM Aglet Workbench.

Example (Telescript). General Magic's Telescript is an interesting communication language for implementing agent-based information services in heterogeneous networks. Rather than replacing a programming language, Telescript complements conventional languages by adding constructs for naming, for path finding and constructs for access control in distributed applications. In general, Telescript agents are interpreted and thus need a specific execution environment, the Magic Cap. By this means, security risks (e.g., virus attacks or unrestricted resource usage), are reduced, and the portability of systems developed with Telescript is drastically increased.

A typical application domain is teleshopping (White 1994a), where agents migrate through the network searching for articles on their shopping lists. They collect information, deliver electronically available quotations and can even order for the user. In this context, the term nomadic agent is used increasingly.

Telescript supports special commands for migration: **go** initiates a migration; **meet** starts the process where two agents, e.g., a user agent and a service provider agent, "meet" within the network in order to settle a shared transaction. The command **send** creates copies of the original agent and distributes these copies to all relevant network locations (e.g., to nodes where products necessary to satisfy a predefined shopping list are offered). According to White (1994b), the Telescript agents migrate between computers including even PDAs (personal digital assistants) using all kinds of different transport protocols.

The problem for Telescript agents of locating and addressing the destination computers is solved in different ways: If the destination is already known as providing the requested Telescript service, then simply its name or network address is used. This is the case whenever the requesting agent has been created by the provider itself or when the agent has been made aware of the relevant network address during prior network shopping tasks. Otherwise, the agent may query electronic address books which list all Telescript service providers.

Example (Tabriz AgentWare). Telescript was not a commercial success which is why General Magic changed its strategy in the summer of 1996 towards the use of the world wide web as the platform for mobile agents. The Magic Cap execution environment was replaced by Tabriz AgentWare.

Example (IBM Aglet Workbench). The so-called Aglet Workbench was developed by IBM Research. As opposed to conventional Java Applets, which load only executable program code (from a server) onto a client machine, an Aglet carries both the respective data and the execution state along with the Java program code. Aglet based agents can migrate at any time between computers. Such Aglet based agents can be considered as mobile CORBA objects (see Sect. 1.6.4). Thus, together with GMD Fokus and The Open Group, IBM has presented standardization plans to the Object Management Group (OMG); see GMD Fokus (1996). These plans favor Java and the Aglet Workbench, discarding any standardization attempts made by General Magic.[5]

Veracity, benevolence and rationality. Veracity is another agent feature. It is assumed that agents do not knowingly communicate false information.

An agent's benevolence is also important for the achievement of complex goals: The agent does not have conflicting subgoals. It will always try to perform its task or to achieve its subgoals with all the means available to it.

An agent acts rationally. Based on its internal state and the local knowledge, an agent will always work towards achieving its goal, rather than working against it.

Learning. As we have seen in the example of Telescript agents, the aspect of learning can be essential for agents (e.g., learning about the location of a provider, learning about efficient paths to providers, etc). A learning agent can easily adapt to a changing environment by extending and modifying its behavior according to its own experience (e.g., by adding new rules or by changing existing rules).

A user agent learns either by interacting with other agents (e.g., by proactively querying the other agents' knowledge bases), or by communicating with the user. In the latter case the learning may be based on user feedback, explicit user programming by examples, or else by observing user interactions with the application (see Fig. 9.3).

Example (Open Sesame!). Open Sesame! by Charles River Analytics, Cambridge, Massachusetts, USA, is a commercial user agent which detects and learns often repeated human activities, such as "each Monday, around 9 a.m., the user starts his email application and processes his electronic mail" or "after files have been discarded, the garbage is often emptied". Derived from the constructed profile information, Open Sesame! creates a list of propositions. In the aforementioned examples, this list could read: "Would you like me to start the email application each Monday at 9 a.m.?" or "Would you like me to empty the garbage whenever something has been discarded?". The learning algorithms of Open Sesame! works well. However, the proposals derived from the learned information are mostly unusable. A nine months study conducted at Zurich University (Hoyle and Lueg 1997) revealed that the proposals made by Open Sesame! did not really ease the workload. Out of 129 proposals, only two were immediately accepted by the users! (Some other proposals were stored for later inspection. Moreover, both accepted proposals had to be manually adapted.)

[5] Early in 1997, General Magic also decided in favor of a Java solution and it joined standardization attempts of IBM, GMD Fokus and The Open Group.

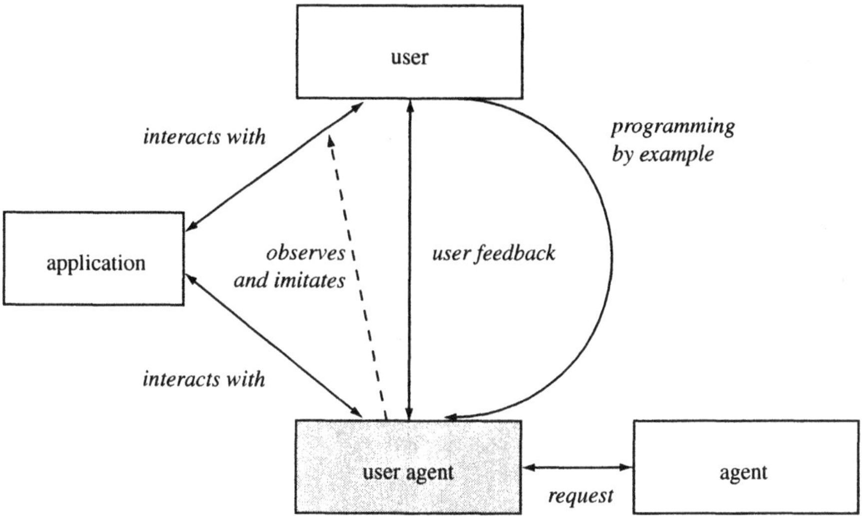

Fig. 9.3. Learning of a user agent

The "failure" of Open Sesame! as a learning user agent was not due to the implemented learning algorithm, but to the choice of the application environment. A desktop environment does not appear to be an appropriate place for user agents. The systems MessageWorld, Firefly and WiseWire have chosen other more promising environments.

Example (MessageWorld). The system MessageWorld designed by Apple Computer realizes a user agent that sorts and displays the flow of incoming and already stored email messages according to user profiles and user "interests". Messages are managed in different online databases. Rose et al. (1995) discuss the rendezvous mechanism which is applied to find and retrieve the relevant messages. After reading an email message the user specifies its value, by pressing either the thumbs-up button (i.e., the message was interesting), or the thumbs-down button (i.e., the message was not of any interest). Based on the correlation of user profiles the system assigns user specific values of interest to still unread messages.

Example (Firefly). The Firefly system from MIT (Massachusetts Institute of Technology, Cambridge, USA) – commercialized by Firefly Networks Inc. (now owned by Microsoft) – utilizes learning user agents for a popular Internet application, finding persons sharing an interest in film, literature or music. New users are questioned by Firefly agents with respect to their preferences in these fields utilizing that information to create user profiles. Agents correlate the profiles in order to identify users with similar taste and then to introduce them to each other anonymously. Firefly also makes recommendations for new entries into a user's profile (like new films, books, or CDs) found in the profile of other users of similar taste. User feedback on agent recommendations enables Firefly to improve a user profile over time.

Example (WiseWire). The system WiseWire designed by Empirical Media utilizes learning user agents for similar applications.[6] Like Firefly, the system creates a user profile with incremental refinement and improvement through user feedback. WiseWire focuses on reader preferences and generates so-called personal newspapers, that is newspapers designed in accordance with an individual user profile. The news material is gathered within the Internet (e.g., Usenet articles). Users sharing interests can be introduced to each other.

The examples above presented only a few possible applications of learning agents concentrating mainly on learning of user intentions. For other applications, learning algorithms, and knowledge representations suitable for learning, the reader is referred to the reading list at the end of this chapter.

9.3 Modeling

The preceding discussion demonstrated that an agent can act/react, communicate with other agents (and the user), and cooperate "intelligently" with other agents during a problem solving process. This last feature is especially important for multiagent systems, since in this case several agents have to cooperate and coordinate their actions in order to achieve the solution of the overall problem.

Example (cooperation among scientists). According to Kornfeld and Hewitt (1981) the cooperation among scientists can be viewed as a model for distributed problem solving processes. It has four characteristics:

1. *Monotony*: Scientists publish their findings. These are added into the common knowledge pool (e.g., libraries). Past findings remain in storage even if they have been contradicted by recent research.
2. *Commutativity*: Scientists are interested in their field both before and after findings relevant to them have been published.
3. *Parallelism*: Scientists work concurrently on common research areas. They influence each other (e.g., at workshops and conferences).
4. *Pluralism*: There is no central agency deciding on the value of publications and research results.

In practice monotony and commutativity are often not dealt with sufficiently resulting in "reinventing the wheel". That is due to research findings sometimes getting lost or being published in a false context, as well as the fact that it is often easier to redo another scientist's work and publish it as "brand new" than it is to do completely unique research.

[6] http://www.wisewire.com; now under the Lycos umbrella.

The cooperation among scientists and the identified four characteristics may serve as a guideline for the integration of cooperation into multiagent systems.

9.3.1 Distributed problem solving

The area of Distributed Problem Solving (DPS) developed various approaches which allow distributed (semi)autonomous agents to cooperate in order to solve complex problems and accomplish tasks which might not be solvable by one individual system. From the problem solving point of view, distribution implies the decomposition of the problem into a set of subproblems and the dissemination of the subproblems to the appropriate agents which solve them autonomously and concurrently. The final solution of the global problem can be generated by composing the solutions of the subproblems. Thus, agents can be viewed as problem solvers which cooperate to generate the solution of the global problem. They must coordinate their knowledge, goals, skills and execution plans.

The distribution of a problem among several problem solvers raises the following three questions:

1. How can a problem description be divided into subproblems which are then distributed among the available problem solvers? This question is closely related to that of allocating subproblems and synthesizing subresults into an overall result. Moreover, the decomposition is influenced by causal and temporal interdependencies among the subproblems.
2. How can the sufficiency of the knowledge available for triggering the (sub)problem solving process be determined?
3. How can the distributed problem solving process be efficiently organized, despite communication and coordination overhead? After all, decomposition and distribution of work only makes sense if
   - the overall problem is solved better by several agents than by one, e.g., it is faster, less expensive, etc.;
   - only the partition into subproblems enables a solution, since subproblems generally require less knowledge and/or less resources.

First attempts at solving these issues will be discussed in the following sections.

9.3.2 Agent model

There exist a variety of models describing the generic structure of an agent. One of the most prominent ones is the insect model (see Fig. 9.4) presented in Haugeneder (1994); see also Deen (1994).

An agent exchanges information with its environment (the user, other agents) via communication channels and the communicator.

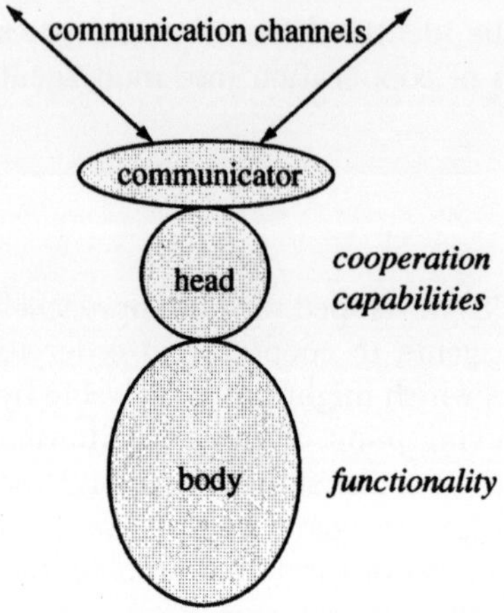

Fig. 9.4. Generic agent model

The head encapsulates the cooperation capabilities of the agent; it is the mediator between the agent's functionality and the problem solving context. The head maintains knowledge about the agent's capabilities (e.g., the scope of its competence), other agents' skills (often there is only partial information available), the current task/problem, the problem hierarchy (e.g., the overall goal and the subproblems), as well as the communication protocols at the application level.

The body encompasses the actual agent functionality.

9.3.3 Conceptual framework

The conceptual framework which may be applied to model the different phases of the agent's problem solving process (see Fig. 9.5) consists of four basic elements: goals, plans, tasks and the functionality required for task execution.

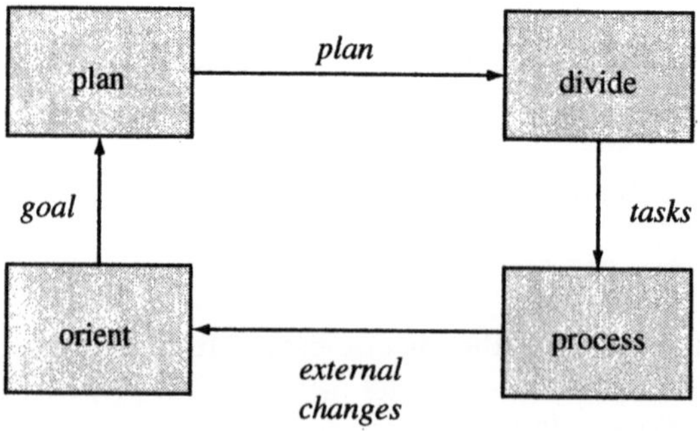

Fig. 9.5. Phases of an agent during problem solving

In the beginning, the agent typically analyzes its current state especially with respect to dependencies on external influences which change dynamically. The problem solving process may be triggered either externally or internally. In the former case, the agent receives a goal proposition (e.g., by another agent), and evaluates whether or not the proposed goal is compatible with its own goals. The agent may negotiate with the proposing agent to refine the original goal. Preconditions stated by the user or a change of the agent's state can result in an internal activation of the problem solving process. Active goals are achieved either conjunctively (i.e., all goals must be achieved), or disjunctively (i.e., the achievement of one goal will suffice). Moreover, goals, both conjunctive and disjunctive, can be subdivided into subgoals for processing.

After orientation, an agent plans its moves for reaching the goal. Already existing plans can be retrieved from a plan library, or a new one can be constructed by using forward or backward inferencing. In the former case, the agents starts from its current state and determines a path towards the goal, whereas in the latter case the agent construes a plan based on a path from the goal towards the current state. In both cases, several executable plans are feasible.

The research community developed a variety of different planning algorithms (partial planning, means-ends planning, hierarchical planning, or conditional planning).

During the next phase, the agent selects a workable plan and divides it into smaller steps and subtasks. The selected plan may include tasks which must be performed by other agents.

Finally, during the last phase the agent processes all subtasks assigned to itself. In general, processing will cause external changes to the world state resulting in a renewed agent orientation, thus influencing the identification of new or the refinement of existing goals. Some agent systems also handle partial plans which require a repeated alternation between the planning and the processing phase. This approach is known as "plan a little bit, execute a little bit".

Figure 9.6 describes the data flow within the agent between the four phases of the problem solving process.

9.3.4 Layer concept

According to M. v. Bechtolsheim (1993) agents can be modeled along two dimensions defining three layers for each dimension (see Fig. 9.7):

1. The behavioral dimension differentiates the layers according to the procedural interactions between agents. It facilitates the identification of functionality which an agent must have in order to make its autonomous behavior possible, at the same time supporting cooperative goal-oriented work on a common problem.

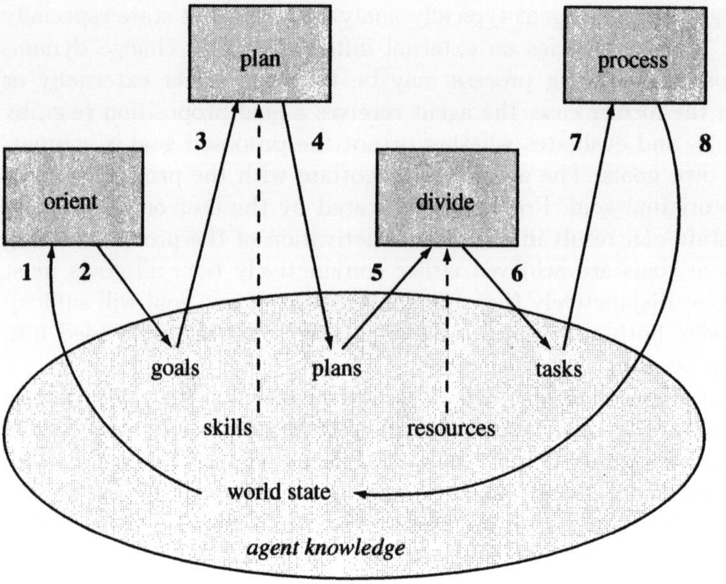

1. The world state provides input information when the problem solving process is triggered.
2. Orientation results in a set of active goals to be achieved.
3. Besides the agent's skills, the planning process also accepts the active goals as input.
4. Plans are constructed.
5. A plan is selected.
6. Plan selection and knowledge about available resources enable the specification of tasks.
7. Tasks are processed.
8. Processing modifies the agent's view of the world state.

Fig. 9.6. Data flow within an agent

The behavioral dimension distinguishes between the layers orientation, planning, and coordination which have already been discussed within the conceptual framework for modeling the phases of an agent (see Sect. 9.3.3).

2. The structural dimension describes different levels of abstraction of the agent functionality and its embedding into a multiagent system. Within the structural dimension, there are three layers:
   - The interaction layer provides the basic infrastructure for communication. It encompasses the agent's ability to contact other agents and exchange messages with them.
     The agent's internal actions are often decoupled from message handling enabling asynchronous communication (i.e., sending and receiving of messages occurs concurrently with the execution of agent functions).

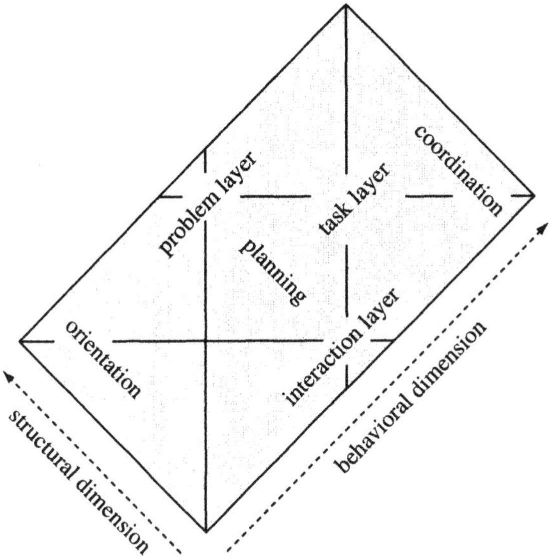

Fig. 9.7. Layered architecture of an agent

- The task layer encompasses the agent's skills to process or delegate tasks. The semantics of the messages depends on the problem domain of the current tasks. Request and result are important message types. Functional aspects of this layer include task decomposition, task processing and the combination of subtask results.
- The problem layer includes the agent's ability of handling and solving problems. Agents have a knowledge base and a functional unit, the so-called inference engine, for drawing conclusions from facts and rules. In this layer, message types are defined from the perspective of the problem domain.

Teufel et al. (1995) use the 3C model known for classifying groupware to categorize the degree of agent interaction according to the structural dimension:

1. Communication is the message exchange between multiple agents on the interaction layer.
2. Coordination refers to those aspects of communication utilized for the coordination of task-oriented agent actions. Most of the coordination takes place on the task layer.
3. Cooperation refers to aspects of communication needed for the negotiation and agreement of shared goals. Parts of cooperation can be assigned to the problem layer.

9.4 Cooperation among Agents

The phenomenon of cooperation which is well-established in the human environment may also be applied to agent interaction. The level of interaction ranges from coexistence, hostility, self-interest and benevolence to self-denial. If agents merely coexist, they solve their problems independently of each other, never interacting, while in the case of hostility they even counteract each other. In the case of self-interest agents discontinue cooperation if they no longer benefit from it. True cooperative behavior starts with benevolence where agents cooperate as long as it has no negative impact for themselves. The extreme of self-denial puts cooperation before a consideration of negative impacts on the agent's own interests.

Research in distributed artificial intelligence focuses on self-interest and benevolence.

9.4.1 Cooperation by (semi) structured messages

In general, cooperation between agents is based on explicit communication (i.e., agents send messages to transfer knowledge and requests). The basic message types in the context of distributed problem solving are requests and answers. The message content which is in most cases restricted to textual information, can range from values, formal and informal descriptions, to constraints. Conventional email systems prescribe only the structure of the message header, whereas the format of the message content is left to the user. For multiagent systems this approach is unreasonable because an unstructured message content would require a quite complex implementation of the agent's communicator and head in order to interpret free form messages correctly.

Classification. According to the internal structure of the message content, messages are nonstructured, semistructured, or structured:

- The textual message content of unstructured messages is free in format. Since the message content has been formulated for a human reader, the agent would require natural language processing for automated text interpretation.
- In a semistructured message the message content is only partly free in format. That portion of the message content whose structure is well-defined can be automatically interpreted by agents without natural language processing.
- The content of a structured message is completely predefined in format and is only intended for agent consumption; the messages are often not in human-readable form.

Example (Semistructured message). The following example shows a semistructured message announcing a meeting. The fields Meeting time, Location and Duration allow only values of a predefined format in order to enable automatic interpretation by calendar agents (e.g., entering the meeting into an electronic calendar). The field Topic contains free format text and will not be interpreted by the agents. It is intended for the human reader.

Meeting time: *Do, Jan 12th, 1999, 10:30*
Location: *G101*
Duration: *1 hour*
Topic: ...

Semiformal system. Semistructured messages are based on the notion of a semiformal system (Malone 1989) which:

1. represents and interprets information that is formally specified,
2. permits the human to create and interpret formal information informally,
3. allows the borderline between the formal interpretation by the computer and the informal interpretation by the user to be easily changed.

Semiformal systems are especially useful in heterogeneous environments where there is no clear separation between human tasks and agent tasks. They support the coexistence of humans and agents in the same environment. For example, some people use personal agents to cooperate in the distributed meeting scheduling process, while other people perform the required requests manually. Thus, semiformal systems facilitate a smooth transition from a purely human-oriented environment to a completely agent-based environment.

Key concepts of semiformal systems are the representation of passive information by semistructured objects, the storage of semistructured objects in fields and the processing of semistructured objects by agents. Semistructured objects can specify both messages as well as tasks, human roles and user profile information. Fields capturing semistructured objects can easily be adapted to a new environment by the user. Within agents the automatic processing of semistructured objects is often specified by active rules.

Example (Semiformal system for message filtering with rules).
An example for a system which uses semistructured messages is Object Lens (Malone and Lai 1988) which provides intelligent filtering and dissemination of emails. Agents filter emails according to predefined rules. The following semistructured message will be used to demonstrate the usage of such rules.

To: *project team* /* message header */
From: *project manager*
Date: *Jan 8th, 1999, 12:20:35* /* Time of announcement; it is automatically generated, similar to email */
/* In conventional electronic mail systems, only the message header is structured and subdivided into fields. In semiformal systems also parts of the message content itself are structured and divided into fields. */

Type: *meeting announcement*
Location: *G101*
Day: *Thursday*
Time: *Jan 12th 1999, 10:30*
Duration: *1 hour*
Agenda: ...

Code fragment (Rule 1). Rule 1 deletes the announcement of a meeting taking place on a Monday or Friday.

```
if ((Type of message N = 'meeting announcement') and
    (Day of message N ∈ {'Monday', 'Friday'}))
then delete message N;
```

Code fragment (Rule 2). Rule 2 marks messages sent by the project manager as important.

```
if (From of message N = 'project manager')
then Characteristic := 'important';
```

Code fragment (Rule 3). Rule 3 files all 'important' meeting announcements in the folder for important announcements.

```
if ((Type of message N = 'meeting announcement') and
    (Characteristic ='important'))
then move message N to "Folder for important announcements";
```

Code fragment (Applying of rules). On arrival of a message, the three rules will be applied according to their linear order.

```
receive(message N)
    int numrules := 3;      /* number of available rules          */
    for i := 1 to numrules do apply rule i;
```

During rule processing the execution of later rules are influenced by the results and side-effects of earlier rules. In our example, Rule 2 assigns the value 'important' to the field Characteristic, and thus, influences the execution of Rule 3. Furthermore, the user may customize and adapt the rules to his personal needs.

Filtering functions. Rule-based message filtering is of high practical value and a variety of commercial email readers already support email filtering functionality. We distinguish between cognitive filtering, social filtering and economic filtering.

- Cognitive filtering selects messages based on the receiver's interest specified by his user profile. On receipt of a message the message content is matched against the user profile, e.g., does the message content include certain keywords. Depending on the result of the match the message may be filed in one of the appropriate folders or even be discarded.

- Social filtering selects messages based on personal and organizational relationships. The main focus is on the sender of a message. For example, if a message originated with the boss, the filtering agent interprets it as important and assigns the highest priority to it.
- Economic filtering applies cost-value functions to classify incoming messages. For example, long messages requiring a lot of disk space might have less value than short messages.

9.4.2 Cooperation strategies

A number of different cooperation strategies between agents have been proposed ranging from strongly hierarchical master-slave relationships, to the less hierarchical contract net protocol (Smith 1980), to the sharing of common goals. We distinguish between five major types of cooperation:

1. *Accidental cooperation:* Agents act independently of each other and are unaware that they implicitly support the goals and actions of one or more agents of the group. An agent's actions can support another agent without having explicitly requested the assistance.
2. *Master-slave cooperation:* As the name already suggests, one agent, the master, delegates a task for execution to another agent, the slave. This type of cooperation models a strong hierarchical relationship with the master agent being in total control of the delegated task and the duration of the relationship.
3. *One-way cooperation:* If an agent requests another agent's support, yet leaves it full autonomy about its positive or negative decision to help or not, then this is called one-way cooperation.
4. *Reciprocal cooperation:* Reciprocal cooperation provides advantages for both agents involved in the cooperation. Both agents decide autonomously on the continuation of cooperation by exchanging information.
5. *Sharing common goals:* In this case agents not only exchange information with respect to their individual tasks and problems, but they also communicate their goals. The cooperating agents follow shared goals when pursuing the problem solving activities.

Cooperation based on sharing common goals. In a multiagent system, the problem solving phases of the different agents influence each other when the agents pursue the common goal. Thus, the cooperative distributed problem solving process can be interpreted as the distribution of goals, plans and tasks across multiple agents. The common goal and the plan achieving the goal are determined by negotiations between the participating agents. No agent constructs a local plan without first negotiating with the other agents.

Figure 9.8 illustrates the fundamental phases within a multiagent system during the cooperation intended to achieve a common goal.

Despite the fact that during the phases *orient* and *plan* multiple agents are involved, both phases must lead to results which are acceptable to all

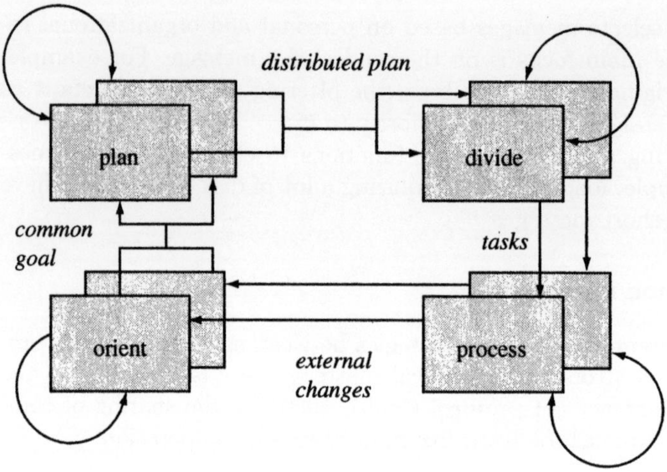

Fig. 9.8. Phases of a multi agent system sharing common goals

cooperating agents. While orientation provides a common goal, the planning phase results in a distributed plan to which all agents have to commit. On the other hand the subsequent phases *divide* and *process* deliver agent specific achievements. In the first case each agent divides its overall task into smaller subtasks, while in the latter case each agent processes all its subtasks triggering thus, agent-specific external changes.

9.4.3 Cooperation methods

Depending on the type of interaction, multiagent systems may support one or several cooperation methods.

The cooperation method *request data* (see Fig. 9.9) distinguishes between agents consuming information and agents providing information. If the consumer agent has desired information locally available within its knowledge base, then this local information is used. Otherwise, an information provider is instructed to search for the requested information and deliver it to the information consumer.

In the case of the cooperation method *update data* (see Fig. 9.10), an agent (periodically) supplies information which is then processed by the information consumer to update his own knowledge base. The (periodical) information is automatically delivered to the consumer agent without any explicit request message. This method seems particularly suitable for the conveyance of sensor data; if the sensor data change the new value is automatically forwarded to the agent which processes these data, e.g., a robotics agent planning a robot's movements or actions.

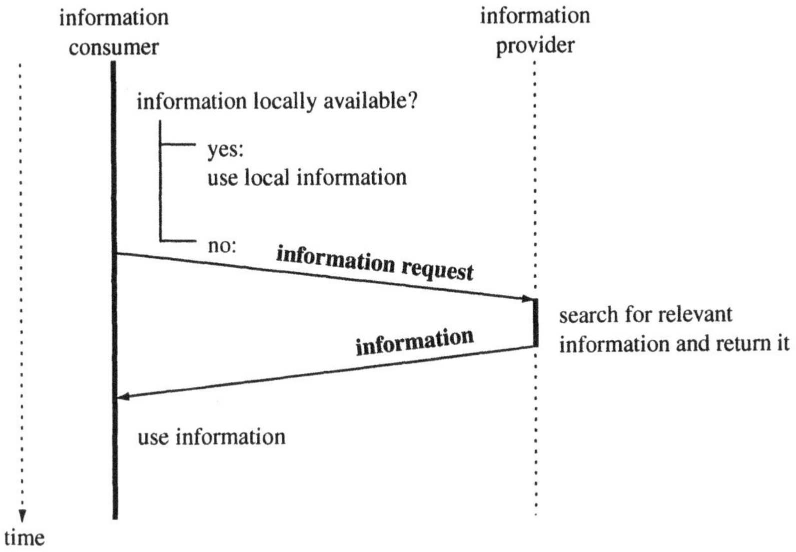

Fig. 9.9. Cooperation method request data

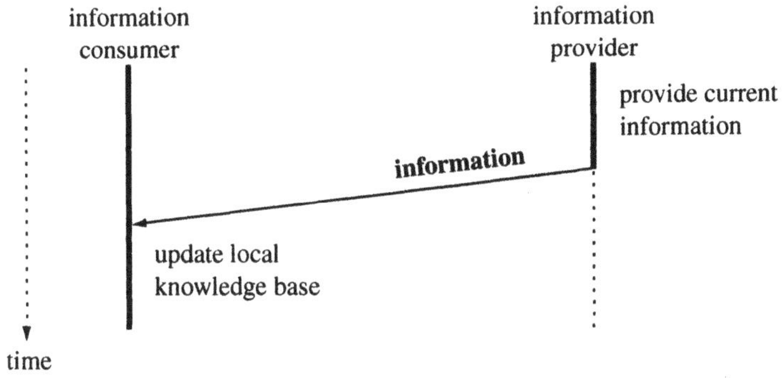

Fig. 9.10. Cooperation method update data

The cooperation method *trial and error* (see Fig. 9.11) allows the delegation of a task to another agent for execution. The method consists of three phases:

1. The initiator prepares the task description and the execution constraints. If an error occurs, the task is terminated and the local environment is cleaned up.
2. If task preparation is completed successfully then the initiator sends a task execution request to the selected contracting agent.
3. After the contractor has performed the task and transmitted the results, the initiating agent checks the results. If this evaluation is negative then the task is listed as a failure and it must eventually be repeated using

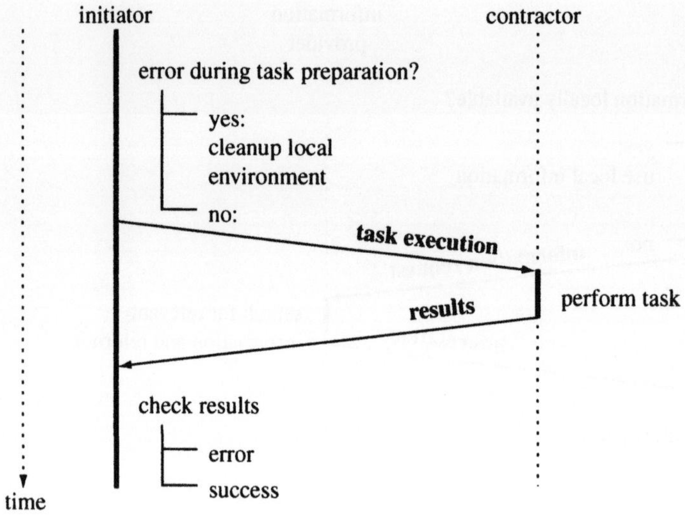

Fig. 9.11. Cooperation method trial and error

a modified task description or context. Otherwise, the task is executed successfully.

The cooperation method *safe trial and error* (see Fig. 9.12) is an extension of the method *trial and error*. The initiator coordinates the task to be delegated with the selected contracting agent who explicitly must commit itself. If the contracting agent rejects such a commitment the task delegation is canceled and the initiator might determine another contractor. In the case of the contractor's consent, the initiator prepares the task execution. Should an error occur, then in addition to the local cleanup the contractor is notified to withdraw its commitment. The task is terminated. If the task preparation did not cause any error then the remaining procedure is analogous to that described as phases 2 and 3 of method *trial and error*.

Besides the four cooperation methods mentioned above, there are several other, much more complex methods, such as the negotiation among agents, the delegation of a task to one of several bidders, or the joint voting of several agents offering different solutions to the same problem.

9.4.4 Communication types

The cooperation and coordination among agents requires the exchange of information. In addition to the zero communication (i.e., no explicit communication takes place), there might be simple communication or communication based on conversations.

- The situation of zero-communication might be of interest during network partitionings. Since agents cannot communicate with each other by ex-

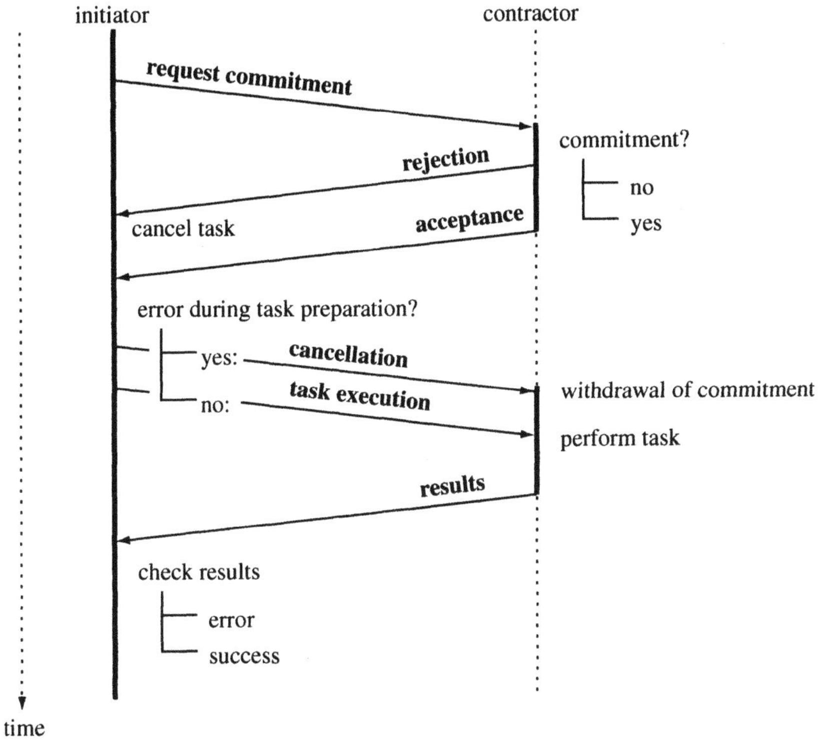

Fig. 9.12. Cooperation method safe trial and error

changing messages they attempt to deduce other agent's intents rationally by using the available information with decision matrices taken from game theory. The advantage of zero-communication is the omission of any communication overhead. However, since the local decision does not take into account any state changes of the remote agents, the goals and the plans of agents might no longer be consistent (i.e., different agents might pursue different goals).

- Simple communication restricts agent interaction to a finite set of well-defined information signals which are exchanged via a simple communication protocol.
- In the case of conversation-based communication, agent interaction is well-formalized by predefined message types (see the KQML performatives on p. 417).

The following section discusses one prominent example of this communication type, the contract net protocol.

9.5 The Contract Net Protocol

The contract net protocol was one of the first approaches to provide a general framework for distributed problem solving by a multiagent system (Smith 1980). It supports an application level protocol for conversation-based communication between problem solving agents and facilitates distributed control during the problem solving effort. Special emphasis is put on

- localizing those agents which are eligible for solving the available subproblems
- the negotiation between agents for the information exchange with respect to subproblem descriptions, required agent capabilities and subproblem solutions.

The main elements of the problem solving process are the assignment and the processing of (sub)tasks necessary to achieve the overall goal. The protocol distinguishes between two agent roles, the manager who tries to delegate a task, and the bidder who applies for performing the task. If multiple bidders are available and they support the required functionality the manager negotiates with the bidders until a suitable agent is determined to which the (sub)task is then assigned. These roles are not permanently assigned to agents, and they may change during the problem solving process. For example, the bidder of a contracted task might decompose it into smaller subtasks which it then delegates to other agents, thus becoming a manager.

The contract net protocol allows task distribution among agents. It may be compared with the announcement of a building project and the collecting of bids of different building constructors.

9.5.1 Basic concepts of the contract net protocol

The interaction between the manager and the set of bidders is based on the following fundamental concepts:

- There is no centralized control for task assignment and task execution.
- Information exchange occurs in both directions which means that the information flows both from the manager agent to the bidding agents and vice versa.
- Each partner evaluates the information from its own local perspective. A mutual selection mechanism ensures the agreement of both, the manager and the selected bidder. Selection is pluralistic (see Sect. 9.3); there is no central agency deciding on the value of the individual bids.
- The contract net protocol uses only structured messages. Task announcement, task bid and task assignment are the primary message types applied during the negotiation process. Furthermore, the protocol supports other message types, such as request, acknowledgement, termination and report.

Each negotiation process has five distinctive phases:
1. Task announcement by the manager;
2. Bids submitted by one or several bidders;
3. Selection of one bid by the manager;
4. Task assignment by manager;
5. Task execution by the selected bidder.

9.5.2 Task announcement phase

At the initiation of a new task the manager constructs a task announcement message incorporating fields, such as task description, required qualification of the bidding agent in order to be eligible, and the requested format of the bid. Additional fields are the deadline for submitting a bid as well as other criteria to be met by a bidding agent. For example, if the manager announces the task of reviewing a journal article then one of the additional criteria might be the reviewer's experience (i.e., the number of articles the agent has already reviewed for the journal). The field values of a task announcement message must follow a well-defined and fixed syntax in order to allow for agents' automatic interpretation and processing; thus, the contract net protocol handles only structured messages.

The task description enables a potential bidder to evaluate the task's priority in comparison with other announced tasks. Furthermore, the required qualification specified in the task announcement message, gives a potential bidder an indication of whether or not it is qualified for the task. In the latter case it will refrain from submitting a bid, thus reducing the network load by eliminating bids of ineligible agents.

The content and the format of a bid is prescribed by the manager. It serves as a guideline for both the manager and potential bidders, and it facilitates the comparison of different bids. Bids submitted after the deadline are generally discarded by the manager. However, it is not necessary to exactly synchronize all clocks within the multiagent system; the worst that might happen is the selection of a suboptimum, but still eligible bid by the manager.

The task announcement message may be sent

- to a selected bidding agent (point-to-point),
- to a group of potential bidders (multicast) whose capabilities the manager might know from earlier problem solving processes,
- to all potential bidding agents within the network (broadcast).

Example (Task announcement message). Suppose the task to be announced is the review of an article submitted for publication in a journal. The editorial board (i.e., the manager agent) distributes the task announcement via multicast to all reviewers known to the editorial board. The announcement message includes the task description and the required qualification of the reviewer.

To: *reviewers* /* multicast to all reviewers known to the journal */
From: *editorial board*
Date: *Dec 1 1999, 08:00:52*
/* time of announcement; it is automatically generated, similar to email */
Type: *task announcement*
Contract: *22-3-1* /* internal task number */
Deadline for bid: *Dec 17 1999, 17:00*
/* task description */
Review: *article name and number*
Deadline for submission: *Feb 1 2000*
/* deadline for the submission of the review */
/* qualification of eligible bidders */
Knowledge domain: *research area of the article*
/* The knowledge scope of the reviewer must match the research area of the article. */
Language skills: *English* /* only English-speaking reviewers are eligible */
/* additional information: to be specified by the potential reviewer */
Name: /* name of reviewer */
Knowledge domain: /* knowledge domain of the reviewer */
Language skills: /* language skills of the reviewer */
Submission date: /* date by which the reviewer assumes he will complete and submit his review */
Number of reviews: /* number of reviews already done for the journal */

9.5.3 Bid creation phase

The internal processing structure of a bidder is outlined in Fig. 9.13.

The process *contract* accepts task announcements addressed to the bidding agent. If the bidder fails to meet the requirements then the announcement is immediately discarded. Otherwise, the agent creates a bid making sure that the bid if accepted can be executed in time. There are two possible ways to create a bid:

1. The process *contract* waits until the process *execute* has finished all running tasks which means that *contract* remains idle as long as the bidder is busy.
2. The processes *contract* and *execute* run in parallel.
   Internal planning is necessary before *contract* can generate and submit a bid.

Example (Task bid). A potential reviewer makes a bid to review a submitted journal article. The bid contains a detailed description of his background.

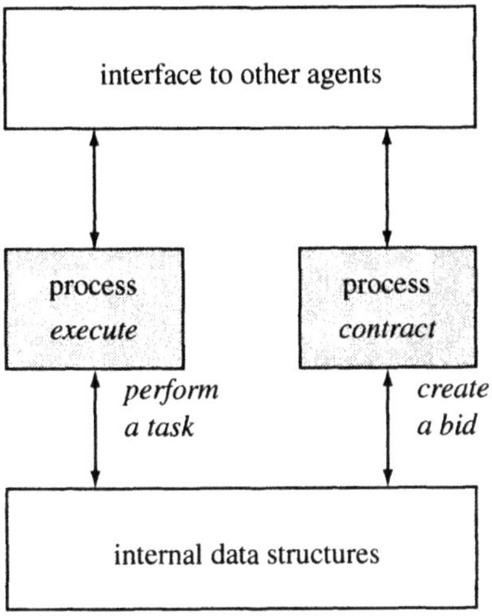

Fig. 9.13. Architecture of a bidding agent

To: *editorial board*
From: *reviewer*
Date: *Dec 5 1999, 10:00:04* /* time of bid submission; it is automatically generated, similar to email */
Type: *task bid*
Contract: *22-3-1*
Bid expiration: *Dec 10 1999* /* description of the bidding agent */
Name: *G. U. Tachter*
Knowledge domain: ...
Language skills: *English*
Submission date: *Jan 15 2000*
Number of reviews: *10* /* The bid can also contain additional fields in which the bidder requires more information with respect to the review. This information will be useful to him if he is assigned the task */
Formatting: /* Additional information on the required format of the review; this information is to be provided by the manager, i.e., the editorial board */

9.5.4 Bid selection phase

The manager decides whether or not a bid is satisfactory, and when the task should be assigned to a selected bidder. The decision may depend on the time at which the manager evaluates the received bids:

1. *immediately after receiving a bid:* If the bid N_A meets the required criteria (e.g., the submission date, the number of reviews) and the bid is still valid then the task is assigned to the bidder.

Code fragment (**evaluate_bid**).

```
global review limit := 5;      /* minimum number of reviews that a bidder
                                  should have supplied prior to the current
                                  one for the journal                      */
evaluate_bid (message N_A)
  if ( (Submission date of message N_A ≤ deadline) and
     (Number of reviews of message N_A ≥ review limit) and
     (Bid expiration of message N_A ≥ today))
  then return N_A;             /* assign task                              */
  else return nil;             /* do not assign task                       */
```

2. *after several bids have been received:* In this case, the incoming bids are added to a queue **SEQ** N **of message**. As soon as the queue has a certain length, the best bid is selected from the queue. "Best" – as shown by the following code fragment – may mean that the review will take the least time.

Code fragment (**select_bid**).

```
global review limit := 5;
select_bid (SEQ N of message)
                        /* N is the sequence of bids received            */
  int i = 1;
  int j;
  message bid = nil;
  while ((bid = nil) and (i ≤ last of SEQ N)) do
    if ( (Number of reviews of message N_i ≥ review limit) and
       (Bid expiration of message N_i ≥ today))
    then offer := N_i
    else i := i + 1;
  for j := i + 1 to last of SEQ N do
    if ( (Number of reviews of message N_j < review limit) or
       (Bid expiration of message N_j < today)) then continue;
                        /* the reviewer of bid N_j does not meet the criteria,
                           or else his bid has already expired            */
    else if (Submission date of message N_j
                < Submission date of bid)
      then bid := N_j;     /* search for bid which has the earliest possi-
                              ble submission of the review                */
  if ((bid = nil) or (submission date of bid > deadline))
  then return nil;         /* there is no bid satisfying the deadline spec-
                              ified by the manager agent; the task is not
                              assigned                                     */
  else return bid;         /* assign task; the bid meets the deadline for
                              the submission of the review; the task is
                              assigned to the selected bidder              */
```

3. *after the deadline for submitting bids has been expired:* The selection process is similar to the previous code fragment **select_bid**.

If the deadline for bids expires without receiving any satisfactory bids then the manager agent can either resend the task announcement (probably with less demanding qualification requirements) or assign the task to the best bidder, even though this bid had previously not been considered eligible. However, the manager can also wait for late arriving bids or decide to cancel the task.

9.5.5 Task assignment phase

After a bid has been selected, an assignment message together with the additional information requested in the bid is sent to the bidding agent who thus becomes the contractor for the task.

Reasons for lack of any bids can be: all potential bidders are currently busy with other tasks, or else qualification requirements are so high that no bidding agent is able to satisfy them. Immediate reply is a possible solution to that problem meaning that the manager requests in the task announcement potential bidders to send an immediate return message specifying the reasons why they are not currently submitting any bid. If a bidder replies that he is busy the manager may decide to resend the announcement later. Otherwise, if the bidder does not meet the requirements, the manager may relax the qualification requirements in order to attract bids.

9.5.6 Task execution phase

Figure 9.14 depicts the state transitions of the contract net protocol from the contractor's perspective. If the contracting agent processes the task alone, then the states *announced*, *assigned* and *suspended* are dropped. All activities necessary for task processing are then executed in the state *ready*.

9.5.7 Assessment of the contract net protocol

The contract net protocol is an opportunistic protocol for distributed problem solving based on negotiations between agents (see Fig. 9.15). Available tasks are allocated by mutual selection between the manager and the bidding agent. A potential bidder selects from the received task announcements while the manager chooses the best bid received.

The task allocation of the contract net protocol is in contrast with the master-slave mechanism where the manager has all the decision making power; only he determines the agent which will perform the task while the performing agent cannot select or reject the allocated task. Blackboard systems are the other extreme with only the performing agent deciding which task it will execute. The manager has no selection possibility.

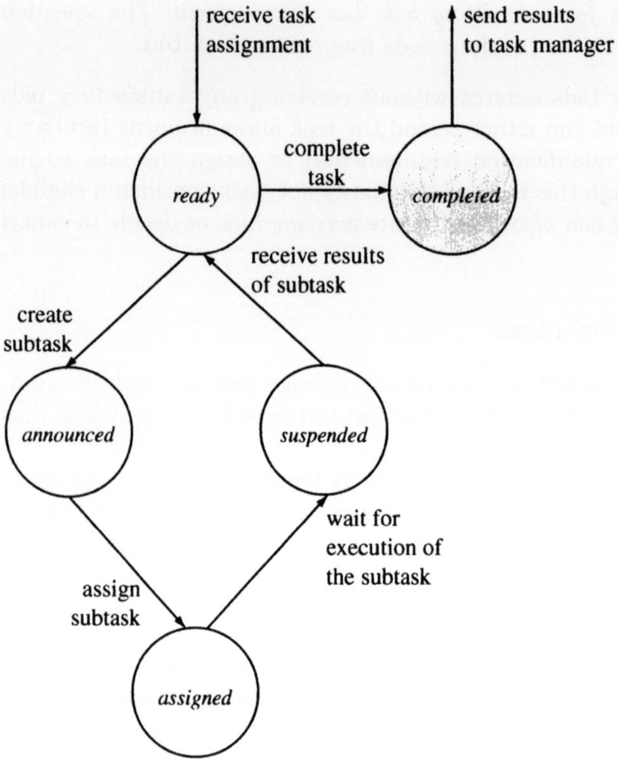

Fig. 9.14. State transitions of the contract net protocol

The applicability of the contract net protocol depends on the task characteristics. It is especially suitable for tasks which agents can automatically decompose into smaller subtasks. However, the subtasks must still be complex enough to make all the communication overhead worth the effort. Major emphasis is given to the local decision, and the selection is based on negotiations among agents. Overall the contract net protocol improves the information exchange between agents.

9.6 Agent-based Information Brokering

This section will discuss a second important area of distributed problem solving: the agent-based information brokering. There are a number of similarities with the contract net protocol. However, the negotiation process is more formal, and due to the formal specification language the description of (sub)problems is a lot more flexible.

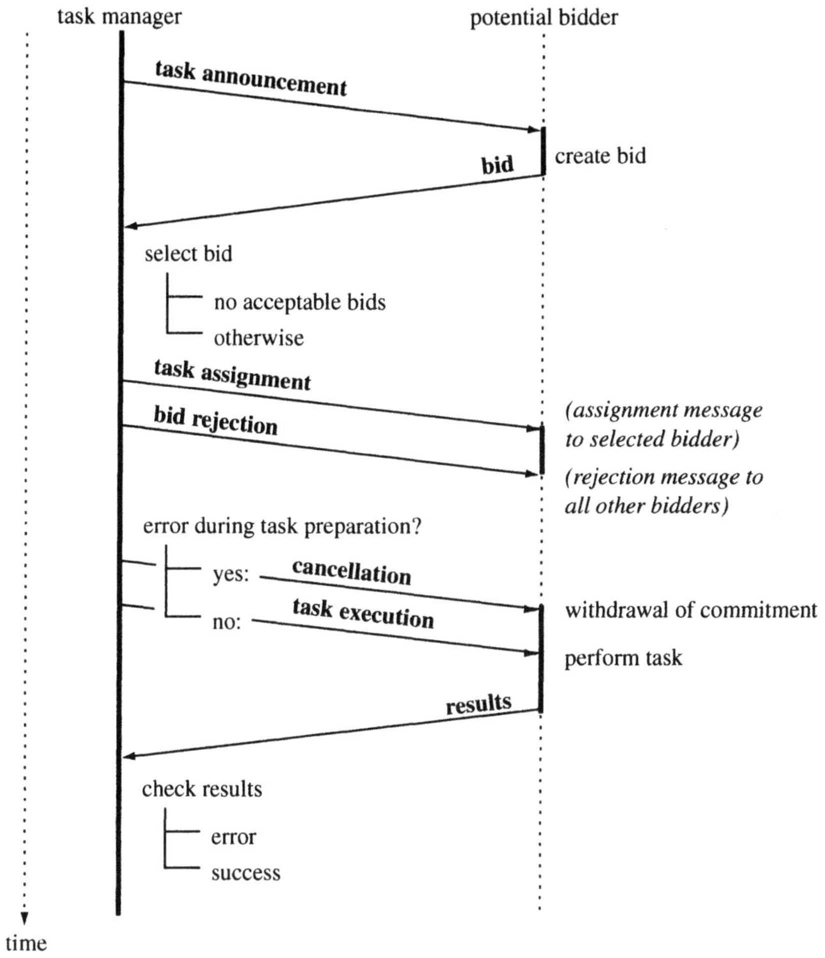

Fig. 9.15. Agent cooperation of the contract net protocol

9.6.1 Systems of agent-based information brokering

An agent-based information brokering system encompasses conceptually several subsystems that perform the following tasks:

1. *Localizing information sources:* One of the major problems currently is the lack of standardized metainformation describing the individual information sources, the content they manage as well as the interface to access it. Also, a complete and correct exploitation (e.g., of all available world wide web pages), is hampered by frequent modifications of content and structure. Index/search services do only statistical interpretation and management of metainformation.

2. *Searching in information sources:* Most information sources use a different syntax for specifying queries, thus queries cannot be reused with multiple information sources.
3. *Retrieving relevant information:* Different information services often use incompatible ranking algorithms for evaluating and prioritizing the identified information.
4. *Generating, recommending and providing applicable knowledge:* A problem for this task is the lack of any systematic methodology for information brokering across multiple, heterogeneous groups.

The problems associated with these tasks are well-known. First attempts to solve these open issues and to standardize interfaces and metainformation have already been made.

Example (STARTS). At Stanford University, Palo Alto, California, USA, providers of information services and managers of information sources started negotiations in 1995, aimed at solving the first three problems listed above. The initial companies to participate in the STARTS project (Gravano et al. 1997) were Fulcrum, Infoseek, PLS, Verity and WAIS. By 1996, Excite, HP, Microsoft Network and Netscape had joined in.

Localizing information sources. The rapid growth of the Internet and the growing importance of Internet applications, such as the world wide web, Wide-Area Information Servers (WAIS) (Kahle and Medlar 1991), gopher systems and countless unstructured data collections, call for innovative mechanisms for efficient localization of relevant information sources. Barbara and Clifton (1992) write:

> "... a large percentage of valuable information is not stored in such systems[7], but as a wide variety of unstructured and semistructured data such as electronic mail, documents, files and spreadsheets. In addition, applications must deal with heterogeneous services such as an electronic library, an airline reservation system or a weather information system. Many times even just locating these services can be an overwhelming task."

Currently, some promising index/search services are being tested and evaluated within the Internet.

- The system INQUERY (Callan et al. 1992, 1995) is currently being developed at the University of Massachusetts in Amherst, USA. It first calculates the appropriateness of the available heterogeneous information sources with respect to a given query. Then it chooses the best fitting sources and conducts the search processing.

---

[7] Referring here to conventional databases.

- The system gGLOSS[8] (Gravano and Garcia-Molina 1995) developed at Stanford University, Palo Alto, California, USA, addresses a similar idea. It keeps sophisticated statistics on available information sources to determine an estimate of which information sources are most appropriate for a given query. The search process is performed through a ranked list of information sources.

  INQUERY and gGLOSS foster and refine an approach which has already been successfully applied in WAIS, the provision of metainformation on stored data. Both systems provide their indexes dynamically and are tailored to individual needs, via a single query. The indexes guide individual searches across the set of selected sources.
- The system ALIWEB[9] summarizes information about the available sources and provides them as static metainformation.
- The system Archie (Emtage and Deutsch 1992) periodically contacts a set of registered Internet file servers to create a file index which serves as a point of entry for queries.

Furthermore, there are available a variety of user agents to facilitate and enhance navigation in the world wide web. Among them are: Folio Web Retriever by Folio Corp., FreeLoader by Freeloader Inc., Metz Netriever by Metz Software Inc., Smart Bookmarks by FirstFloor Inc., The PointCast Network by Pointcast Inc., WebEx by Traveling Software Inc. and Web Whacker by ForeFront.

Search in information sources. All index/search services aim at finding relevant data satisfying the given query (recall), and only the given query (precision).[10]

The Internet already provides numerous index/search services for homogeneous information sources (Obraczka et al. 1993), all of which have more or less good values for recall and precision. Among many others, we know:

- Veronica[11] for gopher databases;
- AllTheWeb[12], Alta Vista[13], Lycos[14], Northern Light[15] and Yahoo[16], for web documents (HTML format).

[8] generalized Glossary-Of-Servers Server
[9] http://aliweb.emnet.co.uk/
[10] Let s be a query and $B(s)$ be all relevant data (with respect to s) available in the information source. $D(s)$ are the data found by processing the query s and $RD(s)$ ($\subset D(s)$) the actually relevant data of query s. Recall measures the portion of the relevant data found, i.e. $recall(s) = RD(s)/B(s)$. Precision measures which subset of the found documents is actually relevant, i.e., $precision(s) = RD(s)/D(s)$.
[11] gopher://gopher.unr.edu/11/veronica
[12] http://www.alltheweb.com/
[13] http://www.altavista.com/
[14] http://www.lycos.com/
[15] http://www.northernlight.com/
[16] http://www.yahoo.com/

Furthermore, there are a large number of index/search services for online databases, e.g., the service NCSTRL.[17]

As soon as appropriate index/search services were implemented, intelligent agents, e.g., Harvest (Bowman et al. 1994a), started to exploit these services. The following list provides an overview of the requirements which an agent-based information brokering system must meet.

1. *Information specification:* The system must support searches in a possibly continuous information flow according to predefined criteria. For example, an agent listening in on news channels extracts those messages which deal with prime rate changes. By changing the criteria the user may dynamically adapt the agent behavior.
2. *Information to be excluded:* In vast information spaces a user often does not know exactly what to look for or what the search process will actually render (i.e., how many results will a query return). It may therefore be necessary to exclude certain kinds of information (e.g., by specifying the following problem description: "find all books by Umberto Eco which are non fiction" rather than "find all books by Umberto Eco").
3. *Dynamic scope of competence and learning:* The scope of an agent should be dynamically adapted as the problem description is incrementally refined (Borghoff et al. 1996b). Furthermore, an agent should maintain a history of previous queries and their results. Subsequent queries may build upon the results of earlier queries. Let us assume that query "find all books by Umberto Eco which are non fiction" is followed by the query "find all literary essays by Umberto Eco". Of course, all literary essays have already been identified and retrieved as part of the processing of the first query. The second query need only extract the relevant data from the agent's history list and return them as the result of the second query.
4. *Cooperation:* During the problem solving process, cooperation between the agents as well as the users should be supported.
5. *Interagent communication:* During the problem solving process, communication between cooperating agents should be flexible enough to adapt to changing goals or modifications to the agent's environment.

Retrieval of relevant information. Despite the support of the aforementioned systems (see also Fikes et al. 1995), the user is often overwhelmed by the vastness of the information sources, especially in the Internet. It is very difficult to identify and retrieve relevant information, and use it for one's own purpose.

Harvest (Bowman et al. 1994a) exploits as an index/search service, both Glimpse (Manber and Wu 1994) and Nebula (Bowman et al. 1994b).

The project TSIMMIS (Chawathe et al. 1994) retrieves information units from a variety of heterogeneous information sources for which special wrappers have been implemented. Through these wrappers, heteroge-

[17] http://www.ncstrl.org

neous information sources appear to be homogeneous. Furthermore, TSIMMIS adds additional semantics to the retrieved information units to enhance query processing. The latter aspect of TSIMMIS is closely related with the Constraint-Based Knowledge Brokers, which we will discuss in detail shortly.

Other information brokering services (e.g., metasearch engines) are All-in-one Search,[18] Ariadne by FU Berlin, Germany,[19] EchoSearch by Iconovex,[20] Garlic by IBM, iFind by Inference Corp.,[21] MetaCrawler by the University of Washington, Seattle, Washington, ProFusion by the University of Kansas, Lawrence, Kansas, SavvySearch by the Colorado State University,[22] Fort Collins, Colorado, and WebCompass by Quarterdeck (now aquired by Symantec)[23].

Generation, recommendation and provision of applicable knowledge. Agents often filter and sort the query results according to user-defined criteria. Besides simple filtering, the automatic generation of abstracts, language analysis (i.e., determine the language of a given document), and semantic text analysis play an important role. Work on these topics has been restricted to research laboratories. However, some consortiums[24] have already been founded to tackle these problems and develop commercially applicable solutions (e.g., solutions for knowledge management). Autonomy, Inc.[25] is developing a powerful knowledge management system which integrates sophisticated algorithms for text analysis and which supports information filtering according to user profiles.

The following examples illustrate the provision and recommendation of knowledge for information brokering across multiple, heterogeneous groups. All examples are based on the following fact (Kautz et al. 1997a):

> "The difficulty of finding information on the world wide web ... has led to the development and deployment of various search engines and indexing techniques. However, many information-gathering tasks are better handled by finding a referral to a human expert rather than by simply interacting with online information sources."

Example (Learning group). As part of a seminar the participants may collaboratively identify and retrieve the relevant documents applying some of

[18] http://www.allonesearch.com/

[19] http://ariadne.inf.fu-berlin.de:8000/

[20] http://www.iconovex.com/products/echosearch/echos.htm

[21] http://www.inferencefind.com/

[22] http://www.savvysearch.com/

[23] http://www.qdeck.com/qdeck/products/webcompass/

[24] The consortium for the KRAFT project (universities of Aberdeen, Wales, Cardiff and Liverpool, as well as the British Telecom; see also http://www.csd.abdn.ac.uk/~apreece/Research/KRAFT/), and the MeDoc consortium (Gesellschaft für Informatik (GI), Springer and Fachinformationszentrum Karlsruhe; see http://medoc.informatik.tu-muenchen.de/).

[25] http://www.autonomy.com/

the aforementioned information brokering services (e.g., Internet search engines). The retrieved documents as well as the final seminar papers represent the seminar results which are made publicly available. Later on, a second group (group 2) which may be composed of students writing their master theses can reuse the seminar results. If a query of group 2 overlaps with a query of the seminar group the search results of the seminar group are immediately reutilized and provided to group 2 without actually performing an additional search; the previously retrieved documents are immediately accessible to group 2. Only knowledge domains which were not already covered by queries of the seminar group result in actual information searches.

Example (Jasper). Jasper, developed by the British Telecom Laboratories, is a simple agent-based information brokering service for collaborating groups. Jasper agents search the world wide web, store and recommend information units. As in Firefly or WiseWire, group members with similar interests are informed on the latest "discoveries" (e.g., by sending an email message). Besides the usual information about documents (URL, document title, creation/modification time), Jasper agents also create and manage additional metainformation, such as key words and abstracts which facilitate the categorization of documents.

Example (GroupLens). GroupLens, developed by Konstan et al. (1997) is a recommender system for Usenet articles. The ratings of the person himself as well as of other users are the basis for recommending or rejecting an article. The user interface might only display recommended articles, thus reducing the cognitive overload of the user. So-called rating servers (also known as Better Bit Bureaus) collect evaluations and distribute them according to user-specific profiles. The motto is (Resnick et al. 1994b):

> "The rating servers predict scores based on the heuristic that people who agreed in the past will probably agree again."

Other recommender systems are Fab (Balabanovic and Shoham 1997), Phoaks (Terveen et al. 1997), ReferralWeb (Kautz et al. 1997b) and Siteseer (Rucker and Polanco 1997).

Example (Embedding of queries into a recommender system). The Knowledge Pump system extends recommendations (and user notifications) to search results as well as ongoing search activities (see Fig. 9.16); see also Grasso et al. (1998) and Glance et al. (1998).

Example (Group topics in Alta Vista and Verity). An important aspect of information brokering across multiple groups deals with the provision of so-called group topics. They support a structured orientation within a large information space. Group topics are either created dynamically, based on individual queries, or else statically for a specific user group. In the first case, the group topics are extracted from the actual search results. For example,

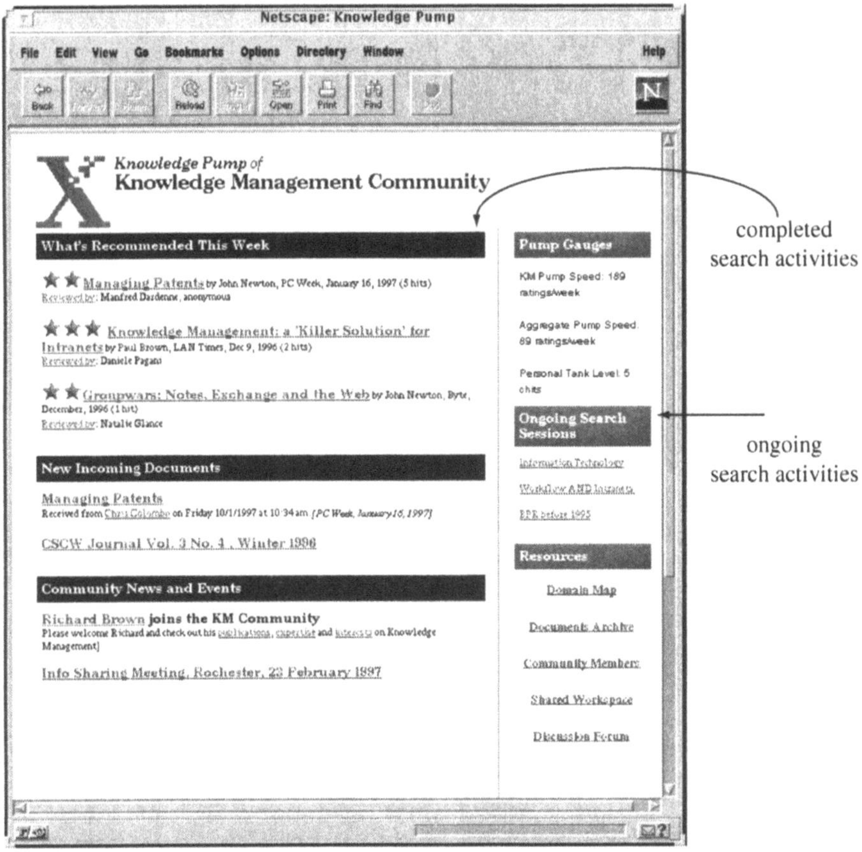

Fig. 9.16. Knowledge Pump's recommendations of search activities

Alta Vista generates search-specific topics graphs out of the words repeatedly occurring in the search results (see Fig. 9.17). Remarkably, Alta Vista works without an externally predefined ontology, instead selecting the relationships from the retrieved data alone. Consequently, the topics graph is very much dependent on the data quality.

The topics first allow for a better orientation within the information space as defined by the search and second they facilitate the refinement or coarsening of the query specification.

Statically predefined topics graphs are specified by experts and then made available to other users. First approaches can be found in the so-called topic-trees by Verity.[26]

[26] http://www.verity.com

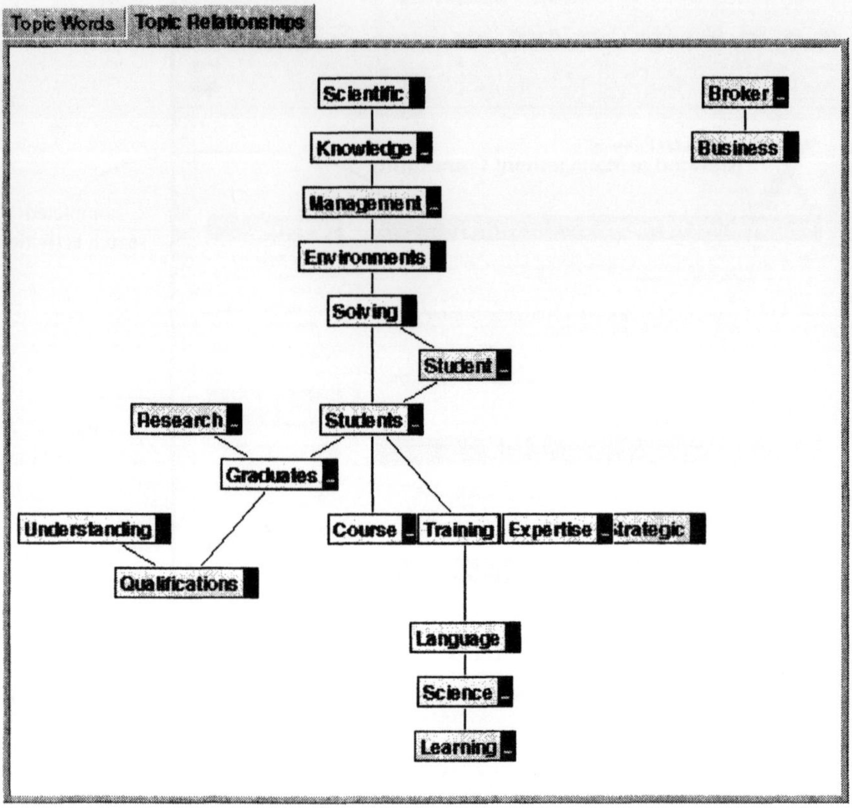

Fig. 9.17. Alta Vistas topics graph automatically generated from the search for information on "knowledge brokers"

9.6.2 Constraint-Based Knowledge Brokers

The Xerox Research Centre Europe in Grenoble, France, has developed the model of Constraint-Based Knowledge Brokers (CBKBs) which exploits constraints to support knowledge-intensive tasks executed by concurrent agents, and views the management and manipulation of information in distributed environments as a form of distributed problem solving (see Andreoli et al. 1994–1997a).[27] Constraints are used both for the specification of the information and the dynamic management of the agent's scope of competence.

CBKB agents explicitly separate aspects of local problem solving, based on computations specific to a single agent, from aspects of global problem solving, derived from the interaction of different agents. On the one

[27] http://www.xrce.xerox.com/research/ct/projects/cbkb/home.html.
A commercial version has recently been released by Xerox Multilingual and Knowledge Management Solutions (MKMS) under the name of *askOnce*; see also http://www.xerox-emea.com/askOnce/index.htm.

hand, the cooperation between agents is based on explicit communication (i.e., agents send messages to transfer knowledge and requests). The message content can range from values, formal and informal descriptions, to constraints. On the other hand, the system supports implicit communication during query processing, and thus it facilitates information brokering across multiple groups (e.g., an agent may investigate the history of previous group processes and exploit the search results generated as part of these processes).

The agents involved in distributed problem solving recursively decompose a given problem into smaller subproblems until a single agent can process it and compute the appropriate solutions for it. In order to enable automatic decomposition, problem descriptions should already contain "potential breakpoints".

Generator. The CBKB model formalizes the problem-subproblem relationship. The functionality of a CBKB agent includes the dynamic creation of new, specialized agents for solving subproblems as well as a generator. Intuitively, a generator defines the decomposition of a given problem into subproblems and the composition of the subproblem solutions into the final solution of the problem.

Given an abstract domain of values $\mathcal{D}$, representing pieces of knowledge which are manipulated by agents. A generator is a mapping $\mathcal{D}^n \mapsto \wp(\mathcal{D})$, which produces new pieces of knowledge from existing ones. The set of generators of all involved agents identifies a subset of the abstract knowledge domain which is stable under these generators, that is, if the arguments of the generator are within the subset, the generator result is also within the same subset.

Definition 9.6.1 (Γ-stable). *Let E be a subset of the abstract knowledge domain and Γ a set of generators. E is Γ-stable if: $\forall g \in \Gamma$, $\forall a_1, \ldots, a_n \in E$, $g(a_1, \ldots, a_n) \subset E$.*

The class of stable sets is closed under intersection, so that it has a smallest element in the sense of inclusion, given by the intersection of all stable sets. The minimal stable set, also called the minimal model, represents the intended semantics of the set of generators (Andreoli et al. 1994).

For the computation of the minimal model, we can use a traditional fixpoint approach, as the following mapping indicates:

$$\begin{array}{l} T : \wp(\mathcal{D}) \mapsto \wp(\mathcal{D}) \\ \forall E \in \wp(\mathcal{D}), T(E) = \bigcup_{g \in \Gamma,\ a_1, \ldots, a_n \in E} g(a_1, \ldots, a_n). \end{array} \tag{9.1}$$

The minimal model M is the smallest fixpoint of T:

$$M = \bigcup_{n \in \aleph} T^n(\emptyset). \tag{9.2}$$

The mapping T supports an incremental computation of the minimal model using the following recursive rule: $E_0 = \emptyset$ and $E_{n+1} = T(E_n)$.

The argument a_i, $i \in \{1, \ldots, n\}$ of the generator g represents a solution for the i-th subproblem. a_i may be either a value which was computed or retrieved from a database by the agent responsible for the subproblem, or else a constraint, e.g., $0 < a_i \leq 10$.

The arguments $a_1, \ldots, a_n$ represent the breakpoints within the initial problem specification for the automatic decomposition into subproblems. The special argument a_0 refers to the result of the agent computation (i.e., to the solution of the overall problem which is be solved by the agent).

The number n of arguments for the generator g specifies the number of subproblems created by the agent. The agent has the arity n and is called *broker/n*. The arity n is only of local importance; it solely depends on the number of subproblems of the decomposed initial problem. The agent which sent the original problem specification has no knowledge of the number of subproblems created by the broker/n. With respect to the decomposition of problems and the composition of subanswers brokers act as autonomous agents. Thus, it is possible for a broker/n to send a problem description to a broker/m in which $n < m$.

The generator g of the broker B composes answers to the original problem r out of the subanswers to subproblems. For an individual subproblem several contacted agents may provide multiple subanswers which are forwarded independently to broker B. Even multiple answers from a single agent may be received by the broker B at different times. Upon receipt of a subanswer the generator g of the broker B attempts to compose an answer to the problem r out of the newly received and already previously received subanswers. The resulting answer will be checked by broker B against the initial constraint of r in order to decide if it represents a valid answer. If there are multiple subanswers available for certain subproblems the generator g will construct all possible combinations to compose answers for the problem r.

Example (Decomposition of a problem description). Suppose the broker/2 decomposed the initial problem r into two subproblems r_1 and r_2. For r_1 the broker/2 received two answers, and for r_2 three answers. The generator g of broker/2 will construct a solution space consisting of six potential solutions for r. By checking the initial constraints of r only valid solutions are extracted from the solution space and propagated to the agent which requested the solution of r.

The process of checking the solutions of a problem and determining whether or not they satisfy the constraints is called constraint solving. Prasad et al. (1995) proposed a negotiation-driven multiagent retrieval approach where inconsistencies between different subanswers were dynamically resolved.

Scope of competence. We define an agent's scope of competence as a subset of the knowledge domain which does not overlap with problem descriptions of already solved problems. In other words, an agent's scope of competence encompasses the complement of those elements of the minimal model which the agent has already generated. The problem allocation depends on the agents' scopes. A problem is assigned to that agent which, due to its current scope, is able to solve, at least partially, the problem.

In the following, Ψ is an agent's scope and Φ a problem description. The agent creates a specialized agent S which is responsible for exploring the subset $\Psi \cap \Phi$ in order to create the appropriate solutions. Henceforth, the original agent has the reduced scope $\Psi \cap \neg\Phi$, with $\neg\Phi$ being the complement of Φ. All future problem requests concerning the scope of the specialized agent S will be directly processed by S. By reusing former results, redundant work can be avoided. Furthermore, scope decomposition avoids the creation of agent replicas which would all solve the same problem. Thus, infinite loops during recursive problem solving cannot occur.

Formal problem description. The simple forward chaining of the CBKB model can be refined by taking into consideration the interdependencies between input and output of several generators. We assume that an agent knows the interdependency between input and output of the local generator. Thus, the formal problem descriptions provide a top-down filtering on the set of values which a generator creates as possible solutions during problem solving. An agent knows how to decompose a problem into subproblems, and how to combine subanswers into solutions for the initial problem. The mechanism for combining subanswers which were computed by other agents we will present below.

In order to cooperate, agents must understand each other. This means that all problem requests, and also all the answers to the problem requests, must be formulated in a common language even if the agents perform local translations. The CBKB model uses a single formalism, the so-called feature constraints, to specify problems, answers and the scope of agents.

In simple terms, feature constraints are multisets of attribute-value pairs (Aït-Kaci et al. 1994). Between attribute-value pairs, interdependencies can be defined. Furthermore, relations ($>$, $<$, $=$, $\neq$, *substring of* etc.), and variables are allowed for value entries. As the following code fragment illustrates a query request for operas by Richard Wagner can be formulated as a feature constraint. The expected result is an opera. In the code fragments the problem domains are highlighted by bold print and the attributes by italics.

Code fragment (Request for information on operas).

```
O                         /* O is the so-called constraint variable; a result as-
                             signment to O must satisfy the following require-
                             ments.                                          */
   O: opera,              /* request domain                                  */
   O: composer ⟶ K, K: 'Richard Wagner'
```

The CBKB model applies the predicate **split** to refine the scopes of agents. The operation divides an agent's scope into two new domains. One of these domains is defined by the received problem request and it represents the scope of the agent specialist which handles the request. The other domain represents the refined, and thus smaller scope of the original agent.

Typically, at system initialization a set of initial agents is provided. Each of these agents has a predefined scope covering a subset of the selected knowledge domain. The sizes of the predefined scopes are application dependent and they may range from very specialized constraints to general descriptions of a constraint space covering the minimal model. By processing problem requests new agents and agent specialists are cloned. Each of the newly cloned agents handles only a subset of their parent scope. This results in a continuous refinement of the scopes until the requested subset of the domain is handled by an agent specialist. In the extreme case, after repeated scope refinements the system contains only agent specialists.

Scope splitting requires[28] a special representation of feature constraints as well as an adaptable, efficient mechanism for constraint solving. Andreoli et al. (1997a) introduce signed feature constraints which allow limited use of negation and incorporates the expressiveness for the kind of scope splitting mentioned above.

Definition 9.6.2 (signed feature constraint). *A signed feature constraint Ψ is a tuple $\langle x + \Phi_0 - \Phi_1 \ldots - \Phi_n \rangle$, with x a variable and $\Phi_0 \ldots \Phi_n$ feature constraints.*

Ψ is defined as follows:

- *Suppose X_0 is the set of all free variables in Φ_0 except variable x;*
- *For each $k = 1, \ldots, n$ let X_k be the set of all free variables in Φ_k (but not in Φ_0) except variable x;*

$$\Psi = \exists X_0 \; (\Phi_0 \wedge \bigwedge_{k=1}^{n} \neg(\exists X_k \; \Phi_k)) \tag{9.3}$$

x is the only free variable in Ψ. It is called the constraint variable of Ψ. The Φ_k, $k = 1, \ldots, n$, represent the information excluded from the scope.

Example (Scope splitting). Assume the agent's scope is represented as a signed feature constraint. Furthermore, the agent processes requests concerning opera information. A query specifies a composer's name, and the agent returns the list of all opera titles written by this composer. Assume further that the agent need not generate subproblems to generate a solution (i.e., the arguments $a_1, \ldots, a_n$ are not needed). Instead, the agent searches an attached opera database in order to answer requests. The initial scope of the agent is specified by the following code fragement.

[28] Andreoli et al. (1995) discuss this topic in more detail.

Code fragment (initial scope of an opera agent).

```
X                       /* constraint variable of the scope              */
+                       /* it follows Φ0                                  */
  X: a0 ⟶ O,            /* the expected result is an opera title         */
  O: opera              /* the agent is initially responsible for all possible
                           operas                                         */
```

If the agent receives the problem description "find all operas by Richard Wagner" (see p. 455 for the constraint specification), it spawns an agent specialist in charge of exploring the operas of Richard Wagner.

Code fragment (Scope of the Wagner specialist).

```
X                       /* constraint variable                           */
+                       /* it follows Φ0                                  */
  X : a0 ⟶ O,
  O : opera,
  X : a0 ⟶ O',
  O': opera,            /* Note the variable renaming. For simplification and
                           also in order to remain as close as possible to the
                           definition of scope splitting, we neglect aspects of
                           scope normalization                            */
  O': composer ⟶ K, K : 'Richard Wagner'
```

The original agent continues with the following, reduced scope.

Code fragment (reduced scope of the original agent).

```
X                       /* constraint variable                           */
+                       /* it follows Φ0                                  */
  X: a0 ⟶ O,
  O: opera,
-                       /* it follows Φ1                                  */
  X: a0 ⟶ O,
  O: opera,
  O: composer ⟶ K, K: 'Richard Wagner'
                        /* This indicates that the agent is responsible for all
                           operas except those composed by Richard Wag-
                           ner. The "excluded information" Φ1 is symbolized
                           by the "-"; see also Definition 9.6.2.         */
```

As outlined in Fig. 9.18 the agent specialized on operas of Wagner searches an attached opera database and returns the results to the requester. The following code fragment illustrates that the reply is an element of the knowledge domain.

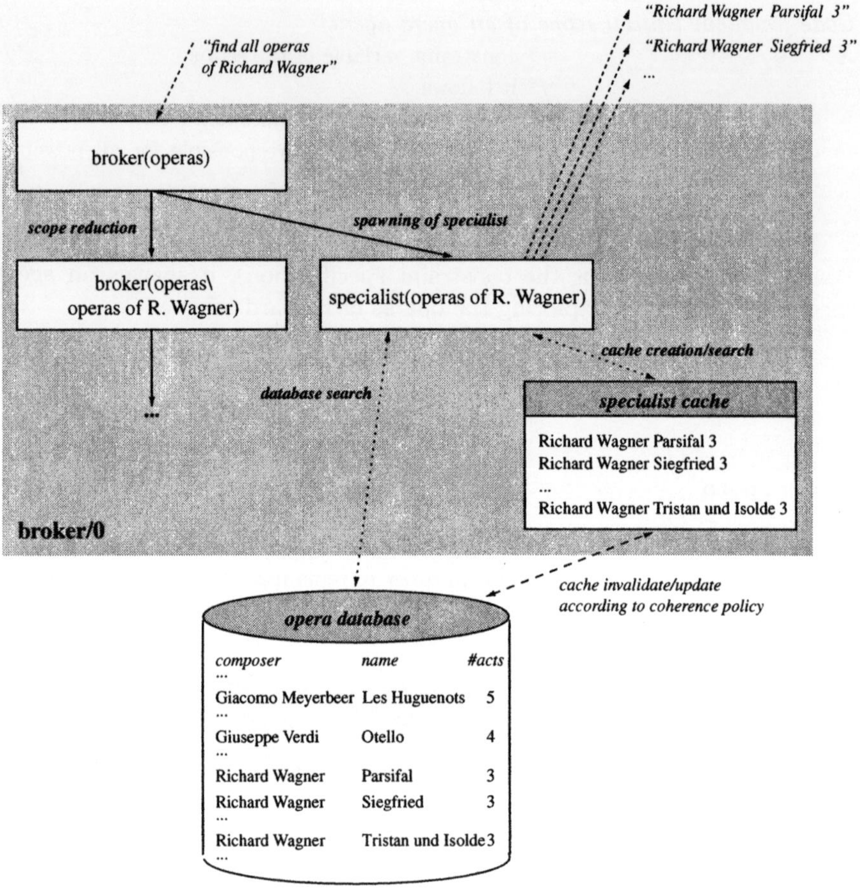

Fig. 9.18. Scope splitting and creation of a specialized agent

Code fragment (result example for an opera request).

O /* constraint variable */

O: **opera**,

O: *composer* $\longrightarrow K$, K: 'Richard Wagner',

/* The problem description encompasses the problem solution, the so-called entailment. */

O: *name* $\longrightarrow N$, N: 'Parsifal',

O: *number_act* $\longrightarrow A$, A: 3

/* The set of result attributes (here names and number of opera acts) depends on the information available in the attached database. */

This agent specialist on Wagner remains active (i.e., whenever another request concerning Wagner operas is submitted, it reuses the already collected results and returns them as an answer of the request). The original agent, due to its scope reduction, will no longer react to requests concerning Wagner operas.

Code fragment (Different opera request).

```
O                          /* constraint variable                  */
   O: opera,
   O: composer ⟶ K, K: 'Giuseppe Verdi',
   O: number_acts ⟶ A, A: 3
```

If the opera agent receives the new request "find all operas by Guiseppe Verdi with three acts" (provided the opera database has entries for act information), it reduces the original scope even further and spawns a new agent specialist on three-act Verdi operas.

Code fragment (further scope refinement of opera agent).

```
X                          /* constraint variable                  */
+                          /* it follows Φ0                        */
   X: a0 ⟶ O,
   O: opera,
-                          /* it follows Φ1                        */
   X: a0 ⟶ O,
   O: opera,
   O: composer ⟶ K, K: 'Richard Wagner'
-                          /* it follows Φ2                        */
   X: a0 ⟶ O,
   O: opera,
   O: composer ⟶ K, K: 'Giuseppe Verdi',
   O: number_acts ⟶ A, A: 3
```

Now, we can demonstrate another characteristics of the approach: Imagine a subsequent request "find all operas by Guiseppe Verdi". This request will be answered by two agent specialists: First, the old Verdi agent specialist for three-act operas will answer (reusing its already collected information). Second, a newly created "specialist" for all Verdi operas not having three acts will answer. The requester of the last request will, due to earlier requests, get answers from two different specialists.

Due to the scope splitting mechanism, redundant work is avoided. Already generated solutions for the overlapping part of the problem domain are reused; in the previous case, the three-act operas of Verdi.

9.6.3 Protocols

Independent of the selected application environment, the CBKB model supports two different agent interaction protocols, the request/subrequest protocol and the local caching protocol. For both protocols, we give an implementation in L0 (see Sect. 1.6.6, S. 54ff.).

Request/subrequest protocol. The request/subrequest protocol applies the findings of grammar analysis (Pereira and Warren 1983) and of database research (Vielle 1986).

Each (sub)problem request carries a unique identifier that is added to all answers of the original request. In this way, requester and requestee are directly linked. Information is provided only if requested, and is sent only to those agents that have explicitly requested it.

Besides the identifier, a request also contains the formal problem description which is represented as a constraint on the problem domain. Similar to the contract net protocol, the receiving agent decomposes the problem description into subproblems which are then submitted as subrequests in the same way as the initial request. New unique identifiers are assigned to the subrequests so that the subsolutions can be collected and used within the problem solving process of the initial request.

Code fragment (Request/Subrequest protocol).

broker(W_0)

@ request(Id,W)

@ **split**(W_0,W,W_1,W_2) /* Suppose, W_0 is the current agent's scope and W the formal problem description of the request. The predicate **split**(W_0,W,W_1,W_2) generates two new scopes W_1 and W_2, with: $W_1 = W_0 \cap W$ and $W_2 = W_0 \cap \neg W$. */

@ **init**(W_1,S) /* The predicate **init**(W_1,S) utilizes the current, reduced scope $W_1 \in \mathcal{D}$ of the specialized agent in order to initialize constraint store $S \in \mathcal{D}^{n+1}$. */

<>- broker(W_2) & agent @ request(Id,W) @ const(S).

/* The following rules apply to all n arguments. In the following we list the rules for the k-th argument as an example. */

const(S)

@ free$_k$ /* During initialization the token free$_k$ is set for all arguments of the agent. */

@ **trigger**$_k$(S) /* The predicate **trigger**$_k$(S) checks whether the constraint store S is sufficient for the argument k. If the threshold conditions of the argument are satisfied the associated subrequest is triggered and sent to other agents and agent specialists. The threshold mechanism will be discussed below in more detail. */

@ **seek**$_k$(S,W) /* The predicate **seek**$_k$(S,W) extracts (by projection) from the constraint store $S \in \mathcal{D}^{n+1}$ a formal subproblem description $W \in \mathcal{D}$ for the k-th subproblem, i.e., $W = \pi_k < S >$. For Saraswat (1989), **trigger**$_k$ and **seek**$_k$ are components of the language construct **ask**. */

@ ^request(Id,W) /* The agent specialist sends a request for the k-th subproblem, wherein the subproblem is formally described by W. Since the identifier Id is not instantiated at that time, it is assigned a new, unique value (by the L0 run time system). In KQML, the performative **ask-all** would be the equivalent. */

<>- const(S) @ wait$_k$(Id) @ request(Id,W).

const(S)

@ wait$_k$(Id) @ answer(Id,X)

@ **ins**$_k$(X,S,Sx) /* The predicate **ins**$_k$(X,S,Sx) inserts the solution $X \in \mathcal{D}$ of the k-th subproblem into the current constraint store $S \in \mathcal{D}^{n+1}$. The constraint store extended by X is called Sx. **ins**$_k$ checks the consistency and, if necessary, simplifies the constraints of Sx. This process is also called constraint solving. Saraswat (1989) uses the language construct **tell**. */

<>- const(S) @ wait$_k$(Id) & const(Sx) @ bound$_k$(X).

arity$_n$ /* The agent specialist inputs the subsolution data $X_1, \ldots, X_n$ into the generator with n being the arity of the agent specialist. This arity equals the number of arguments, that is, the number of subproblems for which the agent specialist must find subsolutions in order to solve the initial request W. */

@ bound$_1$(X_1) @ ... @ bound$_n$(X_n)

<>- tuple$_n$($X_1, \ldots, X_n$).

tuple$_n$($X_1, \ldots, X_n$) /* Generator. */

@ compute from subsolutions $X_1, \ldots, X_n$ the m (≥ 1) solutions L_1 to L_m

<>- res(L_1) @ ... @ res(L_m).

agent

@ res(X)

<>- agent & cache(X).

cache(X)

@ request(Id,W)

@ **sat**(X,W) /* The predicate **sat**(X,W) checks if the solution X satisfies the original problem description W. */

@ ^answer(Id,X) /* The agent specialist returns the solution X. In KQML, this would be the performative **tell** */

<>- cache(X).

The predicate **ins**$_k$ implements the monotony characteristic of agent systems (see Sect. 9.3): A subsolution is only incorporated into the current constraint store if it does not contradict former results. Thus, this "monitored monotony" differs from the scientific approach where often new results are not checked with respect to old results.

Local caching protocol. As opposed to the request/subrequest protocol, the local caching protocol does not link requesters and requestees. As soon as a solution for a particular subproblem is available, it is broadcast to all existing agents. Neither requests nor answers have an identifier assigned.

As before, an agent takes the problem description and decomposes it into subproblems. However, as a consequence of prior problem solutions, for some of the subproblems solutions may already be known to the agent, thus available solutions are reused. The descriptions of yet unsolved subproblems are submitted as subrequests in the same way as the initial request (i.e., again without an identifier).

In this way, we obtain a situation of local caching of information for all existing agents, thus decreasing the overall amount of network traffic, just as we avoid the regeneration of the same requests from different requesters. On the other hand, agents may store information which never gets used. Various studies (Arcelli et al. 1995, Borghoff et al. 1998) on the reusability of knowledge have analyzed this phenomenon for certain application domains.

The local caching protocol reflects the commutativity characteristic of multiagent systems (see Sect. 9.3): Agents are interested in a (sub)problem both before and after (sub)solutions have been broadcasted.

Code fragment (local caching protocol).

broker(W_0)
  @ request(W)   /* The request has no identifier. */
  @ **split**(W_0,W,W_1,W_2) @ **init**(W_1,S)
  <>- broker(W_2) & agent @ request(W) @ const(S).

/* The following rules apply for all n arguments. As above, only the rules for the k-th argument are introduced. */

const(S)
  @ free$_k$
  @ **no_answer_sat**$_k$($\mathcal{X}$,S)   /* The predicate **no_answer_sat**$_k$($\mathcal{X}$,S) checks if none of the available solutions $X \in \mathcal{X}$ represent a solution for argument k. */
  @ **trigger**$_k$(S) @ **seek**$_k$(S,W) @ ^request(W)
  <>- const(S) @ request(W).

const(S)
  @ answer(X) @ **seek**$_k$(S,W) @ **sat**(X,W) @ **ins**$_k$(X,S,Sx)
  <>- const(S) & const(Sx) @ bound$_k$(X).

arity$_n$
  @ bound$_1$(X_1) @ ... @ bound$_n$(X_n)
  <>- tuple$_n$($X_1, \ldots, X_n$).

tuple$_n$($X_1, \ldots, X_n$)
  @ compute from subsolutions $X_1, \ldots, X_n$ the m (≥ 1) solutions L_1 to L_m
  <>- res(L_1) @ ... @ res(L_m).

```
agent
   @ res(X)
   <>- agent & cache(X).
cache(X)
   @ request(W) @ sat(X,W)
   @ ^answer(X)          /* The solution is posted without identifier, thus it
                            can be used by all agents.                      */
   <>- cache(X).
```

9.6.4 Agent processing

As mentioned before, an agent's main tasks are the communication with other agents, i.e., sending and receiving messages, and the reaction upon receipt of messages (which may be either requests or answers to requests). The typical processing of a request submitted to an agent (broker/n) is, by and large, accomplished through the following steps:

1. checking the problem description of the request with respect to the scope of the agent. In the case of a match, the problem description is accepted and the local problem solving process is triggered.
2. exploring the subset of the agent's scope that intersects with the constraint given in the problem description and spawning an agent specialist handling the subset currently under exploration. The original agent itself continues to be in charge of the reduced scope which is derived from the old scope without including the scope of the agent specialist.
3. applying dependencies to each of the agent's arguments of the generator function g in order to simplify the problem description into subproblems.
4. checking the conditions to verify for which of the arguments the simplified problem description can already be submitted as a subrequest. The conditions, called threshold conditions will be discussed below.
5. submitting these subrequests in the same way as the initial request, i.e., with an identifier when using the request/subrequest protocol, or without when using the local caching protocol.
6. updating the local constraint store upon receipt of answers to these subrequests. Other arguments of g may reach their threshold conditions and be submitted as in Step 5.

Once a combination of answers satisfies the initial request (after applying the agent's generator function), a solution is found. This solution is then sent to the initial requester, when using the request/subrequest protocol (see the user interface in Fig. 9.19), or to all agents in the case of the local caching protocol. In addition to the scope splitting mechanisms where the creation of redundant agent specialists is avoided, local caching is of special interest when subproblems overlap. Redundant work is reduced by communicating relevant results in advance. As stated in Oates et al. (1994), it is also interesting to

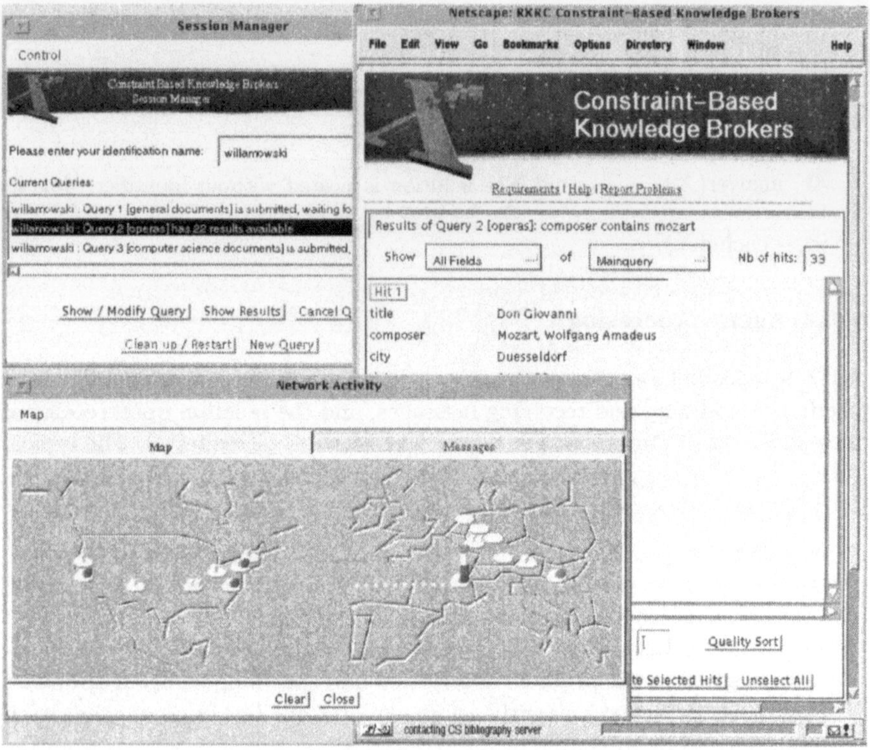

Fig. 9.19. User interface of the CBKB system during a asynchronous search

see that a solution or even a partial solution generated by an agent might facilitate (by focusing or constraining) the problem solving of another agent. For example, due to an unsolicited solution to a subproblem, a threshold could be satisfied and a (possibly more refined) subrequest could be launched.

The aforementioned steps illustrate the processing of a broker/n providing solutions to a request. A broker/n generates solutions out of n subanswers, thus it extends the functionality of other agents. Synthesizing and combining answers is only possible when there are agents in the CBKB model that do not further decompose the problem description into subproblems, but answer a request immediately by other means. This can be achieved by agents with the arity 0, called *broker/0*. A typical example of a broker/0 might be an agent which handles queries to an attached database or an agent which contacts some information service providers in the Internet. A major advantage of a broker/0 for collaborative work lies in the communication with users during problem solving, and thus the use of manual intervention to solve the received request.

A broker/0 reacts to an incoming request as described in Steps 1 and 2. However, instead of Steps 3–6, the simplification of the problem description into subproblems, a broker/0 may initiate the following actions:

- The broker/0 interacts with users and distributes the task associated with the request for manual execution. If multiple users are available the agent may apply the contract net protocol to select the best bidders and assign the task to them. A converter transforms the internal representation of the formal problem description into structured messages required by the contract net protocol. Furthermore, the converter also maps the answer message of a bidder into a broker/0-processable constraint. Instead of applying only the procedure **select_bid**, the broker/0 checks the satisfiability of all answers of the bidders (this is analogous to **evaluate_bid**; see p. 442). Those answers satisfying the problem description are added to the (agent-local) constraint store.
- The broker/0 searches information sources (e.g., local or remote databases, WWW servers, etc.), and retrieves the matching information. Wrappers (Chidlovskii et al. 1997, 1998; Chidlovskii and Borghoff 1998) convert the constraints of the CBKB model to the appropriate query languages of the information sources; see also the TSIMMIS project.
- The broker/0 activates an external application (e.g., by starting a calculation task within a spreadsheet application).
- The broker/0 starts a process that evaluates certain broker-internal data.

Of course, this is just a small selection of possible actions a broker/0 may use to compute solutions to a request. A broker/0 forms the basis for searches over, most probably, heterogeneous information sources. It also provides the interface to external tools and applications. Thus, the CBKB model can smoothly be integrated into an already existing application environment without changing legacy applications.

The following example of a distributed problem solving application illustrates the interaction between a broker/3 and several brokers/0 using multiple information sources.

Example (complex problem description). People interested in classical music may wish to extend their private libraries by the following selection:

"Find all books by non-German authors titled after a Wagner opera".

Applying the feature constraints of the CBKB model we get the following formalized problem description, constraining the variable X:

Code fragment (complex problem description).

X /* constraint variable */

X: **problem**,
X: *find_opera* $\longrightarrow O$,
X: *find_book* $\longrightarrow B$,

X: *check_person* $\longrightarrow P$,
O: **opera**, /* knowledge domain for a_1 */
O: *name* $\longrightarrow T$,
O: *composer* $\longrightarrow K$, K: 'Richard Wagner',
B: **book**, /* knowledge domain for a_2 */
B: *title* $\longrightarrow T$,
B: *author* $\longrightarrow PN$,
P: **person**, /* knowledge domain for a_3 */
P: *name* $\longrightarrow PN$,
P: *nationality* $\longrightarrow N$, $N \neq D$, D: 'German'

In order to answer this request, a broker/3 decomposes the problem into three subproblems assigning them to a broker/0 for operas, a broker/0 for books and a broker/0 for nationalities. The results of these brokers/0 are combined by the broker/3 to generate the solutions of the original request. The initial scope of broker/3 is listed below.

Code fragment (initial scope of broker/3).

Y /* constraint variable */
$+$ /* it follows Φ_0 */
Y: $a_0 \longrightarrow X$,
Y: $a_1 \longrightarrow O$, /* request to a broker/0 for operas */
Y: $a_2 \longrightarrow B$, /* request to a broker/0 for books */
Y: $a_3 \longrightarrow P$, /* request to a broker/0 for checking a person's nationality */
X: **problem**,
X: *find_opera* $\longrightarrow O$,
X: *find_book* $\longrightarrow B$,
X: *check_person* $\longrightarrow P$,
O: **opera**,
B: **book**,
P: **person**

The agent specialist cloned by broker/3 may decompose the problem domain into the following requests: First, using the "potential breakpoint" a_1:

"Find all operas by Richard Wagner."

This request may involve a first broker/0 that searches a marketing server installed at the city of Bayreuth, Germany. Upon receipt of replies to this initial request, the agent specialist extracts for every opera O the name T, e.g., Parsifal, Siegfried, Tristan und Isolde etc., and submits a second request of the form ("breakpoint" a_2):

"Find all books titled T."

This request involves a second broker/0 that executes a script to contact a relevant service provider that may reside within the world wide web (e.g., the Library of Congress). If Telescript's visions (White 1994a) become real it should also be possible to attach a Telescript engine to such a broker/0. Upon receipt of answers to this second request, the agent specialist extracts for every book B the author P (e.g., for the title "Parsifal", book authors are Piotr Bednarski, Friedrich Oberkogler, Hans-Jürgen Syberberg, Peter Vansittart etc.), and submits a third request of the form ("breakpoint" a_3):

"Check the nationality of author P."

This request involves a third broker/0 that sends a query to a commercial Who's-Who server to get information on the author's nationality. Upon receipt of an answer N (assuming a person has only one nationality), the agent specialist feeds its generator with O, B and N to generate a result that is returned to the requester. If N is not German a solution is found and the particular book B is returned as an answer.

The following solution represents a correct answer to the request and thus an element of the minimal model:

Vansittart, Peter. Parsifal : a novel / Peter Vansittart. London : P. Owen ; Chester Springs, PA : U.S. distributor, Dufour Editions, 1988.

The final aspect of agent processing discussed here refers to the life span of agents. As already mentioned above a set of initial agents is provided at system startup. By processing requests the system creates new agent specialists and modifies the scopes of already existing agents. An agent's life span is application-dependent and may range from an individual user query to a session, or to persistent existence. In the first case, agents are only created for the handling of the initial user query. After the final answer has been generated all agents are terminated. The reuse of cached information is usually very low. In the second case, agents live until the session is explicitly terminated. Requests within a session may lead to an increased number of agents.[29] Within a session the results of previous requests may be reused to generate the answers of new requests. In the last case, agents are persistent. Agents exist until they are explicitly removed from the system (e.g., the predefined lifetime of an agent expires). Thus, agents are similar to demons in operating system environments. Again, agents reuse cached results of previous requests (Chidlovskii and Borghoff 1998, 2000).

Interdependencies between subproblems. The support of interdependencies among subproblems provides an efficient approach to prune the search space for agents. Interdependencies may be used to model the order of submitting subrequests and thus, the order of handling of subproblems. For example, an interdependency might specify that the subrequests are to be handled in

[29] Based on a merging strategy for agent scopes, Andreoli et al. (1997b) present first ideas on how to dynamically reduce the number of agents within a session.

sequential order, i.e., the subrequest k (argument k of g) may only be sent after the answers of subrequest $k-1$ (argument $k-1$ of g) have been received. Thus, interdependencies provide a powerful mechanism for modeling causal and temporal relationships between subproblems.

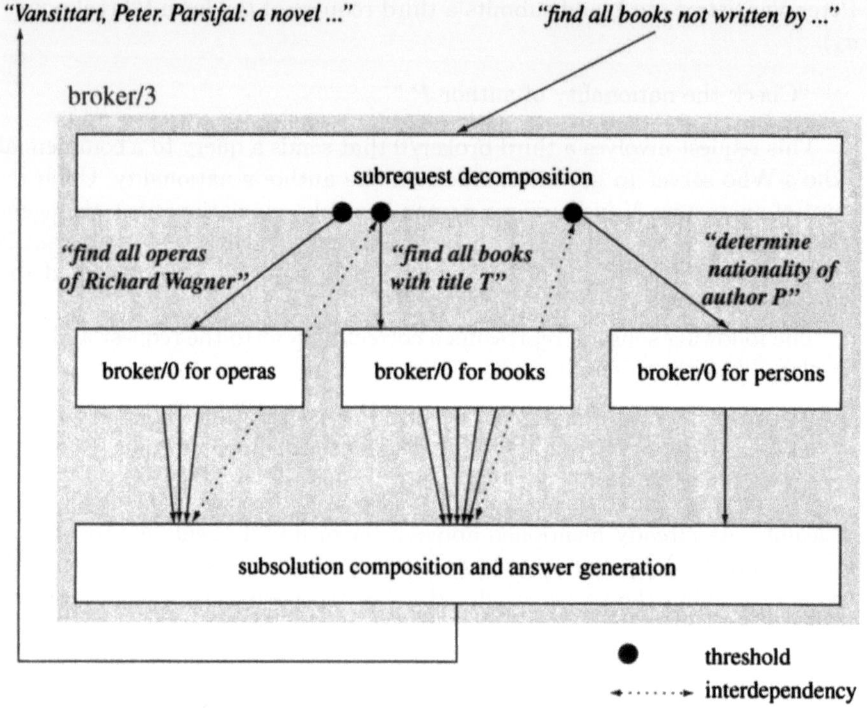

Fig. 9.20. Interdependencies within an agent-based information brokerage service

The opera example on p. 465 already used interdependencies: the name of an opera and the title of the book must coincide, that is O: *name* $\longrightarrow T$ and B: *title* $\longrightarrow T$. Another interdependency constraint forcing the coincidence of the author of the book and the person's name, that is B: *author* $\longrightarrow PN$ and P: *name* $\longrightarrow PN$.

Thresholds. As opposed to interdependencies which are part of the formal problem description or the scope specification, thresholds are explicitly associated with each argument of the agent's generator. They are based on an entailment test which checks whether or not an argument entails a given feature constraint (see the predicates $\mathbf{trigger}_k(S)$ in the code fragments on p. 460 and p. 462). Whenever a threshold condition of an argument is satisfied the associated subrequest is triggered and sent to other brokers and agent specialists. Thus, an agent explicitly recognizes whether or not the constraint store contains enough knowledge to initiate the solution processing for a certain (sub)problem.

Example (Threshold conditions). As Fig. 9.20 illustrates, it makes no sense to request information on a book without the knowledge of its title, or to query the nationality of an unknown person. Using the threshold mechanism and the interdependency constraint broker/3 implements an argument ordering scheme. A request for argument a_1 (Wagner operas) is sent first, a request for argument a_2 (books with relevant title T) is sent whenever an answer for the first request arrives and the value of T is defined. Analogously, the request for argument a_3 (an author's nationality) depends on the answers received for the argument a_2.

For a description of the architectural framework of the CBKB prototype implementation and detailed discussions on adaptation mechanisms, i.e., converting the constraints of the CBKB system into queries of the external information sources as well as the conversion of the query results back into constraints, the reader is referred to Borghoff and Schlichter (1996) und Chidlovskii et al. (1997). Borghoff et al. (1996c, 1997b) elucidate the usage of information brokering services within the context of document management.

9.7 Distributed Meeting Scheduling

This section introduces a third important domain of distributed problem solving: the distributed, agent-based meeting scheduling. Scheduling of meetings is an inherently distributed process. Negotiations on when to schedule a meeting can be interpreted as a distributed search and problem solving process. Meeting scheduling involves the following issues:

- *When should the meeting take place?* The initiator usually has certain ideas on when the meeting should take place. There are three possibilities at the start of the negotiation: He proposes a certain date and time, he proposes several alternatives to select from, or he has no concrete idea and therefore specifies only a time frame for the meeting.
- *How long should the meeting last?*
- *Who should participate?* In this context it is important to decide whether or not all parties concerned are equally important to the meeting or if participants can be classified according to their importance to the meeting (e.g., essential, or desired but not required).
- *Where shall we meet?*

Since there is no optimum algorithm applicable in all possible situations handling the complexity of the problem solving process, quite frequently common techniques of artificial intelligence, such as heuristics, are applied. Intelligent agents have knowledge about a person's interests and priorities. Agents perform organizational routine work as part of meeting scheduling. They filter and manage information, and answer requests for meeting scheduling. If each person has his private electronic calendar which is managed by his own personal agent the meeting scheduling process is improved by transferring some routine planning work from the user to the agent. Agents may work in parallel, thus reducing the scheduling time, increasing the reliability by interpreting consistent calendars, and providing some protection of private entries.

Agents communicate with each other to exchange scheduling information from their perspective (e.g., proposal for date and time, or acceptance of proposed time). The common protocol used by the agents can be considered as a generalization of the contract net protocol, which was discussed earlier in this book. The role of an agent engaged in the meeting scheduling process can be either that of a host, or that of an invitee. After initiating the meeting scheduling process the host coordinates the negotiation progress. Thus, its role is similar to that of the manager in the contract net protocol. The host sends the meeting announcement together with possible time alternatives to all invitees. Negotiations may require several rounds of interaction between the host and all invitees, until finally an agreement is reached, or else the meeting is canceled.

In practice, automatic meeting scheduling has proven to be fairly difficult. An obstacle is that all users must maintain an electronic calendar which has to be updated carefully, since otherwise automatic scheduling will not be possible. As Grudin (1990) remarks there has been a disparity between users of this type of groupware. Only few users benefit from automatic meeting scheduling; typically, these are the people initiating the meetings. Others often have considerably more work. Based on field studies Lange (1992) concludes that the following criteria have to be met in order to use electronic group calendars successfully for automatic meeting scheduling:

- The intended usage must be clearly defined.
- Some users should be selected and serve as champions to accept the groupware system and encourage others to become users as well.
- The work procedures must be updated in order to apply the functionality of the groupware system most successfully without requiring additional work by the users.
- The groupware system must support different types of users and different ways of interacting with the system.

For research and commercial environments, a variety of electronic meeting scheduling systems have been developed and used, some with much and some with little success. The support of these systems ranges from simple management of meeting times to agents automatically scheduling meetings for the user. Interesting meeting scheduling systems are CaLANdar (Grehan et al. 1991), CAP II (Bocionek et al. 1993), CSSA (Mattern and Sturm 1989),

MPCAL (Greif and Sarin 1987), On Time (Campbell 1992), TVS (Woitass 1990) and VS (Beard et al. 1990).

Based on the work of Sen and Durfee (1991b) we will give a formal definition of the meeting scheduling problem and introduce the possible use of agents and heuristics.

9.7.1 Formal definition of the meeting scheduling problem

Given a set of n meetings and k participants (hosts and invitees). The scheduling problem is defined as the pair (A, M) where

$A = \{1, \ldots, k\}$ is the set of involved agents and

$M = \{m_1, \ldots, m_n\}$ is the set of meetings to be scheduled. During the scheduling process overlapping meetings must be taken into account.

Meeting specification. According to Sen and Durfee a meeting m_i is defined by the following tuple:

$m_i = (A_i, h_i, l_i, p_i, \tau_i, \sigma_i, d_i, T_i)$, where

- $A_i \subseteq A$: the set of meeting participants;
- $h_i \in A_i$: the host of the meeting;
- $l_i \in \{1, 2, \ldots\}$: the duration of the meeting, e.g., in hours;
- $p_i \in \{1, 2, \ldots\}$: the priority assigned to the meeting;
- $\tau_i = (D_i, H_i)$: the meeting starting time preferred by the host h_i. (D_i, H_i) represents the pair (date, hour): If both components are specified, then the scheduled time is restricted. In this case, the invitees cannot choose between alternatives. If one component is **nil**, then the meeting is semiconstrained, and for both components being **nil**, it is unconstrained;
- $\sigma_i = (D_{\sigma_i}, H_{\sigma_i})$: the deadline for the meeting, i.e., the latest possible starting time for m_i; it serves as additional information for invitees when they propose alternative meeting times;
- $d_i = (D_{d_i}, H_{d_i})$: the latest possible time for scheduling the meeting; this is the deadline for a decision on whether or not the meeting can take place or must be canceled;
- T_i: the time interval for which the meeting m_i is finally scheduled consisting of an ordered set of points in time $\{(D_{m_i}, H_{m_i}), \ldots, (D_{m_i}, H_{m_i} + l_i - 1)\}$; (D_{m_i}, H_{m_i}) represents the meeting start, whereas $(D_{m_i}, H_{m_i} + l_i - 1)$ specifies the meeting end.

In the case of computing the cost of the scheduling process (e.g., to determine the time it took from the meeting initiation to the final scheduling), the following additional information is of interest:

- $a_i = (D_{a_i}, H_{a_i})$: exact time of meeting initiation by agent h_i; that is the time at which the agent h_i was assigned the task of scheduling the meeting m_i.
- $f_i = (D_{f_i}, H_{f_i})$: time of final decision (by agent h_i) whether or not the meeting m_i was scheduled or canceled.

Calendar representation of an agent. Each user has his own personal calendar managed by the respective agent. In the following we assume $j \in A$ to be this agent.

A personal calendar consists of an ordered set of points in time together with additional information on whether or not a certain time slot has already been filled, i.e., a point in time has been assigned to a meeting either preliminary if the scheduling process is not completed yet, or marked as approved if the scheduling process has been completed successfully:

$$C_j = \{(D_s, 0, \chi_{s,0}), (D_s, 1, \chi_{s,1}), \ldots, (D_s, L-1, \chi_{s,L-1}), (D_{s+1}, 0, \chi_{s+1,0}), \ldots, (D_e, 0, \chi_{e,0}), \ldots, (D_e, L-1, \chi_{e,L-1})\},$$

where

- D_s: starting date of calendar;
- D_e: end date of calendar;
- L: number of time slots per working day, e.g., the number of hours;
- $\chi_{x,y} = \begin{cases} m_i & \text{if meeting } m_i \text{ involves the agent } j \in A_i \text{ and } (D_x, y) \in T_i \\ \textbf{nil} & \text{else} \end{cases}$

A meeting m_i is agreed upon with agent j if:

$$\forall j : \{j \in A_i \text{ and } \forall y, z : \{(D_y, H_z) \in T_i \text{ and } (D_y, H_z, m_i) \in C_j\}\} \tag{9.4}$$

Constraints for meeting scheduling. The negotiation between the agents must satisfy the following constraints:

1. $a_i < d_i$: The meeting initiation must occur before the latest possible time of scheduling the meeting;
2. $f_i \leq d_i$: The decision whether or not a meeting is arranged or cancelled must occur before the latest possible scheduling time;
3. $f_i < (D_{m_i}, H_{m_i})$: The final decision on the meeting time must lie before the meeting actually takes place;
4. If $D_i \neq \textbf{nil}$, then $D_i = D_{m_i}$ must be true, i.e., scheduling is constrained with respect to the date;
5. If $H_i \neq \textbf{nil}$, then $H_i = H_{m_i}$ must be true, i.e., scheduling is constrained with respect to the hour;
6. The meeting time slots are contiguous (i.e., a meeting cannot be decomposed into several disconnected time intervals). Thus, a single meeting cannot extend across several days with interruptions for other meetings. Long, disconnected meetings must be realized as several individual meetings;
7. Given $M_j \subseteq M$ the set of scheduled meetings for the agent j, then the following is true:
   $\forall x, y : \{m_x \in M_j, m_y \in M_j, x \neq y : T_x \cap T_y = \emptyset\}$
   An agent j cannot attend multiple meetings at the same time;
8. h_i is responsible for meeting m_i: h_i triggers the scheduling process, negotiates with the invitees about meeting time and decides eventually whether or not the meeting m_i can take place or must be canceled;

9. An agent j has only access to its private calendar (i.e., agent j cannot directly read agent k's private calendar, or enter meeting times). Agent j must obtain all relevant information by communicating with other agents.

9.7.2 Scheduling process

Similar to the contract net protocol and the CBKB model, the scheduling process is also based on a multistage, decentralized negotiation protocol. The host h_i is the coordinator deciding whether or not the meeting will take place, and, if it takes place, deciding the final meeting time. In general, the invitees interact only with the host h_i and they do not communicate among themselves. In the following we will give a brief outline of the steps involved in the scheduling process:

1. On receipt of the request to schedule the meeting m_i the host h_i determines first the appropriate time intervals in its private calendar which satisfy the requirements of m_i (e.g., date or hour constraints). If the scheduling is unconstrained h_i determines the earliest possible meeting time.
   If no appropriate time interval can be found, the meeting is canceled; otherwise, the scheduling process continues. If the host is the only participant, it finalizes the meeting time, or else it sends a meeting announcement to all participants. This invitation will include one or several proposal for the meeting time.
2. Upon receipt of a meeting announcement, the invited agent j matches the proposed time with the available times in its private calendar. The invitee returns a bid to h_i which may either be a subset of the times listed in the meeting announcement, or else suggest new time intervals. The latter case is called a counter proposal.
3. h_i collects the bids of all contacted agents and evaluates them with respect to overlapping slots. If a common time interval can be identified, the host decides on an agreeable meeting time and confirms it to all invitees.
   If no common time interval can be found, the host h_i will repeat the process computing new proposals which depend on the received bids, and sending a new announcement to all invitees. Previously reserved times must be erased. All invitees will continue with Step 2.
4. The invited agent j receives the confirmed time interval from the host h_i. The agent j performs another check to see if the interval is still available and, if so, it marks the associated time slots as reserved.

9.7.3 Scheduling model

Each meeting m_i involves agents of the agent set A_i. The steps of the agent $j \in A_i$ with respect to m_i is specified by the finite state transition diagram

M_{ij}. Figure 9.21 depicts such a state transition diagram; see also the work of Sen and Durfee (1991b).

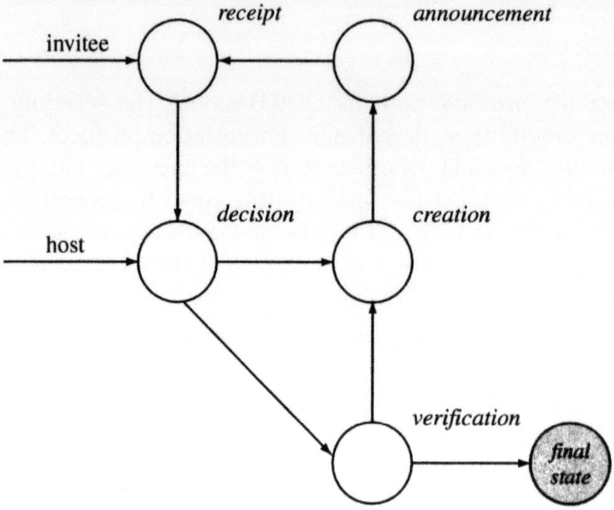

Fig. 9.21. Finite state transition diagram for meeting scheduling

The finite state transition diagram M_{ij} encompasses the following states with different initial states for host and invitees:

- *Decision:* The agent evaluates all generated or received proposals and decides whether or not there is a consensus between all involved agents on a common time interval, or else if new proposals have to be created. If a common time interval exists, it is verified with respect to already existing entries in the private calendar.
- *Creation:* The agent generates new proposals, either as an announcement or as counter proposals.
- *Announcement:* The host sends its proposals to all other cooperating agents, while invitees return the proposals only to the host.
- *Receipt:* The agent receives proposals; these can be both announcements or counter proposals.
- *Verification:* The agent verifies the mutually agreed upon meeting time with the already existing entries in its private calendar.
- *Final state:* State in which a meeting is either agreed upon or canceled.

State transitions of an agent depend on the communication with other agents as well as the information stored in the local calendar.

9.7.4 Strategies

In general, the scheduling problem is an allocation problem which may be solved by heuristics. We will now introduce some strategies which the host and the invitees may apply during the scheduling process.

Announcement strategies. The host applies one of following strategies to determine the way the meeting is to be announced to the other participants. The announcement may include only one best possible meeting or a number of possible times rated "suitable" by the host:

- *best possible meeting time:* Only the best possible time from the host's viewpoint is forwarded to all invitees (e.g., earliest possible meeting time according to the host's private calendar).
- *suitable meeting times:* Several meeting times favored by the host are sent as proposals to the invitees. This strategy requires usually fewer iterations between host and invitees, and thus, it is more efficient with respect to the communication traffic.

Bid strategies. Based on the meeting announcement, these strategies determine the extent to which information is provided by the invitees to the host. It can be a simple acceptance or rejection of the proposed meeting time, or else a list of alternative times if the proposed meeting time is not acceptable:

- *yes-no:* The invited agent returns yes or no with respect to the proposed meeting time; the CAP-II-system (Bocionek et al. 1993) supports two additional answers: possibly and unfavorable time. In the former case, the invited agent is unable to decide whether or not to enter the meeting into the calendar. Additional information by the user associated with the invited agent might be necessary. In the latter case, the invited agent informs the host that his user is basically interested in attending the meeting, but that he is busy at the proposed meeting time.
- *Alternatives:* If the proposed meeting time is not convenient, then the invitee can suggest alternatives in the form of counter proposals resulting in less iterations within the scheduling process.

Acceptance strategies. These strategies determine how the private calendar is managed and how conflicting invitations are dealt with:

- *accepted:* Whenever an agent agrees with the meeting time, it marks the associated time interval as blocked in the calendar, even before the final approval of all participants. This can cause poor utilization of the available time intervals if several meetings have to be canceled because of conflicting times.
- *reserved:* The time interval is only marked as reserved in the private calendar; later meeting requests may overwrite this reservation. The agent may use priorities to select between conflicting meetings. After the final

approval of all participants the reserved time interval becomes a blocked time interval.

- *not accepted:* The time interval will not be blocked in the private calendar until the final approval for the meeting is received. Thus, the agent may return positive answers to multiple meeting requests for the same time interval.

This model of distributed meeting scheduling only distinguishes between two types of agents: host and invitee. Other frequently occurring organizational roles, such as project leader or team member are irrelevant.

Sen and Durfee (1991b) evaluated the behavior of the individual strategies using analytical methods. For example, for a meeting announcement, the strategy "best possible meeting time" usually requires more iterations than the strategy "suitable meeting times". The difference becomes especially apparent for meetings with long duration times. Experimental research using simulations has validated these analytical computations. Other criteria for the analysis of a meeting scheduling model were communication costs and the success rate for arranging meetings.

The approach of Sen and Durfee, as described above, views meeting scheduling as an inherently distributed search process. The focus is on the negotiation between the meeting participants of the appropriate meeting time. Glezer and Yadav (1999) define a new conceptual model which also addresses issues such as group composition and the meeting content planning.

9.8 Actor Model

The actor model was initially introduced in the 1970s by Hewitt (1986) at MIT (Massachusetts Institute of Technology, Cambridge, USA). His idea has gained significant support in the field of Artificial Intelligence. We will outline the main issues of the actor model, since we believe it might be relevant for some future agent programming in groupware environments.

Among the fundamental aspects in the design of concurrent systems are shared resources with changing states, dynamic reconfiguration due to the system evolution, and inherent parallelism which should be explicitly represented in the program.

Basic constructs of the actor model are the actors themselves and message exchanges between the actors. The latter construct is similar to message passing in object-oriented systems.

9.8.1 Actor definition

Definition 9.8.1 (Actor). *An actor is an active agent which carries out its actions on receipt of messages. Among these actions are the following:*

- *sending messages to themselves or to other actors. The delivery of a message is nondeterministic. Messages are buffered, and consequently recursions are possible.*
- *creating new actors.*
- *specifying a replacement behavior, i.e., the actor behaves afterwards differently when new messages arrive resulting in a dynamic system evolution.*

Each actor has a unique identifier used for message addressing. An actor's identifier can be forwarded to other actors which provides the mechanism for dynamic system reconfiguration. For example, on receiving the message N the actor A specifies the actor B as its replacement actor. All subsequent messages to the identifier A are automatically forwarded to B. The replacement actor does not affect the behavior of the original actor A.

Pipelining of actions. The actor code does not contain any variables to which different values may be assigned. This facilitates the pipelining of actions, since there are no data interdependencies.

The actors and the message communication describe the system dynamics. A program consisting of multiple actors is described by a collection of declarations, in particular, using behavior definitions, commands for creating actors, as well as commands for exchanging messages between actors. A behavior definition contains an identifier, a list of known actors, and a script. The script specifies the actor's behavior and consists of a collection of commands.

9.8.2 Generic actor system

Actor systems are implemented by using the actor programming language Act3. In the following we use a BNF notation to illustrate the specification of an actor system. The parenthesis in Act3 have to be interpreted as LISP parenthesis. The symbols *, [,], | and ::= have the standardized BNF meanings.

actor system ::= behavior definition* (command*)
behavior definition ::= (**define** (id ([(**with** identifier (pattern))]*)
communication handler*))
communication handler ::= (**communication** pattern **do** command*)
command ::= let-command | conditional-command |
send-command | become-command

A let-command binds an expression to an identifier, thus representing a temporary variable. A conditional-command, the **if**-command, provides a mechanism for branching; the send-command **send** supports the sending of a message. The become-command specifies the replacement actor.

9.8.3 Example for an actor system

The factorial program (Hewitt 1986) is specified on a very low level. The language Act3 contains constructs which simplify the program specification significantly.

Code fragment (Behavior definition for the factorial example).

```
(define (Factorial() )
  (communication (a doit (with agent ≡ m) (with number ≡ n)) do
    (become Factorial)
                          /* the actor replaces itself          */
    (if (= n 0) (then (send m 1))
    (else (let (x = (new FaculAgent (with agent m) (with number n)))
      (send Factorial (a do (with agent x)
        (with number n-1))))))))
(define FaculAgent (with agent ≡ m) (with number ≡ n))
  (communication (a number k) do (send m n × k)))
```

Factorial and *FaculAgent* are behavioral definitions which turn into agents during the program execution. Figure 9.22 illustrates the dynamic process for computing the factorial of 2.

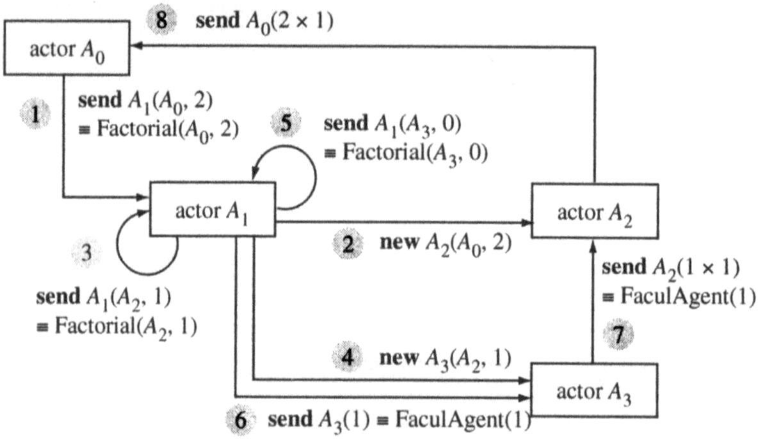

Fig. 9.22. Dynamic process for Factorial(2)

The actor A_1 whose behavior is characterized by the factorial definition, is created in Step 1. The parameters specify that 2! should be computed and the result forwarded to actor A_0. In Step 2, actor A_2 is generated. Its behavior is characterized as follows: Multiply the number received in a message with n (here 2). Step 3 sends a message back to itself, requiring the computation of factorial $n-1$ (here 1). In Step 4, A_1 creates the new actor A_3, the behavior of which is equivalent to A_2. A_3 computes 1!, A_2 computes the factorial of 2. Step 5 again sends a message back to itself (i.e., to the actor A_1) including a notice that the factorial of $n-1$ (here 0) should be computed. Now the execution of A_1 sends a message to actor A_3 in Step 6 requesting the computation of factorial 1 and subsequently the message to actor A_2 of both the result and the request to compute the factorial of 2. In Step 8, the final result of the factorial computation is returned back to the original actor A_0.

The actors A_1, A_2 and A_3 are executed autonomously. Thus, the processing time can be reduced by creating multiple actors, depending on the problem.

9.9 Further Reading

This chapter could only provide an introduction to computer-supported cooperation using agents. Thus, it does not replace relevant works on the subject of agent modeling and the programming of agent systems. The important field of intelligent agents has merely been touched.

The field of distributed artificial intelligence, which plays a central role in the programming of intelligent agents, is presented at length by Bond and Gasser (1988) and Russell and Norvig (1995). M. v. Bechtolsheim (1993) deals with distributed problem solving and agent systems. Descriptions of the BDI architecture can be found in Rao and Georgeff (1991). The interested reader can find a relevant summary of intelligent systems in the December 1996 issue of *IEEE Expert*. We also recommend the web page (http://www.cs.umbc.edu/agents/) provided by T. Finin at the University of Maryland Baltimore County (UMBC), USA. Other agent-related URLs can be found at http://www.cs.bris.ac.uk/~varsamos/agents.html. A collection of important works on software agents can be found in Bradshaw (1997), and aspects of mobile agents are closely investigated by A. Rothermel and Popescu-Zeletin (1997). The Foundation for Intelligent Physical Agents (FIPA) aims at improving the interoperability within and across agent based applications (http://www.fipa.org/). It defines specifications of generic agent technologies, such as an agent communication language which is similar to KQML, mechanisms for agent naming and agent management. A constraint-based description language for agents querying sources on the Web as well as an interaction model, again based on constraints and on the notion of so-called virtual answers, is proposed by Andreoli and Borghoff (2000).

We also wish to refer the interested reader to the proceedings of the conferences on *MultiAgent Systems* and on *Practical Application of Intelligent Agents and MultiAgent Technology*.

The March 1997 and the March 1999 issue of *Communications of the ACM* included a detailed discussion of recommender systems and multiagent systems, respectively.

The so-called knowledge management is introduced in the books by Nonaka and Takeuchi (1995) and Sveiby (1997). Information technologies for knowledge management can be found in Borghoff and Pareschi (1998).

References

ABBADI, A. EL, SKEEN, D., CHRISTIAN, F. (1985): An Efficient, Fault-Tolerant Algorithm for Replicated Data Management. Proc. 4th ACM SIGACT/SIGMOD Symp. on the Principles of Database Systems, Portland, OR. pp. 215–229

ABBOTT, K. R., SARIN, S. K. (1994): Experiences with Workflow Management: Issues for the next Generation. In: Furuta, R., Neuwirth, C. (eds.): Proc. 5th Int. Conf. on Computer-Supported Cooperative Work, Chapel Hill, NC. New York: SIGCHI/SIGOIS ACM, pp. 113–120

ACETTA, M., BARON, R., BOLOSKY, W., GOLUB, D., RASHID, R., TEVANIAN, A., YOUNG, M. (1986): Mach: A New Kernel Foundation for Unix Development. Proc. Usenix Conf. Summer '86, Atlanta, GA. Berkeley, CA: Usenix Association, pp. 93–113

ACKERMAN, M . S., MCDONALD, D. W. (1996): Answer Garden 2: Merging Organizational Memory with Collaborative Help. In: Ackerman, M. S. (ed.): Proc. 7th Int. Conf. on Computer-Supported Cooperative Work, Boston, MA. New York: SIGCHI/SIGOIS ACM, pp. 97–105

ACKERMAN, M. S., PALEN, L. (1996): The Zephyr Help Instance: Promoting Ongoing Activity Indicators: Interface Components for CSCW Systems. Proc. ACM CHI'96 Conf. on Human Factors in Computing Systems. New York: ACM Press, pp. 268–275

ACKERMAN, M. S., STARR, B. (1996): Social Activity Indicators for Groupware. IEEE Computer **29**:6, 37–44

ACKERMAN, M. S. (1994): Augmenting the Organizational Memory: A Field Study of Answer Garden. In: Furuta, R., Neuwirth, C. (eds.): Proc. 5th Int. Conf. on Computer-Supported Cooperative Work, Chapel Hill, NC. New York: SIGCHI/SIGOIS ACM, pp. 243–252

ADAM, N. R., TEWARI, R. (1991): Regeneration with Virtual Copies for Replicated Databases. Proc. 11th IEEE Int. Conf. on Distributed Computing Systems, Arlington, TX. Los Alamitos, CA: IEEE Computer Society Press, pp. 429–436

AGHA, G., CALLSEN, C. J. (1993): ActorSpace: An Open Distributed Programming Paradigm. Proc. 4th ACM SIGPLAN Symp. on Principles and Practice of Parallel Programming, San Diego, CA. ACM SIGPLAN Notices **28**:7, pp. 23–32

AGHA, G. A. (1986): Actors: A Model of Concurrent Computation in Distributed Systems. Cambridge, MA: MIT Press

AGRAWAL, D., ABBADI, A. EL (1991): An Efficient and Fault-Tolerant Solution for Distributed Mutual Exclusion. ACM Transactions on Computer Systems **9**:1, 1–20

AGRAWAL, G., JALOTE, P. (1995): Coding-Based Replication Schemes for Distributed Systems. IEEE Transactions on Parallel and Distributed Systems **6**:3, 240–251

AHAMAD, M., AMMAR, M. H. (1989): Performance Characterization of Quorum-Consensus Algorithms for Replicated Data. IEEE Transactions on Software Engineering **SE–15**:4, 492–496

AHUJA, S. R., ENSOR, J. R., HORN, D. N. (1988): The Rapport Multimedia Conferencing System. Proc. Conf. on Office Information Systems, Palo Alto, CA. New York: ACM, pp. 1–8

AÏT-KACI, H., PODELSKI, A., SMOLKA, G. (1994): A Feature-Based Constraint-System for Logic Programming with Entailment. Theoretical Computer Science **122**, 263–283

AKOKA, J. (1980): Design of Optimal Distributed Database Systems. Proc. 1st Int. Symp. on Distributed Data Base, Paris, France. pp. 229–245

AKSCYN, R. M., MCCRACKEN, D. L., YODER, E. A. (1988): KMS: A Distributed Hypermedia System for Managing Knowledge in Organizations. Communications of the ACM **31**:7, 820–835

ALMES, G. T., BLACK, A. P., LAZOWSKA, E. D., NOE, J. D. (1985): The Eden System: A Technical Review. IEEE Transactions on Software Engineering **SE–11**:1, 43–58

ALSBERG, P. A., DAY, J. D. (1976): A Principle for Resilient Sharing of Distributed Resources. Proc. 2nd IEEE Int. Conf. on Software Engineering. Los Alamitos, CA: IEEE Computer Society Press, pp. 562–570

ANANDA, A. L., TAY, B. H., KOH, E. K. (1992): A Survey of Asynchronous Remote Procedure Calls. ACM SIGOPS Operating Systems Review **26**:2, 92–109

ANDREOLI, J.-M., BORGHOFF, U. M. (2000): Virtual Answers for Query Refinement in Information Retrieval. Proc. 2nd Int. Conf. on the Practical Application of Constraint Technologies and Logic Programming (PACLP'2000), Manchester, UK. Blackpool, UK: The Practical Application Company Ltd., pp. 233–252

ANDREOLI, J.-M., PARESCHI, R. (1991): Communication as Fair Distribution of Knowledge. Proc. Conf. on Object-Oriented Programming Systems, Languages and Applications (OOPSLA '91), Phoenix, AZ. ACM SIGPLAN Notices **26**:11, pp. 212–229

ANDREOLI, J.-M., CIANCARINI, P., PARESCHI, R. (1992): Interaction Abstract Machines. In: Agha, G. A., Yonezawa, A., Wegner, P. (eds.): Research Directions in Concurrent Object-Oriented Programming. Cambridge, MA: MIT Press, pp. 257–280

ANDREOLI, J.-M., BORGHOFF, U. M., PARESCHI, R. (1994): Constraint-Based Knowledge Brokers. In: Hong, H. (ed.): Proc. 1st Int. Symp. on Parallel Symbolic Computation (PASCO '94), Hagenberg/Linz, Austria. Lecture Notes Series in Computing **5**, Singapore, New Jersey, London, Hong Kong: World Scientific, pp. 1–11

ANDREOLI, J.-M., BORGHOFF, U. M., PARESCHI, R., SCHLICHTER, J. H. (1995): Constraint Agents for the Information Age. J. Universal Computer Science **1**:12, 762–789. Electronic version: http://www.iicm.edu/jucs

ANDREOLI, J.-M., BORGHOFF, U. M., PARESCHI, R. (1996): The Constraint-Based Knowledge Broker Model: Semantics, Implementation and Analysis. J. Symbolic Computation **21**:4, 635–667

ANDREOLI, J-M., HANKIN, C., LEMETAYER, D., eds. (1996): Coordination Programming: Mechanisms, Models and Semantics. London: Imperial College Press

ANDREOLI, J.-M., BORGHOFF, U. M., PARESCHI, R. (1997): Signed Feature Constraint Solving. Proc. 3rd Int. Conf. on the Practical Application of Constraint Technology (PACT '97), London, UK. Blackpool, UK: The Practical Application Company Ltd, pp. 35–46

ANDREOLI, J.-M., BORGHOFF, U. M., PARESCHI, R., BISTARELLI, S., MONTANARI, U., ROSSI, F. (1997): Constraints and Agents for a Decentralized Network Infrastructure. In: Freuder, E. C. (ed.): Proc. Int. AAAI Workshop on Constraints and Agents, Providence, RI. Menlo Park, CA: AAAI Press, pp. 39–44

ANDREWS, G. R., SCHLICHTING, R. D., HAYES, R., PURDIN, T. (1987): The Design of the Saguaro Distributed Operating System. IEEE Transactions on Software Engineering **SE–13**:1, 104–118

APPELT, W. (1989): Normen im Bereich der Dokumentverarbeitung. Informatik-Spektrum **12**:6, 321–330. (in German)

APPLEGATE, L. M. ET AL. (1986): A Group Decision Support System for Idea Generation and Issue Analysis in Organization Planning. Proc. 1st Int. Conf. on Computer-Supported Cooperative Work. New York: SIGCHI/SIGOIS ACM, pp. 16–34

ARCELLI, F., BORGHOFF, U. M., FORMATO, F., PARESCHI, R. (1995): Tuning Constraint-Based Communication in Distributed Problem Solving. Proc. 1st Int. Workshop on Concurrent Constraint Programming (CCP '95), Venice, Italy

AUSTIN, J. (1962): How to Do Things with Words. London, UK: Oxford Univ. Press

BAECKER, R. M., eds. (1993): Groupware and Computer-Supported Cooperative Work. San Mateo, CA: Morgan Kaufmann

BAIR, J. H. (1989): Supporting Cooperative Work with Computers: Addressing Meeting Mania. IEEE Intellectual Leverage Digest of Papers, COMPCON '89

BALABANOVIC, M., SHOHAM, Y. (1997): Fab: Content-Based, Collaborative Recommendations. Communications of the ACM **40**:3, 66–72

BALABANOVIC, M., SHOHAN, Y. (1997): Fab: Content-Based, Collaborative Recommendation. Communications of the ACM **40**:3, 66–72. http://fab.stanford.edu/

BALKOVICH, E., LERMAN, S., PARMELEE, R. P. (1985): Computing in Higher Education: The Athena Experience. IEEE Computer **18**:11, 112–125

BANÂTRE, J.-P., MÉTAYER, D. LE (1990): The Gamma Model and its Discipline of Programming. Science of Computer Programming **15**, 55–77

BANCILHON, F., KIM, W., KORTH, H. (1985): A Model for CAD Transactions. Proc. 11th Int. Conf. on Very Large Data Bases. Los Altos, CA: Morgan Kaufmann, pp. 25–33

BANERJEE, J., CHOU, H.-T., GARZA, J. F., KIM, W., WOELK, D., BALLOU, N., KIM, H.-J. (1987): Data Model Issues for Object-Oriented Applications. ACM Transactions on Office Information Systems **5**, 3–26

BANNON, L. J., SCHMIDT, K. (1991): CSCW: Four Characters in Search of a Context. In: Bowers, J. M., Benford, S. D. (eds.): Studies in Computer Supported Cooperative Work. Amsterdam: North-Holland, pp. 3–16

BARBARA, D., CLIFTON, C. (1992): Information Brokers: Sharing Knowledge in a Heterogeneous Distributed System. Technical Report MITL–TR–31–92. Matsushita Information Technology Lab., Princeton, NJ

BARBARA, D., GARCIA-MOLINA, H. (1987): The Reliability of Voting Mechanisms. IEEE Transactions on Computers **C–36**:10, 1197–1208

BARBARA, D., GARCIA-MOLINA, H. (1990): The Case of Controlled Inconsistency in Replicated Data. In: Cabrera, L.-F., Pâris, J.-F. (eds.): Proc. IEEE Workshop on Management of Replicated Data, Houston, TX. Los Alamitos, CA: IEEE Computer Society Press, pp. 35–42

BARBARA, D., GARCIA-MOLINA, H., SPAUSTER, A. (1986): Policies for Dynamic Vote Reassignment. Proc. 6th Int. Conf. on Distributed Computing Systems, Cambridge, MA. Los Alamitos, CA: IEEE Computer Society Press, pp. 37–44

BARBARA, D., GARCIA-MOLINA, H., SPAUSTER, A. (1989): Increasing Availability under Mutual Exclusion Constraints with Dynamic Vote Reassignment. ACM Transactions on Computer Systems **7**:4, 394–426

BARGHOUTI, N. S., KAISER, G. E. (1991): Concurrency Control in Advanced Database Applications. ACM Computing Surveys **23**:3, 269–317

BEARD, D. ET AL. (1990): A Visual Calendar for Scheduling Group Meetings. Proc. 3rd Int. Conf. on Computer-Supported Cooperative Work, Los Angeles, CA. New York: SIGCHI/SIGOIS ACM, pp. 279–290

BENTLEY, R., HORSTMANN, T., SIKKEL, K., TREVOR, J. (1995): Supporting Collaborative Information Sharing with the WWW: The BSCW Shared Workspace System. Proc. of the 4th Int. World Wide Web Conf. O'Reilly & Associates, In., pp. 63–73

BERNSTEIN, P. A., GOODMAN, N. (1984): An Algorithm for Concurrency Control and Recovery in Replicated Distributed Databases. ACM Transactions on Database Systems **9**:4, 596–615

BERNSTEIN, P. A., HADZILACOS, V., GOODMAN, N. (1987): Concurrency Control and Recovery in Database Systems. Reading, MA: Addison-Wesley

BERRY, G., BOUDOL, G. (1990): The Chemical Abstract Machine. Proc. 17th ACM SIGACT/SIGPLAN Annual Symp. on Principles of Programming Languages, San Francisco, CA. pp. 81–94

BIER, E. A., FREEMAN, S. (1991): MMM: A User Interface Architecture for Shared Editors on a Single Screen. Proc. 4th ACM Symp. on User Interface Software and Technology, Hilton Head, SC. New York: SIGGRAPH/SIGCHI ACM, pp. 79–86

BIRMAN, K. P. (1993): The Process Group Approach to Reliable Distributed Computing. Communications of the ACM **36**:12, 37–53

BIRRELL, A. D., NELSON, B. J. (1984): Implementing Remote Procedure Calls. ACM Transactions on Computer Systems **2**:1, 39–59

BLACK, A. P., HUTCHINSON, N. C., JUL, E., LEVY, H. M. (1986): Object Structure in the Emerald System. In: Meyrowitz, N. (ed.): Proc. 1st Conf. on Object-Oriented Programming Systems, Languages and Applications (OOPSLA '86), Portland, OR. ACM SIGPLAN Notices **21**:11, pp. 78–86

BLOCH, J. J., DANIELS, D. S., SPECTOR, A. Z. (1987): A Weighted Voting Algorithm for Replicated Directories. J. ACM **34**:4, 859–909

BLY, S. A., HARRISON, S. R., IRWIN, S. (1993): Media Spaces: Bringing People together in a Video, Audio and Computing Environment. Communications of the ACM **36**:1, 28–47

BOCIONEK, S. ET AL. (1993): CAP II: Making the Calendar Apprentice an Agent. Technical Report. Dept. of Computer Science, Carnegie Mellon Univ., Pittsburgh, PA

BOCK, G. E., MARCA, D. A. (1995): Designing Groupware. New York: McGraw-Hill

BOND, A. H., GASSER, L., eds. (1988): Readings in Distributed Artificial Intelligence. San Mateo, CA: Morgan Kaufmann

BORENSTEIN, N., EVERHART, C., ROSENBERG, J., STOOLER, A. (1988): A Multimedia Message System for Andrew. Proc. Usenix Conf. Winter '88, Dallas, TX. Berkeley, CA: Usenix Association

BORGHOFF, U. M., OBERMAIER, R. (1991): Simulation von Votierungsverfahren in verteilten Datenbanksystemen. In: Tavangarian, D. (ed.): Proc. 7th Symp. Simulationstechnik (ASIM '91), Hagen, Germany. Fortschritte in der Simulationstechnik **4**, Braunschweig: Vieweg, pp. 458–462. (in German)

BORGHOFF, U. M., PARESCHI, R., eds. (1998): Information Technology for Knowledge Management. Berlin, Heidelberg, New York: Springer-Verlag

BORGHOFF, U. M., SCHLICHTER, J. H. (1996): On Combining the Knowledge of Heterogeneous Information Repositories. J. Universal Computer Science **2**:7, 515–532. Electronic version: http://www.iicm.edu/jucs

BORGHOFF, U. M., TEEGE, G. (1993): Application of Collaborative Editing to Software-Engineering Projects. ACM SIGSOFT Software Engineering Notes **18**:3, A-56–64

BORGHOFF, U. M., TEEGE, G. (1993): Structure Management in the Collaborative Multimedia Editing System IRIS. In: Chua, T.-S., Kunii, T. L. (eds.): Proc. 1st Int. Conf. on Multi-Media Modeling (MMM '93), Singapore. Singapore, New Jersey, London, Hong Kong: World Scientific, pp. 159–173

BORGHOFF, U. M., BOTTONI, P., MUSSIO, P., PARESCHI, R. (1996): A Systemic Metaphor of Multi-Agent Coordination in Living Systems. In: Javor, A., Lehmann, A., Molnar, I. (eds.): Proc. 10th Europ. Simulation Multiconf. (ESM '96), Budapest, Hungary. San Diego, CA: The Society for Computer Simulation, pp. 245–253

BORGHOFF, U. M., CHEVALIER, P.-Y., WILLAMOWSKI, J. (1996): Adaptive Refinement of Search Patterns for Distributed Information Gathering. In: Verbraeck, A. (ed.): Proc. Int. Conf. EuroMedia/WEBTEC '96, London, UK. San Diego, CA: The Society for Computer Simulation, pp. 5–12

BORGHOFF, U. M., PARESCHI, R., KARCH, H., NÖHMEIER, M., SCHLICHTER, J. H. (1996): Constraint-Based Information Gathering for a Network Publication System. Proc. 1st Int. Conf. on the Practical Application of Intelligent Agents and Multi-Agent Technology (PAAM '96), London, UK. Blackpool, UK: The Practical Application Company Ltd, pp. 45–59

BORGHOFF, U. M., BOTTONI, P., MUSSIO, P., PARESCHI, R. (1997): Reflective Agents for Adaptive Workflows. Proc. 2nd Int. Conf. on the Practical Application of Intelligent Agents and Multi-Agent Technology (PAAM '97), London, UK. Blackpool, UK: The Practical Application Company Ltd, pp. 405–420

BORGHOFF, U. M., HILF, E. R., PARESCHI, R., SEVERIENS, T., STAMERJOHANNS, H., WILLAMOWSKI, J. (1997): Agent-Based Document Retrieval for the European Physicists: A Project Overview. Proc. 2nd Int. Conf. on the Practical Application of Intelligent Agents and Multi-Agent Technology (PAAM '97), London, UK. Blackpool, UK: The Practical Application Company Ltd, pp. 271–285

BORGHOFF, U. M., PARESCHI, R., ARCELLI, F., FORMATO, F. (1998): Constraint-Based Protocols for Distributed Problem Solving. Science of Computer Programming **30**, 201–225

BORGHOFF, U. M. (1990): Voting and Relocation Strategies Preserving Consistency among Replicated Files. In: Abiteboul, S., Kanellakis, P. C. (eds.): Proc. 3rd Int. Conf. on Database Theory (ICDT '90), Paris, France. Lecture Notes in Computer Science **470**. Berlin: Springer-Verlag, pp. 318–332

BORGHOFF, U. M. (1992): Catalogue of Distributed File/Operating Systems. Berlin, Heidelberg, New York: Springer-Verlag

BOWEN, D. (1991): Open Distributed Processing. Computer Networks and ISDN Systems **23**:1-3, 195–201

BOWMAN, C. M., DANZIG, P. B., HARDY, D. R., MANBER, U., SCHWARTZ, M. F. (1994): The Harvest Information Discovery and Access System. Proc. 2nd Int. World-Wide Web Conf., Chicago, IL. pp. 763–771

BOWMAN, C. M., DHARAP, C., BARUAH, M., CAMARGO, B., POTTI, S. (1994): A File System for Information Management. Proc. Int. Conf. on Intelligent Information Management Systems, Washington, DC

BRACHMAN, B. J., CHANSON, S. T. (1989): A Hierarchical Solution for Application Level Store-and- Forward Deadlock Prevention. Proc. ACM SIGCOMM Symp. in Communications Architectures and Protocols, Austin, TX. ACM SIGCOMM Computer Communication Review **19**:4, pp. 25–32

BRADSHAW, J. M., eds. (1997): Software Agents. Menlo Park, CA: AAAI Press, Cambridge, MA, London, U. K.: MIT Press

BRATMAN, M. E., ISRAEL, D. J., POLLACK, M. E. (1988): Plans and Resource-Bounded Practical Reasoning. Computational Intelligence **4**, 349–355

BROOKS, R. A. (1991): Intelligence without Representation. Artificial Intelligence **47**, 139–159

BROWN, H. M., SEDGEWICK, R. (1984): A System for Algorithm Animation. Computer Graphics **18**:3, 177–186

BROWNBRIDGE, D. R., MARSHALL, L. F., RANDELL, B. (1982): The Newcastle Connection or Unixes of the World Unite. Software – Practice and Experience **12**:12, 1147–1162. also in: Shrivastava S. K. (ed.): Reliable Computer Systems. Collected Papers of the Newcastle Reliability Project, 1985. Berlin, Heidelberg, New York: Springer-Verlag, pp. 532–549

BULLEN, C. V., BENNET, J. L. (1991): Groupware in Practice: An Interpretation of Work Experiences. In: Dunlop, C., Kling, R. (eds.): Computerization and Controversy: Value Conflicts and Social Choices. London: Academic Press, pp. 257–287

BUSH, V. (1945): As We May Think. Atlantic Monthly **176**:1, 101–108

BUSSLER, C., JABLONSKI, S. (1994): Implementing Agent Coordination for Workflow Management Systems Using Active Database Systems. Proc. IEEE RIDE 4th Int. Workshop on Research Issues in Data Engineering, Houston, TX. Los Alamitos, CA: IEEE Computer Society Press, pp. 53–61

CALLAN, J. P., CROFT, W. B., HARDING, S. M. (1992): The Inquery Retrieval System. Proc. 3rd Int. Conf. on Database and Expert Systems Applications. pp. 78–83

CALLAN, J. P., LU, Z., CROFT, W. B. (1995): Searching Distributed Collections with Inference Networks. Proc. 18th ACM SIGIR Conf. on Research and Development in Information Retrieval, Seattle, WA

CAMPBELL, B., GOODMAN, J. M. (1988): HAM: A Genaral Pupose Hypertext Abstract Machine. Communications of the ACM **31**:7, 856–861

CAMPBELL, D. S. (1992): Calendering and Group Scheduling. In: Coleman, D. (ed.): Proc. Groupware'92. Los Altos, CA: Morgan Kaufmann, pp. 388–390

CARROLL, J. L., LONG, D. D. E. (1989): The Effect of Failure and Repair Distribution on Consistency Protocols for Replicated Data Objects. Proc. 22nd Annual Simulation Symp., Tampa, FL. pp. 47–60

CARROLL, J. L., LONG, D. D. E., PÂRIS, J.-F. (1987): Block-level Consistency of Replicated Files. Proc. 7th IEEE Int. Conf. on Distributed Computing Systems, Berlin, Germany. Los Alamitos, CA: IEEE Computer Society Press, pp. 146–153

CASEY, R. G. (1972): Allocation of Copies of a File in an Information Network. Proc. Spring Joint Computer Conf. **40**. Arlington, VA: AFIPS Press, pp. 617–625

CHAFFEY, D. (1998): Groupware, Workflow and Intranets: Reengineering the Enterprise with Collaborative Software. Bedford, MA: Digital Press

CHAKRAVARTHY, S., KARLAPALEM, E., NAVATHE, S. B., TANAKA, A (1992): Database Supported Cooperative Problem Solving. Technical Report UF-CIS-TR-92-046. Univ. of Florida, Gainsville, FL

CHANDY, K. M., MISRA, J. (1988): Parallel Program Design: A Foundation. Reading, MA: Addison-Wesley

CHAWATHE, S., GARCIA-MOLINA, H., HAMMER, J., IRELAND, K., PAPAKONSTANTINOU, Y., ULLMAN, J., WIDOM, J. (1994): The Tsimmis Project: Integration of Heterogeneous Information Sources. Proc. IPSJ Conf., Tokyo, Japan. Los Alamitos, CA: IEEE Computer Society Press

CHERITON, D. (1988): The V Distributed System. Communications of the ACM **31**:3, 314–333

CHEUNG, S. Y., AHAMAD, M., AMMAR, M. H. (1989): Optimizing Vote and Quorum Assignments for Reading and Writing Replicated Data. IEEE Transactions on Knowledge and Data Engineering **1**:3, 387–397

CHEUNG, S. Y., AHAMAD, M., AMMAR, M. H. (1990): Multi-Dimensional Voting: A General Method for Implementing Synchronization in Distributed Systems. Proc. 10th IEEE Int. Conf. on Distributed Computing Systems, Paris, France. Los Alamitos, CA: IEEE Computer Society Press, pp. 362–369

CHEUNG, S. Y., AMMAR, M. H., AHAMAD, M. (1992): The Grid Protocol: A High Performance Scheme for Maintaining Replicated Data. IEEE Transactions on Knowledge and Data Engineering **4**:6, 582–592

CHIDLOVSKII, B., BORGHOFF, U. M. (1998): Query Translation for Distributed Information Gathering on the Web. In: Eaglestone, B., Desai, B. C., Shao, J. (eds.): Proc. 2nd IEEE Int. Database Engineering and Application Symp. (IDEAS'98), Cardiff, UK. Los Alamitos, CA: IEEE Comp. Soc. Press, pp. 214–223

CHIDLOVSKII, B., BORGHOFF, U. M. (1998): Signature File Methods for Semantic Query Caching. In: Nikolaou, C., Stephanidis, C. (eds.): Proc. 2nd Europ. Conf. on Research and Advanced Technology for Digital Libraries (ECDL'98), Heraklion, Greece. Lecture Notes in Computer Science **1513**. Berlin, Heidelberg, New York: Springer-Verlag, pp. 479–498

CHIDLOVSKII, B., BORGHOFF, U. M. (2000): Semantic Caching of Web Queries. The International Journal on Very Large Data Bases **9**:1, 2–17

CHIDLOVSKII, B., BORGHOFF, U. M., CHEVALIER, P.-Y. (1997): Towards Sophisticated Wrapping of Web-based Information Repositories. Proc. 5th Int. RIAO Conf. on Computer-Assisted Information Searching on the Internet, Montreal, Canada. pp. 123–135

CHIDLOVSKII, B., BORGHOFF, U. M., CHEVALIER, P.-Y. (1998): Boolean Query Translation for Brokerage on the Web. In: Verbraeck, A. (ed.): Proc. Int. Conf. EuroMedia/WEBTEC '98, Leicester, UK. San Diego, CA: The Society for Computer Simulation, pp. 37–44

CHU, W. W. (1969): Optimal File Allocation in a Multiple Computer System. IEEE Transactions on Computers **C–18**:10, 885–889

CHU, W. W. (1973): Optimal File Allocation in a Computer Network. In: Abramson, N., Kuo, F. F. (eds.): Computer Communication Systems. Englewood Cliffs, NJ: Prentice-Hall, pp. 82–84

COFFMAN, E. G., GELENBE, E., PLATEAU, B. (1981): Optimization of the Number of Copies of Files in a Distributed Database. IEEE Transactions on Software Engineering **SE–7**:1, 78–84

COHEN, E. G., GOODLAD, J. I. (1994): Designing Groupwork: Strategies for the Heterogeneous Classroom. Teachers College Press

COLE, F., BROWN, H. (1991): ODA Extensions for Quality and Flexibility. Computer Networks and ISDN Systems **21**, 221–230

COLEMAN, D., KHANNA, R., eds. (1995): Groupware Technology and Applications. Upper Saddle River: Prentice-Hall

CONDON, C. (1993): The Computer won't let me: Cooperation, Conflict and the Ownership of Information. In: Easterbrook, S. (ed.): CSCW: Cooperation or Conflict. London: Springer-Verlag

CONEN, W., NEUMANN, G., eds. (1998): Coordination Technology for Collaborative Applications: Organizations, Processes and Agents. Lecture Notes in Computer Science **1364**. Berlin, Heidelberg, New York: Springer-Verlag

CONKLIN, J., BEGEMAN, M. L. (1988): gIBIS: A Hypertext Tool for Exploratory Policy Discussion. Proc. 2nd Int. Conf. on Computer-Supported Cooperative Work, Portland, OR. New York: SIGCHI/SIGOIS ACM, pp. 140–152

CONKLIN, J. (1987): Hypertext: An Introduction and Survey. IEEE Computer **20**:9, 17–41

COOPER, L. (1963): Location-Allocation Problems. Operation Research **11**:3, 331–343

CORBIN, J. R. (1991): The Art of Distributed Applications. Berlin, Heidelberg, New York: Springer-Verlag

COULOURIS, G., DOLLIMORE, J., KINDBERG, T. (1994): Distributed Systems: Concepts and Design. Reading, MA: Addison-Wesley

CRABTREE, A., O'BRIEN, J., TWIDALE, M. B., NICHOLS, D. M. (1997): Talking in the Library: Implications for the Design of Digital Libraries. Proc. 2nd Int. Conf. on Digital Libraries, Philadelphia, PA

CROWLEY, T., MILAZZO, P., BAKER, E., FORSDICK, H., TOMLINSON, R. (1990): MMConf: An Infrastructure for Building Shared Multimedia Applications. Proc. 3rd Int. Conf. on Computer-Supported Cooperative Work, Los Angeles, CA. New York: SIGCHI/SIGOIS ACM, pp. 329–342

DANIELSEN, T., PANKOKE-BABATZ, U., PRINZ, W., PATEL, A., PAYS, P. A., SMAALAND, K., SPETH, R. (1986): The AMIGO Project: Advanced Group Communication Model for Computer-Based Communication Environment. In: Peterson, D. (ed.): Proc. 1st Int. Conf. on Computer-Supported Cooperative Work, Austin, TX. New York: SIGCHI/SIGOIS ACM, pp. 115–142

DASGUPTA, P., LEBLANC, R. J., APPELBE, W. F. (1988): The Clouds Distributed Operating System. Proc. 8th IEEE Int. Conf. on Distributed Computing Systems, San Jose, CA. Los Alamitos, CA: IEEE Computer Society Press, pp. 1–9

DAVĈEV, D., BURKHARD, W. A. (1985): Consistency and Recovery Control for Replicated Files. Proc. 10th ACM Symp. on Operating Systems Principles, Orcas Island, WA. ACM SIGOPS Operating Systems Review **19**:5, pp. 87–96

DAVIDSON, S. B. (1984): Optimism and Consistency in Partitioned Distributed Database Systems. ACM Transactions on Database Systems **9**:3, 456–481

DE CINDIO, F., DE MICHELIS, G., SIMONE, C. (1988): The Communication Disciplines of CHAOS. Concurrency and Nets. New York: Springer-Verlag pp. 115–139

DEAN, M. A., SANDS, R. E., SCHANTZ, R. E. (1987): Canonical Data Representation in the Cronus Distributed Operating System. Proc. IEEE INFOCOM, San Francisco, CA. Los Alamitos, CA: IEEE Computer Society Press, pp. 814–819

DEEN, S. M., eds. (1994): IMAGINE: A Framework for Building Multi Agent Systems. Keele, U. K.: Univ. Keele

DELISLE, N. M., SCHWARTZ, M. D. (1986): Neptune: A Hypertext System for CAD Applications. In: Zaniolo, C. (ed.): Proc. ACM SIGMOD Int. Conf. on Management of Data, Washington, DC. ACM SIGMOD Record, **15**:2, pp. 132–143

DENNIS, A. R. (1994): Electronic Support for large Groups. Journal of Organizational Computing **4**:2, 177–197

DIAPER, D., SANGER, C., eds. (1993): CSCW in Practice: An Introduction and Case Studies. London: Springer-Verlag

DOURISH, P., BLY, S. (1992): Portholes: Supporting Awareness in a Distributed Work Group. Proc. of ACM INTERCHI'92 Conf. on Human Factors in Computing Systems. pp. 514–547

DOURISH, P. (1995): Developing a Reflective Model of Collaborative Systems. ACM Transactions on Computer-Human Interaction **2**:1, 40–63

DOURISH, P. (1998): Using Metalevel Techniques in a Flexible Toolkit for CSCW Applications. ACM Transactions on Computer-Human Interaction **5**:2, 109–155

DOWDY, L. W., FOSTER, D. V. (1982): Comparative Models of the File Assignment Problem. ACM Computing Surveys **14**:2, 287–313

EBERLE, H., SCHMUTZ, H. (1986): NOS Kernels for Heterogeneous Environments. In: Müller, G., Blanc, R. P. (eds.): Proc. Int. Seminar on Networking in Open Systems, Oberlech, Austria. Lecture Notes in Computer Science **248**. Berlin, Heidelberg, New York: Springer-Verlag, pp. 270–295

EFROYMSON, M. A., RAY, T. L. (1966): A Branch-bound Algorithm for Plant Location. Operation Research **14**:3, 361–368

ELLIS, C., BERNAL, M. (1982): OfficeTalk-D: An Experimental Office Information System. Proc. 1st ACM SIGOA Conf., Philadelphia, PA. pp. 131 – 140

ELLIS, C. A., GIBBS, S. J. (1989): Concurrency Control in Groupware Systems. In: Clifford, J., Lindsay, B., Maier, D. (eds.): Proc. ACM SIGMOD Int. Conf. on Management of Data, Portland, OR. ACM SIGMOD Record, **18**:2, pp. 399–407

ELLIS, C. A., WAINER, J. (1994): Goal-Based Models of Collaboration. Collaborative Computing **1**:1, 61–86

ELLIS, C. A., GIBBS, S. J., REIN, G. L. (1990): Design and Use of a Group Editor. In: Cockton, G. (ed.): Engineering for Human Computer Interaction. Amsterdam: North-Holland, pp. 13–25

ELLIS, C. A., GIBBS, S. J., REIN, G. L. (1991): Groupware – Some Issues and Experiences. Communications of the ACM **34**:1, 38–58

EMTAGE, A., DEUTSCH, P. (1992): Archie: An Electronic Directory Service for the Internet. Proc. Usenix Conf. Winter '92, Sunset Beach, CA. Berkeley, CA: Usenix Association, pp. 93–110

ENGELBART, D. C., ENGLISH, W. K. (1968): A Research Center for Augmenting Human Intellect. Proc. Fall Joint Computing Conf. Washington, DC: Thompson Book Co., pp. 395–410

ENGELBART, D. C. (1982): Toward High-Performance Knowledge Workers. Proc. Office Automation Conf. Digest. Arlington, VA: AFIPS Press, pp. 279–290

EVELAND, J. D., BIKSON, T. K. (1988): Work Group Structures and Computer Support: A Field Experiment. ACM Transactions on Office Information Systems **6**:4, 354–379

FEINER, S., NAGY, S., V. DAM, A. (1982): An Experimental System for Creating and Presenting Interactive Graphical Documents. ACM Transactions on Graphics **1**:1, 59–77

FELDMAN, E. (1966): Warehouse Location under Continuous Economies of Scale. Management Science **12**:9, 670–684

FERWAGNER, T., WANG, Y., LEWE, H., KRCMAR, H. (1991): Experiences in Designing the Hohenheim CATeam Room. In: Bowers, J. M., Benford, S. D. (eds.): Studies in Computer-Supported Cooperative Work. Amsterdam: North-Holland, pp. 251–265

FIKES, R., ENGELMORE, R., FARQUHAR, A., PRATT, W. (1995): Network-Based Information Brokers. Proc. AAAI Spring Symp. Series on Information Gathering from Distributed Heterogeneous Environments, Stanford, CA

FININ, T., FRITZSON, R., MCKAY, D., MCENTIRE, R. (1994): KQML: A Language and Protocol for Knowledge and Information Exchange. In: Fuchi, K., Yokoi, T. (eds.): Knowledge Building and Knowledge Sharing. Ohmsha and IOS Press

FISH, R. S., KRAUT, R. E., LELAND, M. D. P. (1988): Quilt: A Collaborative Tool for Cooperative Writing. In: Allen, R. B. (ed.): Proc. ACM SIGOIS/IEEE TC-OA Conf. on Office Information Systems, Palo Alto, CA. ACM SIGOIS Bulletin, **9**:2&3, pp. 30–37

FLORES, F., GRAVES, M., HARTFIELD, B., WINOGRAD, T. (1988): Computer Systems and the Design of Organizational Interaction. ACM Transactions on Office Information Systems **6**:2, 153–172

FLOWER, L., HAYES, J. R. (1981): A Cognitive Process Theory of Writing. College Composition and Communication **32**:4, 365–381

FOUNDATION, OPEN SOFTWARE (1992): Introduction to OSF DCE. Englewood Cliffs, NJ: Prentice Hall

FUCHS, L., PANKOKE-BABBATZ, U., PRINZ, W. (1995): Supporting Cooperative Awareness with Local Event Mechanisms: The Groupdesk System. Proc. 4th Europ. Conf. on Computer-Supported Cooperative Work. Dordrecht: Kluwer, pp. 247–262

FURUTA, R., STOTTS, P. D. (1994): Interpreted Collaboration Protocols and their use in Groupware Prototyping. Proc. 5th Int. Conf. on Computer-Supported Cooperative Work, Chapel Hill, NC. New York: SIGCHI/SIGOIS ACM, pp. 121–131

GARCIA-MOLINA, H., BARBARA, D. (1984): Optimizing the Reliability Provided by Voting Mechanisms. Proc. 4th IEEE Int. Conf. on Distributed Computing Systems, San Francisco, CA. Los Alamitos, CA: IEEE Computer Society Press, pp. 340–346

GARCIA-MOLINA, H., BARBARA, D. (1985): How to Assign Votes in a Distributed System. J. ACM **32**:4, 841–860

GAVISH, B., PIRKUL, H. (1986): Computer and Database Location in Distributed Computer Systems. IEEE Transactions on Computers **C–35**:7, 583–590

GELENBE, E. (1985): On the Availability of a Distributed Computer System with Failing Components. Proc. ACM SIGMETRICS Conf. on Measurement and Modeling of Computer Systems, Austin, TX. ACM SIGMETRICS Performance Evaluation Review, **13**, pp. 6–13

GELERNTER, D. (1985): Generative Communication in Linda. ACM Transactions on Programming Languages and Systems **7**:1, 80–112

GIBBS, SIMON J., ARAPIS, CONSTANTIN, BREITENEDER, CHRISTIAN J. (1999): TELEPORT – Towards Immersive Copresence. Multimedia Systems **7**:3, 214–221

GIBBS, S. J. (1989): CSCW and Software Engineering. In: Tsichritzis, D. (ed.): Object-Oriented Development, Chap. **4**, Univ. of Geneva, Switzerland. pp. 31–40

GIBBS, S. J. (1989): LIZA: An Extensible Groupware Toolkit. Proc. ACM SIGCHI '89 Conf. on Human Factors in Computing Systems, Austin, TX. New York: ACM SIGCHI, pp. 29–35

GIFFORD, D. K., NEEDHAM, R. M., SCHROEDER, M. D. (1988): The Cedar File System. Communications of the ACM **31**:3, 288–298

GIFFORD, D. K. (1979): Weighted Voting for Replicated Data. Proc. 7th ACM Symp. on Operating Systems Principles, Pacific Grove, CA. ACM SIGOPS Operating Systems Review **13**:5, pp. 150–162

GLANCE, N., PAGANI, D., PARESCHI, R. (1996): Generalized Process Structure Grammars (GPSG) for Flexible Representations of Work. In: Ackerman, M. S. (ed.): Proc. 7th Int. Conf. on Computer-Supported Cooperative Work, Boston,

MA. New York: SIGCHI/SIGOIS ACM, pp. 180–189

GLANCE, N., ARREGUI, D., DARDENNE, M. (1998): Knowledge Pump: Supporting the Flow and Use of Knowledge. In: Borghoff and Pareschi (1998). pp. 35–51

GLANCE, N., GRASSO, A., BORGHOFF, U. M., SNOWDON, D., WILLAMOWSKI, J. (1999): Supporting Collaborative Information Activities in Networked Communities. In: Bullinger, H.-J., Ziegler, J. (eds.): Proc. 8th Int. Conf. on Human-Computer Interaction (HCI '99), Munich, Germany. Mahwah, NJ: Laurence Erlbaum Associates, pp. 422–426

GLEZER, CHANAN, YADAV, SURYA B. (1999): A conceptual model of an intelligent meeting-scheduler. Journal of Organizational Computing and Electronic Commerce **9**:4, 233–251

GMD FOKUS, THE OPEN GROUP, IBM (1996): Mobile Agent Facility Specification. Object Management Group. OMG TC Document cf/96-12-01

GOLDBERG, D., NICHOLS, D., OKI, B. M., TERRY, D. (1992): Using Collaborative Filtering to Weave an Information Tapestry. Communications of the ACM **35**:12, 61–70

GOODMAN, N., SKEEN, D., CHAN, A., DAYAL, U., FOX, S., RIES, D. (1983): A Recovery Algorithm for a Distributed Database System. Proc. 2nd ACM SIGACT/SIGMOD Symp. on Principles of Database Systems

GOODMAN, D. (1987): The Complete HyperCard Handbook. New York: Bantam Books

GOSCINSKI, A. M. (1991): Distributed Operating Systems: The Logical Design. Reading, MA: Addison-Wesley

GRASSO, M. A., BORGHOFF, U. M., GLANCE, N., WILLAMOWSKI, J. (1998): Collaborative Information Gathering. In: Verbraeck, A. (ed.): Proc. Int. Conf. EuroMedia/WEBTEC '98, Leicester, UK. San Diego, CA: The Society for Computer Simulation, pp. 65–72

GRAVANO, L., GARCIA-MOLINA, H. (1995): Generalizing Gloss to Vector-Space Databases and Broker Hierarchies. In: Dayal, U., Gray, P. M. D., Nishio, S. (eds.): Proc. 21st Int. Conf. on Very Large Data Bases, Zurich, Switzerland. San Francisco, CA: Morgan Kaufmann, pp. 78–89

GRAVANO, L., CHANG, C.-C., GARCIA-MOLINA, H., PAEPCKE, A. (1997): STARTS: Stanford Proposal for Internet Meta-Searching. Proc. ACM SIGMOD Int. Conf. on Management of Data. ACM SIGMOD Record, **26**

GREENBERG, S., GUTWIN, C., COCKBURN, A. (1996): Using Distortion-Oriented Displays to Support Workspace Awareness. Technical Report. Dept. of Computer Science, Univ. of Calgary, Canada

GREENBERG, S. (1991): Computer-Supported Cooperative Work and Groupware: An Introduction to the Special Issues. Int. J. Man-Machine Studies **34**:2

GREENHALGH, CHRIS, BENFORD, STEVE (1995): Virtual Reality Tele-conferencing: Implementation and Experience. Proc. 4th Europ. Conf. on Computer-Supported Cooperative Work. Dordrecht: Kluwer, pp. 165–180

GREHAN, R. ET AL. (1991): Getting Groups on Schedule. BYTE pp. 250–264

GREIF, I., SARIN, S. K. (1987): Data Sharing in Group Work. ACM Transactions on Office Information Systems **5**:2, 187–211

GREIF, I., SELIGER, R., WEIHL, W. (1986): Atomic Data Abstractions in a Distributed Collaborative Editing System (Extended Abstract). Proc. 13th ACM SIGACT/SIGPLAN Annual Symp. on Principles of Programming Languages, St. Petersburg Beach, FL. New York: ACM, pp. 160–172

GREIF, I. (1988): Computer-Supported Cooperative Work: A Book of Readings. San Mateo, CA: Morgan Kaufmann

GROENBAEK, K. ET AL. (1994): Cooperative Hypermedia Systems: A Dexter-based Architecture. Communications of the ACM **37**:2, 65–74

GRUDIN, J. (1988): Why CSCW Applications fail: Problems in the Design and Evaluation of Organizational Interfaces. Proc. 2nd Int. Conf. on Computer-Supported Cooperative Work, Portland, OR. New York: SIGCHI/SIGOIS ACM, pp. 85–93

GRUDIN, J. (1990): Groupware and Cooperative Work: Problems and Prospects. In: Laurel, B. (ed.): The Art of Human-Computer Interface Design. New York: Addison-Wesley, pp. 171–185

GRUDIN, J. (1991): CSCW: The Convergence of two Development Contexts. Proc. ACM SIGCHI'91 Conf. on Human Factors in Computing Systems, New Orleans, LA. New York: ACM SIGCHI, pp. 91–97

GRUDIN, J. (1994): CSCW: History and Focus. IEEE Computer **27**:5, 19–26

GRUDIN, J. (1994): Groupware and Social Dynamics: Eight Challenges for Developers. Communications of the ACM **37**:1, 92–105

HAAKE, J. M., STREITZ, N. A. (1996): Hypermedia Structures and the Division of Labor in Meeting Room Collaboration. In: Ackerman, M. S. (ed.): Proc. 7th Int. Conf. on Computer-Supported Cooperative Work, Boston, MA. New York: SIGCHI/SIGOIS ACM, pp. 170–179

HAAKE, J. M., WILSON, B. (1992): Supporting Collaborative Writing of Hyperdocuments in SEPIA. In: Turner, J., Kraut, R. E. (eds.): Proc. 4th Int. Conf. on Computer-Supported Cooperative Work, Toronto, Canada. New York: SIGCHI/SIGOIS ACM, pp. 138–146

HAHN, U., JARKE, M., EHERER, S., KREPLIN, K. (1991): CoAUTHOR: A Hypermedia Group Authoring Environment. In: Bowers, J. M., Benford, S. D. (eds.): Studies in Computer-Supported Cooperative Work. Amsterdam: North-Holland, pp. 79–100

HALASZ, F., SCHWARTZ, M. (1994): The Dexter Hypertext Reference Model. Communications of the ACM **37**:2, 30–39

HALASZ, F. G., MORAN, T. P., TRIGG, R. H. (1987): NoteCards in a Nutshell. In: Carroll, J. M., Tanner, P. P. (eds.): Proc. ACM SIGCHI+GI '87 Conf. on Human Factors in Computing Systems and Graphics Interface, Toronto, Canada. New York: ACM, pp. 45–52

HALASZ, F. G. (1988): Reflections on NoteCards: Seven Issues for the Next Generation of Hypermedia Systems. Communications of the ACM **31**:7, 836–852

HAMMER, M., CHAMPY, J. (1995): Business Reengineering. Campus

HAREL, D. (1987): Statecharts: A Visual Formalism for Complex Systems. Science of Computer Programming **8**, 231–274

HARRISON, W. H., OSSHER, H., SWEENEY, P. F. (1990): Coordinating Concurrent Development. Proc. 3rd Int. Conf. on Computer-Supported Cooperative Work, Los Angeles, CA. New York: SIGCHI/SIGOIS ACM, pp. 157–168

HÄRTIG, H., KÜHNHAUSER, W., LUX, W., STREICH, H., GOOS, G. (1986): Structure of the BirliX Operating System. Proc. Europ. Unix Systems User Group Conf. Autumn '86, Manchester, UK. Buntingford Herts, UK: EUUG, pp. 433–449

HASHIM, S. H. (1991): WHAT: An Argumentative Groupware Approach for Organizing and Documenting Research Activities. Journal of Organizational Computing **1**:3, 275–302

HAUGENEDER, H., eds. (1994): IMAGINE: Final Project Report. IMAGINE Technical Report Series

HAZEMI, R., HAILES, S., WILBUR, S., eds. (1998): The Digital University: Reinventing the Academy. London: Springer-Verlag

HEGERING, H.-G., ABECK, S. (1994): Integrated Network and Systems Management. Bonn, Paris: Addison-Wesley

HELAL, A. A., HEDDAYA, A. A., BHARGAVA, B. B. (1996): Replication Techniques in Distributed Systems. Series on Advances in Database Systems **4**. Dordrecht: Kluwer

HENNESSY, P., KREIFELTS, T., EHRLICH, U. (1992): Distributed Work Management: Activity Coordination within the EuroCoOp Project. Computer Communications, Butterworth-Heinemann **15**:8, 477–488

HERLIHY, M. P. (1987): Dynamic Quorum Adjustment for Partitioned Data. ACM Transactions on Database Systems **12**:2, 170–194

HEWITT, C. (1986): Offices are Open Systems. ACM Transactions on Office Information Systems **4**:3, 271–287

HILL, W. C., HOLLAN, J. D., WROBLEWSKI, D., MCCANDLESS, T. (1992): Edit Wear and Read Wear. In: Bauersfeld, P., Bennett, J., Lynch, G. (eds.): Proc. ACM SIGCHI '92 Conf. on Human Factors in Computing Systems, Monterey, CA. New York: ACM SIGCHI, pp. 3–9

HILL, W. C., STEAD, L., ROSENSTEIN, M., FURNAS, G. (1995): Recommending and Evaluating Choices in a Virtual Community of Use. Proc. ACM CHI'95 Conf. on Human Factors in Computing Systems, Denver, CO. New York: ACM Press, pp. 194–201

HILTZ, S. R., TUROFF, M. (1978): The Network Nation: Human Communication via Computer. Reading, MA: Addison-Wesley

HOGG, J. (1985): Intelligent Message Systems. In: Tsichritzis, D. (ed.): Office Automation, **6**. Berlin, Heidelberg, New York: Springer-Verlag, pp. 113–133

HOPPE, H. U., ZAO, J. (1994): C-TORI: An Interface for Cooperative Database Retrieval. In: Karagiannis, D. (ed.): Database and Expert Systems Applications. Berlin, Heidelberg, New York: Springer-Verlag, pp. 103–113

HOSCHKA, P., BUTSCHER, B., STREITZ, N. (1993): Telecooperation and Telepresence: Technical Challenges of a Government Distributed between Bonn and Berlin. Informatization and the Public Sector **2**:4, 269–299

HOYLE, M. A., LUEG, C. (1997): Open Sesame!: A Look at Personal Assistants. Proc. 2nd Int. Conf. on the Practical Application of Intelligent Agents and Multi-Agent Technology (PAAM '97), London, UK. Blackpool, UK: The Practical Application Company Ltd, pp. 51–60

HUANG, C.-L., LI, V. O. K. (1989): Missing-Partition Dynamic Voting Scheme for Replicated Database Systems. Proc. 9th IEEE Int. Conf. on Distributed Computing Systems, Newport Beach, CA. Los Alamitos, CA: IEEE Computer Society Press, pp. 579–586

HUANG, C.-L., LI, V. O. K. (1990): Regeneration-Based Multiversion Dynamic Voting Scheme for Replicated Database Systems. Proc. 10th IEEE Int. Conf. on Distributed Computing Systems, Paris, France. Los Alamitos, CA: IEEE Computer Society Press, pp. 370–377

HUBERMAN, B. A., KAMINSKY, M. (1996): Beehive: A System for Cooperative Filtering and Sharing of Information. Technical Report. Xerox PARC

HUGHES, J., RANDALL, D., SHAPIRO, D. (1991): CSCW: Discipline or Paradigm. In: Bannon, L., Robinson, M., Schmidt, K. (eds.): Proc. 2nd Europ. Conf. on Computer-Supported Cooperative Work, Amsterdam, The Netherlands. Dordrecht: Kluwer, pp. 325–336

HUNTER, D., BAILEY, A., TAYLOR, B. (1995): The Art of Facilitation: How to Create Group Synergy. Fisher Books

HUNTER, D., BAILEY, A., TAYLOR, B. (1999): The Essence of Facilitation. Tandem/ Fisher Books

IBARAKI, T., KAMEDA, T. (1993): A Theory of Coteries: Mutual Exclusion in Distributed Systems. IEEE Transactions on Parallel and Distributed Systems **4**:7, 779–794

IBARAKI, T., KATOH, N. (1988): Resource Allocation Problems – Algorithmic Approaches. Cambridge, MA, London, UK: MIT Press

IGBARIA, M., TAN, M., eds. (1998): The Virtual Workplace. Hershey, London: Idea Group Publishing

IRANI, K. B., KHABBAZ, N. G. (1979): A Model for a Combined Communication Network Design and File Allocation for Distributed Databases. Proc. 1st IEEE Int. Conf. on Distributed Computing Systems. Los Alamitos, CA: IEEE Computer Society Press

ISHIDA, T., ISBISTER, K., eds. (2000): Digital Cities: Technologies, Experiences and Future Perspectives. Lecture Notes in Computer Science **1765**. Berlin, Heidelberg, New York: Springer-Verlag

ISHIDA, T., eds. (1998): Community Computing: Collaboration over Global Information Networks. New York: John Wiley & Sons, Inc.

ISHIDA, T., eds. (1999): Community Computing and Support Systems: Social Interaction in Networked Communities. Lecture Notes in Computer Science **1519**. Berlin, Heidelberg, New York: Springer-Verlag

ISHII, H., MIYAKE, N. (1991): Toward an Open Shared Workspace: Computer and Video Fusion Approach of Teamworkstation. Communications of the ACM **34**:12, 37–50

ISHII, H., KOBAYASHI, M., GRUDIN, J. (1992): Integration of Interpersonal Space and Shared Workspace: ClearBoard Design and Experiments. In: Turner, J., Kraut, R. E. (eds.): Proc. 4th Int. Conf. on Computer-Supported Cooperative Work, Toronto, Canada. New York: SIGCHI/SIGOIS ACM, pp. 33–42

ISO, 8879 (1986): Information Processing – Text and Office Systems – Standard Generalized Markup Language (SGML). Int. Organization for Standardization: ISO IS

ISO, 8613 (1988): Information Processing – Text and Office Systems – Office Document Architecture (ODA) and Interchange Format. Int. Organization for Standardization: ISO IS Parts 1,2,4–8

JABLONSKI, S., BUSSLER, C. (1996): Workflow Management – Modeling, Concepts, Architecture and Implementation. International Thomson Computer Press

JABLONSKI, S., BÖHM, M., SCHULZE, W., eds. (1997): Workflow Management – Entwicklung von Anwendungen und Systemen. Heidelberg: dpunkt.verlag. (in German)

JABLONSKI, S. (1994): MOBILE: A Modular Workflow Model and Architecture. Proc. of the 4th Int. Working Conf. on Dynamic Modeling and Information Systems, Noordwijkerhout, NL

JABLONSKI, S. (1995): Workflow-Management-Systeme: Modellierung und Architektur. Menlo Park, CA: International Thomson Computer Press. (in German)

JACKSON, M., TWADDLE, G. (1997): Business Process Implementation: Building Workflow Systems. Reading, MA: Addison-Wesley

JAJODIA, S., MUTCHLER, D. (1987): Dynamic Voting. Proc. ACM SIGMOD Int. Conf. on Management of Data, San Francisco, CA. ACM SIGMOD Record, **16**:3, pp. 227–238

JAJODIA, S., MUTCHLER, D. (1987): Enhancements to the Voting Algorithm. Proc. 13th Int. Conf. on Very Large Data Bases, Brighton, UK. Los Altos, CA: Morgan Kaufmann, pp. 399–405

JESSUP, L. M., VALACICH, J. S., eds. (1993): Group Support Systems: New Perspectives. New York: Macmillan Publ. Comp.

JOHANSEN, R. ET AL. (1991): Leading Business Teams. Reading, MA: Addison-Wesley

JOHANSEN, R. (1988): Groupware: Computer Support for Business Teams. New York: Free Press

JOHANSEN, R. (1991): Groupware: Future Directions and Wild Cards. Journal of Organizational Computing **1**:2, 219–227

JOOSTEN, S., AUSSEMS, G., DUITSHOF, M., HUFFMEIJER, R., MULDER, E. (1994): WA-12: An Empirical Study about the Practice of Workflow Management. Univ. of Twente, Centre for Teleinformatics and Information Technology

KAELBLING, L. P., ROSENSCHEIN, S. J. (1990): Action and Planning in Embedded Agents. In: Maes, P. (ed.): Designing Autonomous Agents. Cambridge, MA: MIT Press, pp. 35–48

KAHLE, B., MEDLAR, A. (1991): An Information System for Corporate Users: Wide Area Information Servers. Connexions: The Interoperability Report **5**:11, 2–9

KAISER, G. E., KAPLAN, S. M., MICALLEF, J. (1987): Multiuser, Distributed Language-Based Environments. IEEE Software **4**:6, 58–67

KARBE, B., RAMSPERGER, N., WEISS, P. (1990): Support of Cooperative Work by Electronic Circulation Folders. In: Lochovsky, F. H., Allen, R. B. (eds.): Proc. Conf. of Office Information Systems, Cambridge, MA. New York: ACM Press, pp. 109–117

KAUTZ, H., SELMAN, B., SHAH, M. (1997): The Hidden Web. AI Magazine pp. 27–36

KAUTZ, H., SELMAN, B., SHAH, M. (1997): ReferralWeb: Combining Social Networks and Collaborative Filtering. Communications of the ACM **40**:3, 63–65

KAWELL, L., BECKHARDT, S., HALVORSEN, T., OZZIE, R., GREIF, I. (1988): Replicated Document Management in a Group Communication System. Proc. 2nd Int. Conf. on Computer-Supported Cooperative Work, Portland, OR. New York: SIGCHI/SIGOIS ACM

KENT, S. T. (1993): Internet Privacy Enhanced Mail. Communications of the ACM **36**:8, 48–60

KHOSHAFIAN, S., BUCKIEWICZ, M. (1995): Introduction to Groupware, Workflow, and Workgroup Computing. New York: John Wiley & Sons, Inc.

KISER, A. G. (1998): Masterful Facilitation: Becoming a Catalyst for Meaningful Change. AMACOM

KNISTER, M. J., PRAKASH, A. (1990): DistEdit: A Distributed Toolkit for Supporting Multiple Group Editors. Proc. 3rd Int. Conf. on Computer-Supported Cooperative Work, Los Angeles, CA. New York: SIGCHI/SIGOIS ACM, pp. 343–355

KOCH, M. (1995): Design Issues and Model for a Distributed Multi-user Editor. Computer Supported Cooperative Work – An International Journal **3**:3/4, 359–378

KOCH, M. (1997): Kooperation bei der Dokumentenbearbeitung. Wiesbaden: Deutscher Universitäts Verlag. (in German)

KONSTAN, J. A., MILLER, B. N., MALTZ, D., HERLOCKER, J. L., GORDON, L. R., RIEDL, J. (1997): GroupLens: Applying Collaborative Filtering to Usenet News. Communications of the ACM **40**:3, 77–87

KORNFELD, W. A., HEWITT, C. E. (1981): The Scientific Community Metaphor. IEEE Transactions on Systems, Man and Cybernetics **11**:1, 24–33

KOSZAREK, J. L., LINDSTROM, T. L., ENSOR, J. R., AHUJA, S. R. (1990): A Multi-User Document Review Tool. In: Gibbs, S., Verrijn-Stuart, A. A. (eds.): Proc. IFIP Conf. WG 8.4 Conf. on Multi-User Interfaces and Applications, Heraklion, Greece. Amsterdam: North-Holland, pp. 207–214

KRCMAR, H. (1991): Computer Supported Cooperative Work. In: Bullinger, H.-J. (ed.): Human Aspects in Computing: Design and Use of Interactive Systems and Information Management, Amsterdam, The Netherlands. pp. 1113–1117

KREIFELTS, T., HINRICHS, E., KLEIN, K. H., SEUFFERT, P., WOETZEL, G. (1991): Experiences with the DOMINO Office Procedure System. In: Bannon, L., Robinson, M., Schmidt, K. (eds.): Proc. 2nd Europ. Conf. on Computer-Supported Cooperative Work, Amsterdam, The Netherlands. Dordrecht: Kluwer, pp. 117–130

KRONENBERG, N. P., LEVY, H. M., STRECKER, W. D. (1986): VAXclusters: A Closely-Coupled Distributed System. ACM Transactions on Computer Systems **4**:2, 130–146

KUHLEN, R. (1991): Hypertext: Ein nicht-lineares Medium zwischen Buch und Wissensbank. Berlin, Heidelberg, New York: Springer-Verlag. (in German)

KUMAR, A., SEGEV, A. (1989): Optimizing and Evaluation Algorithms for Replicated Data Concurrency Control. Proc. 9th IEEE Int. Conf. on Distributed Computing Systems, Newport Beach, CA. Los Alamitos, CA: IEEE Computer Society Press, pp. 101–109

KUMAR, A. (1990): Performance Analysis of a Hierarchical Quorum Consensus Algorithm for Replicated Objects. Proc. 10th IEEE Int. Conf. on Distributed Computing Systems, Paris, France. Los Alamitos, CA: IEEE Computer Society Press, pp. 378–385

KUMAR, A. (1991): Hierarchical Quorum Consensus: A New Algorithm for Managing Replicated Data. IEEE Transactions on Computers **C–40**:9, 996–1004

KUMAR, V., eds. (1995): Performance of Concurrency Mechanisms in Centralized Data. Englewood Cliffs, NJ: Prentice-Hall

LAI, K.-Y., MALONE, T. W., YU, K.-C. (1988): Object Lens: A Spreadsheet for Cooperative Work. ACM Transactions on Office Information Systems **6**:4, 332–353

LAMPORT, L. (1978): Reliability Issues for Fully Replicated Distributed Databases. Computer Networks **2**, 95–114

LAMPORT, L. (1978): Time, Clocks, and the Ordering of Events in a Distributed System. Communications of the ACM **21**:7, 558–565

LANGE, B. M. (1992): Electronic Group Calendaring: Experiences and Expectations. In: Coleman, D. (ed.): Proc. Groupware'92. Los Altos, CA: Morgan Kaufmann, pp. 428–432

LANING, L. J., LEONARD, M. S. (1983): File Allocation in a Distributed Computer Communication Network. IEEE Transactions on Computers **C–32**:3, 232–244

LEAVITT, H. (1958): Managerial Psychology. Chicago

LELAND, M. D. P., FISH, R. S., KRAUT, R. E. (1988): Collaborative Document Production Using Quilt. Proc. 2nd Int. Conf. on Computer-Supported Cooperative Work, Portland, OR. New York: SIGCHI/SIGOIS ACM, pp. 206–215

LENNON, JENNIFER A. (1997): Hypermedia Systems and Applications: World Wide Web and beyond. Berlin, Heidelberg, New York: Springer-Verlag

LEVIN, K. D., MORGAN, H. L. (1975): Optimizing Distributed Data Bases – A Framework for Research. Proc. AFIPS Nat. Computer Conf. **44**. Arlington, VA: AFIPS Press, pp. 473–478

LEVINE, P. H. (1987): The Apollo DOMAIN Distributed File System. In: Paker, Y., Banâtre, J.-P., Bozyigit, M. (eds.): Distributed Operating Systems: Theory and Practice. Berlin, Heidelberg, New York: Springer-Verlag, pp. 241–260. NATO ASI series Vol. F28

LEWE, H., KRCMAR, H. (1991): Groupware. Informatik-Spektrum **14**:6, 345–348

LEWE, H., KRCMAR, H. (1993): Computer Aided Team mit GroupSystems: Erfahrungen aus dem praktischen Einsatz. Wirtschaftsinformatik **35**:2, 111–119

LEWIS, B., HODGES, J. (1988): Shared Books: Collaborative Publication Management for an Office Information System. In: Allen, R. B. (ed.): Proc. Conf. on Office Information Systems, Palo Alto, CA. ACM SIGOIS, **9**:2&3, pp. 197–204

LILJA, D. J. (1993): Cache Coherence in Large-Scale Shared-Memory Multiprocessors: Issues and Comparisons. ACM Computing Surveys **25**:3, 303–338

LISKOV, B., CURTIS, D., JOHNSON, P., SCHEIFLER, R. (1987): Implementation of Argus. Proc. 11th ACM Symp. on Operating Systems Principles, Austin, TX. ACM SIGOPS Operating Systems Review **21**:5, pp. 111–122

LISKOV, B. (1985): The Argus Language and System. In: Paul, M., Siegert, H.-J. (eds.): Proc. Advanced Course on Distributed Systems – Methods and Tools for Specification, Munich, Germany. Lecture Notes in Computer Science **190**. Berlin, Heidelberg, New York: Springer- Verlag, pp. 343–430

LISKOV, B. (1988): Distributed Programming in Argus. Communications of the ACM **31**:3, 300–312

LISKOV, B. (1993): Replication Algorithms for Highly-Available Systems. In: Spies, P. P. (ed.): Proc. EURO-ARCH '93, Munich, Germany. Informatik aktuell. Berlin, Heidelberg, New York: Springer-Verlag, pp. 211–224

LITMAN, A. (1986): Dunix – A Distributed Unix System. Proc. Europ. Unix Systems User Group Conf. Autumn '86, Manchester, UK. Buntingford Herts, UK: EUUG, pp. 23–31. ACM SIGOPS Operating Systems Review **22**:1, 42–50, Jan. 1988

LONG, D. D. E., PÂRIS, J.-F. (1987): On Improving the Availability of Replicated Files. Proc. 6th IEEE Symp. on Reliability in Distributed Software and Database Systems, Williamsburg, VA. Los Alamitos, CA: IEEE Computer Society Press, pp. 77–83

LONG, D. D. E., PÂRIS, J.-F. (1988): A Realistic Evaluation of Optimistic Dynamic Voting. Proc. 7th Symp. on Reliable Distributed Systems. pp. 129–137

LONG, D. D. E., PÂRIS, J.-F. (1989): Regeneration Protocols for Replicated Objects. Proc. 5th IEEE Int. Conf. on Data Engineering. Los Alamitos, CA: IEEE Computer Society Press, pp. 538–545

LONG, D. D. E., PÂRIS, J.-F. (1990): Voting with Regenerable Volatile Witnesses. Technical Report UCSC/CRL 90/09. Dept. of Computer and Information Science, Univ. of California, Santa Cruz, CA

LONG, D. D. E., CARROLL, J. L., STEWART, K. (1989): The Reliability of Regeneration-Based Replica Control Protocols. Proc. 9th IEEE Int. Conf. on Distributed Computing Systems, Newport Beach, CA. Los Alamitos, CA: IEEE Computer Society Press, pp. 465–473

LUBICH, H., PLATTNER, B. (1990): A Proposed Model and Functionality Definition for a Collaborative Editing and Conferencing System. In: Gibbs, S., Verrijn-Stuart, A. A. (eds.): Proc. IFIP Conf. WG 8.4 Conf. on Multi-User Interfaces and Applications, Heraklion, Greece. Amsterdam: North-Holland, pp. 215–232

LYNCH, N., MERRITT, M., WEIHL, W., FEKETE, A. (1994): Atomic Transactions. San Mateo, CA: Morgan Kaufmann

LYONS, T. (1991): Network Computing System Tutorial. Englewood Cliffs, NJ: Prentice-Hall

MACEDONIA, M. R., BRUTZMAN, D. P. (1994): MBone Provides Audio and Video across the Internet. IEEE Computer **27**:4, 30–36

MAEKAWA, M., OLDEHOEFT, A. E., OLDEHOEFT, R. R. (1987): Operating Systems – Advanced Concepts. Benjamin/Cummings Publ. Company

MAGEEL, J., KRAMER, J. (1999): Concurrency: State Models and Java Programs. New York: John Wiley & Sons, Inc.

MAHMOUD, S., RIORDON, J. S. (1976): Optimal Allocation of Resources in Distributed Information Networks. ACM Transactions on Database Systems **1**:1, 66–78

MALONE, T. W., CROWSTON, K. (1990): What is Coordination Theory and How can it help Design Cooperative Work Systems. Proc. 3rd Int. Conf. on

Computer-Supported Cooperative Work, Los Angeles, CA. New York: SIGCHI/SIGOIS ACM, pp. 357–370
MALONE, T.W., CROWSTON, K. (1992): Toward an Interdisciplinary Theory of Coordination. Technical Report CCS TR 120. Sloan School of Management, MIT, Cambridge, MA
MALONE, T. W., CROWSTON, K. (1994): The Interdisciplinary Study of Coordination. ACM Computing Surveys **26**:1, 87–119
MALONE, T. W., LAI, K.-Y. (1988): Object Lens: A Spreadsheet for Cooperative Work. Proc. 2nd Int. Conf. on Computer-Supported Cooperative Work, Portland, OR. New York: SIGCHI/SIGOIS ACM
MALONE, T. W., GRANT, K. R., LAI, K.-Y., RAO, R., ROSENBLITT, D. (1987): Semistructured Messages are Surprisingly Useful for Computer- Supported Coordination. ACM Transactions on Office Information Systems **5**:2, 115–131
MALONE, T. W., CROWSTON, K., LEE, J., PENTLAND, B., DELLAROCAS, C., WYNER, G., QUIMBY, J., OSBORNE, C., BERNSTEIN, A. (1997): Tools for Inventing Organizations: Toward a Handbook of Organizational Processes. Technical Report CCS Working Paper 198. Cambridge: MIT-Sloan School
MALONE, T. W. (1989): Semiformal Systems and Shared Object Spaces. Groupware Technology Workshop, Palo Alto, CA
MALTZ, D., EHRLICH, K. (1995): Pointing the Way: Active Collaborative Filtering. Proc. Conf. on Computer-Human Interaction. New York: ACM Press, pp. 202–209
MANBER, U., WU, S. (1994): Glimpse: A Tool to Search Trough Entire File Systems. Proc. Usenix Conf. Winter '94, San Francisco, CA. Berkeley, CA: Usenix Association, pp. 23–32
MANTEI, M. (1989): Observations of Executives using a Computerized Supported Meeting Environment. International Journal of Decision Support Systems **5**, 153–166
MARCA, D., BOCK, G., eds. (1992): Groupware: Software for Computer Supported Cooperative Work. Los Alamitos, CA: IEEE Computer Society Press
MARK, G., HAAKE, J. M., STREITZ, N. A. (1995): The Use of Hypermedia in Group Problem Solving: An Evaluation of the DOLPHIN Electronic Meeting Room Environment. In: Marmolin, H., Sundblad, Y., Schmidt, K. (eds.): Proc. 4th Europ. Conf. on Computer-Supported Cooperative Work, Stockholm, Sweden. Dordrecht: Kluwer, pp. 197–213
MARSHAK, R. T. (1995): Rethinking Workflow – Part II: Routine Processing vs. Exception Handling. Workgroup Computing Report **18**:4, 2
MARSHAK, R. T. (1995): Workflow: Applying Automation to Group Processes. In: Coleman, D., Khanna, R. (eds.): Groupware Technology and Applications, Upper Saddle River, NJ. Englewood Cliffs, NJ: Prentice-Hall, pp. 71–97
MATSUOKA, S., TAURA, K., YONEZAWA, A. (1993): Highly Efficient and Encapsulated Re-use of Synchronization Code in Concurrent Object-Oriented Languages. In: Paepcke, A. (ed.): Proc. Conf. on Object-Oriented Programming Systems, Languages and Applications (OOPSLA '93). ACM Press, pp. 109–126
MATTERN, F., STURM, P. (1989): An Automatic Distributed Calendar and Appointment System. Microprocessing and Microprogramming **27**, 455–462
MCCARTHY, J. C., BLUESTEIN, W. M. (1991): The Computing Strategy Report: Workflow's Progress. Cambridge, MA: Forrester Research Inc.
MCGRATH, JOSEPH E. (1993): Methods for the Study of Groups. In: Baecker, R. M. (ed.): Groupware and Computer-Supported Cooperative Work. San Mateo, CA: Morgan Kaufmann, pp. 200–204
MEDINA-MORA, R., WINOGRAD, T., FLORES, R., FLORES, F. (1992): The ActionWorkflow Approach to Workflow Management Technology. In: Turner, J.,

Kraut, R. E. (eds.): Proc. 4th Int. Conf. on Computer-Supported Cooperative Work, Toronto, Canada. New York: SIGCHI/SIGOIS ACM, pp. 281–288

MEYROWITZ, N. (1986): Intermedia: The Architecture and Construction of an Object- Oriented Hypermedia System and Applications Framework. In: Meyrowitz, N. (ed.): Proc. 1st Conf. on Object-Oriented Programming Systems, Languages and Applications (OOPSLA '86), Portland, OR. ACM SIGPLAN Notices **21**:11, pp. 186–201

MILNER, R. (1995): Communication and Concurrency. Englewood Cliffs, NJ: Prentice-Hall

MINOURA, T., WIEDERHOLD, G. (1982): Resilient Extended True-Copy Token Scheme for a Distributed Database System. IEEE Transactions on Software Engineering **SE–8**:3, 173–189

MOSER, L. E., KAPUR, V., MELLIAR-SMITH, P. M. (1990): Probabilistic Language Analysis of Weighted Voting Algorithms. Proc. ACM SIGMETRICS Conf. on Measurement and Modeling of Computer Systems, Boulder, CO. ACM SIGMETRICS Performance Evaluation Review **18**:1, pp. 67–73

MÜHLHÄUSER, M., SCHILL, A. (1992): Software Engineering für verteilte Anwendungen. Berlin, Heidelberg, New York: Springer-Verlag. (in German)

MULLENDER, S., eds. (1993): Distributed Systems. New York: ACM Press

MYNATT, E.D., ADLER, A., O'DAY, V.L. (1997): Design for Network Communities. Proc. ACM SIGCHI'97 Conf. on Human Factors in Computing Systems, Atlanta, GA. New York: ACM SIGCHI, pp. 210–217

NAKANISHI, HIDEYUKI, YOSHIDA, CHIKARA, NISHIMURA, TOSHIKAZU, ISHIDA, TORU (1999): FreeWalk: A 3D Virtual Space for Casual Meetings. IEEE Multimedia **6**:2, 20–28

NASTANSKY, L. (1994): Approaching the Groupware Challenge in Higher Education – The UniTeach 2000 Framework: Visions about the Redesign of Teaching and Learning Processes. ZfB-Ergänzungsheft (Zeitschrift für Betriebswirtschaft): **2**, 121–138

NECHES, R., FIKES, R., FININ, T. (1991): Enabling Technology for Knowledge Sharing. AI Magazine **12**:3, 36–56

NEILSEN, M. L., MIZUNO, M. (1992): Coterie Join Algorithm. IEEE Transactions on Parallel and Distributed Systems **3**:5, 582–590

NEJMEH, B. A. (1994): Internet: A Strategic Tool for the Software Enterprise. Communications of the ACM **37**:11, 23–27

NELSON, M. N., OUSTERHOUT, J. K. (1988): Copy-on-Write for Sprite. Proc. Usenix Conf. Summer '88, San Francisco, CA. Berkeley, CA: Usenix Association, pp. 187–201

NELSON, M. N., WELCH, B. B., OUSTERHOUT, J. K. (1988): Caching in the Sprite Network File System. ACM Transactions on Computer Systems **6**:1, 134–154

NELSON, J. ET AL. (1991): The Role of the PODA Project in the Adoption and Development of ODA. Computer Networks and ISDN Systems **21**, 175–185

NELSON, T. H. (1967): Getting it out of our System. In: Schechter, G. (ed.): Information Retrieval: A Critical Review. Washington, DC: Thompson Books

NELSON, T. H. (1980): Replacing the Printed Word: A Complete Literary System. In: Lavington, S. H. (ed.): Information Processing **80**. North-Holland Publ. Comp., IFIP, pp. 1013–1023

NELSON, T. H. (1981): Literary Machines. Swartmore, PA: T. H. Nelson

NEUWIRTH, C. M., KAUFER, D. S., CHANDHOK, R., MORRIS, J. H. (1990): Issues in the Design of Computer Support for Co- Authoring and Commenting. Proc. 3rd Int. Conf. on Computer-Supported Cooperative Work, Los Angeles, CA. New York: SIGCHI/SIGOIS ACM, pp. 183–195

NEWMAN-WOLFE, R. E., PELIMUHANDIRAM, H. K. (1991): MACE: A Fine Grained Concurrent Editor. Proc. ACM SIGOIS Conf. on Organizational Computing Systems, Atlanta, GA. New York: SIGOIS ACM, pp. 240–254

NICOL, J. R., BLAIR, G. S., SHEPHERD, W. D., WALPOLE, J. (1988): An Approach to Multiple Copy Update Based on Immutability. Distributed Processing, pp. 537–550

NICOL, J. R., BLAIR, G. S., WALPOLE, J. (1988): A Model to Support Consistency and Availability in Distributed Systems Architectures. Proc. IEEE Workshop on Future Trends of Distributed Computing Systems in the '90s, Hong Kong. Los Alamitos, CA: IEEE Computer Society Press, pp. 418–425

NIELSEN, J. (1990): Hypertext and Hypermedia. London, New York, San Diego: Academic Press

NOE, J. D., ANDREASSIAN, A. (1987): Effectiveness of Replication in Distributed Computer Networks. Proc. 7th IEEE Int. Conf. on Distributed Computing Systems, Berlin, Germany. Los Alamitos, CA: IEEE Computer Society Press, pp. 508–513

NONAKA, I., TAKEUCHI, H. (1995): The Knowledge Creating Company: How Japanese Companies Create the Dynamics of Innovation. New York: Oxford Univ. Press

NOTKIN, D., BLACK, A. P., LAZOWSKA, E. D., LEVY, H. M., SANISLO, J., ZAHORJAN, J. (1988): Interconnecting Heterogeneous Computer Systems. Communications of the ACM **31**:3, 258–274

NUNAMAKER, J. F., DENNIS, A. R., VALACICH, J. S., VOGEL, D. R., GEORGE, J. F. (1991): Electronic Meeting Systems to Support Group Work. Communications of the ACM **34**:7, 40–61

OATES, T., PRASAD, M. V. N., LESSER, V. R. (1994): Cooperative Information Gathering: A Distributed Problem Solving Approach. Technical Report TR-94-66. Dept. of Computer Science, Univ. of Massachusetts, Amherst, MA

OBRACZKA, K., DANZIG, P. B., LI, S.-H. (1993): Internet Resource Discovery Services. IEEE Computer **26**:9, 8–22

O'DAY, V., JEFFRIES, R. (1993): Information Artisans: Patterns of Result Sharing By Information Searchers. In: Kaplan, S. (ed.): Proc. ACM SIGOIS/IEEECS TC-OA Conf. on Organizational Computing Systems (COOCS '93), Milpitas, CA. New York: ACM, pp. 98–107

OLSON, M. H., BLY, S. A. (1991): The Portland Experience: A Report on a Distributed Research Group. Int. J. Man-Machine Studies **34**, 211–228

OMG, CORBA (1995): The Common Object Request Broker: Architecture and Specification. Object Management Group and X/Open. OMG Document Rev. 2.0; X/Open Prelim. Spec. of ORB component of CAE

OPPER, S. (1988): A Groupware Toolbox. Byte

ORFALI, R., HARKEY, D., EDWARDS, J. (1996): The Essential Distributed Objects Survival Guide. New York: John Wiley & Sons, Inc.

OUSTERHOUT, J. K. (1987): Position Statement for Sprite: The File System as the Center of a Network Operating System. Proc. 1st IEEE Workshop on Workstation Operating Systems, Cambridge, MA. Los Alamitos, CA: IEEE Computer Society Press

PANKOKE-BABATZ, U., eds. (1989): Computer-Based Group Communication: The Amigo Activity Model. Ellis Horwood

PÂRIS, J.-F., LONG, D. D. E. (1988): Efficient Dynamic Voting Algorithms. Proc. 4th IEEE Int. Conf. on Data Engineering, Los Angeles, CA. Los Alamitos, CA: IEEE Computer Society Press, pp. 268–275

PÂRIS, J.-F. (1989): Voting with Bystanders. Proc. 9th IEEE Int. Conf. on Distributed Computing Systems, Newport Beach, CA. Los Alamitos, CA: IEEE

Computer Society Press, pp. 394–401

PÂRIS, J.-F. (1990): Efficient Voting Protocols with Witnesses. In: Abiteboul, S., Kanellakis, P. C. (eds.): Proc. 3rd Int. Conf. on Database Theory (ICDT '90), Paris, France. Lecture Notes in Computer Science **470**. Berlin, Heidelberg, New York: Springer- Verlag, pp. 305–317

PATTIPATI, K. R., WOLF, J. L. (1990): A File Assignment Problem Model for Extended Local Area Network Environments. Proc. 10th IEEE Int. Conf. on Distributed Computing Systems, Paris, France. Los Alamitos, CA: IEEE Computer Society Press, pp. 554–561

PENDERGAST, M. O., VOGEL, D. (1990): Design and Implementation of a PC/LAN-Based Multi-User Text Editor. In: Gibbs, S., Verrijn-Stuart, A. A. (eds.): Proc. IFIP Conf. WG 8.4 Conf. on Multi-User Interfaces and Applications, Heraklion, Greece. Amsterdam: North-Holland, pp. 195–206

PENTLAND, B. T. (1994): Process Grammars: A Generative Approach to Process Redesign. Technical Report CCS Working Paper 178. MIT-Sloan School

PEREIRA, F. C. N., WARREN, D. H. D. (1983): Parsing as Deduction. Proc. 21st Annual Meeting of the Association for Computational Linguistics, MIT, Cambridge, MA

PETROVIC, O. (1992): Empirical Research in Electronic Meeting Systems: A Demand Side Approach. Journal of Organizational Computing **2**:3&4, 263–275

PIEPENBURG, U. (1991): Ein Konzept von Kooperation und die technische Unterstützung kooperativer Prozesse. In: Oberquelle, H. (ed.): Kooperative Arbeit und Computerunterstützung. Stuttgart: Verlag für Angewandte Psychologie, pp. 79–98. (in German)

PONG, F., DUBOIS, M. (1997): Verifikation Techniques for Cache Coherence Protocols. ACM Computing Surveys **29**:1, 82–126

POPEK, G. J., WALKER, B. J., eds. (1985): The Locus Distributed System Architecture. Cambridge, MA, London, UK: MIT Press

POYSSICK, G., HANNAFORD, S. (1996): Workflow Reengineering. Hayden Books

PRAKASH, A., KNISTER, M. J. (1992): Undoing Actions in Collaborative Work. In: Turner, J., Kraut, R. E. (eds.): Proc. 4th Int. Conf. on Computer-Supported Cooperative Work, Toronto, Canada. New York: SIGCHI/SIGOIS ACM, pp. 273–280

PRASAD, M. V. N., LESSER, V. R., LANDER, S. (1995): Retrieval and Reasoning in Distributed Case Bases. Technical Report TR-95-27. Dept. of Computer Science, Univ. of Massachusetts, Amherst, MA

PRESS, L. (1992): Lotus Notes (Groupware) in Context. Journal of Organizational Computing **2**:3&4, 315–319

PRINZ, W., KOLVENBACH, S. (1996): Support for Workflows in a Ministerial Environment. In: Ackermann, M. S. (ed.): Proc. 7th Int. Conf. on Computer-Supported Cooperative Work, Boston, MA. New York: SIGCHI/SIGOIS ACM, pp. 199–208

PU, C., LEFF, A. (1991): Replica Control in Distributed Systems: An Asynchronous Approach. In: Clifford, J., King, R. (eds.): Proc. ACM SIGMOD Int. Conf. on Management of Data, Denver, CO. ACM SIGMOD Record, **20**:2, pp. 377–386

PU, C., NOE, J. D., PROUDFOOT, A. (1986): Regeneration of Replicated Objects: A Technique and its Eden Implementation. Proc. 2nd IEEE Int. Conf. on Data Engineering. Los Alamitos, CA: IEEE Computer Society Press, pp. 175–187

PUTZ, G. B. (1998): Facilitation Skills: Helping Groups Make Decisions. Deep Space Technology Co.

RABIN, M. O. (1989): Efficient Dispersal of Information for Security, Load Balancing and Fault-Tolerance. J. ACM **36**:2, 335–348

RADA, R., eds. (1996): Groupware and Authoring. London: Academic Press

RAJ, R. K., TEMPERO, E. D., LEVY, H. M., HUTCHINSON, N. C., BLACK, A. P., JUL, E. (1991): Emerald: A General-Purpose Programming Language. Software – Practice and Experience **21**:1, 91–118

RAMAMOORTHY, C. V., WAH, B. W. (1983): The Isomorphism of Simple File Allocation. IEEE Transactions on Computers **C–32**:3, 221–232

RAO, A. S., GEORGEFF, M. P. (1991): Modeling Agents within a BDI-Architecture. Proc. 2nd Int. Conf. on Principles of Knowledge Representation and Reasoning (KR'91), Cambridge, MA. Los Altos, CA: Morgan Kaufmann, pp. 473–484

RAPAPORT, M. (1991): Computer Mediated Communications. New York: John Wiley & Sons, Inc.

RASHID, R. F., ROBERTSON, G. G. (1981): Accent: A Communication Oriented Network Operating System Kernel. Proc. 8th ACM Symp. on Operating Systems Principles, Pacific Grove, CA. ACM SIGOPS Operating Systems Review **15**:5, pp. 64–75

REES, F., HOLT, M., eds. (1998): The Facilitator Excellence Handbook: Helping People Work Creatively and Productively Together. Pfeiffer & Co

REICHWALD, R., MÖSLEIN, K., SACHENBACHER, H., ENGLBERGER, H., OLDENBURG, S. (1998): Telekooperation – Verteilte Arbeits- und Organisationsformen. Berlin: Springer-Verlag. (in German)

REIN, G. J., ELLIS, C. A. (1991): rIBIS: A Real-Time Group Hypertext System. Int. J. Man-Machine Studies **34**, 349–367

RESNICK, P., IACOVOU, N., SUCHAK, M., BERGSTROM, P., RIEDL, J. (1994): GroupLens: An Open Architecture for Collaborative Filtering of Netnews. Proc. Conf. on Computer-Supported Cooperative Work, Chapel Hill, NC. New York: ACM Press, pp. 175–186

RESNICK, P., IACOVOU, N., SUCHAK, M., BERGSTROM, P., RIEDL, J. (1994): GroupLens: An Open Architecture for Collaborative Filtering of Netnews. In: Furuta, R., Neuwirth, C. (eds.): Proc. 5th Int. Conf. on Computer-Supported Cooperative Work, Chapel Hill, NC. New York: SIGCHI/SIGOIS ACM, pp. 175–186

RIFKIN, A. P., FORBES, M. P., HAMILTON, R. L., SABRIO, M., SHAH, S., YUEH, K. (1986): RFS Architectural Overview. EUUGN **6**:2, 13–23

RITTEL, H., WEBBER, M. (1973): Dilemmas in an general Theory of Planning. Policy Sciences **4**

ROBERTSON, G., MCCRACKEN, D. L., NEWELL, A. (1981): The ZOG Approach to Man-Machine Communication. Int. J. Man-Machine Studies **14**, 461–488

RODDEN, T. A., BLAIR, G. S. (1991): CSCW and Distributed Systems: The Problem of Control. In: Bannon, L., Robinson, M., Schmidt, K. (eds.): Proc. 2nd Europ. Conf. on Computer-Supported Cooperative Work, Amsterdam, The Netherlands. Dordrecht: Kluwer, pp. 49–64

ROMAN, G-C., CUNNINGHAM, H. C. (1990): Mixed Programming Metaphors in a Shared Dataspace Model of Concurrency. IEEE Transactions on Software Engineering **SE–16**:12, 1361–1373

ROSCOE, A. W. (1997): Theory and Practice of Concurrency. Englewood Cliffs, NJ: Prentice-Hall

ROSE, D. E., BORNSTEIN, J. J., TIENE, K. (1995): MessageWorld: A new Approach to Facilitating Asynchronous Group Communication. In: Pissinou, N., Silberschatz, A., Park, E. K., Makki, K. (eds.): Proc. 4th Int. Conf. on Information and Knowledge Management (CIKM '95), Baltimore, MD. New York: ACM Press, pp. 266–273

ROSENBERG, J., SHERMAN, M., MARKS, A., AKKERHUIS, J. (1991): Some Comments on Using ODA. Computer Networks and ISDN Systems **21**, 211–220

ROTHERMEL, K., POPESCU-ZELETIN, R., eds. (1997): Proc. 1st Int. Workskop on Mobile Agents, MA'97. Lecture Notes in Computer Science **1219**. Berlin, Heidelberg, New York: Springer- Verlag

RUCKER, J., POLANCO, M. J. (1997): Siteseer: Personalized Navigation for the Web. Communications of the ACM **40**:3, 73–76

RÜDEBUSCH, T., MÜHLHÄUSER, M. (1991): Ein Unterstützungssystem für Gruppenarbeit in verteilten Systemen. In: Effelsberg, W., Meuer, H. W., Müller, G. (eds.): Proc. 7th GI/ITG Conf. – Communication in Distributed Systems, Mannheim, Germany. Informatik-Fachberichte **267**. Berlin, Heidelberg, New York: Springer-Verlag, pp. 464–478. (in German)

RUSSELL, S., NORVIG, P. (1995): Artificial Intelligence: A Modern Approach. Englewood Cliffs, NJ: Prentice-Hall

SANTOS, A. (1995): Multimedia and Groupware for Editing. Berlin, Heidelberg, New York: Springer-Verlag

SARASWAT, V. A. (1989): Concurrent Constraint Programming Languages. Dissertation. Carnegie-Mellon Univ., Pittsburg, PA

SATYANARAYANAN, M., HOWARD, J. H., NICHOLS, D. A., SIDEBOTHAM, R. N., SPECTOR, A. Z., WEST, M. J. (1985): The ITC Distributed File System: Principles and Design. Proc. 10th ACM Symp. on Operating Systems Principles, Orcas Island, WA. ACM SIGOPS Operating Systems Review **19**:5, pp. 35–50

SATYANARAYANAN, M. (1990): Scalable, Secure, and Highly Available Distributed File Access. IEEE Computer **23**:5, 9–22

SCHANTZ, R. E., THOMAS, R. H., BONO, G. (1986): The Architecture of the Cronus Distributed Operating System. Proc. 6th IEEE Int. Conf. on Distributed Computing Systems, Cambridge, MA. Los Alamitos, CA: IEEE Computer Society Press, pp. 250–259

SCHLICHTER, J. H., BORGHOFF, U. M. (1992): Concurrency Control for Multiuser Editors (position paper). Proc. ACM CSCW '92 Workshop on Tools and Technologies for CSCW, Toronto, Canada. ACM SIGOIS Bulletin, **13**:4

SCHLICHTER, J., KOCH, M., BÜRGER, M. (1998): Workspace Awareness for Distributed Teams. In: Conen, W., Neumann, G. (eds.): Coordination Technology for Collaborative Applications – Organizations, Processes and Agents. Lecture Notes in Computer Science **1364**. Berlin, Heidelberg, New York: Springer-Verlag, pp. 197–218

SCHNEIDER, G., SCHELLER-HOUY, A., SCHWEITZER, J. (1996): Vom Workflow-Management-System zur Vorgangsbearbeitungsplattform mit integrierter Telecooperation. In: Krcmar, H., Lewe, H., Schwabe, G. (eds.): Deutsche Computer Supported Cooperative Work, DCSCW'96. Heidelberg: Springer-Verlag, pp. 293–306. (in German)

SCHROEDER, M. D., BIRRELL, A. D., NEEDHAM, R. M. (1984): Experience with Grapevine: The Growth of a Distributed System. ACM Transactions on Computer Systems **2**:1, 3–23

SCHWARZ, R. M. (1994): The Skilled Facilitator: Practical Wisdom for Developing Effective Groups. Jossey-Bass Publishers

SEARLE, J. R. (1969): Speech Acts: An Essay in the Philosophy of Language. Cambridge, UK: Cambridge Univ. Press

SEARLE, J. R., eds. (1979): Expression and Meaning: Studies in the Theory of Speech Acts. Cambridge, UK: Cambridge Univ. Press

SEN, S., DURFEE, E. H. (1991): A Formal Study of Distributed Meeting Scheduling: Preliminary Results. Proc. Conf. on Organizational Computing Systems, Atlanta, GA. New York: SIGOIS ACM, pp. 55–68

SEN, S., DURFEE, E. H. (1991): A Formal Study of Distributed Meeting Scheduling: Preliminary Results. In: de Jong, P. (ed.): Proc. Conf. on Organizational

Computing Systems, Atlanta, GA. New York: SIGOIS ACM, pp. 55–68

SHANNON, C. E. (1948): A Mathematical Theory of Communication. Bell Syst. Techn. J. **27**:3, 379–423, 623–656

SHAPIRO, M. (1986): SOS: A Distributed Object-Oriented Operating System. Proc. 2nd ACM SIGOPS Europ. Workshop on Making Distributed Systems Work, Amsterdam, The Netherlands. ACM SIGOPS Operating Systems Review **21**:1, 49–84, Jan. 1987

SHARDANAND, U., MAES, P. (1995): Social Information Filtering: Algorithms for Automating Word of Mouth. Proc. Conf. on Computer-Human Interaction. New York: ACM Press. Also see: http://www.firefly.com

SHARPLES, M., eds. (1993): Computer supported collaborative writing. London: Springer-Verlag

SHEPHERD, A., MAYER, N., KUCHINSKY, A. (1990): Strudel: An Extensible Electronic Conversation Toolkit. Proc. 3rd Int. Conf. on Computer-Supported Cooperative Work, Los Angeles, CA. New York: SIGCHI/SIGOIS ACM, pp. 93–104

SHETH, A., RUSINKIEWICZ, M. (1990): Management of Interdependent Data: Specifying Dependency and Consistency Requirements. In: Cabrera, L.-F., Pâris, J.-F. (eds.): Proc. IEEE Workshop on Management of Replicated Data, Houston, TX. Los Alamitos, CA: IEEE Computer Society Press, pp. 133–136

SHNEIDERMAN, B. (1987): User Interface Design and Evaluation for an Electronic Encyclopedia. Technical Report CS–TR–1819. Dept. of Computer Science, Univ. of Maryland, College Park, MD

SHOHAM, Y. (1993): Agent-oriented Programming. Artificial Intelligence **60**:1, 51–92

SKARRA, A. H. (1988): Concurrency Control for Cooperating Transactions in an Object-Oriented Database. In: Agha, G. A., Wegner, P., Yonezawa, A. (eds.): Proc. ACM SIGPLAN Workshop on Object-Based Concurrent Programming, San Diego, CA. ACM SIGPLAN Notices, **24**:4, 1989, pp. 145–147

SMITH, R. G. (1980): The Contract Net Protocol: High-Level Communication and Control in a Distributed Problem Solver. IEEE Transactions on Computers **c-29**:12

SMITH, J. B. (1986): WE: A Writing Environment for Professionals. Technical Report 86–025. Dept. of Computer Science, Univ. of North Carolina, Chapel Hill, NC

SMITH, D. E. (1999): Knowledge, Groupware and the Internet. Butterworth-Heinemann

SPICELEY, A. (1991): ODA Profiles: Application and Developement. Computer Networks and ISDN Systems **21**, 165–173

STALLING, WILLIAM (1998): Principles and Practice. Englewood Cliffs, NJ: Prentice Hall

STEFIK, M., BOBROW, D. G., FOSTER, G., LANNING, S., TATAR, D. (1987): WYSIWIS Revised: Early Experiences with Multiuser Interfaces. ACM Transactions on Office Information Systems **5**:2, 147–167

STEFIK, M., FOSTER, G., BOBROW, D. G., KAHN, K., LANNING, S., SUCHMAN, L. (1987): Beyond the Chalkboard: Computer Support for Collaboration and Problem Solving in Meetings. Communications of the ACM **30**:1, 32–47

STEINMETZ, R., NAHRSTEDT, K. (1998): Multimedia: Computing, Communications and Applications. Englewood Cliffs, NJ: Prentice Hall

STOTTS, P. D., FURUTA, R. (1989): Petri-Net-Based Hypertext: Document Structure with Browsing Semantics. ACM Transactions on Information Systems **7**:1, 3–29

STREITZ, N. A., HAAKE, J. M., HANNEMANN, J., LEMKE, A., SCHULER, W., SCHUETT, H., THUERING, M. (1992): SEPIA: A Cooperative Hypermedia Authoring Environment. Proc. 4th ACM Europ. Conf. on Hypertext (ECHT '92), Milan, Italy. pp. 11–22

STREITZ, N. A., GEISSLER, J., HAAKE, J. M., HOL, J. (1994): DOLPHIN: Integrated Meeting Support across LiveBoards, Local and Remote Desktop Environments. In: Furuta, R., Neuwirth, C. (eds.): Proc. 5th Int. Conf. on Computer-Supported Cooperative Work, Chapel Hill, NC. New York: SIGCHI/SIGOIS ACM, pp. 345–358

STREITZ, N. A., REXROTH, P., HOLMER, T. (1997): Does Roomware Matter? Investigating the Role of Personal and Public Information Devices and their Combination in Meeting Room Collaboration. Proc. 5th Europ. Conf. on Computer-Supported Cooperative Work, Lancaster, UK. Dordrecht: Kluwer

STREITZ, N. A., GEISSLER, J., HOLMER, T. (1998): Roomware for Cooperative Buildings: Integrated Design of Architectural Spaces and Information Spaces. In: Streitz et al. (1998b). pp. 4–21

STREITZ, N. A., KONOMI, S., BURKHARDT, H.-J., eds. (1998): Cooperative Buildings – Integrating Information, Organization, and Architecture, 1st Int. Workshop CoBuild'98. Lecture Notes in Computer Science **1370**. Berlin, Heidelberg, New York: Springer-Verlag

STURGIS, H. E., MITCHELL, J. G., ISRAEL, J. (1980): Issues in the Design and Use of a Distributed File System. ACM SIGOPS Operating Systems Review **14**:3, 55–69

SUMITA, U., SHENG, O. R. L. (1988): Analysis of Query Processing in Distributed Database Systems with Fully Replicated Files: A Hierarchical Approach. Performance Evaluation **8**, 223–238

SVEIBY, K. E. (1997): The New Organizational Wealth: Managing and Measuring Knowledge-Based Assets. San Francisco, CA: Berrett-Koehler Publ.

SVOBODOVA, L. (1984): File Servers for Network-Based Distributed Systems. ACM Computing Surveys **16**:4, 353–398

SWENSON, K. D., MAXWELL, R. J., MATSUMOTO, T., SAGHARI, T., IRWIN, K. (1994): A Business Process Environment Supporting Collaborative Planning. Collaborative Computing **1**:1, 15–34

SWINEHART, D. C. ET AL. (1986): A Structural View of the Cedar Programming Environment. ACM Transactions on Programming Languages and Systems **8**:4, 419–490

TANENBAUM, A. S., V. RENESSE, R. (1985): Distributed Operating Systems. ACM Computing Surveys **17**:4, 419–470

TANENBAUM, A. S., KAASHOEK, M. F., V. RENESSE, R., BAL, H. E. (1991): The Amoeba Distributed Operating System: A Status Report. Computer Communications, Butterworth-Heinemann **14**:6, 324–335

TANENBAUM, A. S. (1992): Modern Operating Systems. Englewood Cliffs, NJ: Prentice-Hall

TANENBAUM, A. S. (1996): Computer Networks. Englewood Cliffs, NJ: Prentice-Hall

TANG, J., NATARAJAN, N. (1993): Obtaining Coteries that Optimize the Availability of Replicated Databases. IEEE Transactions on Knowledge and Data Engineering **5**:2, 309–321

TANG, J. (1990): Voting Class – An Approach to Achieving High Availability for Replicated Data. In: Agrawal, R., Bell, D. (eds.): Proc. 2nd Int. Symp. on Databases in Parallel and Distributed Systems, Dublin, Ireland. Los Alamitos, CA: IEEE Computer Society Press, pp. 146–156

TANG, J. C. (1991): Findings from Observational Studies of Collaborative Work. Int. J. Man-Machine Studies **34**, 143–160

TATAR, D. G., FOSTER, G., BOBROW, D. B. (1991): Design for Conversation: Lessons from Cognoter. Int. J. Man-Machine Studies **34**, 185–209

TAY, B. H., ANANDA, A. L. (1990): A Survey of Remote Procedure Calls. ACM SIGOPS Operating Systems Review **24**:3, 68–79

TEEGE, G., KOCH, M. (1994): Integrating Access and Collaboration for Multimedia Applications. In: Brusilowsky, P. (ed.): Proc. East-west Int. Conf. on Multimedia, Hypermedia, and Virtual Reality (MHVR'94), Moskow. Int. Center for Scientific Information, pp. 170–176

TEEGE, G. (1993): The Activity Support System TACTS. Technical Report TUM–I 9306. Inst. für Informatik, Techn. Univ. München, Munich, Germany

TEEGE, G. (1996): Object-Oriented Activity Support: A Model for Integrated CSCW Systems. Computer Supported Cooperative Work – An International Journal **5**:1, 93–124

TERVEEN, L., HILL, W., AMENTO, B., MCDONALD, D., CRETER, J. (1997): PHOAKS: A System for Sharing Recommendations. Communications of the ACM **40**:3, 59–62

TEUFEL, S., SAUTER, C., MÜHLHERR, T., BAUKNECHT, K. (1995): Computerunterstützte Gruppenarbeit. Bonn: Addison-Wesley. (in German)

THACHER, C. ET AL. (1979): Alto: A Personal Computer. Technical Report CLS–79–11. Xerox Palo Alto Research Center, Palo Alto, CA

THOMAS, R. H. (1979): A Majority Consensus Approach to Concurrency Control for Multiple Copy Databases. ACM Transactions on Database Systems **4**:2, 180–209

TICHY, W. F. (1984): Towards a Distributed File System. Proc. Usenix Conf. Summer '84, Salt Lake City, UT. Berkeley, CA: Usenix Association, pp. 87–97

TONG, Z., KAIN, R. Y. (1988): Vote Assignments in Weighted Voting Mechanisms. Proc. 7th Symp. on Reliable Distributed Systems. pp. 138–143

TREVOR, J., KOCH, T., WÖTZEL, G. (1997): MetaWeb: Bringing Synchronous Groupware to the World Wide Web. Proc. 5th Europ. Conf. on Computer-Supported Cooperative Work, Lancaster, UK. Dordrecht: Kluwer

TRIGG, R. H., WEISER, M. (1986): TEXTNET: A Network-Based Approach to Text Handling. ACM Transactions on Office Information Systems **4**:1, 1–23

TRIPATHI, A. (1987): NEXUS Distributed Operating System. Tutorial No. 4, IEEE Int. Conf. on Distributed Computing Systems, Berlin, Germany. Los Alamitos, CA: IEEE Computer Society Press, pp. 142–159

TUROFF, M., HILTZ, S. R. (1982): Computer Support for Group Versus Individual Decisions. IEEE Transactions on Communications **30**:1, 105–118

TWIDALE, M. B., NICHOLS, D. M., SMITH, G., TREVOR, J. (1995): Supporting Collaborative Learning during Information Searching. Proc. Computer Support for Cooperative Learning (CSCL'95), Bloomington, IN. pp. 367–374

TWIDALE, M. B., NICHOLS, D. M., PAICE, C. (1997): Browsing is a Collaborative Process. Information Processing & Management **6**:33, 761–783

V. BECHTOLSHEIM, M. (1993): Agentensysteme: Verteiltes Problemlösen mit Expertensystemen. Braunschweig: Vieweg. (in German)

V. RENESSE, R., TANENBAUM, A. S. (1988): Voting with Ghosts. Proc. 8th IEEE Int. Conf. on Distributed Computing Systems, San Jose, CA. Los Alamitos, CA: IEEE Computer Society Press, pp. 456–462

VALACICH, J. S., DENNIS, A. R., NUNAMAKER, J. F. (1991): Electronic Meeting Support: the GroupSystems Concept. Int. J. Man-Machine Studies **34**, 261–282

VIELLE, L. (1986): Recursive Axioms in Deductive Databases: The Query-Subquery Approach. In: Kerschberg, L. (ed.): Proc. 1st Conf. on Expert Database Systems, Menlo Park, CA. Benjamin/Cummings Publ. Company

VOSSEN, G., BECKER, J., eds. (1996): Geschäftsprozessmodellierung und Workflow-Management. Menlo Park, CA: International Thomson Computer Press. (in German)

WAH, B. W. (1984): File Placement on Distributed Computer Systems. IEEE Computer **17**:1, 23–33

WALKER, J. H. (1985): The Document Examiner. ACM SIGGRAPH Video Review: An Edited Compilation from SIG CHI '85 Conf. on Human Factors in Computing Systems. New York: ACM

WALPOLE, J., BARBER, A., BLAIR, G. S., NICOL, J. R. (1990): Software Development Environment Transactions: Their Implementation and Use in Cosmos. Proc. 23rd IEEE Hawaii Int. Conf. on System Sciences, Hawaii, HI. Los Alamitos, CA: IEEE Computer Society Press, pp. 493–502

WAYNER, P. (1994): Agents Away. Byte pp. 113–118

WELLINGS, A. J. (1985): The PULSE Project. Proc. ACM SIGOPS Workshop on Operating Systems in Computer Networks, Rüschlikon, Switzerland. ACM SIGOPS Operating Systems Review **19**:2, 6–40, Apr. 1985

WEST, A. (1985): The SUN Network File System, NFS – Business Overview. Technical Report. SUN Microsystems, Inc., Mountain View, CA

WHITE, J. E. (1994): Telescript Technology: Scenes from the Electronic Marketplace. General Magic White Paper

WHITE, J. E. (1994): Telescript Technology: The Foundation for the Electronic Marketplace. General Magic White Paper

WIEDERHOLD, G., QIAN, X. (1987): Modeling Asynchrony in Distributed Databases. Proc. 3rd IEEE Int. Conf. on Data Engineering, Los Angeles, CA. Los Alamitos, CA: IEEE Computer Society Press, pp. 246–250

WIEDERHOLD, G., QIAN, X. (1990): Consistency Control of Replicated Data in Federated Databases. In: Cabrera, L.-F., Pâris, J.-F. (eds.): Proc. IEEE Workshop on Management of Replicated Data, Houston, TX. Los Alamitos, CA: IEEE Computer Society Press, pp. 130–132

WILBUR, S. B., YOUNG, R. E. (1988): The COSMOS Project: A Multi-Disciplinary Approach to Design for Computer Supported Group Working. In: Speth, R. (ed.): Proc. EUTECO '88 Conf. – Research into Networks and Distributed Applications, Vienna, Austria. Amsterdam: North-Holland

WILSON, P. (1991): Computer Supported Cooperative Work. Oxford, UK: Intellect Books

WINOGRAD, T., FLORES, F. (1986): Understanding Computers and Cognition: A New Foundation for Design. Norwood, NJ: Ablex

WINOGRAD, T. (1988): A Language/Action Perspective on the Design of Cooperative Work. Human Computer Interaction **3**:1, 3–30

WINOGRAD, T. (1989): Groupware: The Next Wave or Just Another Advertising Slogan. IEEE Intellectual Leverage Digest of Papers, COMPCON '89

WOITASS, M. (1990): Coordination of Intelligent Office Systems – Applied to Meeting Scheduling. In: Gibbs, S., Verrijn-Stuart, A. A. (eds.): Proc. IFIP Conf. WG 8.4 Conf. on Multi-User Interfaces and Applications, Heraklion, Greece. Amsterdam: North-Holland

WOOLDRIDGE, M., JENNINGS, N. R. (1995): Intelligent Agents: Theory and Practice. Knowledge Engineering Review **10**:2, 115–152

YAKEMOVIC, K., CONKLIN, E. (1990): Report on a Development Project Use of an Issue-Based Information System. Proc. 3rd Int. Conf. on Computer-Supported Cooperative Work, Los Angeles, CA. New York: ACM, pp. 105–118

YANKELOVICH, N., MEYROWITZ, N. (1985): Reading and Writing the Electronic Book. IEEE Computer **18**:10, 15–30

YEH, S., ELLIS, C. A., EGE, A., KORTH, H. (1987): Performance Analysis of Two Concurrency Control Schemas for Design Environments. Technical Report STP–036–87. MCC, Austin, TX

YOKOTE, Y. (1992): The Apertos Reflective Operating System: The Concept and its Implementation. ACM SIGPLAN Notices **27**:10, 414–434

ZIMMERMAN, A. L., EVANS, C. J. (1992): Facilitation: From Discussion to Decision. Interax Corporation

ZISMANN (1977): Representation, Specification and Automation of Office Procedures. PhD Thesis. Wharton School, Philadelphia, PA.

List of Figures

List of Tables

Index

MIX
Papier aus verantwortungsvollen Quellen
Paper from responsible sources
FSC® C105338

If you have any concerns about our products,
you can contact us on
ProductSafety@springernature.com

In case Publisher is established outside the EU,
the EU authorized representative is:
Springer Nature Customer Service Center GmbH
Europaplatz 3, 69115 Heidelberg, Germany

Printed by Libri Plureos GmbH
in Hamburg, Germany